THE *LIT DE JUSTICE*
OF THE KINGS OF FRANCE

Studies presented to the International Commission for the History of Representative and Parliamentary Institutions

LXV

Etudes presentées à la Commission Internationale pour l'histoire des Assemblées d'Etats

THE *LIT DE JUSTICE* OF THE KINGS OF FRANCE

Constitutional Ideology in Legend,

Ritual, and Discourse

Sarah Hanley

PRINCETON UNIVERSITY PRESS
Princeton, New Jersey

For
Kathleen Madden
Lynn Madden
Mark Madden
with respect and affection

CONTENTS

List of Figures ix

Preface xi

Abbreviations, Orthography, Dating xiv

Introduction: Whither the Ancient French Constitution? 3

I The Judicial Monarchy in French Constitutional Ideology:
The Royal *Séance* and the *"lit de justice"* in the Later
Middle Ages 14
    The Royal *Séance* and the *"lit de justice"* 1366-1413 14
    The Royal *Entrée* and the *"lit de justice"* 1414-1483 27
    The Revival of the Royal *Séance* 1484-1526 42

II The Juristic Monarchy in French Constitutional Ideology:
The Ceremonial *Lit de Justice* Assemblies of 1527 48
    The *Lit de Justice* Assembly of July 1527 51
    The *Lit de Justice* Assembly of December 1527 72

III Confirmation of French Hegemony in a Constitutional
Forum: The *Lit de Justice* Assembly of 1537 86
    Public Law Writ in Discourse 89

IV Fact and Fiction in Historical Research: Jean du Tillet's
Reconstruction of the French Constitution 102
    Constitutional Theory in the *Recueil des roys de France* 112
    Revision of Du Tillet's Theory in the Memorandum of 1560 121

V A Polarized View of the French Constitution: History
Debated and Ceremony Modified at Mid Century 126
    A Historical-Rhetorical Debate in the Royal *Séance* of 1549 127
    The Royal *Séances* of 1551, 1552, and 1558 133

VI The Question of Legislative Capacity: Problems of
Regency Government 144
    Chancellor Michel de L'Hôpital's Theory of the Legislator-
King 146
    Parlement's Theory of the Legislative Tutor 153

VII The Royal Stance on the French Constitution: The
Majority *Lit de Justice* Assembly of 1563 160
    Public Law Writ in Ritual and Discourse 172

VIII   The Reversal of Parisian Parlementary Procedure:
         Reaction to the Majority *Lit de Justice* Assembly of 1563   183
         The *Lit de Justice* Assemblies of 1564 and 1565   198
         The Majority *Lit de Justice* Celebrations of 1614, 1651, and
            1723   204

  IX   A Conservative Constitutional Course: The Royal *Séance*
         and the *Lit de Justice* Assembly 1569-1597   209
         The Royal *Séances* of 1580, 1581, and 1583   212
         The *Lit de Justice* Assembly of 1597   223

   X   The Dynastic Monarchy in French Constitutional
         Ideology: The Inaugural *Lit de Justice* Assembly of 1610   231
         The Neglected Constitutional Dimension   243

  XI   A Revision of Constitutional Ideology: The Coronation
         Entrée to Reims in 1610   254
         Historical Projects and Ceremonial Programs   267

 XII   The Articulation of Dynastic Right and Legislative
         Authority: *Lit de Justice* Assemblies 1614-1641   281
         The Inaugural Plan for 1643   295

XIII   The Absolutist Monarchy in French Constitutional
         Ideology: The Royal *Séance* and the *Lit de Justice*
         Assembly 1643-1713   307
         Minority *Lit de Justice* Assemblies in 1645 and 1648   315
         The Waning of the *Lit de Justice* Assembly 1652-1713   321

 XIV   Epilogue: The Bourbon Cult of Rulership at the Turn of
         the Eighteenth Century   329
         The Revival of *Lit de Justice* Assemblies in 1715, 1718, and
            1723   333
         Whither the Ancient French Constitution?   341

         Table One: The Legend of the *Lit de Justice* Assembly   345
         Table Two: The *Lit de Justice* Assembly in the *Recueil des roys
            de France* of Jean du Tillet (ed. 1607)   353
         Bibliography
            Manuscripts   355
            Printed Works   357
         Index   373

LIST OF FIGURES

1. Philip VI: Trial of Robert (III) of Artois held in the Louvre in 1332. Miniature, anonymous, in "Procès de Robert (III) Artois, Comte de Beaumont," B.N. ms. fr. 18437, fol. 2r.   36
2. Charles V: Jean Corbechon presenting his manuscript. Miniature, anonymous, in "Barthélemy l'Anglais, Livre des proprietéz des choses, translaté par frere Jehan Corbechon," B.N. ms. fr. 22532, fol. 9r, a fifteenth-century portrayal of a book dedication of 1372.   38
3. Charles VII: Trial of Jean (II), Duke of Alençon, held at Vendôme in 1458. Miniature, attributed to Jean Fouquet, frontispiece in "Le Cas des Nobles Hommes et Femmes malheureux," Bayrische Staatsbibliothek, Munich, Cod. Gal. 369.   40
4. Francis I: Confirming offices in the Parlement of Toulouse in 1515. Engraving, anonymous, frontispiece in Nicolas Bertrand, *Opus de Tholosanorum gestis ab urbe condita* (Toulouse, 1515).   60
5. The king in majesty. Engraving, anonymous, in Claude de Seyssel, *La Grant monarchie de France* (Paris, 1519), B. Arsenal.   62
6. Charles IX: Majority *Lit de Justice* held in the Parlement of Rouen in 1563. Engraving, anonymous, B.N. Département des Estampes.   162
7. Louis XIII: Inaugural *Lit de Justice* held in the Convent of the Augustinians, Paris, in 1610. Drawing, anonymous, B.N. Département des Estampes.   237
8. Louis XIII and the Queen Regent Marie de Médicis in 1610. Engraving executed in 1610 by Nicolas de Mathonière from a design of François Quesnel, B.N. Département des Estampes.   250
9. Louis XIII: The French phoenix, Louis the Just. Design of P.L.D. Gartres, B.N. ms. fr. 23061, fol. 25r.   265
10. Louis XIII: Majority *Lit de Justice* held in the Grand-chambre of the Parlement of Paris in 1614. Engraving, anonymous, B.N. ms. fr. 6391, fol. 98r.   285
11. Louis XIII: Plan of the Majority *Lit de Justice* held in the Grand-chambre of the Parlement of Paris in 1614. Engraving by Nicolas de Mathonière, B.N. Département des Estampes;

B.N. ms. fr. 6391, fol. 97r; and B.N. ms. Collection Cinq Cents
Colbert 212, fol. 145r. 286

12. Louis XIV: Inaugural *Lit de Justice* held in the Grand-chambre
of the Parlement of Paris in 1643. Engraving, anonymous,
B.N. Département des Estampes, Bouchot Pd., fol. 32r; and
B.N. ms. Clairambault 718, fols. 154v-155r. 309

13. Louis XIV: Majority *Lit de Justice* held in the Grand-chambre
of the Parlement of Paris in 1651. Engraving of Antoine
Herisset from a design of Delamonce, B.N. Département des
Estampes. Published in Jean-Aymar Piganiol de la Force,
Nouvelle description de la France (Paris, 1718), I, 27. 318

14. Louis XV: Inaugural *Lit de Justice* held in the Grand-chambre
of the Parlement of Paris in 1715. Engraving of François de
Poilly from a design of Delamonce, B.N. Département des
Estampes, Collection Hennin, LXXXVII, fol. 38r; and B.N.
ms. Clairambault 719, fols. 594v-595r. Published in *Extrait des
registres de Parlement de jeudy 12 Septembre 1715 . . . Louis XV
du nom tenant son Lict de Justice en son Parlement* (Paris, 1715)
[B.N. Réserve, Fol. Lb38.1872]. Displayed in the Musée Carnavalet, Paris [D.7013]. 334

15. Louis XV: Plan of the Inaugural *Lit de Justice* held in the
Grand-chambre of the Parlement of Paris in 1715. Engraving
of François de Poilly, B.N. Département des Estampes; and
B.N. ms. Clairambault 719, fol. 593r. Also in B. Mazarine ms.
2349 (head of volume), and A.N. KK 1429, fol. 214r. Published
in *Extrait des registres de Parlement de jeudy 12 Septembre 1715
. . . Louis XV du nom tenant son Lict de Justice en son Parlement*
(Paris, 1715) [B.N. Réserve Fol. Lb38.1872]. 336

16. Louis XV: Majority *Lit de Justice* held in the Grand-chambre
of the Parlement of Paris in 1723. Engraving of A. Maillot,
B.N. Département des Estampes; and Collection Hennin,
LXXXXI, fol. 3r, A.N. KK 1429, fol. 277r. 338

PREFACE

ONE LOOK at the historical underpinnings of the *Lit de Justice* of the Kings of France recalls the Heraclitean paradox of "time and the river": one cannot "stand in the same place twice" amidst the fluvial tides of history. That paradox points to the epistemological dilemma which haunts these pages, where historical fictions and facts are sorted out. It is apparent that the fictive medieval origins of the *Lit de Justice* assembly were not produced by sixteenth-century rhetoricians, who were accused of valuing eloquence over truth, or by chroniclers, who were accused of weighting facts and fables equally. That fiction was deduced by historians, who consciously avoided the shifting sands of rhetorical prose and chronicle lore for the sure ground of ancient documents that were signed, dated, and deposited in archives. The fiction was turned into a legend by seventeenth-century historians, who conscientiously verified that documentary evidence and then contributed new sources to the thesis. And the legend was confirmed by eighteenth-century historians, who reviewed that history of the *Lit de Justice* in order to comprehend the pristine origins of the assembly. In early modern France the powerful force of historicism, nominalist and philological in conception, bred in its adherents a new mode of perception and a surety of purpose which shaped the *mentalité* of the times. Compiled through painstaking research, the corpus of knowledge about the *Lit de Justice* which they created offered a new way of apprehending reality, eventually assumed a truth of its own, and was passed to posterity with a scholarly imprimatur.

Turning to the same paradox in the twentieth century, the problem of time and space is no less acute. It is still the puzzling task of cultural translation—the extraction of meaning from one system, the expression of it in another—which may at times confound historical explanation. As in the earlier centuries, this approach to the *Lit de Justice* is historical, but befitting the conceptual diversity of modern thought, history is given a helping hand here. The present reading of these events from various texts and contexts, gestures and symbols, suggests that French constitutional ideologies were propagated in *Lit de Justice* assemblies through legend, ritual, and discourse from the early sixteenth to the mid-seventeenth century while the historicist *mentalité* held sway. Repeating

those historians of earlier centuries, though far less sure about apprehending reality, I have concluded also that the historical argument presented here now rests on its own.

This study came into its own largely through the interest and gen-
erosity of colleagues. By far the greatest tribute is paid to Lawrence M.
Bryant, Ralph E. Giesey, and Richard A. Jackson, whose works on the
French Royal *Entrée*, Funeral, and Coronation are closely related to the
Lit de Justice. For over a decade on two continents we have pursued
similar scholarly interests and shared a deep and abiding friendship. I
have profited in untold ways from the stimulating ideas and skeptical
questions posed by them at many critical junctures in this work. I am
also indebted to Eve Borsook, Natalie Zemon Davis, John H. Elliott,
Albert N. Hamscher, Donald R. Kelley, Joseph Klaits, J. Russell Major,
Orest Ranum, Nancy Lyman Roelker, John H. M. Salmon, and William
F. Church for reading and commenting on my work at various stages.
Most of the judicious insights gained from such labors are now part of
this book.

I take pleasure in expressing my gratitude to the Shelby Cullom Davis
Center for Historical Studies, Princeton University, and to Lawrence
Stone, the director of the Center, for my rewarding year as a Davis
Fellow, 1980-1981. It was my good fortune to share the fine intellectual
camaraderie of Davis Fellows Baruch Knei-Paz and Gerald M. Sider
while putting the finishing touches on this work. Similarly, I express
appreciation to my colleagues at the University of Iowa for supporting
my research and writing and for preserving an academic community in
which teaching and scholarship are recognized partners, and to my
colleagues in the History Department for epitomizing that tradition.

I am grateful to Lucette Valensi and Jean-Claude Schmitt for introducing parts of this work to French colleagues through the *Annales*
journal in 1982 and to Emmanuel Le Roy Ladurie for introducing me
to the colloquium on *Les Monarchies*, Université de Paris, in 1981. Likewise, I salute the archivists, librarians, and staffs of the Bibliothèque
Mazarine, Bibliothèque de la Ville de Paris, Bibliothèque de l'Institut
de France, and especially the Bibliothèque Nationale and Archives Nationales, who made available the antiquarian treatises, manuscripts, registers of Parlement, and engravings which constitute the heart of this
book.

My final thanks are for the editors and staff of Princeton University
Press: Lewis Bateman and R. Miriam Brokaw perceived a book in the

offing at the outset, William Hively accomplished the transformation with intelligence and precision, and Laury Egan framed the images with artistic expertise.

Sarah Hanley
Iowa City, 1982

ABBREVIATIONS

A.N.	Archives Nationales, Paris
B. Mazarine	Bibliothèque Mazarine, Paris
B.N.	Bibliothèque Nationale, Paris
B.V.P.	Bibliothèque de la Ville de Paris
Institut de France	Bibliothèque de l'Institut de France, Paris

Orthography. When rendered from the original document, passages retain their original spelling in quotations and in titles. All titles cited in the footnotes and the Bibliography also retain their original spelling.

Dating. All dates have been converted from the old style (dating the new year from Easter) to the new style.

THE *LIT DE JUSTICE*
OF THE KINGS OF FRANCE

INTRODUCTION: WHITHER THE
ANCIENT FRENCH CONSTITUTION?

IN THE mid-eighteenth century the *parlementaire* Louis-Adrien Le Paige passionately decried the perverted format of the contemporary *Lit de Justice* assembly.

> You ask me what a *Lit de Justice* is? I will tell you! In its origins and according to its true nature, a *Lit de Justice* [assembly] is a solemn session of the king in the Parlement [of Paris] which is convoked to deliberate on important affairs of state. It is a tradition which originated in ancient general assemblies held in earlier times. . . . [But today] the convocation of a *Lit de Justice* [assembly] is an occasion of mourning for the nation. . . .[1]

In this lively précis on French constitutional history, Le Paige cited the sixteenth- and seventeeth-century works of Jean du Tillet, *Recueil des roys de France, leurs couronne et maison*, and Pierre Dupuy, *Traité de la majorité de nos rois et des régences du royaume*, sketched the fortunes of the *Lit de Justice* assembly, and raised questions about its place in French history. Convoked by the monarch, this constitutional forum allied king, princes, peers, nobles, Crown officers, and *parlementaires* in a body which represented the nation and deliberated upon affairs of state. The procedure of consultation ordained that the opinion of each order was voiced, heard, and considered by the king preceding his rendition of a final decision. Sometimes known by different names in the past, these solemn *Lits de Justice* were an integral part of the French constitution and provided a fount of national wisdom from which monarchs could draw tried and true "maxims of the kingdom" for proper governance.[2]

[1] Louis-Adrien Le Paige, *Réflexions d'un citoyen sur les Lits de Justice par L-A Le Paige* (n.p., n.d. [c. 1787]), pp. 5-12, first published as *Lettre sur les Lits de Justice, 18 Août 1756* (n.p., n.d.).

[2] Ibid. Le Paige considered all great assemblies as *Lit de Justice* assemblies from time immemorial, whether they were called "*Champ de Mars, Champ de Mai, Placités Généraux, Cours Plénières, plein Parlement, Grand Conseil*," or finally, "*Lit de Justice*." On Le Paige, see John M. J. Rogister, "Louis-Adrien Lepaige and the attack on *De l'esprit* and the *Encyclopédie* in 1759," *The English Historical Review*, XCII (July 1977), 522-539.

Moving from this glowing description of the past to the gloomy contemporary scene, Le Paige depicted the present *Lit de Justice* assembly as a mere shadow of its former self. He criticized procedures which required that opinions be rendered secretly through the chancellor rather than publicly to the monarch, castigated the forced registration of legislation in Parlement, insinuated that the assembly no longer functioned as a representative of the three Estates, and portrayed the king as a mere spectator who simply reiterated decisions already deliberated upon outside the *Lit de Justice*. This neglect of traditional constitutional practice, consultation and deliberation among the *grands du royaume* and the Parlement in the *Lit de Justice* assembly, resulted in faulty legislation upheld by a monarch who was ignorant of the weighty problems facing the kingdom. The convocation of a *Lit de Justice* assembly, Le Paige concluded, now marked a day of national mourning, because it underscored the loss of the pristine ancient assembly and its replacement by a perverted contemporary version.[3]

This rendition of the relationship between the *Lit de Justice* assembly and French constitutional tradition takes liberty with historical verities, but it exemplifies the type of complaint, endemic in the late decades of the ancien régime, which formed the conventional image of the *Lit de Justice* in French historiography.[4] As Crown and Parlement took the roles of political adversaries in a legislative arena in the eighteenth century, the ensuing conflicts were cast in terms of procedure, the efficacy of royal *Lits de Justice* versus that of parlementary remonstrances. Whenever Parlement resisted the registration of a royal edict and returned a remonstrance, the monarch could force registration by convoking a *Lit de Justice*; the king presiding there epitomized the *living law*, and royal legislation was registered immediately without deliberation by the Court. Thus, the *Lit de Justice* assembly, one of the most celebrated and controversial public forums of the ancien régime, is usually defined as a

---

[3] Ibid.

[4] For discussion of those conflicts, consult Ernest D. Glasson, *Le Parlement de Paris, son rôle politique depuis le règne de Charles VII jusqu'à la révolution* (Paris, 1901), II; Franklin L. Ford, *Robe and Sword: The Regrouping of the French Aristocracy after Louis XIV* (Cambridge, Mass., 1953); Joseph H. Shennan, *The Parlement of Paris* (Ithaca, 1968); Jean Egret, *Louis XV et l'opposition parlementaire, 1715-1774* (Paris, 1970), and *The French Prerevolution, 1787-1788*, trans. Wesley D. Camp (Chicago, 1977); William Doyle, "The Parlements of France and the Breakdown of the Old Regime," *French Historical Studies*, VI, 4 (Fall 1970), 415-458; and David Hudson, "The Parlementary Crisis of 1763 in France and its Consequences," *Canadian Journal of History*, VII (Apr. 1972), 97-117.

ceremonial appearance of the king in Parlement used chiefly to exercise absolute royal power.[5]

This view of the *Lit de Justice* as an absolutist weapon used to preempt or quell remonstrances of Parlement and the view of remonstrance as the Court's antidote for it, reflects fairly accurately the circumstances of the later eighteenth century. Following a hiatus of almost half a century, the *Lit de Justice* was revived in 1715 without benefit of accompanying regulations on legislative procedure. The resulting confusion over the proper function of the *Lit de Justice* left Louis XV and Louis XVI to tangle with Parlement regularly in a refashioned legislative arena still called the *Lit de Justice*.[6] During those decades the assemblies were held not only to force the registration of laws but also to reiterate the principle that legislation promulgated in a *Lit de Justice* required immediate registration. At the same time Parlement drew up remonstrances attacking not only the legality of measures registered that way but also the validity of the assemblies themselves. The inability of the *Lit de Justice* and remonstrance to function effectively as legislative channels left a vacuum which exacerbated mounting political quarrels, stymied the legislative process at times, and culminated with the suspension of Parlement in 1788 and the convocation of an Estates General in 1789 for the first time in one hundred and seventy-five years. It was in this tempestuous era, the decades just preceding the French Revolution, that Louis-Adrien Le

[5] The standard dictionaries of institutions contain articles to that effect: Adolphe Chéruel, *Dictionnaire historique des institutions, moeurs et coutumes de la France* (Paris, 1855), II, 670-673; Marcel Marion, *Dictionnaire des institutions de la France aux XVIIe et XVIIIe siècles* (Paris, 1923), pp. 336-338; Gaston Zeller, *Les Institutions de la France au XVIe siècle* (Paris, 1948), pp. 156-160; and Roger Doucet, *Les Institutions de la France au XVIe siècle* (Paris, 1948), I, 186. The same view appears in older monographs: Charles Desmaze, *Le Parlement de Paris, son organisation, ses premiers présidents et procureurs généreaux . . .* (Paris, 1859); J.J.M. Blondel, *Mémoires du Parlement de Paris . . .* (Paris, 1803 [?]), quoting passages verbatim from Louis-Adrien Le Paige (n. 1 above); Ernest D. Glasson, *Le Parlement de Paris, I and II;* Édouard Maugis, *Histoire du Parlement de Paris de l'avènement des rois Valois à la mort d'Henri IV* (Paris, 1913-1916), I, II, and III; Shennan, *The Parlement of Paris*; and Roland Mousnier, *The Institutions of France under the Absolute Monarchy, 1598-1789* (Chicago, 1979), I, 757, retains that definition in the glossary.

[6] Egret, *Louis XV et l'opposition parlementaire*, pp. 45-49, shows how the conflict escalated between 1756 and 1788. Most of the remonstrances treated by Jules Flammermont, *Remontrances du Parlement de Paris au XVIIIe siècle* (Paris, 1888-1898), consider the period after 1750.

Paige drew upon a historical legend about the *Lit de Justice* in order to criticize its deplorable malfunction in contemporary times.

Throughout the nineteenth and early twentieth centuries, scholars who wrote formidable political and institutional histories of the Parlement of Paris adopted this view of the *Lit de Justice* as an ancient French tradition founded in the later fourteenth or early fifteenth century, and they presumed in addition that Parlement's "right of remonstrance" (*droit de remontrance*) also emerged in those early times as the opposing element of legislative procedure.[7] Convinced of the medieval historical roots of both the *Lit de Justice* and remonstrance, they supposed that the two had been incompatible since medieval times.[8] This historical legacy defining the *Lit de Justice* assembly as an absolutist weapon was bequeathed to posterity and has remained impervious to critical evaluation over these many decades. The political and institutional history of the Parlement of Paris has been well studied and is not the central concern of this work. Rather this inquiry focuses on the history of the *Lit de Justice* assembly itself: the actual convocation of those events, the rise of a legend legitimizing them, the ceremonial ritual and the modes of discourse elaborated in the proceedings, and the shifts in constitutional ideology reflected therein.

[7] In addition to works cited in n. 5 above, see Ennemond Fayard, *Aperçu historique sur le Parlement de Paris* (Paris, 1876-1878), and Félix Aubert, *Le Parlement de Paris, de Philippe le Bel à Charles VII (1314-1422)* (Paris, 1886), especially I, 196-197, which cites the Royal *Séance* of Charles V in 1369 as "the first *Lit de Justice*." Particularly influential in propagating the fiction of a medieval *Lit de Justice* assembly and a *droit de remontrance* is Maugis, *Histoire du Parlement*, I, 22, 120, 524, and 628, adjudging the *Lit de Justice* a "customary ceremony" by 1581; and ibid., I, 631, summing up the evolution of a "right of remonstrance" beginning in the fifteenth century. Among other works which adhere to the legend of the *Lit de Justice* are Doucet, *Étude sur le gouvernement de François Ier dans ses rapports avec le Parlement de Paris* (Paris, 1921-1926); Robert J. Knecht, *Francis I and Absolute Monarchy* (London Historical Association, 1969), and *Francis I* (Cambridge, 1982); and Simon H. Cuttler, *The Law of Treason and Treason Trials in Later Medieval France* (Cambridge, 1981), although the legend has become so pervasive by the twentieth century that there is no point in listing all examples here. For a convincing argument against the very early origin of remonstrance as a legislative procedure, see Christopher W. Stocker, "The Politics of the Parlement of Paris in 1525," *French Historical Studies*, VIII (Fall 1973), 191-212; and for the Court's interest in judicial reform, ibid., "Office and Justice: Louis XI and the Parlement of Paris (1465-1476)," *Mediaeval Studies*, XXXVII (1975), 360-386.

[8] Consult the works in n. 5 above.

This study is informed by a triad of interpretive propositions. The first proposition holds that the interaction of two historical processes, the repeated convocation of *Lit de Justice* assemblies and the invention of a legend about them, stimulated constitutional discourse and provided a public forum in which constitutional ideologies were articulated. Those intertwined processes are shown in Table One, which plots both the historical and legendary developments. The historical record of the *Lit de Justice* assembly is reconstructed vertically in Columns A to C, and its legendary life is charted horizontally across Columns D to Z. On the historical side of the picture, Column A lists by date appearances of the king in Parlement from the fourteenth through the seventeenth centuries which were mentioned by antiquarians and manuscript compilers of early modern times.[9] Next, Column B cites the primary sources for these events, the registers of the Parlement of Paris (Series X1a in the Archives Nationales),[10] and Column C gives the secondary sources, copies of the registers (Series U, Collection Le Nain, Archives Nationales) when the originals are missing.[11] When the phrase *"lit de justice"* actually appears in conjunction with an event, the citation in Column B remains un-bracketed; when the phrase does not appear, the citation is bracketed. Finally, when a dated session in Column A is adjudged a *Lit de Justice* assembly according to the criteria of this investigation, the date is set in italic type with an asterisk to the left (✱).

On the legendary side of the picture, Columns D to Z chart chron-ologically the published antiquarian treatises and the anonymous man-uscript compilations (fully identified in the Bibliography) which listed *Lit de Justice* assemblies or commented on them between the sixteenth and eighteenth centuries.[12] Those works identify royal visits to Parlement either as Royal *Séances* (✸) or as *Lit de Justice* assemblies (●) in agreement

[9] Column A terminates at 1713, the last visit of Louis XIV to the Grand-chambre of Parlement.

[10] For a complete list of the nine categories of civil registers, see the manuscript sources listed in the Bibliography for Table One. In order to track down one alleged event, it was often necessary to consult several of these depots. For the organization of A.N. Série X, consult Monique Langlois, "Le Parlement de Paris," *Guide des recherches dans les fonds judiciares de l'ancien régime* (Paris, 1958), pp. 66-160.

[11] For the volumes of the Le Nain collection used here, see the manuscript sources listed in the Bibligraphy for Table One. Le Nain made these copies toward the end of the seventeenth century.

[12] For the published antiquarian treatises and the manuscript compilations the estimated date of completion drawn from internal evidence is given.

with or in opposition to the registers of Parlement.[13] When the commentators in Columns D to Z (who discussed the *Lit de Justice* over time) are compared with the sources in Columns A to C (which actually recorded the events themselves), the pattern that emerges gives form to two interesting observations. First, the table reveals the appearance in the sixteenth century of a historical fiction about the *Lit de Justice* which rooted its origins in medieval times, and it charts the subsequent steady growth in the seventeenth century of this legend, which firmly established the assembly as a pillar of the French constitution. Second, the table reveals the existence of a mutual relationship between the events themselves (known correctly or incorrectly as *Lit de Justice* assemblies) and the legend developed about them. Keeping apace throughout the seventeenth century, the avid research of the new antiquarians matched the growing prominence of the assembly.[14]

The evidence in Table One suggests the following hypotheses about the *Lit de Justice* of the kings of France. First, the *Lit de Justice* assembly (a constitutional forum) did not exist before 1527, despite the fact that commentators in later times insisted upon its medieval origins. Second, the first three *Lit de Justice* assemblies in French history actually appeared in 1527 and 1537, but the assembly was convoked rarely during the rest of that century, just once for the unprecedented Majority *Lit de Justice* of 1563, then only four times more up to 1610. Third, these eight *Lit de Justice* assemblies of the sixteenth century were clearly distinguished from Royal *Séances* (honorary visits), which were held in Parlement more frequently in that century. Fourth, the twenty royal visits to Parlement from 1610 to 1643 were designated uniformly as *Lit de Justice* assemblies, so the sixteenth-century distinction observed between the *Lit de Justice* and the Royal *Séance* was erased in the early seventeenth century. Fifth, nineteen of the twenty-four royal visits to Parlement from 1643 through 1713 were *Lit de Justice* assemblies, the other five Royal *Séances*, so the distinction was blurred in the later seventeenth century.

As for the legend of the *Lit de Justice*, the evidence in Table One highlights three additional points. First, the seminal antiquarian scholarship of Jean du Tillet (Column D) not only introduced the historical fiction of a medieval *Lit de Justice* but also served as an indispensable source for that legend in the next century. Second, the new surge of

[13] The title Royal *Séance* has been adopted here to categorize sessions not specified by title but treated as ordinary royal visits to Parlement; the title *Lit de Justice* has been traced carefully through the sources.

[14] Compare the entries in Columns B and C with those in Columns D to Z.

historical research undertaken by the antiquarians Bernard de La Roche-Flavin (Column E), Pierre Dupuy (Column O), Théodore and Denys Godefroy (Column P), and by many manuscript compilers in the 1620's, 1630's, and 1640's transformed the historical fiction of the *Lit de Justice* into a national legend. Since those later writers automatically severed the sixteenth-century distinction between Royal *Séances* (honorary) and *Lit de Justice* assemblies (constitutional), they "discovered" (or rather invented) a host of new examples to support the burgeoning legend. Third, the seductive seventeenth-century legend affixed the *Lit de Justice* to the ancient French constitution, a vantage point from which it was contemplated historically in the eighteenth century and one from which it has never been dislodged.

The second intrepretive proposition holds that the ritual (ceremonial configuration and procedural format) observed in *Lits de Justice* defined and disseminated precepts of French Public Law (or working axioms of government) in a national forum convoked for that purpose.[15] In the past the function of ceremony in French constitutional history has been treated with indifference, an attitude succinctly expressed by one historian who warned that "Nothing will be said about the solemn ceremonies in which the majesty of the monarch is manifested before the eyes of the crowd: Coronations, *Entrées* to cities, *Lits de Justice*, etc. The details are only of picturesque and anecdotal interest."[16] To the contrary, recent scholarship shows the French propensity to propagate precepts of Public Law through the agency of ceremony in the Royal Funeral, Coronation, *Entrée*, and *Lit de Justice*;[17] and the latter assembly provided the national

[15] Consult Sarah Hanley, "The *Lit de Justice* and the Fundamental Law," *The Sixteenth Century Journal*, VII, 1 (Apr. 1976), 3-14; "Constitutional Ideology in France: Legend, Ritual, and Discourse in the *Lit de Justice* Assembly, 1527-1641," in *Rites of Power: Symbolism, Ritual and Politics since the Middle Ages*, ed. Sean Wilentz (forthcoming); and "L'Idéologie constitutionelle en France: Le Lit de Justice," *Annales: Économies, Sociétés, Civilisations*, no. 1 (Jan.-Fév. 1982), pp. 32-63.

[16] Zeller, *Institutions de la France*, p. 100.

[17] In addition to n. 15 above, consult Ralph E. Giesey, *The Royal Funeral Ceremony in Renaissance France* (Geneva, 1960), and "The Presidents of Parlement at the Royal Funeral," *The Sixteenth Century Journal*, VII, 1 (Apr. 1976), 25-34; Richard A. Jackson, *Vivat rex: Une histoire des sacres et couronnements en France, 1364-1825* (forthcoming), and "The Sleeping King," *Bibliothèque d'Humanisme et Renaissance*, XXXI (Sept. 1969), 527-551; Lawrence M. Bryant, *The French Royal Entry Ceremony: Politics, Society, and Art in Renaissance Paris* (Ann Arbor, University Microfilms, 1978), and "*Parlementaire* Political Theory in the Parisian Royal Entry Ceremony," *The Sixteenth Century Journal*, VII, 1

forum most admirably suited for that purpose. In pertinent places throughout this study, therefore, the ceremonial ritual of the *Lit de Justice* is recapitulated carefully in order to sort out the structures of significance, or levels of inference and implication,[18] through which constitutional axioms were articulated symbolically in the sixteenth and seventeenth centuries. That ritual was manifested in two basic forms: first, the ceremonial configuration which was outlined by the archaeological disposition of the Grand-chambre (Palais de Justice) of the Parlement of Paris (reproduced on occasion in other locations), the type of seating plan employed there, and the particular habits worn by attendants; and second, the procedural format which was organized by prescribed protocol, special privileges, and the order assigned for consultation. These underlying structures of meaning contained in the ritual of the *Lit de Justice* reveal a panoply of ceremonial symbols, or an alternative language molded from space, gesture, and symbol rather than word, which outlined the French constitution in the *Lit de Justice* assembly.

The third interpretive proposition holds that the modes of discourse, or vocabularies, encountered in the writings and speeches of kings, chancellors, *parlementaires*, and others at *Lits de Justice* and Royal *Séances* shed light on the *mentalité* of the participants and the institutions which they molded,[19] on the ties between constitutional practice and theory and the ideologies which emerged.[20] Since these modes of discourse warrant close

---

(Apr. 1976), 15-24. For an excellent study in a different setting, see Edward Muir, *Civic Ritual in Renaissance Venice* (Princeton, 1981).

[18] On the importance of symbolism in reconstructing a cultural system, see Clifford Geertz, "Thick Description: Toward an Interpretive Theory of Culture," and "Ideology as a Cultural System," in *The Interpretation of Cultures* (New York, 1973), pp. 3-30 and 193-233; and *Negara: The Theatre State in Nineteenth-Century Bali* (Princeton, 1980).

[19] On the critical alliance of contextual and lexical elements, consult the works of John G. A. Pocock, "Languages and their Implications: The Transformation of the Study of Political Thought," in *Politics, Language and Time: Essays on Political Thought and History* (New York, 1973), pp. 3-41; *The Machiavellian Moment: Florentine Political Thought and the Atlantic Republican Tradition* (Princeton, 1975); and consult Quentin Skinner, *The Foundations of Modern Political Thought* (Cambridge, 1978), I and II; "Conventions and the Understanding of Speech Acts," *The Philosophical Quarterly*, XX, 79 (Apr. 1970), 118-138; "Some Problems in the Analysis of Political Thought and Action," *Political Theory*, II, 3 (Aug. 1974), 277-303.

[20] On the study of political thought as a history of ideologies, see Skinner, *Foundations of Modern Political Thought*, I and II; for the problem of ideology and the process of history, see Donald R. Kelley, *The Beginning of Ideology:*

attention, the sources whenever accessible are identified, dated, and analyzed in context. The evidence shows how innovative vocabularies were formulated (from private-law maxims, classical and juridical metaphors, biogenetic doctrines, popular proverbs, and historical legends) in order to express precise French constitutional precepts in *Lit de Justice* assemblies decades before such precepts were discussed in the writings of theorists. These modes of discourse coalesced in time to form a new language of French Public Law and diverged over time to propagate variants of constitutional ideology.

From this investigation of the *Lit de Justice* through event and legend, ritual and discourse, one can reconstruct the constitutional ideologies which fashioned juristic, dynastic, and absolutist monarchies in early modern France; identify the frames of constitutional reference which produced both consensus and conflict between the royal party and the Parlement of Paris in those centuries; and trace the demise of the *Lit de Justice* at the royal behest in the late seventeenth century and its anachronistic revival at the turn of the eighteenth century.

Throughout this study there looms large in the foreground the enormous weight of historiographical tradition as shaped by the particular *mentalité* of modern historians and by the interpretive concepts they have employed. As befits most historical problems, the processes of continuity and change are interwoven in the story of the *Lit de Justice*. Yet in this case one is struck straightaway by the sheer durability of the legend of the *Lit de Justice* from the sixteenth through the eighteenth centuries and beyond. In part the legendary life of the *Lit de Justice* resulted from the subscription of early modern historians to the idea of substantialistic likeness, a concept which tended to level the historical differences between contemporary and ancient institutions. Convinced that the roots of contemporary French institutions lay in the medieval past, they searched in effect for the acorns from which the tall oaks had grown. This type of constitutional antiquarianism, justifying contemporary practices by "discovering" historical precedents for them, was rife in early modern France, and it was that sleuthing into the national past which fostered the growth of modern historical scholarship.[21] On the whole the anti-

---

Consciousness and Society in the French Reformation (Cambridge, 1981); and for the study of ideology in culture, see Geertz, "Ideology as a Cultural System."

[21] This genre of research is discussed by Kelley, *Foundations of Modern Historical Scholarship: Language, Law, and History in the French Renaissance* (New York, 1970); Pocock, *The Ancient Constitution and the Feudal Law: A Study of English Historical Thought in the Seventeenth Century* (Cambridge, 1957); "The

quarians' published treatises, which were more conservative in alleging royal sessions in Parlement as *Lit de Justice* assemblies, produced historical scholarship superior to that of the numerous manuscript compilations, which tended to avoid complex distinctions across the board.[22] Nevertheless, all these avid sleuths in the end presumed medieval origins for the *Lit de Justice* assembly. This resort in early modern times to the substantialistic fallacy helps explain the initiation of the historical fiction of the *Lit de Justice* assembly in the sixteenth century, the elaboration of that fiction into a legend in the seventeenth century, and the unabated propagation of the legend in the eighteenth century, but it does not explain its longevity in the nineteenth and twentieth centuries. The following hypothesis may explain that phenomenon. Since the later nineteenth century modern scholars have had access to most of the printed treatises and the manuscript collections of the Bibliothèque Nationale, the Archives Nationales, and the other major collections which are compiled here in Table One. Between the two types of sources, it was probably the numerous manuscript compilations (representing research conducted by Crown officers, *parlementaires*, chancellors, and other officials) which drew most attention, and those manuscripts conveyed the impression that there were many more *Lits de Justice* convoked than antiquarians such as Du Tillet, Dupuy, and the Godefroys recorded in their published treatises. More than likely those scholars treated the quasi-official manuscript sources as prima facie evidence of the extant belief that the *Lit de Justice* was an event common to medieval and early modern times alike. Fortified by the sheer weight of such abundant evidence, historians accepted the conclusion of the well-worn legend, that the ancient French constitution had comprehended a *Lit de Justice*, and then they pursued fruitful research in other directions.

As bequeathed to us, therefore, the intriguing legend about the *Lit de Justice* assembly could only be exposed by eschewing the uncritical acceptance of such sources, sorting out and dating the collections of manuscripts, comparing the antiquarian treatises with manuscript compilations, and verifying all events alleged as *Lits de Justice* against the

---

Origins of Study of the Past: A Comparative Approach," *Comparative Studies in Society and History*, IV (1961-1962), 209-246; Ralph E. Giesey, *If Not, Not: The Oath of the Aragonese and the Legendary Laws of Sobrarbe* (Princeton, 1968); Giesey and John H. M. Salmon, *Francogallia by François Hotman*; and George Huppert, *The Idea of Perfect History: Historical Erudition and Historical Philosophy in Renaissance France* (Urbana, 1970).

[22] Compare the two types of scholarship in Table One.

original entries in the registers of Parlement. In turn, once unearthed, the centuries-old legend of the *Lit de Justice*, which helped fashion the institution itself, provides a new vantage point from which to interpret the *Lit de Justice* assembly in French history. Brought back in this manner to the question which was posed at the outset, "You ask me what a *Lit de Justice* is?" one must perforce reconsider that provocative query.

I

THE JUDICIAL MONARCHY IN FRENCH CONSTITUTIONAL IDEOLOGY: THE ROYAL *SÉANCE* AND THE *"LIT DE JUSTICE"* IN THE LATER MIDDLE AGES

> Today the council met in the Tournelle Criminelle because the Grand-chambre was occupied to set up the *lit de justice*. ... That same day the king ... held his *lit de justice* in his chamber of Parlement. *Nicolas de Baye (1413)*

IN EARLY MODERN FRANCE the historical imagination was struck by the richness of the nation's past as antiquarians and legists studied archival sources in search of the ancient constitution. The resulting reconstruction of the French constitution, outlined in the early sixteenth century by Jean du Tillet and elaborated in the early seventeenth century by a host of disciples, produced a critical typology of royal visits to the Parlement of Paris which distinguished between Royal *Séances* (honorary visits) and *Lits de Justice* (constitutional sessions), creating the historical fiction of a medieval *Lit de Justice* assembly. On the basis of that fiction certain assumptions about chronology arose, suggesting that French constitutional history could be divided into stages: glorious decades when Royal *Séances* and *Lit de Justice* assemblies flourished (the 1360's to 1413) followed by a dark lull when the tradition was suppressed (from 1414 to 1483); interim decades when the Royal *Séance* was revived (from 1484 to 1526) followed by a French constitutional renaissance when the *Lit de Justice* assembly reappeared (from 1527). Yet when one turns to the registers of Parlement, which supplied most of the evidence for this early modern thesis, and to the literary allusions and chronicle lore which also supported it, the historical case for the medieval *Lit de Justice* assembly vanishes along with the periodization based on that fiction.

THE ROYAL *Séance* AND THE *"lit de justice"* 1366-1413

The language used to record Royal *Séances* in the Parlement of Paris during the fourteenth and fifteenth centuries falls into two patterns: a

traditional one (the majority of events) which either simply acknowledged the king's presence or noted that the king was seated in his "royal
majesty" (or "magnificence"),[1] and an innovative one (only six events)
which associated Royal *Séances* inexplicably with a *lit de justice*.[2] It is the
puzzle of the new vocabulary, its origins and context, which requires
attention. This tale of two centuries begins in the 1360's. Two years after
Charles V moved the Royal Household from the turbulent premises of
the Palais de Justice to the quiet quarters of the Hôtel Saint-Pol (1364),
he appointed the Parlement of Paris as guardian of the paraphernalia
which was used to cordon off royal space in the Grand-chambre of the
palace during his visits there. An inventory written by a clerk of Parlement in 1366 described that paraphernalia and its transfer.

> During the council session on Friday, 24 July 1366, the king's *valet
> de chambre*, Guillaume de Feuilloy, brought to the Parlement in
> the name of the king a canopy, a cover, a backdrop, and four new
> velvet pillows, all embroidered with golden fleurs-de-lis and the
> arms of France, in order [that Parlement] hang and place [these
> items] in the chamber of Parlement [the Grand-chambre] when it
> pleased the king to come there. And these items were delivered to
> Alfondet Le Clerc, usher in Parlement, who took them into his
> safekeeping on behalf of Parlement, to store [them] and to hang
> them when required to do so.[3]

[1] "... le Roy en sa personne seant en sa majesté tenu son Parlement ...,"
A.N. X1a 1470, fol. 1r (15 Nov. 1372); "... le Roy tint son Parlement ... Le
Roy en sa majesté royale ...," Théodore [and Denys] Godefroy, *Le Cérémonial
françois* (Paris, 1649), II, 431 (9 Dec. 1378) [Reg. Parl.]; "... le Roy nostre sire
tint son Parlement en la chambre de Parlement à Paris ... le Roy nostre sire
estoit assis en sa majesté royale, en la maniere qu'il a accoustumé quant il sied
pour justice," ibid., II, 432 (9 Dec. 1378) [Reg. Parl., Plaidoiries]; "... le Roy
nostre sire a esté en Parlement en sa majesté royalle ...," A.N. U 2015 (Le
Nain), fol. 217v (9 July 1386). For additional examples, see below, nn. 28 and
29.
[2] The critical events took place in 1387, 1392, 1396, 1407, and twice in 1413,
and are discussed below.
[3] "Du Vendredy xxiv jour de juillet M.C.C.C.LXVI, au conseil. Ce jour
Guillaume de Feuilloy valet de chambre du Roy apporta au Parlement de par
le Roy, un ciel, une couverture et un chevecier, avec quatre oreillers tous neufs
de velvet, semez de fleurs de lis d'or aux armes de France, pour tendre et asseoir
en la chambre du Parlement, quant il plaira au Roy d'y venir; toutes lesquelles
choses ont esté baillées a Alfondet Le Clerc, huissier du Parlement, lequel les
a pris en garde de par le Parlement pour les visiter et tendre quant mestier
sera"; A.N. X1a 1469, fol. 146v (24 July 1366).

No particular name was used by the parlementary clerk to characterize that drapery paraphernalia (canopy, backdrop, cover, and four pillows) placed in the charge of the parlementary usher Feuilloy, but within the next twenty-five years the phrase *lit de justice* appeared precisely for that purpose.

Between 1388 and 1413 three ushers in Parlement wrote detailed expense accounts which recorded the duties they performed to prepare the Grand-chambre of Parlement for Royal *Séances* and the monies they dispensed for the costs incurred.[4] The accounts reveal that ushers arranged for a variety of chores, such as cleaning the Grand-chambre and moving furnishings, and were charged with constructing the *lit de justice* and removing it after the *Séance*.[5] In the usually lengthy interim between Royal *Séances*, moreover, they arranged for the storage and repair of the drapery paraphernalia and the wooden scaffold of the *lit de justice*.[6] One particularly interesting account of 1396 kept by Raoul Le Noir recorded the duties performed and costs expended for Charles VI's Royal *Séance* held that same year, and it provides information crucial for the definition of a medieval *lit de justice*.

> [Wages] for a locksmith in order to make a key for the chest in which the decorative draperies (*draps de parement*) for the *lit de justice* are [kept] and to make new wards for the lock of the said chest ... for which lock the first key was delivered by Guillaume de Feuilloy [royal valet] ... and was lost. ... [Wages] for Ernoulet Le Clerc [parlementary usher] for a locksmith in order to make some small locks ... to put in the place of two other locks which were detached and removed when the king was in the palace during the fête held for the Queen of England. ... Wages for two pages for two days in order to carry the small benches outside the parquet of Parlement and to carry the wooden scaffold (*couche de bois*)

---

[4] A.N. KK 336 (Comptes de l'Hussier), fols. 1r-224r, expense accounts from 1388 to 1419. The ushers are Jehan Baure, Raoul Le Noir, and Pierre Belle.

[5] A.N. KK 336, fols. 1r (1388), 6v, 7r (1390), 10r (1394), 22r (1396), 165r, 165v, 168v, 173r, 174r (1413), giving the following expressions: "Et pour fere le lict de justice"; "pour achever le chaliz du lit de justice"; and "vi varles qui osterrent le lit de justice"; "le lit de justice a este deffaiz"; and finally, "ledit lit de justice fu tenu" (also see n. 24 below).

[6] A.N. KK 336, fols. 21v, 22r (1396), 53v (1400), 55r (1401), 168v (1413), using the following expressions: "draps de parement (or parements) du lit de justice," and "couche de bois (or chaliz) du lit de justice."

[inside] in order to make the *lit de justice* when the king enters Parlement for the trial of Monsieur Pierre de Craon. . . .[7]

This passage affords a good picture of the medieval *lit de justice*. First, the "decorative draperies for the *lit de justice*" are identified as those which were delivered to Parlement in 1366 by Charles V's valet, Guillaume de Feuilloy; so they consisted of a canopy, backdrop, cover, and pillows. Second, a "wooden scaffold" was placed inside the parquet of Parlement "to make a *lit de justice*"; so the draperies covered that rough item. Third, two elements constituted a *lit de justice*, draperies and scaffold; so the phrase *lit de justice* for parlementary ushers must have signified the majestically canopied and draped scaffold which cordoned off space for the king in Parlement.

Earlier in the fourteenth century, between 1318 and 1345 at least, this type of drapery paraphernalia was handled by chamberlains of the Royal Household, not by ushers in Parlement. Apparently at that time there was no distinction made between the draperies which were used in the Royal Household to make the "*lit*"[8] (that is, the canopied structure over

[7] "A un serrurier pour avoir fait une clef pour le coffre ou quel sont les draps de parement du lict de justice et pour faire nouvelles gardes en la serure dudit coffre ... de laquelle serure la premiere clef fu bailler Guillaume du Feuilloy et fut par luy perdu ... A Ernoulet Le Clerc serrurier pour avoir fait des serruries menues ... mettre en lieu de deux autres serrures qui furent destachees et emportees quant le Roy fu au palais a lad. feste de la Royne d'Engleterre ... A deux varles pour leur salaire de deux journees pour porter les petis bancs, hors du parc de parlement et a porter la couche de bois pour faire le lict de justice quant le Roy fu en parlement pour le fait de Messr. Pierre de Craon ...''; A.N. KK 336, fols. 22r-22v (13 Mar. 1396). Edgard Boutaric, *Recherches archéologiques sur le Palais de Justice de Paris, principalement sur la partie consacrée au Parlement depuis l'origine jusqu'à la mort de Charles VI (1422)* (Paris, 1862), XXVIII, 58, reprints parts of this passage but gives no archival citation for it, cites the wrong folios and the old-style date (1395) from the expense account, and quotes the passage with six words missing. Boutaric comments that when the king came to the palace for a *Lit de Justice* assembly he sat "sur un lit ou divan, richement orné: les ornements ou parements de ce lit restaient au Palais," propagating the fiction of a medieval *Lit de Justice* assembly and the notion that the *lit*, or *lit de justice* was a couchlike seat, rather than the drapery paraphernalia. These opinions were incorporated into the work of many modern historians, including Aubert, *Parlement de Paris*, pp. 196-200.

[8] "Nous ordenons ... nos chambellains, que nulle personne mesconqüe ... ne entre en nostre garde-robe, ne mettent main, ne soient à nostre lit faire, et qu'on n'i suffre mettre draps estranges"; *Ordonnances des roys de France de la troisième race*, Eusèbe de Laurière et al., eds. (Paris, 1723-1849), I, 668-669 (16 Nov. 1318).

the *chambre*, or bed, of the king),[9] and the draperies which were used in Parlement to construct the "*lit* of the king" (that is, the canopied apparatus over the draped wooden scaffold).[10] Yet after 1366, when

[9] Household records of the fourteenth and fifteenth centuries reveal the elements comprising a household *chambre*, or bedchamber, and help to identify the *lit*. A *chambre* was constructed out of a canopy, a backdrop, and curtains which were hung upon a *lit*, or frame, supplying an overhead covering for the *couche*, or platform. Thus the *lit* alone consisted of a frame supporting canopy, backdrop, and curtains. But the words *lit* and *chambre* were not interchangeable in medieval times: *chambre* signified the whole bedchamber, including structural members (*lit* and *couche*) and cloth materials (canopy, backdrop, curtains, bedclothes); while *lit* denoted just the frame supporting the inner hangings. Consult Louis Claude Douët-d'Arcq, *Comptes de l'argenterie des rois de France au XIVe siècle* (Paris, 1851), pp. 109, 112-113, 115, 118, and 358; *Nouveau recueil de comptes de l'argenterie des rois de France* (Paris, 1874), pp. 21-22; *Comptes de l'hôtel des rois de France aux XIVe et XVe siècles* (Paris, 1865), pp. 85-93, for descriptions of *chambres*. A classic example appears in Léon-Emmanuel Laborde, *Les Ducs de Bourgogne: Études sur les lettres, les arts et l'industrie pendant le XVe siècle* (Paris, 1849), I, 237. The inventory of goods of Nicolas de Baye, clerk of Parlement, *Journal de Nicolas de Baye, greffier du Parlement de Paris, 1400-1417,* ed. Alexandre Tuetey, *Société de l'histoire de France* (Paris, 1885), I, ix and lxiv, itemizes *lits* as "le lit de la couche de ladicte chambre." By the seventeenth century this etymology was already obscure; see Jean Nicot, *Dictionnaire françois-latin* (Paris, 1584), and Nicot and Aimar de Ranconet, *Thresor de la langue francoyse, tant ancienne que moderne* (Paris, 1606); and consult Edmond Huguet, *Dictionnaire de la langue française du seizième siècle* (Paris, 1961), V. Nineteenth-century glossators tried to rectify the obscurity; see Auguste Scheler, ed., *Oeuvres de Froissart: Glossaire* (Brussels, 1874), XIX, 74; Lucien Favre, ed. of Jean Baptiste La Curne de Sainte-Palaye, *Dictionnaire historique de l'ancien langage françois* (Paris, 1877), III, 341, n. 2; and Frédéric Godefroy, *Dictionnaire de l'ancienne langue française* (Paris, 1889), II, 45. But modern dictionaries let the above-mentioned etymological suggestions slip by them; see Émile Littré, *Dictionnaire de la langue française* (Paris, 1968); Adolf Tobler and Erhard Lommatzsch, *Altfranzösisches Wörterbuch* (Berlin, 1936), II, 190-191; and Walther von Wartburg, *Französisches etymologisches Wörterbuch* (Bonn, 1940), II, i, 130-137. The resulting obscurity surrounding *chambre* and *lit* made possible errors such as that of Boutaric and Aubert (n. 7 above).

[10] In the parlementary milieu there were important ordinances "touchant le Parlement" which were issued to regulate protocol during Royal *Séances*. Ordering that the space in front of the royal tribunal must remain empty to guarantee privacy when the king converses with those whom he summons, a regulation of 1318 states: "Que nul ne se parte de son siege, ne ne viegne soier de lez *le lict du Roy*, les chambellains exceptez, ne ne viegne conseiller à luy, se il ne l'appelle"; *Ordonnances des roys de France*, I, 673-677 (17 Nov. 1318) [italics added]. A copy of this regulation in A.N. U 2013 (Le Nain), fols. 466r-469r, is dated 7 November 1318 and contains an additional note, fol. 466r, which

Charles V made the historic deposit of the latter drapery paraphernalia with the Parlement of Paris precisely for use in Royal *Séances*, the name *lit de justice* emerged to distinguish those furnishings controlled thenceforth by the ushers in Parlement from others overseen by chamberlains in the Royal Household.[11] Moreover, in the same decades that the phrase *lit de justice* became popular among ushers of Parlement charged with erecting the drapery paraphernalia, it appeared also among clerks of Parlement charged with recording Royal *Séances* in the registers. It is clear from the ushers' expense accounts that they worked closely with the clerks. Both Jean Willequin, clerk of Parlement from 1390 to 1400, and Nicolas de Baye, clerk from 1400 to 1416, sent missives to the ushers from time to time and probably presented their expense accounts to the king for collection.[12] As it turned out, therefore, it was the ushers and clerks of Parlement who introduced the name *lit de justice* (drapery paraphernalia) into the parlementary milieu, a phrase which no doubt clarified daily business for them at the time, but which greatly confused matters for posterity.

In early modern times the confusion of constitutional antiquarians over the discovery of a medieval *Lit de Justice* assembly stemmed from the fact that the strange phrase *lit de justice*, jargon understood by parlementary ushers and clerks, appeared in the registers of Parlement when the clerks Jean Willequin and Nicolas de Baye wrote the minutes for the six Royal *Séances* of 1387, 1392, 1396, 1407, and 1413 (May and September). Alongside the ushers' expense accounts, perusal of the clerks' texts in the following contexts provides the best clue for unraveling the historical puzzle of the medieval *lit de justice*. On 2 March 1387 Charles

---

states that "Ce est l'ordonnance que li Roys faict pour son Parlement," as well as a comment which notes that "Celle ordonnance est tirée d'un rouleant en parchemin escrit du mesme temps qu'elle a esté faicte lequel est en les mains de Monsr. d'Erouval [Sieur d'Herouval]"; and the copy given reproduces the text on fol. 468v with the substitution of *"le lic le Roy"* for the phrase in italics above. In the same context a regulation of 1345 repeats the above almost verbatim: "Que nul ne se parte de son siege ne ne viegne seoir deles *le lit le Roy* les chambellans exceptez ne ne viegne conseiller a luy se il ne l'appelle"; A.N. X1a 8602, fol. 14r (11 Mar. 1345), printed in *Ordonnances des roys de France*, II, 219-228, from Jacques Joly, *Trois livres des offices de France* (Paris, 1638), I, cxxxvi.

[11] Note that the ordinances of 1318 and 1345 show royal chamberlains still in charge of the drapery paraphernalia (n. 10 above).

[12] A.N. KK 336, fols. 15r (1395), 23r (1396), and 54v (1400) for Willequin; and fols. 86r (1404), 118v-119v (1407-1408), 175r (1413), 188r (1414), 196v, 204r (1415), and 204r (1416) for De Baye.

VI heard a case in the Parlement of Paris against Charles II, King of Navarre, tried posthumously for the crime of treason, or *lèse-majesté*. Records of the *Séance* differ, for the *conseil* register of Parlement noted that "... the king our lord was in his Parlement in his royal majesty ..."[13] whereas the *criminel* register stated that "The king our lord was in Parlement in state and was holding his royal tribunal in his chamber [which was] decorated in the customary manner with draperies of his arms and [with] the *lit de justice*."[14] Five years later, on 3 December 1392, Charles VI presided in Parlement over a Royal *Séance* which confirmed the ordinance on royal majority and succession promulgated by his father Charles V in 1375, and the text of the register reported that "... the king in person held the Parlement in his magnificence, and the *lit* [was] made in the chamber."[15] A few years after, on 10 April 1396, Charles VI went to Parlement for the trial of a royal official, Pierre de Craon, charged with the attempted assassination of Olivier de Clisson, one of the "Marmousets" who advised the king, and the registers of Parlement stated that "... the king came to the palace where the *lit de justice* was set up, and the king held his council. ..."[16] In this particular circumstance, we know already, from the usher Le Noir's expense account of 1396, that this *lit de justice* consisted of drapery paraphernalia covering a scaffold. Over a decade later, on 26 December 1407, Charles VI sat in the Parlement of Paris when problems of regency and succession were treated and the majority ordinance of 1375 was confirmed. This

[13] "... fut le Roy nostre sire en son Parlement en sa majeste royalle ...";
A.N. X1a 1473, fol. 293v (2 Mar. 1387), reprinted in Aubert, *Parlement de Paris*, pp. 198-199, as "marche roiale" instead of "majeste royalle." Charles (II), King of Navarre, had died on 1 January 1387. Cuttler, *The Law of Treason*, pp. 99-100, mistakenly cites this trial as a *Lit de Justice*.

[14] "... fut le Roy nostre sire en Parlement en estat, tenant son siege royal en sa chambre paree des draps de ses armes et du lit de justice en la maniere accoustumees ..."; A.N. U 790 [4 unnumbered folios] (2 Mar. 1387), a sixteenth-century document in the same handwriting as another in the collection signed by Jean du Tillet, which appears in Godefroy, *Cérémonial françois*, II, 437, with slight variations. The passage is copied in A.N. U 960, U 425, and B.N. Clairambault 715 substituting *"lis"* for *lit*; and in U 819 (Procès célèbres), a collection of materials on trials, substituting *"lieu"* for *lit*.

[15] "... le Roy tint en sa personne le Parlement en sa magnificence et fait le lit en la chambre ..."; A.N. X1a 1477, fol. 14r (3 Dec. 1392). For the ordinance, see *Ordonnances des roys de France*, VII, 530-538.

[16] "... le Roy vint au Palais et fu dressé le lit de justice et tient le Roy son conseil ..."; A.N. X1a 4784, fol. 87r (10 Apr. 1396). The text appears in Aubert, *Parlement de Paris*, II, 199, n. 3, as "fu drecié."

time the new clerk Nicolas de Baye wrote the phrase *lit de justice* in the text of the ordinance which was promulgated there: "Given and read aloud publicly in the Grand-chambre of our Parlement in Paris where the *lit de justice* was set up. . . . [Given] by the king holding his Parlement. . . ."[17]

Throughout these registers, whether the minutes were written by Willequin or De Baye, the vocabulary reveals two distinct patterns: when the clerks indicated the procedure which was underway in the *Séances*, they stated that the king was "holding" his Parlement or council or tribunal; but when they designated the furnishing (i.e., the draped scaffold) "made" or "set up" for the *Séances*, they employed the name *lit de justice*. These sources of 1387, 1392, 1396, and 1407 from registers of Parlement thus support the contention that the fourteenth-century phrase *lit de justice* simply signified a canopied and draped apparatus used in Parlement to cordon off royal space, nothing more. Before the decade was over, however, there were subtle semantic changes in the offing which would cause considerable confusion in later centuries.

Twice in the year 1413 the clerk De Baye recorded Royal *Séances* in a manner which struck a slightly different tone and immediately caught the eye of antiquarians a century later. On 26-27 May 1413 Charles VI presided in Parlement over the registration of the Cabochien ordinance, legislation which would be annulled later in September under the sway of new advisers. On both days the proceedings were recorded in the *conseil* registers of Parlement as follows: ". . . the king our lord in person [and] in the presence of the dauphin . . . [list of persons present] . . . held his *lit de justice* in this place, and parts of certain ordinances were read . . ." (26 May).[18] The *plaidoiries* register for those dates recorded the *Séance*

---

[17] "Données et leuës publiquement, et à haulte voix, en la grant chambre de nostre Parlement à Paris, où estoit drecié le lit de justice . . . Par le Roy tenant son Parlement . . ."; *Ordonnances des roys de France*, IX, 269 (26 Dec. 1407) and reproduced with slight variations by Pierre Dupuy, *Traité de la majorité de nos rois et des régences du royaume, avec les preuves tirées tant du Tresor des Chartes du roy que des registres du parlement, ensemble un traité des prééminences du Parlement de Paris* (Paris, 1655), p. 216 [Trésor des Chartes, no. 14]. Note that Enguerran de Monstrelet, *La Chronique d'Enguerran de Monstrelet*, ed. L. Douet-d'Arcq, *Société de l'histoire de France* (Paris, 1857), I, xxxvii, 170, presumes that the three Estates share in governance during minority.

[18] ". . . le Roy nostre sire en sa personne, presens messeigneurs le dauphin . . . [other notable persons listed] . . . a tenu son lit de justice ceans, et ont esté leues parties de certeinnes ordonnances . . ."; A.N. X1a 1479, fol. 243v (26 May 1413). The corresponding entry is cited in De Baye, *Journal*, II, 114-115. The entry

in the same manner,[19] and the clerk De Baye rendered the critical passages into Latin for his personal journal.[20] Just three months later De Baye repeated this semantic nuance in records of another Royal *Séance*. On 5 September 1413, when Charles VI issued royal letters in Parlement revoking the Cabochien ordinance of May as well as earlier edicts, De Baye's record of the session included the phrase in both forms on the contiguous lines of one passage.

> Today the council met in the Tournelle Criminelle because the Grand-chambre was occupied to set up the *lit de justice* and to decorate it [the Grand-chambre], ... [list of persons present]. That same day the king, our sire, in the presence of [list of persons] ... held his *lit de justice* in his chamber of Parlement.[21]

Again the *plaidoiries* register recorded the *Séance* in the same way, and the clerk rendered the passage into Latin in his journal.[22] In addition the *ordonnance* register of Parlement, which recorded two royal letters revoking earlier edicts, one written in French and the other in Latin, also conflated the two meanings of *lit de justice*.[23]

---

for the next day reads: "Tant à matin que après disner tint le Roy nostre sire, presens les nommez ou jour precedent, son lit de justice, et furent leues ... les ordonnances ..."; A.N. X1a 1479, fol. 244r (27 May 1413). It is also cited in De Baye, *Journal*, II, 115-116.

[19] "Cedit jour [au conseil] le Roy en sa personne ... a tenu le lit de justice pour faire lire certeinnes ordonnances ..."; A.N. X1a 4789, fol. 458v (26 May 1413). Note that Maugis, *Histoire du Parlement*, I, 524, n. 2, when speaking in the text about *Lit de Justice* assemblies, incorrectly dates the year as 1412 and interprets "a tenu son lit de justice" as evidence that this in fact was a *Lit de Justice* assembly. He cites the event as one of those great political assemblies which effected a kind of "consentement publique" for the promulgation of ordinances. The entry for the next day reads: "Tint le Roy nostre sire ... sont lit de justice ..."; A.N. X1a 4789, fol. 458v (27 May 1413).

[20] De Baye, *Journal (Mémorial)*, II, 304, makes a Latin rendition from the French as follows: "xxviiª maii, illo anno, tenuit Rex lectum justicie. ..."

[21] "Jour furent au conseil en la tournelle criminelle pour ce que la grant chambre estoit occupée a drecier le lit de justice ... et la parer ... [list of persons]. Cedit jour le Roy, nostre sire, presens ... [list of persons] tint son lit de justice en sa chambre de Parlement ..."; A.N. X1a 1479, fol. 263r-v (5 Sept. 1413).

[22] "Ce jour [au conseil] le Roy ... tint en la cour et en la chambre de son Parlement son lit de justice ..."; A.N. X1a 4789, fol. 514v (5 Sept. 1413). De Baye, *Journal (Mémorial)*, II, 306, noted that "Rex tenuit lectum justicie. ..."

[23] One version reads: "Nous estans en nostre Parlement tenans le lit de justice ... [revocation of previous letters] ... Donne en la chambre de nostre Parlement à Paris ou estoit le lit de justice ... par le Roy tenant son lit de justice en sa

There is no doubt that Nicolas de Baye introduced a semantic change into this vocabulary. He acknowledged the *lit de justice* as drapery paraphernalia, consonant with the vocabulary of earlier registers, but stated too that the king "held" his *lit de justice*, rather than his Parlement, suggesting for the first time that the draped apparatus signaled the special judicial jurisdiction of the Parisian Court. Alongside the clerk's minutes, the usher Pierre Belle's expense account of 1413 also produced this semantic nuance. He noted that benches had been removed from the parquet of Parlement "where the said *lit de justice* was made" and returned after "the *lit de justice* was taken down." In the next breath he recounted the damage done to the benches by the enormous crowd present "during the time that the said *lit de justice* was held."[24] Thus, even in the narrow context of Belle's expense account, references to the *lit de justice* denoted either the drapery paraphernalia set up (that is, affixed or hung) in the Grand-chambre or a judicial session convoked there; and in the official registers of Parlement, De Baye's usage suggested that a *"lit de justice"* was a special parlementary session.[25] The clerk Nicolas de Baye, who was caught in 1413 along with other *parlementaires* in the struggle for political power waged between competing royal advisers,[26] was known to all as an inordinately zealous guardian of both

---

cour de Parlement"; A.N. X1a 8602, fol. 286v (5 Sept. 1413), published in *Ordonnances des roys de France*, X, 167-170. The other version reads: "Datum Parisis in dicti nostri parlementi camera ... Signat. per Regem suum in parlementi camera justicie lectum tenentem"; A.N. X1a 8602, fol. 285r (5 Sept. 1413), published in *Ordonnances des roys de France*, X, 170-173.

[24] A.N. KK 336, fols. 165r-v (1413). Following the Royal *Séance* of May 1413 this account was written: "Pour avoir oste les bancs du parquet de Parlement ou ledit lit de justice a este faiz et ... remis in lez place apres ce que y'cellui lit de justice a este deffaiz. Item pour avoir refait l'un des petits bancs ou soient lez advocats pour ce qu'il fu rompus par lez gens qui estoyent dessus durant le temps que ledit lit de justice fu tenu pour la grant presse du peuple qui lors y estoit pour ce."

[25] De Baye seemed aware of a distinction between Royal *Séances* held in the Grand-chambre of Parlement and royal sessions held elsewhere with Parlement in attendance, because he did not associate a *lit de justice* with the sessions of 23 August 1404 held in the Hôtel Saint-Pol, or 31 December 1409 held in the Salle Saint-Louis (see below, n. 29); De Baye, *Journal*, I, 113-114, and 305-307.

[26] Charles VI's bouts of illness and the conflict among the Burgundians (the duke, dissident French princes, and Parisian merchants in revolt) and the Armagnacs (the Duke of Orléans and other princes) is well documented; see Ernest Lavisse, ed., *Histoire de France depuis les origines jusqu'à la révolution* (Paris, 1900-1911), IV, 1, 288-308, 339-351, and Gaston J. Dodu, *Les Valois: Histoire d'une maison royale (1328-1589)* (Paris, 1934).

the registers and the prerogatives of the Parlement of Paris.[27] It it not surprising, therefore, that he stretched the phrase *lit de justice* ever so slightly to emphasize the special jurisdiction of the Parisian Court in those unsettled days. Since French kings after 1413 did not visit the Grand-chambre of Parlement again until 1484, the introduction of De Baye's semantic nuance bore no immediate consequences. It would not even be historically important except for the fact that historians in the sixteenth and seventeenth centuries found these passages in the registers of Parlement which referred to a *lit de justice*, interpreted them as evidence for the medieval origins of the *Lit de Justice* assembly, bemoaned the disappearance of that institution in the fifteenth and early sixteenth centuries, and presumed that they had revived that ancient *Lit de Justice* assembly in 1527.

What has been uncovered here is the development of a new vocabulary of short duration, not a constitutional assembly of ancient origin. In the fourteenth century there were many other Royal *Séances* held in Parlement to treat important affairs of state, such as those of 9-11 May 1369, which functioned as a meeting of Estates; 21 May 1375, where Charles V's famous ordinance on majority and succession was registered; and 9-10 December 1378, when the trial of a peer was conducted. Yet the vocabulary of those *Séances* fell into the traditional pattern, simply noting on some occasions that the king was "holding his Parlement," on others that he appeared in "royal majesty" (or "magnificence"), that is, surrounded by drapery paraphernalia which cordoned off royal space not only in the Grand-chambre of Parlement[28] but also in other locations

[27] De Baye spent the first six months in office, November 1402 to May 1403, reading registers to familiarize himself with the "stile de Parlement" and wrote more than six hundred folios in registers for *Séances* in the Grand-chambre, as well as other sessions in the Hôtel Saint-Pol and other places; De Baye, *Journal*, I, vi-ix, 2, 50-51, and 63-64. The clerk also made extracts from the registers of Parlement as far back as 1365 for his personal collection; ibid., *Journal (Memorial)*, II, 281, n. 1. Guarding registers from theft and damage, he locked them up in cabinets in the Tournelle Civile and even walled up the entrance on one occasion to prevent damage or theft when royal chamberlains were sent to lodge there during a visit of Charles VI. Finally, he saw to the renovation of seats and benches in the Grand-chambre and arranged to hang Jean de Virelay's newly painted crucifixion tableau on the north wall, and he placed appropriate texts from prophets, philosophers, and poets along those walls for the edification of *parlementaires*; ibid., *Journal*, I, xiv-xvi, and 335. For the tableau of Virelay placed in the Grand-chambre on 6 January 1406, see Aubert, *Parlement de Paris*, appendix I, pp. 394-395.

[28] Consult A.N. X1a 1469, fols. 341v-343r (9-11 May 1369); A.N. X1a 1470, fols. 145r-148r (21 May 1375), and the ordinance on the same date, A.N. X1a

such as the Hôtel Saint-Pol, the Salle Saint-Louis of the Palais de Justice, and the Louvre.[29] Indeed, a perfect example of the simultaneous existence of the two phrases used to signify the draped thronal apparatus appears in the Royal *Séance* of 1387, where "royal majesty" was employed by one clerk and *"lit de justice"* was adopted by another. In summary, it seems that the phrase *lit de justice* first appeared in expense accounts kept by parlementary ushers during the 1360's in order to clarify their new charge; that the name then was appropriated for minutes of Royal *Séances* written between 1387 and 1413 by clerks of Parlement Jean Willequin and Nicolas de Baye to signify the construction of the majestic draped apparatus delimiting royal space in the Grand-chambre; and that the meaning of the phrase finally was stretched by Nicolas de Baye to denote a special judicial session situated within the jurisdiction of the Parlement of Paris. Indeed, unlike its undiscriminating rival term "royal majesty," which signaled the majestic appearance of the king for royal sessions held in locations other than the Parlement of Paris, the phrase *lit de justice* in both its forms was associated only with Royal *Séances* held in the Grand-chambre of the Parlement of Paris, as the examples of 1387, 1392, 1396, 1407, and 1413 show. In the end, therefore, the phrase *lit de justice* was originated by parlementary ushers to describe important new duties and attained brief prominence through the whim of parlementary clerks, not for any constitutional reason.

Turning from the registers of Parlement to some literary works which mentioned a *lit de justice* in the late Middle Ages, there is further support for this contention. The allegorical poem *Le Roman des deduis* was completed around 1377 by Gaces de La Buigne, royal chaplain of Charles V.[30] He recounted the monarch's rendition of a judgment given in the

---

8602, fol. 77v; A.N. X1a 1471, between fols. 133v-137r (9-10 Dec. 1378). Note that all of these sessions would be considered *Lit de Justice* assemblies by constitutional antiquarians later (see Table One). A perusal of other *Séances* in the Grand-chambre bears this out. See A.N. X1a 1470, fol. 1r (15 Nov. 1372); A.N. X1a 1470, fols. 192v-193r (5 Feb. 1376); A.N. X1a 1470, fols. 243v-245r (28-31 Jan. 1377); A.N. X1a 1473, fols. 145v-148r (9 July 1386); A.N. X1a 1475, fols. 75v-82r (22 June 1390); A.N. X1a 1479, fol. 187r (7 Jan. 1412).

[29] For sessions in the Louvre: A.N. X1a 1470, fols. 237r-238r (18 Nov. 1376); A.N. X1a 1470, fol. 234r (27 Feb. 1377). For sessions in the Hôtel Saint-Pol: A.N. U 2016 (Le Nain), fol. 139r (7 Sept. 1394); A.N. X1a 1478, fol. 172v (23 Aug. 1404). For sessions in the Grande Salle and the Salle Saint-Louis: A.N. X1a 1479, fols. 42v-43r (5 Sept. 1408), and A.N. X1a 4788, fol. 394v (31 Dec. 1409). On the typical expressions used, see above, n. 1.

[30] Gaces de La Buigne, *Le Roman des deduis*, ed. Ake Blomqvist, *Studia Romanica Holmiensia* (Karlshamn, 1951), III, introduction and p. 4 for the dating. La Buigne (c. 1328-1380) pictures the monarch attended by nobles, *avocats*, and

Parlement of Paris and noted that the chamber of Parlement was decorated with "noble ornaments" and that "the *lit de justice* was made
there due to the solemnity of the occasion."[31] Another work, *Le Miroir
de mariage* of Eustache Deschamps, *écuyer* under Charles V and Charles
VI, recalled the regency of Queen Blanche of Castile during the minority
of Louis IX in the thirteenth century. Deschamps imagined a parlementary session in which the queen regent, on behalf of the young king,
appealed to the great nobles of the realm to end civil disorder.

> Blanche, daughter of the king of Castile
> Mother of Saint Louis, the king
> Of France, placed in array
> A handsome *lit* richly decorated
> Which was made in Parlement;
> The king was placed there in the middle of the *couche*,
> And then she herself began
> To address those in attendance.
>
> . . . .
>
> It was ordained that in remembrance
> Of that miracle and that peace
> The *lit* would always be made hereafter
> In all places where consecrated kings hold
>   forth for judgment,
> And for this reason they still prepare it
> And they call it a *lit de justice*,
> Which is a fit reminder
> That it is always the duty of the king
> Either to come to his Parlement,
> Or to sit for justice elsewhere.[32]

---

special councillors, Reason, Prudence, Truth, Law, Justice, and Loyalty, to judge
the question of whether hunting with dogs or falcons is preferred as a sporting
pastime.

[31] "Le roy est en son siege alé, / . . . En la chambre de parlement, / Paré de
noble parement / . . . Le lit de justice y fu fait / Pour la solempnité du fait . . . ;
La Buigne, *Roman des deduis*, lines 5299-5316 (Blomqvist, *Studia*, III, 278-279).
The miniature portraying the king sitting under a canopy, *Roman des deduis*,
introduction, is reproduced from B.N. ms. fr. 1614, fol. 1r.

[32] "Blanche, fille au roy de Castelle, / Mere de saint Loys, le roy / De France,
fist mettre en arroy / Un beau lit richement paré, / Ou droit parlement estoré; /
La mist le roy en mi la couche, / Et puis commança de sa bouche / A dire a
tous les assistens . . . / Fut establi qu'en remembrance / De ce miracle et celle

Both Deschamps and La Buigne, contemporaries at the royal court, treated the *lit de justice* as a draped apparatus which defined royal space in Parlement, and Deschamps further suggested that this *lit de justice* had become a symbol throughout the land for royal justice.

THE ROYAL *Entrée* AND THE *"lit de justice"* 1414-1483

The idea that the draped apparatus (*lit de justice*) symbolized royal justice remained alive during the early fifteenth century even after Royal *Séances* in the Parlement of Paris ceased. The Royal *Séances* held by Charles VI in 1413 were the last of such sessions convoked in the Grand-chambre for over seventy years. From 1416 to 1437 the kingdom of France was fractured and along with it the Parlement of Paris. The Parisian Court in 1416 was split into two rival factions, one at Poitiers secured by French forces, the other at Paris occupied by Anglo-Burgundian troops. Before his death in 1422 Charles VI visited the loyal Parlement at Poitiers once in 1416,[33] but he never attended the rump Court at Paris.[34] The situation

paix / Seroit li liz a tousjours mais / En tous lieus ou les roys seroient / Pour jugement et qui tendroient / De France la saincte couronne, / Fais, et pour ce encor on l'ordonne / Et l'appell' on lit de justice, / Qui est a remembrer propice / Toute fois que roys proprement / Doit venir en son parlement / Ou qu'il siet pour justice aillours"; Eustache Deschamps, *Le Miroir de mariage*, lines 9434-9441 and 9522-9533, in *Oeuvres complètes de Eustache Deschamps*, ed. Le Marquis de Queux de Saint-Hilaire (Paris, 1894), IX, lxxxi, 304-305 and 307. Eustache Deschamps (c. 1320-1406?) here has *Folie* speaking satirically about the virtues of women. Some decades later Christine de Pisan, *Le Livre des fais et bonnes meurs de sage roy Charles V*, ed. Suzanne Solente, *Société de l'histoire de France* (Paris, 1936), I, 62, describes the *"lit de justice"* as royal space in the Palais de Justice where the king sits in order "to hold justice."

[33] A.N. U 513 (Le Nain, table), p. 342 [fol. 326] (8 Aug. 1416), indicates that the session was held "pour demander au Parlement de Poictiers son advis." On this Parlement at Poitiers, consult Maugis, *Histoire du Parlement*, pp. 49-61.

[34] The critical assembly of 23 December 1420, when the English and French kings sat together and publicly announced the disinheritance and banishment of the dauphin (the future Charles VII) took place outside of the Grand-chambre of the Parlement of Paris in the Hôtel Saint-Pol; see Monstrelet, *Chronique* (Paris, 1860), IV, ccxxxii, 15-20, and Jean Le Févre, *Chronique de Jean Le Févre*, ed. François Morand, *Société de l'histoire de France* (Paris, 1881), II, 23, neither of which mentions a *"lit de justice."* Nevertheless, modern biographers of Charles VII, Gaston du Fresne Beaucourt, *Histoire de Charles VII* (Paris, 1881), I, 217, and Malcolm G. A. Vale, *Charles VII* (London, 1974), p. 31, maintain that Charles VI held a *Lit de Justice* on that occasion.

was similiar during part of the next reign, for Charles VII (1422-1461) was not in Paris between 1416 and 1437. Although he managed a delayed Coronation with the help of Joan of Arc in 1429, Parlement was still divided and the capital city remained in English hands until 1436. The French king visited the Parlement at Poitiers in 1431,[35] but it was the English king Henry VI who sat in the other Parlement at Paris that year.[36] After recovering Paris, Charles VII made an *Entrée* there in 1437 and reestablished the Parlement at Paris in 1438. Still, during the rest of his reign the king never visited the Grand-chambre of the Parlement in the Palais de Justice, not even to oversee the promulgation of the great ordinance on the reformation of justice in 1454.[37] Following the cessation of Royal *Séances* after 1413, therefore, the phrase *lit de justice* disappeared from descriptive accounts in the registers of Parlement, as the journal of Clément de Fauquembergue, clerk of Parlement from 1417 to 1435, shows.[38]

At the same time chroniclers picked up the phrase *lit de justice*, and it probably had some currency in the streets of Paris as well. Several chronicles recounted Parisian *Entrées* which featured tableaux set up at the Châtelet (the city tribunal of the provost of Paris) displaying a *lit de justice*. Much earlier Jean Froissart had described an elaborate *tableau vivant* which was staged there during the post-Coronation *Entrée* of Isabel of Bavaria in 1389 and which accommodated a *lit de justice*.

[35] A.N. U 513 (Le Nain, table), p. 342 [fol. 326] (8 May 1431), notes that "Le Parlement fut en la maison du Roy à Poictiers, pour le jugement du Procès de d'Amboise convaincu de crime de l'Eze Majesté."

[36] The young English king, who made his *Entrée* to Paris on 2 December, sat in the Parlement at Paris to receive oaths of office and preside over the reading of ordinances, and the registers stated that ". . . le Roy tint le Parlement . . ."; A.N. X1a 1481, fols. 47v-50v (21 Dec. 1431), and X1a 4796, fols. 294v-296r (21 Dec. 1431), the former account also in the journal of the clerk of Parlement, Clément de Fauquembergue, *Journal de Clément de Fauquembergue*, ed. Alexandre Teutey, *Société de l'histoire de France* (Paris, 1915), III, 26. Fauquembergue was *greffier* from 1417-1435.

[37] The loss or damage of many sets of parlementary registers, including some made in the reigns of Charles VII and Louis XI, leave a void in the body of evidence: *Conseil* for 1443-1458 and 1462-1469; *Plaidoiries* for 1428-1432, 1457-1460, and 1484-1485; and the *Après-dinées* for 1458. Still, A.N. U 513 (Le Nain, table) records no Royal *Séances* either for Charles VII or Louis XI, and the biographies of both kings, Beaucourt, *Histoire de Charles VII*, and Pierre Champion, *Louis XI* (Paris, 1927), reveal no *Séances*. Likewise, neither Maugis, *Histoire du Parlement*, I, 70-71, nor Glasson, *Parlement de Paris*, find Royal *Séances* in these reigns.

[38] Fauquembergue, *Journal* (Paris, 1903 and 1915), I-II, and III.

At the entrance of the Châtelet was a wooden castle ... and in that castle [there was] a decorated *lit* set up and curtained as richly in every way as for the *chambre* of the king, and this *lit* was called the *lit de justice*; and there in that *lit* reclined a figure impersonating Saint Anne. Level with that castle ... was an ... arbor.... And from that woods or arbor emerged a white stag [with golden antlers and a crown-shaped golden collar around its neck, and the stag turned to] the *lit de justice*. There also emerged out of the woods and from the arbor a lion and an eagle ... which approached that stag and the *lit de justice*. Then twelve young maidens wearing golden caps and holding unsheathed swords also emerged from the woods and arbor and placed themselves between the stag and the lion and eagle, demonstrating that by the sword they wished to safeguard the stag and the *lit de justice*.[39]

No doubt this *lit de justice*, described as a draped enclosure, symbolized royal justice, or judicial kingship, especially for viewers in the streets of Paris who were familiar with the white stag which stood across from the Grand-chambre in the Palais de Justice.[40] Since Jean (II) Juvénal des Ursins retold the story of this tableau in the early fifteenth century, the symbolic images were passed to another generation.[41]

[39] "A la porte du Chastelet de Paris avoit ung chastel ... de bois ... et sur ce chastel ung lit paré, ordonné et encourtiné aussi richement de toutes choses, comme pour la chambre le roy, et estoit ce lit appellé le lit de justice; et là en ce lit par figure et par personnage se gésoit madame sainte Anne. Ou plain de ce chastel ... avoit une ... ramée ... Et de ce bois ou ramée ... yssi ung blanc cerf delés [A esles d'or et couronné au col d'une grande couronne d'or, et s'adrescha le cerf] le lit de justice. D'autre part yssirent hors du bois et de la ramée ung lion et ung aigle ... et approchoient ce cherf et le lit de justice. Lors partirent du bois et de la ramée jeunes pucelles environ douze très-richement parées en chappelets d'or, tenant espées toutes nues en leurs mains, et se mirent entre le cerf et l'aigle et le lion, et monstroient que à l'espée elles vouloient garder le cerf et le lit de justice ..."; Jean Froissart, *Oeuvres de Froissart*, ed. Kervyn de Lettenhove (Brussels, 1872), XIV, 10-11, who records the date of the *Entrée* as 20 August 1389, while registers of Parlement, A.N. X1a 1474, fol. 326r, report 22 August but give no details.

[40] The stag (*cerf, cherf*) stood in the Grande Salle of the Palais de Justice in close proximity to the Grand-chambre. On the evolution of the stag as a symbol of justice, see Jean Guerout, "Le Palais de la Cité à Paris des Origines à 1417," *Fédération des sociétés historiques et archéologiques de Paris et de l'Ile de France, Mémoires* (Paris, 1950), II, 135-136. Marcel Thibault, *Isabeau de Bavière* (Paris, 1903), pp. 143-144, takes a different view, maintaining that Saint Anne represents justice.

[41] Jean (II) Juvénal des Ursins, *Histoire de Charles VI, roy de France*, eds.

Even amidst the battles between English and French for control of northern France in the 1430's, Parisian *Entrée* tableaux were placed in front of the Châtelet and displayed the *lit de justice* as a symbol for royal justice, although not necessarily French royal justice. Celebrating victory over Paris in 1431, the nine-year-old English king Henry VI during his *Entrée* to the city saw at the Châtelet a tableau portraying a young king (his age) royally garbed and enthroned in a *lit de justice*. Two anonymous chronicles described that tableau: one said it contained a *"lit de justice"*;[42] the other said it contained a "high scaffold, richly adorned and hung with fine tapestry ... [with] a satin canopy and backdrop bearing the arms of France and England. ..."[43] The French displayed their rejoinder to the English tableau six years later in 1437, after Charles VII recovered the capital city. The chronicler Enguerran de Monstrelet described the religious mysteries dramatized along the *Entrée* route and the *lit de justice* which had been set up in the tableau outside the Châtelet.

Just before the Châtelet was the Annunciation enacted by the angel with shepherds singing *Gloria in excelsis Deo*. Beneath the entrance was the *lit de justice*—divine law, natural law, and human law. And on the other side near the butcher shop was the [Last] Judgment— paradise and hell. And in the middle was the Archangel Michael weighing souls.[44]

Joseph-François Michaud et Jean J. F. Poujoulat, *Nouvelle collection des mémoires pour servir à l'histoire de France* (Paris, 1836), 1ʳᵉ série, II, 378.

[42] "... devant le Chastellet où avoit moult bel mystere; car là avoit droit encontre le Chastellet à venir de front le lit de justice; là avoit un enffent du grant du Roy (de la grandeur du Roy) et de son aage, vestu en estat royal, hausse vermeille et chapperon fourré, deux couronnes pendans qui estoient très-riches à veoir à ung chascun sa sur sa teste ..."; *Journal d'un Bourgeois de Paris, sous le règne de Charles VII*, eds. Michaud and Poujoulat, *Nouvelle collection des mémoires* (Paris, 1837), 1ʳᵉ série, III, 266 (2 Dec. 1431).

[43] "... A l'encontre du Chastellet de Paris, avoit haulx escarfaulx, moult richement aornez et tenduz de moult riche tappisserie; et la estoit un enfant, representant la personne du roy, assiz en un faudestuer; et derrier et au dessus de lui avoit un ciel et dossier de satin armoyé des armes de France et d'Angleterre ... Et dessus lui, deux couronnes en air ..."; Bernard Guenée and Françoise Lehoux, *Les Entrées royales françaises de 1328 à 1515* (Paris, 1968), XI, B, p. 68 (2 Dec. 1431). The account of Monstrelet, *Chronique* (Paris, 1861), V, cix, 4, does not mention a *lit de justice* and does not contain additional description.

[44] "Devant le Chastelet, estoit l'Annunciacion faite par l'angle aux pastouriaus, chantant *Gloria in excelsis Deo*. Et au dessoubz de la porte estoit le lit de justice, la loy divine, la loy de nature et la loy humaine. Et à l'autre costé, contre la boucherie, estoient le jugement, paradis et enfer. Et ou milieu estoit saint Michiel

As seen through these chronicles, the medieval *lit de justice* survived the demise of Royal *Séances* for a quarter of a century in the form of a visual symbol. It represented the ubiquitous concept of justice, albeit unconnected with Parlement, which epitomized the judicial monarchy. The survival of the phrase *lit de justice* to symbolize royal justice in these tableaux is curious, for the route of that transformation is unclear. Few of the chroniclers who recounted events of the fourteenth and early fifteenth centuries took special notice of Royal *Séances* held in the Grand-chambre of the Parlement of Paris. The four who did comment on them, the chronicler of Saint-Denis, Jean Le Févre, Jean (II) Juvénal des Ursins, and Enguerran de Monstrelet, knew the Royal *Séances* of 1407 and 1413 (May and September) held in the Grand-chambre of the Parlement of Paris. But even so they did not distinguish those *Séances* from royal sessions held in other locations, and they did not impute special historical significance either to Royal *Séances* as a genre or to the *lit de justice* which was associated with them.[45] Perhaps this chronicle tradition was spun

---

l'Angle, qui pesoit les âmes"; Monstrelet, *Chronique*, V, ccxix, 303, and the text also in Guenée, *Entrées royales*, VII, C, p. 77 (12 Nov. 1437). Another source, the Herald Berry, noted that this tableau displayed "la justice du Roy"; Guenée, *Entrées royales*, VII, B, p. 77, erroneously dated by the Herald as 8 November.

[45] The chronicler of Saint-Denis offered the phrase *lit de justice* in a variety of semantic poses, associating it indiscriminately with Royal *Séances* of 1413 (May and September) held in the Grand-chambre of Parlement, as well as to a session of 1409 held in the Salle Saint-Louis; *Chronique du religieux de Saint-Denys, contenant le règne de Charles VI, de 1380 à 1422*, ed. Louis F. Bellaguet, *Collection de documents inédits sur l'histoire de France* (Paris, 1842), 1re série, VI, pt. 5, bk. xxxiv, chap. xxxix, p. 192 (26 and 27 May 1413); ibid., pp. 192-194 (5 Sept. 1413); and another comment on the *Séance* of May, ibid., chap. xxxv, p. 152 (Aug. 1413). Compare the above with the account for 1409, ibid., pt. 4, bk. xxx, chap. xvii, p. 282 (31 Dec. 1409). Jean Le Févre (c. 1396-1468), the one chronicler who cited an original source, De Baye's ordinance of 1413 (September), took no notice of the phrase *lit de justice* in that text. Le Févre discussed the *Séances* of 1413, misdating the September event, but he never mentioned a *lit de justice*. What is more, he introduced an error into the text of the ordinance when he copied it, stating that the king was "holding his place (*lieu*) of justice," rather than his *lit de justice*; *Chronique de Jean Le Févre* (Paris, 1876), I, xxxv, 85 (26 May 1413); ibid., I, xxxviii, 110 and 116 (5 Sept. 1413), mistakenly dating the event as 8 September and the ordinance as 12 September. Jean (II) Juvénal des Ursins (1388-1473) was puzzled by the phrase *lit de justice*, associating it perhaps with Parisian *Entrée* tableaux, because he mused about "a kind of *lit de justice*" having been held in 1407 (misdated as 28 December) and 1413 (May); Juvénal des Ursins, *Histoire de Charles VI* (Paris, 1836), II, 445 (26 Dec. 1407); ibid., 483 (27 May 1413). Finally, Monstrelet wrote about the *Séances* of 1407

from a different thread, street pageants or *Entrées* staged earlier than Froissart's example of 1389 but left undocumented. In any case, the *lit de justice* of the Parisian streets outlived that of the Parisian Parlement in the fifteenth century.

In the later decades of his reign Charles VII developed an administration innovation in government, the Grand Conseil,[46] to which cases were sometimes evoked from the Parlement of Paris. At times that body comprehended peers and *parlementaires*, but it could not function as a Court of peers to try criminal cases as had the Royal *Séance*. When the question of a treason trial arose in the 1450's, therefore, a revival of the Royal *Séance* in Parlement seemed in the offing. Accused of the crime of *lèse-majesté* for conspiring with the English, Jean (II), Duke of Alençon and peer of France, refused in 1456 to recognize the hearing ordered by Charles VII and demanded a trial in a Court of peers presided over by the king. Apparently the procedure for such trials was questioned, because Parlement was ordered to search through the Court's registers for precedents. Returning a legal opinion on 20 April 1458, the *parlementaires* stated that peers of France accused of a criminal offense must be tried in the presence of the king assisted by other peers, and they cited the trials of Robert (III) of Artois (1332) (Figure 1), Jean (IV) of Montfort (1378), and Charles (II), King of Navarre (1387) as evidence for that opinion.[47] In 1458 it seemed probable, therefore, that Charles VII would revive the Royal *Séance* in the Grand-chambre of the Parlement of Paris.

---

and 1413 (May and September) but did not associate them with a *lit de justice* and did not distinguish them from the session of 1407 held in the Salle Saint-Louis; *Chronique du religieux*, I, xxxvii, 170 (26 Dec. 1407); ibid., II, civ, 362 (26 May 1413); ibid., II, cvii, 403 (5 Sept. 1413), but misdated as 8 September. Compare the above with the session of 1409; ibid., II, lix, 54-57 (31 Dec. 1409). For a study of how chroniclers fashioned royal myths which contributed to the formation of national identity in France, see Gabrielle M. Spiegel, *The Chronicle Tradition of Saint-Denis* (Leyden, 1978).

[46] Beaucourt, *Charles VII*, VI, 354, discusses the evolution of the Grand Conseil as an administrative organ.

[47] Ibid., VI, 179-198. The decision noted that if certain peers refused to respond to the convocation the king must proceed in their absence, since his presence in the process was indispensable. For the trial of 1387, see above, nn. 13 and 14; for the trial of 1378, see A.N. X1a 1471, fols. 133v-137r; for the trial of 1332, see A.N. U 787 (Procès célèbre) and Figure 1 below. For recent work on treason trials, see Cuttler, *The Law of Treason*, which shows how the French adopted Roman Law (*Julia maiestatis* and *Quisquis*) as the written authority for the French law of treason. Here the trial of 1387 is mistakenly cited as a *Lit de Justice*; ibid., pp. 98-99.

In fact he did not. The king summoned the peers and the Parlement of Paris for the trial of Alençon, but the assembly was slated first for 1 June in the city of Montargis outside of Paris and then was moved south in August to Vendôme.[48]

On 26 August 1458, five days after his *Entrée* to the city of Vendôme, Charles VII convened the assembly in the Château of Vendôme for the treason trial; some weeks later, on 10 October, the guilty verdict was pronounced there.[49] The inordinate magnificence of that assembly, immortalized in a miniature attributed to Jean Fouquet (Figure 3), reflected a fierce Franco-Burgundian rivalry carried out on ceremonial and jurisdictional fronts from the 1450's through the 1480's.[50] Surely the gran-

[48] Beaucourt, *Charles VII*, VI, 179-198.

[49] Ibid. The registers of Parlement yield no information; for other sources, see nn. 53-55 below. Chastellain noted that the Parlement of Paris was there in a body down to the very last clerk, so that all judicial actions ceased in Paris; *Oeuvres de Georges Chastellain*, ed. Kervyn de Lettenhove (Brussels, 1864), III, xciii, 467. For the trial, consult Beaucourt, *Charles VII*, VI, 4-59, citing B.N. ms. fr. 18441, fols. 1r-125v, which mentions no *Lit de Justice* assembly.

[50] Burgundians developed elaborate "duke in majesty" ceremonies rivaling those of monarchs and unlikely to endear the Valois dukes to their relatives in Paris. Olivier de La Marche (1426-1501), chamberlain at the Burgundian ducal palace, noted ceremonial occasions when Duke Philip the Good (1396-1476) "was seated on a bench decorated with tapestry, pillows, and canopy and surrounded by his nobles . . ."; *Mémoires d'Olivier de La Marche*, eds. Henri Beaune and J. d'Arbaumont, *Société de l'histoire de France* (Paris, 1884), II, 24. At times the duke was seated on a platform raised six steps; Pierre Clement, *Les Grands hommes de la Bourgogne* (Paris, 1966), p. 49. The seat from which he gave audiences in the presence of princes of the blood was described as "a high chair richly decorated with tapestry and a golden drape . . ."; Dodu, *Les Valois*, p. 213, n. 3. Although in 1454 Charles VII had never seen the Burgundian duke Philip the Good, French envy of ducal grandeur ran high, according to Chastellain, who visited the French court and remarked on the seething rivalry wrought by the elaborate Burgundian ceremonial; *Oeuvres*, III, 18-19. When Duke Charles the Bold (1433-1477) held public audiences after dispensing justice, he sat on the third level of a platform covered with expensive tapestry "in his chair lavishly decorated by a canopied drape," with a small stool at his feet; La Marche, *Mémoires* (Paris, 1888), IV, 5, 158-189. Jurisdiction was also a problem. Burgundians usurped French royal privileges, such as ennoblement and the powers of pardon and coinage, and they refused to execute some *arrêts* of the Parlement of Paris; see Beaucourt, *Charles VII*, V, 224-225; VI, 276-285; and Le P. Urbain Plancher, *Histoire générale et particulière de Bourgogne* (Dijon, 1781), IV, ccxxxv-ccxxxvi, where Parlement complains that injunctions are not obeyed in the lands of Burgundy. Following his retrieval of the Duchy of Burgundy in 1478, Louis XI agreed that Parlement would send cases concerning

deur impressed those in attendance, but it was also meant to impress the two missing persons: the dauphin (the future Louis XI, estranged from the king since 1447), whose seat in the assembly was reserved and left empty; and the peer Philip the Good, Duke of Burgundy, who sent an ambassador in his stead.[51]

The Vendôme assembly of 1458 looms large in the legend concocted later about the ancient origins of the *Lit de Justice* assembly; so the question of its status is important, albeit insoluble. The *parlementaires* checked precedents for this assembly in the registers and cited the treason trial of 1387 in the legal opinion; so they could have come across the phrase *lit de justice* in those minutes. Yet by this time, almost a half century after the suppression of the Royal *Séance* (along with the *lit de justice*), it is unlikely that clerks of Court still comprehended that term. The extant registers of Parlement either contain no entry for that date or have entries which are damaged and unreadable; so those sources are silent.[52] Moreover, the ones remaining, four contemporary chronicles, present conflicting evidence. On the one hand, two accounts, one by Jehan de Wavrin, the other unidentified, used the traditional vocabulary: both reported that the king sat in his "judiciary tribunal" or in his "high royal tribunal," but mentioned no *lit de justice*.[53] On the other hand, the two other accounts followed the innovative pattern: the royal historiographer Jean Chartier noted that the king intended "to hold his *lit de justice*, or *convencions*," at Vendôme,[54] and the Burgundian chronicler

---

Burgundians to the Parlement of Burgundy; see Champion, *Louis XI*, II, 285, and *Ordonnances de roys de France*, XVIII, 368.

[51] Beaucourt, *Charles VII*, VI, 180-185.

[52] A.N. X1a 1484 gives no record of the trial, and A.N. X1a 4806 is unreadable due to fire and water damage. A.N. X1a 8605, fol. 190r-v, gives the orders to move the trial to Vendôme.

[53] The first record is published in Godefroy, *Cérémonial françois*, II, 441-443 (10 Oct. 1458), identified as [Extract des Chroniques d'Angleterre ... finissent l'an 1471 mises par écrit par Jean Sieur de Forestel, Chevalier du Pays de Hainaut]. That source is Jehan de Wavrin, Seigneur du Forestel (fl. 1415-1471), *Anchiennes cronicques d'Engleterre*, ed. Émilie Dupont (Paris, 1859), II; it contains no account of the events in 1458. The second record is published by Godefroy, *Cérémonial françois*, II, 448-449 (10 Oct. 1458), identified as [Extract d'une chronique manuscrite de la Bib. du Prés. de Thou ...]. Note that Mathieu d'Escouchy, *Chronique de Mathieu d'Escouchy*, ed. Gaston Du Fresne de Beaucourt, *Société de l'histoire de France* (Paris, 1863), nouv. ed., II, cxlvii, 357-361, mentions no *lit de justice* in 1458. A collection of some of these documents is contained in A.N. U 822 (Procès célèbre), but no *lit de justice* is discussed.

[54] Jean Chartier, *Chronique de Charles VII*, ed. Vallet de Viriville (Paris, 1858),

Georges Chastellain stated that the defendant would be placed "under the *lit de justice*" for sentencing.[55] As applied here by some contemporary chroniclers, ignored by others, the phrase *lit de justice* by 1458 signaled both the draped canopy itself and the judicial jurisdiction of the French king in the Parlement of Paris. The phrase *lit de justice* thus survived the demise of Royal *Séances*, for it was used in chronicle lore about Parisian *Entrées* to symbolize the concept of royal justice as portrayed in street tableaux; and then the phrase resurfaced in chronicles of the mid-fifteenth century to emphasize French royal jurisdiction in the face of Burgundian pretensions. Finally, the iconography of scenes which portrayed the king in Parlement suggests that artists, as well as parlementary ushers and clerks, came to appreciate the symbolic significance of the prominent drapery paraphernalia.

There are three iconographical representations presented here, two miniatures and one illumination, which show the king sitting with the Parlement of Paris in the fourteenth and fifteenth centuries. The first representation, a miniature, was executed shortly after the event and depicts the trial of Robert (III) of Artois in 1332 presided over by Philip VI in the palace of the Louvre (Figure 1).[56] Although the miniature is

---

III, chap. 284, p. 90. Godefroy reprints this extract but does not identify the author as Chartier and substitutes the words "et Assemblée" for "ou convencions"; Godefroy, *Cérémonial françois*, II, 444-448 [Autre relation du mesme Lict de Justice, 10 Oct. 1458]. Chartier spoke not about the trial itself but about the first summons convoking the assembly at Montargis. Jean Chartier was appointed historiographer of the king on 18 November 1437; *Chronique*, I, viii. Cuttler, *The Law of Treason*, p. 103, mistakenly cites the trial as a *Lit de Justice*, as does Giesey, *The Juristic Basis of Dynastic Right to the French Throne*, Transactions of the American Philosophical Society, LI, 5 (Philadelphia, 1961), p. 28, misdated as 1457.

[55] Chastellain, *Oeuvres*, III, lxxxii, 422-423; lxxxiv, 428-429, alleging that the Duke of Burgundy and the dauphin would have been indicted along with Alençon if found culpable. Here the magnificent thronal apparatus and tapestried chamber, as well as the ranked seating order is described in detail; ibid., III, xciv, 477-478. At the turn of the sixteenth century, Claude de Seyssel referred to this assembly as a *Lit de Justice*; see *Les Louenges du roy Louys XIIe de ce nom*, in *La Langue française au seizième siècle*, ed. Peter Rickard (Cambridge, 1968), pp. 65-68.

[56] For this miniature (anonymous), see "Procès de Robert (III) Artois, comte de Beaumont"; B.N. ms. fr. 18437, fol. 2r, a fourteenth-century manuscript; it was probably executed around 1337. The absence of a canopy caused a seventeenth-century copyist of this miniature to emend the original by adding not only a canopy and backdrop but also a rug covering the scaffold; see the engraving executed by a copyist of Roger de Gagnières in Bernard de Mont-

1. Philip VI: Trial of Robert (III) of Artois held in the Louvre, 1332.

extraordinary as a very early portrayal of a specific historical event of this type, the image is schematic: it lacks perspective, provides little archaeological detail, and uses blazons of arms to identify attendants. Still, the essential elements are represented: the king at the apex, lay and ecclesiastical peers to the right and left, bound prisoners representing Artois in the middle, and *parlementaires* presenting arguments below. The crowned Philip VI sits in solitary splendor on a benchlike seat, a *chaise curule*, which is partly covered by his royal robes, but the canopy and backdrop, or *"lit* of the king" mentioned as early as 1318 and again in 1345, is missing.[57] In place of the missing drapery apparatus, the anonymous miniaturist provided a crown and royal robes of fleurs-de-lis to designate the sovereignty of the French king.

The second representation, an illumination, was executed in the fifteenth century and served as a frontispiece for the *Livre des proprietez des choses*, a French translation of Bartholomaeus Anglicus' encyclopedia. It portrays the Augustinian friar Jean Corbechon presenting his French translation of that compendium to Charles V in 1372 during a session of Parlement (Figure 2).[58] In royal space defined by a canopy and back-

---

faucon, *Les Monumens de la monarchie françoise* (Paris, 1730), II, 246, plate xliv. In addition Montfaucon also interspersed his own Latin version of the event with the Latin chronicle of Guillaume de Nangis in a confusing manner which allows the reader to assume that the ancient chronicle called this trial *"justitiae lectum."* In fact *Chronique Latine de Guillaume de Nangis de 1113 à 1300 avec les continuations de cette chronique de 1300 à 1368*, ed. Hercule Géraud, *Société de l'histoire de France* (Paris, 1843), nouv. ed., II, 124-133, recounts solemn publication of the *arrêt* and never mentions *justitiae lectum*.

[57] For those documents, see above, n. 10.

[58] This illumination (anonymous) appears in "Barthélemy l'Anglais, Livre des proprietéz des choses, translaté par frere Jehan Corbechon," B.N. ms. fr. 22532, fol. 9r, a fifteenth-century manuscript. The image depicts a book presentation in a parlementary assembly. A detailed copy of this picture taken from the Gagnières collection is published by Montfaucon, *Monumens* (Paris, 1731), III, plate viii, who fails to mention that it was painted not in 1372 but in the fifteenth century (ibid., 34-35) and thus misleads Vale, *Charles VII*, p. 206, who did not see the original and concluded incorrectly that the Corbechon illumination provided a stylistic device for the Fouquet miniature of 1458. Montfaucon, *Monumens*, III, 34-35, perpetuated the legend by designating the assembly a *Lit de Justice*, but he was unsure of the historical event it represented. Perplexed at the ambiance in Parlement, he noted that if this *Lit de Justice* assembly was truly held, then we cannot believe that the king called it just to receive Corbechon's book. Rather, the king, who must have had other pressing business, simply paid the friar the honor of receiving his book the same day. As shown in A.N. X1a 1470, fol. 1r (15 Nov. 1372), Charles V did hold a Royal *Séance*

2. Charles V: Jean Corbechon presenting his manuscript (1372).

drop, Charles V sits in a hieratic pose on an elevated seat at the apex of a diamond-shaped construct enclosed by draperies and a wooden railing; and councillors are seated to the right and left inside the parquet. Yet at same time the king is fully costumed in royal robes, crown, and scepter.[59] Thus the anonymous artist here not only employed the draperies to designate sovereignty but also costumed the monarch in his regalia to emphasize the point.

The third representation, a miniature attributed to Jean Fouquet, was executed a month after the event and depicts the trial of Jean (II), Duke of Alençon, presided over by Charles VII at Vendôme in 1458 (Figure 3).[60] Fouquet provides a very accurate portrayal of that scene replete with archaeological details, correct seating arrangements, and faithful portraits of king and attendants. Charles VII is garbed in a hat and robe, the kind of habit worn in his portrait (also attributed to Fouquet) which hangs in the museum of the Louvre.[61] There is no doubt that royal sovereignty in this image is signaled by the draped apparatus constructed around the king: the luxurious winged-stag wall tapestries and wooden barriers define the limits of an improvised chamber swathed in royal blue and golden fleurs-de-lis, and the canopy and backdrop of fleurs-de-lis which hangs over the raised scaffold where the king sits delimits royal space within that larger diamond.[62]

---

in the Grand-chambre in that year, but Corbechon is not mentioned in the registers for the event.

[59] Since the regalia was deposited at Saint-Denis and removed only for the Coronation, it is unlikely the king was garbed in that manner either in 1332 (see above, n. 56 and Figure 1) or in 1372. On the royal regalia, see Percy E. Schramm, *Der König von Frankreich* (Weimar, 1960), p. 133.

[60] This miniature attributed to Jean Fouquet appears as a frontispiece of "Le Cas des nobles hommes et femmes malheureux," Bayrische Staatsbibliothek, Munich, Cod. Gal. 369, which is a French translation by Laurent de Premierfait of Boccaccio's *De casibus virorum illustrium*. Apparently the miniature was commissioned by Laurens Girard, a royal officer of Charles VII, and was finished 24 November 1458; see Le Comte Paul Durrieu, *Le Boccace de Munich* (Munich, 1909).

[61] For that portrait, see Beaucourt, *Charles VII*, VI (album), or Vale, *Charles VII*, plate 1.

[62] For a description of the winged-stag (*cerf volant*) tapestries and covers for seats and benches sewn with the king's arms which were confiscated by Charles VII from Jacques Coeur in 1451, see the inventory of Jean Dauvet (c. 1400-1471), Michel Mollat, ed., *Les Affaires de Jacques Coeur. Journal du Procureur Dauvet* (Paris, 1953), II, 506. Note that the symbolism of the winged stag with a crown around its neck (royal justice) is similar to that portrayed in the *Entrée* tableau of 1389 (see above, n. 39).

3. Charles VII: Trial of Jean (II), Duke of Alençon, held at Vendôme, 1458.

In the iconographical progression of these three images, the importance of the canopied paraphernalia is instructive. The schematic image of the Artois trial of 1332 placed Philip VI crowned and royally robed on a very bare stage, and the fictional scene (made in the fifteenth century) of Corbechon's presentation of 1372 produced a crowned and sceptred Charles V surrounded by the draped thronal apparatus. But the realistic representation of the Alençon trial of 1458 provided a faithful replica of the uncostumed Charles VII framed by the magnificent canopied apparatus which signified the monarch's sovereignty in a highly ceremonial fashion—grand enough to put the Burgundians on notice. In all of the ceremonial decoration, however, the royal seat itself played no significant role whatever. In this secular symbolic panoply, it was the drapery paraphernalia crowned by the prominent canopy, long an emblem of authority in imperial and ecclesiastical circles, which displayed the monarch as chief judge (*premier justicier*) exercising the royal *dignité* and was named briefly the *lit de justice*.[63]

For a variety of reasons, French kings did not visit the Grand-chambre of the Parlement of Paris after 1414, and such absence remained the royal norm for some decades. Although it is true that the relations of Louis XI (1461-1483) with Parlement were not particularly amicable, his absence from the Grand-chambre cannot be attributed to spite. For almost half a century monarchs had not visited Parlement in the Palais de Justice, and Louis XI personally abhorred ceremony in any form. Hence, his continued neglect of the Royal *Séance* issued from custom and preference.[64] At the same time, the themes of Royal *Entrée* tableaux

[63] According to Schramm, *König von Frankreich*, I, 215-217, and II, 131-133, kings of France sat in various types of chairs or heightened tribunals among peers but had no special throne, not even for the Coronation at Reims; hence in France "a throne ... has no fixed form and no special legal significance." That opinion is borne out by Janos M. Bak, "Medieval Symbology of the State: Percy E. Schramm's Contribution," *Viator*, IV (1973), 33-63. On the use of canopies to signal sovereignty, consult Schramm, *Herrschaftszeichen und Staatssymbolik* (Stuttgart, 1956), III, 722-727; Kantorowicz, "The 'King's Advent' and the Enigmatic Panels in the Doors of Santa Sabina," *Selected Studies* (New York, 1965), pp. 37-75, plate 20, figs. 45 and 46; and Guenée, *Entrées royales*, pp. 13-15. Also consult Giesey, *Royal Funeral Ceremony*, plates 6, 8, and 14, for canopies in Funeral ceremonies where the continuity of the *dignité* was signified.

[64] The king conducted business with Parlement chiefly by letters of instruction and through his chancellor, promulgating legislation which assured tenure of office to *parlementaires* but replacing recalcitrant officers with obedient ones when necessary. Consult Maugis, *Histoire du Parlement*, I, 80-99, and Champion, *Louis XI*, II, 88 and 167-168. Louis XI did attempt to force several members

changed significantly. The *lit de justice* tableaux of 1389 and 1437 had used draped thronal paraphernalia to signify royal justice in an abstract or allegorical form, whereas genealogical tableaux (*tentes* or *pavillons*) from 1476 to 1498 used this paraphernalia to portray specific kings (Pharamond, Charlemagne, Saint Louis, Charles V, and reigning kings Louis XI and Charles VIII) as judges dispensing royal justice.[65] During his Coronation *Entrée* to Reims in May 1484 Charles VIII witnessed the most trenchant of these novel tableaux—the one depicting Pharamond (the first French king) eliciting the Salic Law from four wise men.[66] Then Charles VIII made his post-Coronation *Entrée* to Paris in July 1484 and witnessed a tableau at the Châtelet featuring him (by impersonation) seated in a scene where French justice figured as a chief part of the royal Crown.[67] In this milieu, publicly displaying the king in his judicial role, Charles VIII suddenly convoked a Royal *Séance* in the Grand-chambre of the Parlement of Paris, the first session of its kind in seventy-one years.

THE REVIVAL OF THE ROYAL *Séance* 1484-1526

The accession of Charles VIII (1483-1498) precipitated a crisis in 1483. Before his death Louis XI had designated Anne of Beaujeu (Charles' sister) as regent for the young king. Anne secured that regency despite vigorous opposition from powerful nobles, including Louis, Duke of Orléans (later Louis XII), and in the process both contenders courted Parlement for support.[68] Thus on 20 July 1484 Charles VIII held a Royal *Séance* in the Parlement of Paris, the first since 1413. Although no record remains in the *conseil* registers of Parlement, a note in the *plaidoiries*

---

of the Parlement of Paris to attend a meeting of the Estates at Tours (19 January 1484), but those appointed as deputies never left Paris and so did not attend; Maugis, *Histoire du Parlement*, I, 656.

[65] For the *Entrées* of Louis XI and Charles VIII, consult Guenée, *Entrées royales*, and for a discussion of the constitutional elements of Parisian examples, see Bryant, *French Royal Entry Ceremony*.

[66] The importance of imputing juristic sanction to the royal *dignité* at a Coronation in this manner has been discussed by Giesey, *Juristic Basis of Dynastic Right*, pp. 19-20.

[67] See Guenée, *Entrées royales*, pp. 96-119.

[68] Glasson, *Parlement de Paris*, I, 10-13, and Maugis, *Histoire du Parlement*, I, 100-118.

registers stated that "... our king sat under the *lit de justice* ... ,"[69] a reference no doubt to the canopy and draperies which had just been set up in the Grand-chambre by parlementary ushers much out of practice. Yet, by now the phrase had slipped out of the clerks' vocabulary, because it did not figure in any other accounts of Royal *Séances* for the rest of the century and some decades after. In February 1487 Charles VIII held another *Séance* in the Grand-chambre of Parlement, a treason trial for the accused Louis, Duke of Orléans, and Francis I, Duke of Brittany. The pertinent registers of Parlement mentioned no *lit de justice*,[70] but a contemporary chronicler, Guillaume de Jaligny, stated that "the king held the *lit de justice*."[71] Charles VIII held four more *Séances* in the Grand-chambre before the end of his reign,[72] and then Louis XII (1498-1515), not to be outdone, convoked seven *Séances* in Parlement during his tenure.[73]

During this vigorous revival of Royal *Séances*, the minutes of parlementary clerks mentioned no *lit de justice*, not even in registers for the important legislative sessions of July 1493 and June 1499 in which royal ordinances on justice were promulgated. The *parlementaires* were duly impressed with the revival of Royal *Séances* befitting judicial kingship during these years. Taking advantage of the king's presence, they began

[69] "... Rex sedit sub lecto justiciae ...'; A.N. X1a 4825, fol. 256r (20 July 1484). The session is incorrectly dated as 20 March in A.N. U 2175 (Le Nain), fol. 219v.

[70] A.N. X1a 1495, fols. 102v-109v (19-21 Feb. 1487).

[71] "La Cour de Parlement fust preparée et les sieges faiz pour tenir le lit de justice et au jour de l'adjournment, le Roy tint [son] lit de justice et furent appellez les princes du sang et pairs de France"; B.N. ms. fr. 23285, fol. 29r (Feb. 1487). This account is printed in Godefroy, *Cérémonial françois*, II, 450. Although Jaligny states that there is an account in the registers of Parlement (fol. 31v), the assembly is not recorded there.

[72] Those *Séances* are as follows: (1) A.N. U 2179 (Le Nain), fol. 285v (20 Feb. 1492); (2) A.N. X1a 4835, fols. 140v-153v (5, 7 Feb. 1493); (3) A.N. X1a 1500, fols. 88v-97v (22, 25 Feb. 1493); and (4) A.N. X1a 1500, fols. 260r-265r (8, 9, 11 July 1493).

[73] Those *Séances* are as follows: (1) A.N. X1a 1504, fols. 130v-133v (7 July 1498), incorrectly cited as 5 July in A.N. U 2181 (Le Nain), fols. 378r-386r. In line with the legend, this session is described by Maugis, *Histoire du Parlement*, I, 129, as "the first *Lit de Justice* of Louis XII." (2) A.N. X1a 1504, fols. 319v ff. (13 June 1499); (3) A.N. U 2182 (Le Nain), fols. 382r-389v (5 Dec. 1504); (4) A.N. U 2182 (Le Nain), fols. 390v-400r, and U 2168, fols. 19v-20v (16 Dec. 1504); (5) A.N. U 2182 (Le Nain), fols. 401v-408v, and U 2169, fols. 22r-v (2 Jan. 1505); (6) A.N. U 2168 (Le Nain), fols. 34r-v (12 Nov. 1508); and (7) A.N. X1a 4855, fols. 185v-192v (31 May 1513).

to stress the Court's role as the supreme Court of France by likening the Grand-chambre ("the true tribunal and throne of the king") to the "Senate of Rome" (composed of one hundred officers),[74] and they pointed to documents such as Charles VIII's royal letters of confirmation (1483), which reaffirmed the sovereign jurisdiction of the Parlement of Paris (vis-à-vis foreign pretensions), to support that claim. Later on, historians who looked back and "discovered" *Lit de Justice* assemblies in these very decades referred to these royal letters as proof that such assemblies had been irrevocably located in the Grand-chambre of the Parlement of Paris,[75] but those misconceived allegations arose from false historical conceptions about the medieval *lit de justice*.

At the turn of the sixteenth century Louis XII completely renovated the Grand-chambre of Parlement and replaced the old drapery paraphernalia (the *lit de justice*) with new items. First, the renovation produced a stunning gilded room with finely carved oak ceilings and walls and benches covered with blue velvet and golden fleurs-de-lis.[76] Second, the

[74] "Item et est ladite Cour le vray siège et trône du roy, constituée et ordonée de cent personnes, dont il est le premier et le chef, ad instar du Sénat de Rome . . ."; A.N. X1a 9323, no. 85 (8 July 1489), cited in Maugis, *Histoire du Parlement*, I, 371, n. 1; and in the same vein where comparison of the Parlement to the "Senat du Rome où est son tribunal et trone royal . . ." is made; A.N. X1a 1504, fol. 137r (7 July 1498), a *Séance* which Maugis, *Histoire du Parlement*, I, 120, calls a *Lit de Justice*.

[75] Most surely the document referred to was the following statement of Charles VIII: ". . . la cour de Parlement qui est la cour souveraine et capital de nostre royaume . . . discuter et determiner en souveraine ressort les matieres qui touchant les droit de nous et de la mesme de France. Aussi les causes des peers . . . et autres grant causes . . . et toutes les appelleront qui sont interjettees en icelle et pour punir et corriger tous abbuz faiz soubz couleur de justice·en laquelle nostre cour de Parlement ont toutfois coustume . . ."; A.N. X1a 1491, fols. 2r-4v (20 Sept. 1483). It is produced with errors and omissions by Dupuy, *Traité de la majorité*, p. 562 (misdated as April 1485). Using this evidence for proof, Dupuy alleged that by royal command *Lits de Justice* must be held in the Parlement of Paris; ibid. That allegation was repeated by Le Nain, who thought the letters of command were written in 1475 and 1483, but he provides no documentation; A.N. U 513, p. 343 [fol. 327]. The source of confusion for Dupuy, Le Nain, and others was the seductive fiction of the medieval *Lit de Justice* assembly, well entrenched by the seventeenth century. In this document they both misinterpreted the medieval phrase *couleur de justice* (since in fact *couleur* is barely readable in the register), which denoted justice exercised under false pretences. They thought it read *"lit de justice"* and drew the erroneous conclusions.

[76] Shennan, *Parlement of Paris*, p. 107. The renovation was probably completed

new draperies consisted of a canopy, two large drapes, and five pillows (items similar to those deposited with Parlement by Charles V in 1366) and were embroidered with the emblem of Louis XII, fleurs-de-lis, porcupines, and crowned *LL*'s.[77] In earlier centuries the visual focus had

around 1511 and included the famous painting *Le Retable du Parlement* (now in the Museum of the Louvre [RF. 2065]), which was executed in the mid-fifteenth century. On the provenance of the painting, see Albert Chatelet, "Le Retable du Parlement de Paris," *Art de France* (Paris, 1964), pp. 60-69. In the series of tableaux included here, *Le Retable du Parlement* appears in Figures 6, 7, 10, 14, and 16.

[77] An inventory of Parlement written a half century later describes this drapery apparatus which Francis II ordered removed from Parlement's charge and delivered to Orléans for use at a meeting of the Estates General; A.N. X1a 1596, fols. 43r-43v (29 Nov. 1560): "... a este enjoint a M. Claude Bernyer l'ung des quatre notaires de la Cour de ceans faire description par Inventaire du ciel et parement de siege du Roy suivant la lettre missive dudict Seigneur ... le xxvii de ce mois ... ciel et parement delivrer a P. le Gendre garde des meubles du Roy a Paris pour ... porter a Orleans et se charger du part rapport et qui a este faict suivant ... INVENTAIRE faict par moy Claude Bernyer l'ung des 4 nottaires de la Cour de ceans ... des meubles bailles a P. le Gendre garde des meubles du Roy a Paris qui s'est charge de les faire porter a Orleans pour le fait des estatz qui y doibvent estre tenues et rapporter en d'icelles cour. Une piece de veloux cramoisy violet contenant six les de largeur seme de fleurs de liz enrichia tout a l'entour de porczespicz LL couronnees sur veloux rouge cramoisy servant de partout en laquelle ni a aucun de fauts des fleurs de liz d'or. ITEM une aultre piece de veloux cramoisy violet contenant six les de largeur aussy seme de fleurs de liz d'or enriche de tous costez de porczespicz et LL couronnees sur veloux cramoisy rouge servant de queue en laquelle n'y a aucun de fauts des autres fleurs de liz. ITEM l'un petit ciel de veloux cramoisy violet contenant trois les de largeur seme de fleurs de liz d'or garny de quatre parties assavoir deux desdictes partes garnies de deux costez de fleurs de liz dont l'ung desdict costez est enrichy y de porczespicz et LL couronnees de soye violette et porczespicz d'or des deux costez. L'une desdictes autres partes garnie d'un costez de fleurs de liz de porczespicz et LL couronnees et l'aultre coste de ladict parte enrichy de demy aulne de fleurs de liz seulement frange de soye violette porczespicz d'or d'un coste seulement. La quatorziesme parte simple garnys d'un coste de fleurs de liz porczespicz et LL couronnees frange de soye violette et porczespicz d'or d'un coste en laquelle n'y a de fault des fleurs de liz. ITEM cinq carreaux de veloux cramoisy violet garny d'un coste de fleurs de liz et a chacun d'iceux ung porczespicz et une L couronnee et n'y a faute des fleurs de liz. Tous lesquelles meubles ont este mis dans ung garde robbe servant a deux clefs et baillez audit le Gendre lequel s'en est charger." These draperies were presumably the ones used by Francis I in the *Lit de Justice* assembly, because the command issued by Francis II two days before the inventory was made stated: "We note in Estates General of this kingdom which were held in the times of preceding kings that the tribunal where our prede-

rested upon the draped apparatus (briefly called the *lit de justice*) which decorated the Grand-chambre. Now at the turn of the sixteenth century that focus shifted to the gilded Grand-chambre itself swathed in blue velvet and golden fleurs-de-lis, that is, the larger diamond-shaped spatial complex which contained the draperies.

Following his two predecessors Francis I (1515-1547) held six Royal *Séances* in the Grand-chambre of Parlement for a variety of purposes, and the registers simply noted that the king was present in the Court. On 14 March 1515 Francis I held an honorary *Séance*, the first visit to Parlement following the post-Coronation *Entrée* to Paris (15 February), and he exhorted the Court that day to administer royal justice properly;[78] two weeks later, on 29 March, he attended a judicial pleading conducted in the Court.[79] Then, in the wake of a quarrel with Parlement over unregistered royal decrees, the king held a *Séance* on 5 February 1517 to compel the *parlementaires* to register the Concordat of Bologna swiftly, a remarkably unsuccessful ploy considering that the Court took another year to follow through.[80] Here it is important to note that Francis I tried to press Parlement to register the Concordat not at a *Lit de Justice* assembly, as historians contend, but at a Royal *Séance*. That procedure should induce early on some skepticism about the supposed link between the *Lit de Justice* assembly and the forced registration of royal legislation in the sixteenth century.[81] Francis I held two *Séances* in the Grand-chambre on 15 February 1522 and 30 June 1523, preliminary judicial hearings on indictments against Charles of Austria (the new emperor Charles V), vassal of the French king as Count of Flanders and Artois, for dereliction.[82] Finally, the king held a *Séance* on 8-9 March 1524, a

cessors have been seated has been decorated with a furnishing of blue velvet sewn with fleurs-de-lis which ordinarily served in our Court of Parlement when we held our *Lit de Justice* [assembly] there"; A.N. X1a 1596, fols. 40r-41r (27 Nov. 1560).

[78] A.N. X1a 1518, fols. 96r-100v (14 Mar. 1515). The records for these six *Séances* state that "... le Roy est venu en sa cour ... ," or describe "... le Roy seant en sa cour...."

[79] A.N. X1a 4858, fols. 326v-332v (29 Mar. 1515).

[80] A.N. X1a 1519, fols. 52v-56r (5 Feb. 1522). The Concordat was finally registered on 22 March 1518; Maugis, *Histoire du Parlement*, I, 139; Shennan, *Parlement of Paris*, pp. 192-196.

[81] In making the argument for "absolute monarchy" at this early date, Knecht, *Francis I and Absolute Monarchy*, p. 14, calls this *Séance* a *Lit de Justice*.

[82] A.N. X1a 1524, fols. 95r-97r (15 Feb. 1522); and X1a 1525, fols. 275v-277r (30 June 1523).

preliminary hearing on charges against Charles (II), Duke of Bourbon, for the crime of treason (*lèse-majesté*), and during that session he denied the primacy of the Parisian Parlement in France by negating its likeness to the Senate in Rome.[83]

ALTHOUGH historians with different preconceptions about the ancient constitution later interpreted the phrase *lit de justice* as the title of an ancient constitutional assembly, the name actually emerged in circumstances far more mundane and signified something quite different. The phrase *lit de justice* was connected with Royal *Séances* in the vocabulary of the late middle ages only for a few decades, between 1387 and 1413; it barely survived in chronicle lore thereafter, and it was never incorporated into a language of public discourse in those centuries. Far from indicating an ancient constitutional assembly, as maintained later by constitutional antiquarians, the rare phrase *lit de justice* simply signified the draped apparatus which defined royal space when the king sat as chief judge during *Séances* in Parlement, and the phrase just briefly signaled parlementary jurisidiction. Thus it is the trivial nature of that phrase in the fourteenth, fifteenth, and early decades of the sixteenth centuries, as opposed to the constitutional importance imposed upon it later, which strikes an ironical chord. The Royal *Séance* was a parlementary session characteristic of the judicial monarchy in an era when judicial and legislative functions, molded together under the rubric of "royal justice," were not clearly delineated. By joining king and Parlement on occasion as a body, *vivant et animé*, in the Grand-chambre, the *Séance* symbolized French justice. In the early sixteenth century, however, the combined pressures of renaissance ceremonial splendor, Franco-imperial rivalry, and antiquarian visions brought into being the *Lit de Justice* assembly, an extraordinary public forum which was associated with a different constitutional ideology.

[83] A.N. X1a 1526, fols. 130r-131v (8-9 Mar. 1524), a *Séance* which Doucet, *Étude sur le gouvernement de François Ier*, I, 304-317, calls a *Lit de Justice*.

II

THE JURISTIC MONARCHY IN FRENCH CONSTITUTIONAL IDEOLOGY: THE CEREMONIAL *LIT DE JUSTICE* ASSEMBLIES OF 1527

> ... he could act on his own recognizance in this matter,
> [but] he did not wish to proceed without first revealing it
> to his subjects. For that purpose he decided to assemble
> them not in the form of Estates, but by way of this forum
> which is the *Lit de Justice* [assembly].   *Francis I (1527)*

CONTRARY TO historical suppositions about its ancient origins, the *Lit de Justice* assembly first appeared in the early sixteenth century, not in the fourteenth century, and was clearly distinguished on constitutional grounds from the Royal *Séance*, the usual type of parlementary session held in the Grand-chambre of Parlement and attended by the king. Likewise, contrary to historical opinion casting the *Lit de Justice* assembly primarily as a political tool used against parlementary remonstrances,[1] it was convoked in the sixteenth century mainly to treat specific matters related to Public Law. It is the purpose of the next few chapters to redress the historiographical balance by pointing out the functional distinction made between *Lit de Justice* assemblies and Royal *Séances* in the sixteenth century and by focusing upon the specific constitutional issues that gave rise to the *Lits de Justice*. The stance thus adopted is not meant to suggest that the political contests associated with *Lit de Justice* assemblies and also with Royal *Séances* in that era were unimportant, but it aims at shifting the weight of historical interpretation of the *Lit de Justice* away

[1] For instance, discussing the events of 1515-1518 (before the *Lit de Justice* assembly had made its appearance), Shennan, *Parlement of Paris*, p. 194, notes that the legal forms used to negate Parlement's judgments, according to Claude de Seyssel, were *lettres de jussion* or *Lits de Justice*. But in fact Seyssel, *La Monarchie de France*, ed. Jacques Poujol (Paris, 1961), did not speak of a *Lit de Justice* in those terms. In addition, Knecht, *Francis I and Absolute Monarchy*, pp. 9 and 14, considers the *Lit de Justice* assembly (which is not distinguished from the Royal *Séances* which he is discussing) as an absolutist weapon and extends the legend by dubbing the Royal *Séance* of 5 February 1517 a *Lit de Justice*.

from the political arena in order to illuminate the peculiar origins and uneven development of the assembly as a constitutional forum.

At the very outset of the investigation the picture is confused by two simultaneous but incongruent strands of thought regarding the *Lit de Justice* which were operative during the sixteenth century: a growing adherence to the historical fiction about the antiquity of the assembly together with a lack of consensus regarding its essential nature. At the close of that century, for instance, Bernard de La Roche-Flavin, a Toulousan antiquarian and *parlementaire*, copied excerpts taken from the registers of Parlement for the *Lit de Justice* assembly of July 1527 out of a treatise written decades earlier by a clerk of the Parlement of Paris, Jean du Tillet. Impressed by the magnificient ceremonial procedure and the vast array of attendants, La Roche-Flavin declared that this assembly should "serve as an example and as a formulary for similar occasions," because it represents the greatest and most solemn *Lit de Justice* assembly ever held.[2] That comment was laced with a subtle contradiction. La Roche-Flavin assumed that the *Lit de Justice* of July 1527 was part of an established historical tradition and discussed that tradition at length; yet at the same time he suggested that standards should be set for the ceremony performed in future *Lits de Justice* and alluded to current confusion about procedure in such assemblies. This antithetical characterization of the *Lit de Justice* as a historical French practice, but an unregulated procedure, attests to the interest in the assembly and the curiosity about its origins which prevailed in the late sixteenth century.

Actually the first three *Lit de Justice* assemblies in French history were convoked within a decade by Francis I, two in 1527, a third in 1537. The issues treated in all of them involved, directly or indirectly, a conflict between the French king and the Holy Roman Emperor. Following the Coronation of Charles, Duke of Burgundy (1500-1558), as Charles I, King of Spain in 1516, the new Spanish king outmaneuvered his French competitor Francis I in a bid for the imperial office and was elected as emperor in 1519. For over a quarter of a century afterward Emperor Charles V and King Francis I were locked in a bitter contest set amidst the general turmoil afflicting almost all of western Europe. During the early rounds of this contest, French interests suffered a series of setbacks: the treasonous defection of Charles (II), Duke of Bourbon, greatest of

---

[2] Bernard de La Roche-Flavin, *Treze livres des Parlemens de France* (Bordeaux, 1617), VII, ii, 384, conflates all descriptive elements for the three sessions (24, 26, and 27 July 1527) and identifies Jean du Tillet as his source. In this volume there is an error in pagination, skipping from 202 to 234.

the French nobles, from French to imperial ranks in 1523; the humiliating capture of Francis I at Pavia in 1525 and his long imprisonment in Spain; and finally the reluctant decision of Francis I to sign the Treaty of Madrid in 1526, a document drawn by an emperor intent upon securing French territory and signed by a French king destined to renege on its provisions after securing his own release.[3]

The ascendance of the emperor in this political rivalry spurred the newly freed French king to publicize his own authority and grandeur, because the defection of the Duke of Bourbon, the terms of the Treaty of Madrid, and the question regarding the suzerainty of emperor or king all touched French Public Law. This international conflict thus provided some impetus for the convocation of a trio of extraordinary assemblies in the Parlement of Paris, attended by the king and designated for the first time in French history as *Lit de Justice* assemblies. There were other considerations as well. Most notably, antiquarians had begun to search within archival repositories, especially the registers of Parlement, for the historical foundations of the French constitution and to reconstruct a history of French institutions. Thus, the timely coalescence of severe international crises and incipient constitutional antiquarianism brought forth the first three *Lit de Justice* assemblies in French history in 1527 and 1537 and fired the very early debates about the French constitution.

In weighing the evidence pertaining to this trio of *Lit de Justice* assemblies, one is struck at once by their extraordinary nature. On all three occasions the king sat magnificently enthroned in the Parlement of Paris and acted as a legislator, guardian of the French constitution. Conducting treason trials or heading an advisory body, he pronounced judgments on questions of serious constitutional import, that is, matters which touched the Public Law of the French monarchy.[4] Futhermore, unlike the few Royal *Séances* of the fourteenth and fifteenth centuries which were associated with the *lit de justice* (drapery paraphernalia), each of these first three sixteenth-century sessions was designated officially as a *Lit de Justice* (assembly) in the registers of Parlement by two chief clerks of Court, Séraphin du Tillet and Jean du Tillet. Finally, the extraordinary nature of these first three *Lits de Justice* was underscored

---

[3] For a good general account, see Knecht, *Francis I*, chaps. 10-14.

[4] Here the terms "French Public Law," "Public Law of the French monarchy," or "ancient constitution," are used rather than "Fundamental Law," a narrow term peculiar to the seventeenth century, or "Constitutional Law," suggesting more cohesion of the French constitution than was enjoyed in early modern times.

from the late 1520's through the 1550's by the disagreement between royal advisers who cast them in a special category and *parlementaires* who tried to keep them within the bounds of the traditional Royal *Séance* in Parlement. These suppositions depart in great measure from those usually set forth regarding the *Lit de Justice* in French history. Hence it is necessary in this chapter and the next to reconstruct in some detail the convocation of the first three *Lits de Justice*: first, to establish the constitutional nexus of their origin and note their official designation as *Lit de Justice* assemblies; second, to point out the innovative ritual and the peculiar mode of discourse elicited there; and third, to discuss the growing tension surrounding the appearance and differentiation of *Lit de Justice* assemblies from ordinary Royal *Séances* held in the Parlement of Paris.

The *Lit de Justice* Assembly of July 1527

The first *Lit de Justice* assembly was convoked by Francis I in the Grand-chambre of the Parlement of Paris and remained in session for three days, 24, 26, and 27 July 1527.[5] It was convened for the trial of a peer of France accused of the crime of treason, *lèse-majesté*. The case involved the maintenance of the royal domain, so it fell under the Law of In-alienability, the Public Law of the French monarchy. In this case one of the most powerful of the French nobles, Charles (II), Duke of Bourbon, was accused of treason because of his defection from French ranks in 1522 to serve imperial forces. Since Bourbon had been killed in May 1527 during the sack of Rome, the trial was held posthumously.[6] Ac-

---

[5] A.N. X1a 1530, fols. 349r-359r (24 July 1527), fols. 359r-360v (26 July), and fols. 361r-364v (27 July). Jean du Tillet, *Recueil des grands*, pp. 81-86, contains extracts of the three sessions; for the full citation on Du Tillet's antiquarian compendium, see below, Chap. IV, n. 3. Godefroy, *Cérémonial françois* [Reg. Parl.], II, 463-474, gives part of the civil register for 24 July but extracts of criminal registers for 26 and 27 July (written by the pleadings clerk, Nicolas Malon, who did not entitle the session a *Lit de Justice*). In a confusing manner the Godefroys appended two paragraphs from the civil register of 27 July to their account for that day, one which reiterates that the king was "holding his *Lit de Justice*"; ibid., 476-477.

[6] A preliminary hearing against Bourbon was held on 8 and 9 March 1524, "le Roy presidant en icelle," from which *arrêts* of default were issued; A.N. X1a 1526, fols. 130r-131v. Extracts from the hearing appear in Du Tillet, *Recueil des grands*, p. 81, and Godefroy, *Cérémonial françois* [Reg. Parl.], II, 455-462. No verdict on Bourbon's culpability for *lèse-majesté* was reached in this *Séance*; see

cording to some, French kings were obliged to sit as chief judge in a Court of peers if the fortunes of one was at stake; kings had done so in medieval *Séances* held in the Louvre (1332), the Grand-chambre of the Palais de Justice (1378, 1387, 1487), and outside Paris at Vendôme (1458). Yet this trial of July 1527 was the first of the lot adjudged officially as a *Lit de Justice* assembly.

Francis I, enthroned in a magnificent setting in the Grand-chambre of the Parlement of Paris, was attended by an impressive body of persons. The scene was described in the registers of Parlement by the chief clerk (*greffier civil*) of Parlement, Séraphin du Tillet, as follows:

> Holding his *Lit de Justice* [assembly] in the parquet of Parlement, the king was in his tribunal and royal throne [which was] elevated by seven steps and covered with blue velvet cloth embroidered with golden fleurs-de-lis [with] a canopy of the same material above; and there were four large pillows of the same [material] around and behind the said lord and under his feet.[7]

Running at angles to the right and left of the throne there were elevated tiers of seats, and below them in the parquet, or floor of the Grand-chambre inside the railing, there were other benches and seats which filled the inner perimeters of the parquet. At the right hand of the king in the high seats were two lay peers and five other nobles; at the left in the high seats were three ecclesiastical peers and one archbishop. To the right in the lower rows of the high seats were nine *maîtres des requêtes* of the Hôtel du Roi; to the left three presidents of Parlement. Reclining on the steps leading down from the throne were three royal officers, the grand chamberlain, the first chamberlain, and the provost of Paris holding a white baton. Kneeling in the parquet at the bottom of the seven-

---

Doucet, *Étude sur le gouvernement de François Ier* (Paris, 1921), I, 304-317. Note that Doucet mistakenly cites the *Séance* of 9 March as a *Lit de Justice* assembly, an error repeated by Knecht, *Francis I*, p. 157.

[7] "Le Roy estoit en son siege et trosne royal ou parquet de parlement tenant son Lict de Justice pour monter auquel y avoit sept degrez couverts d'un tapis de veloux bleu seme de fleurs de liz d'or en facon de broderie et au dessus ung ciel de mesmes. Et a l'entour derriere ledit seigneur et soubz ses pieds y avoit quatre grant carraulx de mesme"; A.N. X1a 1530, fol. 349v (24 July 1527), fol. 359r (26 July), and fol. 361r (27 July), all substantially the same. Note that the word *parquet* refers to the floor of the Grand-chambre inside the railings, not to the seat of the king as in earlier times; compare its use in ibid., fol. 349v, with earlier usage adduced by Charles Du Fresne Du Cange, *Glossarium mediae et infimae latinitatis* (Paris, 1883).

step dais were two ushers of the Chambre du Roi, each holding a staff. And at the foot of the throne was the chancellor in a special chair decorated with blue velvet cloth embroidered with fleurs-de-lis like that covering the royal dais and canopy.[8]

In the parquet below were benches and seats for seventy-five councillors of Parlement. The chief clerk of Parlement was at his desk, along with two other clerks and two notaries in front of the presidents and councillors in the upper part of the parquet. Seated behind the councillors in the lower part of the parquet were numerous gentlemen of the Chambre du Roi, some *maîtres* and other gentlemen of the Hôtel du Roi. Finally, sitting on small stools behind them were two knights and one captain of the French royal bodyguard, and guarding the door of the Grand-chambre, some lieutenants of the French royal bodyguard. As this large entourage (around one hundred and twenty people) awaited the arrival of the king, one of the ecclesiastical peers took the oath of a peer of France before the Parlement of Paris in order to exercise the office during the trial. The session opened on the morning of 24 July when Francis I was enthroned under the canopy upon the seven-step dais "holding his *Lit de Justice* [assembly]." Some time between the arrival of the king and the opening of the assembly, the *parlementaires* requested permission to address the king, because Chancellor Antoine Duprat conferred aside with Francis I and then allowed the Court that privilege. At their places the presidents, councillors, and other officers of Parlement knelt as a body before the king, and Francis I hastily ordered them to rise for the first president's address.[9]

President Charles Guillart delivered a learned humanist oration to the assembled group. Comparing French governance to admirable ancient polities and admonishing French kings to preserve the ancient constitution, he spelled out some lessons for contemporaries to heed. He adduced historical examples from biblical, Greek, and Roman sources to discuss the general nature of public office in ancient times. Then he invoked special maxims from the language of medieval jurists and philosophers to discuss the French royal *dignité* and its relation to the constitution. Guillart described the French body politic, head and members, as a *mystical body* (*corps mystique, soit en chef ou membres*) and the king in his royal *dignité* (under the canopy) as the *living and animate law* (*droit vivant et animé*), naturally above the law but bound by reason to

[8] A.N. X1a 1530, fols. 349r-359r (24 July 1527).
[9] Ibid.

observe it, and he stated that "... all law (*droit*), natural, divine, canon, and civil," obliges those who exercise the royal office to render justice and equity to subjects. Defining the king as the *tutor*, or administrator, of the kingdom (*chose publique*), the president located the Parlement of Paris in this body politic, or system of justice, as the supreme Court and condemned justice made under false pretences (*couleur de justice*) in the Grand Conseil. Guillart told the king,

> The true seat of your throne is this place [the Grand-chambre].... Your Court [the Parlement of Paris] has always been the most reputed and sovereign of France.... Just as in the world there is but one sun, ... so also in France there is but one sovereign justice [Parlement of Paris].[10]

Having portrayed king and Parlement through sun imagery as unique consorts in governance and the Grand-chambre as the royal throne, the president turned to French institutional history to support his stand.

According to President Guillart the ancient "parlement" was originally a public assembly similar to the Estates. It was an itinerant body composed of judges from different parts of the kingdom and convoked at the king's pleasure two or three times a year to travel about the kingdom dispensing royal justice. However, due to the difficulties of convoking such a diverse body and the expenses involved, Philip IV (1285-1314) in concert with the "estates" decreed that one Parlement would be located permanently in Paris and convoked regularly thereafter. This shift of procedure whereby the "Court of the Parlement of France" became a stationary body composed of appointed members, rather than an itinerant body, created a new institution, the Parlement of Paris, which thenceforth operated according to parlementary procedure, not royal whim, and served as the supreme Court of France. For over a century this new institution functioned smoothly until Louis XI (1461-1483) rudely contravened tradition by establishing the Grand Conseil and arbitrarily removing cases out of Parlement's proper jurisdiction and into the hands of that Council. Fortunately, Charles VIII (1483-1498) during the Estates at Tours (February 1484) curtailed such irregular practices, and Louis XII (1498-1515) concurred by steadfastly observing the institutionalized

---

[10] For Charles Guillart's speech, A.N. X1a 1530, fols. 350v-357v (27 July 1527); printed with some errors in Godefroy, *Cérémonial françois* [Reg. Parl.], II, 465-474. He drew the notion of *tutorship* from Cicero, *Offices*, I, rather than from the famous Roman Law source, *Digest* 4, 6, 22, 2. Guillart became first president of Parlement in 1508; Maugis, *Histoire du Parlement*, III, 115.

procedure of the Parlement of Paris countenanced by French tradition.[11] This review of French institutional history accomplished, Guillart turned to contemporary practices.

The earlier didactic tone of his message changed into one of passionate indictment. With considerable bitterness, President Guillart cited the impropriety, even illegality, of royal orders which tampered with parlementary procedure, particularly procedure regarding the Court's composition and jurisdiction, and he set forth grievances, or remonstrances, against specific royal policies in effect: the creation and sale of judicial offices in the Court and the transfer of judicial cases from the Parlement of Paris to the Grand Conseil. Concluding his address with rhetorical flourishes flattering to Francis I, the president had barely resumed his place when the king abruptly arose from his seat under the canopy, walked down the seven steps of the dais, and stalked out of the Grand-chambre followed soon after by the royal retinue.[12]

Deserted in this precipitous manner, the *parlementaires* considered the assembly prorogued, or even adjourned, and they too eventually vacated the Grand-chambre. In the meantime Francis I went to the Salle Verte, another chamber in the Palais de Justice, and conferred there with members of his Council (Conseil Étroit) until around noon. Just after noontime the chief clerk of Parlement, Séraphin du Tillet, was informed by the provost of Paris, Jean de La Barre, that the king ordered him to assemble the presidents and councillors of Parlement at two o'clock in the Grand-chambre. Du Tillet sent the appropriate summons to the *parlementaires*, but the provost upon returning at three o'clock to the Grand-chambre found three presidents but only twelve or fifteen councillors present. The absent councillors were summoned again, and by four o'clock more councillors augmented the group. The provost presented this contingent of *parlementaires* royal orders to appear before the king, and they went straightaway to the Salle Verte, where the king was holding his Council. With an angry gesture Francis I brought forth a royal edict which prohibited Parlement from interfering in affairs of state and commanded on the spot that the edict be read and registered forthwith in the Conseil Étroit, the Courts of Parlement, and the Grand Conseil. At the close of the reading the *parlementaires* attempted to confer together in order to make a response, or remonstrance, to the king, but Francis refused to countenance such a move and hurriedly left the room

[11] A.N. X1a 1530, fols. 350v-357v (27 July 1527).

[12] A.N. X1a 1530, fols. 354v-357v (24 July 1527). Details of the king's departure are not recorded.

accompanied by his Council. Rebuffed in such a brusque manner, the *parlementaires* returned alone to the Grand-chambre, and the registers of Parlement report that "nothing else was done" in that rump session, although in fact the clerk did write down the text of the royal edict in the registers.[13] Prorogued by the king's defection on the morning of 24 July, the *Lit de Justice* assembly was not convened again for two more days. In the intervening time tempers cooled. During the dawn hours of 26 July, just preceding reconvention of the *Lit de Justice*, Francis I reinstated several *parlementaires* who had been suspended from office by royal order in 1526. The former black sheep, thus exonerated, rejoined the fold to await the arrival of the king in the Grand-chambre. The next session began on that conciliatory note.[14]

The second session of the *Lit de Justice* opened on 26 July. Two records of that assembly survive. One was made by the chief clerk Séraphin du Tillet, who recorded the assembly as a *Lit de Justice*, the other by a criminal clerk, Nicolas Malon, who treated it as a Royal *Séance*.[15] Considerable confusion attended the opening as the king altered the composition of the assembly. Three lords joined the nobles and peers in the elevated rows of seats to his right, and the two royal ushers stationed at the foot of the dais were requested to leave after their presence at the trial was declared improper. The nine *maîtres des requêtes* of the Hôtel du Roi (in lower seats to the right of the king) were placed to the left, and their seats were taken by nine royal bailiffs and seneschals, two of whom had been seated on stools behind parlementary councillors in the lower end of the Grand-chambre. Francis I insisted that these nine officers must assist in the judgment of Bourbon because they could

[13] A.N. X1a 1530, fols. 358r-359r (24 July 1527). François-André Isambert et al., eds., *Recueil général des anciennes lois françaises depuis l'an 420 jusqu'à la révolution de 1789* (1821-1833), XII, 279-280, uses registers to publish the edict but changes the wording of the text and omits passages.

[14] A.N. X1a 1530, fols. 359r-359v (26 July 1527). First President Charles Guillart had requested their reinstatement in his speech on 24 July. The pardoned *parlementaires* were Christophe Hennequin, councillor in 1504, François Disque, councillor in 1507, Nicole Le Coq, councillor in 1515, and M. François Roger, *procureur général*; for dates of office, Maugis, *Histoire du Parlement*, III, 140, 143, 159. The *parlementaires* had been suspended from office since 1526 for their part in Parlement's quarrel with the queen regent Louise of Savoy and Chancellor Antoine Duprat. For details of the political contest, see Shennan, *Parlement of Paris*, pp. 198-200, and Knecht, *Francis I*, chaps. 12 and 13.

[15] A.N. X1a 1530, fols. 359r-360v (26 July 1527), written by Du Tillet; and Godefroy, *Cérémonial françois* [Reg. Parl.], II, 474-476, Malon's account.

provide witness of the alleged transgressions. He admitted that none of them had ever been part of the official body of the Court but assured the *parlementaires* that the presence of those officers in the *Lit de Justice* would not constitute a precedent for the future. Finally, a host of other royal retainers joined the enormous crowd already seated, and some more archers of the king's guards joined the lieutenants already stationed at the doors of the Grand-chambre accompanied now by the provost of the Hôtel du Roi.[16] If a rough count was taken of attendants finally ensconced in the *Lit de Justice* assembly of 26 July, the number of participants would have risen from around one hundred and twenty to well over one hundred and fifty, maybe even two hundred, a huge parlementary assembly by contemporary standards.

Since Francis I had prorogued the *Lit de Justice* on 24 July right on the heels of President Guillart's speech, the treason trial did not take place until this second session, 26 July, when the Court deliberated on the charges and rendered a verdict finding Charles of Bourbon guilty of the "crimes of felony, rebellion, and *lèse-majesté*." Reenacting an altered version of the judicial procedure used at medieval trials of peers, the Court summoned the defendant publicly in the following manner. The first usher of Parlement called aloud at the *barre du parlement* (the bar enclosing the parquet of the Grand-chambre), the *table de marbre* (the marble table in the Grande Salle), and the *pierre de marbre* (the marble staircase of the Grande Salle) for Charles of Bourbon (or his representative) to appear before the Court for judgment and thereafter reported back to the assembly in the Grand-chambre that neither Bourbon (nor his representative) had responded. On that negative note the case rested.[17]

The third and final session of the *Lit de Justice* was convened on 27 July to pronounce publicly the official *arrêt* issued against Bourbon.[18] Once again confusion reigned as the composition of the assembly was altered and ceremonial innovations were introduced. On this day the three presidents of Parlement were vested in red robes for the pronouncement of the *arrêt* and sat as before to the left of the king below the ecclesiastical peers, while the chancellor sat alone at the foot of the royal dais in a chair decorated with cloth material matching that of the throne and dais. The ushers of the Chambre du Roi were excluded from the assembly, as on the day before, but to this session there were added

[16] A.N. X1a 1530, fols. 359r-360v (26 July 1527).

[17] Ibid. Although Bourbon was deceased, his legal representatives could have appeared.

[18] Ibid., fols. 361r-364v (27 July 1527).

two ambassadors, who sat in the lower rows of elevated seats to the right of the king (where the nine bailiffs and seneschals had been the day before) and one archbishop and two bishops, who sat in the same places to the left. The provost of Paris, still holding a white baton, had left the lower steps of the throne and occupied instead a seat guarding the entry of the parquet inside the Grand-chambre. Some marshals of France were added to benches in the rear of the lower portion of the parquet, and the bailiffs and seneschals were moved to this same area.[19]

Just before Francis I's arrival a captain of the French guards brought an order from him specifying that all princes, ambassadors, and other lords present would assist at the public reading of the *arrêt* despite the fact that they were neither peers of France nor official members of the body of the Court, a dispensation which was accorded for that act only and incurred no precedent. Francis I arrived, sat under the canopy in the throne, and opened the *Lit de Justice* assembly. Then and there he announced that there were not enough lay peers present and named a prince of the blood as a peer of France, expressly stipulating that the new peer would act in that capacity only at the reading of this particular *arrêt* and that the appointment set no precedent. The new lay peer then moved to join the other two peers in the elevated seats to the right of the king. Finally, the doors of the Grand-chambre were opened for public pronouncement of the *arrêt* against Bourbon, and a crowd of people, subjects of Francis I and foreign visitors, crowded into the room between the door and the bar of the parquet to witness the sentencing. When this session was underway, according to the registers of Du Tillet, the king was "holding his *Lit de Justice*" and the Court was "presided over by the king with all chambers assembled and graced with a sufficient number of peers." The sentence against Bourbon was pronounced publicly: from the parquet of the Grand-chambre first and from the entry of the parquet after, Chancellor Duprat and the criminal clerk Malon, respectively, read the *arrêt* issued against "Monsieur Bourbon" for "felony, rebellion, and *lèse-majesté*," which ordered among other things that all domainal property (*biens feodaux*) formerly held by Bourbon reverted summarily to the Crown of France. Following public pronouncement of the *arrèt*, the *Lit de Justice* assembly of July 1527 was adjourned.[20]

ONCE THE SOURCES for the assembly of 24, 26, and 27 July 1527 are reviewed, keeping in mind that it was the first *Lit de Justice* ever con-

[19] Ibid.

[20] Ibid. The *arrêt* against Bourbon is published in Godefroy, *Cérémonial français*, II, 477-478, and Isambert, *Recueil général des anciennes lois*, XII, 280-282.

vened, suspicions about its extraordinary nature are confirmed. Writing in the registers of Parlement, the chief clerk, Séraphin du Tillet, designated the assembly itself as a *"Lit de Justice,"* for he recorded that Francis I was "holding his *Lit de Justice*" and described throne, canopy, and draperies as entities separate from the *Lit de Justice* assembly. For the first time, then, the title *Lit de Justice* signified a special assembly dissociated from the drapery apparatus that the name *lit de justice* had signaled two centuries earlier. Alongside this semantic shift of title, procedural in tone, the ritual of the *Lit de Justice* cast the assembly as a special genre of parlementary session wherein the king presided as legislator, guardian of the French constitution, in contrast to Royal *Séances* wherein the king acted as chief judge. Finally, the whole purpose of convoking a *Lit de Justice* assembly, as opposed to a Royal *Séance*, was to separate issues of Public Law (or constitutional law) from ordinary judicial business, as befit the ideology of juristic monarchy. This *mentalité*, which produced the grounds for distinguishing the *Lit de Justice* (as a constitutional forum) from the Royal *Séance* (as an honorary session), was formed by constitutional and historical suppositions which were not shared by all. Consequently, a mounting crescendo of concern among the *parlementaires*, who did not subscribe to the new view, can be detected throughout the proceedings.

Parlement was alarmed by the ceremonial ritual, which combined both tradition and innovation. In terms of ceremonial configuration (archaeology, seating, habits), the setting was certainly astounding. There in the Grand-chambre, which had been transformed by Louis XII from a room waxed gray with time into a brilliant site of blue and gold, the parquet was arranged in the diamond shape which featured the king under the canopy at the top focal point, the same archaeological arrangement observed in the iconography of earlier Royal *Séances* held in the Louvre, the Grand-chambre, and the Château of Vendôme. There are two early engravings which depict Francis I in parlementary poses, but they present visual images which are historically and iconographically misleading. One shows the king crowned, sceptred, and enthroned under a canopy in a Royal *Séance* of 1515 purportedly held in the Parlement of Toulouse (Figure 4).[21] The other shows a simpler version of the same type of scene with a king flanked by advisers, but no location or date is

---

[21] The engraving (anonymous) in Figure 4 served as a frontispiece in Nicolas Bertrand, *Opus de Tholosanorum gestis ab urbe condita* (Toulouse, 1515), and depicts Francis I confirming offices in the Parlement of Toulouse at a session supposedly held in 1515. The artist added the regalia here and in Figure 5, as in the earlier examples (Figures 1 and 2).

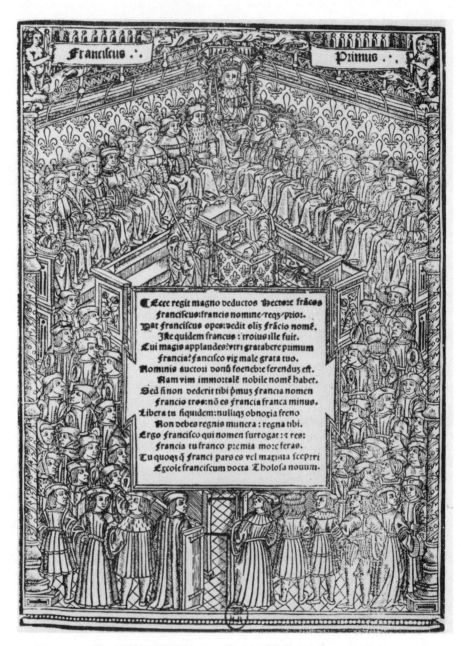

4. Francis I: Confirming offices in the Parlement of Toulouse, 1515.

specified (Figure 5).[22] There is no evidence that Francis I used the new drapery paraphernalia (designed for Louis XII) in his earlier Royal *Séances* held between 1515 and 1524,[23] but it is certain that those furnishings (canopy, five pillows, two large drapes; all embroidered with fleurs-de-lis, porcupines, and crowned *LL*'s) were requisitioned for this *Lit de Justice* of July 1527. Francis I was enthroned more ostentatiously than ever before, because that luxurious drapery paraphernalia harbored the king on an inordinately high dais elevated above the rest of the parquet by seven steps and designated for the first time in registers of Parlement as a "royal throne."[24] This reference to a "royal throne" where the king sat in the Grand-chambre of the Palais de Justice is unusual.[25] Although a "throne" was mentioned in parlementary circles in the late fifteenth century, the allusion was metaphorical, signaling not the royal seat itself but the whole Grand-chambre or larger spatial complex joining king and Parlement. The metaphor appeared in a parlementary remonstrance prepared for Charles VIII in 1489 which described Parlement as the "true tribunal and throne of the king," likening it to the one-hundred-member Roman Senate of ancient times, and the same type of metaphor was repeated in 1498.[26]

In contrast to this early parlementary vision of king and Parlement in consort, the high dais used in 1527 effectively isolated the royal throne

[22] The engraving (anonymous) in Figure 5 appears in Claude de Seyssel, *La Grant monarchie de France* (Paris, 1519), B. Arsenal.

[23] For those sources, see above, Chap. I, nn. 78-83.

[24] The whole question of the transmission of lavish ceremonial practices in European courts from the fifteenth through the seventeenth centuries needs to be studied. In the later fifteenth century the Burgundians, spurred by the Franco-Burgundian rivalry of that age, raised the duke's dais by six steps to underscore ducal grandeur. The Franco-imperial rivalry of the sixteenth century surely influenced this seven-step innovation. Antiquarians were interested in ceremonial practices, particularly enthronement, and cited scriptural and historical examples of rulers elevated on platforms raised by six steps, as the biblical king Solomon and the Roman emperor Aurelian; consult for example, Louis d'Orléans, *Les Ouvertures des Parlements faictes par les roys de France, tenant leur Lict de Justice* (Lyon, 1620; first ed., Paris, 1607), chap. XIX, pp. 237-248, and La Roche-Flavin, *Treze livres des Parlemens*, IV, v-viii, 284.

[25] Often before 1500 and frequently after, the word "throne" signified the heavens or the firmament and designated the seat of God or the angels, Old Testament kings or popes, a theological or ecclesiastical context; consult Godefroy, *Dictionnaire*, VIII, and the *Complément*, IX; Littré, *Dictionnaire*; and Huguet, *Dictionnaire de la langue française du seizième siècle*, VII.

[26] For those metaphors, see above, Chap. I, n. 74, quoting *parlementaires* in 1489 and 1498.

5. The king in majesty.

and, by association, the king from the body at large, producing an image of the French royal *dignité* in the exercise of sovereignty more akin to papal or imperial office. One cannot be sure whence this highly elevated thronal improvisation derived: from antiquarian imagination, or from ecclesiastical sources, or even from Francis I's observation of Spanish ceremony during his captivity several years before. But its construction certainly reflected a royal determination to salvage French political face and fortune amidst mounting international pressures. One step in that direction was to invest the *Lit de Justice* assembly with the grandeur appropriate for a French constitutional forum.

In terms of ceremonial configuration the seating plan and the habits worn also introduced unforeseen novelties. Francis I presided over an inordinately large group that day. Both the elevated seats and those in the parquet overflowed with royal retainers (princes and lords, ambassadors, royal officers and councillors, Royal Household officials, bailiffs and seneschals, and a host of visiting dignitaries) who ordinarily would not have been allowed to sit in Parlement's Grand-chambre in an advisory capacity, let alone exercise the privileges accorded some of them by the king in this *Lit de Justice*. Equally disturbing was the nuance regarding habits. The king's chancellor Antoine Duprat, detested by the *parlementaires* because of earlier disagreements,[27] was favored over the presidents during the public reading of the *arrêt* against Bourbon on 27 July. On that day the presidents of Parlement were arrayed in ceremonial red robes, a habit donned since the fourteenth century for public ceremonies such as Royal Funerals and *Entrées*, as well as for the promulgation of *arrêts* in the Court. The costume spelled out Parlement's constitutional role in the French polity, because the red-robed presidents signified the perpetuity of royal justice, hallmark of the immortal royal *dignité*.[28] Yet

[27] On these disagreements, see Shennan, *Parlement of Paris*, pp. 198-200.

[28] See Giesey, *Royal Funeral Ceremony*, chap. V, and "The Presidents of Parlement at the Royal Funeral," pp. 25-34; and Bryant, "*Parlementaire* Political Theory in the Parisian Royal Entry Ceremony," pp. 15-24. Jules E. J. Quicherat, *Histoire du costume en France depuis les temps les plus reculés jusqu'à la fin du XVIIᵉ siècle* (Paris, 1877), pp. 322ff., makes two incorrect assumptions: that *parlementaires* wore red robes in daily sessions of the Court and that they wore them at all *Lits de Justice*. For a study of such costumes, noting black as the daily habit of Parlement in the sixteenth century, see Jean Dauvillier, "Histoire des costumes des gens de justice dans notre ancienne France," in *Recueil des Mémoires et travaux: Mélanges Robert Aubenas* (*La Société d'histoire du droit et des institutions des anciens pays de droit écrit*, Fascicule IX, 1974), pp. 229-240.

here at the *Lit de Justice* the ceremonial focus was not allowed to rest on Parlement; attention was shifted instead to the king's chancellor, who was seated majestically at the foot of the royal dais in a chair decorated with material matching that of the throne. The inversion of ceremonial symbolism incurred by this shift of focus harbored constitutional implications. More or less wrapped within an extension of the royal thronal trappings, Chancellor Duprat was displayed in the *Lit de Justice* as the representative of royal justice, overshadowing the red-robed presidents of Parlement. Unable to counter this ceremonial inversion in the *Lit de Justice* of 1527, yet ever zealous to preserve its own status, Parlement concentrated on another ceremonial front. For the Funeral ceremony of Francis I in 1547, the Court took pains to formulate its constitutional role succinctly and, garbed in red robes, acted out that role in ritual.[29]

In addition to the innovative ceremonial configuration, the ritual of the *Lit de Justice* of July 1527 also introduced procedural novelties. As for protocol followed there, the Parlement of Paris knelt before the king as a body on 24 July just preceding the president's address, a gesture which symbolized its unique corporate status vis-à-vis other groups there. Yet Francis I with undue haste commanded the Court to rise immediately, and they faced an inordinately high throne in this ceremonial milieu. As for the privileges extended, the king insisted on 27 July that bailiffs and seneschals would give opinions during the judgment of the Duke of Bourbon, since they had witnessed the criminal acts in question; and he demanded that visiting ambassadors, princes, and lords also participate in the public reading of the *arrêt* against the defendant. Finally, the presence of two lay peers had sufficed on 26 July for the actual trial, but on 27 July the king arbitrarily declared that number insufficient for the reading of the *arrêt* and created a peer for a day by elevating a prince of the blood to that office.

The ceremonial ambiance of this *Lit de Justice* assembly probably struck contemporaries (as it did later generations) as an exceedingly

---

Actually the *parlementaires* only wore red robes for the last session of the first *Lit de Justice* of July 1527, when the *arrêt* was issued, and did not don such habits for the second *Lit de Justice* of December 1527; and they wore red robes for some *Séances* in which *arrêts* were pronounced.

[29] Giesey, *Royal Funeral Ceremony*, chaps. I and V, which recount the inordinately lavish ritual organized for Francis I; and the description of Parlement as exempt from mourning at the Funeral and garbed in red robes "because they are the chief and sovereign administrators of justice under the authority of the kings . . . and *Crown and Justice never die*" (p. 60).

magnificent setting which afforded a truly imperial stage from which to broadcast the constitutional precepts associated with juristic kingship. But at the time the resentful *parlementaires*, ordered to attend an assembly in the Grand-chambre billed as a *Lit de Justice*, not a Royal *Séance*, and ceremonially orchestrated by the royal baton, contested some of the novel practices. Evidently the *parlementaires* had searched through registers of Parlement for procedural precedents of note: some evidence on parlementary history was gathered for President Guillart's speech; the procedure used to summon the defendant Bourbon was a modified version of that used in trials for *lèse-majesté* held in 1378, 1387, and 1487;[30] proof was alleged which required peers to take an oath of office before assisting in Parlement at treason trials and which denied ushers of the Royal Household seats at such events; and royal premises denying the setting of precedents were extracted for some infractions of parlementary protocol. Still, the concerted efforts of the *parlementaires* to challenge lapses from parlementary procedure were only marginally successful. They maintained the privilege of deliberation at the trial; therefore, the proceedings took three days to complete, and they wore black robes for the preliminary hearing (24 and 26 July), red robes for the final judgment (27 July). They also required one peer to take the oath of office, but the king countermanded that concession by creating a third peer without benefit of oath, casting doubt about any right of Parlement to enforce such regulations. On the whole, however, the concessions actually wrung from Francis I—the maintenance of deliberations, the removal of royal ushers from the Grand-chambre, and the extraction of royal promises denying certain precedents—were minor in comparison with the king's introduction of the new *Lit de Justice* assembly itself to the Grand-chambre. The *parlementaires* certainly recognized the danger posed to the integrity of the Court's procedure: if the fledgling *Lit de Justice* comprehended constitutional matters, then the customary Royal *Séance* was demeaned in the process. That is why their spokesman President

---

[30] On the procedure for summoning defendants earlier (at the doors of the Grand-chambre, at the *table de marbre*, at the staircase, and at the doors of the Palais de Justice) for the trial of 1378, see A.N. X1a 1471, fols. 133v ff., and Godefroy, *Cérémonial françois* [Reg. Parl.], II, 433; for the trial of 1387, see A.N. X1a 1473, fols. 293v-297r, and Godefroy, *Cérémonial françois* [Reg. Parl.], II, 436; for the trial of 1487, see A.N. X1a 1495, fols. 102v-109v, and Godefroy, *Cérémonial françois* [Jaligny chronicle], II, 451, which mentions the *table de marbre* only.

Guillart acknowledged the constitutional nature of the issue at hand but refused to acknowledge the session underway as a *Lit de Justice* assembly.

Formulating a mode of discourse which linked together medieval legal and philosophical principles, President Guillart defined the relationship between Crown and subjects in the *chose publique* and firmly anchored the Parlement of Paris in the governance of the polity. When Guillart interpreted the symbolism of royal enthronement (a public manifestation of the royal *dignité*) in the Grand-chambre of Parlement, he defined the king as the *living and animate law* bound by reason and equity, thus advancing the medieval jurists' notions of the prince as the *lex animata* (the living law) who was both *legibus solutus* and *ratione alligatus* (technically above the laws but bound by reason to observe them).[31] When Guillart envisaged the body politic, he spoke of a *mystical body* composed of king and subjects with the king functioning as *tutor*, or administrator, of that body.[32] When Guillart imagined an institutional

[31] For the emergence of the Roman Law concept of the king as the *lex animata* [*Corpus Juris Civilis, Novels* 105], viewing the prince as the living image of justice rather than grace, accompanying the development of law-centered polities rather than liturgical ones, see Ernst H. Kantorowicz, *The King's Two Bodies: A Study in Medieval Political Theology* (Princeton, 1957), pp. 126-143. For the notion that the prince is *legibus solutus* but *ratione alligatus* [*Corpus Juris Civilis, Code* 1, 14, 4], see ibid., pp. 105-107; and for the same notion (inviting the idea of limiting legislative power), expressed as *rex supra legem* but *debitor justitiae* [*Corpus Juris Canonici*, Innocent III: c. 11, X, 2, 2], see ibid., p. 163. Note that the Parlement of Paris used the *debtor of justice* image in a remonstrance of 1489: ". . . they [kings of France] hold their kingdom from God and recognize no sovereign other than God . . . they are *debtors of justice* . . . and have ordained a throne of justice (*solium judicii*), that is to say, a sovereign Court, the Court of the Parlement of Paris about which it is written, 'The king who sits in his throne of justice (*solio judicii*) dissipates all evil' "; A.N. X1a 9323, no. 85 (July 1489), cited in Maugis, *Histoire du Parlement*, I, 374, n. 1. For this theme, see Adhémar Esmein, "La maxime *Princeps legibus solutus est* dans l'ancien droit public français," *Essays in Legal History*, ed. P. Vinogradoff (Oxford, 1913), pp. 201-214.

[32] For discussion of the organological notion of the "body politic," or *mystical body*, transformed into a juristic notion after the twelfth century, see Kantorowicz, *King's Two Bodies*, pp. 15, 193-232, 253-258, 447-550. In France the notion was expressed as the *civic and mystical body* by Jean de Terre Rouge; see ibid., 220-223, and Giesey, "The French Estates and the *Corpus Mysticum Regni*," *Album Helen Maud Cam* (*Études présentées à la Commission Internationale pour l'histoire des Assemblées d'États*, 1960, XXIII, 153-171). Terre Rouge's work was in the hands of Guillaume Benedicti around 1500, then published in 1526, and his ideas were common in sixteenth-century France; Giesey, *Juristic Basis of Dynastic Right*, pp. 12-17. We should note, however, that the idea appeared in parlementary circles earlier when a remonstrance of 1489 designated the Royal

bridge between head and members of the *chose publique*, he fastened upon the Parlement of Paris institutionalized in the late thirteenth century as the supreme Court of France and by implication upon the traditional Royal *Séance* held in the Grand-chambre. Finally, when Guillart reviewed present royal transgressions against parlementary procedure, he launched a bitter indictment against two infractions, the venality of office and the jurisdictional pretences of the Grand Conseil.[33] It is important to remember that this speech concentrated on one main theme, the invidious royal transgression of Parlement's procedure, for that transgression is what the Court feared most and protested against overtly and covertly at this assembly. Further analysis of the president's speech, which caused the precipitous interruption of the *Lit de Justice* on 24 July when the king stalked out, brings one full circle in understanding this confusing set of events.

If President Guillart's speech is read carefully in light of the fact that it was tendered at the first *Lit de Justice* assembly ever convened in France, a session which flouted parlementary procedure, one is obliged to challenge current interpretations of this event. Two main points are usually made by historians to account for the peculiar circumstances surrounding this *Lit de Justice* assembly: first, that on 24 July President Guillart put forth a radical constitutional claim for the Court's stature

Séance in Parlement (king, peers, Crown officers, and *parlementaires*) in the Grand-chambre as "... *ung corps mistique* ... représentans le personne du roy ..."; cited in Maugis, *Histoire du Parlement*, I, 37. The notion of *tutorship*, derived from Roman Law (for example, *Digest* 26, 7, 3, and 4, 6, 22, 2) and classical sources (such as Cicero, *Offices*, I, and Plato, *Laws*, VII), was discussed avidly by legists in the mid and later sixteenth century (including Guillaume Budé, Pierre Rebuffi, and René Choppin). It was connected with the idea of representation associated with the maxim *quod omnes tangit* (see n. 55 below) and with French Public Law (inalienability of the domain). Ultimately at stake in the discussion, however, was the question of what agency, if any, served as a co-tutor (peers, Royal Council, Estates, Parlement), and obviously the Parlement of Paris wished to fill the bill. The idea of *tutorship* played an important role in the development of resistance right by the *monarchomaques* in the later sixteenth century; see Giesey, "The Monarchomach Triumvirs: Hotman, Beza and Mornay, *"Bibliothèque d'Humanisme et Renaissance*, XXXII (1970), 41-46, treating the *Vindicia contra tyrannos*; Hanley, "The *Discours Politiques* in Monarchomaque Ideology: Resistance Right in Sixteenth-Century France," *Annali della Facoltà de Scienze Politiche*, XIX, *Quaderni di storia*, 7, 1982-1983; and ibid., introduction to *Discours politiques des diverses puissances* (forthcoming).

[33] On the creation of offices in Parlement by Francis I, see Mousnier, *La Vénalité des offices sous Henri IV et Louis XIII* (Rouen, 1945), pp. 20-71.

in the polity by stating that Parlement was in origin a public assembly which held its power from the nation; and second, that Francis I reacted angrily to this courageous speech, humiliating Parlement at the *Lit de Justice* by forcing the registration of an edict regulating the Court's behavior.[34] The first point is misleading. Guillart did not extol the ancient origins of Parlement. He bemoaned those early times as a period which spelled dependency and instability for "parlements" cursed with ambulatory status, and he credited Philip IV with correcting that deplorable condition by institutionalizing the Court at the end of the thirteenth century as the Parlement of Paris. Far from musing upon unreliable recollections about ancient origins, the first president seized upon a precise historical moment (in his ken) when the Parlement of Paris was legally inaugurated as an institution and invested with procedural autonomy. The contemporary strength of Parlement, from his vantage point, lay in that procedural autonomy. It is within this institutional framework that Guillart made overt complaints, or remonstrances, against specific violations of procedure.[35]

Yet even if the president's stress on Parlement's procedural autonomy, rather than its ancient origins, is admitted, it is still difficult to account for the jarring intensity with which that message sounded in the ears of Francis I that morning. Other *parlementaires* had tendered remonstrances to French kings regarding practices inimical to the Court's rules, especially from the end of the fifteenth century, without incurring immediate royal wrath; and Francis I had clashed with Parlement on a variety of problems during earlier Royal *Séances* without proroguing those sessions in anger.[36] The question therefore remains as to why the

[34] For this interpretation, see Maugis, *Histoire du Parlement*, I, 568-586; Doucet, *Étude sur le gouvernement de François Ier*, II, 251-258; Shennan, *Parlement of Paris*, p. 200; and Knecht, *Francis I and Absolute Monarchy*, pp. 21-22.

[35] Guillart's attribution of Parlement's origins to the reign of Philip IV in the early fourteenth century was supported later by legists such as Étienne Pasquier, *Des recherches de la France, livre premier et second* [1581], ed. Léon Feugère, in *Oeuvres choisies* (Paris, 1849), I, 55-56, and Bernard de Girard Du Haillan, *De l'estat et succez des affaires de France* (Paris, 1571), fols. 86v-88r. Modern historians suggest 1345 as the date when the Parlement of Paris became a permanent institution; see Maugis, *Histoire du Parlement*, I, 1, citing the great ordinances of 1343 and 1345 for evidence, and Shennan, *Parlement of Paris*, pp. 24-28.

[36] Consult Stocker, "Office and Justice," and "The Politics of the Parlement of Paris in 1525," pp. 191-212, which note that the *parlementaires'* major concern was with maintaining the institution of the Parlement of Paris as the primary seat of royal justice (in order to secure the status of judicial offices) and not with protesting against the so-called "absolutism" of Francis I.

Court's attempt to take a stand on the procedural issue at this particular assembly caused the untoward actions of Francis I.

As previously noted, Parlement's request to address the king was not fully anticipated and was granted begrudgingly. What did Francis I expect to hear once the floor was given to President Charles Guillart? No doubt the king expected to bask in the president's historical analogies likening the vigor and justice of ancient polities to French governance and to receive general exhortations, or remonstrances, regarding the exercise of justice. Guillart did provide such rhetoric. But the king did not expect to encounter a challenge to the extraordinary *Lit de Justice* assembly underway. The president explicitly cited procedural grievances regarding the venality of office and shifts of judicial jurisdiction, but at the same time implicitly indicted the king's convocation of the *Lit de Justice* in place of a Royal *Séance* as royal interference with institutionalized parlementary procedure. It is Guillart's stony silence, not his rhetoric, which accounts for the precipitous action of the king in proroguing the *Lit de Justice*. Throughout the entire discourse the president never once referred to the assembly as a *Lit de Justice*, an omission all the more suspect when one recalls that the assembly was officially designated as such in registers of Parlement, that it was organized by royal fiat, and that the concern of Parlement over this extraordinary assembly was evident throughout the proceedings. In fact the hollow resonance of President Guillart's silence contained an ominous insinuation: that a type of parlementary assembly now called *"Lit de Justice"* was unknown in the annals of parlementary history and, by inference, that Francis I was tampering illegally with standard parlementary procedure by instituting this new format in place of the traditional Royal *Séance*. Thus in retrospect the conjecture can be made that Francis I could not abide Parlement's covert refusal to acknowledge the extraordinary session as a *Lit de Justice* assembly, because that refusal implied that the Royal *Séance* alone constituted proper procedure for royal visits to the Grand-chambre of the Parlement of Paris. This reassessment of President Guillart's main theme and the king's reaction to it leads to the correction of the second point in question.

It is alleged by historians that Francis I during this *Lit de Justice* assembly forced the registration of an edict odious to Parlement. Yet the case was quite the contrary. The royal edict which regulated the discipline of Parlement was not registered anywhere in the presence of the king and certainly not in the *Lit de Justice* assembly. After Francis I prorogued the *Lit de Justice* abruptly on 24 July, he went straightaway with his

Council (Conseil Étroit) to the Salle Verte. Several hours later he summoned a contingent of *parlementaires* to appear before him in that chamber. It was during that ad hoc session held in the Salle Verte that Francis I issued the edict regulating Parlement's behavior and ordered its registration in the Conseil Étroit, the Courts of Parlement, and the Grand Conseil. But the king did not personally witness its registration, because he left the Salle Verte immediately after the edict was introduced and before the presidents could reply, and he did not return to the Grand-chambre with the *parlementaires*. Francis I acted to protect the constitutional aura of the *Lit de Justice* assembly that day by registering the edict regulating Parlement's behavior elsewhere. Indeed the force of his intentions is all the more compelling when one considers first that the Parlement of Paris during its rump session back in the Grand-chambre on 24 July did not read the royal edict aloud, as befits registration, but simply wrote it in the registers; and second that on 27 July Francis I adjourned the final session of the *Lit de Justice* assembly and left the Grand-chambre before that royal edict of 24 July, signed by him, was presented to the Court by the secretary, Jean Robertet, and then registered.[37] That royal edict, read in the Salle Verte on the afternoon of 24 July and registered in Parlement after the king left on 27 July, stated among other things that Parlement must seek annual confirmation of its authority from the king (denying its institutional autonomy); that Parlement was forbidden to meddle in affairs of state (that is, constitutional matters, which were the provenance of the *Lit de Justice*); that the cognizance of Parlement encompassed the sphere of judicial business only (effecting a separation of functions, constitutional and judicial); and that the king controlled the registers of Parlement and could remove or cross out entries made in them (announcing royal control of the greatest repository of constitutional precedents in France).[38] These regulations

[37] See Maugis, *Histoire du Parlement*, I, 580-584, which recounts the odd sequence of events on 27 July.

[38] For the text of the edict, see A.N. X1a 1530, fol. 363v (27 July 1527); it was printed in *Recueil de lettres patentes concernant la discipline du Parlement* (n.p., n.d., compiled in 1770 or after), pp. 1-4. This Edict of 1527 also forbade Parlement jurisdiction over ecclesiastical benefices and reversed specific decisions made by the Court during the quarrel with the regent Louise of Savoy and Chancellor Duprat two years before. Note that Francis I probably did not intend to promulgate this edict in July 1527, because it had been drawn up almost a year before, only to be dredged up in this provocative situation following Guillart's speech. As for registration of the Edict of 1527 in Parlement, the king ordered the clerk, Séraphin du Tillet, to bring the registers to him within fifteen

underlined the legitimacy of the *Lit de Justice*, which Francis I had convoked to treat matters involving the Public Law of the French monarchy.

This investigation brings to the fore several factors heretofore neglected or obscured by the unwarranted attention given the precipitous quarrel which erupted after Guillart's speech on the morning of 24 July. To begin with, the first *Lit de Justice* assembly in French history was convoked amidst extraordinary ceremonial grandeur to effect a constitutional purpose, that is, to preserve the royal domain protected by the Law of Inalienability by holding a legal trial against a peer of France accused of the crime of *lèse-majesté*. Although that trial was preempted for one day by the quarrel between king and Parlement, it was resumed again and accomplished in the two days which followed; therefore, it is misleading to inflate the importance of a political quarrel to proportions which overwhelm the crucial constitutional matter at stake. Second, Francis I recessed the *Lit de Justice* in anger following President Guillart's speech on 24 July because of the covert refusal of the first president, speaking for Parlement, to acknowledge the *Lit de Justice* assembly as a venerable constitutional forum different from a Royal *Séance*. Guillart did not make a radical claim for Parlement's origins in time immemorial, as is usually held, but touted instead the procedural autonomy of a Parlement of Paris institutionalized at the turn of the fourteenth century, suggesting obliquely that the *Lit de Justice* assembly itself flouted parlementary procedure. Third, Francis I did order the registration of an edict regulating the discipline of Parlement later in the afternoon of 24 July, but he did so only after recessing the *Lit de Justice* assembly and moving from the Grand-chambre to the Salle Verte. Moreover, he neither remained in the Salle Verte nor returned to the Grand-chambre to oversee the registration of that edict. In other words, the king took pains to dissociate a willful act of royal legislation from the other event, the *Lit de Justice* assembly. Finally, the edict was duly registered on 27 July in the Parlement of Paris only after Francis I had adjourned the *Lit de Justice* assembly and left the Grand-chambre. It is incorrect, therefore, to link the forced registration of a royal edict with a *Lit de Justice* in July 1527 and then to construe such action as a royal victory over a humiliated Parlement of Paris. Rather, one should shift the focus, for

days with minutes of the above-mentioned quarrel removed, and he threatened the clerk with privation of office for failure to comply. The important question regarding control of these registers thus was raised in 1527 and would be raised again in 1563 and 1668.

the moment at least, to envisage the first *Lit de Justice* assembly in French history as a magnificent ceremonial event organized by Francis I and his advisers in the wake of Franco-imperial rivalry and constitutional antiquarianism, for these historical and constitutional aspects of the first *Lit de Justice* also characterized the second and the third, which followed soon after.

THE *Lit de Justice* ASSEMBLY OF DECEMBER 1527

Convoked by Francis I in the Grand-chambre of the Parlement of Paris, the second *Lit de Justice* assembly remained in session for two days, 16 and 20 December 1527.[39] It was convened to discuss the royal proposal to annul the Treaty of Madrid for a new peace treaty consonant with the Law of Inalienability, a tenet of the Public Law of the French monarchy.[40] While a prisoner of the emperor Charles V in Spain, Francis I had signed the Treaty of Madrid in 1526 to secure his release, and the document was registered by the Parlement of Paris and other Courts in France. By that treaty the French would lose control of the important duchy of Burgundy, as well as other properties ceded by the agreement. Once safely back in France, therefore, the king decided to annul the Treaty of Madrid.[41] The *Lit de Justice* assembly was used to publicize the constitutional case against the treaty and to secure a network of national support for its rescission. This assembly was not abruptly interrupted by a peripheral quarrel as was the first *Lit de Justice*, but there were some internal delays which vexed Francis I and slowed down the proceedings.

The assembly opened on 16 December, and the ritual observed there conformed for the most part, except for the absence of red robes, to that followed in the first *Lit de Justice*. The monarch was seated on a royal

[39] A.N. X1a 1531, fols. 26v-33v [recess, fols. 33v-46r] and 46r-53v (16 and 20 Dec. 1527); Godefroy, *Cérémonial françois* [Reg. Parl.], II, 478-501; and his comments on the recess, ibid., 488-490 (17 and 18 Dec.). The account of Isambert, *Recueil général des anciennes lois*, XII, 285-295 (16 Dec.), 295-296 (18 Dec.), and 297-301 (20 Dec.), is totally garbled with inaccurate transcriptions and improper dates. Doucet, *Institutions de la France*, I, 183, n. 2, calls this *Lit de Justice* an Assembly of Notables.

[40] The Law of Inalienability was involved in the first *Lit de Justice* of July 1527 and would figure in the third one of 1537 as well.

[41] Consult Knecht, *Francis I*, chaps. 12-14. For the treaty, see *Ordonnances des rois de France, règne de François Ier*, IV, 185-186.

throne canopied, draped, and set upon a seven-step dais, the attendants we're seated in the diamond-shaped construct, and the assembly was designated officially as a *"Lit de Justice"* by the clerk of Court Séraphin du Tillet.[42] This time, however, the composition of the assembly excluded the numerous household officials and foreign dignitaries present before and instead added to the scene many participants with seemingly representative functions. Besides king, peers, royal officers, Parisian *parlementaires*, and other guests, the second *Lit de Justice* assembly included persons not ordinarily given access to the Grand-chambre: some princes and knights, provincial *parlementaires*, archbishops and bishops of Paris and other cities, the provost of merchants and mayors of Paris, and some gentlemen, all of whom were deputized by the king to attend. In addition to those seated in the parquet of the Grand-chambre, Queen Louise of Savoy (mother of Francis I), accompanied by several other women, also attended the opening session of this *Lit de Justice*; and they were seated on a small platform partly enclosed with latticework and situated next to the parquet. Since the number of regulars and deputies seated there probably reached over two hundred, swelling the entourage far beyond seating capacity, additional benches were brought in at the last minute to accommodate the overflow.[43]

Before he came to the Grand-chambre Francis I sent a message to the *parlementaires* announcing that the ceremonial ritual fashioned for the assembly would not prejudice any prerogatives of the Parlement of Paris in the future, even though the seating plan included persons who were not members of the body of the Court of Parlement. Nevertheless, a noisy argument erupted among archbishops vying for precedence, and it was stilled only when the chancellor, on the advice of presidents and others, reiterated that the seating arrangement entailed no precedent. Once enthroned in the Grand-chambre, Francis I spoke aside to Chancellor Antoine Duprat. Then the chancellor order the captain of the guards to remove from the chamber all persons who were not deputized as representatives to the assembly except the *avocat* and the *procureur général* of the king (*gens du roi*). Finally, the chancellor exacted an oath from the deputies, who with hands raised swore not to reveal the substance of the matters to be discussed. Before a group thus solemnly sworn

---

[42] A.N. X1a 1531, fols. 26v-33v (16 Dec.). The opening description, exactly like that of July 1527, likens this assembly to that one. The *parlementaires* wore red robes on 27 July 1527 (though not on 24 or 26 July), but they did not wear that habit on either day of this assembly.

[43] Ibid.

to secrecy, "the king, seated in his royal tribunal holding his *Lit de Justice* [assembly]," addressed the deputies personally. He pointed out the consultative, or advisory, nature of the *Lit de Justice* underway.[44] As recounted by the clerk of Parlement, Séraphin du Tillet, the king explained

> [First] that out of the good will he bears toward his subjects and the *chose publique* of the kingdom of France, he convoked this assembly to discharge the duty of his office by revealing to them recent events and by relating to them his principal affairs. [Second] that even though the grave matter at hand had been deliberated upon previously, he intended to honor his subjects ... by seeking their opinions and resolutions. Thus even though he had consulted several high dignitaries and other important persons and found that he could act on his own recognizance in this matter, he did not wish to proceed without first revealing it to his subjects. [Third] to that end he decided to assemble them not in the form of Estates but by way of this forum which is the *Lit de Justice* [assembly], hoping that from them he would receive help, comfort, and aid, as well as good and loyal counsel according to their consciences, for the good of him, his kingdom and the *chose publique*.[45]

Prejudicing the review in his favor, Francis I recounted a series of recent crises in international relations, peace and war, alliances and betrayals, and the treason of Charles of Bourbon. Then he shifted back to the constitutional tone struck in his opening remarks. The king placed a critical constitutional issue squarely before the assembly. Should the French king adhere to provisions contained in the Treaty of Madrid, requiring alienation of Crown lands including the Duchy of Burgundy and the counties of Flanders and Artois, to the emperor Charles V, or failing to comply, should he return to captivity in Spain as required by the treaty? Francis I reminded them that the treaty, which flouted French Public Law, had been signed under duress. Yet even now he would rather return to prison in Spain than dismember the kingdom and endanger the *chose publique*. Dramatically espousing his loyal adherence to the Law of Inalienability, a tenet of the Salic Law, Francis I ordered the grand master on the spot to exhibit an edict which had been drawn up during his imprisonment to facilitate the coronation of the dauphin had the king not been released from Spain. To be sure, he was finally

[44] Ibid.
[45] For the king's speech, A.N. X1a 1531, fols. 29r-32v (16 Dec. 1527); reprinted in Godefroy, *Cérémonial françois* [Reg. Parl.], II, 481-487.

released, but the situation now was even more complicated due to the fact that his two sons were held hostage by the Spanish in his stead in order to assure French compliance with the Treaty of Madrid. At this critical juncture, therefore, he had decided voluntarily to seek the counsel of this assembly on the matter, an issue of "urgent necessity" which entailed peace or war for the kingdom and affected the French constitution itself.[46]

Francis I told those present of the alliance which he had secured with King Henry VIII of England and of their mutual determination to seek peace. He proposed, as a solution to the present Franco-imperial dilemma, the immediate negotiation of a new peace treaty with Charles V. In the main the new treaty would offer a ransom payment to Charles V in return for his abandonment of the claim to French territory and for his release of the two royal hostages. But the success of such a peace treaty would depend on the ability to raise ransom monies throughout the kingdom of France. According to the clerk's minutes, Francis I stressed his wish to discharge the duty of his office properly by seeking the "opinion of the assembly" on

> ... a matter which touches not only the said lord and his children but also the entire universal monarchy of the kingdom, the liberty and conservation of the king, princes, and subjects, and the *chose publique* ... which is the kingdom of France....[47]

That request for counsel in the *Lit de Justice* was acknowledged by the deputies in a format remarkably reminiscent of the Estates; that is to say, three persons spoke separately, one for the Church, one for the Nobility, and one for the Parlement of Paris, provincial Parlements, and the City of Paris. Yet a bit later, when the king ordered these groups to discuss his proposal elsewhere during a recess and requested advice on his remonstrances within a few days, the reporting format suddenly changed, separating the Parlements from the City of Paris. As a result, when the *Lit de Justice* of 16 December was recessed, not three but four groups (the Church, the Nobility, the City of Paris, and the Parlements) assembled elsewhere to discuss the proposal.[48]

[46] Ibid.
[47] Ibid.
[48] A.N. X1a 1531, fols. 32v-33r (16 Dec. 1527). Parlement denied that it was represented in meetings of the Estates or that the Estates expressed opinions of the Court; see William F. Church, *Constitutional Thought in Sixteenth-Century France* (New York, 1969), p. 139, n. 49.

Immediately following the close of the first session of the *Lit de Justice* assembly on 16 December the Parisian and provincial deputies for the Church discussed the proposal together and appointed the Cardinal of Bourbon as their spokesman. It is likely that the deputies for the Nobility and the City of Paris also acted swiftly. But on 17 December the seven Parlements still had not discussed the proposal and seemed to be dead-locked on a procedural point involving the format for discussion. In the face of this delay Chancellor Duprat visited the Courts and urged their immediate action. He sharply reminded them that they had been re-quested only to counsel the king on the specific royal proposal just set forth: replacement of the Treaty of Madrid with a new peace treaty consonant with Public Law. Evidently a compromise was effected, be-cause shortly after this meeting the Parlements each went their separate ways for purposes of discussion. The Parlement of Paris held a plenary session in the Grand-chambre, and each of the provincial Parlements (Toulouse, Bordeaux, Rouen, Dijon, Grenoble, Aix-en-Provence) assem-bled elsewhere. Then on 18 December all the Parlements were reunited in the Grand-chambre, rendered their separate responses, and designated the first president of the Parlement of Paris, Jean (II) de Selve, as their spokesman.[49]

The *Lit de Justice* assembly reconvened on 20 December 1527, and the king in his "royal tribunal holding his *Lit de Justice* [assembly]" heard the advice presented from the four groups.[50] First the Cardinal of Bour-bon spoke for the Church, then the Duke of Vendôme for the Nobility, and each addressed the king immediately from a standing position. President Jean (II) de Selve spoke for the Parlements, and the provost of merchants for the City of Paris, but before either representative began speaking, he knelt in front of the throne until commanded to rise by the king. The four groups were of like mind: they advised against the return of Francis I to captivity, upheld the French Public Law of Inal-ienability making any cession of Burgundy illegal, and agreed on the necessity to raise the proposed ransom monies throughout the kingdom in order to free the dauphin and his brother. The responses made by the Church, the Nobility, and the City of Paris were exceedingly short, but President De Selve, speaking for the Parlement of Paris and the

---

[49] For events during the recess, see A.N. X1a 1531, fols. 33v-46r (16, 17, and 18 December 1527); recounted in Godefroy, *Cérémonial français* [Reg. Parl.], II, 488-490. The account as published in Isambert, *Recueil général des anciennes lois*, XII, 285-305, is full of errors.

[50] A.N. X1a 1531, fols. 46r-53v (20 Dec. 1527).

provincial Parlements, presented a detailed legal opinion on French Public Law to the assembly. Amidst a litany of axioms reminiscent of the "king's two bodies," the president characterized the body politic as a *mystical body* and the king as the *spouse of the kingdom*; reaffirmed the validity of the Public Law of the French monarchy, in particular the Salic Law and its provision against the alienation of any part of the royal domain; and set forth three main constitutional and legal arguments justifying abrogation of the Treaty of Madrid by the French.

> [First point: return of the monarch to captivity.] Nature abhors the separation of the body from the head, which deprives it of life; likewise the French people, who comprise the *mystical body* of which the said lord is the head, deprived of him ... would be without life ... for the kingdom is in the king and the king is in the kingdom. ... [Second point: alienation of the Duchy of Burgundy.] That matter has been debated in this assembly comprised of great and notable persons, and no one is of the opinion that the said lord is obliged ... either to cede the Duchy of Burgundy or to uphold the Treaty of Madrid.... And there is nothing in the opinions of the Doctors [in the law] who have ruled on similiar cases, such as Baldus de Ubaldus [d. 1477], Petrus de Ancharano [d. 1416], Franciscus Zabarella [d. 1417], Dominicus de Sancto Germiniano [fl. 1407-1409], Alexander Tartagna de Imola [d. 1477], Franciscus de Accoltis de Aretrio [d. 1486], Philippus Decius [d. c. 1537], to indicate that the said lord is obliged [to observe the Treaty of Madrid].... As far as the Duchy of Burgundy itself, there are reasons why the said lord cannot cede it ... , [one] because it is the first peerage of France, which is inalienable and cannot be separated from the Crown ... , [and two] the said lord cannot cede it because he is obliged to maintain the [Public] Laws of the Crown which are common to him as head and to his people and subjects as members. Apropos of that *a marriage is made between the said lord and his said subjects*, and the law of that marriage which the said lord must keep is to uphold and to maintain the [Public] Laws of his Crown, not the least of which is the Salic Law which has been maintained over time as a holy and just law and according to which the [Public] Laws of the Crown are themselves inalienable ... the kingdom is in the king and the king is in the kingdom and cannot permit his kingdom to be divided.... [Third point: peace treaty and ransom] ... everyone agrees that the said lord must seek peace and must

raise the ransom ... because the ... dauphin and the Duke of Orléans are natural children of the said lord and are also children of the French people and of the *chose publique* [and are] born to govern and to rule.... The common conclusion of this Court and the other sovereign courts which are present here is that clearly the said lord can raise from the Estates of his kingdom the sum required ... for the ransom of the king ... and for the delivery ... of ... his children as hostages held in his stead....[51]

Alluding to the "necessity" of the times which dictated swift action for the preservation of the *chose publique*, the president suggested that provincial officials be informed of the decisions made that day and that ransom monies be raised as soon as possible for the good of all concerned.[52] The king acknowledged the responses of each of the four groups, reiterated his promise to maintain the royal domain intact, and thanked those present for their counsel on behalf of the "welfare and utility of the kingdom." Francis I then retired from the Grand-chambre, and the *Lit de Justice* assembly was adjourned.[53]

As WITH the first assembly, a review of the sources for this second *Lit de Justice* of 16 and 20 December 1527 confirms its extraordinary nature. It was a constitutional assembly designed to reaffirm precepts of French Public Law through ritual and discourse. The clerk of Court, Séraphin du Tillet, designated the assembly as a *Lit de Justice* in the registers of Parlement to distinguish it from a Royal *Séance*, and the king actually likened the *Lit de Justice* assembly to a meeting of the Estates. Although Francis I was quite aware that the ritual instituted for the *Lit de Justice* contravened some rules observed in *Séances*, he maintained the ceremonial novelties to emphasize the special juristic character of the assembly in which the king acted as guardian of Public Law. Once again the ceremonial configuration and procedural format underscored the extraordinary nature of the assembly. The king was enthroned beneath a canopy on a high dais in the top corner of the diamond-shaped construct; the *parlementaires* were displaced from seats usually occupied in *Séances*

[51] Ibid. [italics added], for President De Selve's speech; recounted in Godefroy, *Cérémonial françois* [Reg. Parl.], II, 493-499. The abbreviated names of legists cited in the speech are rendered here fully with dates. Jean (II) de Selve became president in 1520; Maugis, *Histoire du Parlement*, III, 148-149.

[52] A.N. X1a 1531, fols. 46r-53v (20 Dec. 1527).

[53] Ibid.

because deputies ordinarily denied access to the Grand-chambre were present; and the king attempted to combine the City officials and the Parlements (Parisian and provincial) into a Third Estate during deliberations. It appears that red robes were not prescribed for the *parlementaires*, because they were clad in black, but the seating of attendants was determined beforehand and controlled by means of deputation, and Queen Louise of Savoy was present on the first day of the assembly. Finally, both sessions of the *Lit de Justice*, 16 and 20 December, were held *in camera*, and the deputies swore an oath of secrecy at the outset. No doubt behind the scenes Parlement voiced complaints, because the king reaffirmed the Court's customary prerogatives and forbid future allegations of precedent based on ceremonial prescripts followed that day. Nevertheless, signs of friction were in the offing.

The composition of this second *Lit de Justice* of 1527 is perplexing. Clearly Francis I convoked the body with an eye toward representation, because the sworn deputies were drawn by royal order from three Estates (Nobility, Clergy, Parlements and City officials) and from Parisian and provincial locations. Originally the assembly was organized so that a representative for each Estate would reply to the royal request for counsel, but the Parlement of Paris must have refused to countenance its role in the Third Estate. Probably the Court threatened delay, because just before recessing the first session on 16 December the king revamped the reporting procedure to accord separate status to the Parlements. The new format thus separated the *parlementaires* (Parisian and provincial) from the City officials for purposes of reporting and created four orders in the assembly rather than three, that is, the three Estates and the Parlements.[54]

Apparently that significant concession did not quite satisfy the Parisian *parlementaires*. During the recess, they must have objected further to the format set for discussion, that is, the integration of all Parlements together in a single session, because on 17 December the Parlement of Paris evidently refused to meet formally with the provincial Parlements. The delay caused vexation in royal quarters. Francis I sent Chancellor Duprat to meet with the Parlements and remind them of their duty. The chancellor informed the Courts that the other bodies, Church and Nobility, had already taken swift action and were waiting to report, and he reemphasized the consultative nature of the royal charge given them.

[54] Refusing any merger with a Third Estate was parlementary policy; see above, n. 48, and Chap. I, n. 64.

They had been requested to consider only specific points of the new treaty, he said, intimating that they were not to discuss its constitutional validity. For the moment, however, Parlement's delaying tactics proved more effective than royal admonitions, because the Parisian and provincial Parlements were separated for discussion. The Parlement of Paris went to the Grand-chambre; the other Parlements held six separate sessions elsewhere. Following these meetings the seven Parlements met together the next day, 18 December, filed separate opinions, and designated the first president of the Parlement of Paris, Jean (II) de Selve, as their spokesman. There was more at stake in the Parisian Court's recalcitrance than first meets the eye. Its refusal to integrate with the other Parlements gave witness to its superior status as the supreme Court in France. Even more importantly, that refusal stemmed directly from the Parisian Court's intention to assume a unique constitutional role in this *Lit de Justice* assembly. Actually the Parlement of Paris on 17 December intended to deliberate on the constitutional aspects of the issue governed by the Law of Inalienability and then to render a legal commentary on Public Law at the final session of the *Lit de Justice* on 20 December. For that purpose the Parisian Court planned to hold a plenary session in the Grand-chambre, and that is why it refused to meet with representatives of provincial Parlements.

As in the first *Lit de Justice* this kind of conflict involving ceremony and procedure was pivotal to the delicate balance of the larger question: the nature of the *Lit de Justice* assembly itself. Straightaway in the first session of 16 December, Francis I's discourse characterized the assembly as a constitutional forum in which consultation, not consent, was requested from the affected parties. The king formulated the request carefully, invoking language reminiscent of a well-known medieval principle of limited representation, *quod omnes tangit* (what touches all [should be approved of by all]) for that purpose. He told the assembly that since the matter touched all the kingdom, or *chose publique*, he had chosen voluntarily to inform cohorts of the pending plans and to elicit their counsel.[55] Moreover, he had convoked this forum, the *Lit de Justice* assembly, to serve in place of the Estates for the conduct of such con-

[55] The procedural device *quod omnes tangit ab omnibus comprobetur* [*Corpus Juris Civilis, Code* 5, 59, 5, 2, and *Digest* 42, 1, 47], which could be used when joint interests and co-tutorship were involved, was considered a proper summons but did not entail consent; see Gaines Post, *Studies in Medieval Legal Thought: Public Law and the State, 1100-1322* (Princeton, 1964), chaps. III and IV.

stitutional business.[56] The fact is that the king considered the proper maintenance of French Public Law to be a royal prerogative and had already settled the constitutional question by repudiating the Treaty of Madrid for a new treaty which would not flout Public Law. Now he simply issued a proper summons to interested parties, the various orders of the kingdom, to solicit counsel only on the merits of that treaty. Despite these procedural disclaimers, however, the Parlement of Paris ignored the consultative tenor of the king's request and proceeded to rule on constitutional law as if the Parisian Court's charge was unique among the orders. In fact during those five days, 16-20 December 1527, the maneuvering of the Parisian Parlement, both inside and outside of the Grand-chambre, was aimed at attaining official recognition as co-guardian, with the Crown of French Public Law.

The second session of the *Lit de Justice* assembly opened on 20 December, and each of the four groups, the three Estates and the Parlements, advised the king to adopt the new peace treaty which would require the collection of ransom monies to free the royal hostages and prevent the alienation of French lands. The three reports of the Nobility, the Clergy, and the City officials were relatively short. Despite the king's admonitions to the contrary, however, the Parlement of Paris ruled on the constitutional issue, and the first president set forth a detailed legal brief annulling the Treaty of Madrid on the grounds of inalienability. Whether or not Francis I agreed beforehand to hear this legal brief is not known, but he listened with measured politeness to the very end of that long and erudite opinion. Then the king formally thanked all the deputies for their counsel and adjourned the *Lit de Justice* assembly. Francis I had convoked a *Lit de Justice*, not a Royal *Séance* or the Estates, with an eye for staging a ritual that would focus on his role as legislator and guardian of French Public Law, and he intended to effect a separation of functions there. But the Parlement of Paris countered by usurping a constitutional role as co-guardian of Public Law. This ritualized contest over the locus of constitutional prerogative was not resolved in 1527 and would crop up again. In the meantime, however, there was solid agree-

[56] J. Russell Major, *Representative Institutions in Renaissance France, 1421-1559* (Madison, 1960), p. 137, notes the conundrum regarding the nature of this assembly, which cannot be construed as a meeting of Estates. The last line of Francis I's statement seems equivocal; yet he juxtaposed two kinds of public forums, Estates and *Lit de Justice*, so the latter title signified the assembly underway in the Grand-chambre.

ment among the same dissident parties as far as the constitutional problem itself was concerned.

The dissonance sounded over the location of constitutional prerogative contrasted oddly with the resonance heard regarding the precepts of the French constitution, assumptions which were shared by all who were present and propagated for international consumption. The speeches of both king and first president called attention to the public nature of the French polity by differentiating the "king's two bodies," one public and corporate, the other private and familial, and by stressing the "urgent necessity" of this case.[57] It is striking to observe the clarity with which both king and first president focused on French Public Law as the basis for constitutional obligation. The king emphasized several points: the obligation of the monarch to maintain French Public Law, the constitutional nature of the present issue, which "touched the whole kingdom (*chose publique*)," and the voluntary convocation of a consultative *Lit de Justice* assembly with community representation to give counsel on the matter. As pointed out, the very tone of his message, if not the words, surely brought to mind representative notions usually associated with the medieval Roman-canonical maxim *quod onmes tangit*, involving consultation on matters affecting the whole realm. Although not stated verbatim in its familiar form in December 1527, the maxim *q.o.t.*, brandished in English parliamentary circles from medieval times and known to French legal theorists in the later sixteenth century, certainly waxed forth in the tenor of Francis I's invocation at this *Lit de Justice* assembly.[58] This idea of a public polity which rested on specific constitutional foundations stood in sharp contrast to the older notions of individual relations in a feudal nexus. When the king reminded listeners of his right to act

[57] The classic study of the legal concept of the "king's two bodies," separating king and state, is that of Kantorowicz, *King's Two Bodies*, which emphasizes English and continental political theology; the work of Giesey, *Royal Funeral Ceremony*, introduces that concept through a study of ceremony in renaissance France. The French axioms found in the *Lit de Justice* of December 1527 (and again in January 1537) thus complement nicely similar points in Kantorowicz, *King's Two Bodies*, pp. 207-231, 363-364 (*corpus mysticum*); pp. 214-222, 347-358 (the marriage metaphor and inalienability); and pp. 13, 214-223, 437-440 (incorporation of the king in the kingdom). On the use of *necessitas*, see ibid., 235-238, and Post, *Studies in Medieval Legal Thought*, pp. 241-309.

[58] In addition to n. 55 above, see Kantorowicz, *King's Two Bodies*, pp. 170-171, 190, 361-362, and 381; and Giesey, " 'Quod omnes tangit'—a Post Scriptum," *Studia Gratiana*, XV (1972), 319-332, on French usage in the later sixteenth century.

unilaterally, he acknowledged a fading feudal prerogative. But he did not dwell on this aspect of his authority. Instead, he stressed his adherence to French Public Law, his recognition of the consultative principle, his voluntary request for counsel in the discharge of his *dignité*, and thus his decision to convoke a *Lit de Justice* assembly rather than the Estates. In short, the king adopted a constitutional platform befitting juristic kingship.

First President Jean (II) de Selve also emphasized constitutional obligation. At no time, however, did he acknowledge the assembly as a *Lit de Justice*, as distinct from a Royal *Séance*, or admit to the monarch's sole authority in constitutional affairs. But his presentation, like that of the king, emphasized French Public Law, not feudal prerogative, as the basis for deciding the issue posed by the Treaty of Madrid. De Selve presented a litany of axioms reminiscent of the "king's two bodies." He described the structure of the polity as a *mystical body* composed of king and subjects as head and members. "The kingdom is in the king and the king is in the kingdom," he stated, invoking a familiar organological notion of the body politic and mystic that was used to characterize the relationship between the people, or Estates, and the Crown throughout the fifteenth and sixteenth centuries.[59] Then the president introduced a new constitutional image to the French scene by describing that relationship in terms of the king's marriage to his realm. It is worthwhile at this point to repeat a key part of that passage.

> ... he [the king] is obliged to maintain the [Public] Laws of the Crown which are common to him as head and to his people and subjects as members. Apropos of that *a marriage is made between the said lord and his said subjects*, and the law of that marriage which the said lord must keep is to uphold and to maintain the [Public] Laws of his Crown, not the least of which is the Salic Law, which has been maintained over time as a holy and just law and according to which the [Public] Laws of the Crown are themselves inalienable ... [and] the dauphin and the Duke of Orléans ... are children of the French people and of the *chose publique*....[60]

President De Selve's evocation of the marriage metaphor describing the relationship of the king as well as the princes to the kingdom marks a

---

[59] On the *corpus mysticum* and the incorporation of king and kingdom, see above, n. 57, for the juristic models.

[60] For the whole speech, see above, n. 51 [italics added].

very early instance of that juristic rubric in France.[61] It is possible that the president drew his inspiration from a formula elucidated by the medieval jurist Lucas de Penna (1320 – c. 1390), whose maxim illustrated the inalienability of fiscal property and whose works were well known in France in the early sixteenth century.[62] But the crucial twist which De Selve gave the expression made it particularly apropos for this milieu. When the president wed the king and the realm (identifying the dauphin and his brother as the issue of that union), he predicated the duration of that fictive espousal upon the king's successful discharge of his constitutional obligation, that is, upon the monarch's ability to maintain French Public Law unimpaired. Thus in 1527 President De Selve evoked a most unusual image of the French constitution for the time. He proffered the concept of a corporate body politic and described the king's relation to the realm through the marriage metaphor; then he gave a juristic definition of French kingship as a royal *dignité* charged with the maintenance of French Public Law.

' Until now historians have assumed that in France the simplest formulation of this marriage metaphor first appeared in a legal treatise of Charles de Grassaille published in 1538; that the metaphor then found its way into the Coronation ceremonies of 1547 and 1594 connected with the bestowal of the ring; and that its elaborate formulation (likening the domain of the kingdom to the dowry of the marriage) appeared only in the last three decades of the sixteenth century in the writings of legists such as René Choppin, François Hotman, Pierre Grégoire, and Jean Bodin.[63] Yet here the first version of the metaphor (the king as spouse of the kingdom) actually emerged a decade earlier, not in a legal treatise but in a speech rendered by President Jean (II) de Selve during the second *Lit de Justice* assembly of December 1527. Likewise, as will be seen presently, the more complex version of that metaphor (adding the equation of domain and dowry) also appeared several decades earlier than has been supposed, for it first emerged not in the writings of legists

[61] The transfer of this metaphor from canonistic to secular and political thought probably around 1300 is discussed in Kantorowicz, *King's Two Bodies*, pp. 212-232.

[62] Perhaps these French *avocats* were influenced by Lucas de Penna, who used the marriage metaphor in conjunction with the notion of the state as a *corpus mysticum* in his *Commentaria in Tres Libros Codicis*, which was published in France six times during the sixteenth century (first ed., Paris, 1509); discussed in Kantorowicz, *King's Two Bodies*, pp. 221-223.

[63] Ibid., 221-222.

of the late sixteenth century but in a speech set forth during the third *Lit de Justice* assembly of January 1537. Given the appearance of these juristic rubrics at such an early date, the genesis of this genre of constitutional thought must be moved back from the late sixteenth century to the 1520's; and given the linkage of such thought with the extraordinary *Lit de Justice* which appeared at the same time, the constitutional nature of that assembly must be stressed. The second *Lit de Justice* assembly of 1527, as the first, was thus distinguished from the Royal *Séance* on constitutional grounds; and the third *Lit de Justice* of this novel trio would also conform to that pattern.

III

CONFIRMATION OF FRENCH HEGEMONY IN A CONSTITUTIONAL FORUM: THE *LIT DE JUSTICE* ASSEMBLY OF 1537

> ... the king ... is the *husband and political spouse* of the *chose publique* which brings to him at his *sacre* and Coronation the said *domain as the dowry* of his Crown. *Jacques Cappel (1537)*

THE CASE that has been posed thus far, that the *Lit de Justice* assembly appeared first in 1527 and served as an extraordinary constitutional forum, is borne out by the third *Lit de Justice* assembly, convoked by Francis I in the Grand-chambre of the Parlement of Paris on 15 January 1537.[1] It too was convened to discuss a matter involving the disposition of the royal domain and was therefore technically concerned with the Public Law of the French monarchy. Over the decade between the second and third *Lits de Justice*, political relations between Francis I and Emperor Charles V were further strained. Francis I (suzerain of the territories of Flanders and Artois) had much earlier attended two Royal *Séances*, pleadings sessions, in 1522 and 1523, where preliminary charges were brought against Charles V (as count of the Crown lands and vassal of the French king).[2] When the king decided to deprive the emperor of those lands in 1537, he convoked a *Lit de Justice* assembly for that purpose and charged Charles with "notorious felony," another crime of treason within the rubric of *lèse-majesté*. The original record of this assembly made by the chief clerk of Parlement, Jean du Tillet, disappeared from the civil registers of Parlement in the mid-sixteenth century, but an abbreviated version remained in the possession of Du Tillet and a fuller version was found among papers of Barnabé Brisson, a *parlementaire* of the next generation.[3] A second account of the session supplements this

---

[1] For the sources on this assembly, see below, nn. 3 and 4.

[2] A.N. X1a 1524, fols. 95r-97r (15 Feb. 1522), reprinted in Godefroy, *Cérémonial françois* [Reg. Parl.], II, 452-455; and A.N. X1a 1525, fols. 275v-277r (30 June 1523), extracts in Godefroy, *Cérémonial françois* [Reg. Parl.], II, 455-463.

[3] Some of the account from the civil register is contained in Du Tillet, *Recueil des grands*, pp. 93-95 (15 Jan. 1537). A fuller version is found in the papers of Barnabé Brisson (*avocat* in 1575, president of Parlement in 1580); reprinted in

first one, because the clerk of pleadings, Pierre Le Maistre, also made a detailed record of the session that day.[4] Between the two surviving accounts a fairly complete picture of the event emerges.

Arrayed in ceremonial red robes, the Parlement of Paris arrived in the Grand-chambre very early that morning. Straightaway First President Pierre Lizet reported to the Court that a remonstrance had been sent to the king protesting the required red-robed garb for the pending session.[5] Then around eight o'clock the Court hastily dispatched a message to the clerk of pleadings, Pierre Le Maistre, with orders to attend the *Lit de Justice* assembly. He was instructed to proceed at once to the Grande Salle and wait there for an opportune moment to enter the Grand-chambre, to observe the proceedings carefully, and to record not only the opinions given on the case by the king and the Court but also the ceremonial protocol.[6] Suddenly the *procureur général* of the king arrived in the Grand-chambre and announced that there was a person waiting in the Tour Ronde who had produced royal orders to furnish two footstools for the high seats, one for the dauphin, the other for the King of Scotland, and a platform for the queen and her party, who wished to attend the session. The *parlementaires* left the Grand-chambre while those furnishings were installed, waited in the Chambre de la Tournelle, and returned to the Grand-chambre an hour later.[7] Around nine o'clock the pleadings clerk, Pierre Le Maistre, arrived at the entrance of the Grand-chambre and noted that the *parlementaires* were already inside. A parlementary usher on duty told Le Maistre that the Court had been ordered by the king to assemble there.[8] Chancellor Antoine

---

Godefroy, *Cérémonial françois* [Brisson, Reg. Parl.], II, 501-503. These record the same description of royal enthronement as those for the *Lits de Justice* of July and December 1527 and describe this third assembly as a *Lit de Justice*. It is possible that Jean du Tillet borrowed the register account and never returned it (see below, Chap. IV, n. 26).

[4] Le Maistre's account appears in records of the Chambre des Comptes, A.N. P 2306, fols. 353r-413r (15 Jan. 1537), and includes a ceremonial description, the pleading, and the *arrêt*; portions of this account are in Godefroy, *Cérémonial françois* [Le Maistre], II, 503-517.

[5] Godefroy, *Cérémonial françois* [Brisson, Reg. Parl.], II, 501-503 (15 Jan. 1537); and A.N. P 2306 [Le Maistre], fols. 353r-413r, also in Godefroy, *Cérémonial françois* [Le Maistre], II, 503-517.

[6] A.N. P 2306 [Le Maistre], fols. 353r-413r (15 Jan. 1537), also in Godefroy, *Cérémonial françois* [Le Maistre], II, 503-517.

[7] Godefroy, *Cérémonial françois* [Brisson, Reg. Parl.], II, 501-503 (15 Jan. 1537).

[8] A.N. P 2306 [Le Maistre], fols. 353r-413r (15 Jan. 1537), also in Godefroy, *Cérémonial françois* [Le Maistre], II, 503-517.

du Bourg, garbed in a crimson robe and accompanied by several chancellery officers, arrived on the scene and entered the Grand-chambre.[9] The same parlementary usher then complained to Le Maistre that the entrance of chancellery officers flouted parlementary protocol.[10] Inside the Grand-chambre Chancellor Du Bourg addressed the complaints made by the Parlement of Paris regarding the ritual planned for this session. He spoke on behalf of the king as follows: when Francis I and the Royal Council (Conseil Privé) decided two days ago to proceed against Charles of Austria, Count of Flanders [Emperor Charles V], for acts of "notorious felony," Du Bourg inquired of the king whether the assembly would hear the case and adjourn before the final judgment, or hear the case and render a judgment on the spot. The king's reply had been vehement. A verdict would be reached in the *Lit de Justice* assembly that day, he said, and the chancellor was ordered to inform the Court "... that the ceremonial would be strictly enforced, preventing precipitous acts or surprise moves; and that [in this] he only intended to be accorded the proper respect which the making of justice warrants."[11]

Around ten o'clock, following the arrival of some prelates, Le Maistre finally obtained entrance to the assembly and witnessed with surprise the chancellor sitting in the chair especially prepared for him "at the foot of the *lit de justice*." One important disturbance interrupted the seating of this large entourage: the bold but unsuccessful attempt of First President Lizet to claim for the presidents of Parlement the high seats held by ecclesiastical peers.[12] Evidently the *parlementaires* had been drafted into extended ceremonial service, for six councillors of the Court met the royal retinue at Sainte-Chapelle,[13] and then two presidents of Parlement marched from their seats in the Grand-chambre to the gate of the parquet to receive the king.[14] Francis I entered the parquet and was summarily enthroned, apropos of which the pleadings clerk Le Maistre

[9] Godefroy, *Cérémonial françois* [Brisson, Reg. Parl.], II, 501-503 (15 Jan. 1537); and A.N. P 2306 [Le Maistre], fols. 353r-413r, also in Godefroy, *Cérémonial françois* [Le Maistre], II, 503-517. Antoine du Bourg became chancellor in 1535.

[10] A.N. P 2306 [Le Maistre], fols. 353r-413r (15 Jan. 1537), also in Godefroy, *Cérémonial françois* [Le Maistre], II, 503-517.

[11] Godefroy, *Cérémonial françois* [Brisson, Reg. Parl.], II, 501-503 (15 Jan. 1537).

[12] A.N. P 2306 [Le Maistre], fols. 353r-413r (15 Jan. 1537), also in Godefroy, *Cérémonial françois* [Le Maistre], II, 503-517.

[13] Godefroy, *Cérémonial françois* [Brisson, Reg. Parl.], II, 501-503 (15 Jan. 1537).

[14] Ibid. (15 Jan. 1537); and A.N. P 2306 [Le Maistre], fols. 353r-413r, also in Godefroy, *Cérémonial françois* [Le Maistre], II, 503-517.

noted that "the said lord entered Parlement, went up to and sat in the *lit de justice.*"[15]

According to the registers of the clerk of Court, Jean du Tillet, the session was designated as a *"Lit de Justice* [assembly]," and there was in evidence the high canopied royal throne and the diamond-shaped construct filled with a grand array of attendants.[16] However, this time the royal party comprehended not only princes of the blood, lay and ecclesiastical peers, Crown officers, household officers, knights, the provost of Paris, bishops, royal guards, gentlemen, and others, but also the King of Scotland (brother-in-law of the King of France) and the dauphin (the future Henry II). Moreover, Queen Eleanor of Austria (sister of Charles V), accompanied by Marguerite of Angoulême, Queen of Navarre (sister of Francis I), and several other royal princesses entered by a side door and were seated on a platform near the parquet. Finally, the presidents and councillors of the Parlement of Paris, conspicuous as a red-robed body, were seated all around the Grand-chambre. The proceedings began when the doors opened and the parties in the case were called.[17] The *avocats* and *procureur général* (*gens du roi*) knelt before Francis I to request a hearing, and the first usher of Parlement read the writ of complaint: "... a declaration of felony and reversion of fiefs against Charles of Austria, who holds the counties of Flanders, Artois, Charleroi, and other lands and seigneuries from the Crown of France."[18] Chancellor Du Bourg arose from his seat and bowed grandly several times before the king, repeated the request for a hearing and received a positive reply, returned to his seat, and pronounced the proceedings in order.[19]

PUBLIC LAW WRIT IN DISCOURSE

As the *avocat* Jacques Cappel (appearing for the *procureur général*) made ready to speak, the chancellor told the kneeling *avocats* twice to stand

[15] A.N. P 2306 [Le Maistre], fols. 353r-413r (15 Jan. 1537), also in Godefroy, *Cérémonial françois* [Le Maistre], II, 503-517.

[16] Godefroy, *Cérémonial françois* [Brisson, Reg. Parl.], II, 501-503 (15 Jan. 1537).

[17] Godefroy, *Cérémonial françois* [Brisson, Reg. Parl.], II, 501-503 (15 Jan. 1537); and A.N. P 2306 [Le Maistre], fols. 353r-413r, also in Godefroy, *Cérémonial françois* [Le Maistre], II, 503-517.

[18] A.N. P 2306 [Le Maistre], fols. 353r-413r (15 Jan. 1537), also in Godefroy, *Cérémonial françois* [Le Maistre], II, 503-517.

[19] Ibid. [Brisson, Reg. Parl.], II, 501-503 (15 Jan. 1537).

and cover their heads.[20] In opening remarks the *avocat* Cappel spurned the "art of rhetoric" as an archaic style of language that distorts reality and professed a modest type of exhortation. Making liberal use of metaphor, he portrayed the assembly and the king's place in it as follows.

> ... You are as the sun among the planets ... in this noble, illustrious, and wise company of kings and princes of your blood, peers of France, presidents and councillors of your sovereign Court of Parlement, and numerous prelates, which I daresay is a theater and consistory unequaled in all of Europe.... Your people ... see their king sitting in the throne of justice [= the Grand-chambre of the Parlement of Paris] ... due to the *interest* ... he has in this case concerning the public welfare, justice, and reparation for hostile acts ... , [as well as] the preservation of the borders of the kingdom, the domain, and the Laws of your Crown, which you hold, Sire, immediately from God and over which neither you nor your predecessors recognize any other superior.[21]

Then Cappel argued the legal case against Charles. Citing evidence from thirteeth-, fourteenth-, and fifteenth-century documents, he outlined the historical disposition of Flanders, Artois, and other lands. From time immemorial, he maintained, those counties were part of the "domain of the Crown of France"; even after their subinfeudation by Charlemagne (742-814) and Charles the Bald (Charles II, 840-877), the lords and people of those lands were reputed "vassals and subjects of the Crown of France" and were justiciable before the King of France in his Court of Parlement. Cappel recalled for the audience specific points of feudal law regulating such property holdings—the nature of fiefs, the duties of peerage, the

[20] Ibid. (15 Jan. 1537); and A.N. P 2306 [Le Maistre], fols. 353r-413r, also in Godefroy, *Cérémonial françois* [Le Maistre], II, 503-517.

[21] For the speech of Cappel, A.N. P 2306 [Le Maistre], fols. 356v-379v (15 Jan. 1537), also in Godefroy, *Cérémonial françois* [Le Maistre], II, 505-511; and the speech was published later as *Plaidoyez de feu maistre Jacques Cappel, advocat du roy en la Court de Parlement à Paris* (Paris, 1561), fols. 1r-19r [italics added]. We have here a very early example of the linkage of the concept of *interest* with French Public Law. The discussion of Giesey, *"Quod omnes tangit,"* notes the replacement of the formulary q.o.t. with the French concept of *interest* in the late sixteenth century. On the history of the idea consult Albert O. Hirschman, *The Passions and the Interests: Political Arguments for Capitalism before its Triumph* (Princeton, 1977), and Nannerl O. Keohane, *Philosophy and the State in France: The Renaissance to the Enlightenment* (Princeton, 1980). Jacques Cappel became *avocat* in Parlement in 1535; Maugis, *Histoire du Parlement*, III, 333.

place of the oath of fidelity and liege homage in this scheme of property rights—and emphasized in particular the feudal obligation of Charles as Count of Flanders and Artois to protect the French king and Crown.[22]

The *avocat* alleged forthwith that the defendant was guilty of two counts of "notorious felony." Charles had committed acts of felony (invasions, wars, hostilities) against Francis I with conscious intent, crimes which warranted the derogation of feudal privileges. And Charles had acted in contempt of Court by ignoring a legal summons issued by Francis I on 15 February 1522 when the king was sitting in his Court of Parlement attended by princes of the blood, peers of France, and other great lords. Although neither Charles nor his representative had appeared as summoned, the case was heard in the Parlement of Paris on 30 June 1523 with the king and peers present. At this point, Cappel maintained, these acts of felony, compounded by the charge of contempt of Court, were so notorious that it was unnecessary in this case to hold a formal trial. Even though no verdict had been issued against Charles in the earlier hearing, he reasoned, title to the fiefs in question was confiscated automatically from the defendant and reverted naturally to the Crown of France. In the meantime, he alleged, Charles blatantly disregarded his own culpability and continued to commit felonious acts, including the extortion of the treaties of Madrid and Cambrai from Francis I. Cappel insisted that from the outset those treaties were null and void on two counts: first, because sworn contracts or treaties which have been extorted by threats of force or fear of detention (in this case, the imprisonment of either Francis I or his children) are invalid; and second, because any treaty which requires the French king to alienate "heritages of the proper and ancient domain of the [French] Crown" (in this case Flanders and Artois) is illegal.[23] Cappel concluded his "modest exhortation" with a lesson on the French constitution outlined again through metaphor.

> By its nature the Crown is inalienable . . . because according to the Law of France, which is called the Salic [Law], and customary, divine, and positive laws, the sacred patrimony of the Crown, the ancient domain of the prince, cannot be divided among men. [Rather] it is transmitted to the king alone, who is the *husband and political spouse* of the *chose publique* which brings to him at his *sacre* and Coronation the said *domain as the dowry* of his Crown. Kings swear

[22] A.N. P 2306 [Le Maistre], fols. 356v-379v (15 Jan. 1537), also in Godefroy, *Cérémonial françois* [Le Maistre], II, 505-511.

[23] Ibid.

solemnly at their *sacre* and Coronation never to alienate that dowry for any cause whatsoever, because it is itself inalienable.... Consequently, since [Public] Law not only forbids kings the right to alienate the domain but also prohibits the alienation of patrimonial or domainal property itself, and since such prohibition concerns the public welfare, it is obvious that contracts [the treaties of Madrid and Cambrai] which contain clauses of alienation as heretofore mentioned are invalid from start to finish and cannot be validated by consent or oath.[24]

When Jacques Cappel finished pleading the case against Charles, Chancellor Du Bourg ascended the steps of the dais and knelt on one knee before the throne. He conferred with the king for some time before initiating consultation. First, he solicited advice from those in high seats to the right of the king—lay princes and peers, the King of Scotland, the King of Navarre, and the dauphin; then from other princes, Crown officers, and knights. Second, he solicited those in high seats to the left of the king—ecclesiastical peers. Third, he descended from the dais and solicited on the way the grand chamberlain, grand master of the Hôtel du Roi, and admiral. Finally, at the foot of the dais he conferred for a long time with the four presidents of Parlement (sitting in the lower rows of high seats to the left of the king). The chancellor reascended the steps to the throne and reported the opinions to the king, returned below to his own seat and pronounced the verdict against Charles of Austria [Charles V] as Count of Flanders and Artois.[25] In the main the *arrêt* stated that "the king sitting in his Court" and "counselled" by "princes of his blood, peers of France, and other councillors in his said Court" found Charles guilty of "notorious felony" for which crime he was deprived of the counties of Flanders, Artois, and other Crown lands.[26]

A REVIEW of the third *Lit de Justice* assembly of 15 January 1537 shows, as in the two earlier cases of 1527, that the extraordinary nature of this assembly was in contention from the outset. The Parlement of Paris wished to convoke a Royal *Séance* that day; the king intended to convoke

[24] Ibid. [italics added].
[25] Godefroy, *Cérémonial françois* [Brisson, Reg. Parl.], II, 501-503 (15 Jan. 1537); and A.N. P 2306 [Le Maistre], fols. 379v-413r, also in Godefroy, *Cérémonial françois* [Le Maistre], II, 503-517.
[26] Godefroy, *Cérémonial françois* [Brisson, Reg. Parl.], II, 503 (15 Jan. 1537); and A.N. P 2306 [Le Maistre], fol. 413r, also in Godefroy, *Cérémonial françois* [Le Maistre], II, 517.

a *Lit de Justice*. Since the ritual prescribed for the session defined its nature, there was immediate sparring over ceremonial regulations. On the one side, the Parlement of Paris treated the impending session as a Royal *Séance* in which the king would assist as chief judge at a pleading against Charles as in 1522 and 1523. For the *parlementaires* the rendition of a final verdict required a two-day session allowing the Court time for deliberations as a body. Struck by the number of ceremonial innovations pending, they commissioned a second account of the proceedings to supplement that of the chief clerk Jean du Tillet. Hence the pleadings clerk, Pierre Le Maistre, was directed to join the crowd outside and enter the Grand-chambre furtively, once inside to record not only the pleading and *arrêt* given in the case but also the details of ceremonial ritual. In addition, they issued a remonstrance against the royal order requiring the Court to appear in red robes, the habit donned for the formal reading of *arrêts*, and they complained about the invasion of chancellery officials in the chamber. In a last attempt to employ procedure befitting a Royal *Séance*, President Lizet unsuccessfully claimed for the presidents the high seats to the left of the king, which were held by ecclesiastical peers in a *Lit de Justice*. This cast of mind accounts for two reactions of the clerk Le Maistre: his astonishment at seeing Chancellor Du Bourg sitting at the foot of the throne, the place reserved for the pronunciation of final judgment; and his lexical attribution of "*lit de justice*" to the throne itself (usage akin to that of Cappel), a tacit refusal to acknowledge the session as a *Lit de Justice* assembly. Finally, the *parlementaires* certainly objected to consultation in tandem with other groups (forgoing deliberations as a body) and must have been doubly chagrined at placing last in the order of consultation.

On the other side, Francis I intended to hold a *Lit de Justice* assembly, and he had learned the lessons of 1527 well. The king peremptorily informed Parlement (through the chancellor) that the proceedings would entail both the pleading and the final judgment, and he announced forthwith that ceremonial ritual would be strictly prescribed to prevent "precipitous or surprise moves" during the session. Francis I was enthroned under the canopy on the dais seven steps high. The chief clerk of Court, Jean du Tillet (brother of the former clerk, Séraphin), officially recorded the session as a *Lit de Justice* assembly (not a *lit de justice* throne) in the registers of Parlement. In the diamond-shaped construct, the royal family figured prominently. The dauphin (the future Henry II, age eighteen) was seated (somewhat lower) at the right hand of Francis I and thus associated provocatively with the royal *dignité* in the *Lit de*

Justice. Queen Eleanor of Austria and Marguerite, Queen of Navarre, attended the session and were seated on a special platform.[27] The dauphin and the princes of the blood, supplied with special footstools and consulted as a body, were effectively isolated as a special group, an important ceremonial nuance on precedence which was written into law almost four decades later.[28] The royal party was greeted by a parlementary reception committee, several councillors and two presidents, and escorted by the retinue from Sainte-Chapelle to the Grand-chambre. The king was addressed with rather elaborate supplicatory gestures, bowing and genuflecting by the crimson-robed chancellor, kneeling and a baring of heads by the *avocats*. Chancellor Antoine du Bourg brought chancellery officials into the Grand-chambre, flouting parlementary protocol, and sat throughout the proceedings at the foot of the throne whence the verdict was announced.

The procedural format for this trial was similar to that of the first *Lit de Justice* assembly held in July 1527, except that the latter charged the Duke of Bourbon (already deceased) with the crime of high treason, *lèse-majesté*, whereas this trial charged Charles of Austria [Emperor Charles V] with the lesser crime of treason, "notorious felony." In both hearings, therefore, it was actually the property and not the lives of the defendants at stake. The charge of notorious felony brought against Charles in the *Lit de Justice* of 1537 was argued carefully with two legal traditions in mind: one, the feudal law, which mirrored the tie between Francis I and Charles; and the other, French Public Law, which elevated royal authority over imperial power on constitutional grounds. The *avocat* Jacques Cappel bespoke the familiar medieval legal notion, *Rex est imperator in regno suo* (The king is emperor in his own kingdom), popular in French parlementary circles from the fifteenth century, by asserting that ultimate sovereignty belonged to the French king, who held his authority from God and recognized no other superior in temporal matters.[29] In addition he cited precedent from feudal law, as well as com-

---

[27] The queen and her entourage sat in the assembly only during the hearing and not for the verdict.

[28] For the steady growth of the "princes of the blood" as a distinct group vis-à-vis the peers, see Jackson, "Peers of France and Princes of the Blood," *French Historical Studies*, VII, 1 (Spring 1971), 27-46.

[29] On this precept in a parlementary context, see A.N. X1a 1504, fol. 319v (13 June 1499), "... le Roy a plus d'autorite en son royaume que l'Empereur en son empire ..."; and A.N. X1a 4828, fol. 128v (Feb. 1487), "... Le Roy est souverain en son royaume ... [given his] dignite royale ... [and he is] premier justicier...." For discussion of the precept, consult Joseph Declareuil, *Histoire générale du droit français des origines à 1789* (Paris, 1925), pp. 830 ff., recounting

mentaries on it, to establish the fact that Charles in his capacity as count of French lands was the vassal of Francis I. But the *avocat*'s main thesis, the monarch's constitutional obligation to the Crown of France, provided the real guide for legal action that day.

Jacques Cappel repeated the constitutional concept first introduced by President Jean (II) de Selve a decade earlier at the *Lit de Justice* of December 1527 when he described the king's relation to the kingdom in terms of the marriage metaphor. Cappel developed the concept still further, however, first by appending the dowry-domain analogy to that metaphor, then by identifying the Coronation oath as the ceremony which confirmed the transfer of the French domain into the hands of the monarch. This extended version of the marriage metaphor held that

> ... the king ... is the *husband and political spouse* of the *chose publique* which brings to him at his *sacre* and Coronation the said *domain as the dowry* of his Crown. And kings swear solemnly at their *sacre* and Coronation never to alienate that dowry....[30]

Just as De Selve before him, Cappel too molded the marriage metaphor into a French constitutional adage by linking it to the "Law of France," that is, the precept of inalienability contained in the Salic Law.[31] A decade after Cappel's rendition in 1537, which suggested that the Coronation oath legalized this fictive marriage between king and kingdom, that ritual was implicitly expressed in the Coronation order of Henry II in 1547, then explicitly enacted through the rubrics of the Coronation order of Henry IV in 1594.[32] Finally, three decades later Cappel's extended marriage metaphor (linking domain and dowry) was reiterated by a

---

the history of *princeps in suo regno*; Kantorowicz, *King's Two Bodies*, pp. 97-98, 298-299; and Post, *Studies in Medieval Legal Thought*, pp. 247-248, 455-484.

[30] For the full speech, see above, n. 24. Kantorowicz, *King's Two Bodies*, pp. 221-222, thought that Jacques Cappel used this marriage metaphor in a pleading of 1536, but in fact it was given in this *Lit de Justice* of 15 January 1537. Lucas de Penna probably did influence both De Selve and Cappel, as suggested by Kantorowicz, *King's Two Bodies*, pp. 221-222, n. 83.

[31] See Cappel's full speech, above, n. 24. It is this precise scheme connecting the Crown with French Public Law, as opposed to private patrimony and inheritance law, which informed works of legists such as Charles du Moulin at mid century. Church, *Constitutional Thought*, pp. 49-50 and n. 21, discusses this adherence to Public Law.

[32] Now the usage of the marriage metaphor can be dated earlier than the Coronation rubrics. For a discussion of the metaphor and the precept of in-alienability in the context of the Coronation, see Kantorowicz, *King's Two Bodies*, pp. 221-223, n. 83, and Jackson, *Vivat Rex*, who includes antecedents which are not juristic.

Rouennais *avocat* during Charles IX's *Lit de Justice* of 1563. Here at the *Lit de Justice* of 1537, therefore, there emerged from Cappel's pleading a two-pronged constitutional prohibition against alienation of the French domain, one tenet based on the definition of the inalienable domain itself, the other on the regulation of the king's relation to the domain expressed through the marriage metaphor. This constitutional praxis provided a firm basis in French Public Law upon which to rest the case against Charles. As pointed out in the preceding chapter, this whole genre of constitutional thought was first expressed through a mode of discourse fashioned for that purpose and elucidated in *Lit de Justice* assemblies of 1527 and 1537, some time before the appearance of such precepts in legal and theoretical treatises of the later sixteenth century.

According to the discourse of Jacques Cappel in 1537, it was constitutional obligation which moved the French king to prevent alienation of the royal domain. Yet throughout this discussion of the French constitution there was no reference made to the extraordinary *Lit de Justice* assembly underway. Cappel described the king enthroned in the Grand-chambre as "sitting in the throne of justice," a vision in keeping with fifteenth-century parlementary images of the whole Grand-chambre harboring king and Parlement in consort, but not in procedural terms which differentiated two types of parlementary sessions, the *Lit de Justice* assembly and the Royal *Séance*. One can thus detect a dual attitude in the *parlementaires*, the positive side shown in orations which recognized the constitutional nature of the issues at hand, the negative side revealed in the refusal to countenance the assemblies themselves as extraordinary. At first glance the subtle thrust of Parlement's challenge is not obvious, because it took the abstruse form of silence.[33] In 1527 and 1537 the chief clerks, Séraphin and Jean du Tillet, recorded the three sessions as *Lit de Justice* assemblies and Francis I noted the extraordinary nature of the *Lit de Justice* by likening it to the Estates; whereas the disaffected *parlementaires*, Presidents Charles Guillart and Jean (II) de Selve, the *avocat* Jacques Cappel, and the pleadings clerks Nicolas Malon and Pierre Le Maistre, remained mute on that score. In the two instances of July 1527 and January 1537 where more than one record of a *Lit de Justice* assembly survives, the presence of textual discrepancies bears out the above suspicion. In the assembly of July 1527 the chief clerk, Séraphin du Tillet, by royal instruction or antiquarian impulse, recorded the three-day ses-

[33] In the formation of this language of public discourse the silence is especially revealing, because the *parlementaires* were well aware that precedents turned into precepts when written into the registers of Parlement.

sion as a *Lit de Justice*. But the criminal clerk Malon described a "Court in which all chambers were assembled," sufficiently garnished with peers and presided over by the king, who was "in his tribunal and royal throne"—with nary a mention of a *Lit de Justice* assembly. In January 1537 the chief clerk Jean du Tillet, most surely acting out of antiquarian instinct, cast the session as a *Lit de Justice* assembly. But the pleadings clerk Le Maistre noted that Francis I intended to come "in person to his Parlement," recalled the chancellor's chair placed at the foot of the "*lit de justice*," and recounted how the king arrived in the Grand-chambre, went up the steps, and sat in the "*lit de justice*"—a series of statements which used the phrase "*lit de justice*" to signify not a type of assembly but a royal throne. Certainly the fact that the *parlementaires* thought this session should be a Royal *Séance* and ordered Le Maistre at the last minute to record all these ceremonial nuances (in addition to the chief clerk Du Tillet) suggests that the second set of notes was commissioned to counter the official historical records (the registers of the chief clerk of Parlement), which might otherwise legitimize for posterity the *Lit de Justice* assembly. On both these occasions Malon and Le Maistre treated the sessions as Royal *Séances* and admitted no new genre of parlementary assembly named *Lit de Justice*.

In this cast of mind, the tacit refusal to regard the *Lit de Justice* as constitutionally different from the Royal *Séance*, the pleadings clerks were joined by Presidents Guillart and De Selve, and the *avocat* Cappel. The presidents waxed forth with humanist eloquence sustained by biblical and classical history; all three drew upon Roman and Canon Law, Feudal Law, and especially French Public Law to fashion modes of discourse which stressed royal obligation to preserve the Public Law of the French monarchy. The orations welded together a vocabulary of traditional and innovative concepts suitable for constitutional discourse: organological analogies for the French body politic (the *mystical body* of the realm, incorporation of king and kingdom) and expressions of French sovereignty (The king is emperor in his own realm); references to French Public Law as the "Law of France" (the Salic Law and inalienability) and the novel idea of constitutional issues as matters of public *interest*; the innovative marriage metaphor defining the king's relation to the realm (the king as *husband and political spouse* of the kingdom, or *chose publique*, entrusted with the *domain qua dowry*, dauphins as *children of France*, and *tutorship* precepts); and finally the evocative image of the assembly itself (king, peers, royal officers, and *parlementaires* in the Grand-chambre) as a jurisdiction ("throne of justice") wherein the king (as the *lex animata* and *debitor justitiae*) upholds the French constitution. This public discourse, a language framed by royal and parlementary speakers, outlined very early in the sixteenth century important elements of juristic kingship, a system of constitutional ideology which stressed the obligation of the monarch, as holder of the royal *dignité*, to maintain French Public Law. Yet other elements of the same discourse presented different versions of the proper relationship between king and Parlement in this system. Despite the admittedly constitutional nexus of the assemblies, not one of these parlementary orators referred to any of the events as a *Lit de Justice* assembly. Their stark omissions are difficult to abide considering that all were important officers in the Parlement of Paris certainly privy to the procedural dilemma caused by the introduction of the *Lit de Justice* to Parlement's Grand-chambre.

By way of contrast, the royal party distinguished these first three *Lits de Justice* from Royal *Séances* on constitutional grounds. Francis I convoked the *Lit de Justice* to treat French Public Law, introduced a ritual which emphasized its constitutional format and consultative nature, and likened the *Lit de Justice* to a meeting of the Estates. The chief clerks, Séraphin and Jean du Tillet, labeled the assemblies in the registers as *Lits de Justice* and probably did so under the presumption that such sessions represented a revival of ancient French tradition. Those familiar with ancient parlementary meetings would have been satisfied that two of the assemblies (July 1527 and January 1537), trials for treason, followed traditions observed in the trials of 1378, 1387, and 1487, and that the third (December 1527), a consultative assembly, resembled similar sessions held in 1369, 1375, 1392, 1407, and 1413. Contemporary political theory on the French constitution, as outlined by Claude de Seyssel (c. 1450-1520), required the monarch tò maintain Public Law, presented a flexible view of the function of the Estates, and exhorted monarchs to seek consultation in public affairs.[34] Now the introduction of the *Lit de Justice* provided a constitutional forum for that purpose.

Whether they were considered venerable or novel at the time, these *Lit de Justice* assemblies comprehended constitutional matters while leaving judicial business for the Royal *Séance*, and the ritual (ceremonial

---

[34] Seyssel, *La Monarchie de France* (written in 1515, published as *Grand Monarchie de France* in 1519): I, 7, 11 (Public Law); I, 13-28 (Estates); and II, 4-9 (counsel and councils). Seyssel's views on the necessity to convoke assemblies for advice were certainly practiced by Francis I, who tended to experiment with a variety of consultative sessions early in his reign; Major, *Representative Institutions in Renaissance France*, pp. 126-140.

configuration and procedural format) of the *Lit de Justice* relegated Parlement to the position of one corporate group among others. Parlement was summoned to the tones of *quod omnes tangit* to give advice, yet prevented from undertaking deliberations which implied consent. Fully cognizant of this deflation of the Court's role, the *parlementaires* stubbornly refused to countenance the event as different from a Royal *Séance* or to admit that such an assembly had ever existed in the past. Determined to preserve the Royal *Séance* (organized by parlementary procedure) as the unique forum uniting Crown and Parlement in French history, the *parlementaires* made oblique references to a *"lit de justice"* (throne or Grand-chambre) but recognized no *Lit de Justice* (assembly).

Although it is not possible to locate the precise genesis of the historical fiction of the medieval *Lit de Justice* assembly (the notion that the forum constituted a "revival" of French tradition) in the 1520's, some early version of that fiction must have accompanied the convocation of these three *Lits de Justice* in 1527 and 1537. Certainly the full ideological formulation of that fiction, which emerged by mid century, was preceded by isolated forays into the registers of Parlement conducted much earlier. As evidence is fragmentary, the exact course of such early research has not been charted. In the fifteenth century officials connected with the Parlement of Paris (presidents, *avocats*, especially clerks) were perusing registers of Parlement for historical precedents. The clerks Nicolas de Baye and Clément de Fauquembergue, for instance, made collections of documents copied from registers. One *avocat*, Jean Magistri, drew information from the registers for a historical discourse on French institutions (the Crown, the peers, and the Court of Parlement) which was presented to Charles VIII in the Parlement of Paris during a Royal *Séance* held for the trial of a peer in 1487.[35] Others followed suit in the sixteenth century. From the specific historical facts adduced by President Charles Guillart and the *avocat* Jacques Cappel at the *Lit de Justice* assemblies of July 1527 and January 1537, it is clear that they had culled enough evidence from the registers of Parlement to ruminate extensively about the feudal origins and procedural traditions of the Court. Later on the registers of Parlement were cited by legists and historians such as François Baudouin, Guillaume Budé, Charles du Moulin, Pierre Rebuffi, Étienne Pasquier, Bernard du Haillan, Jean Bodin, and others.[36] It is not known whether they read the original sources personally or

[35] Godefroy, *Cérémonial françois* [Jaligny chronicle], II, 450-451.
[36] Kelley, *Foundations of Modern Historical Scholarship*, pp. 216-217.

worked through the chief clerks of the Parlement of Paris.[37] Whatever the case, the greatest access to those records was enjoyed by the clerks of Parlement, who guarded the ancient documents and studied them on occasion, recorded daily proceedings, and added to the storehouse on French constitutional history.

To what extent these early forays into the registers of Parlement contributed to legitimizing the first three *Lit de Justice* assemblies in 1527 and 1537 cannot be known for certain. But at this point one can conjecture that certain advisers who were familiar with French history as told by the registers of Parlement presented the following proposition to Francis I: that the *Lit de Justice* assembly was a venerable constitutional forum which had fallen into disuse for a century or more and that it should be revived in 1527 to broadcast the principles of French Public Law in the face of the formidable imperial threat. Consequently, the clerks of Court, Séraphin and Jean du Tillet, far from writing down nonsensical phrases in the civil registers, probably acted upon intelligent opinion officially countenanced when they entitled the extraordinary sessions of 1527 and 1537 as *"Lit de Justice"* assemblies. If this was the case, then the constitutional validity of the first three assemblies was predicated upon some early version of the fiction of a medieval *Lit de Justice*.

The hypotheses set forth thus far—that the first three *Lit de Justice* assemblies were born of international political crises and nurtured by growing antiquarian suppositions about the ancient constitution; that the royal attempt to delineate two types of parlementary sessions, the *Lit de Justice* (constitutional) and the Royal *Séance* (honorary), was resisted by some *parlementaires*—are borne out by the ambivalence surrounding the *Lit de Justice* in the 1540's. Just four years after he convoked the third *Lit de Justice* in 1537, Francis I appeared uncertain about categorizing any further royal visits to the Grand-chambre of the Parlement of Paris. At one point he rescheduled a visit to Parlement for 25 February 1542 and then abruptly canceled the session.[38] Evidently the question about the type of assembly contemplated, *Lit de Justice* or Royal *Séance*, had intruded upon the scene, because the king immediately ordered the chief clerk of Parlement, Jean du Tillet, to investigate the matter. The king wished to peruse evidence from the registers of Parlement to ascertain

---

[37] Ibid., p. 216, n. 6, noting La Popelinière's complaint that the registers were closed to the public.

[38] A.N. X1a 1548, fol. 271v (25 Feb. 1542): the captain of the guards told the Court that the king was indisposed that day (Saturday) and would come on Monday, but the latter session never took place.

what type of meeting had been convoked in the Court "when he or his predecessors, kings of France, went there in the past to dignify royal justice."[39] Francis I did not visit the Grand-chambre of the Parlement of Paris before his death in 1547, but the order of 1542 addressed to the clerk of Parlement initiated the official research which later developed into an intensive study of the French constitution. A lack of consensus regarding the contemporary function of the *Lit de Justice* assembly thus stimulated new research which eventually led to the ideological rationalization of the assembly as part of the ancient constitution.

[39] Ibid., ". . . de retirer des registres du greffe la forme de la seance dudit Sgr. en icelle Cour quand par cy devant luy ou ses predecesseurs Roys de France y sont venus pour decorer sa justice."

IV

FACT AND FICTION IN HISTORICAL RESEARCH: JEAN DU TILLET'S RECONSTRUCTION OF THE FRENCH CONSTITUTION

> I have concluded that the [historical] argument which I have presented here ... rests on its own compelling force. *Jean du Tillet (1560)*

ALTHOUGH LITTLE is known about the evolution of the clerkship in the Parlement of Paris during the fourteenth and fifteenth centuries,[1] it is clear that the rapid rise in status accorded that office in the early sixteenth century correlated directly with a burgeoning interest in the French historical past. At the forefront of these developments, Jean du Tillet, Sieur de la Bussière (d. 1570), exercised with consummate skill the office of chief clerk (*greffier civil*) of the Parlement of Paris for almost half a century. In 1526 he assumed the office to which he was appointed in 1521 and recorded minutes of parlementary sessions from around the close of the 1520's. During the same decade he studied the French medieval past through the vast collection of ancient documents stored in his parlementary depot and other archives.[2] Working within this milieu, Du Tillet compiled information for a historical treatise, the *Recueil des roys de France, leurs couronne et maison*,[3] as well as other important

---

[1] Gustave Ducoudray, *Les Origines du Parlement de Paris et la justice aux XIIIᵉ et XIVᵉ siècles* (Paris, 1902), chap. X, especially pp. 230-284, traces their emergence from the *notaires* in the mid-fourteenth century whence they were entitled *clercs du greffe* or *greffier*.

[2] Kelley, *Foundations of Modern Historical Scholarship*, pp. 215-238, and "Jean du Tillet, Archivist and Antiquary," *Journal of Modern History*, XXXVIII, 4 (1966), 339-354. A.N. X1a 1520, fol. 308v (11 Aug. 1518), states that the office of *greffier civil* in the Parlement of Paris would become hereditary in the Du Tillet family upon the death of the holder, Nicole Pinchon; see Maugis, *Histoire du Parlement*, I, 184, n. 6.

[3] Jean du Tillet, *Recueil des roys de France, leurs couronne et maison* (Paris, 1607), the most complete edition (referred to hereafter as *Recueil des roys de France*). The work was first published posthumously under the title *Les Mémoires et les recherches* (1577 and 1578), then in a version expanded and titled as above (1580, 1586, 1587, 1588, 1602, 1607, 1618). The edition of 1607 used here contains

studies, published and unpublished, on the Public Law of the French monarchy. Throughout his long career as clerk of Parlement, scholar, and briefly as politician, he firmly believed in the indigenous nature of French laws and institutions, and he set upon a scholarly course to rescue documents recounting that history.[4] In the sixteenth century the treatises written by legal humanists, including the works of his younger brother, placed the revived corpus of Roman Law in historical perspective, and the clerk Du Tillet envisioned a similar revival for the French legal and constitutional tradition.

Functioning in this dual role as clerk of Parlement and scholar, discovering the past and recording the present, Du Tillet became involved very early in historical research. From at least the later 1520's he searched through the registers of Parlement for documents pertinent to public affairs and built a private collection of historical sources. As early as 1530 Du Tillet supplied Francis I with accounts of Royal *Entrées* taken from the registers of Parlement,[5] and in 1541 he gathered information from the registers on royal visits to the Grand-chambre of the Parlement of Paris.[6] In the late 1540's he provided interpretive accounts of Royal Funeral ceremonies,[7] and in 1549 he supplied the historical evidence for Chancellor François Olivier's speech on parlementary history at a Royal *Séance*.[8] Du Tillet retrieved from other archives two fourteenth-century

---

three sections paginated separately: (1) *Recueil des roys de France, leurs couronne et maison* (same title as the whole treatise), pp. 1-456; (2) *Recueil des rangs des grands de France*, pp. 1-130 (both referred to hereafter as *Recueil des roys* and *Recueil des grands*), along with a long discourse, *Contenant les guerres et traictez de paix, tresves et alliances d'entre des rois de France et d'Angleterre (Tome II)*, dated 1606, pp. 131-424; and (3) *Chronique abbreggee des roys de France*, a chronological chart of the bishop Jean du Tillet, brother of the clerk (but bearing the same name), pp. 1-272, along with *Memoire et advis de maistre Jean du Tillet, protonotaire, et secretaire du roy tres-chrestien, greffier de sa Cour de Parlement, sur les libertez de l'Eglise Gallicane*, pp. 273-387, and several other documents. For the importance of this treatise in French historiography, see Kelley, *Foundations of Modern Historical Scholarship*, pp. 215-238, and André Lemaire, *Les Lois fondamentales de la monarchie française d'après les théoriciens de l'ancien régime* (Paris, 1907), 82-91, who give due emphasis to Du Tillet's merits as a founder of the historical school of French law.

[4] Kelley, *Foundations of Modern Historical Scholarship*, pp. 215-238.

[5] A.N. U 2031, fol. 260 (1530), and Godefroy, *Cérémonial françois*, I, 779-780; cited by Bryant, *French Royal Entry Ceremony*, pp. 78-79, n. 47.

[6] See above, Chap. III, n. 39.

[7] Giesey, *Royal Funeral Ceremony*, p. 60, nn. 31 and 32.

[8] See below, Chap. V, nn. 5-8.

documents missing from registers of Parlement and added them in 1545 and 1551 to properly dated places in those registers,[9] and in the 1560's he provided Chancellor Michel de L'Hôpital with archival evidence on the origins of Parlement and French Public Law. At the same time that Du Tillet studied the past, he also recorded contemporary ceremonies (Coronations, *Entrées*, Funerals, Estates, parlementary sessions) in minute detail, with considerable knowledge aforethought of historical precedents.[10] Thus under scholarly auspices some of the legendary lacunae in parlementary registers bemoaned by clerks and kings alike were filled, and detailed contemporary records were kept. Inevitably, current events were influenced by views of the past. Du Tillet's mounting collection of documents was eminently useful in an age which was wont to express precepts of Public Law through ceremony. First circulated in manuscript during the mid decades of the sixteenth century, Du Tillet's collection, after publication, was consulted universally by legists, historians, and others from the sixteenth century to the present.

In the manner of parlementary clerks before him, such as Nicolas de Baye and Clément de Fauquembergue, Jean du Tillet too read many ancient registers of Parlement during his early years in office in order to cultivate his expertise on parlementary procedure and protocol. But Du Tillet stretched the limited historical bounds of his journal-keeping forebears. He sought the key to the French national past, the true ancient

---

[9] A.N. X1a 8602, fol. 210v: here at this folio there are inserted two folios signed by Du Tillet. The second one (fol. 2r-v) is a copy of letters of confirmation of Parlement, 28 April 1364, which a marginal note says were found among the papers of the *greffe civil* and added by order of the king dated April 1545. The first one (fol. 1r-v) is a document of 1366 which was added to the register in 1552. This activity of the clerk seems quite in keeping with the comment of Louis Regnier de La Planche, *Histoire de l'estat de France tant de la république que de la religion sous le règne de François II* (1576). Ed. J.A.C. Buchon. *Choix de chroniques et mémoires sur l'histoire de France* (Paris, 1836), II, 202-421, who states, p. 269, that, "Searching the ancient registers of the Parlement of Paris, Du Tillet began to examine them and finding them worthy of memory, by neglect or ignorance forgotten by historians, proposed to make a collection to serve posterity"; cited in Kelley, *Foundations of Modern Historical Scholarship*, pp. 223-224, n. 24.

[10] On the Coronation, *Recueil des roys*, pp. 259-275, and *Recueil des grands*, pp. 26-27 and 119-120. On the Royal Funeral, *Recueil des roys*, pp. 333-346. On Royal *Entrées*, *Recueil des grands*: pp. 68-70 (Louis XI at Reims, 1461); pp. 97-98 (Henry II to Paris, 1549). On the Estates, *Recueil des grands*: pp. 8, 17, 290 (three Estates of Louis XI at Tours, 1468); p. 23 (Estates of Pepin at Soissons, 744); p. 102 (three Estates of Henry II in Paris, 1558); p. 109 (comment).

constitution, in a variety of documents which were officially signed, sealed, and preserved in archival repositories. These monuments of antiquity, parchment rolls long left in dust and disarray, were direct witnesses to French customs and institutional practices. Du Tillet called attention to the historical method which informed his unique scholarly enterprise. He scoffed openly at tellers of preposterous tales, who insisted on the Trojan rather than Germanic origins of the French,[11] attributed the Salic Law to a legendary King Pharamond,[12] located French institutions such as the twelve peers and the Parlement of Paris in soil trod by Charlemagne,[13] and interpreted the age of majority for French royal succession in terms of civil law rather than French Public Law.[14] In his estimation attempts to unearth French tradition from "fabricated fables committed to short chronicles" created fiction, not fact, whereas his research into the archives presented a true "mirror of the French past."[15] Those who used "the annals and chronicles of France" as a source for historical truth were "standing on shifting sands," he said, and they "should be ashamed to give equal weight to both passages from the annals ... [which are] full of fables and palace gossip, ... and true facts [which are] signed, dated, and taken from charters, titles, and other official sources."[16]

Just as fallacious as chronicle lore in his mind were the unsubstantiated historical injunctions which decorated rhetorical composition. Du Tillet called attention to the difference between rhetoric and history, style and veracity. He roundly complained that

> Today there are people who are so overly refined that they cannot countenance anything [in linguistic usage] which is not perfectly polished and smoothed, and they wish to frighten me into retreating [from this endeavor] because of the coarseness of my style. Such

[11] Du Tillet, *Recueil des grands*, pp. 15, 65-66, and see Kelley, *Foundations of Modern Historical Scholarship*, pp. 229-233. On the Trojan origins of the French, see George C. Huppert, *The Idea of Perfect History*, pp. 72-87.

[12] Du Tillet, *Recueil des roys*, pp. 9-10, calling attention to the feudal and Christian roots of the Salic Law, which he also treated in a separate essay.

[13] Ibid., 363.

[14] See the discussion below and Chap. VI.

[15] Du Tillet, *Recueil des roys de France* (preface), fols. A ii[v]-a iii[r], and within that treatise, *Recueil des roys*, p. 365; and also *Pour l'entière majorité du roy très chrestien contre le légitime conseil malicieusement inventé par les rebelles* (Paris, 1560), fol. d[v].

[16] Ibid.

people consider text rather than context, appearance rather than reality, a situation typical of the ignorant who treat [linguistic] eloquence as authoritative even if it is devoid of veracity. But I have concluded that the [historical] argument which I have presented here needs no artificial ornaments but rests on its own compelling force. . . .[17]

More than likely the offenders included officers of Parlement such as Charles Guillart, Jean (II) de Selve, Jacques Cappel, Pierre Lizet, and others whose skill at fine oratory was admired. They had refused tacitly in 1527 and 1537 and would refuse explicitly in 1549 to acknowledge any substantive difference between Royal *Séances* and *Lit de Justice* assemblies. Their rhetorical stance, based on the translation of *"lit de justice"* as a linguistic metaphor describing the whole Grand-chambre housing king and Parlement, challenged Du Tillet both as a historian of laws and institutions and as the clerk of Parlement convinced that the first three *Lits de Justice* of 1527 and 1537 were revivals of ancient constitutional custom. Stung by such criticism Du Tillet was determined to establish simple truths culled antiquarian-fashion from historical documents in place of tall tales dramatized by linguistic niceties, and that effort determined the outlines of his whole scholarly endeavor.

The suspicion looms ever large that Du Tillet's early research played some part in the decision of Francis I to convoke three *Lit de Justice* assemblies, but the exact dimensions of that influence are not known. Du Tillet was appointed chief clerk of the Parlement of Paris in 1521 but did not gain definite title to that office until May 1526 following litigation against a brother, Séraphin du Tillet, who contested the appointment.[18] The fact that Séraphin was still named as recording clerk

[17] Du Tillet, *Recueil des roys de France* (preface), fols. a iii[r-v]. The vehemence of this passage defending his work might be attributable to accusations made in the 1560's such as that of La Planche, *Histoire de l'estat de France*, who wrote the following about *greffiers*: "There are two types of men called ministers of judges . . . *greffiers* and *sergens*. We can call the *greffiers* butchers of the people. They distort and stretch parchment by excessive tautologies of language, by great bursts of letters written over long intervals . . . [their] clerks are greedy robbers . . . who pillage masters and valets. . . . It is necessary for the good of justice to restrain their salaries . . . and reform their style of writing." Du Tillet, according to La Planche, was not a man of letters; ibid., 373. Du Tillet struck back at such comments in *Recueil des roys*, pp. 277-278.

[18] *Catalogue des actes de François Ier* (Paris, 1887-1908), I, 249-250, no. 1363, reads, "Provisions de l'office de protonotaire et greffier civil du Parlement de Paris, en faveur de Jean du Tillet, sur la resignation de Séraphin du Tillet, son

in both *Lits de Justice* of 1527[19] suggests either that the extraneous terms of the legal settlement delayed Jean's full assumption of office or that research duties connected with the convocation of those extraordinary assemblies forestalled his personal exercise of the clerkship. Whatever the case, further information was needed, as Francis I's order of 1542 shows, to settle the differences of opinion which arose in response to the delineation of Royal *Séances* and *Lits de Justice* in these decades. Du Tillet's early archival forays prepared him well to undertake extensive investigations with explicit goals in mind, a task he began in 1548 when Henry II commissioned him to compile information on great assemblies including the *Lit de Justice*. The text of that royal order read in part as follows:

> We wish to be apprised of the rank and order held in all great and solemn assemblies from the times of our predecessors, kings of France, until the present.... For this reason we send you word to cease and postpone all other duties, and we commission you, as well as others appointed by you, to visit and inspect the registers of our said Court of Parlement which document those events. You are to copy faithfully from those registers extracts of sources which verify the above events, especially those which mention specifically the quality of the assembly and whether or not it was solemn, [that is] in the form of Estates or *Entrées* of previous kings into their cities, or convocations, of the *Lit de la Justice* [assembly] or other solemn assemblies where rank and order was observed and assigned to each; and especially those [sources] which record the dates and the reigns of kings in which they [the events] were convoked. And if you determine that further information and verification regarding the above requires that you peruse other extant registers in our

---

père. Dijon (6 June 1521)" [italics added]. But Séraphin is the brother, not the father of Jean. The father of both is Elie du Tillet, ennobled in 1484, vice-president of the Chambre des Comptes in 1514; see Hervé Pinoteau, "Quelques réflexions sur l'oeuvre de Jean du Tillet et la symbolique royale française," *Archives héraldiques suisses* (Lausanne, LXXe année, 1956), pp. 1-24, for geneological details and analyses of engravings contained in the *Recueil des roys*. Jean du Tillet's title to office was presented to Parlement on 15 June 1521, A.N. X1a 1523, fol. 232v, and 30 May 1522, A.N. X1a 1524, fol. 249v, as noted in *Catalogue des actes de François Ier*.

[19] A.N. X1a 1530, fol. 350r (24 July 1527), also in Godefroy, *Cérémonial français* [Reg. Parl.], II, 464; and A.N. X1a 1531, fol. 28r (16 Dec. 1527), also in Godefroy, *Cérémonial français* [Reg. Parl.], II, 480.

Chambre des Comptes or Trésor des Chartes in the said [City of] Paris, you will appear before the officers of the Chambre des Comptes and the keeper of our said [Trésor des] Chartes whom we command and enjoin to show and present to you as many of the said registers as you request . . . in order that similar extracts may be copied from them. All of the extracts finally collected by you are to be delivered forthwith into the hands of our dear and faithful chancellor [François Olivier] as soon as possible . . . [21 December 1548].[20]

Two conjectures can be made from the text of this research commission. First, Henry II was unsure of what type of parlementary assembly to convoke for his first visit to the Grand-chambre of the Parlement of Paris in 1549 and issued the commission in part to settle that dilemma; and second, by 1548 the *Lit de Justice* already was perceived in royal quarters as a "revival" of ancient French practice, although its perpetrators still entertained some nagging curiosity about its origins. The royal commission of 1548 contained a special request for Du Tillet to deliver information about the *Lit de Justice* swiftly to Chancellor François Olivier, so there was some preoccupation with the imminent question about the type of assembly, Royal *Séance* or *Lit de Justice*, which would be convoked for the king's first visit to Parlement following the Royal *Entrée* to Paris in 1549.[21] In addition, the wording of the commission shows that Henry II thought of the *Lit de Justice* as an ancient public assembly and included it with other solemn public assemblies, such as Royal *Entrées* and Estates. That view was confirmed in 1559 when Francis II, preparing for the upcoming Estates General at Orléans, requisitioned from Parlement the drapery apparatus ordinarily used, as he put it, "when we hold our *Lit de Justice* [assembly] there."[22] Conse-

----

[20] Ibid., I, fol. E iv[r]. The commission was delivered to Du Tillet the next day, 22 December 1548.

[21] On that *Séance*, see Chap. V below.

[22] "Nous avons sceu que en estats generaulx de ce royaume que se sont tenez du temps des Roys nos predecesseurs a este pare du parement de veloux bleu seme de fleurs de liz qui a accoustume servir en nostre Cour de parlement quant nous y tenons nostre lict de justice . . . et pour ce que nous desirons que la mesme façon qui a este gardee a nosdictz predecesseurs . . . soit observee . . ."; A.N. X1a 1596, fols. 40-41 (27 Nov. 1560). For the description of that drapery paraphernalia, see above, Chap. I, n. 77. Apparently it was used for the canopied three-step dais constructed for Charles IX at the Estates General of Orléans (1560-1561) held after the untimely death of Francis II. There was discussion about the *Lit de Justice* at this time, as shown by one *parlementaire*, at least, who argued for the Court's sovereign status as the supreme Court in France

quently, even though the *Lit de Justice* assembly had only recently made its debut in 1527 and 1537 clothed differently from a Royal *Séance*, it was treated in royal circles as a traditional French practice by mid century. At the same time, however, those who mused about the *Lit de Justice* also wished to know much more about its history, and so special orders were issued for further investigation, first by Francis I in 1542 and again by Henry II in 1548.

When Henry II died in 1559 Du Tillet must have sought the immediate renewal of his research commission, because Francis II issued another some time between 1559 and 1560. No doubt the clerk had recounted for the new king the dismal disorder and rapid disintegration of rare documents resting in the Trésor des Chartes, for Francis II commented on that egregious situation and directed Du Tillet to reorganize the vast collections of manuscripts housed in the royal archives so that they would be "... enrolled in good registers with a well-organized index and classification...."[23] As the recipient of these royal commissions Jean du Tillet attained free access to a wide range of state secrets and by his own admission entered all archival doors thus opened to him in the registry of the Parlement of Paris, the Chambre des Comptes, and the Trésor des Chartes. There he looked for all documents which shed light on the Public Law of the French monarchy.[24] In the meantime the challenge of this rapidly growing enterprise was met by augmenting the clerical staff. By 1562 at least fourteen clerks and four notaries assisted in the work of the registry,[25] a group busy with research

---

by pointing out that the kings have "held their *Lit de Justice* [assembly] and Court of Peers" there; A.N. X1a 1583, fol. 379r (5 Dec. 1556).

[23] B.N. ms. fr., n. a. 20256, fol. 55v, contains a copy of this commission signed by Francis II but mistakenly dated 12 May 1562. As pointed out by Kelley, *Foundations of Modern Historical Scholarship*, p. 219, n. 14, the commission is published in Henri Omont, "Jean du Tillet et le Trésor des Chartes (1562)," *Bulletin de la Société de l'histoire de Paris*, XXXI (1904), 79-81, and it is mistakenly ascribed to Francis I in *Catalogue des actes de François Ier*, VII, 453, as well as in Arthur de Boislisle, "Jean du Tillet et le Trésor des Chartes," *Société de l'histoire de France, Annuaire-Bulletin*, X (1873), 106-111.

[24] Godefroy, *Cérémonial françois*, I, fol. E iv^v.

[25] Maugis, *Histoire du Parlement*, I, xvii-xxiii, notes the many complaints about stolen and falsified records in the 1550's and 1560's. The difficulties of keeping registers under lock and key are shown by an incident of 1565: the clerk was informed that printed texts of the Edict of Pacification of January 1562 had been sold publicly even though the original, registered by one clerk alone, was locked in the depot afterward; ibid., I, 545, n. 3. Information contained in registers was critical in controversies of the mid-sixteenth century, including

projects as well as record-keeping. Launched upon the uncharted seas of historiography, Du Tillet on his own recognizance from the late 1520's, and by royal commission between 1542 and 1563, rummaged for almost four decades through vast stores of archival documents. He borrowed rare manuscripts, determined the provenance of many sources, and analyzed the French past directly through them. He did not achieve a tidy reformation of the archives and may even have contributed to the confusion by failing to return certain manuscripts borrowed during his lengthy tenure.[26] Yet in the end he made a chronological compilation of important documents which recounted the history of French Public Law and institutions, and he served as the resident expert on royal ceremony, thus imposing some order upon the chaos.

In the 1560's Jean Du Tillet sought remuneration for this lifetime of scholarly labor. For that purpose he composed a preface for the yet unpublished *Recueil des roys de France* presented to Charles IX in 1566.[27] In that preface he decried the longstanding lack of financial support which had doomed the efforts of his predecessors (such as Girard de Montagu, secretary of Charles V) to compile collections of French historical documents, and he described in some detail for Charles IX his own archival labors.

> Since being installed in office I have searched through countless registers of your Parlement and visited libraries and ecclesiastical repositories in your kingdom. With the permission of the late king, your father [Henry II] ... , I entered the Trésor des Chartes and consulted all [the documents] just as he commanded. On his promise of compensation for the great expenses incurred in such work, I then organized these [documents] in historical form according to the [dates of] reigns: [first], controversies recorded between this

---

the place of the *Lit de Justice* in the ancient constitution, and in one case of 1537 the only account of the *Lit de Justice* remaining was found later in the possession of Barnabé Brisson, president of Parlement in 1580.

[26] Later on Pierre Dupuy, *Traitez touchant les droits du roi très chrestien* (Paris, 1655), p. 1011, complained that "M. du Tillet gained entrance into the archives to examine and to borrow whatever he needed, and this he did with such abandon that the titles he used were not replaced and many were kept by him and lost ..."; cited in Kelley, *Foundations of Modern Historical Scholarship*, p. 220, n. 15. Still, Dupuy admired the clerk greatly for his historical acumen; *Traité de la majorité* (preface), fol. [a iv^v] and p. 314.

[27] Pinoteau, "Quelques réflexions sur l'oeuvre de Jean du Tillet," p. 2, cites that date.

dynasty and its neighbors; [second], references to the domain of the Crown . . . ; and [third], evidence of the laws and ordinances [promulgated] since the Salic [Law]. . . . [Moreover], I compiled in separate collections those [documents] pertaining to royal persons and houses, to the ancient form of governance of the three Estates, and to the regulation of justice in the kingdom [with attention to] changes which have occurred [over time].[28]

This statement recounts two stages in Du Tillet's scholarly enterprise, the original period of research and the final compilation of sources; and it reaffirms the suggestion made earlier that these historical inquiries were undertaken very early in his career. First, Du Tillet's mention of his installation in office refers to his clerkship of 1521, substantiated in 1526; so the visits to registers of Parlement and libraries which followed that appointment represent his activities from the 1520's. The allusion to his extended forays in the Trésor des Chartes at the behest of Henry II recalls the royal commission of 1548 (renewed by Francis II between 1559 and 1560), which made research in other archives possible through the 1560's. Second, Du Tillet's mention of his organization of sources relative to foreign conflicts, the domain of the Crown, the Salic Law and other laws and ordinances suggests that his research supplied evidence to legitimate the three *Lit de Justice* assemblies of Francis I in 1527 and 1537 and to support the constitutional precepts set forth in them. Finally, his emphasis on the historical perspective underlying this compilation of documents on royal affairs, the three Estates, and the regulation of justice refers to the writing of the *Recueil des roys de France*, his great antiquarian treatise.[29] Du Tillet's major contribution to French constitutional theory, the "discovery" of the ancient *Lit de Justice* assembly (a public forum for legislator-kings) is set forth in that treatise. One must turn to the *Recueil des roys de France*, therefore, to comprehend the historical suppositions which supported the convocation of *Lits de*

---

[28] Du Tillet, *Recueil des roys de France* (preface), fol. A ii^v-a iii^r. Kelley *Foundations of Modern Historical Scholarship*, p. 227, cites the preface as addressed to Francis II rather than Charles IX.

[29] Two surviving manuscripts show how he searched through a maze of unindexed documents, made notes to serve as an index, recorded by date references to sources, and either crossed out entries or left them unmarked for inclusion in or deletion from a final comprehensive work; B.N. ms. fr. 1831, sources from 1255-1488; and B.N. ms. fr. 18311, sources from 1468-1523 (fols. 1r-84v), from 1468-1577 (fols. 85r-447v).

Justice in the sixteenth century and to trace the effect of that constitutional theory on later events.

Constitutional Theory in the *Recueil des roys de France*

Jean du Tillet's major historical treatise merits a special place within the tradition of official French historiography. It was first published post-humously under the title *Les Mémoires et les recherches* (editions 1577 and 1578) and was then published in an expanded version entitled *Recueil des roys de France* (editions 1580, 1586, 1587, 1588, 1602, 1607, and 1618) (see Table One, Column D).[30] Two of the subtitled works contained in the *Recueil des roys de France*, the *Recueil des roys* and more importantly the *Recueil des grands*, stand out as excellent examples of scholarly research in the antiquarian mold of early modern times.[31] Later on, they served as prime sources for all scholars whose convictions about the antiquity of the *Lit de Justice* sent them in search of precedents.[32] The writing of the *Recueil des roys* and the *Recueil des grands* probably began in the 1540's or earlier and ended in 1563, the last date mentioned in both.[33] Du Tillet's approach, oriented in legal and historical directions, resembled that of the legal humanists. He purposefully reconstructed past events and customs in order to set forth "knowledge of precedent" and "separate the true and the false from events over thousands of years." He interpreted his data with a sense of historical relativity, accounting for "changes which have occurred" over the ages and distinguishing between laws and institutions still valid and those obsolete.[34] This critical

[30] See above, n. 3, for the full citation. Elie du Tillet, Sire of Gouaix (*grand maître des eaux et forêts*), second son of Jean du Tillet, the clerk, made all the posthumous editions and wrote the supplements; Pinoteau, "Quelques réflexions sur l'oeuvre de Jean du Tillet," p. 3.

[31] Note that in the *Recueil des roys* the pagination skips at p. 112 to p. 143, and in the *Recueil des grands* it skips at p. 89 to p. 92. It should be understood here that the "antiquarian mold" means a type of historical research admirable in the context of early modern France.

[32] Sixteenth- and seventeenth-century writers who developed the full legend of the *Lit de Justice* assembly all leaned heavily on Du Tillet's scholarship; consult Table One and see below, Chap. IX.

[33] Du Tillet, *Recueil des roys*, p. 280, where 17 May 1563 is the last date; and *Recueil des grands*, p. 107, where 17 August 1563 is the last date.

[34] Ibid., *Recueil des roys de France* (preface), fol. a iii[r]; see Kelley, *Foundations of Modern Historical Scholarship*, pp. 226-233, for that citation and a lengthy account of Du Tillet's scholarly investigations, especially his sense of historical

sense of historical relativity resulted in a search for the roots of French institutions which was directed not to a nebulous time immemorial but to a specific historical moment identified by original documents. From that search Du Tillet compiled sources on parlementary sessions attended by the king, analyzed those events in their time, and classified them in two separate categories, Royal *Séances* and *Lit de Justice* assemblies.

The thinly etched outline of Du Tillet's constitutional theory regarding the *Lit de Justice* assembly is barely visible in the *Recueil des grands*, because the antiquarian format of the work (a lengthy compendium of vital facts with scant formal analysis) demands conceptual organization.[35] The following discussion supplies a conceptual framework for the *Recueil des grands* and the companion piece, the *Recueil des roys*, as well as several other published and unpublished works. The salient point to keep in mind is that no thorough compilation of sources relative to royal par- lementary sessions had ever been made before, let alone subjected to historical scrutiny.

In the *Recueil des grands* Du Tillet divided great national assemblies, past and present, into two major categories, "ecclesiastical" assemblies (Coronations and Funerals) and "secular" assemblies (Estates, *Entrées*, parlementary sessions).[36] Clearly, his major concern was with secular events, particularly the parlementary assemblies attended by the king. Du Tillet produced numerous copies of extracts from archival documents dated from 1224 to 1563 which recounted royal visits to Parlement, judicial decisions and royal ordinances registered there, and regulations applied to the Court and its personnel over time; and he pointed especially to Parlement's growing secular orientation.[37] From those materials Du

---

relativity, distinguishing between laws still valid and those obsolete, a view which differs from Church, *Constitutional Thought*, p. 204, who credits historians of this time with studying documents but suggests that they lacked a real sense of historical perspective.

[35] Basically the *Recueil des grands* is divided into three parts: an introduction (pp. 6-22), a collection of documentary sources (pp. 22-109), and a summary (pp. 109-113). The introductory essay discusses the types of notable persons involved in great national assemblies. The long series of documentary sources gives extracts from archival manuscripts and parlementary registers dating from the seventh century to 1563. The summary of sources accounts for differences of rank observed over time by references to historical conditions and is followed by a short commentary denying any right to wear swords in Parlement.

[36] See above, n. 10.

[37] Du Tillet, *Recueil des grands*, pp. 31-108. Lemaire, *Les Lois fondamentales*, p. 83, n. 4, states that Du Tillet intended to analyze "Justice," presumably the

Tillet painted a vivid portrait of the evolution of Parlement: first from around the mid-eleventh century, when the "parlement" was a traveling Court of peers and advisers which was gradually staffed with professional *parlementaires*; then from the mid-fourteenth century, when that "parlement" became a fixed judicial body or supreme Court, the Parlement of Paris, procedurally regulated and located in Paris by Philip VI [1328-1350].[38] To this history of Parlement he bound another hypothesis regarding the simultaneous evolution of a medieval *Lit de Justice* assembly, which was procedurally linked with that specialized judicial body and comprehended the ancient Court of peers.[39] This idea, that the *Lit de Justice* assembly emerged as an institution along with the Parlement of Paris, thoroughly pervades the pages of this vast compilation of sources.

In the *Recueil des grands* one can perceive essentially three stages in Du Tillet's analysis of French constitutional history. In the first stage the clerk copied from registers of Parlement and other archives original sources documenting forty-nine sessions which brought the monarch together with the Parlement between 1310 and 1563 (Table Two).[40] He then separated them into two different groups, using affiliation with the Parlement of Paris as the delineator. Those sessions which were convoked in the Grand-chambre of the Parlement of Paris and seated the monarch and others together with the whole body of Parlement were judged as official royal parlementary sessions; whereas those which were held in other locations and summoned only a contingent of *parlementaires* to the king's presence were considered as ad hoc royal meetings. From his list of forty-nine sessions the clerk discarded the thirteen ad hoc royal sessions held between 1310 and 1559.[41] Thus thirty-seven official royal sessions in Parlement remained to be studied.

Parlement of Paris. There is no separate work of this nature in print or in manuscript, unless we can consider the *Recueil des grands* as the study mentioned.

[38] Du Tillet, *Recueil des grands*, p. 8, and *Recueil des roys*, pp. 365-366 and 376.

[39] In that vein Du Tillet located the origins of the twelve peers of France in the mid-eleventh century, stating that they were created to assist the king at his Coronation and to sit with him to render sovereign justice; and from the mid-fourteenth century the peers would attend the monarch when "he holds his *Lit de Justice* [assembly]"; Du Tillet, *Recueil des roys*, pp. 362-386, especially pp. 364-368.

[40] Du Tillet, *Recueil des grands*, pp. 35-108; and see Table Two below.

[41] One was held in an unidentified location (1310), two in the palace of the Louvre (1332, 1367), seven in the Hôtel Saint-Pol (two in 1366, one each in 1367, 1369, 1374, 1404, and 1412), one outside of Paris in the Château of Vendôme (1458), one in the Salle Saint-Louis of the Palais de Justice (1558), and one in the Convent of the Augustinians (1559). See Table Two below.

In his second stage of analysis Du Tillet studied documents pertinent to the thirty-seven official royal parlementary sessions convoked in the Grand-chambre and procedurally linked with the Parlement of Paris.[42] Although they seemed similar on the surface, they differed in substance, and the historical eye of the clerk fastened upon the dissimilarity. He decided that those official sessions actually constituted two different types of assembly: one type was honorary in purpose because the king simply graced Parlement with his presence during ordinary proceedings; the other type was constitutional in nature because the king treated matters related to French Public Law. Separating them on that basis, he grouped together twenty-five honorary sessions, which he categorized as Royal *Séances* held between 1369 and 1563.[43] Then he concentrated on the remaining twelve sessions.

In his third stage of analysis Du Tillet intensively studied archival documents relevant to the twelve seemingly extraordinary sessions convoked in the Grand-chambre of the Parlement of Paris, which he eventually designated as *Lit de Justice* assemblies, held in 1369, 1375, 1378, 1387, 1392, 1396, 1407, 1413 (2), 1527 (2), and 1537.[44] He found that in all cases (except the one of 1396) issues of constitutional import headed the agenda. And he saw that these assemblies were convoked in two forms, either as Courts of peers, where accused peers of the realm were judged by colleagues, or as consultative bodies, where participants were invited to counsel the king.[45] Du Tillet cited as examples of the first form of *Lit de Justice* (peer trials) three events of December 1378, March 1387, and July 1527, when Charles V, Charles VI, and Francis I assembled princes, peers, royal officers, Council members, and *parlementaires* in the

[42] See Table Two.

[43] Those *Séances* were held in 1369, 1493 (2), 1498, 1499, 1502, 1504 (3), 1505, 1508 (2), 1509, 1515 (2), 1517, 1522, 1523, 1524, 1549, 1551, 1552, 1558, 1559, and 1563. Also, see Table Two below.

[44] See Table Two.

[45] Du Tillet pointed out that peers accused of *lèse-majesté* must be tried in a Court staffed by other peers of the realm and acknowledged the legal opinion of 1458 which required the presence of French monarchs in person at such trials, and he admitted that the evidence was indecisive as to whether or not it was necessary to hold a *Lit de Justice* assembly for judgment against a prince of the blood; *Recueil des grands*, pp. 15, 65-67. He strongly cautioned readers against the false opinion which would extend the authority of peers beyond the judicial sphere to advisory councils, since kings had always appointed public councils to deal with "affairs of state" before and after the founding of the Parlement of Paris in the mid-fourteenth century and peers gave counsel on constitutional matters, including the composition of regencies, only if the king requested it; *Recueil des roys*, p. 367.

Grand-chambre of Parlement to hear charges against peers of the realm—Jean (IV) of Montfort; Charles (II), King of Navarre; and Charles (II), Duke of Bourbon—cases which affected the disposition of the royal domain.[46] Moreover, in a separate essay entitled *Du crime de leze majesty*, a collection of sources on peer trials from 1216 to 1527, he again cited these same three trials as examples of *Lit de Justice* assemblies.[47] Many peer trials are listed in the *Recueil des roys*, *Recueil des grands*, and the essay on *lèse-majesté*, but only those of 1378, 1387, and 1527, which allied the monarch and Parlement in the Grand-chambre, are designated as *Lit de Justice* assemblies. Consequently, Du Tillet's notion of an institutional linkage between the *Lit de Justice* and the Parlement of Paris shows forth clearly in these studies, and this institutional bias accounts for the fact that he never suggested that the trials of Artois (held in the Louvre in 1332) and Alençon (held at Vendôme in 1458) were *Lit de Justice* assemblies.[48] Du Tillet concluded that a variety of assemblies had been employed to try peers of France for treason, but only the *Lit de Justice* was institutionally related to the Parlement of Paris.

Du Tillet cited as examples of the second form of *Lit de Justice* assembly (consultative bodies) eight events of May 1369, May 1375, December 1392, December 1407, May 1413, September 1413, December 1527, and January 1537, when Charles V, Charles VI, and Francis I assembled in the Grand-chambre princes, peers, royal officers, Council members, *parlementaires*, and sometimes persons of the three Estates to give counsel on matters pertaining to the royal domain and problems of succession.[49] He considered such problems at length. Du Tillet professed himself an expert on questions relating to the royal domain,[50] and he also wrote a separate essay on the Salic Law.[51] In addition he joined the volatile political argument over the accession of Francis II (1559-1560), writing tracts on the French Law of Succession which again identified some of these same events as *Lit de Justice* assemblies. Published by Du Tillet in 1560, the two tracts on succession, *Pour la majorité du roy* and *Pour l'entière majorité du roy*, supported the claim of Francis II to rule without

[46] See Table Two.

[47] B.N. ms. fr. 17318 (Du crime de leze majesty), fols. 71r-77v.

[48] Ibid.; see Table Two below.

[49] See Table Two.

[50] See the quotation of Du Tillet, above, n. 28.

[51] B.N. ms. fr. 17294 (Discours sur la loy salique), fol. 215r, which Kelley, *Foundations of Modern Historical Scholarship*, p. 228, n. 32, suggests was an early version of "Des anciens loix des françois" in *Recueil des roys*, pp. 9-10.

an appointed regency.[52] In those tracts he argued that at fifteen years of age Francis had achieved the "age of majority" required by French constitutional law to exercise the royal *dignité*, an opinion opposed by adversaries who claimed that the "age of discretion," even for a monarch, was twenty-five years as specified by civil law.[53] In this fray Du Tillet alone argued on historical grounds, comparing his trustworthy sources, original documents signed, dated, and preserved in national archives, with the "fables and palace gossip" drawn from chronicles by his adversaries.[54]

Du Tillet's historical argument on the age of royal majority rested on two crucial points, both supported by archival evidence contained in the *Receuils*, then still unpublished: first, that Charles V presiding in the Parlement of Paris in May 1375 promulgated the "Law of Majority," which stipulated the right of French monarchs to full rule at the completion of fourteen years of age; and second, that Charles VI confirmed that ordinance in December 1392 and December 1407. What is more, the clerk alleged that these three sessions called to promulgate Public Law were *"Lit de Justice"* assemblies.[55] Du Tillet's adversaries were

---

[52] Du Tillet, *Pour la majorité du roy très chrestien, contre les escrits des rebelles* (Paris, 1560) and *Pour l'entière majorité du roy*. Du Tillet comments on these tracts in *Recueil des roys*, pp. 277-279. He recounts how Francis II and Queen Catherine de Médicis ordered publication of the first tract, how it was attacked by adversaries (the malcontents), and how he countered with publication of the second tract to silence the opposition, mainly the "imposter" [Pierre de La Place], author of *Commentaires de l'estat de la religion et republique*, in *Histoire de l'estat de France*. Later on Pierre Dupuy included the tracts on majority in his treatise, because copies of them were extremely rare; *Traité de la majorité* (preface), fol. [a iv^v], with the tracts on pp. 317-329, 329-347. Kelley, *Foundations of Modern Historical Scholarship*, pp. 224-225, n. 6, points out that Du Tillet's pronouncements on majority acquired legal authority when Chancellor Michel de L'Hôpital inserted the works in the collection of royal ordinances, *Ordonnances des roys de France*, VI, 26-32.

[53] The political stakes were high. If Francis II was truly a "major," then political influence fell to his Council, the powerful Catholic Guise faction. Princes of the blood and peers, including the Protestant Antoine, King of Navarre, would be shunted aside. For a good summary of this contest of 1560, see Kelley, *Foundations of Modern Historical Scholarship*, pp. 223-225.

[54] Du Tillet, *Pour l'entière majorité du roy*, fol. d^v.

[55] For 1375 and 1407, Du Tillet, *Pour la majorité du roy*, pp. 9-13, *Pour l'entière majorité du roy*, fol. d^v (both tracts published later with some errors in Dupuy, *Traité de la majorité*, pp. 317-329 and 329-347), and *Recueil des grands*, pp. 52-58, 60. For regencies in general, see Du Tillet, *Recueil des roys*, pp. 275-281,

astonished at this use of historical proof to support the royal case. He was angrily accused of having sold his pen to the powerful.[56] Yet the accusation was far afield. The clerk could indeed wield a polemical pen, but in the main he wrote as a historian whose collection of ancient documents offered a compelling discovery about the French past: first, that Charles V, acting as constitutional legislator, had legitimately created the Law of Majority to cover circumstances unforeseen in the ancient Salic Law and that Charles VI had confirmed that law; and second, that these legislative activities associated with the Public Law of the French monarchy were carried out in a unique genre of French constitutional assembly, the *Lit de Justice*, convoked by the king for that purpose in the Grand-chambre of the Parlement of Paris. For Du Tillet, therefore, the roots of the juristic monarchy were firmly planted in the later fourteenth century.

According to the theory set forth by Du Tillet in the historical treatises, the *Recueil des grands* and the *Recueil des roys*, supported in his essays on the Salic Law and the crime of *lèse-majesté*, and argued in his tracts, *Pour la majorité du roy* and *Pour l'entière majorité du roy*, there existed in French history twelve *Lit de Justice* assemblies which were called to treat constitutional issues. The evidence he produced substantiated that claim for all the events except one. In addition to alleging constitutional content as the rationale for convoking *Lit de Justice* assemblies, the clerk produced philological evidence to buttress the case.[57] Du Tillet probed the language of the original texts of nine medieval assemblies and copied verbatim excerpts from them for the *Recueil des grands*; therefore, he knew that the innovative pattern of language used in six sources, 1387, 1392, 1396, 1407, and 1413 (2), mentioned a *"lit de justice,"* whereas the traditional pattern of language used in the other three, 1369, 1375, and

---

especially pp. 277-279, and *Recueil des grands*, pp. 120-123. The original ordinance on majority (1375) is published in *Ordonnances des roys de France*, VIII, 518; and the confirmations (1392), ibid., VII, 530-538, and (1407), ibid., IX, 267-269.

[56] For the circumstances of the accusation, see Kelley, *Foundations of Modern Historical Scholarship*, pp. 225-226. The accusation did not spring solely from religious passion, as the acrimonious debate between La Planche and Du Tillet over the office of *greffier* suggests.

[57] Note also how Du Tillet muses about the word "parlement"; *Recueil des roys*, p. 376. On his interest in etymology in general and specific use of philological evidence to support his thesis of the Germanic origins of the French, and on the impact of philology on legal studies of the time, see Kelley, *Foundations of Modern Historical Scholarship*, pp. 229-233, and 241-270.

1378, contained no such allusion.[58] The clerk did not necessarily know about Charles V's transfer of drapery apparatus to the Parlement of Paris in 1366 and had not read the usher's expense account of 1396 dubbing that apparatus as a *"lit de justice,"*[59] so he probably never imagined that the contemporary term referred simply to draperies decorating the royal seat. Musing about the etymological root of *"lit"* in *"lit de justice,"* he toyed with the idea that the term signified the royal throne itself.[60] Yet the thronal explanation did not satisfy Du Tillet as it did others whose suppositions rested on a cursory knowledge of ancient artifacts. Although the phrase *"lit de justice"* was unfamiliar and its provenance uncertain, he detected a slight etymological shift in tone, procedural in meaning, which was sounded by the two texts of 1413.[61] Convinced already that these nine medieval assemblies were constitutional in orientation and now aware that six of the events were also associated with a *"lit de justice"* which in two cases connoted parlementary procedure, Du Tillet ignored other textual discrepancies and bound the assemblies together under the common genre of *Lit de Justice.*[62] In the end, therefore, the clerk was convinced that he had "discovered" the medieval prototypes for the three assemblies of 1527 and 1537 convoked in his own time. Only one of the medieval events, that of April 1396, eluded this fairly taut constitutional theory about the origin of the *Lit de Justice.* How was he to view the trial of Pierre de Craon in 1396? Attended by the monarch

[58] Consult Table Two below.

[59] For those documents, see above, Chap. I, nn. 3 and 7.

[60] The clerk knew about the regulations for use of the drapery paraphernalia in Parlement issued in 1345 (see above, Chap. I, n. 10) and mused about the relation between the *"lict du roy"* in his chamber and that used when "he holds his *lict de justice* [assembly]"; Du Tillet, *Recueil des grands*, p. 20, and *Recueil des roys*, p. 416.

[61] See Table Two below.

[62] By comparing Du Tillet's comments on *Lit de Justice* assemblies in the *Recueil des grands*, *Recueil des roys*, and other works with original sources for the same events which he compiled accurately in the *Recueil des grands*, we can detect the mental process which led him to entitle events as *Lits de Justice* even when original sources mentioned no *lit de justice*. Compare the following: (1) May 1369: discussion in *Recueil des roys*, p. 256, with the original extract from registers of Parlement, *Recueil des grands*, pp. 51-52; (2) May 1375: discussion in *Recueil des roys*, p. 277, *Pour la majorité du roy*, pp. 9-13, and *Pour l'entière majorité du roy*, fol. d^v, with the extract in *Recueil des grands*, pp. 52-53; and (3) December 1378: discussion in *Recueil des grands*, pp. 11, 14, 18, and "Du crime de leze majesty," B.N. ms. fr. 17318, fols. 71r-77v, with the extract from registers in *Recueil des grands*, pp. 53-55.

in the Grand-chambre of the Parlement of Paris, the assembly was convoked not to judge a peer of France but only to treat charges against a royal official. According to Du Tillet's constitutional criterion (the presence of an issue affecting French Public Law), this trial should not have qualified as a *Lit de Justice* assembly; yet the language of the registers mentioned a *"lit de justice"* for that event.[63] To be sure, the phrase was used that very day by parlementary ushers charged with hanging the thronal drapery apparatus, but Du Tillet was not aware of that fact. Hence this event of 1396 remained an anomaly in his scheme, included as a *Lit de Justice* assembly but left unexplained in constitutional terms.

What Jean du Tillet concocted out of this wealth of archival evidence was a tantalizing theory about the unique character of French laws and institutions. Rather than being fixed since time immemorial, they had demonstrated great flexibility in the face of changing historical conditions. He viewed the Parlement of Paris as having evolved in two stages, ambulatory and institutionalized, and correlated the growth of a *Lit de Justice* assembly with the second phase of the Court's development. In those early "parlements," amorphous gatherings bereft of standard procedure, the king sat in Royal *Séances*; but in the Parlement of Paris, institutionalized from the mid-fourteenth century, the king sat in two types of parlementary sessions, Royal *Séances*, ordinary sessions which did not require his presence, and *Lits de Justice*, constitutional assemblies which required the presence of the king, comprehended the Court of peers, and were procedurally tied to the Parlement of Paris. This theory alleged a historical turning point in the mid-fourteenth century, when *Lit de Justice* assemblies appeared and were distinguished from Royal *Séances* on constitutional grounds. To susceptible antiquarian spirits, the new constitutional theory supplied a heady and truthful amalgam of historical precepts too long lost. Thus from Jean du Tillet's careful scholarship there arose the historical fiction of the medieval *Lit de Justice* assembly.

Du Tillet's constitutional theory differed significantly from the view which prevailed among the *parlementaires* in 1527 and 1537, and that theory would be openly debated in 1549. During the decade which witnessed the first three *Lits de Justice*, the *parlementaires* dated the institutionalization of the Parlement of Paris earlier, in the reign of Philip IV (1285-1314); treated the Royal *Séance* as a historical tradition rooted in the birth of the monarchy and common to ancient and modern

[63] Consult Table Two below.

parlementary protocol alike; and placed all royal visits to the Court in a single genre. By virtue of his access to archival resources, his enlarged clerical staff, and his research commissions, however, Jean du Tillet was by far the most privileged participant in this search for ancient laws and institutions. Moreover, his daily function as chief clerk of the Parlement of Paris, inexorably intertwined with his long-term historical research, invested his encyclopedic *Recueil des roys de France* with considerable stature. Yet over time even that formidable treatise, as all historical works, was subjected to considerable revision. In Du Tillet's case the findings were amended in a peculiar fashion even before the posthumous publication of the book.

REVISION OF DU TILLET'S THEORY IN THE MEMORANDUM OF 1560

One of the most interesting instances of outright tampering with historical evidence to suit short-term political circumstances lies in the anonymous memorandum on *Lit de Justice* assemblies which purportedly summarized Du Tillet's constitutional theory.[64] The memorandum was attributed to Du Tillet three quarters of a century after his death,[65] but the internal evidence of the document proves that attribution false. In all probability the memorandum was requisitioned by Chancellor Michel de L'Hôpital around 1560; certainly it was written by a person who interpreted Du Tillet's work with some latitude. First, the anonymous author of the memorandum repeated accurately Du Tillet's theory delineating *Lits de Justice* and Royal *Séances* on constitutional grounds, but failed to date some of the events adduced as evidence. Then he added a new ceremonial guide for the two types of sessions, but skewed the historical evidence to fit that guide. Finally, he added an odd paragraph to his summary which suggested that the *Lit de Justice* assembly could be convoked outside of Paris, an assertion quite contrary to Du Tillet's theory. A recapitulation of the major points set forth in this document shows how Jean du Tillet's data were molded to fit a different context.

[64] Godefroy, *Cérémonial françois*, II, 427-428, published in 1649 with the Godefroys' comments in margins. A manuscript copy of the document, B.N. Cinq Cents Colbert ms. 212, fols. 210r-v and 213r-v (two pages mistakenly inserted between), was found among the papers of Mathieu Molé (1584-1655), a *procureur général* and then president of Parlement, keeper of the Trésor des Chartes and friend of Pierre Dupuy.

[65] Godefroy, *Cérémonial françois*, II, 427, margin notes.

The author of the memorandum of 1560 correctly recounted Du Tillet's distinction between Royal *Séance* and *Lit de Justice*, and he also propagated Du Tillet's historical fiction about the medieval *Lit de Justice* assembly. The memorandum states that royal parlementary sessions fall into two categories, the *Lit de Justice* assembly and the Royal *Séance*, each distinguished by function, the one constitutional and the other honorary. As a result, the *Lit de Justice* is convoked rarely and only for one basic reason, to deal with matters which "universally concern the state of the king," that is, affairs of state, or constitutional matters. Several examples of such events are given: the confirmation by Charles VI of the ordinance on the majority of French kings [a reference to the event of 1407], the agreement made to ransom the sons of Francis I [a reference to the *Lit de Justice* of December 1527], and the rendition of judgments against peers of France, examples of which are legion [a reference probably to the events of 1378, 1387, and the *Lit de Justice* of 1537]. In contrast Royal *Séances* are honorary events which occur when the king comes to the Court for regular pleadings or council sessions.[66]

Besides recounting Du Tillet's constitutional theory regarding the *Lit de Justice*, the author of this document set forth for the first time a guide to ceremonial protocol for the two types of parlementary sessions. According to that new guide, the most elaborate ceremonial procedure is accorded the *Lit de Justice* assembly. There the king sits on a high throne raised above two other tiers of seating, and officers of Parlement wear distinctive red robes.[67] By way of contrast, the protocol for Royal *Séances* is less elaborate. During one type of Royal *Séance*, the pleadings session, the king sits on a high throne and two tiers of seating are used as in

[66] Godefroy, *Cérémonial françois*, II, 427-428, with no dates given for the events in the memorandum.

[67] Ibid., II, 428. The description states: The king sits on a high throne [i.e. raised by seven steps] above the others in the upper rows of seats, princes of the blood, peers, and lords sit at his sides, and ranked on the steps at his feet are the grand chamberlain, first chamberlain, and provost of Paris. In the lower rows of seats inside the parquet the chancellor, presidents, and councillors of Parlement are seated, while ushers holding staffs kneel in the parquet in front of the king. No habit is specified for the monarch or members of the royal party, but officers of Parlement are vested in red robes with presidents in capes and the clerk in a hood. Notes in the margins show that the Godefroys were puzzled by the attribution of red robes. In their time *Lits de Justice* and *Séances* were no longer distinguished, and red robes were first specified for the third *Lit de Justice* of 1537. They were confused and remarked that "sometimes they [*Lits de Justice*] have been in black robes."

the *Lit de Justice*, but officers of Parlement wear black robes.[68] During the other type of Royal *Séance*, the council session, the king sits in a lower decorated chair in the parquet of Parlement flanked by only one seating tier, and officers of Parlement wear black robes.[69] Finally, Royal *Séances* sometimes comprehend both pleadings and council sessions, as those which have followed Parisian *Entrées*, where the king sits "to honor and authorize his justice" [a reference to the *Séances* of 1498, 1515, and 1549].[70] In summary the Royal *Séance* (pleadings and council) does not require the presence of the king for the enactment of judicial business, and so the *parlementaires* wear black robes whether or not the monarch attends those sessions. In contrast the *Lit de Justice* assembly deals with constitutional issues and requires the presence of the king, and so the *parlementaires* in attendance are vested in ceremonial red robes.

In fact, Du Tillet did not point to any such ceremonial distinction in his work, and the association of the *Lit de Justice* and red-robed *parlementaires* is not borne out by the evidence for the two assemblies of 1527. Even so, by 1560 this anonymous author, who was probably well aware of the symbolic significance of red-robed *parlementaires* attending the king, considered that attire necessary for a *Lit de Justice*. During other public ceremonial occasions such as *Entrées* and the Te Deum, the Parlement of Paris donned red robes in processions; and from at least the fifteenth century, presidents of Parlement marched surrounding the crowned effigy of the king at Royal Funerals, not in mourning dress but in red robes, symbolizing the dual immortality of the royal *dignité*

[68] Ibid. The description states: The king is seated in his high seat [i.e. raised several steps], princes of his blood, lay peers, constable, provincial governors, and other great lords invited for the occasion are seated to his right, and the chancellor, presidents of Parlement, cardinals, and ecclesiastical peers are seated to his left. If places remain empty on the other two sides, they are filled by *maîtres des requêtes*, or the oldest councillors according to their rank, and others sit in the low seats in the parquet. Officers of Parlement wear black robes.

[69] Ibid. The description states: The king sits in a lower decorated chair inside the parquet of Parlement, princes of the blood and lay peers sit in low rows of seats to the right of the king beneath the empty high seats, and cardinals and ecclesiastical peers sit in low seats opposite from the Chambre des Enquêtes. The chancellor and presidents of Parlement also sit in low seats to the left of the king below the empty high seats, and the councillors sit both in the seats across from him and in the second set of seats around the parquet. Officers of Parlement dress in black robes and only Council members invested with the right to give their opinions to the king are seated there.

[70] Ibid., with no dates given. The quoted reference follows Du Tillet's comments on post-*Entrée* visits; *Recueil des grands*, pp. 78-79.

and Crown justice. Although the *parlementaires* wore black for ordinary business in Parlement in the sixteenth century,[71] they donned red robes for the reading of *arrêts* in the Grand-chambre; so this new alliance of red-robed *parlementaires* and monarch in the *Lit de Justice* assembly provided a colorful tableau replete with constitutional symbolism befitting the emphasis on the king as constitutional legislator.

In this memorandum the author correctly summarized Du Tillet's constitutional theory and then created a new ceremonial guide for parlementary assemblies. In the end, however, he actually modified the clerk's theory substantially by allowing the convocation of *Lits de Justice* outside of the Grand-chambre of the Parlement of Paris. Judging from the information contained in one short incongruent paragraph of the memorandum, the document was probably solicited in 1560 with an important question in mind: whether or not a *Lit de Justice* assembly could be convoked outside of the Grand-chambre of the Parlement of Paris. The affirmative answer reads as follows:

> The *Lit de Justice* [assembly] of the king is held most often in the Parlement of Paris, which is the Court of the peers. When the said lord decides to hold it in a place other than Paris, he summons his Parlement to the appropriate location; and at times [the *Lit de Justice*] has been transferred to Montargis, Vendôme [1458], and other cities.[72]

That short statement contravenes the evidence which Du Tillet compiled in the *Recueil des roys de France* and other works. The clerk did not characterize the peer trial at Vendôme [a reference to the event of 1458] as a *Lit de Justice* assembly, he did not discuss the abortive summons which preceded it at Montargis, and he did not produce examples of *Lits de Justice* held in provincial Parlements.[73] To the contrary, from beginning to end throughout his works Jean du Tillet maintained a procedural link between the Parlement of Paris and the *Lit de Justice* assembly. That institutional link is shown in the reconstruction of his constitutional theory given above, and it is further confirmed by the

---

[71] Dauvillier, "Histoire des Costumes des Gens de Justice," pp. 230-240.

[72] Godefroy, *Cérémonial françois*, II, 427, with no dates given. In margin notes the Godefroys remarked that since the time of the memorandum "kings have held their *Lit de Justice* [assemblies] in Rouen [a reference to the event of 1563], Bordeaux [a reference to the event of 1564], and Toulouse [a reference to the event of 1565]."

[73] See Table Two below.

important fact that the clerk never recognized the extraordinary assembly convoked at Rouen in 1563 as a *Lit de Justice*.[74] The anonymous memorandum of 1560 could not have been written by Du Tillet: the lack of reference to the important session of Charles V, where the original Majority Ordinance was promulgated (in 1375), the references by name only to events already dated by him, the addition of a new ceremonial guide to parlementary assemblies based on incorrect information, and most importantly the incongruous reference to the convocation of *Lit de Justice* assemblies outside of Paris all point to a different author. Furthermore, if this important document had been written by Du Tillet, it no doubt would have appeared in the *Recueil des roys de France*. In fact, as will be seen, the appearance of this memorandum represents just one leap of historical imagination in a series of leaps which propelled Du Tillet's ideas along a different route later.

In the meantime, between the 1530's and the 1550's Jean du Tillet's reconstruction of the French constitution produced a critical typology of parlementary assemblies which distinguished *Lits de Justice* from Royal *Séances*, rested that distinction on the fiction of the medieval *Lit de Justice*, and thereby produced a proper historical context for Francis I's three *Lits de Justice* of 1527 and 1537, recently convoked. French constitutional history thus told witnessed a golden era when the newly institutionalized Parlement of Paris harbored Royal *Séances* and *Lit de Justice* assemblies (the 1360's to 1414) followed by a dark interval when royal visits to Parlement ceased (from 1414 to 1483); then the interim decades when the Royal *Séance* was revived in Parlement (from 1484 to 1526) capped by the momentous constitutional renaissance presently underway, which was marked by the revival of the *Lit de Justice* assembly in 1527 and 1537. During the 1540's and 1550's, Du Tillet's theory of the ancient constitution rested quite as the clerk imagined "on its own compelling force," and surely it influenced the policy of Henry II regarding the *Lit de Justice* assembly.

[74] Du Tillet, *Recueil des roys*, p. 280, does not refer to the provincial assembly at Rouen (17 August 1563) as a *Lit de Justice*.

V

A POLARIZED VIEW OF THE FRENCH CONSTITUTION: HISTORY DEBATED AND CEREMONY MODIFIED AT MID CENTURY

> From that time [1350's] on there were no affairs of state treated *in the Court* [Parlement of Paris] except by a *special commission*, and the Court concerned itself with justice only according to the terms of the ordinance of King Jean [II]. *François Olivier (1549)*

BETWEEN the late 1520's and the 1550's, the provenance of the *Lit de Justice* assembly was discussed, Jean du Tillet provided the assembly with historical roots and constitutional validity, and in royal circles, at least, the *Lit de Justice* by mid century was treated as a traditional constitutional forum. During the 1540's and 1550's, therefore, it is perplexing to find that the *Lit de Justice* assembly was not convoked while at the same time some of its novel ceremonial attributes were vested in the Royal *Séance*. Although Henry II (1547-1559) did not hold a *Lit de Justice* during his entire reign, he sat in four Royal *Séances* in the Grand-chambre of the Parlement of Paris in 1549, 1551, 1552, and 1558, and all except one were staged in a ceremonial format somewhat similar to the earlier trio of *Lit de Justice* assemblies in 1527 and 1537. The shift of grand ceremony to the Royal *Séance* seems at first to signal a recission of royal policy delineating two categories of parlementary sessions in favor of the opposing parlementary view conflating all royal visits to Parlement into one timeless genre. To the contrary, however, even though Royal *Séances* came to resemble *Lit de Justice* assemblies ceremonially, the rationale which distinguished them on constitutional grounds remained intact until the last decade of the sixteenth century. The fact is that the clerk Jean du Tillet, a perpetrator of this rationale, designated Henry II's parlementary sessions as Royal *Séances* rather than *Lit de Justice* assemblies precisely because pertinent constitutional issues did not appear on the dockets. From 1549 to 1597 ceremonial splendor thus spread out renaissance style to encompass most parlementary sessions, but the *Lit de Justice* remained apart by virtue of its constitutional format. On that score the debate about the provenance and purpose of the *Lit de Justice* persisted until the differences of opinion on the subject, which were muffled in the *Lit de Justice* assemblies of 1527 and 1537, burst into the open at the Royal *Séance* of 1549.

A HISTORICAL-RHETORICAL DEBATE IN THE ROYAL *Séance* OF 1549

Henry II held his first Royal *Séance* in the Grand-chambre of the Parlement of Paris on 2 July 1549, two years after his Coronation and sixteen days after his Royal *Entrée* to Paris.[1] The ritual was regulated by a new officer, the master of ceremonies, and resembled in some aspects the three earlier *Lits de Justice*. The throne for this *Séance* was raised by several steps only; a huge entourage of notables was seated in the diamond-shaped construct; Queen Catherine de Médicis (crowned at Saint-Denis a month earlier), accompanied by some princesses, sat on the side platform; the crimson-robed chancellor occupied a decorated chair at the foot of the throne; and the princes of the blood were given first rank ahead of the peers of France and the *parlementaires*. The *parlementaires* were vested in ceremonial red robes, some councillors and four presidents of Parlement met the king at Sainte-Chapelle and accompanied him to the Grand-chambre, and the *parlementaires* knelt bare-headed before the king preceding the speech of the first president. Yet even though this assembly might have looked to the uninitiated eye like a *Lit de Justice*, the clerk Jean du Tillet recorded the session in the registers of Parlement as a Royal *Séance*, and both the king and the chancellor described it as a royal visit honoring the Parlement of Paris.[2]

According to Du Tillet, Henry II announced in opening remarks that "... having come to this city [Paris], he wished to observe [the proceed-

---

[1] A.N. X1a 1565, fols. 203v-212r (2 July 1549), where the opening description is exactly the same as those of 1527 and 1537 except that the procedural designation, "holding his *Lit de Justice* [assembly]," does not appear, and the throne elevation (denoted earlier as "seven steps") appears here as "several steps." Extracts of the *Séance* are contained in Du Tillet, *Recueil des grands*, pp. 98-99, and in Godefroy, *Cérémonial françois* [Reg. Parl.], II, 518-530, incorrectly entitled as a *Lit de Justice*. Maugis, *Histoire du Parlement*, I, 518, mistakenly cites A.N. X1a 1665 for this date, and I, 593, calls the *Séance* a *Lit de Justice*. Isambert, *Recueil général des anciennes lois*, XIII, 260-262, calls this *Séance* a *Lit de Justice* and cites it as a ceremonial prototype for that of 12 February 1552, which in fact observed no ceremony at all.

[2] A.N. X1a 1565, fols. 203v-212r (2 July 1549).

ings] and to honor his Court [of Parlement] by his presence."[3] Then the king charged the chancellor to address the assembly on his behalf. To begin with Chancellor François Olivier also noted the honorary nature of the *Séance*.

> Having attended to matters pertaining to his state ... the king retired to this city [Paris], capital of his kingdom. . . . Following his *Entrée* and that of the queen amidst the magnificence and grandeur which his royal majesty merits, [the king] wished to visit this place [the Grand-chambre] and this company [the Parlement of Paris], honoring it by his presence and giving authority to the sovereign justice of this Parlement, which is the Court of the peers of France and one of the most ancient Courts and jurisdictions known in Europe, . . . greatly renowned both among subjects of the kingdom and foreigners.[4]

For the rest Olivier related a history of the Parlement of Paris which employed archival evidence similar to that compiled in Du Tillet's two *Recueils* and probably obtained from the clerk, who had been ordered by the royal commission of 1548 to deliver his findings to the chancellor. According to Chancellor Olivier the history of Parlement could be viewed in four distinct stages: the first stage one of conjecture due to the tentative state of historical knowledge about early "parlements," the second stage one of ambulatory parlementary bodies, the third stage one of institutional evolution, and the fourth stage one of specialization in function.

First, Olivier warned that the origin of "parlements" was somewhat obscure, because

> . . . it is not ascertainable either from histories or from ancient records exactly when this Parlement [of Paris] originated and was organized or how the sovereign justice of France was administered in early times; but it is generally conceded that it [the Parlement

---

[3] Ibid., fol. 205r, for the king's remarks.

[4] Ibid., fols. 205r-207v, for the chancellor's speech. The text of the speech was repeated by Chancellor Philippe Hurault de Cheverny, A.N. X1a 1683, fol. 177r (7 Jan. 1584), and it was given singular importance by Dupuy, *Traité de la majorité*, pp. 574-585, who published the whole text. François Olivier, formerly a president of Parlement, was chancellor from May 1545 to January 1551, when due to illness he no longer exercised the office but retained the title and privileges associated with it; Maugis, *Histoire du Parlement*, III, 150, and I, 595-596, nn. 1 and 2.

of Paris] formerly consisted of an assembly of varied persons chosen
by the king, convoked intermittently, and called "parlement."[5]

Second, he recapitulated the uneven growth of the "parlements" at the
first discernable historical stage, when sporadic convocations of ambulatory feudal courts took place during the reigns of Louis IX and Philip
III; then he identified the first attempt to regulate convocations in the
reign of Philip IV.

> From the reign of King Saint Louis [Louis IX, 1226-1270] and that
> of his son Philip [Philip III, 1270-1285], there were convoked in
> times of peace three or four "parlements" per year. Philip the Fair
> [Philip IV, 1285-1314] reduced that number to two "parlements"
> held in peacetime, one held in summer, the other in winter, and
> only one "parlement" held during wartime, [that one] in winter. It
> is certain that during the reign of King Philip [III], son of Saint
> Louis, there was no certain location established for the "parlement"
> and no exact number [of convocations] specified and that there were
> in attendance [in the parlements] numerous great princes and great
> lords or prelates.[6]

Third, Olivier fastened upon the reign of Philip VI as the era in which
there issued from these diffuse "parlements" a recognizable institution,
the Parlement of Paris. That change occurred when a division of chambers (Grand-chambre, Enquêtes, Requêtes) took place and a specified
number of secular *parlementaires* were designated to staff them. Often-
times the king, princes, and peers joined the Court to discuss important
affairs; therefore, the jurisdiction of the Parlement of Paris still comprehended a wide variety of matters, domestic and foreign, private and
public, civil and constitutional.

> It was King Philip of Valois [Philip VI, 1328-1350] who first es-
> tablished the number of *parlementaires* at sixty-five; that is to say,
> twenty for the Grand-chambre and forty for the [Chambre des]
> Enquêtes and five for the [Chambre des] Requêtes. By the year
> 1342 the Grand-chambre was probably augmented to thirty in ad-
> dition to the presidents, while at the same time the *maîtres des
> requêtes* were reduced to four. The authority of the Parlement
> always has been so great that all cases were received and deliberated

[5] A.N. X1a 1565, fols. 205r-207v (2 July 1549).
[6] Ibid.

upon there. [First] churches requested permission of the king in his Parlement to elect bishops following the death of their prelates. [Second] cases between adversaries were settled there . . . , and . . . great foreign princes often submitted voluntarily to the judgment of Parlement. . . . [Third] most ancient ordinances were made in the Parlement either with the king present or another representing him. . . . An ordinance written during the reign of Philip of Valois, given to Parlement and observed carefully over time, specified that it was forbidden to deputize prelates to hold the Parlement, . . . because the king wished to have in his Parlement men who could hear cases continually and without interruption. . . . All evidence certainly points [in those times] to the ancient authority and integrity of the Parlement and of the Court of the peers of France, where the king and the great princes of his kingdom often assisted and deliberated for the most part on matters of importance.[7]

After establishing the institutional roots of the Parlement of Paris around the 1340's and showing the comprehensive nature of the Court's jurisdiction over private and Public Law at that time, Olivier proceeded further to identify a fourth and final stage in Parlement's evolution, the historical moment in the 1350's when the Parlement of Paris became a specialized judicial body and a concomitant separation of powers, judicial and constitutional, took place.

King Jean II [1350-1364] realized that affairs of state were no longer accorded the secrecy due them and that the Parlement [of Paris] was increasingly burdened with judicial affairs, so he decided to limit the cognizance and jurisdiction of Parlement. He ordained that it [Parlement] would rule thenceforth only on cases of the peers of France . . . and [on cases] of persons who by privilege or precedent were heard in the Court of the domain of the king. . . . From that time on there were no affairs of state treated *in the Court* [Parlement of Paris] except by a *special commission*, and the Court concerned itself with justice only according to the terms of the ordinance of King Jean. However, that [separation of functions] did not entail a loss of renown regarding its [Parlement's] integrity. . . . It [Parlement] remained greatly reputable due to the virtue and knowledge of the persons who composed it and the equity of their judgments and due also to the fact that kings, who always have been devotees

[7] Ibid.

of justice, set for themselves the task ... of preserving their subjects from all wrongs and injustices, ... one of the greatest commendations acquired by kings of France.... [As in the case of] King Charles V [a reference to the event of 1375], ... the just and prudent prince is like a *living and speaking law* which serves the administration of justice better than all the written laws and ordinances which are in themselves deaf and mute....[8]

This interpretation of parlementary history was very radical in conception. Chancellor Olivier allowed that originally feudal "parlements" of French kings had treated both private and Public Law, as did the new institution, the Parlement of Paris, at the immediate outset; but then he correlated the first decades of the Court's institutional status with a concomitant shift in its sphere of jurisdiction. Sometime during the 1350's King Jean II issued an ordinance which in effect removed affairs of state, or constitutional matters, from the Parlement's normal jurisdiction, and thereafter the Parlement of Paris functioned to contemporary times solely as a judicial institution and retained only one aspect of its former constitutional role, that is, its judicial function as a Court of peers. By invoking the example of Charles V (who promulgated the Law of Majority in 1375), Olivier juxtaposed the king in the role of legislator to the Parlement of Paris as adjudicator, noting that Parlement's source of authority was not inanimate ordinances but the animate king, that is, the *living and speaking law* of the realm.[9] Finally, once Parlement took up these specialized judicial duties, ruling as the supreme Court on private law, matters of Public Law were treated *in the Court* only by a *special commission*, that is to say, by the convocation of an extraordinary assembly in the Grand-chambre for that purpose. Throughout his speech the chancellor did not mention the *Lit de Justice* assembly by name, but his separation of judicial and constitutional functions, his allotment of judicial cognizance alone to Parlement, his insistence that after the 1350's affairs of state, or constitutional issues, were treated *in the Court* only by a *special commission*, and his use of Charles V as the example certainly suggested that an extraordinary assembly akin to the *Lit de Justice* had

[8] Ibid. [italics added].

[9] Olivier's formulation points to the antithesis between animate king and inanimate law rendered in the late thirteenth century by Aegidius Romanus, *De regimine principum*, and dedicated to the future King Philip IV, a formulation which was repeated by others, including Lucas de Penna, a jurist much read in early sixteenth-century France; see Kantorowicz, *King's Two Bodies*, pp. 134-136, on the earlier usage.

existed in medieval times and could be convoked again whenever constitutional business arose.[10]

The first president of Parlement, Pierre Lizet, spoke after the chancellor and presented the opposing view. Although the *parlementaires* had
shrouded the *Lit de Justice* in conspicuous silence in 1527 and 1537, they
shifted that stand slightly in 1549 by directly confronting the phrase *lit
de justice* in French historical discourse. Yet even though President Lizet
broke the earlier silence of his colleagues, Charles Guillart, Jean (II) de
Selve, and Jacques Cappel, by speaking openly about a *lit de justice*, he
maintained their skeptical stance by refusing to acknowledge it as an
ancient constitutional assembly. To illustrate his interpretation of French
constitutional history, as opposed to Du Tillet's formulation, President
Lizet emphasized linguistic usage. He argued that the medieval phrase
lit de justice was simply a metaphor for the Parlement of Paris.[11] Thus
in his ken kings had sometimes used the phrase *lit de justice* not as a
title for a special assembly but as an allusion to the Court of Parlement
itself ensconced in the Grand-chambre along with the monarch.

> Sire, it is both fitting and proper that your royal majesty, following
> his excellent and triumphant *Entrée* into Paris, follow the laudable
> custom of your royal predecessors and come to this sovereign con-
> sistory, which is your humble and obedient Court of [the] Parlement
> [of Paris], in order to sit in your true royal throne [= the Grand-
> chambre]. When great assemblies or convocations of the peers of
> France were held [in the Court of Parlement], your predecessors
> called it [the Court of Parlement] the *lit de justice*, indicating by
> that reference the presence there of both your royal majesty and
> your subjects. Sire, in it [the Court of Parlement, or the *lit de justice*]
> you effect repose, because when you choose to come here and
> exercise sovereign justice, then by that [exercise of] justice you affirm
> the obedience and subjection owed you by your subjects ... and
> maintain the true repose and tranquillity of your state.... Sire,
> when you honor sovereign justice with your royal presence, you
> maintain concord, union, and the bonds of human society among

[10] A.N. X1a 1565, fols. 205r-207v (2 July 1549).
[11] In this contest over semantics, both Du Tillet and Lizet concentrated on
procedural nuances, and neither connected the medieval *lit de justice* with the
drapery apparatus. Thenceforth the *parlementaires* would maintain Lizet's metaphorical image to link king and Parlement in governance.

your subjects; consequently, it [the Court of Parlement, or the *lit de justice*] is also for them the *lit* where they repose.[12]

Here President Lizet took direct issue with Chancellor Olivier's interpretation of parlementary history. Lizet gave no quarter either to the notion of a historical separation of judicial and constitutional authority or to the possible existence of any *special commission, Lit de Justice* assembly or other, in Parlement which differed constitutionally from an honorary Royal *Séance*. He did not correctly trace the phrase *lit de justice* to the medieval drapery paraphernalia, but he did locate its usage in figurative rather than procedural language. Lizet thus stated explicitly in 1549 the principle that Parlement had harbored implicitly in 1527 and 1537: that historically the phrase *lit de justice* was a metaphor which brought to the mind's eye a vision of the king and the Parlement of Paris conjoined in the Grand-chambre, that is, a traditional Royal *Séance* in which all matters, judicial and constitutional, were comprehended; there was no constitutional separation of functions. In the Royal *Séance* of 1549, therefore, there were finally expressed outright two diametrically opposed views about the locus of constitutional power and by inference the legitimacy of a *Lit de Justice* assembly in the Court. Since no *Lit de Justice* assembly was convoked to treat a constitutional issue for more than a decade, that dispute hung in abeyance until the 1560's. In the meantime Henry II held three more honorary Royal *Séances* in the Grand-chambre of the Parlement of Paris.

THE ROYAL *Séances* OF 1551, 1552, AND 1558

On 12 November 1551 Henry II attended a second Royal *Séance* in Parlement to witness the annual opening of the Court.[13] Before the arrival

[12] A.N. X1a 1565, fols. 207v-210r (2 July 1549), for Lizet's speech. Pierre Lizet, councillor in 1514, *avocat du roi* in 1517, replaced Jean (II) de Selve as first president in 1529; Maugis, *Histoire du Parlement*, III, 148-149, 157, 336; and in July 1551 Lizet was forced to resign and was replaced by Gilles Le Maistre; ibid., I, 234-235, n. 4.

[13] A.N. X1a 1571, fols. 1r-4r (12 Nov. 1551). This account makes no procedural reference to a *Lit de Justice* being held and describes the scene as one where the king was in his "decorated tribunal" elevated by "several steps." The accounts for the next two *Séances* of 1552 and 1558 follow suit. Extracts are contained in Du Tillet, *Recueil des grands*, pp. 99-100, and in Godefroy, *Cérémonial françois* [Reg. Parl.], II, 531-537, mistakenly entitled a *Lit de Justice*.

of the royal retinue, however, First President Gilles Le Maistre and the *avocat* Pierre (I) Séguier, spokesman for the *gens du roi*, argued over the propriety of presenting four remonstrances to the king, three procedural complaints (against the evocation of cases out of Parlement's jurisdiction, the sale of judicial offices, and the appointment of ecclesiastical rather than lay councillors in the Court) and a fourth regarding the distribution of alms to the poor. President Le Maistre spoke vehemently against the presentation of remonstrances, arguing that "on this solemn occasion, when it pleased the king to assist [in Parlement] in order to honor his Court, the making of them [remonstrances] is improper." In addition he noted that the hour was late and the ceremony allowed no time for such action. Séguier disagreed and insisted that the occasion was eminently suitable for presenting remonstrances to the king, whereupon Le Maistre consulted the Court and insisted again that the *gens du roi* seek an audience with Henry II later in the day instead.[14] In this Royal *Séance*, as in that of 1549, the ceremony was elaborate: the king sat in an elevated throne; the *parlementaires* were red-robed; princes of the blood, peers, knights, royal officers, and others were in attendance; the seals-keeper (acting for the chancellor) was seated at the foot of the throne. Two peers of France, the dukes of Guise and Montmorency, took the oath of peers and sat in the high seats, and the Royal *Séance* opened formally with a speech from the first president. President Le Maistre described Henry II enthroned in the Grand-chambre as a Gallican Augustus, the *living law* of the realm and the *debtor of justice*.

> Sire, the two principal duties required of a good king and emperor ... are [the maintenance of] religion and justice.... In this relationship you are the *debtor of justice* by virtue of the obligation sworn at your *sacre*, and your subjects are your creditors, for there are three oaths which you have sworn in your *sacre* and Coronation (which are registered herein), one of which is to render and administer justice to your subjects and to guard the weak from the oppression of the strong. The act of sitting in your Court to acquaint yourself with the administration of justice acquits you of part of your obligation. Sire, we hope that this *Séance*, the opening of Parlement which it has pleased your majesty to attend, will greatly

[14] A.N. X1a 1571, fols. 1r-4r (12 Nov. 1551). Le Maistre became fourth president in 1550, then first president following Jean Bertrand in 1551; Maugis, *Histoire du Parlement*, I, 595-596, nn. 1 and 2, and III, 189, 333. Pierre (I) Séguier was *avocat du roi* in 1550 and later became president in 1554; ibid., III, 190, 333. Maugis does not discuss this *Séance*, but he implies that the remonstrances were presented that day; ibid., I, 225.

serve justice within your kingdom. . . . Sire, you are the *living law* and your presence greatly authorizes the act [of opening Parlement]. . . . In order to salute your joyous arrival within [the Grand-chambre] today, your Court gives to you an acclamation similar to that . . . made by the Roman Senate to the good emperor Alexander Severus upon his arrival in the Senate: Henry, Christian king . . . , our Caesar, our Augustus, our emperor. . . .[15]

Then the *avocat* Pierre (I) Séguier presented only one of the four remonstrances originally proposed in his dispute with President Le Maistre, the innocuous one pertaining to alms for the poor. In response the seals-keeper Jean Bertrand (exercising the function of vice-chancellor) went up to the throne, spoke to the king, and pronounced in favor of the request. At this point in the *Séance* the whole body adjourned to Sainte-Chapelle, next door, to celebrate a special mass of the Holy Spirit, and afterward the Royal *Séance* was reconvened in the Grand-chambre. There the king admonished the Court to administer proper justice in his name, and the first president pledged the obedience of the Court. Finally, the doors of the Grand-chambre were opened and a crowd of spectators was admitted. The new *avocats* took their oaths, filed before the king, and received advice from the seals-keeper regarding the proper practice of their new profession.[16]

On 12 February 1552 Henry II held a third Royal *Séance* in the Grand-chambre of the Parlement of Paris.[17] That *Séance* confounded the grand ceremonial pattern adopted for Royal *Séances* in 1549 and 1551 because

[15] A.N. XIa 1571, fols. 1r-4r (12 Nov. 1551) [italics added].

[16] A.N. XIa 1571, fols. 1r-4r (12 Nov. 1551). When Olivier was discharged from the exercise of the office of chancellor due to illness in 1551, a new office was created, seals-keeper, with the same rights and privileges as that of chancellor. Jean Bertrand, first president of Parlement, who had already taken charge of the seals two years earlier, was appointed to fill that office; Maugis, *Histoire du Parlement*, I, 595-596, nn. 1 and 2, and II, 172. On the creation of the new office and Parlement's remonstrances against it, see Isambert, *Recueil général des anciennes lois*, XIII, pp. 181-182.

[17] A.N. XIa 1571, fols. 278v-283r (12 Feb. 1552). The account denotes a "decorated tribunal" which was elevated by "several steps" but no *Lit de Justice* assembly. Extracts are contained in Du Tillet, *Recueil des grands*, pp. 100-101, and in Godefroy, *Cérémonial françois* [Reg. Parl.], II, 537-545, where the *Séance* is incorrectly entitled a *Lit de Justice*. Isambert, *Recueil général des anciennes lois*, XIII, 260-262, incorrectly entitles the *Séance* a *Lit de Justice* and mistakenly equates the ceremony with that of 28 [i.e. 2] July 1549, which is also incorrectly dubbed a *Lit de Justice*. Shennan, *Parlement of Paris*, p. 205, dates this *Séance* as "early in 1551" rather than 1552.

the king and his retinue dropped in unexpectedly on the Court that day. Around eight o'clock in the morning the seals-keeper Bertrand told the Court that the king, accompanied by provincial governors, knights, the provost of Paris, and councillors of his private Council, wished to visit the Grand-chambre forthwith before attending mass and to sit in Parlement as in council. Consternation abounded in Parlement following this precipitous announcement: for one thing, the *parlementaires* were in black robes; for another, parlementary propriety would be breached in the *Séance* by the entrance of persons ordinarily not allowed there. Acting swiftly, Parlement dispatched the clerk Jean du Tillet to find Constable Anne de Montmorency and ascertain the king's intentions. As he searched through the palace for the constable, Du Tillet encountered Henry II leaving his chamber for the Palais de Justice and reported his charge to the king. After some discussion with the princes and peers beside him, the king made his intentions known. Du Tillet reported to Parlement that "... he [Henry II] commanded me to tell his Court that on this particular occasion he wished only to inform [Parlement] about matters concerning his state and did not intend to seek advice [of the Court] or to assist in a judicial case there; moreover, he intended to have the provincial governors, knights, and provost of Paris enter [the Grand-chambre] and assist in the council [session]."[18]

The *parlementaires* were angry and confused. They sent four presidents to receive the king, but around nine o'clock he entered the Grand-chambre through rear doors and sat in his seat without ever passing by the parquet. Before the *Séance* proceeded the Duke of Aumale took the oath of a peer of France and moved to the high seats; then the king spoke to Parlement. Since the warmongering of Emperor Charles V might require that he leave the kingdom, Henry said, he wished to apprise all persons beforehand of "the affairs of his state." In the event of his absence, Queen Catherine de Médicis, assisted by the dauphin (the future Francis II) and his council, would head the regency government and must be obeyed as his representative. In particular, items sent by the regent to the Court must be dispatched promptly by officers of the Grand-chambre, setting a good example for other Courts. Speaking for the king, Constable Montmorency outlined the fortunes of war and peace in this reign, castigating Emperor Charles V's insidious designs and suggesting vigilance in case of emergency. Replying for the Nobility, Church, and Parlement respectively, Constable Montmorency, the Car-

[18] A.N. X1a 1571, fols. 278v-283r (12 Feb. 1552).

dinal of Bourbon, and President Le Maistre pledged their cooperation to the king in case of emergency, and this very short session closed around ten o'clock.[19]

Five years later, on 15 January 1558, Henry II held a fourth Royal *Séance* in the Parlement of Paris and sat in a grand ceremonial milieu consonant with those of 1549 and 1551.[20] On 5 January, ten days before, the king had convened the Estates General in the Salle Saint-Louis of the Palais de Justice to request emergency war subsidies from deputies of the three Estates,[21] and he invited participants from that meeting, Parisian City officials, presidents of provincial Parlements, and deputies of the three Estates of the kingdom, to join the princes, peers, royal officers, knights, and *parlementaires* in the Grand-chambre for this *Séance*. Just as Francis I had seated Henry as dauphin in the *Lit de Justice* of 1537, Henry II now seated the dauphin (the future Francis II) in this Royal *Séance*, as well as in the Estates General preceding it.[22] In this last Royal *Séance* Henry II published an edict on religion and announced

[19] Ibid. Shennan, *Parlement of Paris*, p. 205, cites this *Séance* as an example of Henry II's harmonious relations with Parlement, but given the conditions outlined here that view does not hold.

[20] A.N. X1a 1587, fols. 14r-17v (15 Jan. 1558). The account describes a "decorated tribunal" elevated by "several steps" but mentions no *Lit de Justice* assembly. An extract is contained in Du Tillet, *Recueil des grands*, pp. 105-106; and in Godefroy, *Cérémonial françois*, II, 545, who mistakenly calls the *Séance* a *Lit de Justice*, omits the proceedings, and refers the reader for details on ceremonial procedure to the "Assembly of Notables" (that is, the meeting of Estates General) of 5 January 1558.

[21] A.N. U 2046 [Le Nain], fols. 227v-232r (5 Jan. 1558, Salle Saint-Louis), makes a point of noting that the tribunal was elevated by seven steps. Extracts are contained in Du Tillet, *Recueil des grands*, pp. 101-105, who notes that the king assembled "men of the three Estates"; also in Godefroy, *Cérémonial françois*, II, 379-382, where the session is called an "Assembly of Notables." Many others in the seventeenth and early eighteenth centuries (see Table One) considered this meeting a *Lit de Justice* assembly. But Major, *Representative Institutions*, pp. 144-147, labels the event an Estates General. Just as in the *Lit de Justice* of December 1527 (which comprehended three Estates) Parlement must have insisted on separating the Third Estate and Parlement in this session, because the king referred to it as a "general convocation of the four Estates." For the edicts given there, see Isambert, *Recueil général des anciennes lois*, XIII, 494-497, 506-509.

[22] On seating at the Estates, consult the sources in n. 21. Note that in 1558 Francis II was fourteen years old, so his presence in the Royal *Séance* as well as the Estates followed the "Law of Majority" discovered by Du Tillet in these decades and propagated by his pamphlets in 1560.

the stunning French defeat of the English at Calais and his imminent departure for that stronghold.[23]

HENRY II's VISITS to Parlement present a conundrum when analyzed in consort with Jean du Tillet's constitutional theory. On the one hand the sessions were designated correctly in the registers of Parlement as Royal *Séances*, because they did not treat constitutional issues. The first *Séance* of 1549 followed a Parisian *Entrée* and was the first visit to Parlement since the Coronation at Reims; the second in 1551 witnessed the annual opening of Parlement; the third in 1552 announced emergency plans already made for a regency; and the fourth in 1558, close on the heels of the Estates General, announced the French military success at Calais and effected the publication of an edict. Furthermore, the honorary purpose of these *Séances* was recognized not only by Du Tillet, Henry II, and Chancellor Olivier but also by Presidents Lizet and Le Maistre. On the other hand, the ceremony observed in three of the *Séances* was considerably enhanced, but that of the fourth was totally neglected. The *Séances* of 1549, 1551, and 1558 were executed in red-robed Parlements with thrones canopied and elevated by several steps (not seven steps) and with ceremonial ritual reminiscent of the *Lit de Justice* assemblies of 1527 and 1537, whereas that of 1552 was conducted in a black-robed Court with no observance of ceremony. These ceremonial irregularities of the mid-sixteenth century were very perplexing for later commentators.[24] It did not occur to them that the venerable *Lit de Justice* "revived" in 1527 was not clearly distinguished at this time by a specific ceremonial program, especially since the misleading memorandum of 1560 provided a ceremonial guide which required red-robed *parlementaires* in a *Lit de Justice*. Yet the faithful accounts written by the Du Tillets in the registers of Parlement show that the grand ceremonial ritual observed in the *Lits de Justice* of 1527 and 1537 abounded with variations. In this milieu of renaissance splendor ceremony was malleable, readily adapted by kings to serve their purposes in Parlement and elsewhere.

Amidst the escalating international rivalries of the mid-sixteenth century, especially the strain between France and the Empire, Henry II was intensely preoccupied with ceremonial grandeur. At every opportunity he extolled on the ceremonial stage the superiority of French royal

[23] A.N. X1a 1587, fols. 14r-17r (15 Jan. 1558). For edicts given there, see Isambert, *Recueil général des anciennes lois*, XIII, 506-509.

[24] For example, see the comments of La Roche-Flavin, above, Chap. II, n. 2, and the Godefroys, above, Chap. IV, n. 67.

authority. Associated as dauphin with Francis I in the *Lit de Justice* assembly of 1537, Henry II as king associated his own son in the same manner in the Royal *Séance* of 1558 and in the Estates General just before the *Séance*. One of the organizers of Francis I's elaborate Funeral ceremony in 1547, Henry as a hidden spectator viewed that ritual in which the lifelike effigy of his father demonstrated the immortality of the French royal *dignité*. The first French king to dramatize in the Coronation the constitutional relationship of king and kingdom through the marriage metaphor (a precept propagated earlier in *Lits de Justice*), Henry II swore as the *spouse of the kingdom* to uphold French Public Law upon the bestowal of the ring at that ceremony in 1547. Through iconographical devices on display at his Parisian *Entrée* of 1549, Henry II was portrayed as the son of the Gallic Hercules (Francis I), and his own royal device was united with an imperial crown to show, as the attendant inscription noted, that "The king of the French knows no superior on earth"[25] (a precept expressed earlier in *Lits de Justice*). There is no doubt that in this ceremonious milieu stressing sovereign authority both national and international, illustrating the nature of the French royal *dignité* and its relation to the Public Law of the French monarchy, and extolling the superiority of the French over the imperial office, the Grand-chambre of the Parlement of Paris provided the perfect setting for the kind of imperious enthronement required to substantiate the French king's image as a French Augustus and the *living law* of the realm.[26] It was during this heated race for international stature, therefore,

[25] *C'est l'ordre qui a este tenu à la nouvelle et joyeuse entrée, que treshault, tresexcellent, & trespuissant prince, le Roy treschrestien Henry deuzieme de ce nom, à faicte en sa bonne ville & cité de Paris, capitale de son royaume, le seizieme jour de juin. M. D. XLIX* (Paris, 1549): pp. 7 and 9 (plate) for the closed imperial crown above the arms of Henry II and the anti-imperial statement quoted; pp. 10 and 11 (plate) and pp. 24 and 28 (plate) for the closed imperial crown identified with the French king; and p. 3 for the Gallic Hercules (Francis I) surrounded by four orders, Nobility, Clergy, Third Estate, and Parlement, giving advice to his son, another anti-imperial allusion, given the fact that Emperor Charles V utilized Hercules for his device. For details on this entry of 1549, consult Bryant, *French Royal Entry Ceremony*, chap. II, especially the competition between Henry II and Philip II of Spain, son of Emperor Charles V, as the French king made a series of provincial entries between 1547 and 1548, following his Coronation, in anticipation of Philip's plans to visit a series of cities in Brabant and the Netherlands.

[26] Comparisons of the king with the emperor were stock remarks made by the Court, royal officials, and others as part of the general anti-imperial propaganda in these centuries. But comparisons of the Parlement of Paris with the

that Henry II introduced ceremonial nuances for the Royal *Séance* in the Grand-chambre: the drapery paraphernalia, the throne raised by three steps, and most especially, the *parlementaires* impressively red-robed.

Still, there is no evidence to show that Henry II shifted ceremonial elements from the *Lit de Justice* to the Royal *Séance* with the intention of conflating the two into one genre. In fact just the opposite is true. It was probably the king's growing acquaintance with Du Tillet's conservative theory, allowing the convocation of *Lit de Justice* assemblies only for issues pertaining to French Public Law, which led to the preservation of that view of the ancient constitution. The wording of Henry II's research commission to Du Tillet shows that the king considered the *Lit de Justice* a constitutional forum. Henry II ordered Du Tillet in 1548 to dispatch swiftly to the chancellor the results of his research on the *Lit de Justice* assembly, so some version of the clerk's findings was available before the king's first visit to the Parlement of Paris in 1549. Du Tillet never formulated a ceremonial guide for the *Lit de Justice*, and he maintained a conservative constitutional stance on the assembly throughout his checkered career. As it turns out, therefore, Henry II did not violate the constitutional function of the *Lit de Justice*. He never convoked it for ordinary visits to the Grand-chambre such as those ceremonious Royal *Séances* of 1549, 1551, and 1558. Moreover, the ceremonial aggrandizement of Royal *Séances* caused no alarm in Parlement as had the convocation of ceremonious *Lit de Justice* assemblies in 1527 and 1537. Whereas the *parlementaires* had stridently opposed the use of ceremony to distinguish the *Lit de Justice* from the Royal *Séance* in 1527 and 1537 because of the separation of constitutional and judicial authority effected by the distinction, they cooperated amiably with the ceremonial enthronement of the monarch in the Royal *Séance*, for it heightened the prestige of the Parlement of Paris.

In this context Parlement's dilemma regarding the presentation of remonstrances in the *Séance* of 1551 and the dismay occasioned by the lack of ceremony for the *Séance* of 1552 is telling. Henry II's relations with the Parlement of Paris were contentious enough,[27] but remonstrances and *lettres de jussion* pertinent to legislation and exchanged almost daily were not connected with Royal *Séances*. The fact that President Le Maistre questioned the propriety of presenting remonstrances in a Royal *Séance* of 1551, that he and the *avocat* Séguier vehemently disagreed on

---

Senate of Rome subtly promoted the Parisian Parlement as the supreme Court in France and a possible co-tutor of the kingdom.

[27] Maugis, *Histoire du Parlement*, I, chap. IX.

the solution to the problem, and that Parlement deliberated on the matter indicates the Court's reluctance to jeopardize the new ceremonial privileges accorded the *Séance*. That reluctance was underscored by the resolution of the issue: Parlement presented only the remonstrance on alms for the poor, which portrayed royal largesse, and suspended the other three procedural remonstrances, which replicated President Guillart's complaints about the infringement of parlementary protocol voiced with dire consequences in 1527. In addition, the fact that Parlement was disturbed by the neglect of ceremony in the Royal *Séance* of 1552 shows the value the Court placed on the newly gained ceremonial privileges. The king's precipitous arrival preempted such preparations as the donning of red robes, and his insulting treatment of the four presidents, sent to greet him only to find he had entered through a rear door, embarrassed the Court. And most importantly, Henry II's insistence on bringing his Council and other guests into the Grand-chambre to announce the regency plan as a *fait accompli* served notice that a Royal *Séance* did not comprehend constitutional matters, despite the *parlementaires'* claim to the contrary.

Henry II's relegation of the *Lit de Justice* assembly to the sidelines did not rule out its future convocation, but the animosity of the *parlementaires* toward such an assembly was deep-seated, as the debate at mid century showed. In the Royal *Séance* of 1549 Chancellor François Olivier and President Pierre Lizet elucidated two different versions of Parlement's history and function, both directly related to unsettled contentions about the novelty or historicity of a *Lit de Justice* assembly. President Lizet reiterated the stance taken by Presidents Guillart and De Selve and the *avocat* Cappel. Parlement was institutionalized during the reign of Philip IV in the late thirteenth century when king and Parlement sat in Royal *Séances* together. As used by Lizet the phrase *lit de justice* was not a procedural term for an assembly but a simple figure of speech which signified the Grand-chambre of the Parlement of Paris filled with notables gathered to treat affairs of state. Consequently the French constitution knew no *Lit de Justice* assembly and witnessed no separation of powers. The rhetorical argument of the *parlementaires* had its convincing aspects, but it paled in contrast to the powerful historical case advanced by the royal party. In his speech Chancellor Olivier followed Jean du Tillet's lead. Parlement achieved institutional status not in the late thirteenth century but around the 1340's. In the next decade, however, the Parlement of Paris became a specialized judicial institution, and then a *special commission*, or *Lit de Justice* assembly, was instituted in the Court to deal with constitutional business. According to Olivier, the French constitution provided for a separation of functions in the 1350's, the judicial left to ordinary sessions of Parlement, the constitutional (or legislative) vested in the *Lit de Justice*. This historical argument harbored devastating implications for the theory of the French constitution. During the forced recess of the *Lit de Justice* of July 1527, Francis I had given an *arrêt* which proclaimed just such a division of powers, and his institution of the *Lit de Justice* assembly supported that claim. Now in the Royal *Séance* of 1549 Chancellor Olivier, speaking for Henry II, provided the historical evidence necessary to substantiate that separation of judicial and constitutional roles and thus legitimize the *Lit de Justice* assembly.

These opposing views of the ancient constitution arose in part as a response to varied pressures: Parlement's unceasing quest for institutional status as the supreme Court of France, on the one hand, and royal pretensions set to ritual during the Franco-imperial contest, on the other. And bound up with these political struggles were the basic intellectual perspectives from which both parties interpreted the French past. Each of the arguments followed a different approach in assessing the development of the ancient constitution: the Parlement focused an eye on the completeness of the past; the royal party nudged the eye toward what is fleeting in time. The parlementary view, that constitutionalized authority was vested in the Royal *Séance* since the late thirteenth century, was rhetorical in orientation. The *parlementaires* analyzed linguistic usage in varied documents including parlementary speeches like those of 1489 and 1498, and they proffered a diachronic view of events which stressed universal likenesses and historical continuity. Conversely, the royal view, that constitutional authority was a royal prerogative exercised in the *Lit de Justice* since the 1350's, was historical in conception. These investigators analyzed signed and sealed documents deposited in archives, and they proffered a synchronic view of events emphasizing change and historical discontinuity. As will be recalled, one of the foremost proponents of the new historical method, which provided the foundations for modern historical scholarship, was Jean du Tillet, who expressed great disdain for the rhetoricians' study of "text rather than context, appearance rather than reality," and insisted on the "compelling force" of historical facts. The rhetorical stance and the historical one presented conflicting theories about the French past which bore directly on contemporary practices. Although the epistemic structure of discourse in these times has been described as an "archaeology of knowledge," where reality was reconstructed through resemblances and apprehended through signifiers,[28] that hypothesis must now be amended. As encountered here, one mode of discourse, parlementary rhetoric, provides the historical evidence to support such a hypothesis, but the other, historical argumentation, directly challenges it. There was no archaeology of knowledge discernible during this period; there were different modes of perception competing for place. By 1559, then, at the close of Henry II's reign, the *Lit de Justice* in theory and practice remained a constitutional assembly rarely convoked, and the Royal *Séance* remained an honorary session but was provided with an eminent new ceremonial format. It was within the ambit of this world, bounded on the one side by royal policy and antiquarian research and on the other by parlementary reservations and rhetorical tradition, that the two opposing theories about a separation of legislative and judicial functions in the French constitution emerged.

[28] See Michel Foucault, *The Order of Things: An Archaeology of the Human Sciences* (New York, 1971), especially chap. II.

VI

THE QUESTION OF LEGISLATIVE CAPACITY: PROBLEMS OF REGENCY GOVERNMENT

> ... the attire [red robes] in which we [the Parlement of Paris] are vested during Royal Funerals shows that since they [kings] do not die in respect to justice, they can never be reputed as minors [in respect to justice]. *Christophe de Thou (1563)*

THE *Lit de Justice* assembly, which was first convoked by Francis I in 1527 and 1537 and then provided with historical legitimacy by Jean du Tillet's research spanning the 1530's, 1540's, and 1550's, actually faded in practice during the latter two decades, yet spawned the historical-rhetorical debate about the ancient constitution at mid century. This paradoxical waxing and waning of practice and theory was further complicated by a tangled web of regency problems and religious wars in the 1560's. Francis II (1559-1560) did not visit the Parlement of Paris during his short reign.[1] Yet the young king's claim to full rulership rested squarely on a historical argument which posited the existence of a medieval *Lit de Justice* assembly. The new king fully acknowledged the convocation of *Lit de Justice* assemblies in the past and swiftly renewed Jean du Tillet's research commission (expired upon the death of Henry II). At his accession, however, debate arose regarding the imposition of a regency government. In part the opposing stands in that debate followed the political commitments of Catholic and Huguenot parties, but the issue itself was constitutional: whether the fifteen-year-old king had already reached his "age of majority" sufficient to rule without benefit of a regency, or remained a minor until the age of twenty-five as required by civil law. Translated into political terms the issue was whether power would fall to the Guise faction in the Royal Council or to the princes

---

[1] Following his Coronation, 18 September 1559, Francis II did not make either a reception *Entrée* or a ceremonial *Entrée* to Paris; see Bryant *French Royal Entry Ceremony*, table 1. For the act regarding the regency given in the Estates General at Orléans on 21 December 1560, see Dupuy, *Traité de la majorité*, pp. 110-113, who flatly denies that the Estates conferred the regency; and Isambert, *Recueil général des anciennes lois*, XIV, 58-60, with no mention of the Estates.

of the blood, that is, Antoine de Bourbon, King of Navarre, in a regency. At that point Jean du Tillet addressed the constitutional question as well as the political one in the two powerful treatises on majority written in 1560, *Pour la majorité du roy* and *Pour l'entière majorité du roy*, which traced the roots of the French constitutional Law of Majority to medieval times. Du Tillet's unique argument was based on a startling historical discovery: that Charles V promulgated a Law of Majority (specifying fourteen years as the legal age of succession) in 1375, that Charles VI confirmed the law in 1392 and 1407, and that these legislative activities, which in effect amended the Public Law of the French monarchy, had taken place in three *Lit de Justice* assemblies convoked for that purpose. This interpretation of French history, which portrayed the French monarch as constitutional legislator in the *Lit de Justice* assembly, supported juristic kingship in general and the independent authority of Francis II in particular. Furthermore, for Francis II this interpretation of the age of discretion had been symbolically celebrated earlier by Henry II's public association of his fourteen-year-old son with the royal *dignité* in the Royal *Séance* of 1558. Not long after Du Tillet's publication of the majority tracts, Chancellor Michel de L'Hôpital corroborated and expanded this view of the legislator-king by his trenchant statements advanced during the next succession.

A grave problem regarding regency government arose with the succession of the ten-year-old king Charles IX (1560-1574), who was truly a minor and ruled with a Regency Council headed by his mother, Queen Catherine de Médicis. Between his Coronation in 1561 and his majority in 1563 the young king held only one Royal *Séance* in the Parlement of Paris. All the while several questions vexed contemporaries. What agency or institution appointed a regent in cases of minority succession? Was full legislative authority vested in a minor king? Could he convoke a *Lit de Justice* assembly? These concerns were translated into one constitutional problem, which focused on the degree of legislative authority accorded a minor king; yet no solution was forthcoming. Given the disputed notions about the French constitution and the legislative process, no resolution was possible. The new version of constitutional history, which advocated a separation of roles and was associated with Francis I's "revival" of the *Lit de Justice*, Jean du Tillet's historical research, and Chancellor François Olivier's rendition of parlementary history, was spurned by the *parlementaires*. At the same time the prevailing theory, which defined the Crown as the source of the law and the Parlement as the executor of the law, failed to spell out the procedural relationship between the two. Was Parlement's use of remonstrance a privilege or an autonomous right, advisory or binding upon the king? This important question remained a point of conflict throughout the ancien régime.[2] The situation was particularly egregious for Charles IX, because Parlement delayed the registration of his edicts in a manner which suggested the legislative incapacity of a minor king and insinuated the tutorship capacity of the Court until royal majority. As a result, Chancellor Michel de L'Hôpital throughout his tenure was forced to defend royal legislative authority and did so in a number of ways. Taken collectively his pronouncements present a comprehensive theory of juristic monarchy in the sixteenth century.

CHANCELLOR MICHEL DE L'HÔPITAL'S THEORY OF THE LEGISLATOR-KING

Chancellor L'Hôpital and the historian-clerk Jean du Tillet maintained close relations in the 1560's. According to L'Hôpital "the esteemed Du Tillet" supplied him with documentary evidence for his treatise on government, *Traité de la réformation de la justice*, which contained a short history of Parlement.[3] There is no doubt that L'Hôpital was influenced by Du Tillet's findings, because he eventually modified early notions about Parlement's history to fit the clerk's scheme. At the outset the chancellor allotted the primary constitutional role to the Estates, a position supporting the royal party's simultaneous efforts to validate the

[2] Consult Church, *Constitutional Thought*, pp. 150-151, and Doucet, *Institutions de la France*, I, 184-185, on the theory of the king as the source of the law and the procedural problem. See the parlementary remonstrance of July 1489, which stated the prerogatives of the Court, and the response of Charles VIII to it; Maugis, *Histoire du Parlement*, I, 374-380.

[3] Michel de L'Hôpital, *Oeuvres inédites de Michel de l'Hospital*, ed. P.J.S. Duféy (Paris, 1825), I, 170-171 (pt. iv). This treatise is divided into seven parts in two volumes: I, 3-406 (pts. i-iv), and II, 1-316 (pts. v-vii). Of greatest interest are the passages on French history, I, 221-406 (pt. iv), especially pp. 231-235 (on judgments of foreigners made in the Parlement of Paris), pp. 246-266 (on feudal justice connected with fiefs, the first ambulatory parlements, and the creation of the Parlement of Paris), and pp. 267-406 (on parlementary regulations and the corruption wrought by the venality of office). Consult Keohane, *Philosophy and the State in France*, pp. 61-66, who notes that some caution should be exercised in using this treatise and suggests that the last five parts of the work may not have been written by the chancellor. L'Hôpital was made chancellor on 30 June 1560 by royal letters verified on 2 July; Isambert, *Recueil général des anciennes lois*, XIV, 33-35.

disputed Estates General called by Francis II in 1559 and implemented by Charles IX in 1560. Just a few years later, however, he adopted Du Tillet's historical theory and propagated the *Lit de Justice* assembly as the major constitutional forum. In the end L'Hôpital's comprehensive view of the French constitution extolled the virtue of indigenous French laws, reaffirmed a separation of functions (monarchical-legislative and parlementary-judicial), located legislative authority in the royal *dignité*, and emphasized the advisory role of institutions in government. As will be seen the chancellor's notion of the legislator-king, which allowed for historical change and the emendation of laws over time, mirrored Du Tillet's notion about the active legislative roles played in *Lits de Justice* by Charles V and Charles VI in medieval times. This new image of the king as legislator entailed shifts of place which symbolized another constitutional view: the French king moved from the foot of the *lit* in the Salle Saint-Louis and from under the oak in the Bois de Vincennes, where Louis IX dispensed justice to subjects, to the *Lit de Justice* assembly in the Grand-chambre of the Parlement of Paris, where Charles V and Charles VI promulgated French Public Law. Translated into constitutional terms, this new image of French kingship linked the royal *dignité* primarily with the legislative prerogative, secondarily with the judicial one. As might be expected, therefore, the constitutional question regarding a separation of functions, which had been articulated by the royal party and opposed by the *parlementaires* at mid century, was reintroduced into public discourse in the opening years of the 1560's.

Despite a great deal of criticism, Charles IX's regency government carried through Francis II's plans for an Estates General at Orléans (1560-1561). In many ways this was a bold move. Contemporaries were not of one mind about the institutional status of the Estates. Oddly enough, some thought that the last meeting of Estates had been held at Tours in the later fifteenth century;[4] others argued about the Estates' precise function, especially whether or not that body was invested with the right to confer the regency.[5] Attempting to refresh historical memory,

---

[4] L'Hôpital, *Oeuvres complètes*, I, 378, where he guesses that the last meeting of the Estates was held "around eighty years ago"; and Du Tillet, *Recueil des grands*, p. 8, and *Recueil des roys*, p. 290, who speaks specifically of only one Estates General held by Louis XI at Tours in 1468. Actually two other Estates General were held after those of 1468 (Tours) and 1484 (Tours): one in May 1506 (Tours) and one in January 1558 (Paris); Major, *Representative Institutions*, p. 152.

[5] Pierre de La Place, *Commentaires de l'estat de la religion et république soubs les rois Henry et François seconds et Charles neufviesme* [ed. 1565], in *Choix de*

Chancellor L'Hôpital recounted his version of French history with specific references to the roles played by the Estates and Parlement. For parts of that story he drew information from passages in Du Tillet's *Pour l'entière majorité du roy* published three months earlier. Nevertheless, at first L'Hôpital's exegesis veered from the clerk's by alleging that the separation of governmental functions, which occurred in ancient times, split the "parlement" into two institutions, the Estates (charged with legislative cognizance) and the Parlement of Paris (charged with judicial business). As L'Hôpital put it,

> It is certain that former kings customarily held the "estates" often, that is, held an assembly of all their subjects or deputies representing them. [The term] "to hold the estates" means simply that the king communicates with his subjects regarding his most important affairs and solicits their advice and counsel . . . , heeding it when reasonable. [When such an assembly took place] in very early times, it was called a "parlement," and that name has been retained in England and Scotland. But [French] kings through the same means [parlements] had cognizance over both general [i.e. public] matters concerning the whole [kingdom] and private matters concerning particulars. Later on, private cases were heard by special judges appointed by the king and established in [an institution] called Parlement, and public and general audiences were reserved for the king's [cognizance] and took the name of Estates.[6]

In 1549 Chancellor Olivier had followed Du Tillet in positing a historical separation of constitutional and judicial functions around the mid-fourteenth century, vesting the former in the *special commission*, or *Lit de Justice*, held in Parlement, the latter in the Court. In 1560 Chancellor L'Hôpital reaffirmed that separation of functions but sifted out a different pair of institutions from the "parlements": the Parlement of Paris, a specialized judicial institution, and the Estates (likened to the Parliaments of England and Scotland), an advisory forum treating constitutional-

---

chroniques et mémoires sur l'histoire de France, ed. J.A.C. Buchon (Paris, 1836), II, 1-201, acknowledges the Law of Majority but says that the Estates have to assemble during a minority; and La Planche, *Histoire de l'estat de France*, II, 202-421, discusses the role of Estates and notes that in minority situations the Estates must be called, criticizing Du Tillet's majority thesis vehemently.

[6] L'Hôpital, *Oeuvres complètes*, I, 378-379; for the whole speech, ibid., I, 375-407 (13 Dec. 1560). The chancellor gave no precise date when the separation of Parlement and Estates occurred.

legislative matters. At this point, therefore, L'Hôpital did not follow Du
Tillet's theory on the *Lit de Justice* to the letter, but within a few years
he returned full-fold to the clerk's position on the place of that assembly
in the ancient constitution.

In the meantime Chancellor L'Hôpital continued to emphasize legal-
hereditary succession and the legislative nature of kingship. In his opening remarks made at the Estates General in 1560, he clearly set forth
that position by rewording a familiar medieval maxim on royal authority.
Linking the office of kingship with the Public Law of the French monarchy, he maintained that "The king holds the Crown from God and
the ancient Law of the kingdom."[7] The chancellor also invested French
kings with the authority to amend laws when necessary for the public
good. During a series of assemblies held in Parlement and presided over
by L'Hôpital in June and July 1561, the chancellor insisted that there
was latitude within the French constitution for kings to amend laws
according to changing dictates of the times, because "the true office of
a king ... is to consider the times and to augment or mitigate the laws
accordingly."[8] To be sure, the monarch should seek counsel in these
actions, the chancellor maintained, but institutions such as the Estates
and Parlement were called only at the discretion of the king and served
strictly in an advisory capacity.[9] Finally, L'Hôpital did not recognize the
superior status of the Parlement of Paris as a supreme Court. Instead
he accorded equal status to all Courts as parts of the whole, arguing that
"If the king could administer his sovereign justice by one Parlement
alone, as was done in earlier times, he would do so. But [in these times]
individual Parlements are only various divisions of the [whole] Parlement

[7] Ibid., I, 389 (13 Dec. 1560). This is an interesting interpolation of the proverb,
"The king holds the Crown from God and the Sword" and is connected with
the other proverb, "The king is emperor in his own kingdom." See André
Bossuat, "Le Formule 'Le Roi est empereur en son royaume,' " *Revue Historique
du Droit Français et Étranger*, 4ᵐᵉ série (July-Sept. 1961), pp. 371-381. The proverb
was stated by Du Tillet, *Recueil des grands*, p. 16; Jean Bodin, *Les Six livres de
la république* (Paris, 1583; first ed. 1576), bk. VI, chap. 5; Jérome Bignon, *La
Grandeur de nos roys et de leur souveraine puissance* (Paris, 1615), pp. 12-14; and
many others throughout the sixteenth and seventeenth centuries.

[8] A.N. X1a 1597, fols. 300v-308r, especially fols. 301r-303r (18 June 1561);
parts printed in Godefroy, *Cérémonial françois* [Reg. Parl.], II, 545-550, especially
p. 548, and L'Hôpital, *Oeuvres complètes*, I, 419-428, especially p. 426.

[9] A.N. X1a 1597, fols. 301r-303r (18 June 1561); parts printed in Godefroy,
Cérémonial françois [Reg. Parl.], II, 545-550. The view was also expressed in an
address to the Estates General at Orléans; L'Hôpital, *Oeuvres complètes*, I, 375-
407 (13 Dec. 1560), especially p. 378.

of the king."[10] This statement limiting institutional authority vis-à-vis royal authority and that of the Parlement of Paris in particular aroused debate immediately.

Chancellor L'Hôpital stated the royal position at the annual opening of the Parlement of Paris on 12 November 1561, and President François de Saint-André countered with an opposing statement. Concentrating first on the function of institutions in government, L'Hôpital maintained the separation of legislative and judicial roles and outlined legislative procedure in keeping with that division. He analyzed the workings of two important institutions, the Royal Council and Parlement, which operated in separate spheres of public activity and required specialized knowledge to perform their respective duties. L'Hôpital maintained that the king in the Royal Council managed affairs of state, that is, constitutional matters, by reference to French Public Law, and those decisions affected the universal interest, or the public good. In contrast Parlement administered justice to subjects in accordance with private law, and those judgments touched particular interests, or cases of subjects. Consequently, the king and Royal Council in making laws must consider the public welfare of the whole kingdom over time, whereas the Parlement in making judgments treats individual cases brought at particular times. Following this division of duties, the chancellor addressed the thorny problem of legislative procedure. He concluded that the king and Royal Council draw edicts and send them to the Court for perusal and registration; that in turn the Court imparts advice, that is, remonstrances, on those edicts for the king to consider. But he insisted that Parlement can never exceed its specialized judicial function by interfering with legislation, that is, by refusing to register royal edicts.[11] According to Chancellor L'Hôpital's analysis, therefore, the respective powers of king and Parlement belonged in legislative and judicial categories, and legislation was a royal prerogative. In this way, the chancellor restated formally in 1561 the view of the French constitution which was propagated in 1527 and 1537 through the three *Lit de Justice* assemblies of Francis I, repeated by Chancellor François Olivier in 1549 on behalf of

---

[10] A.N. X1a 1595, fol. 200v (7 Sept. 1560), cited in Maugis, *Histoire du Parlement*, I, 418.

[11] L'Hôpital, *Oeuvres complètes*, II, 9-18 (12 Nov. 1561). The chancellor always maintained that the king makes laws and the Parlement executes them, reiterating that opinion in the famous Edict of Moulins (February 1566) enunciating judicial reform; see the excellent study of Salmon, *Society in Crisis: France in the Sixteenth Century* (New York, 1975), p. 156, n. 18.

Henry II, and substantiated throughout by Jean du Tillet's constitutional theory. Needless to say, statements such as these stirred opposition: some held that French kings (Charles V included) could not tamper with Public Law without the consent of the Estates;[12] others insisted that it was Parlement which filled that bill.

The response of President François de Saint-André probed at the very heart of this disagreement about the locus of legislative power. The president insisted that Parlement was the king's co-legislator and was obliged to rule on the validity of laws promulgated by monarchs: thus, the registration of laws followed positive conclusions, remonstrances followed negative ones. He boldly asserted that royal laws remained unenforceable without the sanction supplied by registration in the Parlement of Paris, implying that the absence of parlementary remonstrances on royal edicts, not the promulgation of the edicts themselves, created binding laws.[13] According to the parlementary position, therefore, the Court and the king in unison created law since the issuance of law by the monarch and its approval by Parlement constituted a twofold legislative procedure. As a result, the Court's role in legislation was not simply advisory but strictly consensual. Once again, as in 1549, the debate between a chancellor and a president of Parlement articulated two opposing theories regarding a separation of functions. On the one hand, the royal theory separated legislative and judicial functions: the king was legislator, looking outward to the general public good; the *parlementaires* were judges, seeing that justice was rendered to subjects in particular cases. On the other hand, the parlementary theory considered legislation a twofold procedure: legislation was issued by the king but required the sanction of legal wisdom before adoption; the *parlementaires* were not simply judges but executors of the law charged with judging its validity within the body of laws of the realm.

Although amply defined at the opening of the 1560's, Chancellor L'Hôpital's theory of legislative kingship was seriously weakened in practice due to the minority status of Charles IX. Speaking to Parlement in November 1561, L'Hôpital chided those who disobeyed a minor king.

---

[12] Exemplified in La Planche and La Place (see above, n. 5), those views had some credence in medieval times as told by Monstrelet (see above, Chap. I, n. 17), and were thoroughly denounced in the seventeenth century by Dupuy (see above, n. 1).

[13] A.N. X1a 1597, fols. 303r-v (18 June 1561); in L'Hôpital, *Oeuvres complètes*, II, 17-18. Saint-André was made president of Parlement in 1535; Maugis, *Histoire du Parlement*, III, 150.

He reminded the Court that Charles IX and the Regency Council had sought counsel on affairs of state from a wide variety of advisory groups: an Assembly of Notables [Fontainebleau, August 1560], the Estates General [Orléans, December 1560–January 1561], and finally a series of parlementary sessions [June-July 1561] which united persons from all these groups in a common effort to solve serious problems.[14] Up to this point, however, the king had not visited the Grand-chambre of the Parlement of Paris,[15] and there is good reason to suspect that much of the sparring between Court and Royal Council arose on the one side from Parlement's steady insinuation that the presence of the young king in the Court was required for the registration of royal legislation during the king's minority, and on the other side from the Regency Council's adept avoidance of a royal visit to Parlement, which might lend credence to that insinuation. Sometime between 1560 and 1561, on the heels of such subtle harassment, the Regency Council seriously considered the convocation of a *Lit de Justice* assembly. Apparently on 22 May 1561 the Council planned a *Lit de Justice* to be held in the Parlement of Paris on 20 July,[16] then dismissed the plan and toyed instead with the idea of convoking a *Lit de Justice* assembly outside of Paris. During this time, when the possible convocation of a *Lit de Justice* somewhere loomed large, the anonymous memorandum on parlementary assemblies (mistakenly attributed in later years to Jean du Tillet) was solicited, probably around 1560 by L'Hôpital, and was drawn up by a person with a flexible sense of historical interpretation. As we have seen, the anonymous author of the memorandum followed Du Tillet's theory in outlining the respective constitutional and honorary functions of *Lit de Justice* and *Séance*, but in addition he compiled for the first time a ceremonial guide for each and introduced the convenient notion that *Lit de Justice* assemblies could be convoked outside of the Parlement of Paris. As it turned out, Charles IX during his minority finally held one Royal *Séance* in the Grand-chambre of the Parlement but only under duress, as will be seen, and he did not convoke a *Lit de Justice* in those years. In the meantime

[14] L'Hôpital, *Oeuvres complètes*, II, 10-11, without the precise names and dates of the assemblies.

[15] Following his Coronation, 15 May 1561, Charles IX did not make a ceremonial *Entrée* into Paris, but he made a reception *Entrée* to Paris on 6 April 1562 in which Parlement did not participate; consult Bryant, *French Royal Entry Ceremony*, table 1, and pp. 181-182. Moreover, the young king did not visit the Parlement of Paris after that *Entrée*.

[16] A.N. X1a 1597, fols. 203v-205r (22 May 1561).

Chancellor L'Hôpital presided over a series of parlementary assemblies held in the Grand-chambre.

PARLEMENT'S THEORY OF THE LEGISLATIVE TUTOR

The parlementary assemblies of June-July 1561 were composed of numerous groups (princes of the blood and peers, royal officers and councillors, Parlement, clergy, and the university) which sought some means to stem the rising tide of religious revolt in the kingdom.[17] Discussion of that volatile issue moved at a slow pace. It was not until 11 July that the clerk Jean du Tillet read and solicited opinions on a legislative proposal, the Edict of Toleration (Saint-Germain), which confirmed the earlier Edict of Romorantin (1560) and introduced additional peacekeeping measures.[18] The precise results of that vote will never be known, but the royal reaction to it was swift and ominous. On 12 July Du Tillet was summoned to the presence of Charles IX, Queen Regent Catherine de Médicis, the King of Navarre, and other regency officials. He was ordered to submit to the queen a list of the individual votes recorded for and against the edict and warned against keeping a copy of that list himself. Astounded at this command to produce a list disclosing deliberations ordinarily kept secret, Du Tillet requested a written order, and the request was granted forthwith by the queen.[19] This voting list must have exposed Parlement's refusal to countenance the proposed legislation. Although the Court had played a prominent part in the parlementary assemblies from which the edict issued, it consistently delayed action on the legislative measure and finally registered the edict on 31 July only after guardedly stipulating that registration was provisional, a concession

[17] A.N. X1a 1597, fols. 300v-348v (18, 23, and 25-27 June 1561), and fols. 383r-444v (1-5 July 1561). Extracts are in Du Tillet, *Recueil des grands*, pp. 108-109 (9 July 1561); and in Godefroy, *Cérémonial françois* [Reg. Parl.], II, 545-553 (18, 23, 25-26 June, and 11-12, 31 July, 1561).

[18] For the Edict of Saint-Germain (often called the Edict of Toleration, 11 July 1561), see Isambert, *Recueil général des anciennes lois*, XIV, 109-111, which omits the provisional clause; and for the earlier Edict of Romorantin (May 1560), ibid., XIV, 31-33. Note that Isambert considers the assembly of 11 July 1561 (the king not even present) as a *Lit de Justice* assembly. Consult Nicola M. Sutherland, *The Huguenot Struggle for Recognition* (New Haven, 1980), pp. 349-353, for commentary on these edicts.

[19] A.N. X1a 1598 [unnumbered folios] (11-12 July 1561); with extracts in Godefroy, *Cérémonial françois* [Reg. Parl.], II, 551-552.

to "the necessity of the times."[20] Parlement's delaying tactics and provisional registration certainly cast doubt upon the legislative capacity of a minor king. According to a contemporary the Court did in fact consider the edict in force only until the king reached his majority,[21] and Parlement admitted as much regarding another edict issued in 1563. Did the Parlement of Paris wish to insinuate that for legislative purposes Charles IX and his regency government must come in person to the Grand-chambre to oversee the registration of the Edict of Toleration? It would seem so, if the following events are any indication.

The Peace of Amboise ended the first of a series of religious wars that lasted for over thirty years, and the first royal Edict of Pacification (Amboise), issued on 19 March 1563, called for the co-existence of two religions until such time as a "national or general council" could be convened.[22] Charles IX did not come to Parlement on 27 March for the registration of this edict, but he attempted to give it added legislative weight by sending two princes of the blood to witness the process. Upon registration of the edict the princes' names were entered in a subscription on the bottom fold of the document.[23] Despite the presence of the princes, Parlement interpreted the subscription to indicate provisional registration only, that is, registration as law only until a "general or national council" could be held after the majority of the king, and that contention was at the root of the bitter quarrel which took place between king and Parlement six months later, in September 1563.[24] As might be expected the royal party finally capitulated in the face of this consistent negative

[20] A.N. X1a 1598 [unnumbered folios] (30-31 July 1561), with the provisional Latin clause added at the end; portions published including the clause in Godefroy, *Cérémonial françois* [Reg. Parl.], II, 552.

[21] Consult *Mémoires de Claude Haton contenant le récit des événements accomplis de 1553-1582*, ed. Félix Bourquelot, in *Collection de documents inédits sur l'histoire de France*, 1re série (Paris, 1857), VIII, 1, 186ff.

[22] For commentary on the Edict of Amboise (called the Edict of Pacification, 19 March 1563), see Sutherland, *Huguenot Struggle*, pp. 356-357.

[23] The subscription stated: "Lecta publicata et registrata audito Procuratore Generali Regis, in praesentia dominorum Cardinalis à Borbonio, et Ducis Montispenserii ad hoc specialiter per dominum nostrum Regem missorum"; A.N. X1a 1604, fols. 525r-550r (27 March 1563), and also in Dupuy, *Traité de la majorité* [Reg. Parl.], p. 423. Isambert, *Recueil général des anciennes lois*, XIV, 135-140, omits the subscription.

[24] During the conflict of September 1563 (see below, Chap. VIII), Parlement admitted that the edict of March (Amboise) was registered provisionally; Dupuy, *Traité de la majorité* [Reg. Parl.], p. 423.

reception of legislation introduced by a minor king. Charles IX came to Parlement in person for the next round.

On 17 May 1563 Charles IX, still six weeks shy of his thirteenth birthday, held his first Royal *Séance* in the Parlement of Paris. He had come to solicit advice on a proposal to tax the Church without papal approval in order to finance a campaign against the English. Enthroned in the lower decorated seat, the king was attended by an array of notables, including Queen Catherine and the Regency Council, princes of the blood, peers, Crown officers, and *parlementaires* (presidents in red robes, councillors in black).²⁵ Opening the session with a personal statement emphasizing the Court's judicial role and the honorary nature of the *Séance*, Charles IX excused his earlier absence. "Because I became king at such a young age and have been so preoccupied with other [public] affairs ever since, I could not come here sooner to do my duty; that is, to admonish you to administer justice well and honorably before God."²⁶ After announcing his intention to mount a campaign against the English at Le Havre, the king turned the floor over to the chancellor. Recounting part of the contents of the anonymous memorandum of 1560, by now in his hands, Chancellor L'Hôpital summarized the constitutional regulations dividing two types of parlementary assemblies and blamed the young king's neglect of "traditional" ceremonies (probably a reference to the post-Coronation Parisian *Entrée* and the visit to Parlement which followed it) on the "evident necessity" of the times. Then he spoke of the danger to national security if Le Havre remained in English hands, a danger which constituted an undeniable case of legal "necessity" sufficient to override the Church's exemption from taxes. The French Church, he claimed, was only trading some lands (which would have to be alienated to meet the tax) in order to assure its own survival.²⁷

The first president of Parlement, Christophe de Thou, spoke briefly on behalf of Parlement. His opening lines were reminiscent of the par-

²⁵ A.N. X1a 1605, fols. 169v-177v (17 May 1563); with extracts in Du Tillet, *Recueil des grands*, pp. 107-108, the last royal visit to Parlement recorded in this treatise, and in Godefroy, *Cérémonial françois* [Reg. Parl.], II, 553-566.

²⁶ Ibid., all sources.

²⁷ Ibid., all sources. Du Tillet, *Recueil des grands*, suggested that holding Royal *Séances* in Parlement following post-Coronation *Entrées* to Paris had become a tradition. He cited the *Séances* of Louis XII (7 July 1498), p. 78, Francis I (14 March 1515), p. 79, and Henry II (2 July 1549), pp. 98-99. The anonymous memorandum of 1560 picked up those comments word for word, stating that such *Séances* were held "to honor and authorize his justice" following Parisian *Entrées*; see above, Chap. IV, n. 70.

lementary rhetoric of earlier years, and the message suggested again that Parlement along with the Regency Council were co-tutors, who made legislative decisions.

> The officers of your Court cannot hide their joy at seeing before them the image and power of God represented in their king and sovereign lord seated in the throne of his majesty [= the Grand-chambre of the Parlement of Paris] and assisted by the queen [Catherine de Médicis], monsignor [King of Navarre], and other princes of his lineage, peers of France, prelates and lords ... , [a place] eminently suitable for the administration of justice.... Sire, you are very humbly beseeched to visit this place [the Grand-chambre] often and to take pleasure in the fact that you are the ninth king of your name established by the grace of God as King of France ... [and that you] are carrying out your obligations [in that office] as did King Saint Louis, your predecessor, who was also the ninth [king] of his name.... As for the necessity evident in the proposition which your majesty has made through monsieur the chancellor, ... we are all in the same situation ... and as pilot of a [vessel] which is tossed and torn by ill winds, the king as is customary requests counsel of those who are inside....[28]

Du Tillet was ordered by the king, through the chancellor, to read the proposed edict aloud, and the *avocat* Baptiste Dumesnil pleaded the royal case. Dumesnil picked up President De Thou's theme and stressed the minority status of Charles IX by comparing the presence in Parlement of Queen Catherine to the role played by Queen Blanche, regent and mother of Louis IX, and by describing the Regency Council present as "moderators" of the young king's actions. The *avocat* pleaded the case in legal and historical terms, citing passages from Roman Law to show that "necessity knows no law" and referring to earlier acts of French kings consonant with that precept. Dumesnil concluded that the principle of inalienability of Church goods was subordinate to the "imperious commands of extreme necessity" which on this occasion required alienation, albeit without setting any precedent.[29] This Royal *Séance* of 1563

[28] A.N. X1a 1605, fols. 169v-177v (17 May 1563); extracts printed in Godefroy, *Cérémonial françois* [Reg. Parl.], II, 560-561. Here the "two bodies" image of the king as both pilot and passenger recalls Seneca's allusion; *Epistolae morales*, lxxxv, 35. De Thou became first president in 1562 at the death of Gilles Le Maistre; Maugis, *Histoire du Parlement*, III, 216.

[29] A.N. X1a 1605, fols. 169v-177v (17 May 1563); extracts in Godefroy, *Cé-*

was not acrimonious; to the contrary, the session evinced a truce between the regency government and Parlement on the legislative issue. Pressured for two years by Parlement, the Regency Council finally brought the young king to a Royal *Séance* in the Grand-chambre to effect speedy legislative action. Contrary to common supposition, therefore, this Royal *Séance* of May 1563 was specifically convoked to register a royal edict not under the iron hand of the monarch but at the willful insistence of a Parlement intent upon securing for itself during minority kingship a greater legislative role.[30]

The most critical problem still facing Charles IX was the enforcement of the Edict of Pacification registered provisionally by Parlement the preceding March. Catholics suspiciously viewed it as a potential way of validating the existence of two religions in France, and everywhere people armed themselves for another civil war. But by summer the campaign to win Le Havre from the English united Catholic and Huguenot camps temporarily against a common foe, and the ensuing French victory in July boosted the fortunes of the king immeasurably. At the same time the king had entered his fourteenth year, putting the minority issue on a different footing. At this strategic moment, when royal popularity and royal majority merged, Chancellor L'Hôpital seized the opportunity to dramatize the theory of legislative kingship. Charles IX would announce his majority age publicly and issue a second Pacification Edict in his own right in an extraordinary *Lit de Justice* assembly to be held outside of Paris.

The story really begins in a session of the Parlement of Paris which took place on 21 July 1563, two weeks before Charles IX announced the convocation of a *Lit de Justice* in the city of Rouen. The record of deliberations made by the Parlement of Paris for that day does not survive or, more likely, was destroyed right after the session. Judging from the exchanges made between the Parlement and the king afterward, however, the following events were played out. First, the Parlement of Paris was apprised of the impending *Lit de Justice* in Rouen to celebrate the king's majority and was requested to send deputies to that assembly; second, during a closed session Parlement discussed the royal request in highly unfavorable terms and refused to send deputies there; and third,

---

rémonial françois [Reg. Parl.], II, 561-566. Dumesnil became *avocat du roi* in 1556; Maugis, *Histoire du Parlement*, III, 333.

[30] Note that Glasson, *Parlement de Paris*, I, 29, mistakenly assumes this assembly was a *Lit de Justice* and concludes that the principle was established thenceforth that absolute obedience was due a king sitting in his *Lit de Justice*.

these *in camera* deliberations of the Court were revealed to the Regency Council when one among the *parlementaires* reported on this discussion of the king's affairs, particularly opinions regarding the status of his authority since passing the thirteenth year. Whatever the case, the Parlement of Paris realized that its secret deliberations had been exposed and hurriedly dispatched two letters to the king and the regent on 5 August expressing distress that the royal party found the Court's opinions of 21 July unacceptable. If this supplicatory gesture was prompted to stave off the impending *Lit de Justice* assembly, it was too late. Charles IX had announced his intentions the day before. On 4 August 1563, a week after the French had taken the port of Le Havre, the king sent a letter to the city officials of Rouen which announced his intention to make an *Entrée* to the city on 12 August and then hold a *Lit de Justice* assembly in the Parlement of Rouen on 17 August.[31]

In this plan, the royal party was supported by the conclusions of the anonymous memorandum of 1560, which correctly followed Du Tillet's constitutional theory of the *Lit de Justice* but erroneously allowed the convocation of such assemblies outside of the Grand-chambre of the Parlement of Paris. Since the memorandum was drawn up around 1560 and tentative plans for a *Lit de Justice* assembly were made and then dismissed in 1561, it is evident that the royal party had considered convoking a *Lit de Justice* between 1560 and 1563 but had not done so, perhaps for fear of introducing notions about parlementary tutorship of a minor king to the scene. Along those lines, therefore, it is interesting to read the Parisian *parlementaires'* supplicatory letter of 5 August, because the implication of tutorship is indeed there. In that letter First President Christophe de Thou professed distress that the king took umbrage at the Court's discussions of 21 July and astonishment that he charged them with willful disobedience during his minority. In effect there was no reason to convoke such an extraordinary assembly for the purpose of celebrating the royal majority, De Thou told Charles IX, because

> ... even if you [Charles IX] were only one day old, you would be as much a major in respect to justice as if you were thirty years old, since it [justice] is administered in your name by the power God has given you. In addition, the attire [red robes] in which we [the Parlement of Paris] are vested during Royal Funerals shows

[31] Recounted in Dupuy, *Traité de la majorité*, pp. 355-356, who does not give the text of the letter.

that since they [kings] do not die in respect to justice, they can never be reputed as minors [in respect to justice].[32]

Here Parlement stressed the perpetuity of the royal *dignité* as it worked in justice, by implication through the Parlement of Paris, recalling the symbolism of the red-robed presidents in Royal Funerals which portrayed that notion so well. In contrast, Chancellor L'Hôpital would emphasize the perpetuity of justice by linking the immortal royal *dignité* directly to French Public Law, and he would do so at a *Lit de Justice* assembly in the Parlement of Rouen. Realizing full well the dangerous precedent set by the convocation of a *Lit de Justice* outside of the Grand-chambre of the Palais de Justice but unable to prevent the extraordinary event, the Parisian *parlementaires* retreated behind the closed doors of their chambers to plan an effective counter strategy.

THUS FAR the discussion has cast some light upon the theory and practice of the *Lit de Justice* up to the turn of the 1560's: its early transitory appearance in 1527 and 1537 as a constitutional forum and its later mature theoretical articulation between 1542 and 1563 at the very time of its paradoxical failure to figure prominently as a constitutional phenomenon. This paradoxical estrangement of theory and practice lasted for a quarter of a century, and then Jean du Tillet's constitutional theory was reassessed and reemployed in 1563. In the future, however, that theory would no longer be challenged by *parlementaires* anxious to preserve the universal validity of the ancient Royal *Séance* but would be amended anew by royal officials resolved to mold the *Lit de Justice* to fit pressing constitutional needs. When Chancellor Michel de L'Hôpital chose a *Lit de Justice* assembly for the grand ceremony publicizing the king as legislator in August 1563, it was convoked in the Parlement of Rouen, not in the Parlement of Paris; and that action openly challenged the pretensions of the Parisian Parlement to legislative partnership with the monarch. The convocation of the Majority *Lit de Justice* assembly in a provincial Parlement opened a whole new stage in the history of the *Lit de Justice* assembly.

[32] Ibid. [Reg. Parl.], pp. 397-399.

VII

THE ROYAL STANCE ON
THE FRENCH CONSTITUTION:
THE MAJORITY *LIT DE JUSTICE*
ASSEMBLY OF 1563

> ... *the kingdom is never vacant*, because there is continu-
> ity from king to king so that *as soon as the king's eyes close*
> [in death] there is another king ... without awaiting Coro-
> nation, unction, consecration, or any other ceremo-
> nies. *Michel de L'Hôpital (1563)*

THE REAPPEARANCE of the *Lit de Justice* assembly in 1563 reflected both
circumstance and design. The assembly itself was not convoked during
the 1540's and 1550's, yet the new theory of the ancient constitution,
which depended on the *Lit de Justice* assembly for a separation of constitutional and judicial functions, was elaborated in those decades and
integrated into discourse on constitutional ideology. As a result, fortune's
wheel reversed a turn: the "revival" of the *Lit de Justice* in 1527 had
generated its theoretical elaboration; in turn the new theory reactivated
the assembly in 1563, altered somewhat to suit constitutional needs. The
Lit de Justice assembly convoked in the Parlement of Rouen on 17 August
1563 introduced a new ritual to the French scene: a public celebration
of the king's attainment of the legal age of fourteen years required to
rule the kingdom. When the drama had unfolded, it was clear that the
historical script of Jean du Tillet had been freely adapted to serve the
unprecedented Majority *Lit de Justice* of Charles IX.[1] The convocation

---

[1] A full account probably written by the clerk of the Parlement of Rouen
was published in *Description du pays et duché de Normandie, appellée anciennement
Neustrie, de son origine et des limites d'iceluy. Extraict de sa Cronique de Normandie,
non encores imprimée, faicte par feu maistre Jean Nagerel* (Rouen, 1580, also 1578
and 1610), hereafter cited as *Cronique de Normandie* (Cron. de Norm.). The
entire text of *Cronique de Normandie* was published in Dupuy, *Traité de la
majorité*, pp. 356-397, the source cited here. In addition an excerpt from the
proceeding was published separately in 1563: *La Declaration faicte par le roy de
sa majorité tenant son Lict de Justice en sa Cour de Parlement de Rouen: Et
Ordonnance par luy faicte pour le bien et repos public de son royaume: Et ce qu'il
dict en ladicte Cour avant la publication de ladicte ordonnance* (Paris, 1563), which

of a *Lit de Justice* in the provincial Parlement of Rouen broke one of the main tenets of Du Tillet's theory, the institutional affiliation of the *Lit de Justice* assembly with the Parlement of Paris; and it eventually forced the royal and parlementary parties to reach consensus on the historical-rhetorical debate about the nature of the assembly. The Majority *Lit de Justice* also inaugurated a new ceremonial agency. In gesture, word, and symbol the ritual dramatized tenets of French Public Law (legal-hereditary succession and the separation of legislative and judicial functions) and introduced a mode of constitutional discourse which was distinctly French in conception. The event was dramatic for the royal party and the Parlement of Rouen, traumatic for the Parlement of Paris.

Jean du Tillet was conspicously absent from the Rouennais *Lit de Justice*, because the Parlement of Paris did not send a delegation to the assembly; and the registers of the Parisian Court, the prime source for historical precedent, maintained absolute silence that day in respect to the event. The anonymous engraving of the Majority *Lit de Justice* (Figure 6) was executed somewhat later and represents the scene with several inaccuracies. In this series it is valuable nonetheless as the third portrait of an actual dated event showing the French king in a parlementary session and as the first one depicting an official *Lit de Justice* assembly.[2]

Since the event was rife with constitutional symbolism, the ritual and discourse of the Majority *Lit de Justice* assembly warrant special attention.

---

contains the king's speech, the Pacification Edict, and his response to the Parlement of Paris in the debate later. The text of *Cronique de Normandie* was abbreviated, eliminating speeches and the text of legislation, and published by Théodore Godefroy in his early work, *Cérémonial de France* (Paris, 1619), pp. 457-467 (the only *Lit de Justice* assembly listed in that collection). The same abbreviated version was republished by the Godefroys in *Cérémonial françois* (which provides a complete collection of *Lits de Justice*), II, 257-262, and it is accompanied by another augmented version, II, 566-576, giving the first one-third of the proceedings up through Chancellor L'Hôpital's speech. Finally, Isambert, *Recueil général des anciennes lois*, XIV, 147-150, published an incomplete account taken from Dupuy, *Traité de la majorité*. Alfred Franklin, *Les Rois et les gouvernements de la France* (Paris, 1978), p. 69, a manual for names and dates, incorrectly dates the majority as 1564.

[2] B.N. Dépt. des Estampes. There are errors in the engraving: the queen regent is at the left instead of the right of Charles IX, four persons sit at the left instead of two, and no usher stands at the foot of the throne. The fifteenth-century painting, *Le Retable du Parlement*, which remained on the wall to the left of the throne in the Grand-chambre of the Parlement of Paris since Louis XII's renovation at the turn of the sixteenth century, is shown here on the wall of the chamber in the Parlement of Rouen.

6. Charles IX: Majority *Lit de Justice* held in the Parlement of Rouen, 1563.

First, the ceremonial configuration replicated the pattern established in the Parlement of Paris by Francis I's *Lit de Justice* assemblies. The Parlement of Rouen had been warned that the king would come that day "to hold his *Lit de Justice*" and were apprised of the ceremony "accorded him in such acts," so the parties were seated in the judicial chambers of the palace in Rouen in the form observed in Paris except that the regent, Queen Catherine de Médicis, was seated at the right of the king in this assembly.[3] Yet this *Lit de Justice* was affiliated with the Parlement of Rouen rather than Paris, and that crucial deviation from institutional location called into question the Parisian Court's claim to preeminence among Parlements. Second, the procedural format divided the session into two distinct stages which symbolized two different categories of legal action, legislative and judicial, and it dramatized through them the separate roles of Crown and Parlement. Third, the peculiar elements of language contained in the important speech of Chancellor Michel de L'Hôpital fashioned a new system of constitutional discourse fit for elucidating French Public Law. Fourth, the constitutional warp of these proceedings raised the Majority *Lit de Justice* to the status of a succession ceremony which symbolized precepts of French Public Law.

[3] At eight o'clock in the morning the red-robed Parlement of Rouen assembled in the Palace at Rouen to await the arrival of Charles IX. Chancellor Michel de L'Hôpital arrived first, accompanied by members of the Royal Council and several members of the Grand Conseil, and the group was escorted to Parlement's chamber by an honor guard of Rouen *parlementaires*. At ten-thirty Charles IX arrived, accompanied by the royal party (queen regent, princes, peers, and Crown officers) and was escorted to the chamber. There were probably four levels of seating above the ground level of the parquet, and priority of rank was determined by proximity to the king, the most esteemed seats highest and closest to the throne. The king sat in his throne on the highest level, the queen, princes, and peers (lay peers to the king's right, ecclesiastical peers to his left) on the second level, and Crown officers, knights, royal councillors, and *parlementaires* on the third and fourth levels. Some women of the royal court sat in a screened area to the side of the parquet. Precise details about the decoration of the chamber and the royal throne are not recorded, but the seats of the royal party were "tapestried," covered probably with material embroidered with fleurs-de-lis, and most assuredly the throne was canopied, setting off the royal entourage from the red-robed *parlementaires* in a colorful visual fashion. As the doors of the chamber closed, the king holding his *Lit de Justice* [assembly] opened the session; Dupuy, *Traité de la majorité* [Cron. de Norm.], pp. 356-357, 397. Excerpts appear in Godefroy, *Cérémonial de France*, pp. 457-459, and Godefroy, *Cérémonial françois*, II, 566-567. For additional details, see Hanley, "The *Lit de Justice* and the Fundamental Law," pp. 3-14.

THE *Lit de Justice* opened with a focus on royal constitutional and legislative authority. In a voice bristling with hostility, Charles IX declared his majority status and demanded obedience from all subjects. Straightaway he promulgated an ordinance in his own right, a Pacification Edict aimed at enforcing the earlier Edict of Pacification (Amboise) issued in March but registered only provisionally by the Parlement of Paris.

> After all the disorders my kingdom has suffered, it has pleased God to accord me the grace to achieve peace and to rout the English who have held Le Havre de Grace [the port of Le Havre] illegally. I have come into this city [Rouen] to thank God, who has never forsaken either me or my kingdom, and to inform you that I have reached the age of my majority and will tolerate no longer the disobedience toward me which had been manifested amidst these disorders. I issued the Edict of Pacification [Amboise, in March], effective until the general or national council can render a good and holy [plan of] reform, ... and I have now ordered [by the second Pacification Edict] that all those who break or contravene it will be punished as rebels for disobeying my commands. The [second] edict must be kept and observed throughout my kingdom. ... No one can plead ignorance [of it], because I intend to publish the edict in my presence and send it to all my other Courts of Parlement. Hence, those who contravene it will be charged with the crime of *lèse-majesté* and punished as rebels.[4]

Charles IX then turned the floor over to Chancellor L'Hôpital. He gave a long speech replete with historical data culled from Du Tillet's majority tract of 1560,[5] one of the most important statements on French

---

[4] Dupuy, *Traité de la majorité* [Cron. de Norm.], pp. 358-359; excerpts in Godefroy, *Cérémonial françois*, II, 259 and 568. That speech was published the same year in Rouen; see *Receuil de ce que le Roy Charles IX a dict en sa Cour de Parlement de Rouen, declarant sa majorité. Assisté de la royne sa mere, monsieur son frere, et tous les princes de son sang, et officiers de sa couronne, et seigneurs de son conseil, d'esquelz tous il a esté declaré et recogneu pour tel* (Rouen, 1563).

[5] Dupuy, *Traité de la majorité* [Cron. de Norm.], pp. 359-371; also in Godefroy, *Cérémonial françois*, II, 568-576. L'Hôpital played up the importance of the province of Normandy in French history, referring to Rouen and Paris as the "two principal cities of the kingdom." He gave a sketch of the medieval fortunes of the Duchy of Normandy vis-à-vis English and French suzerainty. In this story the English claimed the duchy after William the Conqueror took the English Crown, but Normandy was retrieved in 1204 by Philip (II) Augustus

constitutional history made in the sixteenth century.[6] First, L'Hôpital traced the historical development of the French Law of Succession and showed its legal application to Charles IX.

> I refer now to the declaration of his majority which the king has just made to you. . . . I will speak of the "Majority of the king," a thing [historical phenomenon] unknown to many persons, but as authentic as truth itself. Indeed, our forebears were wise rulers who should be commended [in history] as much for their prudence in making laws and ordinances as for their brave acts in war which histories record. For the moment we will set aside common and ordinary [private] laws associated with governance (*la justice et police*) of the kingdom and discuss two of the greatest and most utilitarian [Public] Laws known to us: one which concerns the institution of the king, the other, the administration of the kingdom. [First, concerning the institution of the king]: in order to prevent the disorder wrought by the space of time left between the death of one king and the institution of a successor, . . . that is, situations marred by interregnum, . . . our wise rulers ordained as an immutable law (*loy perpetuelle*) [the precept] that *the kingdom is never vacant* (*le royaume n'est jamais vacant*), because there is continuity from king to king so that *as soon as the king's eyes close* [in death] there is another king . . . without awaiting Coronation, unction, consecration, or any other ceremonies. [Second, concerning the administration of the kingdom]: the king has already spoken to you about the law which we call the "Law of Majority" made to deal with the administration of the kingdom. . . . That law considers our king a major at fourteen years of age and is unique [to France], not commonly found in other kingdoms and empires. Through it

---

[1180-1223] and Saint Louis (IX) [1226-1270] maintained that French holding by a treaty. Following the Battle of Crécy [1346], however, the English occupied Normandy again and remained even after the Battle of Agincourt [1416]. They were routed for a time by Charles VII [1422-1461] but returned intermittently. At this point, according to L'Hôpital, the English queen had broken a treaty made with Henry II [1547-1559] which guaranteed the English departure from Normandy, and now Charles IX rightly took by force the port of Le Havre and the surrounding area. Many of these historical examples used by the chancellor appeared in Du Tillet, *Pour l'entière majorité*, published three years before.

[6] Lemaire, *Les Lois fondamentales*, pp. 78-81, missed this important speech in his interesting summary of the way L'Hôpital's ideas contributed to a notion of the so-called Fundamental Law of France in the sixteenth century.

the administration of the kingdom is given to the king at the age of fourteen years. . . . And that [Law of Majority] . . . was promulgated by Charles V [in 1375]. . . . Moreover, another law was made in the time of King Charles VI and published in the Parlement of Paris the day after Christmas [1407] . . . which ruled that whatever the age of the king, be it only a year, all affairs would be [conducted] in his name. . . .

Our king has certainly reached that age [the fourteenth year], although he has not completed it. But those who have read the [Roman Law] books know that in cases of preferments [public offices] the law intends that the year begun is considered completed. I will cite the law which is in our books: . . . it is the well-known law *ad rempublicam de munerib[us] et honor[ibus]* in the Pandects [of Justinian] which holds that it is sufficient to have attained and not completed the last year of the age [requirement].[7]

Then L'Hôpital contrasted the joyous celebration of the Majority *Lit de Justice* with the lugubrious and spiritual tones of the two traditional ceremonies of succession, the Royal Funeral and Coronation, and named the Majority *Lit de Justice* as the one ceremony which marked a true renewal of the royal office because the monarch had come of age as legislator.

. . . since our king has reached his age of majority, we should celebrate that occasion as a . . . renewal of reign which is more joyful and pleasing than any of the others. [For instance] the moment of [royal] accession to the Crown holds some sadness because of the recent death of the preceding king still fresh in human memory. The day [of the Royal Funeral] when the heralds cry out at burial "The king is dead" followed immediately by "Long live the king!" is also tinged with sadness. And the day of the Coronation holds more religious ceremonial [significance] than joy. But today [in the *Lit de Justice* assembly] when our king is declared a major . . . everyone is joyful. . . . It behooves us, therefore, to accord him heart-

---

[7] Dupuy, *Traité de la majorité* [Cron. de Norm.], pp. 362-365; also in Godefroy, *Cérémonial françois*, II, 571-572 [italics added]. In the *Corpus Juris Civilis* the *Lex ad rempublicam* in the title *de muneribus et honoribus* [*Digest* 50, 4, 8] speaks of majority at twenty-five years of age but specifies that "entering the twenty-fifth year is regarded as fulfilling it." By 1604 L'Hôpital's legal precedent on majority was famous enough to be included in the marginal gloss on that rubric; *Corpus Juris Civilis*, ed. Jean Vignon (Orléans, 1604).

felt honor and obedience. He is a major, but I do not hesitate to say in the presence of his majesty (who concurs) that he wishes to be considered as a major, acting with the counsel of the queen his mother ... and that of the princes and lords [of the Regency Council]. As a major the king wished to make his *Entrée* into this city [Rouen] to deliver and prescribe the law and order which he intends to maintain during his reign.... He wishes that all his edicts and ordinances be observed and maintained, including the Edict of Pacification of disorder [second Pacification Edict] drawn not by him alone but by the counsel, advice, and deliberation of the queen his mother and the princes and lords of his council.... In addition his majesty wishes that all threats and enmities [among subjects] cease and admonishes ... all his officers, those of his sovereign Courts as well as *baillis*, *sénéschals*, and others, to adminster his justice with equity and without prejudice or passion.[8]

Having explained the king's Majority Declaration and legislative action, Chancellor L'Hôpital delivered a stinging volley of criticism against the French Parlements. He reiterated the separation of legislative and judicial functions, insisted that Parlement must invoke the procedure of remonstrance for royal legislation deemed troublesome instead of willfully interpreting such legislation, stressed the obligation of individual *parlementaires* to inform the king of infractions made by the Court against royal ordinances, and called for specific parlementary reforms.

I speak now directly to you [the Parlements of France] who discharge the justice of the king over which I preside. I am greatly displeased with the disorder which exists in the sphere of justice (*la justice*).... Messieurs, I will not remind you of precepts which teach the art of proper judgment, for you have copious books on that [subject]. Rather I will admonish you solely about the proper comportment which should be observed in the process of making such judgments.... [First, on royal ordinances]: you swear an oath at your reception into office [as members of Parlements] to maintain ordinances and to make [others] maintain them. Do you keep them well? Most are badly kept.... What is worse you act as if you are above the ordinances and not obliged to follow them if they displease you. Messieurs, messieurs, the ordinances should be above you! You are reputed to be sovereigns [sovereign Courts], but the ordinance

[8] Dupuy, *Traité de la majorité* [Cron. de Norm.], pp. 365-366; also in Godefroy, *Cérémonial françois*, II, 572-573.

is the command of the king and you are not superior to the king ... it is necessary that the will of the judge accord with the intention of the legislator. [Instead] the king makes an ordinance and you exceed your authority by interpreting it falsely, contrary to his intention. Judges who do not wish to conform to the legislator are like sailors who throw a ship off course. ... If you find in executing an ordinance that it is too harsh, difficult, or unfit for the region in which you are judges, you must nevertheless observe it until the prince corrects it. You do not have the power to break, change, or vitiate it; you must have recourse to [the procedure of] remonstrance.

[Second, on prejudicial judgments]: Messieurs, take care in making judgments not to act out of favor or prejudice ... toward friends or enemies ... sects or factions ... without considering equity in the case. You are civil judges, not [judges] of life, morals, or religion. You seem to think that cases can be judged on the basis of whether or not one man is a better Christian than another, which is no more relevant to judgment than opinions about which among them is the better poet, orator, painter, artisan.... There have been numerous complaints about this problem, and the king to his regret might find it necessary to remove cases from your cognizance....

[Third, on gifts]: I come now to [the problem of] gifts. Messieurs, you know that justice if exercised properly must be gratuitous ... [the emoluments] which used to be called "spices" (*épices*) in ancient France, when judges took next to nothing from the parties to execute justice, have now undergone a perverse metamorphosis into gold and silver ... and in many places ... a judge now does nothing without money....

[Fourth, on lawsuits]: the true goal of a judge is to settle lawsuits so that, if possible, none are pending. Hence laws which prevent crimes from being committed are better than those which punish them.... But instead judges seek fame not by decreasing litigation but by rendering unclear judgments which engender more conflict: as the saying goes, "lawsuits beget more lawsuits." You have issued some *arrêts* which have engendered litigation more extensive than the original, ... and despite the fact that in these days you are seated all year long in three chambers, lawsuits never seem to diminish.... To be sure, one wishes to make a living by his profession, ... but you would do well to bring order to it [the legal profession].

[Fifth, on secret deliberations]: you complain that malicious persons commit perjury by revealing some of the secret deliberations of the Court to the king. But I consider these informers good men if ... they do not fear being seen and heard [in the act] ... ; [that is], if they do not reveal [secret] opinions [clandestinely] out of ambition or to ingratiate themselves with kings and lords. ... The eye of justice sees all, the king sees and discovers all in the course of time. Do nothing which you would not wish known! ... Those who reveal the judgments of the Court warrant punishment, but those who out of proper zeal and affection reveal infractions committed against the ordinances of the king are not [punishable] and incur no blame. You are required, even your presidents, to remonstrate regarding actions which are contrary to the ordinances and to warn the king about them. In times past there were commissioners of the king and even councillors of the Grand Conseil, called today the Privé Conseil, who entered Parlement specifically in order to listen and report to the king all that went on there. [Moreover], the ordinance enjoins you to hold the *Mercuriales* and to report on them to the king so that the said lord is informed of actions taken against his ordinances and errors committed in his Courts of Parlement. He is duty-bound to make inquiries about the errors of his judges and officers, so do not act as if these admonitions are odd. Your judgments are often reported to the king when they seem prima facie to veer from rectitude and equity ... you should not find that odd, because the greatest [officers], constable, marshals, chancellor of France, render an account to the king daily regarding the exercise of their offices. ... His majesty has the right to know how his justice is administered and whether or not his judges are [properly] discharging their duties. ... You must not feel wronged when held accountable to your king ... from whom you hold your honors and magistracies for an indeterminate length of time (*à titre de précaire*), that is, as long as it pleases him. Unlike other countries, ... your magistracies here [in France] are perpetual, [so] take care not to abuse that [privilege]. ... In summary, obey the king and his ordinances. ... .[9]

[9] Dupuy, *Traité de la majorité* [Cron. de Norm.], pp. 367-371; also in Godefroy, *Cérémonial françois*, II, 573-576. The *Mercuriales* were hearings which Parlements were supposed to conduct on the last Wednesday of every month to assure the proper execution of offices. Note that L'Hôpital's odd remark, "even your presidents" are required to warn the king about parlementary infractions, sug-

Following Chancellor L'Hôpital's speech, the first president of the Parlement of Rouen addressed the *Lit de Justice* assembly. President Antoine de Saint-Anthot delivered an erudite speech on kingship and justice stressing the art of government. He called for the exercise of "political virtue," that is, "civil reason" in the conduct of "affairs of state," and he emphasized the necessity to promulgate good Public Laws to sustain the kingdom. Throughout his exhortation Saint-Anthot maintained a conciliatory tone, made no response to L'Hôpital's criticism of the Parlements, and never mentioned the delicate issue posed by the convocation of this Majority *Lit de Justice* assembly in the Parlement of Rouen rather than the Parlement of Paris.[10]

The chancellor consulted briefly with Charles IX, Queen Catherine de Médicis, and the Regency Council and announced the king's wish that the queen and Royal Council pay homage to him as sovereign. As the queen moved toward the throne, the king stood up, removed his hat, and descended a step to meet her. She declared the administration of the kingdom delivered forthwith into the hands of Charles IX, then knelt and kissed her son in an act of homage. In rank each member of the royal entourage, princes, peers, and Crown officers, went up to the throne, knelt, and kissed the king's hand in similiar acts of homage.[11] Following the homage ritual, underscoring the importance of the Royal Council in regency government, Charles IX concluded this demonstration of his full legislative authority by ordering the Pacification Edict read and registered in the Parlement of Rouen and in the other Courts of Parlement. And it is important to note that the Latin subscription of registration, which appeared by order of the king on the bottom fold of the edict, bore no provisional clause as did that imposed by the Parlement of Paris on the Edict of Pacification the preceding March.[12] In the first stage of the *Lit de Justice* assembly the constitutional and legislative role

gests that *parlementaires* might have accused presidents of reporting matters discussed *in camera* to the king.

[10] Ibid., 371-375. Just before the president spoke, the *parlementaires* knelt as a body before the king, who bade them rise immediately.

[11] Ibid., 376-377. The clerk at Rouen who wrote this account noted that the queen had been made regent by the Estates, a troublesome contention which the royal party would not have countenanced. Later on around 1662 or earlier Chancellor Pierre (III) Séguier remarked on how extraordinary it was that the king arose and went to the queen regent; B.N. ms. fr. 18411, fol. 148v (a margin note).

[12] Dupuy, *Traité de la majorité* [Cron. de Norm.], pp. 377-382, for the edict; and Isambert, *Recueil général des anciennes lois*, XIV, 142-147.

of the Crown was emphasized. The close alliance effected between the king's Majority Declaration (affirming French Public Law) and his promulgation of the second Pacification Edict (creating national law) exemplified that principle.

In contrast to the king's constitutional-legislative role stressed in the first stage, the proper judicial role of the Parlement of Rouen was emphasized in the second part of the session. The king sat as judge while the *parlementaires* evoked the customary laws of Normandy to argue a case in private law, which involved a civil inheritance suit in which two women sought recovery of dowries from their brother. The *avocats* focused upon Charles IX as legislator and judge, characterized the king as tutor of the kingdom, and restated the nature of his relationship to the kingdom through the marriage metaphor encountered in the *Lits de Justice* of 1527 and 1537 (the king as spouse of the kingdom, the domain of the Crown as dowry).[13] Following a summation of the case, the chancellor took counsel from the king, royal party, and *parlementaires*, and the *arrêt* was pronounced in favor of the plaintiffs. The Majority *Lit de Justice* was adjourned when the king, queen, princes, and lords stood up, bowed graciously toward the *parlementaires*, and withdrew from the chambers of the Parlement of Rouen.[14] Thus, by the close of

[13] The *avocat* Brétignières for the plaintiffs noted that his clients "ask for no other judge than the king alone," knowing that "Justice is the end of the law and the law is the work of the prince"; Dupuy, *Traité de la majorité* [Cron. de Norm.], pp. 383-389. This statement following Plutarch, *Ad principem ineruditum*, III, 780E, was given also by Bodin, *République* [1578], p. 118 (cited by Church, *Richelieu*, p. 27, n. 42) and by the *avocat* Jacques de La Guesle in a remonstrance of 21 July 1588, *Les Remonstrances* (Paris, 1611), p. 42 (cited by Kantorowicz, *King's Two Bodies*, p. 499, n. 13). The *avocat* Laurens Bigot (for the king) called attention to regional jurisdiction, the customary law of Normandy, noting that the king in his *Lit de Justice* guards the rights of private citizens just as the law of Normandy protects the king's rights and privileges; Dupuy, *Traité de la majorité* [Cron. de Norm.], pp. 389-392. The *avocat* Guillaume Ango (for the defendant) emphasized French sovereignty, calling Charles IX "emperor and monarch in your kingdom, recognizing God alone as superior," and employed the marriage metaphor to characterize the domain as "the true dowry of the Republic which has no other husband than you, Sire, who holds the office, tutelage, and defense of it [the Republic], your true spouse"; ibid., 392-394.

[14] Dupuy, *Traité de la majorité* [Cron. de Norm.], pp. 382-397. The direct judgment exercised by the king in this case has been described by Doucet, *Institutions de la France*, I, 90, as portraying the principle of *justice retenue* as opposed to *justice déléguée* to emphasize the right of the king to render justice in person. But that characterization takes no note of the important division of

this assembly the new theory of the ancient constitution, separating constitutional-legislative and judicial authority, had been demonstrated once more through the ritual of the *Lit de Justice*.

PUBLIC LAW WRIT IN RITUAL AND DISCOURSE

The organization of the Majority *Lit de Justice* of Rouen was not undertaken precipitously, nor was the planning haphazard.[15] The idea of convoking a *Lit de Justice* for Charles IX had simmered within the Royal Council for three years among persons who were familiar with the *Lits de Justice* of 1527 and 1537 and with the historical conception of the medieval *Lit de Justice* advanced by Jean du Tillet's research, most recently in the majority tracts of 1560. Chancellor L'Hôpital was the person in that Council most knowledgeable about the theory and practice of the *Lit de Justice* assembly, for his chancellery, as that of his predecessor François Olivier, was the official depository for such information following the instructions of Henry II's commission of 1548. In addition L'Hôpital and Du Tillet were brought into daily contact through the duties of their respective offices, and the chancellor acknowledged that the clerk shared historical discoveries with him. Around 1560 the anonymous memorandum on parlementary assemblies was prepared, probably under L'Hôpital's auspices, and close to that time a *Lit de Justice* was planned and abruptly canceled in 1561. As will be recalled, the author of the memorandum correctly recapitulated Du Tillet's constitutional delineation of *Lit de Justice* assemblies and Royal *Séances*, but in addition he composed a new ceremonial guide which required *parlementaires* to don red robes in *Lit de Justice* assemblies and introduced the novel suggestion that *Lit de Justice* assemblies could be convoked outside Paris. Indeed, here just two years later the main injunctions of that memorandum provided a blueprint for the Majority *Lit de Justice* convoked in Rouen. The document stated that *Lit de Justice* assemblies treated

the proceedings to reflect royal constitutional-legislative authority as opposed to parlementary-judicial cognizance.

[15] Historians have disagreed on the direction of this affair. Henri Amphoux, *Michel de L'Hôpital et la liberté de conscience au XVIᵉ siècle* (Paris, 1900), maintains that Queen Catherine de Médicis arranged the events; whereas François Albert-Buisson, *Michel de L'Hôpital* (Paris, 1950), notes the enormous influence of the chancellor on the queen during the early reign of Charles IX. Glasson, *Parlement of Paris*, I, 27-30, suggests that L'Hôpital was responsible for the organization of the *Lit de Justice*, and the evidence set forth here supports that contention.

constitutional issues (matters "universally concerning the state of the king") and cited as one example Charles VI's assembly of 1407 dealing with regency and majority rules; it specified a high throne for the king and red robes for *parlementaires*; it noted that *Lit de Justice* assemblies sometimes followed Royal *Entrées* to various cities; and it suggested that *Lit de Justice* assemblies could be held in provincial locations. All of these elements were present in the Majority *Lit de Justice* of 1563. In all probability Du Tillet never wholly countenanced this convocation of a *Lit de Justice* in a provincial Parlement. Throughout his works the clerk consistently posited a procedural tie between the *Lit de Justice* assembly and the Parlement of Paris, and in the *Recueil des roys de France* he barely mentioned the Rouen assembly of 1563 and never acknowledged it as a *Lit de Justice*. On the horns of this dilemma to the very end, Jean du Tillet, clerk of the Parlement of Paris, exemplified the officeholder described by L'Hôpital as attached to Parlement but beholden to the king, for he was caught between the conflicting demands of Charles IX and the Parisian Court during the bitter controversy which followed the Majority *Lit de Justice* of Rouen.

The ritual of the first Majority *Lit de Justice* was organized carefully to display through gesture, word, and symbol the royal party's view of the ancient constitution. First, both the geographical setting and the ceremonial configuration effectively symbolized institutional relationships. The convocation of the assembly in a provincial Parlement and the promulgation of royal legislation there, rather than in Paris, disarmed the Parisian Court's claim to superior status among Parlements and substantiated L'Hôpital's previously stated view of individual Parlements as separate but equal in status, together forming a single corporate entity beholden to the king. Furthermore, the king's demeanor amply demonstrated the constitutional-legislative role of the monarch. Charles IX personally declared his majority status, underscored his full legislative capacity by issuing an edict, and received the individual acts of homage from the regent and Royal Council, which recognized his change of status. Second, the procedural format confirmed the separation of legislative and judicial functions. The king as legislator promulgated his Majority Declaration which affirmed Public Law and an edict which created national law, whereas the Parlement of Rouen as a judicial body argued a civil suit before the king which was settled according to the customary law of Normandy. Finally, the discourse pronounced in the *Lit de Justice* elucidated the royal view of the French constitution. Charles IX not only issued his Majority Declaration and an edict but also ex-

panded the legal definition of the crime of *lèse-majesté* to include disobedience to royal ordinances promulgated for the nation at large,[16] ex-
emplifying on the spot L'Hôpital's legislator-king. Lest these bold actions
seem arbitrary, the chancellor provided a pithy explanation of their
legitimacy, thereby outlining the ideology of juristic monarchy.

In terms eminently clear for the time Chancellor L'Hôpital discussed
French Public Law as the source of royal legislative authority and depicted legislator-kings at work.[17] Devising an innovative conceptual scheme
for implementing the Law of Succession, he divided the process into
two continuous phases: first, the precise instant at which a successor
legally assumed the office or "seized" the Crown; then the somewhat
later point (much later in minority kingship) at which the king actually
undertook full "administration of the kingdom," that is, fully exercised
the legislative prerogative. He identified two "laws," or axioms, which
governed that time-bound sequence: the precept of *Saisine*, or *"Seizure
of the kingdom,"* which regulated the initial phase (the assumption of
office); and the precept of the *"Majority* of the king," which regulated
the second phase (the renewal of legislative capacity). Chancellor L'Hôpital defined *Seizure* of the kingdom, the first stage of this immutable
law (*loy perpetuelle*), as

> [the precept] that *the kingdom is never vacant* (*le royaume n'est jamais
> vacant*), because there is continuity from king to king so that *as soon
> as the king's eyes close* [in death] [= *mortuus aperit oculos viventis*]
> there is another king ... without awaiting Coronation, unction,
> consecration, or any other ceremonies.[18]

[16] Commenting on the crime of *lèse-majesté*, Francis I's ordinance (1539)
defined the action as one of "conspiring, plotting, or acting against our person,
our children, or the state of our kingdom"; Isambert, *Recueil général des anciennes
lois*, XII, 590. But Charles IX in 1563 connected the crime specifically with
failure to observe royal ordinances. For the steady expansion of the list of offenses
falling under the rubric of *lèse-majesté* and the increased use of that charge
under Louis XIII and Cardinal Richelieu, see Church, *Richelieu and Reason of
State* (Princeton, 1972), especially pt. III on statebuilding; for the medieval
precedents, see Cuttler, *The Law of Treason*, chap. II.

[17] Lemaire, *Les Lois fondamentales*, p. 78, n. 4 (following a rendition of L'Hôpital's *Traité de la réformation de la justice* provided by Duféy, *Oeuvres inédites*,
I, 61), guardedly suggests that the chancellor might have been the first to use
the term "fundamental" to characterize the Salic Law. It is unlikely that L'Hôpital used that expression. He formulated quite a different vocabulary for constitutional discourse, and the term Fundamental Law was associated with the
mode of discourse peculiar to the seventeenth century.

[18] For the whole speech, see above, nn. 7 and 8 [italics added].

L'Hôpital's image of the successor instantly seizing the kingdom "as soon as the king's eyes close" relied upon a medieval proverb from private law, *Mortuus aperit oculos viventis* (The dead opens the eyes of the living), which had been applied earlier in the sixteenth century to cases in private law involving inheritance.[19] But L'Hôpital invested his statement with clear constitutional meaning when he invented a distinctly French expression, *Le royaume n'est jamais vacant* (The kingdom is never vacant), to explain that concept of legal-hereditary succession to the Crown in terms of Public Law. Thus he not only defined kingship in legal terms stressing the continuity of office, as had Jean de Terre Rouge in the fifteenth century,[20] but also advanced a language of French Public Law in which to conduct this constitutional discourse. Chancellor L'Hôpital was not alone in advancing these conceptions of Public Law in terms peculiarly French. Two years earlier, in 1560, the Royal Council (headed by the chancellor) defended the legitimacy of an Estates General held by Charles IX (but convoked by his deceased predecessor Francis II) by arguing that

> ... according to the [Public] Law of the kingdom *royal authority does not die* (*l'autorité royale ne meurt point*), [because] *the dead seizes the living* (*le mort saisit le vif*), and authority passes without interruption from the deceased king [Francis II] to his legitimate successor [Charles IX].[21]

Here L'Hôpital (and the Council) drafted a private-law maxim on inheritance, *Le mort saisit le vif* (The dead seizes [with respect to the

---

[19] The medieval jurist Baldus de Ubaldis (c. 1327-1400) quoted the proverb *Mortuus aperit oculos viventis* to show that one born unfree could become free on the death of his master (*Codex* 7, 15, 3, n. 2, fol. 12). In the early sixteenth century the French jurist André Tiraqueau (d. 1558) quoted it to explain the famous maxim of French private law on inheritance, *Le mort saisit le vif* (The dead seizes [with respect to the inheritance] the living), calling for immediate seizure, or possession, of property by the rightful heir, but he denied that the concept could apply to the assumption of a public office (as the Crown) (in Tiraquella, *De jure primogenitorum*, q. 40, n. 31 [*Tractatus varii*, Frankfurt, 1574, IV, 70, and V, 73]). For a discussion of these notions as applicable to the continuity of office derived from *Dignitas non moritur* (The dignity does not die), consult Kantorowicz, *King's Two Bodies*, pp. 393-394, nn. 267, 268.

[20] For the idea of "simple succession" (that is, legal-hereditary succession) in Jean de Terre Rouge, *Contra rebelles suorum regnum* (Lyons, 1526), see Giesey, *Juristic Basis of Dynastic Right*, pp. 12-17.

[21] Georges Picot, *Histoire des États généreaux considérés au point de vue de leur influence sur le gouvernement de la France de 1355 à 1614* (Paris, 1872), II, 188 [italics added]. The original verbs read "ne mourroit point" and "saissisoit."

inheritance] the living),[22] to describe the French Public Law of Succession and advanced the first known French maxim of Public Law, *L'autorité royale ne meurt point* (Royal authority does not die), to characterize the process. And there is more. Jean du Tillet too explained the French Law of Succession in these terms.

> ... having rejected the ancient habit of counting reigns of the kings of France from the day of their *sacres* and Coronations, we now count them without break from the day that the Crown devolves upon them; and in that respect *the dead seizes the living (le mort saisit le vif)* ... for the Crown devolves upon the next capable [successor] in *the same instant that the king renders his last breath* [= *mortuus aperit oculos viventis*].[23]

Here Du Tillet linked his version of the proverb *Mortuus aperit oculos viventis* (where he substituted the "last breath" for "closed eyes") with the maxim *Le mort saisit le vif* to describe legal-hereditary succession, although he did not provide a French analogue in Public Law for these two related notions. Descended from the medieval maxim *Dignitas non moritur* (The dignity does not die), which illustrated the immortality of office well known in English circles at this time,[24] the two vernacular maxims, *L'autorité royale ne meurt point* and *Le royaume n'est jamais vacant*, neatly spelled out the perpetuity of French royal office beyond the death of the individual incumbent and thus provided a new French system of discourse in Public Law to elucidate the older maxims on succession originally derived from private inheritance law. It has been suggested that the recourse to precepts of private law signaled a "proprietary" notion of kingship and the state.[25] But that suggestion does not take into consideration first, that the discussants at this time had no other appropriate vocabulary from which to draw, and second, that they

[22] The legal maxim from private law *Le mort saisit le vif* circulated among legists in the early sixteenth century following its use by Tiraqueau to denote the idea of the immediate possession of inheritance. For use of the maxim in a feudal context, see Giesey, *Juristic Basis of Dynastic Right*, pp. 7-12.

[23] Du Tillet, *Recueil des roys de France* (Annotations), p. 125 [italics added].

[24] On the development of *Dignitas non moritur* and the clear delineation of the "king's two bodies" in England, see Kantorowicz, *King's Two Bodies*, pp. 383-450.

[25] See Herbert H. Rowen, *The King's State: Proprietary Dynasticism in Early Modern France* (New Brunswick, 1980), chap. II. Contrary to this thesis, it was in fact the pattern of rules governing succession which mitigated against the sense of ownership in the system of juristic monarchy.

were attempting to fashion the best vocabulary available into a suitable language of Public Law. The importance of the emergence of a language of French Public Law around 1560 and the application of that language to the discussion of the Law of Succession in a *Lit de Justice* in 1563 is readily apparent when placed in historical perspective. Before moving in that direction, however, it is necessary to recount Chancellor L'Hô-pital's second precept regulating the French Law of Succession.

Following his exposition on the precept of *Seizure*, the first axiom governing the assumption of office, L'Hôpital turned to the precept of *Majority*, the other axiom regulating full exercise of the royal legislative prerogative during minority kingship. Citing evidence directly from Du Tillet's works, particularly the majority tracts of 1560, the chancellor gave the *Majority* precept historical roots in feudal times.

> The Law of Majority ... considers our king a major at fourteen years of age and is unique [to France]. ... [It] was promulgated by Charles V [in 1375] ... [and] Charles VI [in 1407]. ...[26]

Then he outlined a ceremonial plan to implement that precept. In his critical view none of the traditionally celebrated moments of royal succession could serve as joyous public celebrations renewing kingship. The moment of *Seizure* marked the actual instant of succession to the throne, but that moment was always dolorous given the concomitant death of the predecessor king. The Royal Funeral publicly proclaimed succession to royal office when the heralds' cry *Le roi est mort! Vive le roi!* (The king is dead! Long live the king!) was given at the moment of burial, but the ceremony itself was tinged with funereal gloom. The Coronation ceremony provided confirmation of succession, but it was inherently religious and therefore not suitable for a joyous public celebration. In contrast the *Lit de Justice* assembly, celebrating the king's attainment of majority and legislative capacity, constituted a true public celebration of the renewal of kingship in France. Reasoning thus the chancellor effected a transposition of traditional ceremonial symbolism, denigrating the importance of the Funeral and Coronation in the succession process and raising the Majority *Lit de Justice* high on the gamut of civic ritual.

When placed in historical perspective the emergence of this body of constitutional precepts between 1560 and 1563 constitutes a landmark in French constitutional thought and practice. It has been shown that the

---

[26] Comparison of this speech with Du Tillet's majority tracts shows L'Hôpital's dependance on those works for his evidence.

private-law maxim *Le mort saisit le vif* attained some stature in Public Law when political thinkers such as Guillaume Benedicti, Jean Bodin, and François Hotman associated it with succession to the Crown.[27] But now one must consider the early pronouncements of Du Tillet and L'Hôpital between 1560 and 1563 which not only transferred *Le mort saisit le vif* and its cohort *Mortuus aperit oculos viventis* to the Public Law sphere but also propagated them publicly in a *Lit de Justice* assembly. It has also been suggested that the first French analogue for *Le mort saisit le vif* was the adage *Le roi ne meurt jamais* (The king never dies), a slogan descended from *Dignitas non moritur* (The dignity does not die), and that the adage was commonly used early in the sixteenth century even though it was not published until 1576 by Jean Bodin.[28] Both facets of that assumption must be qualified. First, Bodin's discourse on Public Law read as follows:

> ... as they say, it is certain that *the king never dies* [*le roi ne meurt jamais*], because as soon as one [king] is deceased the nearest male of his lineage is *seized by the kingdom* [= *le mort saisit le vif*] and in possession of it before he is crowned. And [the kingdom] is not deferred by patrimonial succession but by virtue of the Law of the kingdom.[29]

Although here *Le roi ne meurt jamais* serves as the French analogue for *Le mort saisit le vif*, such usage was predated by the maxims *L'autorité royale ne meurt point* and *Le royaume n'est jamais vacant*, which had circulated in the 1560's. Moreover, these earlier analogues (citing *royal authority* and the *kingdom* as immortal) captured the sense of their progenitor *Dignitas non moritur* (The dignity does not die) more precisely than Bodin's adage (citing the *king* as immortal).

[27] Giesey, *Juristic Basis of Dynastic Right*, pp. 10-11, n. 29.

[28] Giesey, *Royal Funeral Ceremony*, pp. 177-183, and Kantorowicz, *King's Two Bodies*, pp. 409-410. For a very early rendition of the metaphor in Burgundy, see Paul Saenger, "Burgundy and the Inalienability of Appanages in the Reign of Louis XI," *French Historical Studies*, X, 1 (Spring 1977), pp. 1-26, where it is attributed to Michel de Pons in the late fifteenth century.

[29] "Car il est certain que *le roy ne meurt jamais*, comme l'on dit, ains si tost que l'un est decedé, le plus proche masle de son estoc *est saisi du royaume* et en possession d'iceluy au paravant qu'l soit couronné"; Jean Bodin, *République*, bk. I, chap. 8. In addition, note that Bodin repeated that assertion: "C'est pourquoy on dit en ce royaume que *le roy ne meurt jamais*: qui est un proverbe ancien, qui monstre bien que le royaume ne fut onques electif ..."; ibid., bk. VI, chap. 5 [italics added].

Second, since there is no textual evidence to support Bodin's elusive suggestion that *Le roi ne meurt jamais* was an ancient French proverb commonly known,[30] the suggestion should not be taken at face value. In the 1560's the language of constitutional discourse maintained the peculiar juristic tone struck by the maxims of L'Hôpital and Du Tillet, which focused on the perpetuity of royal office. The same sense underlay President De Thou's discussion of the royal *dignité* in 1563 when he stated that "the attire [red robes] in which we [the Parlement of Paris] are vested during Royal Funerals shows that ... they [kings] do not die in respect to justice...."[31] And this juristic reference was preserved in the comment made by a *parlementaire* about the succession of Henry III in 1574.

> We find that we are never without a king (*nous ne sommes jamais sans roy*) because *the deceased king opens the eyes of the living* [king] (*roy qui decede aperit oculos viventis*). Although [individual] kings die, the kingdom and justice by which kingdoms are administered and regulated is inviolable. Thus we [Parlement] never change habits [red robes], not even for the death of kings or the change [of reigns].[32]

The mode of discourse employed by Chancellor L'Hôpital, Jean du Tillet, and various *parlementaires* suggests that the ambiguous adage *Le roi ne meurt jamais* did not enter the public discussion of the French constitution throughout most of the sixteenth century, because it did not preserve the precise distinction between the royal office and its corporeal incumbent which was sought at the time.

[30] Giesey, *Royal Funeral Ceremony*, p. 177, and Kantorowicz, *King's Two Bodies*, note that Bodin's allusion *"comme l'on dit"* implies earlier usage, and the second quotation from Bodin might seem at first glance to confirm that opinion (n. 29 above).

[31] For the context of the full quotation, see above, Chap. VI, n. 32. The use of *kings* here in the plural connotes the immortal nature of office (filled by a succession of persons), which was symbolized by the red-robed *parlementaires*.

[32] "Nous trouverons que nous ne sommes jamais sans Roy, que le Roy qui decede *aperit oculos viventis* combien que les Rois soient morts, que le royaume et la justice par laquelle les royaumes son administrez and policez, est inviolable, et aussi pour la mort, et mutation des Rois, nous ne changeons jamais d'habits ... (31 May 1574)"; quoted in Dupuy, *Traité de la majorité*, pp. 449-453 [italics added]. The French Law of Succession is described further as a "loy speciale, singuliere et particuliere de ce royaume laquelle nous avons gardée et observée inviolablement depuis la creation de nos rois successivement ..."; ibid., 450.

In fact, the confusion of the "king's two bodies" which was allowed by Bodin's peculiar rendition of *Le roi ne meurt jamais* was obvious in the later treatment accorded that adage by Charles Loyseau and Antoine Loisel. In 1611 Loisel added Bodin's adage to his fourth compilation of legal maxims, connecting it with slogans from the Royal Funeral.[33] Loyseau explained Bodin's adage within the network of succession concepts discussed here, attached a combined and amended version of L'Hôpital's maxims to them, and then fashioned a new maxim of his own for the lot.[34] In the end, however, Loyseau's amended maxim, *La royauté est tousjours remplie et non jamais vacante* (Royalty is always replenished and never vacant), substituted royalty for the kingdom (*royaume*, or *chose publique*), blurring king and office, in a different mode of discourse which fit the circumstances of the early seventeenth century. Paradoxically, it was the ambiguous nature of *Le roi ne meurt jamais* which accounted both for its failure to enter the constitutional discourse of the sixteenth century and for its success and longevity in the seventeenth century. Standing alone the adage tended to confuse the "king's two bodies," so it was handily adapted by those living in a new era whence the distinction between office and incumbent was rapidly receding.

[33] Antoine Loisel, *Institutes coutumières*, ed. Michel Reulos (Paris, 1935), no. 3, and p. 19: "Le roi ne meurt jamais, ou, le roi est mort, vive le roi." Giesey, *Royal Funeral Ceremony*, p. 182 and n. 22, notes that the previous editions (1607, 1608, and 1609) did not contain this maxim *Le roi ne meurt jamais*, and cites *Ordonnances des rois de France*, I, 32-35, for commentary on the proverb, which he suggests struck a theme tending toward absolutism. In fact that proverb-turned-maxim specifically characterized the new ideology of dynastic monarchy which held sway between the terms of juristic and absolutist monarchies.

[34] "... the first maxim of our French law ... *Le mort saisit le vif* (*The dead seizes the living*), ... ordains that *at the same instant the deceased king renders his last breath* [= *mortuus aperit oculos viventis*], his successor is fully king by an immediate continuation of right and possession, one to the other, there being no conceivable interval of interregnum, just as Roman Law recognized the continuation of right and seigneury *in suis haeredibus, 1. in suis. D. De lib. & post.* [= *Digest* 28, 2, 11]. I say [that the successor is] fully king without awaiting his *sacre*, as Bodin has proven in bk. I, chap. 8, and Parlement has declared by a notable *arrêt* in the year 1498, although Du Tillet notes that formerly the contrary was held. That is why we say in the vernacular that *Le roi ne meurt jamais* (*The king never dies*), that is to say, *La royauté est tousjours remplie et non jamais vacante* (*Royalty is always replenished and never vacant*) [= combining *L'autorité royale ne meurt point* and *Le royaume n'est jamais vacant*]"; Charles Loyseau, *Cinq livres du droit des offices*, I, x, 58, in *Les Oeuvres de Loyseau* (Paris, 1666) [italics added]. This passage (translated differently) is discussed in Giesey, *Royal Funeral Ceremony*, p. 181, n. 17; and *Juristic Basis of Dynastic Right*, p. 11, n. 29.

At this point some revision of the current interpretation of the origin of these constitutional notions on legal-hereditary succession is in order. During the mid decades of the sixteenth century, a new type of discourse on the French Law of Succession surfaced in response to critical questions raised about regency and majority, and that discourse aimed to eliminate the shadow of legislative incapacity hovering over the scene of royal minority. Fashioned from constitutional concepts advanced by Du Tillet and L'Hôpital, that discourse developed in essentially three phases. First, the older legal maxims from private law, *Le mort saisit le vif* and *Mortuus aperit oculos viventis*, were linked together to explicate the process of instantaneous succession in France, and then two new French maxims of Public Law, *L'autorité royale ne meurt point* and *Le royaume n'est jamais vacant* (derived from the medieval maxim *Dignitas non moritur*) were invented as analogues to underline the legal nexus of succession to royal office. Second, the Law of Majority (a legislative amendment of Charles V in 1375) was explained in historical context as a legitimate precept of the ancient constitution, and the *Lit de Justice* assembly was designated as the succession ceremony which best demonstrated these precepts of French Public Law. Third, this network of constitutional axioms on succession was actually demonstrated in the *Lit de Justice* assembly of 1563, which was represented as French historical tradition. Once again the *Lit de Justice* assembly played a prominent part in the articulation of constitutional concepts, for precepts of French Public Law were institutionalized there in ritual and discourse. Just as another constitutional precept, the marriage metaphor defining the monarch's relation to the Crown, appeared much earlier in the sixteenth century than previously assumed and was articulated in the *Lit de Justice* assemblies of 1527 and 1537, so too the first French analogue in Public Law to describe legal succession to royal office, *Le royaume n'est jamais vacant*, appeared at mid century, a decade and a half before Bodin's later ambiguous formulation, and was likewise propagated in the *Lit de Justice* assembly of 1563.

Following this groundbreaking examination of the French Law of Succession in the *Lit de Justice* of 1563, Chancellor L'Hôpital discussed the nature of legislative authority. In 1560 he had insisted that "The king holds the Crown from God and the ancient Law of the kingdom," a precept of juristic monarchy echoed in Bodin's statement that "[the kingdom] is not deferred by patrimonial succession, but by virtue of the Law of the kingdom." Here in 1563 he described the role of the Parlements (whose officers were bound by oath to the king) in the proper exercise of judicial business. From the criticisms which he leveled at the

Courts there issued some startling rules for reform. L'Hôpital demanded that the Courts cease interpreting royal legislation deemed troublesome and adopt instead the procedure of post-registration remonstrance to make objections known to the king. He reminded *parlementaires* that they were bound by solemn oath to observe royal ordinances and concluded that officeholders were ethically obliged to report legislative and procedural infractions to the monarch. He did not question the right of Courts to deliberate *in camera* on certain occasions but denied their power to exclude royal officers appointed to attend those sessions. He called for Parlements to regulate their own behavior by issuing reports to the king from regular fact-finding sessions, or *Mercuriales*, where the cases of *parlementaires* accused of derelictions were heard by cohorts and offenders were held accountable. He reminded them outright that although they were tenured in office, the exercise of their charges depended upon the proper observation and implementation of royal ordinances. These rules bound individual officeholders in Parlements to the king, not to their own institutions, and subjected Parlements to the royal legislative prerogative.

Determined to instigate a wide-ranging program of reform in the 1560's aimed at preserving a society in crisis, L'Hôpital probably inspired the circle of legists who attempted to codify French law.[35] Likewise, his admonitions to the Parlements in 1563 aimed at standardizing the legislative system observed through Parlements across the land, and the organization of the Majority *Lit de Justice* of Rouen epitomized that system. In a swift reaction to this convocation of the Majority *Lit de Justice* in a provincial Parlement, the Parlement of Paris bitterly denounced the assembly. Yet when the Parisian *parlementaires* tested Michel de L'Hôpital's stated rules to the limit in the weeks that followed, they discovered exactly what the chancellor meant by his warning that "the eye of justice sees all, the king sees and discovers all in the course of time."

[35] On this reform movement, see Salmon, *Society in Crisis*, pp. 151-162, with a discussion of L'Hôpital's speech. For the proposed codification, see Giesey and Salmon, *Francogallia by François Hotman* (Cambridge, 1972), pp. 1-45, suggesting that the reformist circle at the library of Fontainebleau (Hotman, De Thou, Dumoulin, and others) took up the idea of codification.

VIII

THE REVERSAL OF PARISIAN PARLEMENTARY PROCEDURE: REACTION TO THE MAJORITY *LIT DE JUSTICE* ASSEMBLY OF 1563

> ... kings of France automatically become majors without
> any formal declaration as soon as they enter the fourteenth
> year of age. But if express ... declaration of this or similar
> ordinances is deemed necessary, then the act must take
> place first in this Court [the Parlement of Paris] ...
> [where] he [the king] customarily holds his *Lit de Justice*
> [assembly]. *Parlement of Paris (1563)*

FROM THE POINT of view of the royal party, the Majority *Lit de Justice* of Rouen established two constitutional precedents: kings could convoke *Lit de Justice* assemblies in any Parlement of France, and the royal legislative prerogative demonstrated in the Majority ceremony signaled the end of regency government. For the Parlement of Rouen, which cooperated amiably in hosting the Majority *Lit de Justice*, the event brought eminence and set a favorable precedent for future location. But for the Parlement of Paris, which did not participate, the convocation of a *Lit de Justice* in a provincial Parlement diluted the Parisian Parlement's claim to preeminence as the supreme Court in France. Countering the affairs in Rouen with consummate boldness, the Parlement of Paris formulated a plan to rescind the constitutional precedents set there and relentlessly pursued that plan to the bitter end. The strategies of Court and king are reconstructed from a scattered series of letters and speeches and from notes interspersed through the registers of the Parlement of Paris. First the Parisian *parlementaires* demanded the deletion of the Majority Declaration from the Ordinance of Rouen in order to void the provincial precedent for Majority *Lits de Justice*. Then they circumscribed the legislative force of the second Pacification Edict in order to deny that national legislation had originated in a provincial Parlement. Finally the Parlement of Paris delayed registration of the ordinance, pressuring the king to visit the Grand-chambre and oversee its publication, in order to attain ceremonial superiority over its provincial rival. Meanwhile,

Charles IX cautiously bided his time on the outskirts of Paris, assisted by an informer inside the Grand-chambre, and countered the Court's every move with equal audacity. At stake was the constitutional validity of the Majority *Lit de Justice* of Rouen as first one side, then the other, tested the limits of dissension in the two months that followed the assembly. Well worth recounting, the tale provides a rare insight into the procedural confusion surrounding the legislative process in the sixteenth century.

On 18 August 1563, the day after the Majority *Lit de Justice* assembly, Charles IX ordered the Parlement of Paris by *lettres patentes* to register the Ordinance of Rouen (consisting of the Majority Declaration and the second Pacification Edict) promulgated in the Parlement of Rouen due to the "necessity of the times."[1] Delivered on 21 August by the royal envoy, the Sieur de Lansac, that order was discussed at length by the *parlementaires*. The Parlement of Paris raised four objections to the ordinance, and two of them, one questioning the constitutional validity of a Majority *Lit de Justice* held in a provincial Parlement, the other the legality of the second Pacification Edict, constituted the very core of Parlement's plan for rescinding the Majority *Lit de Justice* assembly.[2] On the first point regarding the constitutionality of a provincial *Lit de Justice*, the *parlementaires* marshaled two arguments: first, that the convocation of this assembly was unnecessary, since the original royal ordinances on majority (1375, 1392, 1407) did not require kings to make personal declarations of majority in *Lit de Justice* assemblies; and second, that the Majority *Lit de Justice* of Rouen was invalid because even if public pronouncement of a Majority Declaration was dictated by "necessity," that declaration must be made first in the supreme Court, the Parlement of Paris. The rationale supporting these arguments is important. Parlement held that

> ... kings of France automatically become majors without any formal declaration as soon as they enter the fourteenth year of age. But if express publication and declaration of this or similar ordinances is deemed necessary, then the act must take place first in

[1] For the sources on this extended conflict, see A.N. X1a 1606, fols. 138v-441r (18 Aug. to 5 Oct. 1563), contained in Dupuy, *Traité de la majorité* [Reg. Parl.], pp. 405-443, cited here. Dupuy collected a variety of registers, documents, and letters which help to tell the tale when finally sorted out. *La Declaration faicte par le roy de sa majorité* provides the full speech given by Charles IX that day.

[2] Dupuy, *Traité de la majorité* [Reg. Parl.], pp. 405-411.

this Court [Parlement of Paris]. That fact cannot be ignored because this Court is the first of the Courts of the kingdom, the Court of peers, and the seat of the king's sovereign justice (*lit de la justice souverain du roy*). It is the place in which the ordinance concerning the majority was first promulgated by Charles V in the year 1375 ... and afterward ... renewed by Charles VI in the years 1392 and ... 1407, the king holding his *Lit de Justice* [assemblies] in his said Court [on those occasions]. ... He [the king] customarily holds his *Lit de Justice* [assembly] there [in the Parlement of Paris], and as Charles VIII remarked, it [the Court] represents the true and solid image of the majesty and dignity of his justice.[3]

The wording of this passage makes two things strikingly clear: one, that here in 1563 the Parlement of Paris publicly acknowledged the *Lit de Justice* as a constitutional forum for the first time since Francis I's introduction of the assembly in 1527; and two, that the Court adopted Jean du Tillet's historical theory to emphasize the procedural tie between the *Lit de Justice* assembly and the Parlement of Paris.[4] In their bid to void the Majority *Lit de Justice* of Rouen and defend the superior status of the Parlement of Paris, the *parlementaires* conflated the Court's rhetorical version of the *lit de justice* as a metaphor for the Grand-chambre harboring king and Parlement with Du Tillet's historical version of the *Lit de Justice* as an ancient constitutional assembly, thereby terminating the rhetorical-historical debate of former years. On the other point, the legality of a second Pacification Edict, the Parisian *parlementaires* denied that legislation had been promulgated first in the Majority *Lit de Justice* of Rouen. They held that the second Pacification Edict merely affirmed the original Edict of Pacification (March) registered by the Parlement of Paris and still in effect; therefore, they insisted that the second edict

[3] Ibid., 407-409. The reference is to Charles VII but probably should read Charles VIII, because the document cited is similar to that of 1483.

[4] Du Tillet's loyalties must have been divided in this affair, because he always affiliated the *Lit de Justice* assembly with the Parlement of Paris. The clerk might have provided Parisian *parlementaires* with evidence to advance such a case, or else the *parlementaires* simply quoted Du Tillet's tracts on majority which had been published in 1560. A few years later one historian supported Parlement's case, noting that the "*Lit de Justice* [assembly]" held in the "Parlement of Normandy" was "against ancient custom observed by previous kings who performed ceremonies concerning the state of the royal majesty in the Court of peers in Paris"; François Belleforest, *Histoire des neuf roys Charles de France* (Paris, 1568), VI, 100, 1644v.

must be reworded to include the same provisional clause (referring to a future national council to settle the bifurcation of religion) contained in the first. It was late by the time these objections were fully set forth, and so the Court adjourned.[5]

Before deliberations resumed on the morning of 23 August, the king's envoy Lansac addressed the Grand-chambre. Once again he requested speedy action from Parlement on the ordinance, and he repeated Chancellor L'Hôpital's recent admonition that the Parlement of Paris must register the ordinance first, as ordered, and resort to remonstrance afterward. For five more days, the *parlementaires* deliberated.[6] But they were interrupted on 28 August when Lansac returned and presented two royal letters sent special delivery by Charles IX on 26 August which addressed the objections raised by *parlementaires* in closed session just the day before. One letter assured Parlement that the second Pacification Edict would bring peace to the kingdom, not recognize the co-existence of two religions in France as they contended. The other ordered the Parlement of Paris to remain in session until the king arrived in Paris to explain the Rouennais Ordinance fully.[7] From the timing of these letters, it is clear that an informer among the *parlementaires* was keeping the king immediately apprised of specific objections raised during deliberations, a practical demonstration of Chancellor L'Hôpital's warning that "the king sees and discovers all in the course of time." This im-

[5] Dupuy, *Traité de la majorité* [Reg. Parl.], pp. 409-411. The third and fourth points regarding the edict are as follows: Parlement complained that the form of address used on the royal letters ordering registration inverted the customary order by charging the provincial governors and their lieutenants before the Court of Parlement responsible for registration and always named first; and they argued that Parisians should not be included in the order to lay down arms, but in any case the matter was one for City officials to settle, not the Parlement of Paris.

[6] Ibid., 411-412. Lansac gave a grim picture of the state of emergency in Normandy, where the king had replaced captains and governors of cities with Catholics in Rouen, Dieppe, Caen, and lower Normandy. He also warned that a preacher in Paris named Artus Desiré had preached seditiously the day before, telling people that disarming themselves would cause their ruin. On this crisis in Rouen, see Philip Benedict, *Rouen during the Wars of Religion* (Cambridge, 1981).

[7] Dupuy, *Traité de la majorité* [Reg. Parl.], pp. 412-414. The letters were accompanied by one from the queen providing additional reassurance. Touching upon the idea of the king as the *lex animata-debitor justitiae*, First President Christophe de Thou exhorted the king "to live and die in the law," a type of comment repeated in greater detail by President Séguier on 23 September.

mediate access to supposedly *in camera* discussions enabled Charles IX to respond to Parlement's objections even before official remonstrances could be issued and to effect a skillful counter strategy throughout the weeks that followed. Following reception of these letters Parlement continued deliberations, but the precipitous announcement of the king's pending visit and the extension of the session put tremendous pressure on the Court to terminate debate and draw up official remonstrances for presentation. Finally on 1 September Parlement prepared four remonstrances on the Rouennais Ordinance for presentation to the king upon his arrival.[8] Yet as soon as Charles IX received word that remonstrances had been drawn, he reversed his strategy and sent the Court another set of orders on 6 September. The new orders commanded that Parlement deputize a delegation of officers to present the remonstrances directly to the king in the city of Gaillon on the morning of 7 September at the latest. Charles IX did not intend to visit the Grand-chambre of the Parlement of Paris to explain the ordinance after all; instead the *parlementaires* were required to bring the remonstrances to him. The first president of Parlement, Christophe de Thou, led a delegation of two deputies on this mission and the three returned a week later with a full report.[9]

On 15 September, in a session of the Grand-chambre presided over by President François de Saint-André, First President De Thou presented the Parlement of Paris with a report on the seven-day sojourn. As recounted in the registers of Parlement, the deputies left Paris on 7 September and arrived in Vernon on 8 September, where they remained upon hearing that the king was expected there the next day. After Charles IX entered the city on the afternoon of 9 September, the deputies went to greet the king and queen. Apparently they expected a royal audience;

[8] Ibid., 415-416. The remonstrance gave the original objections outlined on 21 August. In addition, the *parlementaires* called attention to the royal error in dating the Edict of Pacification as 7 March (instead of 19 March), and they decided to make remonstrances to both king and queen. Finally, if the king insisted on registering the ordinance notwithstanding the remonstrances, the Court would make further remonstrances against the ordinance based on their "consciences," which disallowed registration.

[9] Ibid., 416-417. The two other *parlementaires* who accompanied De Thou as deputies were Nicole Prévost and Guillaume Viole. Christophe de Thou was an *avocat* of the king and councillor in 1554 and became first president in 1562; Prévost was a councillor in 1534 and became president of the Enquêtes in 1556; and Viole became a councillor in 1550. See Maugis, *Histoire du Parlement*, III, 190, 216, 236; 175, 193; and 201.

instead they were peremptorily ordered by the king to move on to Mantes and await him there and doubly warned by the queen to obey that command. The deputies went to Mantes on 10 September and met with the king the next day. Again they expected to present the remonstrances; once more they were dismissed by the king. He commanded that they return early the next morning for an exchange of remonstrances: he would hear their remonstrances on the ordinance and then present his remonstrances regarding Parlement's disobedience. Ready early on the morning of 12 September to present remonstrances, the deputies waited all day long before the meeting finally took place. A special Royal Council meeting had been called for that purpose, so the deputies presented Parlement's remonstrances to the king and the Royal Council. During that presentation President De Thou repeated the two complaints: that the Majority *Lit de Justice* should have been convoked in the Parlement of Paris, "the place of the majors [= *maior pars*] where kings customarily make such solemn declarations," and that the wording of the second Pacification Edict appeared definitive rather than provisional as the first. Given those serious discrepancies, De Thou said, the Parlement of Paris could not in good "conscience" register the ordinance.[10]

Addressing the deputies himself Charles IX refuted Parlement's remonstrances point by point. First, the king declared that the Majority *Lit de Justice* of Rouen was a legitimate assembly. Echoing the historical view on royal majority originally posed by Jean du Tillet and conveniently amended by the memorandum of 1560 to include provincial Parlements, he declared that the Majority Declaration was issued in Rouen "because my affairs required that action, and I am free to make that declaration wherever it pleases me, as other kings have done."[11] Second, he demanded registration of the ordinance already issued by him in

---

[10] Dupuy, *Traité de la majorité* [Reg. Parl.], pp. 419-420. De Thou also discussed the other two points. He noted that Parlement found the form of address on the royal letters ordering registration unacceptable, because governors of cities appeared before Courts of Parlement (responsible for registration); and he noted that although the law to lay down arms was in itself reasonable it should exclude Parisians who had taken up arms by the king's command for the defense of his state. Parlement again called attention to the royal misdating of the Edict of Pacification as 7 March (instead of 19 March). On the Roman Law concept of the *maior pars* [*Digest* 50, 1, 19], the idea of the "major or saner part" (connected with *quod omnes tangit*), consult Post, *Studies in Medieval Legal Thought*, pp. 175-176.

[11] Dupuy, *Traité de la majorité* [Reg. Parl.], p. 419. This remark is certainly predicated upon the opinion of the anonymous memorandum of 1560.

person. Dismissing the idea that the Parlement of Paris could register a royal edict provisionally, he refused to recognize conditional status for the first Edict of Pacification (March) and disallowed it for the second Pacification Edict as well. Indeed, if any condition bound both edicts, he said, it was the attainment of peace itself which the second edict should ensure. He had considered Parlement's remonstrances, the king reminded them, and now with the advice of the Royal Council he commanded that the Parlement of Paris register the Rouennais Ordinance.[12] In a turnabout Charles IX then ordered Chancellor L'Hôpital to present the deputies with royal remonstrances criticizing the disobedience of the Parlement of Paris, and President De Thou responded to them afterward as best he could.[13] Toward the end of this tense meeting the president questioned the wisdom of extending the session of Parlement, as required by the royal letter of 28 August, since wages were already in arrears. The queen tersely informed him that the king intended Parlement to remain in session only until the ordinance was registered. At this point on 15 September, according to the registers of Parlement, the president concluded his report to the Court.[14]

President De Thou's report on the meeting with the king, queen, and Royal Council can be supplemented by information left out of the registers of Parlement. For one thing, during the meeting on 12 September Jean du Montluc, Bishop of Valence, a royal councillor, provided a formal rebuttal of Parlement's remonstrances against the Rouennais *Lit de Justice* assembly. In a sarcastic tone he parodied the *parlementaires'* use of "conscience" to rationalize the Court's refusal to register royal legislation,

[12] Ibid., 419-420. The king also responded to the other two remonstrances: as for the disputed form of address on royal letters, no precedent would be incurred by the mention of Parlement after provincial governors; as for the laying down of arms, all subjects were to do so immediately.

[13] Ibid., 420-421. The king complained about the following. (1) The deputies were commanded to meet him at Gaillon and showed up in Vernon instead. (De Thou responded that the turmoil due to the armies moving around Gaillon prevented their entrance to the city.) (2) Parlement retained several cases evoked by the king to his Council. (De Thou said that was true but not without cause since Parlement assumed evocations took place at their pleasure.) (3) The Court had given orders to judges, *prévots*, and others and thereby usurped the power of the king. (De Thou admitted this was true but said they had done so out of "necessity.") The queen remarked that given the "necessity of the times" that was excusable. (4) The Court had sealed some documents after the chancellery had refused to seal them. (De Thou replied that he must investigate that matter before responding.)

[14] Ibid., 421.

and he mocked their notions of historical precedent locating the *Lit de Justice* assembly in the Grand-chambre from time immemorial. The real problem, he said, was a difference of opinion between the Parlement and the Royal Council which only the king could resolve. On behalf of the Royal Council the bishop advised the king to maintain control of the location of the *Lit de Justice* and to retain the format of the ordinance exactly as registered in the Parlement of Rouen.[15] For another thing, the king's address to the deputies was much more harsh than the registers of Parlement suggest. That speech, published just a few weeks after the *Lit de Justice*, castigated Parlement's attempt during regency government to gain a greater legislative role and affirmed the theory of a separation of powers. Charles IX told the deputies:

> The kings who preceded me placed you [the Parlement of Paris] in your present station only for the purpose of making justice for subjects.... I must remind you that you are not my tutors or guardians of the kingdom or conservators of my City of Paris, despite the fact that you choose to believe that error.... If you find it difficult to understand the commands I give, you are always welcome to make remonstrances to me as is customary, but not as my governors. And after having made them [remonstrances] and having heard my will, you must obey without further reply.... You seem to think that you are my tutors, but you will find that I do not consider you as such. You are my servants and subjects who must obey me when I command.[16]

Late in the day of 15 September following President De Thou's report the presiding officer in Parlement, President de Saint-André, ordered the clerk to read the two royal letters of the king and queen which had

---

[15] Ibid. [Advis de Monsieur l'Evesque de Valence], pp. 399-404. This document is out of place chronologically in the *preuves* given by Dupuy. It belongs to the section on events of 12 September recalled in President De Thou's report of 15 September (p. 418). For the sake of peace the Bishop of Valence was willing for the moment to tolerate religious "conscience" until a council could be held, but he denied that political (or legal) conscience could defy the royal will. He was particularly irritated at the Court's use of the following clauses in remonstrances: "La Cour ne peur ny doit selon leur conscience enteriner ce qu'il luy a esté mandé," "Nous ne pouvons ne devons selon nos consciences"; and he insisted that neither histories nor registers of Parlement showed that the Parlement of Paris must be treated as "the place of the majors where kings have customarily made such solemn acts."

[16] *La Declaration faicte par le roy de sa majorité*, fols. D ii^v-D iii^v.

been drawn in Mantes on 13 September and sent back with the deputies. Those letters commanded again that the Parlement of Paris register the ordinance forthwith.[17] Repeatedly stymied in its efforts to rescind the Majority *Lit de Justice* assembly (by negating the Majority Declaration and rewording the second Pacification Edict), Parlement quickly retrenched. No further questions were raised about the constitutional validity of the *Lit de Justice* assembly and no further demands were made regarding the inclusion of a conditional provision in the second Pacification Edict. Instead the *parlementaires* shifted tactics and concentrated on the procedural technicalities of registration itself. They argued that the two Edicts of Pacification were examples of "political laws and ordinances made due to the necessity of the times and the demands of [public] affairs," and as such were provisional, not definitive; therefore, if the king really had no intention of allowing two religions to exist in France, he should have no objection to recording the second edict with the same subscription as the first noting the presence of the princes of the blood as witnesses.[18]

Once again apprised of these deliberations that very day by an informer, Charles IX wrote two letters on 15 September, one to the Parlement of Paris, the other to the first president, and both were presented to Parlement on 17 September. The king was furious at the attempted inclusion of a provisional subscription. He reminded Parlement, and more specifically the first president, that the second edict had already been published in a *Lit de Justice* assembly held in the Parlement of Rouen, and he demanded that the Court publish the Rouennais Ordinance in the Parlement of Paris in a "pure and simple manner" without any additional subscription.[19] Blocked again in the effort to transform the second Pacification Edict into a replica of the first, which would have effectively denied that the Majority *Lit de Justice* marked a change in the king's status and that legislation had been promulgated there, the *parlementaires* voted on 17 September as to whether or not the Court would register the second Pacification Edict as ordered without the subscription referring to the princes of the blood. The result of the vote was a division of opinion, a tie of 31 to 31. This *billet de partage*, as it

[17] Dupuy, *Traité de la majorité* [Reg. Parl.], pp. 421-422.

[18] Ibid., 422-423. Here the Pacification Edict given at Rouen on 17 August is mistakenly dated 19 August.

[19] Ibid., 424-425. The reception of the king's letter in Parlement on 17 September is incorrectly dated as 17 June.

was called, was recorded in the clerk's minutes of that meeting in two signed columns which tallied votes by name.[20]

From this point until the end of the controversy the debate between king and Parlement centered upon the Court's *billet de partage*. As might be expected, news of the tie vote was surreptitiously relayed to the king immediately. He demanded to see a copy of the original *partage* which recorded the vote, but Parlement delivered a copy which gave the voting results only and did not specify the voters by name.[21] On 22 September, therefore, Lansac returned to the Parlement of Paris with a royal letter repeating the demand for an exact copy of the original *billet de partage*. Then he withdrew from the Grand-chambre while Parlement discussed a course of action. The Court deputized one officer from each voting faction, Presidents Pierre (I) Séguier and François Dormy, to meet with the king in the city of Meulan and present Parlement's remonstrances regarding the king's demand. The *parlementaires* hoped that Charles IX would be content to see the *partage* without individual names but instructed the deputies to deliver a copy of the original document if he insisted on knowing the exact disposition of the vote. Before the *parlementaires* adjourned Lansac returned to the Grand-chambre with a chilling message: the king found it singularly odd that Parlement refused to register the Rouennais Ordinance after remonstrances had been duly heard and found it strange that Parlement disregarded the authority of the king and Royal Council as a whole, yet insinuated that the presence of two princes of the blood authorized royal laws. In effect, Lansac informed them, Charles IX intended to make an example of this issue involving the legislative process. The first president responded for Parlement. He stated that the first Edict of Pacification (March) sufficed without recourse to a second edict, and that the legality of the second edict was in doubt because the king appeared to confirm therein as a major the legislation which he had promulgated as a minor and which the Court considered provisional. If a second edict was published, the first president maintained, it must be read as the first in order to maintain its provisional character. To be sure, Parlement respected the authority of the Royal Council, but that body constituted just one group of royal

[20] Ibid., 423-426. The column which tallied votes for registration of the Rouennais Edict without the princes of the blood present was signed by First President De Thou; the other against the action by Councillor Violé. Both had traveled to Mantes with the remonstrances.

[21] Ibid., 426-428. The *partage* of 17 September is incorrectly dated as 27 September.

advisers, and the Court wished to have the king and queen present when the Royal Council and the Parlement of Paris together gave opinions dictated from "conscience" without dissension or ill will.[22] Here Parlement finally admitted outright that the question of the status of royal authority in minority loomed large in this debate. Although the Court's suggested remedy was subtle, its direction was clear. In one last effort to salvage ceremonial and legislative supremacy, the Parisian Parlement was pressuring the king, queen, and Royal Council to convoke a *Lit de Justice* assembly in the Parlement of Paris to settle the issue.

The next day, 23 September, Presidents Séguier and Dormy went to Meulan, presented Parlement's remonstrance on the *billet de partage* to the king, and returned to the Grand-chambre on 27 September with the following report recorded in the registers of Parlement. Upon arriving in Meulan the deputies were warned by Chancellor L'Hôpital, the constable, and several other lords that the king was grievously offended by the *partage* and were advised to make immediate amends for Parlement's behavior. At nine o'clock that morning the deputies entered the king's chamber and found Charles IX seated with the princes of the blood and his Council standing around him. Staunchly professing the Court's obedience, the presidents described the state in organological terms as the "Republic of France," a "body politic" with the king as head and the Court as a member "living and dying" with that body. Then they explained the circumstances prompting the *billet de partage* and the procedural nexus within which it arose. The *partage* was a regrettable action, they admitted, occasioned by some *parlementaires* who feared the incursion of the reformed religion in France and could not in "conscience" abide the royal refusal to render the second edict provisional. Because the king wished to see an exact copy of the *partage* including votes tallied by name, the presidents felt compelled to explain the Court's procedure at this time. It had always been Parlement's custom, they said, to take a voice vote which was recorded in writing only when a single chamber of Parlement relayed information to other chambers for judgment. However, once the judgment was made, the written record of individual opinions was always destroyed. In this instance all chambers of Parlement had voted together, but the tie vote produced an impasse which was then recorded in the *billet de partage*. As they explained the procedure, the presidents affected an air of innocence, asserting that the king had

[22] Ibid., 428-430. The royal letter was written 21 September. For the designation of Séguier and Dormy as deputies, see the account for 27 September below.

a perfect right to see the *partage*; yet clearly they found themselves in a difficult situation. The presidents complied with the king's order to present a copy of the original document. But they pointed out the danger of publishing the list because of the "spite, hate, and envy" which might be engendered against *parlementaires* for individual stands taken, and they requested that the king destroy the *billet de partage* immediately after reading it.[23]

Charles IX spoke to the deputies directly. As far as he was concerned the existence of the *billet de partage* supplied direct evidence of Parlement's disobedience to his command ordering publication of the Rouennais Ordinance. He ordered the deputies at once to hand over a copy of the original *partage* to Chancellor L'Hôpital for perusal by the Royal Council. Parlement had better realize, he said, that royal legislative commands must be obeyed. The deputies again professed Parlement's obedience only to be greeted with stony silence as they arose and departed from the king's chamber.[24] Later in the day the deputies made an appeal to some of the lords of the Royal Council but received a sharp reply maintaining the royal position on the separation of duties and the proper role of remonstrance in the legislative process. The royal councillors told the *parlementaires*:

> You act to conserve the honor of your [Parlement's] *partage*; we act to conserve the honor of the state of the king. In general your *partage* is invalid because you lack authority in affairs of state of the king; in particular because it [the *partage*] contradicts the preceding royal decision to verify [the second Pacification Edict]. You cannot thwart that decision by alleging that messieurs the princes must be present [at registration]. . . .[25]

Following this double censure of Parlement by king and Royal Council, the deputies left Meulan for Paris and were overtaken on the road by a messenger bearing a packet from the king to the Parlement of Paris. At this point on 27 September President Séguier ended his report to Parlement on the Meulan meeting. Then the Court read the *lettres closes*,

[23] Ibid., 431-435. Pierre (I) Séguier (who voted for registration of the edict in the *partage*) was *avocat du roi* in 1550, president in 1554; François Dormy (who voted against) was *avocat* in 1545 and a president of the Enquêtes in 1550; see Maugis, *Histoire du Parlement*, pp. 190, 216, and 187, 217.

[24] Dupuy, *Traité de la majorité* [Reg. Parl.], pp. 432-435.

[25] Ibid., 434-435.

lettres patentes, and the *arrêt* (drawn by the king on 24 September) contained in the royal packet.[26]

One of the letters ordered the Parlement of Paris to remain in session until further notice; the other, to execute the king's commands contained in the enclosed *arrêt*.[27] The *arrêt* was an extraordinary document. First, the king dismissed the Court's negative judgment on the Rouennais Ordinance implicit in the *billet de partage* and declared the *partage* invalid because it had been issued by judges whose cognizance did not extend to "affairs of state" in the kingdom. Second, he ordered the Parlement of Paris to register the ordinance immediately without modifications in the presence of all presidents and councillors and threatened the *parlementaires* with suspension of offices for noncompliance. Third, he disallowed Parlement's future interference in "affairs of state," as in the present case, through the continued blockage of royal legislation following remonstrances. Fourth, he ordered the Court to cancel the *billet de partage*, nullifying the deed, and then record the canceled document in the registers of Parlement. Fifth, he commanded that the clerk [Jean du Tillet] register the *arrêt* forthwith and without finding fault.[28] On that same day, 27 September, under threat of suspension of offices, Parlement agreed as instructed to remain in session and to register the royal *arrêt* containing the five commands.[29] Thus on 28 September the disputed ordinance was finally registered by the Parlement of Paris, six weeks after its promulgation at the *Lit de Justice* in the Parlement of Rouen.[30] Still, this action did not end the sparring, because the overriding principle, the locus of legislative prerogative, remained in question due to the Court's treatment of the *arrêt* the day before.

Although the royal *arrêt* had been registered, its fourth provision, instructions to record the canceled *billet de partage* in the registers of Parlement, was deliberately ignored. The Court instead actually deleted that document from the records as if the *partage* had never occurred. In the meantime the king arrived in Paris, was apprised of the dereliction, and summoned the first president on 2 October to explain the deletion. As reported to Parlement on 4 October, First President De Thou tried

---

[26] Ibid., 435.

[27] Ibid., 435 and 437.

[28] Ibid., 436-437. Charles IX spoke of "affairs of state" as "choses qui appartiennent a l'éstat de cedit royaume," and "la connoissance des choses de l'éstat de ce royaume"; and he declared the *partage* "broken, revoked, and worthless."

[29] Ibid., 437-439.

[30] Ibid., 439-440.

to justify the Court's action to the king. It was true that the canceled *billet de partage* had not been recorded, he said, but Parlement thought that the deletion of the document more clearly satisfied the true intention of the king to consign the deed to oblivion. Queen Catherine de Médicis spoke up quickly and countered that excuse. She stated that the king and his Council intended to have the royal *arrêt* executed by Parlement exactly as given and without modification. At this point on 4 October the president concluded his report and turned the floor of the Grand-chambre over to Jean (II) du Tillet, son of the clerk-historian and now *protonotaire* and *greffier civil* of the Parlement of Paris by *survivance* along with his father, who still held the office. Speaking for his father Du Tillet (II) reaffirmed the president's report just given. He recounted that the king, queen, and Royal Council had called Jean du Tillet before them on 3 October and commanded the clerk to inform Parlement of the king's intentions the next morning: that the canceled *billet de partage* must be registered exactly as ordered in the *arrêt*, not simply deleted from the registers, and that the king must be informed by the clerk when the deed was accomplished.[31] In the face of such persistence, the Court deliberated and capitulated rather swiftly: the canceled *billet de partage* would be recorded in the registers of Parlement following the *arrêt* of the king, and the clerk would be sent to Charles IX with the registers as proof of execution.[32]

At long last on 5 October the bitter controversy sparked by the Rouennais *Lit de Justice* reached its weary conclusion as the two clerks Du Tillet, father and son, brought minutes bearing the canceled *billet de partage* to the king. Then Charles IX, Catherine de Médicis, Chancellor L'Hôpital, and the Cardinal of Bourbon read for themselves the caption added by Parlement below the *partage* which stated "canceled by the order of the said Court obeying the will of the king." But they were not satisfied with that formula and insisted that the clerk add the words "following the *arrêt* of the said lord" to the caption. When the Du Tillets explained that Parlement's official record (transferred from the minutes) would not be made for some time, the king ordered that the register be brought to him again for personal verification right after that was done.[33] Apparently that final meeting of king and clerk never took place, because the canceled *billet de partage* is recorded in the registers of Parlement

[31] Ibid., 440-442.
[32] Ibid. Du Tillet was indisposed, and the king allowed his son to speak for him.
[33] Ibid., 442-443.

without that addition to the caption.[34] In retrospect, however, this final act of defiance by Parlement was a weak gesture indeed compared with the gravity of precedents already set. The Parlement of Paris was well aware that Charles IX's Majority *Lit de Justice* of Rouen had undermined its pretensions to supremacy among the Courts of France.

It has been maintained that there existed uncontested in the sixteenth century an official doctrine, or "theory of unity," which held that all the Parlements of France were united under the original and oldest one, the Parlement of Paris, the supreme Court.[35] In retrospect the evidence shows just the opposite to be true. Notions about parlementary unity under Parisian aegis, far from solidified in the sixteenth century, were a source of contention. To be sure, at every opportunity the Parlement of Paris elevated its status in order to set precedents for such supremacy, but there is no reason to believe that those acts achieved the intended goal. In fact, over the decades the Parisian Parlement's claims to supremacy caused a series of conflicts. During the *Lit de Justice* assembly of December 1527 the Parlements, Parisian and provincial, were supposed to deliberate together in one body, but the Parlement of Paris subtly circumvented that procedure to avoid a precedent unfavorable to its quest for superior status. In his addresses to the Parlements of Paris, Rouen, Bordeaux, and Toulouse between 1560 and 1565, L'Hôpital set forth his version of parlementary unity, but his definition leveled all the Courts to one unit headed by the king and pointedly ignored the idea of Parisian supremacy. Most importantly, in 1563 the convocation of a *Lit de Justice* in Rouen and its manner of legitimation afterward disallowed the claim that any one Parlement in France was supreme in constitutional matters and instead located such supremacy in the *Lit de Justice* assembly itself, which could be convoked in any Parlement. Far from being official doctrine in the sixteenth century, the idea of parlementary unity under the Parisian Court was vigorously contested and bound to cause contention in an era given over to the testing of constitutional precepts. At this opportune time, therefore, the royal party continued to press its case for parlemen-

---

[34] A.N. X1a 1606, fols. 330r-331v (17 Sept. 1563).

[35] Maugis, *Histoire du Parlement*, I, 418-419. This case is weak, for Maugis has only three examples, one the speech of L'Hôpital (A.N. X1a 1595, fol. 200v) of 7 September 1560, which has been interpreted differently here (see above, Chap. VI, n. 10); another of 14 October 1549 involving provincial *parlementaires* soliciting a favor from the Parisian Court (A.N. X1a 1566, fol. 177v); and a third much later on 29 December 1580 again involving a deputation from a provincial Court (A.N. X1a 1670, fol. 40r).

tary unity under the supremacy of the *Lit de Justice* assembly. Back in
Paris in October 1563 following the resolution of the Rouennais contro-
versy, Charles IX still did not visit the Parlement of Paris. Instead he
left the capital city for an extended tour of France which featured Royal
Entrées to provincial cities and visits to the provincial Parlements of
Bordeaux and Toulouse.[36]

THE *Lit de Justice* ASSEMBLIES OF 1564 AND 1565

The assemblies held in the Parlements of Bordeaux (11 April 1564) and
Toulouse (1 February 1565) were recorded by the respective clerks of
those Courts as *Lit de Justice* assemblies. The constitutional precedents
already set in Rouen were reaffirmed there: the ritual employed portrayed
the king as legislator and the Parlements as judges, and the speeches of
Charles IX and Chancellor L'Hôpital struck the familiar themes from
Rouen.[37] In the Parlement of Bordeaux Chancellor L'Hôpital pointedly

[36] A contemporary account of the travels of Charles IX in 1564 and 1565
claims that the queen mother planned the voyage to propagandize the cult of
rulership; *Recueil et discours du voyage du roy Charles IX* (Paris, 1566), p. 2.
Historians have accepted that view for the most part, but it was certainly
Chancellor L'Hôpital who directed the performances of the *Lit de Justice* assemblies during that tour. For a description of *Entrées* to cities across France
made at this time, see Victor E. Graham and W. McAllister Johnson, *The Royal
Tour of France by Charles IX and Catherine de Médicis: Festivals and Entries, 1564-
1566* (Toronto, 1979).

[37] For the *Lit de Justice* at Bordeaux, see Godefroy, *Cérémonial françois* [Jacques
de Pontac, clerk], II, 577-586 (11 Apr. 1564). This account of "the king holding
his *Lit de Justice* [assembly]" gives the fullest description of the thronal setting
since the Parisian accounts of 1527 and 1537. Apparently the drapery paraphernalia belonged to the Parlement of Bordeaux. Set at an angle in the corner,
the king's seat (*chaire*) was upholstered in crimson velvet with a cushion of the
same material and two pillows beneath his feet. The canopy was made of a
drape of gold bordered with crimson satin. A crimson tapestry ran underneath
the seat and down the three steps of the dais. To the right of the seat a huge
velvet tapestry was hung from the top of the window to the floor. On the floor
below these high seats the chancellor's seat was covered with black velvet, and
there were two pillows decorated with Turkish tapestry beneath his feet. Catherine de Médicis sat to the right of the king, but she went to her place by some
side stairs and was seated on the dais before the king reached his place. Moreover,
as he went up the center steps to his seat the king made a reverent bow to the
seated queen regent. The princes of the blood preceded the peers in seating,
and all lords wore swords. The précis of the king's speech given in this account

recalled speeches given by chancellors of France on "the institution and the authority of the Parlements" and then addressed a general remonstrance to "Parlements" (at large) criticizing legislative irregularities incurred by Courts whose business was primarily judicial.

> You, messieurs [the Courts of Parlement], are commissioned specifically to execute justice. Do not imagine otherwise! You hold borrowed seats [i.e. offices] and must recognize that you hold them from the king according to legitimate ordinances and that your judgments must follow the law.... The law must be above the judges, not the judges above the law.... When you do not obey his royal ordinances, you remove from him his royal power, which is worse than removing from him his domain.... Even though your expertise is limited to judging [particular] cases, ... you seem to believe that you are wiser than the king. You are certainly not wiser than the king, the queen, and the Royal Council. [How ironic that] he [the king] has achieved peace [in the land] but is at present at war with his Court of Parlement....[38]

L'Hôpital also charged the Bordeaux *parlementaires* with specific faults, for he had taken the trouble to read the registers of that Court. He noted angrily that royal ordinances promulgated three years ago had not been registered yet, found it scandalous that deliberations often ended in brawling, that the Court allowed itself to be intimidated by outsiders, that bribes were taken, that forced marriages to gain inheritances were allowed, and that *parlementaires* lent money at interest to merchants. Dismissing any suggestion that the king did not fully support these admonitions, the chancellor warned again, as in Rouen, that secret deliberations aimed at contravening royal ordinances should and would be revealed in due time to the king. It was the duty of the *parlementaires*, he said, to assist in the administration of the polity but not in "affairs of state," and the king delegates to them the administration of justice

---

sounds as if it replicated the one given at Rouen. The *parlementaires* wore red robes, but unfortunately the long speech of the first president was not recorded. The king as legislator gave his Majority Declaration and the Pacification Edict; the Bordeaux Parlement as judges heard a civil case and gave opinions after the king, queen, and lords in high seats.

[38] Ibid., 581-584. Surely L'Hôpital's references to speeches of other chancellors included the address of Chancellor Olivier in the *Séance* of 1549, and his use of "his Court of Parlement" (in the singular) following admonishment of the "Parlements" (in the plural) again suggested a leveling of the Courts.

to be discharged according to his conscience, not theirs.[39] Nine months later, as told by the clerk of the Parlement of Toulouse, the same scenes and admonitions were reenacted in that Court.[40]

[39] Ibid., 581-586. L'Hôpital made an invidious comparison between the two Parlements of Bordeaux and Toulouse (which he would visit next). Neither was conducted with perfect propriety in relations with outsiders, particularly merchants, he said, for the Parlement of Toulouse acted in a manner "too grave" whereas that of Bordeaux behaved in a manner "too familiar." In the end he would praise the gravity of the former over the familiarity of the latter as serving the king best. The clerk Pontac also included some other interesting details. Apparently the presidents, incensed at the chancellor's accusations, delivered a remonstrance to him on 16 April and requested his presence in Parlement to discuss it. Unfortunately the substance of the complaint is not recorded. L'Hôpital did reply that he had spoken generally without naming culprits although he certainly could do so. He apparently agreed to visit the Court and receive the remonstrance on behalf of the king, but the meeting did not take place until a month later. The day after delivery of the remonstrance (17 April) the presidents were informed by the royal Conseil Privé (in response to Parlement's requests) that the wages of the Courts would not be augmented, that compensation had already been provided for the mace-bearers of the king who announced civil pleadings, and that no compensation would be forthcoming either for the trumpeters or for the master of ceremonies. (The sense of these notes seems to be that the Bordeaux group had provided a sumptuous ceremony, and the king was not willing to assume the whole bill.) Finally, on 18 May, a month later, Chancellor L'Hôpital did appear in the Court and heard the remonstrance, but no details of the session were recorded.

[40] For the *Lit de Justice* at Toulouse, see Godefroy, *Cérémonial françois* [La Roche-Flavin, *Treze livres des Parlemens de France*, bk. IV, chap. I; bk. VII, chap. I, quoting from Toulousan registers], II, 586-591 (1 Feb. 1565). As reported by the unidentified clerk, the Court assembled between 13 and 21 January to discuss ceremonial procedures and insisted on 15 January that remonstrances would be made to the king in this *Lit de Justice*. Apparently this action was disallowed, because on 31 January L'Hôpital attended a special session of the Court to hear remonstrances by the first president. The short account recalls "the king sitting in his *Lit de Justice*" following the "*Lit de Justice* [assemblies] of Paris [an error, for none had been held in Paris for Charles IX], Rouen, and Bordeaux" and describes a high seat covered with a velvet canopy and the queen seated to the king's right. The proceedings followed almost exactly those at Bordeaux. Chancellor L'Hôpital addressed to red-robed *parlementaires* "many remonstrances regarding the state of sovereign justice in this kingdom and . . . complaints made against some members of the Court, exhorting them to maintain . . . the authority of the king which his majesty delegated to them." To these admonitions the first president responded that such charges against *parlementaires* arose from the animosity of persons who wished to slander certain judges. At the end of this account the Godefroys appended another very short record of the assembly describing the procession to the chamber of Parlement; ibid. [unidentified source], 591-592.

From beginning to end the royal view of the French constitution had been disseminated with intelligence and precision, first through ritual and discourse in the *Lit de Justice* at Rouen in 1563 and then at Bordeaux and Toulouse in 1564 and 1565. The program was originally outlined in Du Tillet's historical theory of the *Lit de Justice* convoked in the Parlement of Paris, but the contours of that view were sufficiently enlarged by Chancellor L'Hôpital to encompass provincial Parlements. The royal party wavered not an inch during the long and bitter controversy with the Parlement of Paris over the constitutional validity of the Rouen *Lit de Justice* assembly. In the end, therefore, the Parisian Court's claim to supremacy over the Parlements of France and to co-legislative partnership with the king was dealt a resounding blow in theory and practice by the Majority *Lit de Justice* of 1563.

Judged in relation to the usual interpretations of the *Lit de Justice*, defining that assembly as a royal legislative weapon used to quell remonstrances of the Parlement of Paris, the order and tone of these events is ironically inverted. It was the Parlement of Paris which tried with limited success during Charles IX's minority to force the young king and his Council into the Grand-chambre to oversee royal legislation; and it was the Parlement of Paris which tried without success throughout the controversy over the Rouennais *Lit de Justice* to pressure the royal party into convoking a *Lit de Justice* assembly in the Grand-chambre to register the Ordinance of Rouen. Conversely, during his minority, 1561-1563, Charles IX avoided visiting the Parlement of Paris for legislative purposes and held only one Royal *Séance* there in 1563 under duress. As for the Majority *Lit de Justice* of 1563, it was convoked first and then became the target of remonstrances from the Parlement of Paris, which claimed the *Lit de Justice* as part of the Parisian Court's procedure. Throughout the controversy over the Rouennais *Lit de Justice*, September-October 1563, Charles IX steadfastly avoided overtures from the Parlement of Paris aimed at convoking a *Lit de Justice* in the Grand-chambre to register the disputed ordinance there. As the order of events unfolded in the mid decades of the sixteenth century, therefore, it was the Parlement of Paris, not the king, which introduced the notion that *Lit de Justice* assemblies promulgating legislation belonged in the Grand-chambre; and it was the king and Royal Council which repeatedly disavowed that notion. Finally, the Parlement of Paris officially recognized the *Lit de Justice* assembly for the first time in 1563 and made a strong bid for its exclusive location in the Grand-chambre thereafter, because the assembly had become a pivotal element in the Court's claim to supremacy among the Parlements of France.

It has been assumed that this period, the first half of the sixteenth century, represents one of the most homogeneous in the history of France due to the concordance of governmental policies and theoretical speculation.[41] But that assumption must be reassessed to reflect the turbulent divergence of opinion in those times, brought to light by a close examination of the ceremonial implementation and theoretical elaboration of the controversial *Lit de Justice* assembly. The vigorous dissension reflected the fact that the precedents and precepts set by the legitimation of the *Lit de Justice* were formidable: the validity of the *Lit de Justice* assembly as part of the French constitution; the separation of legislative and judicial powers; the Crown's right to convoke a *Lit de Justice* in any Parlement; the refusal to countenance the Parisian Court's claims to preeminence and co-legislative capacity; and the ceremonial celebration of royal majority evidencing a renewal of the legislative prerogative within a system of legal-hereditary succession. It has also been suggested that constitutional theorists of the period, even Chancellor L'Hôpital, who argued for the king's right to amend obsolete laws, viewed the monarch primarily as a judge and considered the activity of legislation as definitely subordinate to that of adjudication.[42] Yet the opening decades of this period witnessed the full-fledged emergence of the legislator-king enthroned in the *Lit de Justice* to treat constitutional issues touching French Public Law; the chancellors, François Olivier and Michel de L'Hôpital, distinguished the royal legislator from parlementary adjudicators; and this shifting view of French kingship was acted out on the stage of the Majority *Lit de Justice* of 1563, where ritual portrayed the monarch primarily as legislator and secondarily as judge.[43]

[41] Church, *Constitutional Thought*, p. 44.

[42] Ibid., 205-207.

[43] Toward the end of the sixteenth century, Guy de Coquille picked up Chancellor L'Hôpital's orchestration of *Lits de Justice* to emphasize a separation of legislative and judicial powers. He noted that "Parlements are established to exercise justice in particular cases and not to make laws or to have cognizance of affairs of state.... It is true that the king holds in the said Parlements his *Lit de Justice* [assembly] with the peers of France and in them are published and registered edicts and constitutions which kings promulgate. But in [the matter of] edicts and *arrêts* the king alone speaks and recognizes that the Court is his council,... not his consort, in that power to ordain and make laws"; *Discours sur les États de France*, p. 281, quoted in Lemaire, *Les Lois fondamentales*, pp. 145-146, n. 2. Repeating this distinction between the judicial power of Parlements and the legislative power of the king, Coquille refers directly to the statements of Charles IX [and L'Hôpital] in 1563 articulating that separation of powers; see *Discours sur les causes des misères de France*, p. 215, quoted in ibid.

The whole controversy surrounding Charles IX's Majority *Lit de Justice* of Rouen illuminates the deep fissures within the French polity on questions of constitutional import. Between 1527 and 1563 the Parisian Court had steadily refused to acknowledge a constitutional distinction between *Lit de Justice* assemblies and Royal *Séances* held in the Parlement of Paris due to the separation of functions inherent in that distinction. By the mid decades of the sixteenth century, however, Jean du Tillet's theory of the *Lit de Justice* assembly had become part of the language of constitutional discourse and therefore served as a stimulus for convoking the *Lit de Justice* again in 1563. Following the Majority *Lit de Justice* of Rouen in 1563, which demonstrated Du Tillet's theory as reinterpreted by Chancellor L'Hôpital to associate the *Lit de Justice* with provincial Parlements, the Parisian Parlement swiftly changed its stance and officially acknowledged the *Lit de Justice* as part of the ancient French constitution. To that end the Parlement of Paris adopted the very same language of constitutional discourse associated originally with the royal party and Du Tillet: the Court attached the *Lit de Justice* assembly to the ancient constitution and held to the institutional linkage between the *Lit de Justice* assembly and the Parlement of Paris. At the same time the Parisian Court attempted to rescind the Majority *Lit de Justice* of Rouen and to convoke a *Lit de Justice* in the Grand-chambre in order to associate the assembly with the Parlement of Paris and salvage its claim to preeminence over the other Parlements of France. Thus after the *Lit de Justice* of 1563 the grounds of the contest shifted: thenceforth both the royal party and the Parlement of Paris agreed that the ancient constitution comprehended a constitutional forum, the *Lit de Justice* assembly, but disagreed on the question of its institutional location. As time went on the Parlement of Paris continued in language tinged with metaphor and history to picture the Grand-chambre as the seat of the *Lit de Justice* assembly, yet attempted at every turn to remold the ritual format of the *Lit de Justice* which symbolized the separation of legislative and judicial roles. In this first endeavor, that of locating the *Lit de Justice* irrevocably in the Parlement of Paris, the Court would be successful; in the second, that of nullifying a separation of roles, it would engage kings in contest until the French Revolution. From 1563 until the closing years of the sixteenth century, royal policy regulating the rare convocation of *Lit de Justice* assemblies once again adhered very closely to the conser-

and noted by Church, *Constitutional Thought*, pp. 272-302, especially nn. 58 and 59.

vative course originally charted by Jean du Tillet. Before returning to that story, however, it is interesting to observe the Majority *Lit de Justice* later on, when it had become demonstrably traditional rather than arguably innovative.

THE MAJORITY *Lit de Justice* CELEBRATIONS OF 1614, 1651, AND 1723

During the seventeenth and eighteenth centuries three more kings, Louis XIII (1610), Louis XIV (1643), and Louis XV (1715), came to the throne of France as minors and thus celebrated majorities. Louis XIII celebrated his majority on 2 October 1614,[44] and the assembly is depicted by the engraving in Figure 10 and by the seating plan in Figure 11.[45] Louis XIV followed suit on 7 September 1651 and Louis XV on 22 February 1723;[46] and those assemblies are shown by the engravings in Figures 13

[44] A.N. X1a 1866, fols. 1r-11v (2 Oct. 1614). In Godefroy, *Cérémonial françois* [Reg. Parl. and *Mercure françois*, vol. III, pt. II, pp. 579-595, combined], II, 263-273. A portion of Godefroy's account (II, 271-272, from the *Mercure françois*) appears in Dupuy, *Traité de la majorité*, (unnumbered pp. 499 [e-f]), which mistakenly leaves the queen out of the consultation procedure. Printed commentaries on this assembly appeared almost immediately: see Louis Servin, *Action des gens du roy sur la déclaration de Louys XIII, roy de France et de Navarre, seant en son Lict de Justice en sa Cour de Parlement au jour de sa majorité* (Paris, 1615), covering the assembly and including speeches given there. The *avocat* Louis Servin gave the speech in place of the *procureur général* that day. An *avocat* in the Parlement of Tours in 1589, he was transferred to the Parlement of Paris in 1594; Maugis, *Histoire du Parlement*, III, 338, 339. For other accounts, see Pierre de Bernard, *Les Cérémonies qui ont esté observées en la déclaration de la majorité du roy* (Paris, 1614); Jean Baudoin, *Les Feux de joye pour la réjouissance publique par la déclaration de la majorité du roi en sa cour de Parlement de Paris...* (Paris, 1614), and *Discours d'un fidelle françois sur la majorité du roy* (Paris, 1614). See also, *Ordre de la séance tenue au Parlement ... le roi séant en son Lit de Justice, pour la déclaration de sa majorité ...* , in *Mercure françois*, vol. III, pt. II, pp. 579-595, and *L'Ordre et cérémonies observées à la majorité du roi, avec la réception de M. le prince de Condé et la requête des prisonniers de sa majesté* (Paris, 1614).

[45] The assembly and a vignette of the entry procession are in the engraving (anonymous), B.N. ms. fr. 6391, fol. 98r. The seating plan is in the engraving by Nicolas de Mathonière, B.N. Dépt. des Estampes; B.N. ms. fr. 6391, fol. 97r; and B.N. Cinq Cents Colbert ms. 212, fol. 145r.

[46] For Louis XIV the account is missing from the registers of Parlement but is printed in Dupuy, *Traité de la majorité* [Reg. Parl.], pp. 536-541 (7 Sept. 1651, mistakenly dated as 2 Oct.); and also in A.N. U 2103 (Le Nain) [4 unnumbered folios] and fols. 446v-454v. The speeches of the chancellor, first president, and *procureur général* are missing, but Dupuy noted that they did not appear in the

and 16.[47] Supported by a vivid legend which had sprung up about it, the Majority *Lit de Justice* was rationalized in the seventeeth century in theory and practice as French tradition. Unlike the Rouennais Majority of 1563, however, these assemblies were convoked in the Grand-chambre of the Parlement of Paris, attesting to the change of venue accomplished by the Parisian *parlementaires*.[48] The ritual observed was similar in outline to that of 1563, but the later sessions exhibited an ostentatious inflation of royal ceremony which accompanied the denouement of the vigorous constitutional symbolism perceived earlier. Magnificently enthroned under a canopy in the Grand-chambre in these later years, Louis XIII, Louis XIV, and Louis XV presented Majority Declarations which confirmed Chancellor L'Hôpital's contention that the Law of Majority was a facet of the French Law of Succession, part and parcel of the ancient constitution. As Louis XIV put it, "... following the Law of my state, I wish henceforth to undertake the government and administration of it [my state] myself."[49] Just how that "Law" was reinterpreted by 1651

---

registers. For a printed commentary, see *L'Entrée du roy dans son Parlement, pour la déclaration de sa majorité* (Paris, 1651). For Louis XV the account is in A.N. X1a 8441, fols. 339r-368v (22 Feb. 1723), with a summons for the *Lit de Justice* (18 Feb.); ibid., fols. 332r-333r.

[47] For Louis XIV: the engraving of the assembly is by Antoine Herisset from a design of Delamonce; B.N. Dépt. des Estampes; published in Jean-Aymar Piganiol de La Force, *Nouvelle description de la France* (Paris, 1718), I, 27. For Louis XV: the engraving is by A. Maillot; B.N. Dépt. des Estampes; Collection Hennin, LXXXXI, fol. 3r; and A.N. KK 1429, fol. 277r. There is a second unidentified engraving in the collection which differs from this one and apparently was discarded, since the date is left blank in front of "February 1723."

[48] For instance, at the Majority celebration of 1614 the *avocat* Louis Servin likened Louis XIII in his *Lit de Justice* assembly to Charles V promulgating the Law of Majority in 1375, and he recalled that Charles IX and Chancellor L'Hôpital had revived that ancient French tradition in 1563; see Servin, *Action des gens du roy*, pp. 7-15. Similarly, an essay on the Majority celebration of 1651 for Louis XIV spoke of the "laudable custom" of making that Majority Declaration in the Parlement of Paris; see *L'Entrée du roy dans son Parlement*, p. 5. Most treatises of the seventeenth century tended to trace this venerable French custom to Charles V; see, for example, Jacques Corbin, *Le Code Louis XIII, roy de France et Navarre. Contenant ses ordonnances et arrests de ses Cours souveraines ...* (Paris, 1638), pp. 7ff.; Servin, *Action des gens du roy*, 7-15; and *De la nature et qualité du Parlement de Paris et qu'il ne peut estre interdit ny transferé hors de la capitale du royaume, pour quelque cause ny pretexte que se soit* (Paris, 1652), stressing Parisian cognizance.

[49] For Louis XIII: A.N. X1a 1866, fols. 1r-11v (2 Oct. 1614); in Godefroy, *Cérémonial françois* [Reg. Parl.], II, 263-273. The king sent an order to the Court

is discussed later. For now it is notable that by the seventeenth century two important changes had occurred: the Law of Majority, vigorously contested in the 1560's, was incorporated into French Public Law; and its ceremonial partner the Majority *Lit de Justice* of Rouen, bitterly denounced by Parisian *parlementaires*, was moved to Paris.

In these later Majority *Lit de Justice* celebrations held in the Grand-chambre of the Parlement of Paris, Louis XIII, Louis XIV, and Louis XV received gestures of reverence from the royal party, but the perfunctory actions were mere vestiges of the formal acts of homage made to Charles IX in 1563.[50] The sphere of legislative activity was extended as the three kings Louis promulgated several national edicts, in contrast to the single edict pronounced by Charles IX.[51] None of the chancellors here discussed substantive constitutional matters as had L'Hôpital in 1563, because by that time the questions of royal majority and legislative capacity were not at issue. The chancellors sought advice on the edicts promulgated, but the order of consultation varied over the years, reflecting the rise of Bourbon blood princes over the peers and indicating the shifting fortunes of Parlement. Whereas the Parlement of Rouen in 1563 had been consulted third after the king and queen regent and the royal party in high seats, the Parlement of Paris in 1614 briefly gained a coveted second place right after the king and before the queen and royal party. Later on, in 1651 and 1723, a newly ascendant group, the Bourbon blood princes, usurped second place, leaving the *parlementaires* in third place, consulted after the king, regent, and Bourbon princes but before all others in high seats.[52]

Considerable ceremonial pomp and circumstance attended these later

---

"to hang the canopy of the king in the golden Grand-chambre where his majesty must sit in his *Lit de Justice* and decorate the seats with velvet tapestries embroidered with golden fleurs-de-lis, and to place the velvet pillows in the necessary places." For Louis XIV: Dupuy, *Traité de la majorité* [Reg. Parl.], pp. 536-541 (7 Sept. 1651). For Louis XV: A.N. X1a 8441, fols. 339r-368v (22 Feb. 1723). The Majority Declarations were formularies, spoken personally by Louis XIV and Louis XV, spoken by the regent for Louis XIII.

[50] See sources in n. 49. For Louis XIII: the royal party and Parlement knelt before the king from their places. For Louis XIV: the king sent an order prescribing that a bow of "profound reverence" must be given as "a kind of homage" without leaving seats, except for Bourbon blood princes (constituting a special group), who would make that bow in front of the king; B.N. ms. fr. n. a. 9750, fol. 70r. For Louis XV: the procedure followed the latter of 1651.

[51] See sources in n. 49. There were edicts against blasphemy and dueling and edicts confirming peace.

[52] See sources in n. 49.

celebrations. Long processions of sumptuously clothed and jeweled participants, some on horseback, others on foot, marched to the sound of drums and trumpets through the streets of Paris from the Palais Royal and the Louvre to the Palais de Justice; and an enormous entourage was seated on a stage of numerous tiers in the Grand-chambre of the Parlement of Paris.[53] In 1614 these complex ceremonial plans caused quarrels over precedence which stalled the Majority *Lit de Justice* for several days.[54] That disorderly situation was prevented in 1651 and 1723 by royal *arrêts* which strictly ordered the rank and procedure beforehand for both the procession and the assembly.[55] Caustically commenting on this dazzling ceremonial spectacle in 1614 (see Figure 10), one observer remarked that the Grand-chambre of the Parlement of Paris had been transformed from a judicial forum into a "magnificent theater."[56] From all accounts that ceremonial spectacle did indeed overwhelm any constitutional drama performed there. Yet the oppressive hollowness pervading the Grand-chambre during these later Majority *Lit de Justice* celebrations cannot be ascribed solely to ostentatious flair or to the clash and clang of drums and trumpets, for in truth the Royal Majority celebrations of these later decades, unlike that of 1563, marked no constitutional rite of passage. The Majority *Lit de Justice* of Charles IX clearly celebrated the renewal of legislative prerogative, because it was the first *Lit de Justice* held by that king and the occasion upon which he first promulgated an ordinance in his own right. Conversely, the Majority celebrations for Louis XIII,

[53] See sources in n. 49. For Louis XIII: see the description of the sumptuous clothing and jewels, the cannons fired, and the bonfires lighted. For Louis XIV: the elaborate plans sealed and given to the master of ceremonies for the affair indicate an enormous and complex ceremonial program; B.N. ms. fr. 3157. For Louis XV: a letter of the king (16 Feb. 1723) ordered trumpets and drums and placed the master of ceremonies in charge of all details; A.N. K 724, no. 59.

[54] See sources in n. 49. For Louis XIII: in the planning stages there were daily quarrels over protocol and precedence, including the heated argument over whether princesses and women of the royal court would be allowed into Parlement; see Godefroy, *Cérémonial françois* [Reg. Parl.], II, 263-264, 267-268 (25-27, 30 Sept. 1614).

[55] See sources in n. 49. For Louis XIV: the master of ceremonies Saintot specified rank and procedure for the procession and the assembly, and he recorded in his journal that the king gave orders in council that this plan should be presented to Parlement and followed strictly; B.N. ms. fr. 3157. For Louis XV: the master of ceremonies was put in charge of all details decided upon the week before; A.N. K 724, no. 59.

[56] Bernard, *Les Cérémonies qui ont esté observées en la déclaration de la majorité du roy*, p. 6, which describes a dazzling spectacle.

Louis XIV, and Louis XV had been preceded by at least one earlier *Lit de Justice* assembly; so the constitutional theme of renewal was preempted by that interesting turn of events. In the meantime the *Lit de Justice* assembly was convoked twice more in the remaining decades of the sixteenth century.

IX

A CONSERVATIVE CONSTITUTIONAL COURSE: THE ROYAL *SÉANCE* AND THE *LIT DE JUSTICE* ASSEMBLY 1569-1597

> [Sire], since it pleases you to honor this company [the Parlement of Paris] with your presence [in the Royal *Séance*], do us that honor fully by taking counsel on matters which you wish executed ... it is not wise for you to depart from these procedures ... because *observation of the procedures* [themselves] *constitutes one facet of justice.* Achille (I) de Harlay (1583)

AFTER its provincial debut as a Majority celebration in the Parlement of Rouen in 1563 (followed up in Bordeaux and Toulouse in 1564 and 1565), the *Lit de Justice* assembly was held only twice during the remainder of the sixteenth century, both times in the Parlement of Paris. Charles IX convoked the *Lit de Justice* in 1573 and Henry IV in 1597; the first was a legitimate assembly according to prevailing constitutional policy whereas the second was not. The main architects of constitutional policy on the *Lit de Justice*, Chancellor Michel de L'Hôpital and Jean du Tillet, had departed from public life by the 1570's, the former isolated from affairs of state in 1568 (deceased by 1573), the latter semi-retired after 1563 (deceased by 1570). Therefore, it is not clear what official direction, if any, was given that policy during the 1570's and 1580's. Still, by the 1580's a systematic body of information about the *Lit de Justice* had transcended the narrow bounds of the chancellor's office, the official repository from the 1540's, because Jean du Tillet's treatise, *Recueil des roys de France*, was published six times from 1577 to 1588, and the work of the new antiquarians was initiated in the next few decades.

Several years after the provincial sojourns, Charles IX held three Royal *Séances* in the Parlement of Paris in 1569, 1571, and 1572; then he convoked a *Lit de Justice* assembly in 1573. The conscious distinction made between the two types of parlementary sessions is evident, but on two occasions there was some confusion among pleadings clerks, as opposed to chief clerks of the Grand-chambre, who blurred the categories. Apparently Charles IX dropped in on a pleadings session in

Parlement on 1 August 1569, and a pleadings clerk mistakenly noted in his minutes that a *Lit de Justice* had been held there.¹ Yet two years later the king held another Royal *Séance* on 12 March 1571, a week after his *Entrée* to Paris, and the mistake was not repeated.² During that *Séance* Charles IX defined the limitations of Parlement's "state and profession." The king allowed that the Parlement of Paris was "the most ancient [judicial] Court" in France, but insisted firmly upon the distinction between judicial (parlementary) and legislative (royal) roles. He permitted remonstrances from Parlement on legislation, but only when issued immediately and followed by obedience to royal ordinances in the interim. And he declared cognizance of constitutional issues, or "affairs of state," a royal prerogative reserved for the Crown.³ A year later Charles IX hastily assembled notable persons in the Grand-chambre of Parlement on 26 August 1572, three days after the Saint Bartholomew's Day massacres, apparently to sanction that attack on the Huguenots.⁴ That day a pleadings clerk again mistakenly noted that the session was a *Lit de Justice* assembly.⁵ Following these three Royal *Séances*, two of which were

¹ A.N. X1a 5023, fols. 284r-284v (1 Aug. 1569), a pleadings register. Note that except for Le Nain (A.N. U 2205, fols. 262v) this event was not known by any of the antiquarians or compilers; see Table One.

² A.N. X1a 5031, fol. 342r (12 Mar. 1571), a pleadings register. Squeezed in between two lines, a note says that the *cahier* for that day is lost, indicating that the minutes of the *conseil* register are missing. Although correctly recorded as a *Séance* ("the king sitting in his Parlement") in the registers, there was confusion created just three years later when the following account was published: *Harangue du roy Charles IX à messieurs de la Cour de Parlement à Paris, tenant son siège royal et Lict de Justice* (Rouen, 1574). And several decades later the historian and *parlementaire* De Thou thought of this *Séance* as a *Lit de Justice* assembly; *Histoire universelle de Jacques-Auguste de Thou avec la suite par Nicolas Rigault* (The Hague, 1740), IV, 50, pp. 485-487. On this work, see Samuel Kinser, *The Works of Jacques-Auguste de Thou* (The Hague, 1966).

³ Clearly this speech reiterated L'Hôpital's precepts given in 1563, 1564, and 1565; *Harangue du roy Charles IX*, fols. A [ivʳ]-B iiʳ.

⁴ Sutherland, *The Massacre of St. Bartholomew and the European Conflict, 1559-1572* (New York, 1973), chap. XVII.

⁵ A.N. X1a 5039, fol. 219r (26 Aug. 1572), noted: "That day the king being in his Court held his *Lit de Justice....*" But it is very odd that there is no full account of this important meeting in the *conseil* registers of Parlement (X1a 1637). Moreover, here in the *plaidoiries* register there is only a six-line note squeezed into a small space at the bottom of the page. Although written in the same ink and hand as the rest of the page, the note was added later, because it is written in the past tense, and it was not picked up by any of the compilers. Yet in accounts printed later, this *Séance* is labeled a *Lit de Justice*; see De Thou,

recorded incorrectly as *Lit de Justice* assemblies by a pleadings clerk (1569 and 1572),[6] the king convoked his fourth *Lit de Justice* assembly, the only one held in the Grand-chambre of the Parlement of Paris.

In August of 1573 nine princes of the blood had signed a pact allowing Henry (III), Charles IX's brother and heir presumptive, to accept the Polish throne without forfeiting a future claim to the Crown of France. A month later that agreement was solemnized in a *Lit de Justice* of 18 September 1573 because it concerned a constitutional matter, the regulation of succession according to French Public Law.[7] Thus although Charles IX widened the purview of the *Lit de Justice* to include its convocation in provincial Parlements during his reign, he nevertheless kept a constitutional focus on the assembly. All told that king held four *Séances* in the Parlement of Paris in 1563, 1569, 1571, and 1572, and he convoked four *Lit de Justice* assemblies in the Parlements of Rouen, Bordeaux, and Toulouse in 1563, 1564, 1565, and in the Parlement of Paris in 1573, all concerned with the French Law of Succession. When Charles IX died on 30 May 1574, the documents which instituted a regency (until Henry III's return from Poland) clearly stated the precept of legal-hereditary succession, a cornerstone of the juristic monarchy in

---

Histoire universelle, vol. IV, bk. 52, p. 599; Maximilien de Béthune, Duc de Sully, *Mémoires de Sully, principal ministre de Henry-le-Grand* (nouv. ed., Paris, 1814), vol. I, bk. 1, pp. 52-53. A medal was struck to legitimize royal complicity in the massacre, and it showed Charles IX enthroned under a canopy with an inscription on justice; B.N. Médailles, série royale, no. 178 (attributed to Alexandre Olivier), reproduced in Fernand Mazerolle, *Les Médailleurs français du XVe siècle au milieu du XVIIe siècle, Collection de documents inédits sur l'histoire de France* (Paris, 1902), vol. II, no. 164, p. 40. There are some edicts dated 27 August which probably occasioned the *Séance*: one edict which regulated the conduct of the *gendarmerie* and a declaration on the death of Admiral Coligny which prohibited Huguenot gatherings; see *Catalogue général des livres imprimés de la Bibliothèque Nationale. Actes Royaux.*, ed. Albert Isnard (Paris, 1910-1960), I, 417 (nos. 2601 and 2603 ff.).

[6] The *Séances* of 1569, 1571, and 1572 were recorded by pleadings clerks while the chief clerk of the Grand-chambre made no records in the important *conseil* registers.

[7] A.N. X1a 1640, fols. 451v-452r (18 Sept. 1573), stating that the king was "in the Court to hold his *Lit de Justice* [assembly]." The succession pact is reproduced (as registered in A.N. X1a 8630) by Sixte de Bourbon de Parme, *Le Traité d'Utrecht et les lois fondamentales du royaume* (Paris, 1914), pp. 272-273, but the date of the *Lit de Justice* is given incorrectly as 17 September. It appears that Charles IX planned to hold a *Lit de Justice* earlier in 1573, but there is no evidence that it took place; A.N. X1a 1640, fol. 218v (8 Aug. 1573), cited in Maugis, *Histoire du Parlement*, I, 315, n. 1.

the sixteenth century as developed by Du Tillet, L'Hôpital, and others, and demonstrated in that king's *Lit de Justice* assemblies. The Law of Succession was described therein as "... a special Law which is unique and particular to this kingdom and which we have maintained and observed inviolably since the institution of our kings successively...."[8] Although the *Lit de Justice*, provincial or Parisian, attained prominence between 1527 and 1573, it had been convoked rarely, just seven times in forty-six years, and for constitutional business only. In the next two decades its appearance or nonappearance depended upon the successful dissemination of this new theory of the French constitution.

THE ROYAL *Séances* OF 1580, 1581, AND 1583

When the conflicting testimony of contemporaries and the layers of historical error are sorted out, it appears that Henry III (1574-1589) never convoked a *Lit de Justice* assembly. It is necessary to stress this point, because misconceptions connecting the *Lit de Justice* with the forced registration of legislation in his reign have become commonplace.[9] Henry

---

[8] "... loy speciale, singuliere et particuliere de ce royaume laquelle nous avons gardée et observée inviolablement depuis la creation de nos rois successivement ..."; Dupuy, *Traité de la majorité*, p. 450 (31 May 1574).

[9] The following examples give some sense of this confusion. (1) For 8 June 1576: Maugis, *Histoire du Parlement*, I, 251, n. 2, maintains that an "edict was verified in a *Lit de Justice* on 8 June [1576]." But the registers which he cites, A.N. X1a 1652, fols. 159v-192v (1-8 June 1576), do not show either that a *Lit de Justice* was held that day or even that the king was present in the session. On 1 June, the week before, Henry III did announce his intention to come in person to register an edict alienating church goods, correctly reported in Maugis, *Histoire du Parlement*, I, 627-628, n. 3. But the register which he cites, A.N. X1a 1652, fol. 125v (1 June 1576), makes no mention of a *Lit de Justice* assembly; to the contrary, on this day the black-robed precedent for Royal *Séances* (supposedly set by Charles IX on 17 May 1563) was discussed. (2) For 4 July 1580: Maugis, *Histoire du Parlement*, I, 254, n. 1, states that an edict "was published by the authority of a *Lit de Justice*" on that date. But once again the register cited, A.N. X1a 1668, fols. 442ff. (4 July 1580), neither shows that a *Lit de Justice* took place nor gives evidence that the king was present. (3) For 26 July 1580: Shennan, *Parlement of Paris*, pp. 218-219, who cites Maugis as above, introduces a new error by calling this event a *Lit de Justice* even though Maugis does not. (4) For 4 July 1581: Maugis, *Histoire du Parlement*, I, 257, dubs this *Séance* as a *Lit de Justice*. But see the explanation below. (5) For 15 (or 16) June 1586: Lemaire, *Les Lois fondamentales*, p. 148, n. 4, calls this the famous *Lit de Justice* where President Harlay made the important speech on parlementary procedure

III held three Royal *Séances* in 1580, 1581, and 1583, but if the two famous sessions of 1585 and 1586 (regularly hailed as *Lit de Justice* assemblies by historians) ever took place, they were either meetings of the Royal Council (attended by *parlementaires*) or Royal *Séances*. The primacy of the Royal *Séance* at this time cannot be attributed to lack of knowledge about the *Lit de Justice* assembly. To the contrary, information on parlementary assemblies was rapidly disseminated following the publication of Du Tillet's work in 1577,[10] and ceremonial ritual in varied forms interested Henry III at this time. For instance, the king legally accorded the princes of the blood top rank in public ceremonies in 1576,[11] he commissioned a master of ceremonies, Guillaume Pot de Rhodes in 1583 to make a memorandum on ceremonial procedures,[12] and he institutionalized the office of master of ceremonies by 1585.[13] More importantly, the constitutional and ceremonial regulations for parlementary sessions, which had been summarized in the memorandum of 1560, were known to the king, because he discussed Parlement's black-robed pre-

---

(dating the event 15 June); Maugis, *Histoire du Parlement*, III, 329, and Church, *Constitutional Thought*, pp. 153-154, n. 80, (dating the event 16 June) follow suit. But see the explanation below. In general Maugis, *Histoire du Parlement*, I, 602-631, describes the last of the Valois (Henry II, Charles IX, and Henry III) as using "the *Lit de Justice* as a unique means of constraint." Finally Church, *Constitutional Thought*, pp. 150-155, holds that a major grievance against Henry III's reign was his increased use of the *Lit de Justice* to force the registration of edicts, citing an anonymous pamphlet of 1588 (p. 152, n. 77) which more than likely refers to a *Séance* and certainly mentions no *Lit de Justice*.

[10] For the publishing history of the *Recueil des roys de France*, see above, Chap. IV, n. 3, and trace the influence of his sources on later commentators in Table One below.

[11] Consult Jackson, "Peers of France and Princes of the Blood," pp. 27-46, and Giesey, *Juristic Basis of Dynastic Right*, pp. 38-40. For the edict, consult Isambert, *Recueil général des anciennes lois*, XV, 318.

[12] In 1583 a meeting of king, princes, Crown officers, councillors, and *parlementaires* was held at Saint-Germain-en-Laye to discuss the confusion regarding French ceremonial procedures. Henry III was advised to have the master of ceremonies draw up a complete memorandum on the discrepancies and disputes which had occurred at public ceremonies; Godefroy, *Cérémonial françois*, I, e iv^v (1583). It is possible that "Règlemens de la maison du roi (1585)," Louis Cimber and Felix Danjou, *Archives curieuses de l'histoire de France* (1re série, X, 1836), pp. 299-358, represents the modest results of that commission.

[13] The letters commissioning Guillaume Pot, Sieur de Rhodes (2 Jan. 1585) and later François Pot de Rhodes, Sieur du Macquet (24 Feb. 1616) order the masters of ceremonies "to make the dignity and splendor appropriate to our royal grandeur known"; B. Mazarine ms. 2737, fols. 336r-338r.

cedent for the Royal *Séance* and red-robed distinction for the *Lit de Justice*.[14] Finally, there is evidence that Henry III and his ceremonial advisers at one point planned a red-robed *Lit de Justice* assembly, although it was never carried out. Hemmed in by peculiar political circumstances, the king decided on an Estates General rather than a *Lit de Justice* assembly when a constitutional forum was required. In the meantime he drafted the Royal *Séance* as a vehicle for the swift registration of financial edicts and denied Parlement the time to hold separate deliberations in those sessions.

Henry III first visited the Parlement of Paris on 26 July 1580. He had come to register financial edicts, but the one-line note in the registers states only that the king arrived in his Parlement and gives no details about the event.[15] The next year the king held a Royal *Séance* on 4 July 1581 in a black-robed Parlement to register financial edicts, some of which Parlement had not even perused, creating new offices in the Court.[16] Although the king had warned Parlement twice of the im-

[14] A.N. X1a 1652, fol. 125v (1 June 1576).

[15] A.N. X1a 1669, fol. 141v (26 July 1580). There is no record of the event in Godefroy, *Cérémonial françois*, or in A.N. U 2068 (Le Nain), although ibid., fols. 109r-109v (27 July), acknowledges that the king was "sitting in his Parlement the day before." Not a single commentator discusses this event (see Table One below). Two months earlier the king sent a warning to Parlement that "he would come here [the Grand-chambre] to publish some edicts himself in person," but no mention is made of a *Lit de Justice* either by the king or by the first president, who called the impending *Séance* "an extraordinary action"; for this exchange, A.N. U 2068 (Le Nain), fol. 83r (30 Apr. 1580). Likewise, the published version of the edicts makes no mention of a *Lit de Justice*; see *Edict du roy de l'erection d'une deuxiesme chambre aux requestes du palais et de deux présidents et huict conseillers pour la composition d'icelle. Publié en Parlement, le roy y séant, le 26 juillet 1580* (Saint Maur-des-Fossés, 1580). For the edicts, see Isambert, *Recueil général des anciennes lois*, XIV, 478, 484-485. Consult Shennan, *Parlement of Paris*, pp. 218-219, for details on the session, but note that he assumes the *Séance* was a *Lit de Justice* assembly. Henry III did not make a formal *Entrée* to the City of Paris as had predecessors from Philip V in 1317; as a result, there was no post-*Entrée* visit to the Grand-chambre in this reign as in those since Louis XII in 1498.

[16] A.N. X1a 1672, fols. 131r-133v (4 July 1581); and in A.N. U 2068 (Le Nain), fols. 170r-176v, and Godefroy, *Cérémonial françois* [Reg. Parl.], II, 592-594 (3, 4, and 5 July 1581). The metaphorical allusion to the king as "sitting in his *lit de justice* [i.e. Parlement or Grand-chambre]" at the end of the account would cause confusion among later commentators. For the edicts, see Isambert, *Recueil général des anciennes lois*, XIV, 486, 489-499. Consult Maugis, *Histoire du Parlement*, I, 257, 628, but note that he maintains the edicts were registered in a *Lit de Justice*, thereby misleading Shennan, *Parlement of Paris*, p. 216.

pending *Séance*, the Court paid no heed.[17] As a result Parlement was not prepared to defend its position when the king arrived and presented a legal brief to legitimize the action. Henry III defended the registration of financial edicts at a Royal *Séance* by alleging "great and urgent necessity" in the "affairs of the kingdom," the *casus necessitatis*, and that venerable legal principle allowed a temporary suspension of ordinary laws for the defense of the kingdom in a dire emergency.[18] Parlement took refuge in angry silence and refused to render an opinion when Seals-keeper (acting chancellor) Philippe Hurault de Cheverny solicited the Court's advice. Still chafing from the events the next day, the *parlementaires* were determined to record their imposing negative silence. They called the clerk of the Parlement of Paris before them, reviewed his minutes of the *Séance*, and ordered him to write into the record that the presidents and councillors of the Court had advised the chancellor "that they could not deliberate on what they had not even seen."[19]

Henry III held a third Royal *Séance* on 7 March 1583 and again registered edicts creating new judicial offices.[20] As in 1581 these edicts

[17] Apparently the king warned the Court that he intended to come into Parlement and register edicts perused but still unregistered, because four days before the *Séance* Parlement tried to persuade "the king not to come in his Parlement" to register the edicts; A.N. U 2068 (Le Nain), fol. 168r-v (30 June 1581). A similar request was made a week earlier; ibid., fol. 167r-v (23 June 1581). The king issued a second warning to Parlement the day before the *Séance*, stating that "since his Court did not wish to verify the said edict . . . he intended to come in his Parlement tomorrow in order to publish it along with other edicts . . ."; A.N. X1a 1672, fols. 130r-131r (3 July 1581). But there is no mention either in the account itself (see above, n. 16) or in the warnings of a *Lit de Justice* held or pending.

[18] On the *casus necessitatis* as a venerable legal principle, consult Post, *Studies in Medieval Legal Thought*, chap. V, chap. XI, and pp. 558-561; and Kantorowicz, *King's Two Bodies*, pp. 284-291.

[19] A.N. X1a 1672, fols. 131r-133v (4 July 1581); and in A.N. U 2068 (Le Nain), fols. 170r-176v, and Godefroy, *Cérémonial françois* [Reg. Parl.], II, 592-594 (3, 4, and 5 July 1581). Philippe Hurault de Cheverny, *maître des requêtes* in 1563, was made chancellor in 1583; Maugis, *Histoire du Parlement*, III, 203, 219. In the meantime he was seals-keeper (acting chancellor) from September 1578.

[20] A.N. X1a 1679, fols. 387v-389v (7 Mar. 1583), where the account is written in a different hand and ink from the rest of the register and placed there out of order after records for the month of April. In A.N. U 2068 (Le Nain), fols. 291r-293v, "March" is crossed out and "April" is incorrectly inserted. And there are notes in Godefroy, *Cérémonial françois* [unidentified source], II, 595-600. There is no mention of a *Lit de Justice* assembly, but a metaphorical allusion

had been sent to the Parlement of Paris earlier, but apparently the Court presented remonstrances on some and left others unperused. Furious at these stalling tactics the king threatened several times, even that very morning, to come into Parlement and register the edicts. In the face of the Court's delays he finally did just that. During the *Séance* the king again alleged a state of emergency and invoked the principle of *casus necessitatis* to legitimize the action, but this time Parlement countered his compelling legal argument with a constitutional claim. First President Achille (I) de Harlay defined king and Parlement as co-legislators, repeating the same theme, the inviolability of Parlement's institutionalized procedure, which had been introduced by President Guillart in the first *Lit de Justice* of July 1527 and reiterated by President de Saint-André in 1560.[21] But in 1583 Harlay pressed that theme to its ultimate conclusion. Countering the royal invocation of *necessitas*, the first president made the subtle but astounding suggestion that Parlement's legislative registration process fell within the sanctified realm of French Public Law. Harlay told the king,

> Sire, your predecessors have bestowed this honor on your Parlements; [that is], to regulate the scales of justice by counsel and advice. And since they [your predecessors] could exercise absolute power like you, they kept the maxim "Law and Reason" engraved on their spirit so as to subjugate their power to the civility of the laws.... For this same consideration Theopompus established the ephors without whose counsel he could not make any law.... Sire, do not change the customary procedures followed in the distribution of justice or in the publication of edicts. Although they [the laws] derive force only from your authority, you [French kings] have held at all times that they should be deliberated upon and resolved in your Parlement [of Paris].... Sire, these deliberations [of Parlement] are necessary for the good of your service ... because often edicts which you have proposed seem prima facie plausible but actually after examination are found specious because they deviate from your intention ... and are damaging to your subjects. Since it pleases

is used by President Harlay to describe the enthroned king as "sitting in your *lit de justice* [i.e. Parlement or Grand-chambre] ... the true image of God." For the edicts, see Isambert, *Recueil général des anciennes lois*, XIV, 500-504, 509, 514, 520-539. Shennan, *Parlement of Paris*, pp. 218-219, n. 1, discusses this event as a *Lit de Justice*, although his source, Maugis, *Histoire du Parlement*, II, 674-703, does not treat it as such.

[21] Achille (I) de Harlay was made councillor in Parlement in 1558 and president in 1572: Maugis, *Histoire du Parlement*, III, 214, 246.

you to honor this company with your presence, do us that honor fully ... by taking counsel on matters which you wish executed. Once the law is [properly] made, it cannot be disputed or revoked by doubt; to the contrary, it is necessary ... to obey it. Your predecessors have acted in this manner in Parlements ... as the Roman emperors in the senate ..., [and] it is not wise for you to depart from these procedures even if you can do as you please.... [The act of] verification [in the Parlement of Paris] provides the best and easiest means for executing them [the laws] if they have been made through the customary procedures in your Parlement, because *observation of the procedures* [themselves] *constitutes one facet of justice....*[22]

In addition to declaring Parlement's institutionalized procedure a facet of Public Law in this *Séance* of 1583, President Harlay criticized Henry III's invocation of the *casus necessitatis*. Referring to actions taken in the earlier *Séance* of 1581, the president questioned the legality of a "necessity" which was continual rather than temporary in character. He told the king that ". . . we [Parlement] fear that this [case of] necessity, which has not been resolved by the numerous edicts already verified, will not end or diminish, but to the contrary will grow from day to day until it becomes perpetual."[23] Responding to this pointed legal reference distinguishing actual necessity from perpetual or habitual necessity, the king

[22] A.N. X1a 1679, fols. 387v-389v (7 Mar. 1583); and in Godefroy, *Cérémonial françois* [unidentified source], II, 595-600 (the speech, II, 595-599 [italics added]). Note that the legislator-king is described as one who is *legibus solutus* but *ratione alligatus*, above the laws but bound by reason to observe them. Harlay's speech is quoted in Church, *Constitutional Thought*, pp. 153-154, n. 80, but cited incorrectly from Godefroy, *Cérémonial de France* (1619). It has been stated that this radical identification of Parlement's registration procedure with French Public Law was made first in a *Lit de Justice* of 16 June 1586 (a *Séance* discussed below) and that the same theme was repeated in other speeches prepared by Harlay (published later by Guillaume Du Vair); see Church, *Constitutional Thought*, p. 154, nn. 81, 82. But the speech actually was given here in 1583 and then published again in the collection of Du Vair as recounted below.

[23] A.N. X1a 1679, fols. 387v-389v (7 Mar. 1583); and in Godefroy, *Cérémonial françois* [unidentified source], II, 599. On the notion of "perpetual necessity," especially the discussion of Oldradus de Ponte (d. 1335) on the subject, see Kantorowicz, *King's Two Bodies*, pp. 284-291. Actually the *parlementaires* had greeted arguments based on necessity with a jaundiced eye since the late 1550's. Questioning Henry II's plans to sell judicial offices in 1558, President Séguier remarked that "There is a great deal of difference between 'public necessity' which observes no law and 'particular profit' which is subject to law," sentiments also expressed by an *avocat*; Maugis, *Histoire du Parlement*, I, 228-229.

assured the Court that he had already formed a commission "to advise him on the means to make such necessity cease."[24]

Earlier in 1580 Parlement had announced its strict interpretation of the procedural prerogatives at its command for the registration of new laws. President Christophe de Thou boldly maintained first, that the Court considered iterative remonstrances a part of legislative procedure; second, that Parlement would attach written reservations to a given law in the face of irresolvable differences between Court and king; and third, that such reservations would render the law provisional and subject to expiration upon the death of the king. Thus royal legislation unregistered by Parlement could bind subjects in the short term only.[25] When Henry III extended the scope of Royal *Séances* to implement the registration of so-called emergency edicts in 1581 and 1583, therefore, he deliberately challenged Parlement's procedural stance. The king's controversial expedient first brought opposition, then cooperation from the Court. The *parlementaires* were adamantly opposed to the legislative *Séance* of 1581 and refused to participate: they presented no legal brief countering the king's action and kept an uncooperative silence when approached for an opinion on registration. Yet two years later in 1583 the *parlementaires* negotiated a compromise beforehand and cooperated in the *Séance*: they pointedly pronounced the legal limitations of the *casus necessitatis*, and President Harlay boldly claimed stature in Public Law for their legislative procedure, but in the end they rendered an opinion on the edicts when requested to do so. It appears that Parlement was rewarded on the spot for this compromise. Although the uncooperative Court had placed last in the order of consultation at the *Séance* of 1581, the cooperative one attained a coveted first place (immediately following the king and preceding the royal party in the high seats) at the *Séance* of 1583, a formidable, albeit ephemeral, ceremonial precedent. In civic ritual the struc-

[24] A.N. X1a 1679, fols. 387v-389v (7 Mar. 1583); and Godefroy, *Cérémonial françois* [unidentified source], II, 600. According to the *avocat* Augustin (II) de Thou: "After having commanded us [Parlement] several times, even again this morning, to present the edicts read just now to Parlement, your majesty took the trouble to appear here to explain the urgent necessity facing you. Yet as your majesty told us this morning, he has also commissioned persons of probity and integrity to advise him on the means to make such necessity cease." De Thou was made *avocat* in 1569 and president in 1585; Maugis, *Histoire du Parlement*, III, 247, 333.

[25] For De Thou's remarks of 29 January 1580, see Maugis, *Histoire du Parlement*, I, 630, and Church, *Constitutional Thought*, p. 148, n. 70.

ture of public authority was revealed, even fashioned; therefore, Parlement argued for matters of principle, yet acted to attain place.

This round of challenges and counter challenges did not end there. Within the very next year the royal party denounced the claim that Parlement's registration procedure enjoyed status in Public Law. Shading a borrowed history lesson, Chancellor Philippe Huralt de Cheverny delivered a speech to Parlement which was taken word for word from Chancellor Olivier's address of 1549. Parlement was disbarred from cognizance of affairs of state in the mid-fourteenth century, Cheverny insisted, and thenceforth was consulted in constitutional matters only by a *special commission* issued by the king.[26] In 1549 Olivier's original statement underscored the distinction between the *Lit de Justice* (where Public Law was treated) and the Royal *Séance* (where private law was adjudged). But in 1584 Cheverny's version placed emergency financial legislation under affairs of state and drafted the Royal *Séance* as the emergency vehicle, or *special commission*, for implementing that legislation. In this way Henry III forthrightly denied Parlement's invocation of Public Law status for its legislative procedure and adapted the Royal *Séance* as a legislative vehicle capable of emergency action. All the while, however, the *Lit de Justice* assembly was kept in constitutional reserve.

Frequently discussed in historical works but troublesome to account for are two more parlementary sessions of Henry III, one allegedly held on 18 July 1585 registering an edict on religious unity, the other on 15 or 16 June 1586 registering financial edicts creating offices.[27] Apparently Henry III planned to convoke a *Lit de Justice* on 18 July 1585, because Master of Ceremonies Guillaume Pot de Rhodes organized the seating for the assembly in a plan drawn for the session and the Court was expressly ordered to wear red robes for the event.[28] Yet this alleged *Lit de Justice* assembly was not recorded in the registers of Parlement, and the suspicion looms large that it never actually took place.[29] It is possible

[26] A.N. X1a 1683, fol. 177r-v (7 Jan. 1584).

[27] On the confusion surrounding these assemblies, see above, n. 9.

[28] The summons, A.N. U 2071 (Le Nain), fols. 104r-105r (17 July 1585), noted: "... the chancellor explained that the king would come tomorrow in this Court to put the matter [edict revoking former edicts of pacification] in deliberation, so messieurs the presidents and councillors should be vested in their red robes. ... The said lord stated that ... tomorrow he would come in his Parlement ... and that he should be received by his Court in red robes. ..." On the proposed plan drawn for the *Lit de Justice*, see the sketches in A.N. KK 1428, fol. 496v (18 July 1585), and B.N. ms. fr. n. a. 9750, fol. 29v.

[29] There is no account for 18 July 1585 in A.N. X1a 1692 or in A.N. U 2071

at the outset that Henry III considered this an appropriate occasion for the convocation of a *Lit de Justice*, because the edict on religious unity which was registered that day touched, peripherally at least, upon a possible succession crisis due to the status of Henry of Navarre (the future Henry IV), who had become heir presumptive to the Crown following the death of the Duke of Anjou in June 1584.[30] But if the king had been persuaded in July of 1585 to promulgate a much stronger legislative measure on religious unity in an Estates General rather than in a *Lit de Justice*, as he eventually did in 1588, then that decision would have caused the cancellation of this proposed *Lit de Justice* assembly.

The same difficulties attend the alleged assembly of 15 or 16 June 1586. Historians invariably speak of this event as a *Lit de Justice* assembly, interpreting it as a prime example of a *Lit de Justice* used to force the registration of edicts in Parlement and citing it as the moment when President Harlay actually claimed the inviolability of the Court's registration procedure.[31] To be sure, the Parlement of Paris registered a number of financial edicts creating offices on 16 June, one of which provoked a strike of angry *procureurs* attempting to protect the status of their offices.[32] Yet once again there are no official sources which show that a *Lit de Justice* assembly was actually convoked,[33] and President Harlay had already claimed inviolable Public Law status for the Court's registration procedure three years earlier in the Royal *Séance* of 1583. The confusion surrounding this alleged *Lit de Justice* assembly of 1586 arises from the evidence usually cited, not the registers of Parlement but a collection of speeches prepared for the event and gathered by Guillaume du Vair, a councillor in Parlement.[34] The collection itself raises critical

---

(Le Nain); and Godefroy, *Cérémonial françois* [no source], II, 600, provides no account but nevertheless states without evidence that a *"Lit de Justice"* was held "for the revocation of edicts of pacification."

[30] On the edict, see Isambert, *Recueil général des anciennes lois*, XIV, 595.

[31] For some examples of these interpretations, see above, n. 9.

[32] For the edicts, see Isambert, *Recueil général des anciennes lois*, XIV, 597-598, 601-608. On the *procureurs*, ibid., 601-603, and Church, *Constitutional Thought*, p. 152, n. 78, quoting a memoir which describes how the furious officers revolted and refused to hold pleadings sessions.

[33] There is no account for 15 or 16 June 1586 in A.N. X1a 1698 or in A.N. U 2071 (Le Nain). Once again, Godefroy, *Cérémonial françois* [no source], II, 600, provides no account, yet notes without evidence that a *Lit de Justice* was held regarding the registration of edicts creating offices.

[34] Guillaume du Vair, *Actions et traictez oratoires* (Paris, 1911), ed. René Radouant, is a collection of speeches collected by Du Vair including those of

problems: two conflicting dates, 15 and 16 June, are given for the event; and two different locations, the king's Council and Parlement, are cited, leaving historians free to choose the most likely place.[35] As a result of this confusion and the lack of records attesting to the existence of this assembly, the assertion that the session was a *Lit de Justice* held in Parlement is unfounded and the dates of 15 or 16 June remain contradictory.[36] It is quite possible that the speeches of 1586 were prepared for a proposed parlementary assembly of 16 June, probably a Royal *Séance*, but actually given in a meeting of the Royal Council attended by a group of *parlementaires* including the first president; or else that the speeches, prepared for a Royal *Séance* of 16 June which never took place, remained among Du Vair's papers but actually were never given at all.[37] Whether these events of 1585 and 1586 were Royal *Séances* or Royal Council meetings, actually convoked or not, the allegations that they were *Lit de Justice* assemblies cannot be substantiated by the evidence at hand.

In retrospect it is evident that Henry III had good reason not to convoke the *Lit de Justice* in 1585 to address a potential succession problem: he had decided already to tamper with the Law of Succession and could not employ for that purpose a forum which had been charged for decades with maintaining French Public Law. In any case, Parlement was fractured in two by the time the king made his move: one Court

---

President Achille (I) de Harlay. Du Vair was a councillor in Parlement in 1584 (Maugis, *Histoire du Parlement*, III, 267, 277) and seals-keeper under Henry IV.

[35] The editor of Du Vair's collection, René Radouant, shows that places and dates for the assembly of 1586 differed in the various editions of this collection. The first edition of 1586 states that the king was "in his Council the 16th of June"; ibid., xxiii. The editions of 1606, 1625, and 1641 give two variants, one which states that the king was "in his Council the 16th of June," the other that the king was "in Parlement the 15th of June"; ibid., 208 and n. 1. Although the editor admits to some confusion regarding these dates, he maintains without adducing new evidence that "the speeches were pronounced in Parlement and not in the Council of the king ... on 15 June 1586"; ibid.

[36] Ibid., xxiii, n. 1, the assertion of Radouant. In addition, none of the speeches contained in this collection states that the king was holding a *Lit de Justice* assembly: for Henry III's speech, see pp. 208-211; for Chancellor Du Vair, pp. 211-212; for President Harlay, pp. 214-217.

[37] During the sixteenth century the eloquent discourses of *parlementaires* and chancellors required some time for preparation, and surely many were written for future use. That might be the case for another speech of President Harlay, undated in Du Vair's collection but similar to the president's speech actually given in the Royal *Séance* of 1583; ibid., 221-228. Church, *Constitutional Thought*, p. 154, n. 82, cites this speech but does not connect it with the *Séance* of 1583.

recognized by the monarch was gathered at Tours, and a rump Court sat in the Grand-chambre at Paris.[38] Hence the king turned to the Estates General, which had been claimed by some, most recently in the 1560's, as the traditional French forum for treating Public Law.[39] In a move historically unprecedented, the king and deputies at the Estates General of Blois (1588-1589) promulgated a new Public Law, the Edict of Union (1588), which required the maintenance of religious unity under Catholicism in the kingdom.[40] This measure was not promulgated in a *Lit de Justice*, and it violated French Public Law. By virtually excluding the rightful successor Henry of Navarre (a Protestant), the edict annulled legal-hereditary succession, which required assumption of office by the nearest male. When the *parlementaires* (the rump faction in the Grand-chambre) registered the edict, they attempted to legitimize the subversive measure by declaring it a "fundamental and irrevocable law."[41] Fundamental or not, the magnitude of the constitutional disruption posed by the Edict of Union produced a backlash, and *parlementaires* of both factions (Paris and Tours) and legists successfully argued against its acceptance and in favor of retaining legal-hereditary succession.[42] During the sixteenth century the *Lit de Justice* assembly had provided a public forum for maintaining French Public Law, and this contrary action taken by the Estates General failed to undermine that constitutional authority.

It is true that Henry III attempted to extend royal legislative authority,

---

[38] After the "Day of the Barricades," 12 May 1588, Henry III fled to Chartres. The king's recognition of the Parlement at Tours (which included Harlay) created two rival factions, the other still at Paris (which included Du Vair). For details, see Salmon, *Society in Crisis*, pp. 234-257; and Church, *Constitutional Thought*, pp. 134-136. For the edicts disbanding Parlement and other Courts (which apparently were not registered) and transferring Parlement to Tours, see Isambert, *Recueil général des anciennes lois*, XIV, 633-635.

[39] Consult Church, *Constitutional Thought*, pp. 137-139, on the Estates and their connection with Parlement.

[40] See Salmon, *Society in Crisis*, pp. 243-246, on the connection of the Leaguer faction with this meeting. Lemaire, *Les Lois fondamentales*, pp. 137-139, and Church, *Constitutional Thought*, p. 90, n. 29, consider this action in the Estates General (October 1588–January 1589) the only historical example of the creation of a new "Fundamental Law" in the Estates.

[41] For confirmation of the Edict of Union in Parlement, see Isambert, *Recueil général des anciennes lois*, XIV, 629-635; and for a commentary on the edict, see Sutherland, *Huguenot Struggle*, pp. 365-366.

[42] For example, see the arguments of Guy Coquille and Guillaume du Vair; Lemaire, *Les Lois fondamentales*, pp. 142-150, especially p. 143, and Church, *Constitutional Thought*, p. 93, n. 38, and p. 145, n. 63.

first by enlarging the scope of the Royal *Séance* to include the registration of financial edicts in situations of national emergency, then by creating Public Law in the Estates General. Still, it is necessary to emphasize that the *Lit de Justice* assembly played no part in these legislative innovations. In fact throughout the sixteenth century the *Lit de Justice* was not connected with the forced registration of edicts in Parlement. Francis I dissociated the *Lit de Justice* assembly from such registration in 1527; Henry II and Francis II commissioned research on the assembly but never held a *Lit de Justice* during their reigns; Charles IX refused to associate the *Lit de Justice* with ordinary legislative business even under extraordinary pressure from the Parlement of Paris; and Henry III adapted the Royal *Séance*, not the *Lit de Justice*, as a legislative vehicle and bypassed the *Lit de Justice* for the Estates General in order to amend legal-hereditary succession by reference to a "fundamental law." Thus, in the six decades from its appearance under the Valois Francis I to the demise of the last Valois Henry III, the *Lit de Justice* assembly was actually convoked on just seven occasions by two kings, Francis I and Charles IX. Throughout that time, moreover, the distinction between Royal *Séances* (honorary sessions) and *Lits de Justice* (constitutional assemblies) was maintained in theory and practice. A quarter of a century later, however, during the reign of the first Bourbon king, that constitutional focus was distorted.

THE *Lit de Justice* ASSEMBLY OF 1597

Henry IV (1589-1610) came to the throne of France as a Protestant king after the assassination of Henry III in August 1589, and the succession crisis which ensued did not subside until his religious conversion and Coronation at Chartes (not Reims) in February 1594, almost five years later. Amidst the devastating religious and political turmoil of those years, the Catholic League held Paris in its grip and eventually terrorized and alienated even the rump group of *parlementaires* left in the Grand-chambre. In 1593 the Leaguers held an Estates General in Paris (declared illegal by Henry IV) to select a new Catholic king, but it failed and then collapsed in the face of Henry IV's conversion.[43] Threatened with foreign intervention and struggling under a mound of debts, the new king attempted to raise monies through financial edicts which Parlement

[43] Salmon, *Society in Crisis*, pp. 234-273.

persistently refused to register.[44] It has been alleged that Henry IV held numerous *Lit de Justice* assemblies, even that he threatened Parlement with a *Lit de Justice* on the eve of his departure for war in 1595.[45] But there is no evidence to support those allegations. The king did make use of many *lettres de jussion* as had Henry III, and he did send ten edicts to the Court for every one he wished published in this game of cat and mouse. Time and time again he berated the *parlementaires* for irresponsible behavior, reminding them on one occasion that it was the royal sword and troops, not the *arrêts* of red-robed judges, which would halt advancing foreign armies. Still, throughout those years such tirades, some inordinately fierce, were never followed up with royal sanctions against the Court.[46] Along those lines it is misleading to construe as a threat Henry IV's comment (made not long after his Coronation) about holding a *Lit de Justice* in the Parlement of Paris after routing the foreign armies. In all probability the king was stating his intent to give public witness of his legitimate ascension to the French throne, that is, to emphasize his claim to rule by virtue of legal-hereditary succession. Whatever the case at that time, however, a decade later financial crises had soured the whole scene, and the situation turned out quite differently. Besides the unsuccessful attempts to push financial edicts through Parlement, Henry IV also failed just as handily to raise monies through the Estates General of Rouen (1596-1597).[47] It appears that the king finally reacted in total exasperation. He precipitously convoked not a Royal *Séance* (following the pattern of Henry III) but a *Lit de Justice* assembly, the first of its kind, for the purpose of forcing the registration of financial edicts through Parlement.

Henry IV sat in a *Lit de Justice* assembly in the Parlement of Paris on 21 May 1597.[48] The registers show that the Court was warned the

[44] For the steady stream of edicts, see Maugis, *Histoire du Parlement*, II, 243-271, and Shennan, *Parlement of Paris*, pp. 232-236.

[45] Maugis, *Histoire du Parlement*, II, 266, quoting Henry IV's comment to Parlement that following his expulsion of invading armies from the kingdom, "... I will go to hold my *Lit de Justice* [assembly]...." In Maugis' opinion the king used all kinds of threats, including *lettres de jussion* and *Lit de Justice* assemblies.

[46] Ibid., where the lack of royal sanctions is noted.

[47] Shennan, *Parlement of Paris*, pp. 235-236, calls this meeting an Assembly of Notables; but Major, *Representative Institutions*, considers it a restricted Estates General (November 1596–January 1597).

[48] A.N. X1a 1749, fols. 470v-471v (21 May 1597), and Godefroy, *Cérémonial françois* [no source], II, 600-601.

day before to don red robes for the ceremony because the king intended "to hold his *Lit de Justice.*" Mustering the same legal allegations as his predecessor, the *casus necessitatis* (the necessity of war, compounded by Parlement's refusal to verify earlier edicts), the king attempted over Parlement's objections to register edicts raising war monies. For refusing to cooperate in this session, the Court reverted to third place (after the king and royal party) in the order of consultation.[49] Although the political conflict between king and Court on this day has been carefully studied,[50] the proper role of the *Lit de Justice* has not been pointed out. This use of a *Lit de Justice* assembly to register disputed edicts raising war monies was not part of a long tradition; it was an extraordinary action. Moreover, ironically enough, the *Lit de Justice* of 1597 failed to fulfill its new role. Three quarters of a century later, in his study of *Lit de Justice* assemblies, Louis XIV's chancellor, Pierre (III) Séguier, noted with curiosity that "the king [Henry IV] read nine edicts" in the *Lit de Justice* assembly of 1597, "but they are not in the register," a fact borne out in a major compilation of such laws.[51] It appears, therefore, that the *Lit de Justice* assembly roundly failed its first test as a royal legislative weapon. Henry IV thereafter abandoned the Grand-chambre and confronted Parlement on royal grounds, at the palaces of the Tuileries and the Louvre, regarding registration issues.[52]

UNTIL 1563 Jean du Tillet's constitutional theory separating parlementary sessions into constitutional *Lit de Justice* assemblies and ordinary Royal *Séances* proved amazingly resilient. That theory legitimized the first three *Lit de Justice* assemblies and established conservative constitutional guidelines for future convocations in the Parlement of Paris. Francis I held five Royal *Séances* in 1515, 1517, 1522, 1523, and 1524; then he convoked three *Lit de Justice* assemblies in 1527 and 1537 which treated constitutional issues; following that he canceled a proposed visit to Parlement

[49] Ibid., both sources.

[50] Albert Chamberland, *Le Conflit de 1597 entre Henri IV et le Parlement de Paris* (Paris, 1904).

[51] B.N. ms. fr. 18411, fol. 144r. The only document registered that day was a declaration attributing to the Grand-chambre sole authority to register edicts and ordinances; Isambert, *Recueil général des anciennes lois*, XV, 164, n. 1.

[52] On meetings at the palaces, see Maugis, *Histoire du Parlement*, II, 272, and Shennan, *Parlement of Paris*, pp. 236-238. Although *Recueil de lettres patentes concernant la discipline du Parlement*, p. 9, alleges that Henry IV gave a discourse in Parlement on 8 January 1599, the king was not there that day; A.N. X1a 1766, fols. 272r-303v (8 Jan. 1599).

in 1542, ordered Du Tillet to conduct research on royal visits to the Court, and did not visit the Grand-chambre of the Parlement again. Henry II acknowledged the ancient origins of the *Lit de Justice* and commissioned special research on that assembly in 1548; then he held four Royal *Séances* in 1549, 1551, 1552, and 1558, expropriated some ceremonial elements for three of them, and did not convoke a *Lit de Justice* during his entire reign. Francis II did not visit the Parlement of Paris in his short reign, but he too acknowledged the *Lit de Justice* assembly in 1560 and rested his case for majority on the historical existence of a medieval *Lit de Justice* wherein the Law of Majority was promulgated. Finally, Charles IX during his minority, 1561-1563, considered convoking a *Lit de Justice* but in fact held only one Royal *Séance* in the Parlement of Paris under duress in May 1563. Some of the ceremonial attributes of the *Lit de Justice* were adopted off and on for the Royal *Séance* after 1549; then the memorandum of 1560 set ceremonial guidelines which required black-robed and red-robed parlementary garb for the *Séance* and the *Lit de Justice* respectively. All along, however, the conservative constitutional course which Du Tillet originally charted for the *Lit de Justice*, requiring convocation in the Parlement of Paris and the presence of a constitutional issue on the docket, prevailed until 1563.

In that year Charles IX abruptly severed the institutional tie between the *Lit de Justice* and the Parlement of Paris by convoking a Majority *Lit de Justice* in the Parlement of Rouen followed by two more in Bordeaux and Toulouse. Still, even Charles IX reverted once again to Du Tillet's conservative stance when he held three Royal *Séances* in the Parlement of Paris in 1569, 1571, and 1572 and then convoked a *Lit de Justice* there in 1573 concerned with the Law of Succession. Finally, Henry III planned one *Lit de Justice* assembly in 1585 and never convoked it, but he held at least three Royal *Séances* in 1580, 1581, and 1583 where he forced financial edicts through the Parlement of Paris on legal grounds of *necessitas*. The point should be emphasized, therefore, that in the sixteenth century the Royal *Séance*, not the *Lit de Justice*, first served as a legislative weapon to register financial edicts until the year 1597, when Henry IV tried unsuccessfully to draft a *Lit de Justice* assembly for such service.

Now some light can be shed on a vexing matter, the elusive modern theory of "absolutism," which no two historians define in the same manner. The concept has been conspicuously excluded from the discussion thus far, because it distorts historical perspective. When applied without discrimination to Francis I, Henry IV, Louis XIV, as well as others in between and after, the name absolutism becomes nothing more than an empty synonym for monarchy in early modern France.[53] There was no common tie which bound together so-called absolute monarchies over centuries, certainly not the *Lit de Justice* assembly. The discourse of *parlementaires* upholds that contention. In 1583 the word "absolute" applied to royal authority indicated a commonplace, that the French monarch was the source of law: he was the *living law* but also the *debtor of justice*, technically above the law but bound by reason to observe it. In 1632 the *parlementaires* accepted the king's command as "absolute authority" in one breath and in the next secured from him the promise that the absolute command entailed no precedent. When the queen was given "absolute authority" by the regency declaration in 1643, she became head of the Regency Council. Even the feisty *avocat* Omer Talon in the 1640's would not have objected to Louis XIV's demonstration of "absolute power" if the king had reached his majority. The question thus remains for France, as well as for England, whether kings could subscribe to absolutism before modern historians invented that theory.[54] Since the term absolutism in France originally was coined to fit the later reign of Louis XIV,[55] its application to earlier reigns telescopes time, obscuring the particular facets of constitutional ideology which molded varied types of monarchy—juristic, dynastic, and absolutist.

The argument set forth here points to diversity over the centuries, not similarity. In the early sixteenth century the convergence of contemporary practice and historical theory produced the *Lit de Justice*, where

[53] Such allegations are common. Knecht, *Francis I and Absolute Monarchy*, makes this case and ties the *Lit de Justice* to it; ibid., *Francis I* (following Doucet), pp. 360-361, reiterates the charge. Many consider that the reign of Henry IV ushered in absolutism; see Church, *Constitutional Thought*, where strands of constitutionalism and absolutism are interwoven, and Keohane, *Philosophy and the State in France*, which follows that lead; as well as Giesey, *Juristic Basis of Dynastic Right*, Salmon, *Society in Crisis*, and Mousnier, *Institutions of France under the Absolute Monarchy*, I, 640-642.

[54] See the remarks of Conrad S. R. Russell, "Monarchies, Wars, and Estates in England, France, and Spain, c. 1580 – c. 1640," *Legislative Studies Quarterly*, VII, 2 (May 1982), 205-220, which analyzes the pressures on varied "constitutions" brought to bear by the escalating costs of warfare in those years; and the citation of James W. Daly, "The Idea of Absolute Monarchy in Seventeenth Century England," *Historical Journal*, XXI (1978), 227-250, for the meaning of "absolute" in English governance.

[55] The historical definition of the term is discussed by Rowen, "Louis XIV and Absolutism," pp. 302-316, in John C. Rule, ed., *Louis XIV and the Craft of Kingship* (Columbus, 1969).

kings (and on occasion queens), princes and peers, Crown officers, *par-lementaires*, invited guests, and sometimes deputies from the three Estates, discussed French Public Law in the Grand-chambre. The ceremonial ritual and discourse observed there articulated a number of constitutional precepts, most shared, some not. There was general consensus on the juristic distinction between the "king's two bodies"; the definition of the king as political spouse, or tutor, of the *chose publique*; the royal obligation as constitutional legislator to maintain and observe Public Law; the adherence to legal-hereditary succession focused on the royal *dignité* conferred by Public Law. There was endemic conflict over the alleged separation of constitutional functions (royal-legislative, parlementary-judicial); the role of Parlement as co-legislator, or co-tutor, of the realm; and the steady struggle of the Parisian Parlement to establish hegemony as the supreme Court in France. What might have been the institutional corollaries of these interesting developments, which were cut short by decades of civil and religious wars, cannot be known. But the replacement of one maxim, *The kingdom is never vacant*, by another, *The king never dies*, already evident in the later sixteenth century, bespoke the change of constitutional *mentalité* which was in the offing.

Now another seemingly irresolvable dilemma can be explained: the presumed laissez-faire attitude of Parlement toward the purported abuses of the *Lit de Justice* assembly. It has been suggested that the majority of sixteenth-century legists were loath to recognize any royal misuse of *Lits de Justice* to force registration of edicts of Parlement.[56] But the fact is that criticism of the *Lit de Justice* by legists and *parlementaires* was lacking because the assembly had not functioned in that manner during this time. The *Lit de Justice* emerged as a constitutional forum treating Public Law measures in 1527 and 1537, and it acquired historical and theoretical legitimacy in the 1540's and 1550's. The assembly maintained its unique constitutional function in the 1560's and in 1573, and it was retained in constitutional reserve during the 1570's and 1580's, when the Royal *Séance* was drafted to serve as a legislative vehicle. Finally, this whole pattern remained undisturbed until the *Lit de Justice* of Henry IV in 1597. Thus there could be no complaints about the abuse of the *Lit de Justice* as a legislative weapon in the sixteenth century. Such complaints appeared in the later seventeenth century and in the eighteenth century, to be sure, but that was long after the constitutional distinction between *Lits de Justice* and Royal *Séances* had disappeared. At the turn of the sev-

---

[56] Church, *Constitutional Thought*, pp. 150-151.

enteenth century, therefore, it is not surprising to find humanist treatises providing additional luster for the historical reputation of the *Lit de Justice* assembly.

The two treatises of André du Chesne, *Les Antiquitez et recherches . . . des roys de France* and *Les Antiquitez et recherches . . . des huict Parlemens*, were obviously inspired by Du Tillet's work on the *Lit de Justice* as well as his division of subjects into two *Recueils*.[57] Du Chesne ranked the *Lit de Justice* assembly right along with the other public ceremonies, Coronation, *Entrée*, and Funeral;[58] and he reaffirmed the medieval origins of the *Lit de Justice* in the Grand-chambre of the Parlement of Paris.[59] The treatise of Louis d'Orléans, *Ouvertures des Parlements*, portrayed the *Lit de Justice* of the kings of France held in the Parlement of Paris as a unique organ of government housed in the famous Palais de Justice, linked the assembly with the French constitution, and liberally drew proof for his case from Du Tillet's *Recueil des roys de France*.[60] And the treatise of Antoine Arnauld, *La Justice aux pieds du roy*, eulogized the *Lit de Justice* assembly as an ancient French tradition.[61] Yet given the rare convocation of such assemblies and the strict conditions under which they were convoked in the previous decades, crises connected with French Public Law, an astute observer of the scene might have predicted that the *Lit de Justice* would recede from time and mind unless called forth

[57] André du Chesne, *Les Antiquitez et recherches de la grandeur et majesté des roys de France* (Paris, 1609); and *Les Antiquitez et recherches des villes, chasteaux et places plus remarquable de toute la France, divisées en huict livres selon l'ordre et ressort des huict Parlemens* (Paris, 1609).

[58] Du Chesne, *Les Antiquitez et recherches . . . des roys de France*, bk. II, pp. 339-530.

[59] Du Chesne, *Les Antiquitez et recherches . . . des huict Parlemens*, pt. I, bk. I, chaps. I-XIX.

[60] Louis d'Orléans, *Les Ouvertures des Parlements faictes par les roys de France, tenant leur Lict de Justice* (Lyon, 1620), first published in Paris, 1607. For passages on the *Lit de Justice*, pp. 37, 51, 91, 137, 155-156, 160-161, 191, 237, 241-242, 248, 272, 530; and those citing Du Tillet, pp. 155-156, 161-162, 177, 249. For passages recounting the antiquity of French justice and extolling the Palais de Justice as the seat of the *Lit de Justice* assembly, pp. 403-404 (Deuxiesme remonstrance faicte au Parlement de Paris . . . 1590), pp. 399-446, especially p. 50, ". . . la main de justice qu'ils portent avec leur sceptre . . . n'est advenu qu'aux Roys de France, pource que la justice est née avec la France, et a son droict heredital en la terre de France. Il y a des pays qui sont doiiez de choses rares. . . . Aussi n'y atil qu'une France, où s'exercent les vrayes fonctions de la justice."

[61] Antoine Arnauld, *La Justice aux pieds du roy pour les Parlemens de France* (n.p., 1608), sets the theme throughout.

once more with the advent of a major constitutional crisis. On 15 May 1610 that crisis ensued when Henry IV was assassinated and the Crown of France passed to his eight-year-old son, Louis XIII. In the hours immediately following the tragedy a *Lit de Justice* assembly was convoked which broke all established rules for the ceremonial comportment of a new king and triggered a reformulation of French constitutional ideology.

X

THE DYNASTIC MONARCHY IN FRENCH CONSTITUTIONAL IDEOLOGY: THE INAUGURAL *LIT DE JUSTICE* ASSEMBLY OF 1610

> When contemplating you [Louis XIII] it seems that we behold the *living image of the deceased* which assures us that there is not a loss of that great sun [= Henry IV] but rather an eclipse of it whereby its light, no sooner obscured in one place, appears in another [= Louis XIII]. *Achille (I) de Harlay (1610)*

ON 14 MAY 1610 the Parlement of Paris had vacated the Grand-chambre for the post-Coronation festivities of the queen and were assembled in the Convent of the Augustinians when the news of Henry IV's assassination was received.[1] The *parlementaires* were shocked by the dire news and confused by conflicting reports. They sent for First President Achille

[1] Five main sources cover the sequence of events from the death of Henry IV through the proceedings of the *Lit de Justice* assembly. (1) The register of Parlement, A.N. X1a 1829, fols. 226v-233v (15 May 1610), is contained in Dupuy, *Traité de la majorité*, pp. 460-474, cited here. Louis (II) du Tillet, Sieur de Senelles (or Servoles), clerk in Parlement, took the office on 22 January 1610. (2) *Le Mercure françois; ou, La suite de l'histoire de 1605-1644* (Paris, 1605-1644), I, fols. 427r-434v. (3) The report of Jacques Gillot, *Relation faite par maître Jacques Gillot, conseiller d'Eglise à la Grand'chambre du Parlement de Paris, de ce que se passa audit Parlement séant aux Augustins, touchant le régence de la reine Marie de Médicis, mère du roi Louis XIII, les 14 et 15 mai 1610*, eds. Michaud et Poujoulat, *Nouvelle collection des mémoires* (Paris, 1838), XI, 474-484, cited here (published also in Dupuy, *Traité de la majorité*, pp. 475-495). Gillot was confirmed as a councillor in Parlement in 1573; Maugis, *Histoire du Parlement*, III, 245. (4) Nicolas Rigault's continuation of Jacques-Auguste de Thou, *Histoire universelle de Jacques-Auguste de Thou avec la suite par Nicolas Rigault* [bk. III] (The Hague, 1740), X, 288-308. De Thou became a councillor in Parlement in 1579, president in 1595; Rigault was a *parlementaire* and keeper of the royal library, and he added three books to the *Histoire universelle* of De Thou which covered the years 1607-1610. (5) Maximilien de Béthune, Duc de Sully, *Mémoires du Sully, principal ministre de Henri-le-Grand* [bk. XXVIII] (nouv. ed., Paris, 1814), V, 130-144. The Duke of Sully (1560-1641) was a councillor and minister of Henry IV.

(I) de Harlay to assume command of the Court and dispatched the *gens du roi* (Louis Servin and Cardin Le Bret) to confer with Queen Marie de Médicis at the palace of the Louvre. The *gens du roi* met with the royal party at the Louvre and then returned to Parlement. They reported that the queen was in council with Chancellor Nicolas (II) Brulart de Sillery, some princes and lords, including the Duke of Sully, and her eight-year-old son addressed by all as King Louis XIII. They described the dreadful spectacle of Henry IV's body lying on a bed at the Louvre, and the *parlementaires* then and there grieved for the dead king in stunned silence. The *gens du roi* also relayed the queen's wish that Parlement remain assembled "to give advice" if requested and her intention to undertake the regency of the government.[2] The Duke of Epernon and the Duke of Guise then visited Parlement briefly and emphasized the necessity for a swift declaration of the regency.[3] Obviously the *parlementaires* were familiar with the procedure used to declare the two previous regencies (*lettres patentes* issued in the new king's name and sent to Parlement for registration), because they discussed its application in the reigns of Charles IX (legally a minor in 1560) and Henry III (residing in Poland in 1574).[4] Nevertheless, almost immediately after the dukes left and without awaiting further instructions, the Court deliberated on the regency matter and issued the following *arrêt*:

> ... the said Court has declared and does declare the said queen mother of the king [Marie de Médicis] regent in France to have [charge of] the administration of the affairs of the kingdom during the minority of the said lord, her son, with full power and authority.[5]

[2] Dupuy, *Traité de la majorité* [Reg. Parl.], pp. 460-462; Gillot, *Relation*, pp. 474-476, noting that the *gens du roi* also knew that provincial governors had gone to the Louvre to pay homage to the new king and that other lords had been dispatched to keep order in outlying areas (pp. 476-478); De Thou (Rigault), *Histoire universelle*, pp. 288-290. Servin was an *avocat* at the Parlement of Tours, transferred to Paris in 1594, and Le Bret was an *avocat* in 1604; Maugis, *Histoire du Parlement*, III, 338-339, 334.

[3] Gillot, *Relation*, pp. 476-477. The registers of Parlement mention only the Duke of Guise; Dupuy, *Traité de la majorité* [Reg. Parl.], p. 463. Nicolas (II) Brulart, Sieur de Sillery, was confirmed as chancellor on 26 March 1608; Maugis, *Histoire du Parlement*, III, 298.

[4] Gillot, *Relation*, p. 477. For evidence that Parlement knew the usual procedure, see the explanation the Court gave to the Prince of Condé; Dupuy, *Traité de la majorité* [Ce qui se passa au Parlement ... le vingt-troisième juillet 1610], pp. 496-500.

[5] Dupuy, *Traité de la majorité* [Reg. Parl.], p. 462; Gillot, *Relation*, pp. 476-478; De Thou (Rigault), *Histoire universelle*, p. 289-290.

At 6:30 that same evening deputies from Parlement promptly took the regency *arrêt* to the queen at the Louvre.[6] Thus within three hours of Henry IV's death, the Parlement of Paris in a unilateral action proclaimed the regency.

Upon receiving the regency *arrêt* from Parlement, Queen Marie de Médicis sent the deputies back to the Court with a message of appreciation for such prompt action. At the same time she commanded that Parlement remain assembled to give further counsel if necessary.[7] The *parlementaires* remained in session as directed, and a royal messenger soon arrived with further instructions: on the advice of the Royal Council Marie de Médicis intended to bring the king to Parlement the next day to "hold his *Lit de Justice* [assembly] confirming and executing the *arrêt* of regency."[8] The *Lit de Justice* of 15 May would be a solemn ceremony, Parlement was told, so the Court must assemble in the "customary manner." Accepting the command for the *Lit de Justice* without further deliberation, President Harlay ordered the Court to appear in red robes at six o'clock the next morning to receive the king.[9] The red-robed *parlementaires* assembled in the Convent of the Augustinians the next day as commanded. Before the royal party arrived, however, several procedural matters were treated.[10] The *parlementaires* received notice from the queen that she would accompany the young king during the *Lit de Justice* ceremony.[11] They swore in an ecclesiastical councillor as a

---

[6] See the sources in n. 5. The *arrêt* appears also in Isambert, *Recueil général des anciennes lois*, XVI, 3-4.

[7] Dupuy, *Traité de la majorité* [Reg. Parl.], p. 462; Gillot, *Relation*, p. 478; De Thou (Rigault), *Histoire universelle*, pp. 290-291.

[8] Gillot, *Relation*, pp. 477-478; De Thou (Rigault), *Histoire universelle*, pp. 290-291. But the registers of Parlement, Dupuy, *Traité de la majorité* [Reg. Parl.], p. 463, do not mention that the *arrêt* was to be "confirmed" in the *Lit de Justice*. All accounts report simply that the queen was "counseled" or that the decision was made "in Council." But Sully, *Mémoires*, p. 139, was more explicit: "Immediately after seeing the dead king, the first act of Parlement was to defer the regency to the queen mother; as a result they [the Royal Council] decided it was necessary for the king ... to hold his *Lit de Justice* [assembly]...." In addition, the author of *Cérémonies* (see below, Chap. XI, n. 6) admitted that the Royal Council intended to declare Louis XIII as king in the *Lit de Justice*.

[9] Dupuy, *Traité de la majorité* [Reg. Parl.], p. 462; Gillot, *Relation*, pp. 477-478; De Thou (Rigault), *Histoire universelle*, p. 292.

[10] Dupuy, *Traité de la majorité* [Reg. Parl.], p. 464; Gillot, *Relation*, p. 478; De Thou (Rigault), *Histoire universelle*, p. 292.

[11] Gillot, *Relation*, p. 478. Earlier the queen stated only that she would bring Louis XIII to the *Lit de Justice*, not that she would stay for the proceedings (see above, n. 8).

peer despite his lack of qualifications and justified the hasty act on grounds of the grandeur required by the occasion.[12] And the presidents of Parlement conversed secretly with the queen's messenger on a matter which was not divulged by the registers of Parlement.[13]

The arrival of the royal party created a series of difficulties.[14] The most interesting problem, a dispute over seating, occurred when four bishops (all ecclesiastical peers) decided to sit in high seats to the right of the royal throne. President Harlay argued against the move on grounds of ceremonial protocol. In Royal *Séances* they would sit (in the capacity of bishops) in high seats to the right of the king, Harlay said, but in *Lit de Justice* assemblies they must sit (in the capacity of ecclesiastical peers) to the left because seats to the right were reserved for princes of the blood, lay peers, and officers of the Crown. Studiously ignoring President Harlay's admonitions, the bishops seated themselves to the right of the royal throne anyway, loudly proclaiming themselves as "born councillors" of the king. The first president insisted that the four bishops move to the left and tried to dislodge them but the bishops, exuding menacing retorts and gestures of defiance, held fast. Adding to the confusion, four cardinals arrived on the scene, saw that the high seats to the left of the throne (reserved for the bishops) were empty, and quickly took them.[15]

[12] Gillot, *Relation*, p. 478; De Thou (Rigault), *Histoire universelle*, p. 292. The rules required that an ecclesiastical peer must be twenty-five years old and hold the office of an annointed archbishop. The councillor in question fulfilled neither requirement.

[13] Gillot, *Relation*, p. 478.

[14] The Duke of Mayenne (as grand chamberlain) should have been seated below the king on the steps to the throne, but he was seated on a chair in the center of the parquet due to an infirmity which prevented placement on the steps; Gillot, *Relation*, p. 479. The anonymous drawing (Figure 7) portrays this detail correctly. Mayenne's place was taken by the young Duke of Elbeuf (who does not appear in the figure), creating a departure from protocol by seating a child to represent an officer of the Crown; Dupuy, *Traité de la majorité* [Reg. Parl.], p. 464; Gillot, *Relation*, p. 478; *Mercure françois*, I, fol. 427r.

[15] Gillot, *Relation*, pp. 478-479; De Thou (Rigault), *Histoire universelle*, p. 292. This dispute over seating involved others as well. Influenced by the confrontation, the Archbishop of Paris tried to usurp a seat at the right of the throne; confused by the precipitous movements, the anxious constable moved three times searching for a proper place. The registers of Parlement, Dupuy, *Traité de la majorité* [Reg. Parl.], pp. 460-474, did not record the quarrel of the bishops over precedence in the *Lit de Justice*. Later on during the Royal Funeral procession of Henry IV the bishops again contested precedence. Although dressed in mourning and expected to accompany the encoffined body (representing the dead king Henry), they took places by the crowned effigy of Henry IV (rep-

The battle over seating was still being waged when Chancellor Sillery arrived and sat on the bench ahead of the first president to await the arrival of the king.[16] Informed of the seating contest, the chancellor requested two presidents of Parlement to convince the bishops of the impropriety of this dispute and to request that they move to the left. The attempted conciliation failed, and the jostling and arguing continued.[17]

As the king, queen, and royal party entered the parquet of the assembly, accompanied by women of the royal court,[18] some irritated *parlementaires* decried the lapse of procedural rules allowing women inside the parquet.[19] Since the arrival of the royal entourage did not end the heated argument over seating arrangements, this unseemly spectacle greeted the young king as he stood at the foot of the dais.[20] By royal command the bishops were peremptorily ordered to vacate the places at the right of the royal throne. Forced to move, they tacitly accepted the status of ecclesiastical peers by sitting in high seats to the left of the throne but now had to sit after the cardinals and considered the arrangement thoroughly demeaning.[21] When everyone was seated at last in an appointed (or usurped) place, bringing order to the raucous scene,

---

resenting the royal *dignité*), pushing and elbowing the red-robed *parlementaires* accompanying the effigy all the way from the Louvre to Notre Dame one day and from Paris to Saint-Denis the next day. For this incident, consult Giesey, *Royal Funeral Ceremony*, pp. 122-124 and n. 71.

[16] Dupuy, *Traité de la majorité* [Reg. Parl.], p. 465; Gillot, *Relation*, p. 479; De Thou (Rigault), *Histoire universelle*, p. 292. The chancellor was accompanied by five or six *maîtres des requêtes* and preceded by an honor guard of two of the Court's most senior councillors.

[17] Gillot, *Relation*, p. 479; De Thou (Rigault), *Histoire universelle*, p. 292.

[18] Dupuy, *Traité de la majorité* [Reg. Parl.], p. 465; *Mercure françois*, I, fol. 427v; Gillot, *Relation*, p. 479; De Thou (Rigault), *Histoire universelle*, p. 293. Louis XIII rode a small white horse from the Louvre to the Convent of the Augustinians, accompanied by princes, peers, officers of the Crown, and a great number of nobles all on foot, and by the queen in her carriage followed by some princesses and duchesses. The drums of the king's guards warned the Court of his approach, and an honor guard of *parlementaires* (third and fourth presidents, four of the oldest councillors) was sent to the door to greet him. For further comments on the triumphal notes sounded, see the remarks of the author of *Cérémonies* below, n. 51, and Sully, n. 56.

[19] Gillot, *Relation*, p. 479; De Thou (Rigault), *Histoire universelle*, p. 293.

[20] Gillot, *Relation*, p. 479.

[21] De Thou (Rigault), *Histoire universelle*, pp. 292-293, who castigated the cardinals for deliberately taking advantage of the confusion in order to usurp the place of the bishops.

Louis XIII was enthroned under a canopy strewn with golden fleurs-de-lis and Queen Marie de Médicis was seated at his right under the canopy. The king was dressed in violet (or purple) mourning garb and the queen in a black mourning dress and veil.[22] Following Louis XIII's enthronement Chancellor Sillery left the bench of the presidents and occupied his official chair placed at the foot of the royal dais and covered by material extending from the thronal paraphernalia.[23] The anonymous drawing (Figure 7) which was made of this *Lit de Justice* assembly held in the Convent of the Augustinians provides a fairly reasonable replica of the ceremonial configuration and the disposition of the main royal and parlementary officials in attendance.[24]

[22] Dupuy, *Traité de la majorité* [Reg. Parl.], pp. 462-463; *Mercure françois*, I, fol. 427v; Gillot, *Relation*, p. 479, who noted that the king was wearing a pleated cap and that the thronal paraphernalia harked back to Louis XII; and De Thou (Rigault), *Histoire universelle*, p. 293, who identified violet as the mourning color.

[23] Dupuy, *Traité de la majorité* [Reg. Parl.], p. 464; *Mercure françois*, I, fol. 428r; De Thou (Rigault), *Histoire universelle*, p. 293; and Gillot, *Relation*, p. 479, who observed the ceremonial connection of the throne and the chancellor's chair as well as the departure from protocol allowing the Count of Anguien (Louis de Bourbon), a child only four or five years old, to be seated with the royal entourage. The king and queen were seated with lay peers to the right, ecclesiastical peers to the left. At the king's feet the young representative of the grand chamberlain was seated on a pillow, and below the grand chamberlain's representative the provost of Paris reclined.

[24] The watercolor drawing (anonymous), Figure 7, provides a reasonably accurate picture of the scene; B.N. Dépt. des Estampes. The seating arrangements in the drawing correspond fairly well with the account given in the registers of Parlement (Dupuy, *Traité de la majorité*, pp. 462-464). In the high seats to the right of the king ten princes, peers, and officers are listed in the registers, and nine appear in the drawing. In the high seats to the left nine cardinals, archbishops, and bishops are listed in the registers, and ten appear in the drawing. Left out of the scene are the representative of the grand chamberlain and the chancellor's chair at the foot of the throne. The odd seating in the parquet of the Duke of Mayenne, grand chamberlain, is shown. In the drawing, the room in the Convent of the Augustinians looks much like the Grand-chambre of the Palais de Justice in décor, because the walls are covered with tapestries decorated with fleurs-de-lis, crowns, and Louis XII's interlaced initials *LL*. A crew of workers must have spent the night and dawn hours of 14 and 15 May hanging the canopy and tapestries and constructing the thronal apparatus and adjoining high seats, paraphernalia which had to be transported from the Palais de Justice to the Convent of the Augustinians several blocks away. The tapestries were actually hung in the Augustinians that day, as the comments of Gillot (see above, n. 22) and President Harlay (see below, n. 34) reveal. In the

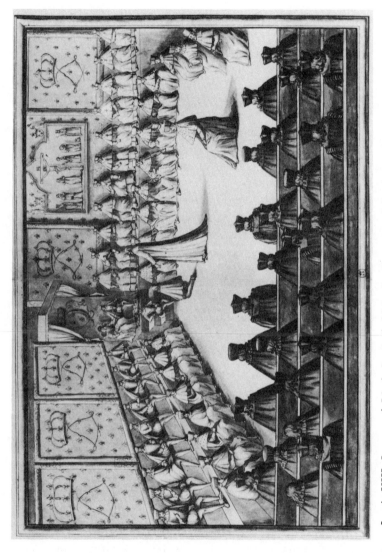

7. Louis XIII: Inaugural *Lit de Justice* held in the Convent of the Augustinians, 1610.

Chancellor Sillery opened the proceedings. He went up the steps of the dais and conferred with the king and queen, returned to his seat, and gave the floor to the queen.[25] Marie de Médicis presented a short address soliciting counsel and advice from those present.

> Messieurs, since God has taken unto himself our good king, my lord, by so tragic an accident, I have brought the king, my son, to you and pray that you attend to him as you must in memory of his father, for yourselves, and for your country. I wish that he follow your good counsel in the conduct of his affairs, and I beg of you to advise him as your consciences direct you.[26]

Following this request for counsel the queen rapidly descended from her seat and managed to reach the middle of the parquet in an attempt to leave the assembly. This surprise action engendered heated debate in the chamber as to whether or not the "Salic Law" forbade the queen's presence beside the king during the proceedings. The *parlementaires* insisted that her presence was appropriate, because she had already been declared regent by the Court's *arrêt* the day before. The queen adamantly refused to remain, but she was hemmed in by a crowd of *parlementaires*, making departure difficult, and eventually returned to her place beside the king.[27]

The young king Louis XIII officially proposed the regency, although the noise in the room made it difficult to hear his childish voice.

> Messieurs, since God has taken unto himself the deceased king, my lord and father, I have come here on the advice and counsel of the queen, my mother, in order to tell you that I wish to follow your good counsel in the conduct of my affairs, hoping that God will give me the grace to profit from the good examples and instructions which I have received from my lord and father. Thus I beg of you

---

drawing the canopy is positioned flatly against the left wall instead of diagonally in the corner. The inclusion here of the famous painting *Le Retable du Parlement*, which decorated the Grand-chambre from the later fifteenth century, is a figment of the artist's imagination.

[25] Gillot, *Relation*, pp. 479-480.

[26] Dupuy, *Traité de la majorité* [Reg. Parl.], pp. 465-466, and repeated in *Mercure françois*, I, fol. 428v. The wording differs slightly in Gillot, *Relation*, pp. 479-480, and De Thou (Rigault), *Histoire universelle*, p. 293.

[27] Ibid., all sources. Figure 7 does not convey the crowded conditions which prevailed in the assembly.

to give me your advice and to deliberate presently on the proposal which I have commanded the chancellor to present to you.[28]

His words echoed the queen's suggestion that the *Lit de Justice* had been summoned to deliberate upon a regency declaration issued by the king enthroned in the assembly. Just as he finished speaking, Marie de Médicis made a second attempt to leave, ostensibly excusing herself while deliberations took place on the royal declaration of the regency. But again her exit was immediately thwarted when President Harlay personally intervened. There would be no deliberations today, Harlay stated, because the queen had been declared regent already by Parlement's *arrêt* given the preceding day, and now that *arrêt* needed only to be published.[29] Once again under duress the queen returned to her seat.

Taking the floor Chancellor Sillery continued the strategy begun by the queen and king. He called attention to the importance of the *Lit de Justice* assembly as the first official act of the new king.

> ... God has taken unto himself the deceased king, and the first action which the king, his son who reigns at present, wished to undertake following the wise advice of the queen his mother, was to visit his Parlement in order to hold his *Lit de Justice* [assembly], an act which gives hope that he will carefully render to his subjects that good justice which is the principal duty of royal office.[30]

The chancellor presented a notion of dynastic succession befitting the problematic accession of a minor. He stated that the power of the deceased Henry IV's active *will* (*volonté*) still had the force of law beyond his death and far outweighed ordinary written testaments. In the presence of witnesses the deceased king had *willed* before his death that the queen would be regent in case of his premature demise, Sillery stated, and that command was being fulfilled in the *Lit de Justice* assembly. Succession to the French throne could not be weakened by the rule of a minor king, the chancellor concluded, because the young monarch would be

[28] Dupuy, *Traité de la majorité* [Reg. Parl.], p. 466, repeated in *Mercure françois*, I, fols. 428v-429r. Gillot, *Relation*, p. 480, notes the king's weak voice, and De Thou (Rigault), *Histoire universelle*, p. 294, gives slightly different wording.

[29] Dupuy, *Traité de la majorité* [Reg. Parl.], p. 466; De Thou (Rigault), *Histoire universelle*, p. 293.

[30] Dupuy, *Traité de la majorité* [Reg. Parl.], p. 467; *Mercure françois*, I, fol. 429r-v; Gillot, *Relation*, p. 480; De Thou (Rigault), *Histoire universelle*, p. 294.

guided by the queen mother acting as regent of the government and agent of the *will* of the deceased king Henry IV.[31]

Following the chancellor's speech, President Harlay addressed Louis XIII enthroned upon the dais.[32]

We who have experienced that miserable accident would be in despair were it not for the consolation that we receive from your presence. When contemplating you it seems that we behold the *living image of the deceased* (*l'image vive du défunt*) which assures us that there is not a loss of that great sun [= Henry IV] but rather an eclipse of it whereby its light, no sooner obscured in one place, appears in another [= Louis XIII].[33]

According to Harlay, Henry IV and Louis XIII both shared the same hereditary "rare virtues," that is, royal qualities necessary for kingship and passed from father to son. Quite rightly, then, since Louis XIII was "successor to the hereditary Crown ... of Henry IV," the *Lit de Justice* functioned simultaneously in two dimensions, as a funereal commemoration for the one and as a celebrative succession ceremony for the other. Louis XIII was enthroned in the *Lit de Justice* assembly under a canopy and in a room decorated with the emblems of Louis XII, his progenitor, Harlay said, and the young king was the thirteenth of that name to convoke a *Lit de Justice* assembly. The first president offered the new king homage and an oath of fidelity on behalf of the Parlement of Paris, and he suggested that a medal be struck with the inscription *Marie de Médicis, sûreté de la France* to honor the new regency.[34] At the close of President Harlay's speech, the chancellor took the floor again.

[31] Ibid., all sources.

[32] The presidents of Parlement knelt before the king to request recognition, but the young Louis XIII neglected to order them to rise and the chancellor corrected the oversight; Gillot, *Relation*, p. 480; De Thou (Rigault), *Histoire universelle*, p. 294.

[33] Dupuy, *Traité de la majorité* [Reg. Parl.], pp. 467-469; *Mercure françois*, I, fols. 429v-431r; Gillot, *Relation*, pp. 480-481; and De Thou (Rigault), *Histoire universelle*, pp. 294-295, who gives a précis only.

[34] Ibid., all sources. Harlay remarked that the chance juxtaposition of the festively decorated City of Paris (awaiting the queen's *Entrée*) and the mournful aura (cast by the assassination) mirrored the dual funereal-celebrative elements of the *Lit de Justice* assembly. On Louis IX as the sub-genearch of the Bourbon line, see Giesey, *Juristic Basis of Dynastic Right*, pp. 36-37. The medal advocated by Harlay was supposed to replicate a coin struck in honor of Helene, wife of the Roman emperor Constantine, engraved with the words *Sûreté de l'Estat*. Kantorowicz, *Oriens Augusti—Lever du Roi*, Dumbarton Oaks Papers, no. 17

Despite President Harlay's firm statement that the session would entail no deliberations because the queen already had been declared regent, Chancellor Sillery solicited opinions on the regency declaration anyway, first from the king and queen, second (in a surprise move) from Parlement, and third from princes, dukes, peers, and Crown officers.[35] Then the chancellor ordered the doors of the chamber opened, and the crowd waiting outside pressed into the overcrowded chamber.[36] The next address was given by the *avocat* Louis Servin. Like the president and chancellor, Servin rationalized the instant succession of a minor king on this occasion. He contrasted the French Law of Succession providing governmental stability with the Roman practice of election allowing chaotic interregna, proffered the example of Queen Blanche of Castile, mother of King Louis IX (Saint Louis) as a prototype for the present regency, and alluded to Louis IX as a progenitor of Louis XIII. Reiterating the view of the president, Servin emphasized the dual funereal-celebrative nature of this *Lit de Justice* assembly wherein last honors for the deceased king were rendered at the same time that the advent of his successor was proclaimed. The continuity of government guaranteed by French dynastic succession was signified by the French fleur-de-lis, he said, which was a visual symbol far more powerful than the fleur-de-lis imprinted on coins of the Roman emperors. Servin praised the Parlement of Paris as the Court of peers and the supreme Court of France; he identified the *Lit de Justice* assembly as the public forum wherein the "first-born" of the royal family, Henry IV's Bourbon successor Louis XIII (descended from Louis IX), was instantly acclaimed king on this day; and he noted that the Parisian Court would send the official announcement of succession to the other provinces in France. Servin explained that Parlement's swift rendition of the regency *arrêt* the day before resulted from an emergency situation and requested that the king, assisted by blood princes, dukes, peers, and Crown officers,

---

(New York, 1963), pp. 119-177, discusses the unsuccessful attempt to interest Henry IV in a project for a medallic history of French kings.

[35] Gillot, *Relation*, pp. 481-482, the only account which gives the order of consultation. De Thou (Rigault), *Histoire universelle*, p. 295, commented that the chancellor insisted upon consultation by orders to emphasize the fact that Parlement did not have the authority to issue a regency *arrêt* independently of the princes and peers. Note that the registers of Parlement, Dupuy, *Traité de la majorité* [Reg. Parl.], p. 470, and *Mercure françois*, I, fol. 431v, delete all mention of consultation.

[36] Dupuy, *Traité de la majorité* [Reg. Parl.], p. 470; *Mercure françois*, I, fol. 431v; Gillot, *Relation*, p. 482; De Thou (Rigault), *Histoire universelle*, p. 295.

now order publication of the regency declaration in all the other sovereign Courts of the kingdom.[37]

Ordinarily the chancellor would have read the royal declaration forthwith, but this day he solicited advice again in a second round of consultation.[38] Then he pronounced the royal regency declaration as follows:

> The king sitting in his *Lit de Justice* [assembly] with the advice of the princes of his blood, other princes, prelates, dukes and peers, and officers of his Crown, upon the request of his *procureur général* has declared and does declare the queen, his mother, regent in France in order to oversee his education and welfare and the administration of the affairs of his kingdom during his minority. The present *arrêt* will be published and registered in all the *baillages, sénéchausées*, and other royal tribunals within the competence of the Court as well as in all the other Courts of Parlement of his kingdom.[39]

At the close of this reading on 15 May President Harlay, amidst a rising swell of protesting murmurs, aggressively challenged the chancellor's failure to include a clause referring to Parlement's previous *arrêt* of 14 May. Affecting an air of innocence, Chancellor Sillery charged the deletion to simple oversight and stated that the clause would be written into the official record of the regency declaration.[40] The disputed clause "con-

---

[37] Dupuy, *Traité de la majorité* [Reg. Parl.], pp. 470-474; *Mercure françois*, I, fols. 432r-434v; Gillot, *Relation*, pp. 482-483. De Thou (Rigault), *Histoire universelle*, p. 295, gives a short version. Servin identified the Roman prototype as that bearing the legend, *L'Esperance Auguste, l'Esperance du Peuple Romain*. On the argument over "elective kingship," see Jackson, "Elective Kingship and Consensus Populi in Sixteenth-Century France," *Journal of Modern History* XXXXIV, 2 (June 1972), pp. 155-171.

[38] Gillot, *Relation*, p. 483; *Mercure françois*, I, fol. 434v; De Thou (Rigault), *Histoire universelle* [Reg. Parl.], p. 295. The registers of Parlement, Dupuy, *Traité de la majorité*, p. 474, omit the second round of advice as well as the first. It is quite likely that the presidents, who wished to claim the Court's *arrêt* as constitutive by avoiding deliberations, remained adamantly silent during both rounds of consultation.

[39] Gillot, *Relation*, pp. 483-484, alone gives an account of the first reading of this *arrêt*. De Thou (Rigault), *Histoire universelle*, p. 294, comments that the chancellor's silence about the earlier *arrêt* insinuated that Parlement did not have the authority to issue the document. The registers of Parlement, Dupuy, *Traité de la majorité* [Reg. Parl.], p. 474, do not record this first reading.

[40] Ibid., all sources. Again the registers of Parlement do not record the president's challenge.

forming with the *arrêt* given in his Court of Parlement yesterday [14 May]" was added to the regency declaration of 15 May, and the document was recorded in the registers of Parlement in that form.[41]

THE NEGLECTED CONSTITUTIONAL DIMENSION

Historical interpretations of these events of 14 and 15 May 1610 are seriously flawed, because the constitutional significance of the *Lit de Justice* itself has been obscured by the interesting political contest over the regency. As the tale usually is told, Parlement issued a regency *arrêt* and confirmed it in a *Lit de Justice*, aggrandizing its power at the expense of a monarchy weakened by minority kingship.[42] Yet when the events are reassessed, collating a number of sources including the registers of Parlement and focusing on the *Lit de Justice* assembly rather than the regency issue, the neglected constitutional dimension looms much larger than the peripheral political contest. At the outset it is important to remember that on the evening of 14 May Parlement's status was precarious. The Court sat isolated and anxious in the Convent of the Augustinians, its institutional tenure technically suspended by the death of the king, while the royal party at the palace of the Louvre formulated decisions of state, including the possible convocation of a *Lit de Justice* assembly, even before the regency was declared. Stymied in this interim position Parlement sent for President Harlay and dispatched the *gens du roi* (Servin and Le Bret) to assess the grave situation at the Louvre. On their return the *gens du roi* relayed to the Court the command of Marie de Médicis to remain in session for consultation, and they probably announced the queen's intention to undertake the regency. More than

[41] The registers of Parlement, Dupuy, *Traité de la majorité* [Reg. Parl.], p. 474, record the final version only. See also *Mercure françois*, I, fol. 434v; Gillot, *Relation*, pp. 483-484, regarding the addition. The text of the *arrêt* appears in Isambert, *Recueil général des anciennes lois*, XVI, 4-5. Note that the final words of Parlement's *arrêt* of 14 May giving the queen "full power and authority" were also omitted on 15 May, but no objections were raised.

[42] For instance, Berthold Zeller, *La Minorité de Louis XIII* (Paris, 1892-1897), I and II, barely notices the *Lit de Justice* assembly yet takes this position; Glasson, *Parlement de Paris*, I, 117-120, who does not consult the registers of Parlement, gives the standard view; and Shennan, *Parlement of Paris*, pp. 241-242, follows that interpretation.

likely they reported also on the royal proposal for a *Lit de Justice* which was under discussion at the Louvre.[43]

The Court's actual discussion of these propositions was not recorded, but the general tenor of Parlement's position was revealed in later actions. First, Parlement surely recognized the important procedural precedent which was set by the royal command to remain in session, that is, royal recognition of the institutional tenure of the Parlement of Paris beyond the death of a king. Parlement had claimed such corporate continuity since the fifteenth century, but the claim remained unacknowledged as new kings upon accession continued to issue *lettres patentes* of confirmation to the Court.[44] Thus when the queen and Royal Council commanded Parlement to remain assembled upon the death of Henry IV, the corporate continuity of that body was implicitly granted in royal quarters for the first time. Second, Parlement offered no objections to the proposed plans for a *Lit de Justice* assembly to acclaim Louis XIII as king. In fact it seized the opportunity to figure prominently as the supreme Court of France and co-tutor of the kingdom in this innovative ceremonial ritual by accepting the convening order without deliberations and cooperating amiably in that ceremony later. Third, Parlement reviewed the procedure for declaring regencies, royal *lettres patentes* sent to the Court for registration, and expected at any moment following the visit of two dukes, Epernon and Guise, to receive those letters from the Louvre. Yet before the requisite letters arrived, the Court deliberately misconstrued the queen's limited mandate for consultation as an order to act on the regency and issued a regency *arrêt* on the spot. The precipitous action reveals a formidable dilemma. Parlement was determined to facilitate plans for a *Lit de Justice*, which would inaugurate the young king within a parlementary nexus, but was loath to allow the promulgation of a regency declaration by a minor king, which would limit the Court's presumed authority as legislative tutor. Acting quite without precedent, therefore, Parlement took advantage of the emergency to

[43] The assumption is warranted, because the *avocat* Servin, one of the *gens du roi* seeking information for Parlement at the Louvre on 14 May, tendered a speech in the assembly the next day.

[44] In fact during the meeting of Francis I and his Conseil Étroit in the Salle Verte on 27 July 1527 after the king's hasty departure from the *Lit de Justice*, a royal *arrêt* was issued which specified that the Parlement of Paris must seek annual confirmation from the king. On the problem of confirmation, also see Giesey, *Royal Funeral Ceremony*, pp. 183-192, and Kantorowicz, *King's Two Bodies*, pp. 415-430.

inflate its role in regency government and issued a regency *arrêt* unilaterally.

The queen and Royal Council must have been astounded to receive the regency *arrêt* from Parlement just three hours after the assassination of the king. Clearly they envisaged the *Lit de Justice* as a kind of inauguration which would acclaim the successor without calling attention to his limited legislative capacity. Despite Parlement's intercession, therefore, the royal party proceeded as planned to convoke a *Lit de Justice* assembly for the next morning, 15 May. Then they planned new tactics for declaring the regency which would annul, or at least neutralize, the effects of Parlement's earlier *arrêt*. As a result, two incompatible themes are interwoven in the proceedings of the *Lit de Justice*: the inauguration of the young king, which elicited accord; and the contest over the regency, which caused dissension.

The question of the regency evoked opposing strategies over a fundamental issue: whether Louis XIII in the *Lit de Justice* assembly actually declared the regency on 15 May or just confirmed Parlement's regency *arrêt* issued the day before. Parlement linked the events of regency and inauguration sequentially and tried to sustain the Court's regency *arrêt* of 14 May in the *Lit de Justice* of 15 May. Conversely, the royal party conflated them and held that the regency *arrêt* must be issued in the Inaugural *Lit de Justice* assembly. The friction was apparent even before the assembly was convened. Marie de Médicis' ambivalence probably reflects the *parlementaires'* insistence that she attend the session as regent. The queen hesitated, consenting at first only to bring the young king to the assembly but deciding at the last moment to attend the ceremony with him. If the mysterious message sent by the queen to the Court before the session announced that she was not attending as regent, the Court ignored the contention. Certainly the behavior of the opposing parties during the *Lit de Justice* revealed the underlying tension. Marie de Médicis wished to identify the Inaugural *Lit de Justice* as the agency naming the regency, so she attempted twice to leave the assembly before deliberations on the regency took place. But the *parlementaires* intended to sustain the Court's regency *arrêt* of the day before, so they thwarted the queen's departure both times and declared her presence as regent proper.

Along those same lines the speeches of the royal party stressed the deliberative aspect of the *Lit de Justice*. The queen, king, and chancellor stated that the young king had convoked the assembly to seek advice on the regency question, which would be settled in the *Lit de Justice* on

15 May. Conversely, Parlement treated the regency as a fait accompli as of 14 May. President Harlay stated that the *Lit de Justice* would not be deliberative, because the queen had been declared regent the day before; and he seconded the point by offering homage and fidelity to the young king and soliciting a medal to commemorate the regency. Chancellor Sillery countered Parlement's assertion by soliciting advice anyway, not once but twice, and he changed the usual order of consultation by approaching the presidents of Parlement second, rather than third, in order to elicit the Court's cooperation.[45] At this point, therefore, the contestants had reached an impasse. Parlement had successfully blocked the queen's departure from the assembly, alleging her status as regent by the Court's prior *arrêt*; and the chancellor had requested consultation on the regency, insinuating that her status was not yet official, pending action in the *Lit de Justice*. The silence of the registers of Parlement underscores the Court's strategy. The clerk did not record that consultation took place in the *Lit de Justice* on 15 May, leaving the distinct impression that the assembly merely confirmed Parlement's prior regency *arrêt*.

The skirmish did not end there. At the close of the *Lit de Justice* Chancellor Sillery made another attempt to annul Parlement's regency *arrêt*. Apparently the *parlementaires* had understood that the Court's *arrêt* of 14 May would be mentioned in the regency declaration of 15 May, but the chancellor deleted that reference from his reading of the royal declaration. Vigorously challenged by President Harlay, the chancellor masked his omission as simple oversight and added the disputed clause to the royal declaration. Again the silence of the registers of Parlement bears witness to the Court's intentions. There is no mention of the argument between chancellor and president over the crucial deletion, and the record shows only the complete text of the final declaration, to which the clause had been added. Parlement thus deliberately left the impression for posterity that the Court's *arrêt* of 14 May had created the regency government in 1610.

Those who are unaware of the crucial main theme of the *Lit de Justice*, the unprecedented public inauguration of a minor king and his immediate exercise of legislative power, have treated the contest over the regency as paramount that day. Yet what strikes the historical imagination is not the contentious opposition between the royal party and the

[45] Note that the registers of Parlement, Dupuy, *Traité de la majorité* [Reg. Parl.], p. 470, and *Mercure françois*, I, fol. 431v, delete mention of consultation. Gillot, *Relation*, pp. 481-482, gives the account.

Parlement over the regency but the harmonious agreement of the two factions to acclaim the young Louis XIII as king in the *Lit de Justice* despite the lack of precedent for such action. Actively supporting the *Lit de Justice*, the *parlementaires* accepted the convening order without deliberations, allowed flagrant deviations from protocol in order to enhance the grandeur of the event, insisted that the four recalcitrant bishops recognize the session as a *Lit de Justice* by sitting at the left as ecclesiastical peers, and evoked the historical fiction of the medieval *Lit de Justice* to legitimize the whole undertaking. Even more importantly, the chancellor, president, and *avocat* all advanced compatible legal-philosophical and historical arguments with dynastic implications which were particularly suitable for the acclamation of a minor king.

Chancellor Sillery set the inaugural tone. He noted that the process of instant succession, father to son, had taken place, and he dubbed the *Lit de Justice* as the first official public act of the new king. To eradicate the legal problem of the king's minority, he maintained that the active *will* (*volonté*) of Henry IV had the force of law beyond his death and identified the *Lit de Justice* as the agency which carried out that *will* by declaring the queen as regent. The chancellor's argument ingeniously adapted medieval legal precepts to suit the moment. Doctrines of Roman Law had claimed that the prince's active *voluntas* inherent in him as a *persona publica* had the power of law. The prince in his corporal person dies, Baldus wrote, but the *dignitas* "seems to will even after his death because ... everything pleases the prince that is done by his judges even after his death, provided they do not act against the law."[46] Furthermore, jurists during previous centuries had agreed that written testaments did not regulate French royal succession, because the Crown devolved through legal-hereditary means, or "simple succession."[47] But Chancellor Sillery's adaptation of these precepts to the cause of dynastic succession failed to preserve the jurists' emphasis on the legal aspects of succession and rooted the active royal *will* in the undying dynastic line rather than in the immortal royal *dignité*. Chancellor Sillery pointed directly to the living child-king Louis XIII actually enthroned in the Inaugural *Lit de Justice* assembly when he spoke of continuity in the dynastic line, and the first president and *avocat* followed suit.

[46] On the concept of a public *voluntas* (Baldus on *Codex* 10, 1, rubr., n. 16, fol. 232v) as part of the movement from liturgical to law-centered kingship, see Kantorowicz, *King's Two Bodies*, pp. 93-97 and 400-419, nn. 296, 349.

[47] Consult Giesey, *Juristic Basis of Dynastic Right*, pp. 12-17, for analysis of that opinion, especially in the work of Jean de Terre Rouge.

President Harlay employed doctrines of a biogenetic stripe to explain the instant succession of a minor king. He signified the uniqueness, or sameness, of Henry IV and Louis XIII as partakers of royal qualities necessary for kingship and described Louis XIII enthroned in the *Lit de Justice* assembly as the *living image of the deceased*. Presenting a powerful metaphorical vision of dynastic continuity, Harlay allowed that passing clouds might cast a shadow over the sun [= Henry IV] in one place, but that sun [= Louis XIII] would nevertheless shine again in another. The president typed the ritual of the *Lit de Justice* as one which witnessed both the demise of Henry IV and the accession of Louis XIII, serving admirably as the ceremonial agency implementing succession. Finally he relied on the fiction of the medieval *Lit de Justice* to portray the assembly as a constitutional tradition and associated thirteen kings Louis with *Lits de Justice* in their times.[48] President Harlay's message rested upon legal-philosophical doctrines of Aristotle and Aquinas, Roman Law and Canon Law, which stressed the biogenetic affinity of father and son, the oneness of the two both in species and in their nature as kings. Staples of dynastic legitimism in medieval times, these notions were familiar in French circles by the fifteenth century, as shown in Jean de Terre Rouge's explanation of the *unigenitus*, the oneness of the predecessor and successor insofar as appropriation of the *dignité* was concerned.[49] But Harlay's reformulation of these ideas obliterated the juristic stress on office in favor of a dynastic focus on blood lineage. It was the physical presence of the *rex juvenis* Louis XIII in the *Lit de Justice* assembly which filled the royal *dignité* immediately by reason of dynastic right and regardless of his minority status.

The speech of the *avocat* Louis Servin completed this trilogy of dynastic themes. Picking up the president's argument, Servin suggested that the *Lit de Justice* assembly, simultaneously funereal and celebrative, was a unique French practice which commemorated the deceased Henry IV and acclaimed his "first-born" successor Louis XIII as king. He intro-

---

[48] In the later sixteenth century the use of sun imagery by jurists and antiquarians to connote the continuity of the king and body politic was popular; for example, see Orléans, *Ouvertures des Parlements*; Arnauld, *La Justice aux pieds du roy*; and André Valladier, *Parénèse royale sur les cérémonies du sacre du très-chrestien Louis XIII, roy de France et de Navarre* (Paris, 1611).

[49] On biogenetic likenesses used to substantiate the undying nature of the *dignité* through dynastic continuity, consult Kantorowicz, *King's Two Bodies*, pp. 328-336, 391-401; for Terre Rouge, see Giesey, *Juristic Basis of Dynastic Right*, pp. 12-17.

duced a genealogical tree for Louis XIII which reached back to Louis IX and used the historical example of Queen Blanche of Castile to validate the present regency. That genealogical lesson was confirmed two weeks later when Marie de Médicis replaced the portrait in the Louvre of Philip VI (a Valois) with that of Louis IX (a Capetian), progenitor of the Bourbons, and a month after that when the royal party tried to reschedule the Coronation to coincide with the fête of Saint Louis.[50] Chancellor Sillery, First President Harlay, and the *avocat* Servin artfully fashioned a new mode of discourse which defined French royal succession as a dynastic process (based on blood lineage), language at odds with the discourse of the 1560's which had defined succession as a legal procedure (characterized by assumption of the *dignité*). Discussion of the French Law of Succession was shifted in this manner from juristic to dynastic grounds, providing a rationale which legitimized the novel Inaugural *Lit de Justice* assembly and a new constitutional ideology.

Two other related incidents underscored the validity of the Inaugural *Lit de Justice*. At the close of the assembly the young king was hailed by the crowd outside shouting *Vive le roi!*[51] although that ceremonial cry customarily heralded a new king only at the moment of his predecessor's burial during the Royal Funeral ceremony. And at Notre Dame Louis XIII took the royal oath to protect the Church just four days after the *Lit de Justice*,[52] even though that oath had been taken by new kings for over two centuries only after the Royal *Entrée* into Paris following the Coronation ceremony. In addition, the important transformation from juristic to dynastic kingship symbolized in the *Lit de Justice* was confirmed by iconographical representations of the event which appeared shortly afterward. An engraving and a medal which were issued to commemorate the accession of Louis XIII and the regency of Marie de Médicis both focused upon the *Lit de Justice* assembly as the moment of inauguration. The engraving (Figure 8) is dated 1610 and was designed by François Quesnel.[53] It portrays the child-king Louis XIII and the

[50] For the portrait replacement, see Godefroy, *Cérémonial françois*, II, 273, and for the rescheduled Coronation ceremony, see below, Chap. XI, n. 8.

[51] *Mercure françois*, I, fol. 434v, and *Les Cérémonies et ordre tenu au sacré et couronnement de la royne Marie de Médicis, royne de France et de Navarre, dans l'Eglise de Sainct Denys le 12 May 1610. (Ensemble la mort du roy et comme monsieur le dauphin à esté declaré roy, et la royne regente par la Cour de Parlement)* (n.p., 1610), pp. 12-14.

[52] Consult Bryant, *French Royal Entry Ceremony*, p. 182, n. 79.

[53] Born in Edinburgh, François Quesnel (1543-1619) worked mainly in France as a portrait painter.

8. Louis XIII and the Queen Regent Marie de Médicis, 1610.

queen regent Marie de Médicis beneath a canopy and backdrop decorated with fleurs-de-lis reminiscent of the *Lit de Justice*, and it shows both as crowned and dressed in ermine-trimmed robes decorated with fleurs-de-lis reminiscent of a Coronation. To the right of Louis a small stand is covered with a cloth decorated with the arms of France, fleurs-de-lis, and interlaced *LL*'s, a replica of Louis XII's device which appeared on the tapestries used in the *Lit de Justice* assembly. The coronation emblems (scepter and *main de justice*) lie in a crossed position on the stand; the young king lightly clasps the scepter in his right hand. The iconography of this scene thus perpetrates the royal view of the *Lit de Justice* as an assembly in which the inauguration and the declaration of regency were conflated. The medal was designed by the great French medalist Guillaume Dupré and cast in 1611.[54] The obverse shows jugate busts of Louis XIII and Marie de Médicis. The reverse portrays a classical scene showing Louis XIII as a naked young *Sol* rising in the early dawn, sun rays flashing from his head, a globe in his left hand. Marie de Médicis in the armor of Minerva sits facing him. She holds thunderbolts in her lowered left hand and an olive branch in her right hand which is poised over the globe in the hand of the young king to signify peace on earth. The legend reads *Oriens Augusti Tutrice Minerva* (The rise of the August One under the tutelage of Minerva), presenting for the first time since antiquity the *Oriens Augusti* inscription derived from ancient Roman coins.[55] As in the Inaugural *Lit de Justice*, where President Harlay's metaphor of a setting and rising sun described the uniqueness of the deceased Henry IV and the reigning Louis XIII, this medal fashioned sun imagery to commemorate the young king's instant accession that day. Moreover, within weeks the artistic imagination would present a complete symbolic rendition of dynastic succession (as evidenced in Louis XIII) by linking the sun and the legendary phoenix (bird of the sun) with the late sixteenth-century Bodinian maxim *The king never dies*.

Despite the program of legend, ritual, discourse, and iconography which was mustered to lend an aura of legitimacy to the Inaugural *Lit de Justice* assembly of 1610, the rude break with French constitutional tradition which it entailed could not be masked totally. The seriousness of such innovation was expressed aptly by the Duke of Sully, a former

[54] Guillaume Dupré (c. 1572-1642) entered the service of Henry IV in 1597.
[55] This iconographical analysis follows Kantorowicz, *Oriens Augusti*, pp. 119-177. The Dupré medal appears in ibid., 42a, as well as Mazerolle, *Médailleurs*, II, no. 663.

minister and close friend of Henry IV. He was aghast at the prospect of participating in the inaugural ceremony and recalled that

> ... the day after the death of the king was chosen for that ceremony [the *Lit de Justice*], and I was entreated ... by the queen to accompany his majesty. I made all kinds of excuses to avoid doing so. I even pretended to be indisposed and unable to get out of bed that day. I felt extreme repugnance at the thought of doing what they required. But it was necessary to comply, the queen having given good reason for such compliance. My grief was heightened by the sound of the drums and musical instruments, but judging that my tearful face appeared improper amidst the cries of joy and gaiety which surrounded me, I made my way through the crowd and was one of the first persons in the chamber of the Augustinians where the Parlement was held.[56]

Sully was not the only one to object to the Inaugural *Lit de Justice*. The four errant bishops (ecclesiastical peers), it will be recalled, refused to recognize the assembly as a *Lit de Justice*, appropriating seats proper for a Royal *Séance* until forced to move by royal command. The dilemma was acute. Louis XIII was enthroned in a *Lit de Justice* assembly and issued a regency declaration just hours after Henry IV's death. Yet Louis, a minor only eight years of age, had not been crowned and anointed, and Henry, the deceased king, had not been buried. No French king had ever held a *Lit de Justice* before his own Coronation since the appearance of that assembly in the early sixteenth century. French kings had not appeared publicly until after the Funeral of their predecessors for at least two hundred and fifty years. And full legislative power was not celebrated by a minor king until he came of age, according to rubrics given in the Majority *Lit de Justice* assembly almost a half century earlier. As a result, the Inaugural *Lit de Justice* of 1610 preempted the former ceremonial program of inauguration (Royal Funeral, Coronation, and Majority *Lit de Justice*) which demonstrated legal-hereditary succession in a juristic monarchy as a procedure subject to French Public Law. What is more, it initiated a bold new inaugural program which supported a different theory of kingship based now on dynastic right.

To be sure, the medieval notion of dynastic legitimism carried over into the sixteenth century.[57] Early on, the dauphin and princes of the

[56] Sully, *Mémoires*, pp. 139-140.
[57] See Kantorowicz, *King's Two Bodies*, pp. 317-336, on the theory of dynastic continuity; Giesey, *Juristic Basis of Dynastic Right*, pp. 38-40, on legal restrictions

blood were elevated as a special "Crown-worthy" group through the principle of *jus sanguinis* or blood right (the hereditary aspect of juristic monarchy) in the rituals of the *Lit de Justice* assembly (1537 and 1573), the Royal *Séance* (1558), and other ceremonies which symbolized that privileged status. The ascendance of Crown heirs was written into law by Henry III's ordinance of 1576 and was confirmed dramatically by Henry IV's triumphal succession to the Crown although twenty-one degrees removed from his predecessor. Nevertheless, this limited conception of blood right should not be confused with the later notion of *mystique du sang*, which became a major tenet of Bourbon kingship in the late seventeenth century. The earlier principle of *jus sanguinis* functioned in league with the Law of Succession, which concentrated on the legal assumption of the *dignité*; whereas the later *mystique du sang* eventually became a law unto itself, which focused on the royal incumbent and his lineage. At this ideological crossroads in 1610, therefore, the Inaugural *Lit de Justice* provided ritual and discourse which suited a dynastic monarchy and signaled the change of constitutional precepts which would legitimize that system in France.

---

which tempered blood right earlier; and Andrew W. Lewis, *Royal Succession in Capetian France: Studies on Familial Order and the State* (Cambridge, 1981) on family strategy regarding hereditary succession.

XI

A REVISION OF CONSTITUTIONAL IDEOLOGY: THE CORONATION *ENTRÉE* TO REIMS IN 1610

> [The successor king] ... is always the most near and capable to succeed among males of the royal blood even if he is still in the womb and not yet born and named.... As a result there has arisen among us the proverb that *the king of France never dies* to which the emblem of our Louis XIII, *Occasum Gallia nescit* (France never knows the setting [sun]), refers. *Nicolas Bergier (c. 1610-1620)*

Louis XIII's extraordinary *Lit de Justice* of 1610, which concurrently inaugurated a minor king and displayed his legislative capacity, effectively modified the French constitution. First, the Inaugural *Lit de Justice* displaced the inaugural program of the sixteenth century, which demonstrated the tenets of juristic monarchy. Second, it stimulated a new wave of historical research on *Lits de Justice* and a programmatic extension of ritual therein. Third, it witnessed the demise of the Royal *Séance* and the amplification of legislative functions in the *Lit de Justice* assembly.

The traditional ceremonial program of inauguration (Royal Funeral, Coronation, and Majority *Lit de Justice*) which had supported the ideology of juristic kingship was rendered obsolete by Louis XIII's *Lit de Justice* of 1610. Early on the Coronation had served as the principle ceremony of royal inauguration, because new reigns until the later thirteenth century began at the moment of Coronation (marked by ecclesiastical consecration) and the problem of the continuity of the realm posed by the "little interregnum" (between accession and Coronation) was rationalized on occasion by the fiction of Christ as the *interrex*. In the year 1270, however, when Louis IX died in Africa with his son Philip III by his side, the new king issued legal documents in his own name without benefit of Coronation investiture. Thenceforth the full exercise of royal authority (along with regnal dating) was severed from the Coronation ceremony. From this time on the Crown devolved upon the new king at the moment of royal accession (marked by the immediate assumption of legal power), and the defect of the little interregnum (now solved legally) soon was corrected ceremonially by the Royal Funeral. The Royal Funeral ceremony provided a lifelike crowned effigy of the deceased monarch to represent the immortality of the royal *dignité* until the burial of the body at Saint-Denis, and the new king made this legal fiction effective by remaining secluded as a private person even though he issued edicts in his own name during that time. The symbolism of the ceremony thus preserved the inaugural role of the Coronation as the first public revelation of the new king.[1] This inaugural system prevailed even during minority succession requiring a regency, and finally the Majority *Lit de Justice* was introduced in 1563 to celebrate the renewal of full legislative capacity for a minor successor already crowned. Following the convocation of Louis XIII's first *Lit de Justice* assembly, however, this tripartite inaugural program was broken on all three fronts.

When preceded by the Inaugural *Lit de Justice*, the Royal Funeral ceremony became a meaningless exercise in constitutional symbolism. The rules of the Funeral ritual required that red-robed presidents of Parlement surround the royal effigy, symbolizing the perpetuity of the royal *dignité* and the continuity of royal justice, while the new king refrained from appearing in public until the removal of that symbolic effigy following the burial of his predecessor at Saint-Denis.[2] But in the *Lit de Justice* of 1610 red-robed presidents of Parlement accompanied the living successor king, who appeared publicly and actualized on the spot the symbolism of that ritual. Enthroned in the Grand-chambre of the Parlement of Paris, Louis XIII was designated as the *living image of the deceased*, a term ordinarily used in the Funeral ritual to designate the effigy of the dead king; afterward in the streets of Paris he was hailed by shouts of *Vive le roi!*, the cry normally given for the first time at the Saint-Denis graveside as the funereal cries *Le roi est mort! . . . Vive le roi!* signaled the rebirth of royal power. Already stripped of constitutional symbolism by the time the Funeral took place in the next weeks, Henry IV's effigy served only as a quaint reminder to spectators of the former *dignité* of the king which was actually manifested now in his living son. The impropriety of holding a *Lit de Justice* to inaugurate the new king before the Royal Funeral had taken place was underscored by

[1] For remarks on how the system functioned, consult Giesey, *Royal Funeral Ceremony*, chaps. IV-X, recounted in Kantorowicz, *King's Two Bodies*, pp. 328-335.

[2] Although it was customary to destroy effigies at burial, an effigy mask constructed for Henry IV's funeral (but bypassed in the competition) remains in the Musée du Carnavalet, Paris.

the reluctance of the Duke of Sully to participate in the assembly. Recounting the scene at the Louvre a few days after the *Lit de Justice* but still during the mourning period for Henry IV, Sully described a palace which had been turned into a theater with two stages: one in the upper state apartments where public mourning was displayed everywhere, the other in the lower apartments where a magnificent décor celebrated the succession of the new king. Sully decried this perverse juxtaposition of joy and grief as a real violation of public order which troubled the few decent subjects still remaining.[3] Recounting the Funeral of Henry IV, the anonymous author of the *Bref discours des pompes, ceremonies, et obseques funebres* illustrated the confusion caused by this neglect of customary protocol. When he described Henry IV's effigy reclining on the bed of state in the Louvre during mourning, he correctly referred to the apparatus as a *lit de parade*. But when he described the effigy on the litter surrounded by red-robed presidents of Parlement as it was carried later in the Funeral procession to Saint-Denis, he mistakenly referred to the apparatus as a *lit de justice*.[4] Thus the lifelike effigy of Henry IV appeared to some not as a symbol of the immortal *dignité* but as a representation of the king enthroned at a *Lit de Justice* assembly and surrounded by red-robed *parlementaires*.[5] Devoid of constitutional symbolism after 1610, the Royal Funeral was also bereft of institutional support. Since Parlement's constitutional role in the Funeral was transferred to the Inaugural *Lit de Justice*, prestigiously located in its own quarters and repeated in the next two reigns for minor kings, the Court allowed the Royal Funeral ceremony to fade away with no objections.

In like manner the Majority *Lit de Justice* assembly was denuded of constitutional vigor by the Inaugural *Lit de Justice*, although it survived as a truncated celebration in the seventeenth century. The Parlement of Paris had argued vehemently against the validity of the ceremony in

[3] Sully, *Mémoires*, pp. 142-144.

[4] *Bref discours des pompes, ceremonies, et obseques funebres de tres-haut, tres-puissant, tres-excellent prince Henry le Grand, par la grace de Dieu roy de France et de Navarre, tres-chrestien, tres-auguste, tres-victorieux et incomparable en magnanimité et clemence, qui trespassa en son Palais du Louvre, le vendredy quatorziesme may mil six cens dix.* [14 May 1610] (n.p., n.d.), pp. 5 and 14-15.

[5] If by 1610 the effigy was no longer viewed as representing the immortal *dignité* but instead was seen as representing the king in the *Lit de Justice* assembly (another version of "king and justice never dies"), then the specific grounds for the bishops' abandonment of the corpse for the effigy (with the presidents of Parlement) in Henry IV's Funeral procession is more clear; see above, Chap. X, n. 15.

1563 because it was held in the Parlement of Rouen, but the situation was different in 1610. Since the Parisian Court boldly issued a regency *arrêt* preceding the Inaugural *Lit de Justice* in order to claim legislative tutorship of a minor king, a Majority *Lit de Justice* convoked in Paris later would have cemented that pretended role by marking its end ceremonially. Logic thus dictated that the Parlement of Paris had a stake in maintaining the Majority *Lit de Justice* in its own quarters. In fact, the Majority rituals for Louis XIII in 1614 (Figure 10), Louis XIV in 1651 (Figure 13), and Louis XV in 1723 (Figure 16) were located in the Grand-chambre of the Parlement of Paris, but they were shorn of a constitutional role by the Inaugural *Lit de Justice* and served only as gala nameday parties.

The Coronation ceremony too suffered a constitutional setback, losing its unique inaugural role to the first *Lit de Justice* of Louis XIII. In 1610 the obstreperous bishops (ecclesiastical peers) drew attention to this departure from Coronation protocol by challenging the format of a *Lit de Justice* for the inauguration. The anonymous author of the *Cérémonies*, who mistakenly confounded the Inaugural *Lit de Justice* with the Coronation ceremony, bore witness to the confusion which resulted. Speaking of the decision of 14 May to hold a *Lit de Justice* assembly, he noted that "It was resolved in the [Royal] Council to lead *Monsieur le dauphin* to Parlement to declare him king." Struck by the inaugural tone of the event, he recalled that

> *Monsieur le dauphin* came on foot, and the crown, scepter, and *main de justice* were carried before him. . . . The people cried *Vive le roi!* . . . The Court [of Parlement] received *Monsieur le dauphin* as king and the queen as regent. Then the scepter and *main de justice* were put in the hands of the *king* [Louis XIII], and all the assembly saluted him *as king*. The ceremonies and the speeches lasted about two hours. Then the king left along with the [royal] court, and he was led on a horse to the Louvre as the people cried out *Vive le roi!*[6]

It is doubtful that the Coronation emblems (crown, scepter, and *main de justice*) were carried in this procession, because they were deposited at Saint-Denis. Yet the illusion of this observer that a kind of Coronation had taken place in the *Lit de Justice* attained additional credibility when Louis XIII just a few days later took the oath (to protect the Church)

---

[6] *Cérémonies*, pp. 12-14 [italics added].

at Notre Dame which was usually taken after the Coronation ceremony. Still, even though the Coronation had been dislodged from the traditional ceremonial spectrum by the Inaugural *Lit de Justice*, its future differed from that of the Royal Funeral and Majority *Lit de Justice*. The Coronation was supported by an alliance of powerful interests, the Church, the City of Reims, and the royal party, groups which for different reasons wished to preserve the Coronation ritual in the new constitutional order. The Church played a major role in the Coronation but acquired no special status in the Inaugural *Lit de Justice*, so it behooved ecclesiastics to maintain the former even in a form somewhat attenuated. The City officials of Reims still chafed at the loss of the Coronation to the City of Chartres sixteen years earlier when Henry IV was crowned, and they were determined to regain it for Reims in 1610. Most importantly the royal party intended to legitimize the *Lit de Justice* of 1610 as a full inauguration allowing no interregum, legal or ceremonial, and seized the opportunity of the Coronation to reassert that principle. Consequently, there arose from this amalgamation of varied interests a new constitutional rationale which provided a place for the Coronation within the changed order of inaugural ceremonies. We can trace the invention of that rationale through the notes of one of its perpetrators.

In the treatise *Le Bouquet royal* Nicolas Bergier, a legist by profession and one of the City officials of Reims commissioned to organize Louis XIII's pre-Coronation *Entrée* there, recorded in detail the program devised for the *Entrée* and commented on the ideological framework which supported it.[7] Beset by a host of difficulties, Louis XIII's Coronation, which was originally planned for 26 July 1610 and rescheduled several times, was held finally on 17 October, the day after the Royal *Entrée* to

---

[7] Nicolas Bergier [and P. de La Salle], *Le Bouquet royal ou le parterre des riches inventions qui ont servy à l'entrée du roy Louis le Juste en sa ville de Reims* (Reims, 1637). Bergier composed the narration of the pre-Coronation *Entrée* (fols. 1r-71v), La Salle that of the Coronation (fols. 72r-88v). The poems written by Jacques Dorat complete the work (fols. 89r-100v). La Salle published the work after Bergier's death (1623), and both were involved officially in the *Entrée* preparations: architecture, sculpture, paintings, thematic devices, and inscriptions (fols. 5v-7v and 10r). The *Entrée* inscriptions were published earlier in *Inscriptions principalles des portes et arcs de triomphe faictz pour l'entrée, sacre et couronnement du roy Louys Treiziesme en sa ville de Reims (par Guillaume Baussonnet, Nicolas Bergier et Jacques Dorat)* (Reims, 1610). Nicolas Bergier was a professor of law and a *syndic* for the City of Reims, an *avocat* in the *siège presidial*, and a historiographer. He was a friend of Pierre Dupuy, Nicolas-Claude Peiresc, and Pomponne de Bellièvre.

Reims.[8] Just a few weeks after the Inaugural *Lit de Justice* (15 May) the officials of Reims began to organize the Coronation *Entrée*, and they were directed in that task over the next five months by a royal contingent in Paris.[9] The symbolism of the royal emblematic device designed for the *Entrée* program was crucial for the whole enterprise, because it confirmed the theme of the earlier *Lit de Justice* and set the theme for the forthcoming Coronation. Designed under royal auspices and sent from Paris to Reims as early as 8 July, the device showed a rising sun, the splendor of its first rays dissipating thick clouds, and bore the inscription *Occasum Gallia nescit* (France never knows the setting [sun]).[10] According to Nicolas Bergier that inscription reminded viewers of "the proverb which has arisen among us that *The king of France never dies*."[11] A variety of father-son themes proliferated throughout the Coronation *Entrée*,[12] and it was explained that in Louis XIII one sees "the king, worthy son of a worthy father, as a new *Orient* [rising sun] elevating

[8] Bergier, *Bouquet royal*, fols. 1r-8v, recounts the planning. On 26 May 1610, just eleven days after the *Lit de Justice*, Louis XIII sent *lettres closes* to Reims scheduling the Coronation for 26 July, two months later. On 5 June the Rémois committee sent a delegation to Paris to inquire about an emblematic device for the *Entrée* and colors for the habits of the participants. On 8 July royal letters arrived in Reims rescheduling the Coronation for 25 August, the *fête* of Saint Louis, namesake of Louis XIII. On 7 August the group at Reims realized that grape harvesting threatened to tie up the labor needed to decorate the city and asked the people in Paris for a delay. The Coronation was rescheduled a third time for 17 October, the date which finally prevailed. Throughout the four months following the *Lit de Justice*, however, the Rémois committee was not sure the Coronation would actually take place there, since strong lobbying was being conducted in Paris by parties favoring other cities for the site. It was early in October before the plans were finally formalized.

[9] Ibid. A delegation from the Rémois committee was in Paris consulting the royal party on the plans, and they took orders from Paris until early October.

[10] Ibid., fol. 42r. The provenance of this well-integrated program of sun imagery, phoenix, and proverb needs investigation. It seem likely that the numismatists and antiquarians in touch with Henry IV's court, such as Guillaume Dupré, Rascas de Bagarris, and Fabri de Peiresc, worked these images out earlier. De Bagarris certainly intended to instigate a history of the reign through medallions. When the unforeseen *Lit de Justice* of 1610 occurred, therefore, there might have been a thematic program in the offing which served that occasion and was carried through the *Entrée* to Reims preceding the Coronation later. For the medallic history proposed by De Bagarris but negated by Henry IV and the medallic program picked up by Louis XIV, see Kantorowicz, *Oriens Augusti*, pp. 119-177.

[11] Bergier, *Bouquet royal*, fol. 55v.

[12] Ibid., fols. 25r-36v, especially fols. 26v and 36r-v; and fols. 51r, 52v-53v.

itself over the horizon of good fortune."[13] The sun emblem and father-son themes of the *Entrée* recalled the metaphorical sun imagery expounded in the *Lit de Justice* assembly and portrayed by Dupré's medal commemorating the event. The Coronation *Entrée* at Reims also reflected the conjoined theme of mourning and triumph which had characterized the Inaugural *Lit de Justice*.[14] Those marching in procession before the royal party wore mourning as in the *Lit de Justice*.[15] Upon entering Reims Louis XIII was acclaimed by shouts of *Vive le roi!* along with the sounds of drums and fifes, firing cannon, and ringing bells reminiscent of the post-inaugural convoy in Paris from the Palais de Justice to the Louvre.[16] Thus the iconographical and ceremonial arrangement of the Coronation *Entrée* deliberately linked the forthcoming Coronation with the *Lit de Justice* in thematic terms emphasizing dynastic succession. Furthermore, the program devised for the *Entrée* at Reims also spelled out for viewers the precepts governing the French system of dynastic succession which had been realized in the *Lit de Justice* assembly.

There were two related tableaux featured at the *Entrée*, both of which portrayed the Inaugural *Lit de Justice* assembly and the Coronation ceremony as related stages in the ceremonial program of dynastic succession. The first tableau recalled the *Lit de Justice* assembly of 15 May in Paris. It showed Louis XIII's entrance into the Convent of the Augustinians, and the words *Rege designato* (He is designated king) were inscribed on the arch over the scene. The second tableau depicted Louis XIII's *Entrée* to Reims that same day in preparation for his Coronation, and the words *Regno suscepto* (He receives the kingdom) were inscribed on the arch. According to Bergier, the first tableau reminded viewers that the young Louis XIII was designated King of France in the *Lit de Justice* immediately upon the death of his father, and the second tableau reminded them that Louis XIII's Coronation would confirm that designation by uniting king and royalty (*royauté*).[17] Discussing the iconog-

[13] Ibid., fol. 7r.

[14] Ibid., fols. 6v, 17r, 20v-21r, 37r-39r, 91v, and 93v.

[15] Ibid., fols. 20v-21r. The king was dressed in a violet cloak, his white horse caparisoned with matching colors. The royal party, including princes of the blood, other princes, dukes, counts, great lords, and gentlemen, were vested in mourning garb.

[16] Ibid., fols. 17r, 37r-39r.

[17] Ibid., fols. 53v-57v. Other tableaux in the *Entrée* celebrated Louis XIII's birth and baptism; ibid., fol. 53v. All of Bergier's references to the event of 15 May, which he clearly viewed as an inauguration, are denoted as *Lit de Justice* here, although he uses expressions such as "the celebrated act," "the first act,"

raphy of the tableaux, Bergier cautiously qualified the role of both succession ceremonies. The Inaugural *Lit de Justice* did not constitute the king but served as a "demonstrative ceremony" whereby the successor publicly "signifies his capability to succeed to the Crown under the ancient laws and constitutions of the kingdom (*royaume*)." Likewise the Coronation did not provide the King of France with any new right because "birth makes him king."[18] To clarify these definitions Bergier drafted the marriage metaphor (which had originally signified the inalienability of the realm) into the service of dynastic succession. He stated that the Coronation served as "a kind of sacrament through which the king is made the *husband of the kingdom* (*royaume*), which he marries that day by the ring ... placed on his finger as a sign of spiritual marriage."[19] For Bergier's scheme this marriage metaphor, which substituted the *royaume* for the *chose publique* and never mentioned kingdom qua dowry, was extended to encompass the *Lit de Justice* and explained the dual ceremonial facets of succession perfectly.

> By the first act [the Inaugural *Lit de Justice*] in which he [the successor king] is declared and designated King of France, *he betrothes royalty* which [Public] *Law and Nature* give him, and by [the second act] the Coronation, he marries it.[20]

Whereas sixteenth-century juristic ideology held that the royal *dignité* was conferred upon the hereditary successor by virtue of French Public Law and that the act was realized ceremonially in the traditional inaugural program (Royal Funeral, Coronation, and Majority), this redefinition of the system suggested that royalty was conferred through [Public] Law and Nature and was confirmed ceremonially by the new two-stage inauguration, *Lit de Justice* and Coronation.

There is no doubt that Rémois and Parisian cohorts designed an ideological framework for the Coronation *Entrée* program which would legitimize the *Lit de Justice* of 15 May as an inaugural ceremony and elucidate for the public the new dynastic precepts which governed the "Salic Law," as they called the Law of Succession.[21] A careful reading of those notes, furthermore, reveals that the new ideology was formulated

---

"the ceremony," "the assembly" to describe the Inaugural *Lit de Justice*; ibid., fols. 56v and 57v.

[18] Ibid., fol. 56v.

[19] Ibid., fols. 56v-57r.

[20] Ibid., fol. 57r [italicis added].

[21] Ibid., fol. 55r.

by amending the constitutional ideology of the 1550's and 1560's to suit the situation in 1610. From the text of Chancellor L'Hôpital's speech on the Law of Succession given at the Majority *Lit de Justice* in 1563,[22] Nicolas Bergier copied almost word for word L'Hôpital's two precepts regulating French succession, *Seizure* (governing the institution of the king) and *Majority* (governing the administration of the kingdom). To explain the origins of the axiom on *Majority*, Bergier repeated the historical thesis advanced by Jean du Tillet and Chancellor L'Hôpital regarding Charles V's promulgation of the Law of Majority in a *Lit de Justice* of 1375.[23] To explain the axiom on *Seizure*, however, Bergier first repeated L'Hôpital's words exactly and then added a new interpolation to the passage which skewed L'Hôpital's original text beyond recognition. Bergier began with L'Hôpital's remarks:

> ... our wise rulers ordained as an immutable law (*loy perpetuelle*) [the precept that] *the kingdom is never vacant (le royaume n'est jamais vacant)*, because there is continuity from king to king so that *as soon as the king's eyes close* [in death] [= *mortuus aperit oculos viventis*] there is another king ... without awaiting Coronation, unction, consecration, or any other ceremonies....

But Bergier continued by characterizing the successor as the one

> who is always recognized as the most near and capable to succeed among males of the royal blood even if he is still in the womb and not yet born and named.... As a result there has arisen among us the proverb that *the king of France never dies (le roi de France ne meurt jamais)* to which the emblem of our Louis XIII, *Occasum Gallia nescit* (France never knows the setting [sun]), refers.[24]

As pointed out earlier Chancellor L'Hôpital characterized the first stage in the French Law of Succession, *Seizure*, as a procedure subject to French Public Law. He invented a French maxim, *The kingdom is*

[22] Bergier, *Bouquet royal*, fol. 55r-v. Bergier referred to the Majority *Lit de Justice* of 1563 but did not mention borrowing verbatim from L'Hôpital's speech given there.

[23] Ibid., fols. 55v-56r. He thus held that French kings are capable of administering the kingdom at the age of fourteen according to the law promulgated by Charles V in the fourteenth century, confirmed by Charles VI in the fifteenth century, and implemented publicly by Charles IX in the Majority *Lit de Justice* of the sixteenth century.

[24] Ibid., fol. 55r-v [italics added]. For the corresponding passage in L'Hôpital's speech of 1563, see above, Chap. VII, n. 7.

never vacant, to explain that legal precept of succession which was based on the continuity of royal office. Conversely, Bergier submerged L'Hôpital's legal definition beneath a principle of dynastic right conferred by Law and Nature and enjoyed even by a successor "still in the womb and not yet born and named." He subtly equated the kingdom with royalty and employed the odd Bodinian proverb, *The king [of France] never dies*, to define this new view of dynastic succession which was based on the immortality of the Bourbon dynasty. And he deftly allied the older marriage metaphor to that dynastic axiom in a manner which transformed the ring-bestowing rubric of the Coronation from a ritual signifying the inalienability of the realm into one turning the kingdom over to the Bourbon dynasty. The scheme devised by the Parisian and Rémois *Entrée* planners and outlined in Bergier's treatise thus redefined legal-hereditary succession to reflect the new view of dynastic kingship in France. Outlined in the early seventeenth century, this notion of dynastic right would be transformed later in the seventeenth century into a Bourbon *mystique du sang*.

To complete the symbolism of dynastic succession evident in the Inaugural *Lit de Justice* and the Coronation *Entrée* of Louis XIII, the phoenix was displayed prominently in the *Entrée* program. The second tableau portrayed a young phoenix being reborn from his own ashes and extending his wings to take first flight, and the words *Vivit morte refecta* (Death restores his life) were inscribed on the scene.[25] In the same refrain Jacques Dorat, another organizer of the *Entrée*, presented Louis XIII with the keys to the City of Reims and a poem written for the occasion. The pages of Dorat's poem bore the sun emblem and the inscription *Occasum Gallia nescit*, and the poem itself likened the symbolism of the instantly reborn phoenix to the meaning of the proverb *The king never dies*.

> The French lily of immortal seed
> Does not recognize the accident of death.
>
> . . . .
> Determining that like the bird of the sun [phoenix],
> The death of one gives birth to the other
>
> . . . .
> Since kings in France do not die.[26]

[25] Bergier, *Bouquet royal*, fol. 58r.
[26] Ibid., fol. 89v. This theme of regeneration also employed the French lily, recalling Servin's speech earlier in the Inaugural *Lit de Justice*.

The phoenix metaphor was based on ancient and medieval lore of the solitary phoenix, mythical bird of the sun who at the end of his life set his nest afire and fanned the flames with his wings, giving birth to the new phoenix from the glowing cinders. In medieval times the metaphor served well to explain notions of inheritance in private law because it signified the idea of *perpetuitas* by identifying the deceased with the living successor, an idea supported by popular legal maxims such as *Mortuus aperit oculos viventis* and *Le mort saisit le vif* already discussed. At that time the phoenix metaphor briefly entered the realm of Public Law when theorists adopted it to explain dynastic legitimism, but it was bypassed throughout most of the sixteenth century when commentors fashioned a mode of discourse aimed at stressing legal rather than hereditary aspects of succession.[27] Following the Inaugural *Lit de Justice* assembly of 1610, however, the alliance of the phoenix metaphor with the Bodinian proverb *The king never dies* generated a whole new mode of discourse which moved away from the medieval idea of dynastic legitimism and the sixteenth-century focus on Public Law to characterize instead the new precepts of dynastic right. No wonder then that phoenix imagery was associated with the young king Louis XIII for some time. In 1611 he was called "the young phoenix" (*le pétit phoenix*) whose living image gave proof that in France "The king does not die" (*le roi n'est pas mort*).[28] A bit later in the reign he was designated as "the sun of France" (*sol Franciae*), a "French phoenix" (*phoenix Francorum*), in an anagram (Figure 9) which played upon the ideas of divine law and French law.[29] Finally the convoluted phoenix-like expression "The king dies but another is born" (*Le roi meurt mais un autre est né*) signaled the same idea of Bourbon corporeal succession to the Crown of France.[30] In this vein

[27] On this medieval use of the phoenix myth to propagate a legal fiction, consult Kantorowicz, *King's Two Bodies*, pp. 388-401.

[28] Valladier, *Parénèse royale*, pp. 15-16. See also the discussion of this theme renewed in B.N. ms. fr. 23061, fols. 319v-320r, where the following explanation is given: "At the Royal Funeral the French shout *Vive le roy!* to emphasize that the person of the king dies, not the office; thus only the French monarchy is characterized by the phoenix because the death of one king signals the birth of the next."

[29] B.N. ms. fr. 23061, fol. 25r (purportedly the design of P.L.D. Gartres). The *"phoenix francorum"* allusion is to the right and just below the middle portion of the circle.

[30] B.N. ms. fr. 23061, fols. 344v-346r, where a discussion of the uniqueness of the phoenix is given. The materials drawn together here suggest that propagandists intended to associate the Bourbon dynasty with the phoenix; see

9. Louis XIII: The French phoenix, Louis the Just.

Loisel's addition of the proverb *Le roi ne meurt jamais* to his fourth compendium was timely indeed, and Loyseau's refashioned maxim of Public Law, *La royauté est toujours remplie et non jamais vacante*, symbolized the new dynastic monarchy.[31] It is true that the themes of phoenix and sun were used later to characterize dynastic right at the accession of Louis XIV,[32] but they were derived from this ceremonial ritual established three decades earlier at the accession of Louis XIII in 1610.[33]

Once again precepts of the French constitution were reflected in ritual. When the alliance of the Salic Law and royal succession was first forged publicly, the precept was featured in the Royal *Entrée* program of Charles VIII to Reims in 1484.[34] When the relationship between the Law of Majority and French Public Law was first spelled out, the precept was propagated in the Majority *Lit de Justice* of 1563. Now when the new alliance of the Salic Law and dynastic right occurred, that precept made its public debut first at the Inaugural *Lit de Justice*, then in the *Entrée* program of Louis XIII to Reims in 1610. Furthermore, within this context of dynastic blood succession, another ritual, the fiction of the "Sleeping King" (related to the Coronation ceremony), was also amended to fit the circumstances. When used in 1561 to depict the young Charles IX as "sleeping," that ceremony probably referred specifically to his minority status. Yet when applied in 1610 to Louis XIII, the ritual suggested that the child-king had been "sleeping" while Henry IV was alive but that he awakened to full rulership capacity immediately upon his father's death.[35] As amended, therefore, the ritual of the Sleeping King also promoted the principles of dynastic succession which had been promulgated in the Inaugural *Lit de Justice* at Paris and propagated for the public at large in the Coronation *Entrée* at Reims.

---

designs for medals portraying Henry IV and the phoenix, fols. 10r-15r, as well as the two allusions mentioned above.

[31] For the full context, see above, Chap. VII, nn. 33 and 34.

[32] The examples for Louis XIV are discussed by Giesey, *Royal Funeral Ceremony*, pp. 191-192, fig. 18, and Kantorowicz, *King's Two Bodies*, pp. 413-414, fig. 24. Louis Marin, *Le Portrait du roi* (Paris, 1981), pp. 123-124, also connects the phoenix with Louis XIV's accession. Unaware of the dynastic provenance of the image in 1610 for inaugural purposes, Marin places the phoenix within a theological paradigm.

[33] In addition to the examples given above, note that the jeton struck for Louis XIV in 1643 (figs. 18 and 24 cited in n. 32 above) picked up the iconography of the pre-Coronation *Entrée* tableau devised for Louis XIII in 1610.

[34] Giesey, *Juristic Basis of Dynastic Right*, pp. 19-20.

[35] For a description of that ritual, see Jackson, "The Sleeping King," pp. 527-551.

Following the Inaugural *Lit de Justice* of 1610, the ideological framework which supported juristic monarchy was revised and the ceremonial program which implemented succession was revamped to support that revision. The earlier legal-hereditary notion of succession, which declared the royal office separate from the incumbent and defined succession as a process regulated by French Public Law, was replaced with the dynastic idea of royal office, which conflated office and incumbent, wed the office to the Bourbon dynasty, and made succession a matter of dynastic blood right transferred seminally at conception. Moreover, a new mode of discourse accompanied this shift in constitutional ideology. Whereas juristic kingship was characterized in the sixteenth century by the maxims *The kingdom is never vacant* and *Royal authority does not die*, dynastic kingship was characterized in 1610 by the maxim *The king never dies*, which was resurrected precisely for that purpose in league with phoenix and sun metaphors, and *Royalty is always replenished and never vacant*, which explained that maxim in its new context. Admirably fit for elucidating the theme of the Inaugural *Lit de Justice* (which implemented dynastic succession) and the Coronation (which confirmed it) in 1610, *The king never dies* along with other dynastic motifs (sun imagery, phoenix lore, biogenetic likenesses, and the convoluted marriage metaphor) moved directly into public discourse as the harbinger of a new dynastic ideology supported by a reinterpretation of French Public Law. Besides introducing a new set of ideological tenets which defined French kingship as dynastic in nature, the Inaugural *Lit de Justice* effectively expanded the legislative function of kingship, which had been stressed under the juristic monarchy. By the first decade of the seventeenth century, therefore, French Public Law was redefined to accommodate a newly forged amalgamation of dynastic right and legislative authority, tenets expressed first in the Inaugural *Lit de Justice* of Louis XIII and again in the many *Lit de Justice* assemblies which followed. This inflation of royal legislative power will be discussed in the next chapter after recalling two other phenomena which contributed greatly to the prominence of the *Lit de Justice* assembly in the seventeenth century: the new wave of historical research and the organization of ceremonial programs.

HISTORICAL PROJECTS AND CEREMONIAL PROGRAMS

The ceremonial presentation of Bourbon dynastic ideology perpetrated in the Inaugural *Lit de Justice* of 1610 impressed contemporaries, and a second stage of historical research was initiated almost immediately. The new antiquarians and compilers whose works issued from the 1620's through the 1640's produced the grand legend of the *Lit de Justice* which is plotted here (Table One) up to the eighteenth century. At the same time a programmatic extension of ritual for the assembly was devised by the ceremonial masters, professional directors attuned to royal grandeur. The second stage in the legendary life of the assembly stood squarely upon Jean du Tillet's earlier fiction of the medieval *Lit de Justice* set forth in the *Recueil des roys de France* (see Table One, Column D) and published nine times from 1577 to 1618. But in addition the new antiquarians avidly tracked down almost every *Lit de Justice* (fictional and authentic) in the French past (see Table One), noted the functions of those sessions, traced the ceremonial prerogatives allotted therein, and launched still another constitutional rationale for the assembly. This second stage of research coincided with Louis XIII's increased convocation of such assemblies in the Grand-chambre of the Parlement of Paris, and the vital interests of both king and Parlement thus became wedded to the past and future fortunes of the ritual. In the opening decades of the seventeenth century the seeds for this legend were already planted in humanist treatises by André du Chesne, Louis d'Orléans, and Antoine Arnauld which ranked the French system of governance along with the best of antiquity and the *Lit de Justice* as an ancient French institution. No doubt inspired by the extraordinary Inaugural *Lit de Justice* performed in the Parlement of Paris by Louis XIII, a new spate of treatises appeared. Foremost among such works was the historical treatise of Bernard de La Roche-Flavin, *Treze livres des Parlemens de France*, which cited dated events and entire passages verbatim from Du Tillet's work on the *Lit de Justice* (see Table One, Column E). La Roche-Flavin portrayed the French constitution as embodied in the *Lit de Justice* in Parlement, where *Rex* and *Lex* reposed together for the common good of the kingdom.[36] This graphic image of *Rex* and *Lex* in the *Lit de Justice*

---

[36] La Roche-Flavin, *Treze livres des Parlemens de France*, quoted Orléans' famous passage (see above, Chap. IX, n. 60) verbatim but added the important clause [in italics] below, emphasizing the role of Parlements, so that the last line reads "... où s'exercent les vrayes fonctions de la justice, *et principalement és Parlemens* ...."; IV, xv, 285. For the image of *Rex et Lex*, IV, ix, 284. The author's vision of the *Lit de Justice* is discussed in IV, i-v, 283; IV, viii-ix, 284; IV, xv, 285; and VII, iii, 384-385. He was reprimanded and fined for his strong pro-Parlement stance. La Roche-Flavin copied passages from Jean du Tillet and cites the clerk's work in VII, ii, 384.

permeated the assemblies of the 1620's and 1630's, where Louis XIII fulfilled a variety of public functions in sessions held more regularly than ever before.

The renewed historical enterprise of the seventeenth century produced the voluminous results which fashioned the legend shown in Table One: first, because the *Lit de Justice*, past and present, was scrutinized over time from all sides; and second, because these new investigators, convinced of the antiquity of the *Lit de Justice*, presumed that Royal *Séances* from the fourteenth through the sixteenth centuries were *Lit de Justice* assemblies and thus discovered (or invented) more assemblies than ever actually existed.[37] Jérome (I) Bignon compiled thousands of extracts from registers of Parlement covering the years 1499-1600, conducted a search on ceremonial prerogatives, and wrote a monograph extolling the Parlement of Paris as the royal seat of government.[38] President Achille (I) de Harlay, who delivered a speech on dynasticism at the Inaugural *Lit de Justice* of 1610, may have initiated the manuscript collection on *Lit de Justice* assemblies which was owned and then updated by his successor (see Table One, Column M),[39] and Julien Peleus extolled the role of the presidents of Parlement in *Lit de Justice* assemblies.[40] Louis Servin, who also delivered an inaugural speech in 1610, wrote a monograph which discussed the fortuitous alliance of king and parlement in the *Lit de Justice* assembly,[41] and Jacques Corbin published a monograph which elucidated a parlementary vision of the Grand-chambre as a great ceremonial stage for king and Court engaged as partners in constitutional

[37] Note in Table One the steady attribution of the title *Lit de Justice* to sessions which were actually Royal *Séances*.

[38] A.N. U 492 (Table alphabetique des choses remarquables contenues dans les registres du conseil [du Parlement] du XVIᵉ siècle, attribuée à Jérome Bignon, avocat général), one volume of 1,459 folios which list varied topics including parlementary sessions. Bignon noted items from registers of Parlement which correspond now to A.N. X1a 1505-1766 (1499-1600). He also published *La Grandeur de nos roys*, stressing royal over papal prerogatives, as well as other treatises noting ceremonies at the papal court. Bignon was *avocat général* in 1625 and grand master of the library of the king in 1642.

[39] The manuscripts were owned by Achille (III) de Harlay; B.N. ms. fr. 16511 and 16512 (see Columns M and U in Table One). There were also other volumes in the latter's collection; B.N. ms. fr. 16579 and 16513.

[40] Peleus, *Premier président du Parlement*, eulogizing president, Parlement, and *Lit de Justice*.

[41] Servin, *Action des gens du roy*, extolling the role of the *avocats* at Louis XIII's Inaugural *Lit de Justice*.

affairs.[42] Finally, the manuscript compilation made by Jean (V) Le Nain (over five hundred volumes strong) included one hundred and fifteen volumes of extracts from the registers of Parlement on royal visits to Parlement, and that work exemplifies the thoroughness of this whole endeavor (see Table One, Column C).[43] The prodigious efforts of the new investigators, anonymous manuscript compilers and published antiquarians, to locate every *Lit de Justice* in French history matched the prominence of the assembly itself in the seventeenth century.

Struck by this same wave of historical curiosity attuned to actual practice, Louis XIII and Louis XIV directly commissioned research on the *Lit de Justice* assembly. At the outset Cardinal Richelieu issued royal commissions for archival research on the *Lit de Justice*; later on Pierre (III) Séguier commented on some of the findings produced by that effort. The main recipients of these commissions, Pierre Dupuy and Théodore Godefroy, collected and studied archival materials for decades throughout both reigns. As early as 1615 Dupuy and Godefroy were commissioned to make an inventory of manuscripts in the Trésor des Chartes.[44] In the next twelve years Godefroy published two preliminary treatises, *Le Cérémonial de France* and *L'Ordre et cérémonies observées aux mariages de France et d'Espagne*.[45] In 1623 and again in 1629 Dupuy was commissioned to investigate royal prerogatives, and that charge was renewed in 1633 and 1644.[46] Finally, Godefroy was commissioned anew in 1631 to conduct an enormous research project on ceremonial assemblies.[47] The results of this whole enterprise were impressive.

The *Traité de la majorité* of Pierre Dupuy was published posthumously (with the assistance of his brother Jacques). That study recounted the origin and function of the *Lit de Justice*, especially its prominence in succession crises (see Table One, Column O), and acknowledged the

---

[42] Jacques Corbin, *Le Code Louis XIII*.

[43] A.N. U 513 (Le Nain, table) and U 2000-2115 (Le Nain), volumes dealing specifically with royal visits to Parlement from 1260 to 1669.

[44] B.N. ms. Dupuy, vols. 162-169 and 171, form that inventory. On the commission (23 May 1615), see Isambert, *Recueil général des anciennes lois*, XVI, 76.

[45] Théodore Godefroy, *Le Cérémonial de France* (1619), and *L'Ordre et cérémonies observées aux mariages de France et d'Espagne* (Paris, 1627).

[46] B.N. ms. Dupuy, 404, fol. 2r (31 Jan. 1623), and fol. 3r (1629). For renewals of the commission, B.N. ms. fr. 18275, fols. 286r-287r and 290r.

[47] See Denis-Charles Godefroy-Ménilglaise, *Les Savants Godefroy, mémoires d'une famille pendant les XVIe, XVIIe et XVIIIe siècles* (Paris, 1873), p. 128, which discusses the commission.

great debt owed to the historical labors of Jean du Tillet.[48] It is readily apparent that seventeenth-century antiquarians owed a great debt to their precursors; it is not so apparent that they subtly reinterpreted the earlier juristic rubrics of French Public Law to suit different times. Dupuy provides a case in point. Like his cohorts, Loyseau and Bergier, Dupuy adapted the juristic mode of discourse on Public Law, which had been developed by Du Tillet, L'Hôpital, and others, to suit a new context. Dupuy actually opened his treatise with the following lines:

> In France one holds as a reliable and undoubted law that *the kingdom is never vacant* (*le royaume n'est jamais vacant*), that there is continuity from king to king, that *the dead seizes the living* (*le mort saisit le vif*), and that we have a king as soon as the other is dead [=*mortuus aperit oculis viventis*] without awaiting Coronation, unction, consecration, or any other ceremony.[49]

He also recounted the history of the Law of Majority promulgated in the *Lit de Justice* by Charles V in 1375, noting that it is "... unique [to France] not commonly found in other kingdoms . . . ," and must be observed.[50]

This message has a ring of authenticity. Yet from the rationale which informed Dupuy's conclusions, one can see at first hand the same shift from juristic to dynastic ideology which accompanied the ritual of the

[48] Dupuy, *Traité de la majorité* (1655) consists of a preface, twelve chapters, and two appended treatises. Chap. I (pp. 1-8) treats the French Law of Majority, chap. II (pp. 9-13), the *sacre* of kings; chaps. III-XII (pp. 14-122) treat regencies and regents. The first long appended treatise (pp. 125-554) provides *preuves* for these chapters, the second short one (pp. 557-585) discusses the historical role of the Parlement of Paris. The preface (a iii^r–c^r) acknowledges the influence of Du Tillet (fol. a iv^v and pp. 3, 17, 112) and the inclusion of his two tracts on majority (pp. 313-347), and expresses appreciation to Monsieur Vyon, Sieur d'Herouval, royal councillor and *auditeur* in the Chambre des Comptes (see above, Chap. I, n. 10, for Herouval's connection with Le Nain). For a recent study of the legal nexus of regency government, see Harriet Lightman, *Sons and Mothers: Queens and Minor Kings in French Constitutional Law* (Ann Arbor, University Microfilms, 1980).

[49] Dupuy, *Traité de la majorité*, pp. 1-13. Compare this passage with the renditions of L'Hôpital in 1563 and Bergier in 1610. Many sections of this treatise and that of Bergier, *Le Bouquet royal*, are exactly alike. Since Dupuy had the sources at his disposal, which were published along with his commentary, it is possible that Bergier borrowed from a manuscript version of this work.

[50] Ibid. See the views of other theorists of Fundamental Law in Lemaire, *Les Lois fondamentales*, chap. III.

Inaugural *Lit de Justice*, the *Entrée* of 1610, and the musings of Loyseau. Dupuy no longer treated the king's relation to the kingdom (*royaume*, or *chose publique*) primarily in terms of what was constitutional (that is, legal). Rather, he spoke of the king's association with royalty (*royauté*, or dynasty) mainly in terms of what was constitutional (that is, "fundamental" and natural). He thus pointed out with historical surety that the French "hold as a Fundamental Law (*Loy Fondamentale*) that *Le mort saisit le vif* and that *Le roy ne meurt point en France*."[51] Although the concept of "fundamental law" has been thought to have a continuity of its own, one should observe first, that the subtle linguistic shift from the amorphous earlier terms, such as "Loy de France," "Loy perpetuelle," and "Loy speciale [et] singulière," to the specific term "Loy Fondamentale," occurred in the early seventeenth century; and second, that the shift was part of a new mode of discourse which signaled the appearance of another constitutional ideology. In sixteenth-century discourse the Public Law of the kingdom was on the docket; in seventeeth-century discourse the Fundamental Law of royalty filled that bill. Finally, these dynastic cues were picked up by the *parlementaires*, who had helped to mold the innovative inaugural, and influenced their views on the perpetuity of individual officeholders in the Court.

At the same time that the *Lit de Justice* propagated precepts of dynastic monarchy, the historical fiction about it developed into a full-scale legend. As a result, knowledge about the ceremonial ritual of the *Lit de Justice* was eagerly sought on all fronts. Théodore Godefroy and his fraternal collaborator Denys Godefroy published *Le Cérémonial françois*, a study of various genres of royal ritual including the *Lit de Justice* (see Table One, Column P). They acknowledged Du Tillet as the first historian commissioned for such research and thanked Dupuy and the masters of ceremonies, Nicolas Saintot and his brother, for supplying pertinent manuscripts.[52] The magnitude of this second wave of research is im-

[51] Dupuy, *Traité de la majorité*, pp. 1-13.

[52] See Godefroy, *Cérémonial françois*, I and II. Vol. II contains accounts of *Lit de Justice* assemblies. Reproduced in the preface are two research commissions, one for Du Tillet in 1548 and one for the master of ceremonies in 1583 (I, e iv^v). Dupuy and the Saintots are cited for having supplied sources for the work (I, e iii^v). According to the Godefroys (I, e ii^r), a third volume was planned. It was never published, and materials for it are in Institut de France, Collection Godefroy mss. 379-483 (106 folios). An outline for another volume using some unpublished materials of the Godefroys was published by François-Antoine Jolly, *Projet d'un nouveau cérémonial françois, augmenté d'un grand nombre de*

mediately apparent when the contents of the early work by Théodore Godefroy are compared with those of the new treatise. Whereas the first small quarto edition of 1619 recorded only the Majority *Lit de Justice* assembly of 1563, the two-volume folio edition of 1649 contained a whole section of 223 pages devoted to *Lit de Justice* assemblies held between 1369 and 1648 and embellished with the authors' marginal notes on ceremonial precedent.[53]

As we have seen, chancellors had been collecting and disseminating information on the *Lit de Justice* since 1548. During the first stage of historical inquiry in the 1540's and 1550's Chancellor François Olivier used Du Tillet's findings to comment on parlementary assemblies during the Royal *Séance* of 1549, and later Chancellor Michel de L'Hôpital reinterpreted that evidence to support convocation of the Majority *Lit de Justice* in Rouen. Likewise, during this second stage of inquiry in the 1620's, 1630's, and 1640's Chancellor Pierre (III) Séguier collected information on the *Lit de Justice*, and he elaborated not only constitutional theory but also ceremonial protocol in regard to the assembly. In the very year (1633) that Séguier became seals-keeper (acting chancellor), Pierre Dupuy sent him a letter which discussed the delivery of manuscripts treating royal prerogatives, including some volumes promised by Godefroy earlier.[54] Séguier benefited directly from the work of the two antiquarians at a most auspicious moment. During the 1630's and 1640's he collected an enormous number of manuscripts containing extracts from registers of Parlement, and some of those volumes dealt specifically with *Lit de Justice* assemblies (see Table One, Column R).[55] Those sources did not gather dust on the bookshelves of the chancellery. Séguier studied

---

pièces qui n'ont pas publiées par M. Godefroy (Paris, 1746), but the work was never completed; see B.N. ms. fr. suppl. 11185.

[53] Compare Godefroy, *Cérémonial de France*, pp. 457-467, with *Cérémonial françois*, II, 427-650.

[54] B.N. ms. fr. 17367, fol. 390r (20 May 1633), and B.N. ms. fr. 18843-18883 for the volumes which Godefroy sent to Séguier. On these volumes, see Léopold Delisle, *Le Cabinet des manuscrits de la Bibliothèque Impériale (Nationale)* (Paris, 1874), II, 78-99. Pierre (III) Séguier was president in Parlement in 1624, seals-keeper in 1633, and chancellor in 1635.

[55] Consult B.N. ms. fr. 18411, fols. 116r-144v and 146r-156v; B.N. ms. fr. 18522, fols. 1r-257r; B.N. ms. fr. 18410, fols. 1r-439r; and Column R in Table One. Séguier also corresponded with foreign agents who bought books and manuscripts for him, and his library was superior to that of the king. Although most of the printed material was lost in a fire of 1794, many of the manuscripts survive; Delisle, *Cabinet des manuscrits*, II, 78-99, and René Kerviler, *Le Chancelier Pierre Séguier* (Paris, 1874), pp. 158-164.

the volumes pertinent to *Lit de Justice* assemblies carefully, writing comments in the margins on the historical and constitutional nature of the assembly; and he put such information to practical use during his contest with the *parlementaires* over oaths of office in 1643. All these factors, Séguier's close relationship with the Godefroys and Dupuy, his possession of source material on the *Lit de Justice*, and his curiosity about the assembly as a constitutional forum, point to the chancellor's influence on the fortunes of the assembly.

Besides producing a historical legend about the *Lit de Justice*, the new research in the seventeenth century led to speculation about certain functions of the assembly which resembled those of the Estates General. Although the antiquarian nature of the work (long on examples, short on analysis) leaves the evidence in conceptual disarray, some fairly obvious conclusions can be drawn from it. The exemplary proofs which are piled up and accompanied by terse notes in published works and in manuscript compilations suggest two conclusions: first, that contemporaries viewed the *Lit de Justice* as a constitutional forum fit not only for propagating Fundamental Law but also for raising extraordinary revenues, a duty formerly associated with the Estates General; and second, that contemporaries were aware that some *Lit de Justice* assemblies had employed a procedure for consultation (by orders) similar to that of the Estates General. As a result, in the mid-seventeenth century there was conjecture about the relationship between these two institutions, *Lit de Justice* and Estates, which differed markedly from earlier speculation on the subject. At times in the sixteenth century queries had been raised about the relationship between them. Francis I had announced that the *Lit de Justice* of 1527 (December) was convoked instead of the three Estates; President Charles Guillart had stated in the *Lit de Justice* of 1527 (July) that the Parlement of Paris had originated in a convention of "estates," and L'Hôpital in the 1560's had seen the early "estates" and "parlements" as the same body before their institutional separation. At times during parlementary assemblies consultation had proceeded by orders (Nobility, Clergy, and Third Estate), as in the Royal *Séances* of 1369 and 1552 and the *Lit de Justice* of 1527 (December), and the three Estates had been present in the *Séance* of 1558. Still, Parlement had always refused union with the Third Estate for purposes of deliberation as in the *Lit de Justice* of 1527 (December), when the Court insisted on its separate status, and even in the Estates of 1558, which Henry II described as a "general convocation of the four Estates," presumably the three and Parlement. Despite that refusal, however, the Court had not denied historical affinity with the Estates. Parlement had described itself in 1563 as an "abridged form of the three Estates, the image and replica of all the orders of the kingdom,"[56] and had argued following the Majority *Lit de Justice* in Rouen that same year that all legislation must be verified first in the Parlement of Paris, the institution which represents the Estates General.[57] Indeed, political theorists, the Parlement, spokesmen for the orders in the Estates General, and even the king had allowed that the Parlement of Paris was a kind of permanent representative of the Estates General.[58] To be sure, the origins of these institutions were not at all clearly perceived. In order to avoid misinterpretation, therefore, these sixteenth-century comments must be weighed carefully, first because they focused on the Parlement of Paris, not the *Lit de Justice*, and second because they did not actually equate the Court with the Estates. In those decades when the Estates General still flourished, the connection sometimes posited between the Parlement of Paris and the Estates was one which simply viewed Parlement (a body with institutional continuity) as the representative of the Estates General (a body convoked sporadically) when the latter was dispersed, nothing more.

Conversely, during the seventeenth century, which witnessed the demise of the Estates General after 1615 and the Assembly of Notables after 1626,[59] conclusions drawn from such historical conjecture differed. Cardinal Richelieu, a deputy to the last Estates General meeting (1614-1615), viewed that institution with utter disdain; similarly, Chancellor Séguier put little stock in such meetings. Within this vacuum, therefore, speculation arose in high places which tended to equate the *Lit de Justice* assembly with the Estates. The notion of such an equation received additional support from new evidence at hand. The legend of the *Lit de Justice* provided a new pool of sources for study. It subsumed almost all Royal *Séances* under the *Lit de Justice* category, and some of those *Séances*, along with authentic *Lits de Justice*, seemed to have absorbed functions of the Estates. At the same time Richelieu strengthened the

[56] A.N. X1a 1605, fol. 321r (18 June 1563). Note that Maugis, *Histoire du Parlement*, I, xiv, misprinted the date as 1593, an error repeated by Church, *Constitutional Thought*, p. 138, n. 47.

[57] A.N. X1a 1606, fol. 159r (21 Aug. 1563).

[58] Church, *Constitutional Thought*, pp. 137-139, and Julian Franklin, *Jean Bodin and the Rise of Absolutist Theory* (Cambridge, 1973), pp. 20-22.

[59] For representative assemblies, national and provincial, see Major, *Representative Government in Early Modern France* (New Haven, 1980), pp. 403-415 and 501-509.

legislative format of the *Lit de Justice*, an auspicious forum for implementing a policy of *raison d'état* and in that vein Séguier actually turned
to the *Lit de Justice* as a substitute for the Estates.[60] Contemplating
alternatives, Chancellor Séguier wrote scattered notes in the margins of
a manuscript on *Lit de Justice* assemblies, which commented on the role
of the Estates in French history.[61] Curious about the constitutional nature
of Charles V's important assembly of 1369, which included the three
Estates and raised revenues,[62] and influenced by the legend of the *Lit
de Justice* as well, Séguier offered the following explanation for its odd
format. In 1369 Charles V attempted to assemble the three Estates to
solicit war monies and failed, so he pursued a different course of action.
The king decided instead to treat all great affairs of state in the Parlement,
opting for a smaller consultative body, and he convoked the *Lit de Justice*
assembly of 9, 10, and 11 May 1369 for that purpose.[63] Since Séguier
thought that the assembly of 1369 resembled a meeting of Estates more
than a *Lit de Justice*, he presumed that the function of the one had been
assumed by the other. Adducing further proof for that hypothesis, the
chancellor noted the same institutional interplay in the *Lit de Justice* of
1527 (December) where the method of differentiating orders in the
Estates was used in the consultation phase of the *Lit de Justice*. In a
sweeping indictment he concluded that the Estates had been ineffective
since the fourteenth century, and he insinuated that the *Lit de Justice*
assembly on occasion had assumed the functions of the Estates.[64] Al-

[60] Both were blamed for making radical changes in the format of the *Lit de
Justice*; see Institut de France, Collection Godefroy ms. 395, fols. 288v-290r;
Omer Talon, *Mémoires de feu M. Omer Talon, avocat général en la cour de
Parlement de Paris* (The Hague, 1732), XXX, p. 21; and Kerviler, *Chancelier
Pierre Séguier*, p. 54. For the emerging theory and practice of *raison d'état*, see
Church, *Richelieu and Reason of State*.

[61] B.N. ms. fr. 18411, fols. 146r-154r, the folios studied.

[62] This session amounted to an Estates General convened in Parlement, the
first of three occasions in fourteenth-century France when Estates and Parlement
held a joint assembly to prepare the country for war subsidies. Charles V thus
broke from French tradition separating judicial and consultative assemblies; see
John B. Henneman, *Royal Taxation in Fourteenth Century France: The Captivity
and Ransom of John II, 1356-1370* (Philadelphia, 1976), pp. 254-270.

[63] B.N. ms. fr. 18411, fol. 146r. We know that the session of 1369 was a Royal
Séance, but Jean du Tillet listed it as a *Lit de Justice* in the *Recueil des grands*
(see Table Two, below). Following Du Tillet virtually all antiquarians and
manuscript compilers adopted that attribution, creating for the event a legendary
life in the seventeenth century (see Table One).

[64] B.N. ms. fr. 18411, fol. 154r.

though Chancellor Séguier's marginal notes reveal a certain perplexity, they nevertheless suggest that he seriously considered the *Lit de Justice* as an alternative to the Estates in the early seventeenth century. Séguier was not alone in holding such views. The influential author of *De la souveraineté du roy*, Cardin Le Bret, former *parlementaire*, Royal Council member, and confidante of Richelieu, registered strong opinions on the royal right to effect emergency taxation and the parlementary obligation to register such measures, in effect bypassing the Estates.[65]

At the same time that the *Lit de Justice* was exalted in this manner, trials of peers were removed from its purview. As noted earlier, according to parlementary opinion cited in the fifteenth century (preceding the trial of Alençon in the Royal *Séance* of 1458), reiterated by Jean du Tillet in the sixteenth century, and substantiated by the trial of Bourbon in the *Lit de Justice* of July 1527, French kings were required to attend the trial of a peer of the realm. During the reign of Louis XIII, however, those trials were conducted in ad hoc parlementary sessions, and the king was not present. Once again Le Bret might have influenced this change of policy. He sat as judge at the peer trials of 1632, 1639, and 1642, and he presented the fullest discussion to date on the crime of *lèse-majesté* in his treatise on sovereignty.[66] By the early decades of the seventeenth century, the place of the *Lit de Justice* in the French constitution was reinterpreted. Now the *Lit de Justice* comprehended taxation, assuming powers formerly associated with the Estates; and peer trials were adjudicated outside the *Lit de Justice*, erasing the last vestiges of the king's judicial role and expanding the legislative one.

Although the case cannot be pressed too far, it seems that this equation of *Lit de Justice* and Estates appealed also to some *parlementaires*, who

---

[65] Cardin Le Bret, *De la souveraineté du roy* (Paris, 1632), which is discussed in Church, *Richelieu and Reason of State*, pp. 268-276. On the problems of finance in general, see Julian Dent, *Crisis in Finance: Crown, Financiers and Society in Seventeenth-Century France* (Newton Abbot, 1973), who draws a social profile of the financiers whose capital came not from commerce but from state finances; and Richard Bonney, *The King's Debts: Finance and Politics in France, 1589-1661* (Oxford, 1981), who focuses on the inefficiency of deficit financing, the parasitic nature of the system on the French economy, and the inability to effect reform in wartime.

[66] On the trials, see Richard Bonney, *Political Change in France under Richelieu and Mazarin, 1624-1661* (Oxford, 1978), pp. 114-116; and especially, Church, *Richelieu and Reason of State*, pp. 179-184, 235-236, and 304-334, who notes the increasing number of crimes classified as *lèse-majesté*; and ibid., 268-276, which recounts Le Bret's legal discussion of that crime.

turned the theory to the advantage of the Court. Following the decline of Parlement's constitutional role in the Royal Funeral ceremony after 1610, the Court fastened upon the *Lit de Justice* as the ritual successor. In line with the evocative image of *Rex* and *Lex* reposing in the *Lit de Justice*, other eloquent spokesmen for the *parlementaires* culled passages from the registers of Parlement to confirm the Court's claim to represent the monarch and conjured up visions of the *Lit de Justice* assembly in the Grand-chambre as the "theater of France," the "sanctuary of justice," and even the "moderator of the edicts and the will of the prince."[67] Proclaiming that the Parlement of Paris (not the Estates) was "an institution as ancient as the monarchy, the place where the king has his *Lit de Justice* [assembly] . . . , the great tribunal denoted as *Judicium Francorum*," the *parlementaires* by mid century had reinterpreted French history. They argued for Parlement's hegemony over the Estates General, since the latter was obliged to observe the Court's *arrêts*,[68] and they were alleging outright by 1664 Parlement's superiority over the Estates.[69] If we allow that the idea of substituting the *Lit de Justice* for the Estates lingered about in the seventeenth century, it is not surprising to find that one *parlementaire* validated Louis XIV's legislative action in the Inaugural *Lit de Justice* of 1643 by referring to the presence of Bourbon blood princes and the three Estates of the kingdom. These heady allegations were overshadowed later in the century by the Sun King but surfaced again in Parlement's polemical literature of the 1730's. Later in the eighteenth century they were repeated by Louis-Adrien Le Paige, who certainly saw the *Lit de Justice* as comprehending the three Estates, and they were echoed now and then right up to the end when Parlement was disbanded and the Estates were called in 1788.[70]

[67] Comments like these of Peleus, *Premier président du Parlement*, pp. 8, 11, 12, and 20, are scattered through other works such as Orléans, *Ouvertures des Parlements*; La Roche-Flavin, *Treze livres des Parlemens de France*; Servin, *Action des gens du roy*; Bignon, *La Grandeur de nos roys*; and Corbin, *Code Louis XIII*; as well as scores of "remonstrances" (i.e. speeches) prepared for delivery in Parlement. Perhaps the prototype of this genre is Du Chesne's two treatises, *Les Antiquitez et recherches . . . des roys de France* and *Les Antiquitez et recherches . . . des huict Parlemens* discussed above. The "public interest" directs civil governments, Pierre Picault later argued, so the king cannot rule without Parlement; *Traité des Parlements ou États Généraux* (Cologne, 1679).

[68] A.N. K 695 (16.6), *Les Veritables maximes du gouvernement de la France* (1652), a published pamphlet, pp. 21-22.

[69] Institut de France, Collection Godefroy ms. 395, fol. 294r.

[70] In 1732 the treatise *Judicium francorum*, modeled on the *Veritables maximes*

In addition to this resurgence of antiquarian legend-making about the *Lit de Justice* and the tendency to equate the assembly with the Estates General, the ceremonial program of the *Lit de Justice* flourished with ever greater grandeur and precision in the seventeenth century, as already noted regarding Majority celebrations. Whereas the constitutional nature of the issues was of paramount importance in sixteenth-century *Lit de Justice* assemblies, now the ceremonial configuration assumed preeminence as a system of conventions which defined public authority. Early in the sixteenth century kings depended upon the knowledge of clerks of Parlement to organize their rare convocations of *Lit de Justice* assemblies. Later they appointed other officers ad hoc to plan specific parlementary sessions. Finally they regularized the office of master of ceremonies in 1585. In contrast, by the mid decades of the seventeenth century, the grand master of ceremonies, supported by the master of ceremonies and the aide of ceremonies, headed a bureau of professional experts who worked under royal auspices and regulated royal ceremonies. From the records left by Guillaume Pot de Rhodes, François Pot de Rhodes, the famous Nicolas Saintot, and Michel Ancel Desgranges during the reigns of Henry III, Louis XIII, Louis XIV, and Louis XV, the meteoric rise of that office can be discerned.[71] The grand master of ceremonies provided memoranda on protocol when requested by the king, received royal orders for *Lit de Justice* assemblies, issued formal convocation notices to Parlement and other attendants, drew up precise seating plans and rules for the sessions, appointed aides to direct proceedings there, and supplied antiquarians with historical data on such

---

of 1652 (see n. 68), was published; and around 1770 another pamphlet, *Recueil de lettres patentes*, p. 47, blamed that treatise for supporting Parlement's pretensions. For a discussion of that charge, see Ford, *Robe and Sword*, p. 93. Finally, the notions of Le Paige, *Réflexions*, renew the same allegations (see above, Introduction, n. 3); and the extensive work of Henri de Boulainvilliers, *Lettres sur les anciens Parlements de France que l'on nomme États-Généraux* (London, 1753), sets them in perspective.

[71] There is a large collection of manuscripts on ceremony which have never been thoroughly studied. The Godefroys left materials for a third volume, which was not published (see above, n. 52). The extensive collection of Brienne, B.N. ms. fr. n. a. 6972-7328 (see Table One, Column I), first in the hands of Richelieu, then Mazarin, became part of the royal library after 1661. The manuscripts of Master of Ceremonies Saintot are scattered through several collections in B.N. ms. fr. 14117-14120, 13017, 15524, 16633, 20821, and B.N. ms. fr. n. a. 3122, 3156. A collection of manuscripts was made by Master of Ceremonies Desgranges, B. Mazarine mss. 2737-2753. On fol. 1r of each of the first six volumes, Desgranges noted that he had copied Saintot's registers and then returned them.

assemblies. This group of experts kept detailed records of the sessions, provided a new repository for documents regarding *Lit de Justice* assemblies and other ceremonies, and probably arranged for the publication of posters, engravings, and pamphlets depicting and recounting the events, publications that appeared with increasing frequency in the seventeenth century.[72] Since the French monarchy until late in the seventeenth century had no official throne room outside of the Grand-chambre of the Palais de Justice, the king's appearance in Parlement was the most celebrated ceremony in the kingdom, for unlike the Coronation or even *Entrées* to cities it was an event repeated regularly. Consequently, Parlement too was caught up in the heights of ceremonial grandeur associated with the *Lit de Justice* and failed to perceive that the ceremonial program itself would eventually absorb the *Lit de Justice* assembly. In the meantime, the ritual of the *Lit de Justice* provided a powerful device for shaping constitutional policy, because it promoted both the new dynastic ideology and the legislative authority of the Bourbons.

[72] For original royal letters to masters of ceremonies bearing orders for ceremonial events, consult A.N. KK 1448, fols. 20r-209v. Besides the records in the ceremonial register of the masters, consult, for example, B.N. ms. fr. n. a. 9744, fols. 1r-33r, for a type of memorandum on ceremony drawn expressly for the king. There was a plan drawn for a proposed session of 1585 (see above, Chap. IX, n. 28). The plan printed for the Majority in 1614 appears in Figure 11. There was a plan probably drawn by Master of Ceremonies Rhodes for a *Lit de Justice* of 1616 (see below, Chap. XII, n. 10). The plan for the inauguration of 1715 appears in Figure 15.

XII

THE ARTICULATION OF DYNASTIC RIGHT AND LEGISLATIVE AUTHORITY: *LIT DE JUSTICE* ASSEMBLIES 1614-1641

> ... the Bourbon blood princes ... and the cardinals ...
> quickly joined the king [Louis XIII] *under the canopy* and
> presented advice from there as a separate order. *Lit de
> Justice assembly (1632)*

IN THE *Lit de Justice* of 1610 the Parlement of Paris sought prominence
on two fronts, as the primary inaugural institution and as the legislative
tutor of a minor king. To realize those ends, the Court willingly implemented the royal inauguration but issued a preemptive regency *arrêt*
to limit royal legislative capacity. Yet in the long run the ceremonial
demonstration of dynastic kingship carried out in the *Lit de Justice*,
repeated in the Coronation *Entrée*, and rationalized by legend-makers
stamped the emerging system of dynastic monarchy with a strong legislative hue. Starkly dramatic thenceforth was the royal alliance of dynastic right and legislative authority in *Lits de Justice*; caught in the
juncture was the Parlement of Paris, which actively supported the former
but tried to temper the latter. Parlement supported the ideology of
dynastic right because it buttressed the Court's own growing dynastic
conception of parlementary office. That new concept was reflected in
regulations on officeholding and exemplified in social alignments. The
earlier system of simple *survivance* was replaced with that of the *droit
annuel* (*paulette*, 1604) which encouraged the hereditary transmission of
office.[1] Eventually the parlementary officeholding enterprise took on a

---

[1] On early inheritance practices in Parlement, see Françoise Autrand, *Naissance d'un grand corps de l'état: Les gens du Parlement de Paris, 1345-1454* (Paris,
1981); and in a civic setting, see Barbara Diefendorf, *Paris City Councillors in
the Sixteenth Century: The Politics of Patrimony* (Princeton, 1983). Salmon, *Society
in Crisis*, pp. 318-326, recounts the two sides of the question as argued by Sully
and Pomponne de Bellièvre. On venality in general, see Mousnier, *La Vénalité
des offices*, who sees the system of venality as supporting royal power, and his
Institutions de la France, II, 319-365, where he notes that for *parlementaires* in
the sixteenth and seventeenth centuries venality stimulated social ascension. For
discussion of the *droit annuel* (*paulette*) and its connection with the social com-

dynastic dimension of its own: legally considered as *"propres"* in family succession, offices provided one prop for dynastic officialdom; united in a tightly knit corporation, Parisian *parlementaires* identified themselves as a *noblesse de robe*.[2] Whereas Parlement in the sixteenth century had claimed perpetuity as a corporate body beyond the death of a king, *parlementaires* in the seventeenth century claimed perpetuity both as a corporate body and as individual family proprietors of offices within that body.[3] Thus the ideology of dynastic kingship legitimized the aspirations of *parlementaire* families and fit the Court's notion of the right order of things. Conversely, Parlement resisted the articulation of royal legislative power in *Lits de Justice* because it seriously undermined the Court's alleged co-legislative function in the polity. Yet at this point the *Lit de Justice* assembly brought enormous prestige to the Court. Consequently, even though the use of the assembly as a royal legislative vehicle jarred Parlement's notion of right order, the Court issued no disclaimers at first. To be sure, Louis XIII did not convoke another *Lit de Justice* while still a minor, but he virtually requisitioned the Grand-chambre of the Parlement of Paris as a royal throne room in later years.

In the course of Louis XIII's reign the character of the *Lit de Justice* assembly changed in practice and theory. For one thing, that king convoked more parlementary assemblies than all others put together. In the

---

position of Parlement, see Albert N. Hamscher, *The Parlement of Paris after the Fronde, 1653-1673* (Pittsburgh, 1976), who notes that Parlement could and did give powerful opposition to the Crown even after the *Fronde* because Louis XIV had maintained the system of venality intact. As an excellent corrective to works which ignore the importance of female hypergamy on social stratification, see Carolyn C. Lougee, *Le Paradis des Femmes: Women, Salons, and Social Stratification in Seventeenth-Century France* (Princeton, 1976), pp. 113-170.

[2] Giesey, "Rules of Inheritance and Strategies of Mobility in Prerevolutionary France," *American Historical Review*, LXXXII, 2 (Apr. 1977), pp. 271-289, shows how parlementary offices, which were transmitted by inheritance through the *paulette* and provided regular revenue as did *rentes*, were viewed as fictive immovables in the law and considered as *propres* in family succession, creating a "Dynastic Officialdom." A. Lloyd Moote, *The Revolt of the Judges: The Parlement of Paris and the Fronde, 1643-1652* (Princeton, 1971), shows how risky it was to tamper with venality and notes that the mode of officeholding figured in the crises of the *Fronde*. Since the family background of the *parlementaires* was magisterial, according to Hamscher, *Parlement of Paris after the Fronde*, pp. 32-61, the group did indeed become a closely knit corporation.

[3] Peleus, *Premier président*, p. 23, describes Parlement as a perpetual institution (whose members do not wear mourning on the death of a king), where authority is vested "n'est pas seulement en corps, mais aussi en chacun des membres, officiers et ministres."

thirty-three years between 1610 and 1643 there were twenty sessions convoked, three in provincial Parlements, seventeen in the Parlement of Paris; and every one was designated officially as a *Lit de Justice* whether matters treated therein were constitutional or honorary, judicial or legislative. As a result, the constitutional distinction between *Lit de Justice* and Royal *Séance* observed from 1527 to 1597 disappeared.[4] For another thing, the historical research of the new antiquarians and manuscript compilers, conducted on a grand scale now, transformed the modest sixteenth-century historical fiction of the *Lit de Justice* into a national legend which commanded public attention and rationalized the new system of dynastic monarchy.[5] Finally, the ostentatious ceremonial programs newly devised by masters of ceremonies provided a grand stage upon which this fortuitous union of dynastic right and legislative power was realized, at first with some consensus, later amidst a rising tide of criticism.

At the outset the conflict was minimized. The Parlement of Paris cooperated with the programmatic inflation of ceremonial grandeur in the *Lit de Justice* for good reason: performance of the ritual in the Grandchambre brought the Court great status by associating Crown and Parlement in governance, and the king granted the Parlement an impressive ceremonial prerogative, first place in consultation, for almost a decade from 1620 to 1629.[6] Yet at the same time Parlement attempted at every turn to widen its sphere of legislative influence in the assembly and to stem other ceremonial innovations which undermined that position. In 1615 the Court insisted upon its right to deliberate on laws, ordinances,

---

[4] Table One records the failure to distinguish between the two parlementary assemblies during this reign. In the registers of Parlement, moreover, bold titles identify the sessions as *Lit de Justice* assemblies, and the summonses which were issued for the events precede each account there. The three assemblies of 1615 (Bordeaux), 1620 (Rouen), and 1620 (Bordeaux) provoked no ire in the Parlement of Paris because the Inaugural and Majority ceremonies were firmly anchored in the Parisian Court.

[5] For that transformation at a glance, see Table One.

[6] Godefroy, *Cérémonial françois* [unidentified source], II, 609-613 (11 July 1620, Rouen), and *Mercure françois*, VI, 293-294, when Parlement took first place in consultation. Of the twenty *Lits de Justice* held by Louis XIII, fifteen are discussed below. The five which are not treated here in detail are recorded in the registers of Parlement as follows: (1) A.N. X1a 1909, fols. 18r-110r (4 July 1620); (2) A.N. X1a 1929, fols. 167v-170v (18 Mar. 1622); (3) A.N. X1a 1967, fols. 36v-39r (6 Mar. 1626), and the summons (5 Mar.), fol. 27r; (4) A.N. X1a 1982, fols. 567r-574v (28 June 1627); and (5) A.N. X1a 2044, fols. 344r-350r (13 Aug. 1631), and the summons (12 Aug.), fols. 332v-333r.

and peace treaties, and also on the creation of offices. Vying with the Estates General recently dismissed, Parlement claimed for itself historical origins contemporary with the monarchy (an institution "born with the state") and thereafter declared, throughout the ancien régime, that it was the representative of the nation.[7] That same year Parlement moved from theoretical pronouncements to practical action: the Court brazenly attempted to convoke an assembly of princes, peers, and *parlementaires* in the Grand-chambre (a Court of peers without the king) to discuss affairs of state, an attempt stopped short by the Royal Council.[8] In turn over the next few decades the Crown acted to restrict Parlement's sphere of cognizance, first by manipulating ceremonial ritual in the *Lit de Justice* in a way which limited the Court's authority, then by issuing legal counterparts for those earlier ceremonial regulations. From the convocation of the Majority *Lit de Justice* in 1614, ritual was expanded and standardized throughout the kingdom. First, the ceremony was extended spatially outside the walls of the Grand-chambre to include lavish entry and departure processions graced by sumptuously dressed royal participants marching or riding to the triumphant notes of drums, trumpets, and fifes. That extension of pomp and circumstance, already discussed for the Majority celebration of 1614 (Figures 10 and 11) set the tone for such processions throughout the century. Second, ceremony was amplified substantively during the assembly itself inside the Grand-chambre. Parlement harbored a dual reaction toward these innovations: the king could append ceremonial accretions to his dramatic arrival and departure outside of the Palais de Justice, but he should not tamper with the Court's ceremonial customs inside the Grand-chambre. It was in fact inside the parquet where the most interesting novelties were introduced.

In the ritual of Louis XIII's *Lits de Justice*, there stood in bold relief two critical elements which supported Bourbon kingship: dynastic right and legislative power. On the dynastic side there was a steady ceremonial elevation of the king and Bourbon Crown-worthy males. At the *Lit de Justice* of 1615 in Bordeaux the narrow corner of the chamber containing the throne apparatus was enlarged and decorated splendidly for Louis XIII, and the *parlementaires* were pressured into deputizing some presidents and councillors to accompany the king as practiced in the Parle-

---

[7] Glasson, *Parlement de Paris*, I, 123-126; and Shennan, *Parlement of Paris*, p. 244, who cites the date incorrectly as 1616.

[8] Ibid., both sources, regarding the attempt to convoke a Court of peers; see also Isambert, *Recueil général des anciennes lois*, XVI, 61-76.

HERAVS' DARME S· LARRIVEE DV ROYAV PALAIS·MONSIEVR
FRERE DV ROY

10. Louis XIII: Majority *Lit de Justice* held in the Grand-chambre of the Parlement of Paris, 1614.

ORDRE DE LA SEANCE TENVE AV
PARLEMENT, LE ROY SEANT EN SON LICT DE
IVSTICE, POVR LA DECLARATION DE SA MAIORITE'.

Le deuxiesme d'Octobre, l'an de grace mil six cens quatorze.

LE ROY.

LA ROYNE
Marguerite.

Mᵉ de Sourdis. | Mᵉ du Perron. | Mᵉ de la Roche Foucaud. | Mᵉ de Bonzic.
Mᵉˢ les Cardinaux au lieu des Pairs d'Eglise par la volonté du Roy.

Mᵉ de Verdun. | Mᵉ du Blanc. | Mʳ Seguier. | Mᵉ de Hacquenille. | Mʳ le Ley. | Mᵉ Lefcalopier Mesnil.

Mᵉˢ les Presidens de la Cour en robbes rouges & mortier d'or.

Madame la Presidente
Verdun.

Monsieur de Pontaines
Chastandrey.

Mada. de Conty. | Mad. de Boissons. | Mad. de Guyse.

Mad. de Elboeuf. | M. le Cont. d'Auverg.

Mes Dames les Princesses.

Plusieurs Seigneurs debout
parez de diamans &
de pierreries.

Messieurs les Cardinaux au lieu des Pairs d'Eglise par la volonté du Roy.

Messieurs les Princes & Pairs laics.

Messieurs les Marefchaux de France.

Messieurs les Confeillers de la Cour en robbes rouges.

Messieurs les Confeillers d'Eftat en robbes de foye | Messieurs les Evefques & Confeillers d'Eftat d'eipee.

Messieurs les Chevaliers de l'Ordre & Confeillers d'Eftat d'eipee.

Monsieur de Rhodes
Gr. M. des Ceremonies.

Messieurs les Secretaires d'Eftat, Bailly du Palais, & Precepteur du Roy.
De Lomenie, Puyfieux, De Scaus, Pontchartrain, De Beaumont.
Messieurs des Requeftes, de la fuitte de Mᵉ le Chancellier.

Greffe Ciuil & Criminel.

Mᵉˢ les Confeillers de la Cour en robbes rouges, Gᵉ. Chambre.
Messieurs les Confeillers de la Cour en robbes rouges.

Messieurs Seruin, Bellieure, le Bret. Gens du Roy.
Messieurs les Confeillers de la Cour en robbes rouges.
Messieurs les Confeillers de la Cour en robbes rouges.
Messieurs les Confeillers de la Cour en robbes rouges.

Monsieur de la Force
Capitaine des Gardes
en quartier.

Le Parquet des
Huissiers.

A PARIS, le 2. d'Octobre 1614.
De l'Imprimerie d'Antoine Champenois, au Griffon d'Or deuant la grand'porte du Palais.

11. Louis XIII: Plan of the Majority *Lit de Justice* held in the Grand-chambre of
the Parlement of Paris, 1614.

ment of Paris.[9] During the *Lit de Justice* of 1616 in Paris and that of 1620 in Rouen the Bourbon blood princes were allotted precedence over other princes, dukes, and peers; moreover, in the latter assembly they were accorded the title of *Monseigneur* to distinguish them from the dukes called *Monsieur* and supplied with ceremonial pillows matching those of the throne paraphernalia.[10] In the assembly of 1620 at Bordeaux the princes were privileged to remain seated with hats on while the king spoke.[11] In the *Lit de Justice* of 1621 the Bourbon blood princes were isolated as a special group for the purpose of consultation.[12] Clearly the Bourbon blood princes were well on the road to becoming a "separate and distinct order" by 1625, as Master of Ceremonies Desgranges would observe when mulling over this situation at the turn of the eighteenth century.[13] Besides elevating the status of Bourbon Crown heirs, Louis XIII accorded special place in the *Lit de Justice* to certain royal officials. The most notable case was that of Cardinal Richelieu, who obtained peer rank in 1627 and sat in that capacity in *Lit de Justice* assemblies from 1629, the same year that the presidents of Parlement lost first place in the order of consultation.[14] The masters of ceremonies also benefited

[9] Godefroy, *Cérémonial françois* [clerk of Court], II, 602-608 (10 Dec. 1615, Bordeaux), and *L'Ordre et cérémonies observées aux mariages* [Marillac], pp. 70-79.

[10] A.N. X1a 1878, fols. 149r-356r (7 Sept. 1616), and the summons (6 Sept.), fol. 145v. See also Godefroy, *Cérémonial françois* [Rhodes], II, 608-609, and *Mercure françois*, IV, 214. B.N. ms. fr. 18431 [unnumbered folios] indicates that a plan was drawn in 1616 by the master of ceremonies, Rhodes, but does not specify day or month. Hand-drawn versions of that plan appear also in B.N. ms. fr. n. a. 7231, fols. 154r and 154v-155r. Sources for 11 July 1620, Rouen, are cited in n. 6 above; and Godefroy, *Cérémonial françois*, II, 609, gives the following description of the thronal paraphernalia: "Suspended above the said seat, which was covered by a drape of black velvet, was the dais or royal canopy, the back and two sides hung with tapestries sewn with golden fleurs-de-lis. The velvet pillow was also sewn with golden fleurs-de-lis, and [there were] other pillows of velvet on the said seat and at the foot [of it], ornaments which are all in the said Court. From the footstool to the lowest step of the parquet there was another Turkish tapestry. The said dais will remain in the same place [in the Parlement of Rouen] as long as the king is in Normandy."

[11] Godefroy, *Cérémonial françois* [Pontac], II, 613-618 (28 Sept. 1620, Bordeaux).

[12] A.N. X1a 1918, fols. 8v-15r (3 Apr. 1621), the summons missing. See also, Godefroy, *Cérémonial françois* [unidentified source], II, 618-625.

[13] B. Mazarine, 2745, fol. 164v.

[14] A.N. X1a 2009, fols. 199v-204v (15 Jan. 1629), and the summons the same morning (15 Jan.), fol. 199r. For the original *lettre de cachet* sent from the king

from special privilege. In 1616 François Pot de Rhodes was required to remove his sword before entering the Grand-chambre to announce a *Lit de Justice*, but by 1635 Nicolas Saintot entered freely with a sword and a baton of authority.[15] Finally, when the seals-keeper (acting chancellor) was accorded deference at the expense of the presidents of Parlement, the bizarre scene recounted below erupted. The Parlement of Paris tried to guard its ceremonial prerogatives as the quest for royal splendor and with it royal authority escalated, and a showdown between king and *parlementaires* was inevitable.

At least two volatile issues came to the fore in this shifting scene, and they provide a rare glimpse into the prevailing *mentalité* which subscribed

---

to Mathieu Molé, see B.N. Cinq Cents Colbert ms. 212. See also, Godefroy, *Cérémonial françois* [Pontcarré, councillor], II, 625; and *Mercure françois*, XV, 7-28, including the speech of the seals-keeper, Michel de Marillac. For Cardinal Richelieu's appointment as peer, consult Isambert, *Recueil général des anciennes lois*, XVI, 198. In an essay, A.N. U 928 (Traité de la cour de Parlement de Paris), this *Lit de Justice* is discussed and reference is made to Du Tillet; fols. 109r-124r. For details on this session, consult Major, *Representative Government*, pp. 515-518.

[15] The privilege of wearing a sword in the Grand-chambre of the Parlement of Paris ran a long and testy course. Originally a prerogative of the king, it was extended to princes, peers, and Crown officers during the absence of the monarch in the mid-sixteenth century; see Du Tillet, *Recueil des grands*, pp. 111-112, recounting arguments over the privilege from 1415 to 1556, and A.N. U 424 (31 Aug. 1551), an extract from registers of Parlement indicating that Henry II allowed the privilege to the above-named in his absence. For the masters of ceremonies it is difficult to fix the exact date of the privilege. In 1616 Rhodes wore the sword when he delivered a royal summons for the *Lit de Justice* of 7 September, but he was denied entrance to the Grand-chambre that day and left rather than remove the sword; A.N. X1a 1878, fols. 145v-149r (6 Sept. 1616), and Mathieu Molé, *Mémoires de Mathieu Molé*, ed. Aimé Champollion-Figeac, *Société de l'histoire de France* (Paris, 1855), I, 125-136, recounting the refusal to remain without the sword. Yet by 1619 Rhodes wore the sword to deliver a summons for the *Lit de Justice* of 12 March; A.N. X1a 1896, fols. 190v-191r (11 Mar.). Finally, by 1635 Saintot was wearing a sword by his side and carrying a baton of authority in his hand to deliver such a summons; Godefroy, *Cérémonial françois* [Saintot], II, 632 (19 Dec. 1635). The privilege was extended to other Courts when the king granted it for entrance to the Chambre des Comptes; A.N. P 2606, fols. 156v-157v (26 Oct. 1637). The *parlementaires* were irritated by the practice but accepted it for fear of offending the king according to a report of 1641; B.N. ms. fr. 23061, fols. 1v-6r. A decade later the entrance of the master of ceremonies, sword at side, baton of command in hand, to the Grand-chambre was an established practice; A.N. KK 1448, fol. 155r-v (26 Sept. 1651).

to a system of ceremonial ritual defining public authority. Just before the *Lit de Justice* of 1632 was convened, Louis XIII sent orders to the Grand-chambre requiring that the presidents of Parlement pay deference to the seals-keeper (acting chancellor) by rising when that officer entered the assembly as they would for the chancellor.[16] Since First President Nicolas Le Jay and President Pierre (III) Séguier balked at implementing the royal order, they were summoned next door to Sainte-Chapelle for an audience with the king. First the presidents argued on the specific merits of the case, complaining that the novel regulation granted a new "prerogative of state" to the seals-keeper which prejudiced the *dignité* of the presidents. Parlementary protocol required that councillors of the Court rise for presidents and that presidents rise for the chancellor (a member of the Court), but protocol did not require such deference for the seals-keeper (not a member of the Court). Next the presidents argued on grounds of principle, claiming that parlementary protocol itself could not be breached. Moving beyond President Harlay's admonitions of 1583, they held that grave changes in parlementary ceremonies such as that just commanded could not be implemented unless deliberated upon beforehand by the whole Court. Extremely irritated by this incident, which delayed the *Lit de Justice* assembly, Louis XIII abruptly commanded "as king and by his absolute authority" that Parlement carry out the new ceremonial regulation. The presidents capitulated on the spot but requested permission to register the "absolute command" as one which entailed no precedent, and the king granted that request. Back in the Grand-chambre the presidents, still determined to hold the line against such encroachment, contrived a ruse to circumvent the order. They stood together pretending to discuss the problem and thus avoided rising for the arrival of the seals-keeper, Charles de L'Aubespine, Marquis of Chateauneuf. As Chateauneuf passed by the standing presidents, a nasty exchange took place in muffled undertones. The presidents were standing not because of any honor due the office of the seals, President Le Jay said, but because the king ordered such deference for that day, and the registers of Parlement would show that the action set no precedent. The seals-keeper responded that he believed the deference was due his charge; the first president retorted that the presidents believed

---

[16] This quarrel dated to the *Lit de Justice* of 1616, when the seals-keeper tried to exact such deference from presidents. For the original letter of the king to Molé warning the presidents of the change in protocol, see B.N. Cinq Cents Colbert ms. 212, fol. 291r.

otherwise.[17] The disclaimer of precedent counted for naught. Pierre (III) Séguier was a president of Parlement when he championed the Court's prerogatives in 1632, but he changed his allegiance as fast as his robes when appointed seals-keeper in the following year. Thus the bizarre scene was repeated in the assemblies of 1633 and 1634: the presidents of Parlement, who were required to stand for the entrance of Séguier, indulged their anger as he passed, whispering into his ear their nasty reservations about forced compliance.[18] This quixotic rite of resistance ended on the morning preceding the *Lit de Justice* of 1635 when Seals-keeper Séguier was appointed chancellor, thereby fending off an imminent fourth quarrel.[19] Clearly the danger to parlementary prerogatives posed by the introduction of new ceremonial regulations to the *Lit de Justice* assembly was a recognized source of contention by the 1630's.

The second issue which came to the fore in the *Lit de Justice* of 1632 concerned the relative positions of king and Parlement as symbolized in ceremonial ritual. During the *Lit de Justice* of 1632 a most astounding reversal of protocol occurred at the moment of consultation. As Seals-keeper Chateauneuf approached Louis XIII to request the order for consultation, the Bourbon blood princes (Condé and Soissons to the king's right) and the cardinals (Richelieu and La Valette to his left) quickly

[17] A.N. X1a 2055, fols. 385r-392v (12 Aug. 1632), and a summons (11 Aug.), fol. 377r. The original *lettre de cachet* from the king to Molé is contained in B.N. Cinq Cents Colbert ms. 212. See also Godefroy, *Cérémonial françois* [unidentified source], II, 626-629 and 629-632; *Mercure françois*, XVIII, 526-536, giving the speech of Seals-keeper Chateauneuf; and *Mémoires de Talon*, XXX, 14. Charles de L'Aubespine, Marquis of Chateauneuf, was seals-keeper from 1630 to 1633, then again in 1650. Le Jay became an *avocat* around 1615, president later.

[18] For the first scene, A.N. X1a 2064, fols. 161r-168r (12 Apr. 1633), and the summons (11 Apr.), fol. 151r. For the original *lettre de cachet* from the king to Molé, see B.N. Cinq Cents Colbert ms. 212. See also *Mercure françois*, XIX, 67; *Mémoires de Molé*, II, 175; and *Mémoires de Talon*, XXX, 21. For the second scene, A.N. X1a 2074, fols. 301r-311r (18 Jan. 1634), and the summons (17 Jan.), fol. 294r-v. For the original *lettre de cachet*, see B.N. Cinq Cents Colbert ms. 212. See also *Mercure françois*, XX, 2-38, including the speech of Cardinal Richelieu; *Mémoires de Molé*, II, 197-206; and *Mémoires de Talon*, XXX, 29. Godefroy, *Cérémonial françois*, II, 632, mentioned both events but published no accounts. For details on this dispute, consult Kerviler, *Chancelier Pierre Séguier*, pp. 36-62.

[19] According to Master of Ceremonies Saintot, a nasty recurrence was narrowly avoided when Séguier was officially installed as chancellor at seven in the morning just preceding the *Lit de Justice* of 20 December 1635; Godefroy, *Cérémonial françois* [Saintot], II, 632-634.

joined the king *under the canopy* and presented advice from there as a separate order. The presidents objected vociferously. When the seals-keeper informed them that the regulation of ceremonial procedure was a royal prerogative, President Le Jay granted that there was nothing left to say and the presidents refused to opine.[20] This extraordinary format for consultation allied Bourbon blood princes and selected royal advisers directly with Louis XIII under the royal canopy and left Parlement to give advice indirectly through a royal officer. That format was employed in every *Lit de Justice* assembly during the rest of the reign (1633, 1634, 1635, and 1641),[21] and it altered the consultation process significantly. In effect Louis XIII used ceremonial procedure to set a devastating precedent allowing Bourbon princes and special advisers a deliberative voice in the *Lit de Justice* but restricting Parlement to a consultative one.

In addition to publicizing Bourbon dynastic right, the ritual of Louis XIII's *Lit de Justice* assemblies expanded royal legislative authority to include fiscal power. In at least fifteen of his twenty *Lit de Justice* assemblies the king sought to register legislation; in six of those sessions the *parlementaires* evoked remonstrances to counter the action.[22] In those years, moreover, when European monarchs were plagued by the escalating costs of warfare and tax revolts,[23] Louis XIII resorted to the sale of offices, many of them in the Courts, and that financial expedient

[20] See n. 17 above for the *Lit de Justice* of 12 August 1632. An unidentified source complained that a novel procedure had been introduced to the assembly: ordinarily the chancellor approached the king first not to solicit his opinion but to receive his command regarding the order of consultation to be followed; hence, if the king gave his opinion first, free deliberations would not be possible; Godefroy, *Cérémonial françois* [unidentified source], II, 629-632. See also *Mémoires de Talon*, XXX, 16. The princes were Henry (II) de Bourbon, Prince of Condé, and Louis de Bourbon, Count of Soissons; and the other cardinal besides Richelieu was Louis de Nogaret d'Épernon, Cardinal of La Valette [italics added].

[21] For citations on the assemblies of 12 April 1633 and 18 January 1634, see n. 18 above; and those of 20 December 1635 and 21 February 1641, nn. 29 and 30 below. The working notes of Godefroy make it clear that this procedure allying persons *under the canopy* was most extraordinary; Institut de France, Collection Godefroy ms. 395.

[22] The important legislative sessions are those of 1610, 1614, 1619, 1620 (July, Rouen), 1620 (February), 1620 (September, Bordeaux), 1621, 1622, 1626, 1627, 1629, 1632, 1633, 1635, and 1641.

[23] See Russell, "Monarchies, Wars, and Estates," pp. 205-220; Bonney, *Political Change in France*, chaps. X-XI; and Salmon, "Venal Office and Popular Sedition in Seventeenth-Century France," *Past and Present*, no. 37 (1967), 21-43.

infuriated officeholders with family stakes in dynastic officialdom. Thus between 1620 and 1641 the line of tension over legislative prerogative was drawn taut, mainly because royal edicts increasingly contained financial measures which affected officeholding. It was in these decades, therefore, that parlementary remonstrances began to appear regularly in the wake of the *Lit de Justice*. In the *Lit de Justice* assembly of 1620 (February), Louis XIII promulgated edicts creating and regulating offices, and three days later some councillors from the Chambre des Enquêtes boldly demanded a plenary session of the Grand-chambre to deliberate on the execution of those edicts.[24] In the assembly of 1620 (September) at Bordeaux, the king presented for registration four edicts dealing with taxation, alleging the *casus necessitatis*, "necessity in the affairs of his majesty," to legitimize the action; but the *parlementaires* still insisted upon deliberating first. When the king then reiterated the order for registration, the *parlementaires* immediately announced their intention to issue remonstrances on two of the four edicts.[25] In the *Lit de Justice* of 1621 Louis XIII promulgated edicts which alienated part of the income from *gabelles* for *rente constitutée*, again alleging the *casus necessitatis*, a situation of "public necessity" arising from the financial distress caused by wars, and suggested that "extraordinary" measures such as this *required* compliance. But again Parlement insisted that it must deliberate on edicts presented for registration, and later the Court drew up remonstrances stating that position. This affair did not end there. Two days later Parlement forbade the clerk to deliver the *arrêt* for registration of the edicts, and the king countered by sending the Prince of Condé to demand obedience to the royal will.[26]

In the assembly of 1629 a similar scene ensued as several edicts were presented and a dispute developed over one of them, the ordinance known as the Code Michaud, which Parlement refused to register without prior deliberation. When the *parlementaires* indicated that they would

[24] A.N. X1a 1905, fols. 291r-293v, with parts omitted and then added at the end of that register, fols. 497v-498r (18 Feb. 1620). Godefroy, *Cérémonial françois* [no source], II, 609, mentions the event but gives no account. On the demand of the Enquêtes, consult A.N. X1a 1905, fols. 302v-310v (21 Feb. 1620). For the edicts registered, see Isambert, *Recueil général des anciennes lois*, XV, 136-139.

[25] For this assembly of 1620, see the sources in n. 11 above.

[26] For this assembly of 1621, see the sources in n. 12 above. On Parlement's refusal to have the *greffier* [Du Tillet] deliver the royal *arrêt* of registration, A.N. X1a 1918, fols. 15r-24v (5 Apr. 1621). Le Bret in *De la souveraineté* argued that the Courts must register fiscal edicts in cases of "urgent necessity"; see Bonney, *Political Change in France*, pp. 115-116.

issue remonstrances on that edict, Seals-keeper Michel de Marillac reminded them that Article 1 of the pending code allowed remonstrances only after the publication of royal edicts and within six months of registration. And it was in this assembly, it should be recalled, that Louis XIII denied Parlement the decade-old prerogative of first place in consultation.[27] As the next decade opened the disputes grew more acrimonious. A Royal Council decree (May 1631) expressly denied Parlement the right to deliberate on royal declarations that involved affairs of state, and Louis XIII supported that separation of jurisdictions with a reminder (January 1632) to *parlementaires* that their charges were strictly judicial, established only to judge cases of royal subjects.[28] The next seven years witnessed no détente in this contest, and actions taken in the last two *Lits de Justice* of the reign only increased hostilities. In the assembly of 1635 the king promulgated numerous edicts, including at least thirteen which created new offices in Parlement, and the same scene was played out: Louis XIII presented edicts for registration on the grounds of *necessitas* (the "necessity of war") on the one side, and Parlement countered with a procedural complaint about the lack of prior deliberations on the other. Once again (as in 1620) some councillors from the Chambre des Enquêtes later demanded a plenary session of the Grand-chambre to deliberate on the edicts despite their registration in the king's presence during the *Lit de Justice*.[29] Finally the king took legal steps to settle the

[27] For the assembly of 1629, see the sources in n. 14 above. On the edicts registered, consult Isambert, *Recueil général des anciennes lois*, XVI, 223-344.

[28] According to Molé, the king said, "You are here only to judge between master Peter and master John, and I intend to keep you in your place; and if you continue your machinations, I shall cut your nails to the quick"; *Mémoires de Molé*, II, 143-144.

[29] A.N. X1a 2101, fols. 506r-511r (20 Dec. 1635), and the summons (19 Dec.), fols. 505r-506r, near the end of the register out of chronological order. See also *Mercure françois*, XXI, 88-89, and Godefroy, *Cérémonial françois* [Saintot], II, 632-634, and ibid. [Reg. Parl.], II, 634-635. Saintot supplied a good description of the thronal paraphernalia: "It is a grand dais of violet velvet sewn with golden fleurs-de-lis, the queue of which reaches the chair of the chancellor and serves to ornament that chair. There are under the feet of the king, behind him, and on both sides, a number of pillows sewn with golden fleurs-de-lis. The grand chamberlain reclines at his feet, and the provost of Paris acts as guard of the parquet on the step going to the high [seats], and the said provost [wears] a sword by his side and [carries] a baton covered with white velvet"; ibid., II, 634. For the edicts, consult Isambert, *Recueil général des anciennes lois*, XVI, 441-450, 460-465.

dispute over the authority of the *Lit de Justice* assembly versus that of Parlement's registration procedure.

The matter was brought to a head in Louis XIII's last *Lit de Justice* assembly in 1641. There the king promulgated a long edict confirming the separation of legislative (royal) and judicial (parlementary) powers, forbidding the Parlements of France any cognizance in affairs of state.[30] The important Edict of 1641 opened with a preamble which provided a historical résumé of royal pronouncements on the separation of powers.[31] The preamble listed a series of regulations which have now been identified in previous chapters: (1) the *arrêt* of Francis I denying Parlement cognizance of affairs of state (which was given in the ad hoc session held during the recess of the first *Lit de Justice* of July 1527); (2) the ordinance of King Jean (in the mid-fourteenth century) which denied Parlement access to affairs of state except by way of a *special commission* or *Lit de Justice* (the doctrine which was stated by Chancellor Olivier in the Royal *Séance* of 1549); (3) the *arrêt* of Charles IX with the same prohibitions (which was issued during the quarrel with Parlement over the *billet de partage* following the Majority *Lit de Justice* of Rouen); and (4) three examples of the same limitations imposed during Louis XIII's own reign (the first, discussed below, condemned Parlement's attempt to convene a Court of peers without the king in 1615, the second and third probably referred to the statements of 1629 and 1631 discussed above). Then the Edict of 1641 set forth procedural regulations which spelled out the relationship between the king's *Lit de Justice* assembly and Parlement's registration process. Those regulations stated that Parlement must register legislation promulgated at a *Lit de Justice* (laws concerning affairs of state) immediately and without deliberation beforehand. Remonstrances were not allowed before registration, and after registration they were permitted once, but only on matters pertaining to execution of the new measure.[32] In this way the *Lit de Justice* was gradually adapted as

---

[30] A.N. X1a 8387 [4 unnumbered folios] (21 Feb. 1641), and the summons (20 Feb.) [2 unnumbered folios]. Godefroy, *Cérémonial françois* [no source], II, 635, mentions the event but gives no account. Note that Glasson's report, *Parlement de Paris*, pp. 167-171, mistakenly gives the date as January. For the Edict of 1641, extremely important in this context, see Isambert, *Recueil général des anciennes lois*, XVI, 529-555.

[31] For the preamble, Isambert, *Recueil général des anciennes lois*, XVI, 529-533.

[32] Ibid., 529-534, preamble and Articles 1-6. The king stipulated in addition that the Court was never allowed to modify legislation or to attach the insulting rider "nous ne devons ni ne pouvons" to its registration notice. Finally, he also suppressed the offices of Parisian *parlementaires* considered offenders.

a vehicle for registering a variety of legislative measures, including financial edicts affecting venal offices and taxation. For several decades this legislative adaptation was accomplished through the symbolism of innovative ceremonial ritual enacted in the assembly; then that legislative authority was confirmed by legal decree. The Edict of 1641 for the first time defined the *Lit de Justice* as a legislative forum and remonstrance as a judicial procedure excluded from the proceedings of that forum.

During the reign of Louis XIII, the ritual of the *Lit de Justice* played a significant role in revising French constitutional ideology. The attendant shift of constitutional focus from the undying *dignité* to its corporeal incumbent, from the *Lit de Justice* as a constitutional forum associating the Crown with the Public Law of the kingdom to one propagating the dynastic right of royalty distinguished seventeenth-century kingship from its renaissance counterpart. Yet the tendency to embody elements of French Public Law in the ceremonial patterns of a baroque age created a host of new problems over the locus of public authority. By the mid-seventeenth century there was apparent a certain ambivalence about the *Lit de Justice* assembly: it was rightly perceived by both king and Parlement as the public agency which supported the ideology and practice of dynasticism in officeholding, but increasingly regarded by Parlement as an agency for registering legislation potentially dangerous for venal officeholders. This ambivalence over the nature of the assembly accounts for the fact that the royal party, served well by the *Lit de Justice*, continued for some decades to rely upon the institution, whereas the Parlement of Paris, intent upon maintaining the prestigious *Lit de Justice*, including the Inaugural and Majority assemblies, in the Grand-chambre but wary of the new legislative prerogative assigned to the assembly, trod an uneven course in the seventeenth century. In these years, therefore, Parlement usually supported the *Lit de Justice* in theory yet sometimes opposed it in practice.

THE INAUGURAL PLAN FOR 1643

During the reign of Louis XIII dynastic ideology was disseminated with expertise by Crown and Parlement. At the end of that reign, however, the king was still haunted by two specters: Parlement's bold attempt to issue a regency *arrêt* unilaterally upon Henry IV's death in 1610 and its attempt to convoke an assembly of princes, dukes and peers, Crown officers, and *parlementaires* (without the king present) in the Grand-chambre to discuss affairs of state in 1615. For over thirty years Louis

XIII harbored tremendous animosity against the Court for such actions undertaken early in his reign. In the meantime, he regulated the ceremonial ritual of the *Lit de Justice* to negate all parlementary claims to unilateral authority, and he condemned Parlement's bold moves (as late as 1641) as usurpations of French Public Law.[33] Aware that the *Lit de Justice* assembly had given public legitimation to the dynastic precepts of French constitutional ideology propagated during his own reign, Louis XIII as the father of a young son (born in 1638) was determined to maintain the assembly as a royal prerogative regardless of the age of the successor king. Since the legislative function of kingship had been emphasized during the institutional development and ideological rationalization of the *Lit de Justice* in the early seventeenth century, the time was now ripe for the king to amend the French constitution to include a formal "Law of Regency" regulating minority succession. In fact an appeal for such a law appeared in the treatise *Commentaires sur l'ordonnance de la majorité des rois* probably published some time between 1638 and 1643.[34] The author called for Louis XIII to follow in the legislative footsteps of Pharamond (who instituted the Salic Law) and Charles V (who instituted the Law of Majority) by promulgating a Law of Regency in the ancient constitutional forum of the *Lit de Justice*.[35] At the same

[33] For condemnation of Parlement's earlier actions, see *Recueil de lettres patentes concernant la discipline du Parlement* (n.p., n.d.), pp. 20-23, and Isambert, *Recueil général des anciennes lois*, XVI, 529-535. For discussion of this dispute, consult Glasson, *Parlement de Paris*, I, 123-125.

[34] *Commentaires sur l'ordonnance de la majorité des rois* (n.p., n.d.). In 1740 Lenglet Dufresnoy alleged that the author of this treatise was "P. Du Puys [i.e. Pierre Dupuy]," but a letter in manuscript attached to this rare book notes that Pierre Dupuy could not have written the work because (among other things) he would not have subscribed to the Trojan origin of the French nor to the dubbing of Antinor as the first French king. Internal evidence referring to the majority of Louis XIII (fol. 77r) and appealing to the king for a new law (fol. 81v) dates this work between 2 October 1614 and 14 May 1643. Given the urgency of the tone, however, it was probably written between 1638, the year of the birth of the dauphin (the future Louis XIV), and 1643, the death of Louis XIII, five years during which the problem of minority succession would have been acute.

[35] *Commentaires*, fols. 47r, 76v-77v, and 81v. The author speaks of the *Lit de Justice* assembly as an ancient French tradition "toujours en la meme forme et solemnité de tout temps observée ... le Roy se transporte en personne en son Parlement, où se seant en son Lict de Justice, accompagné de ses princes, ducs et pairs, officiers de sa Couronne, son conseil, et Parlement ..."; fol. 77r-v. Note that this quote is exactly the same as that rendered in Corbin, *Code Louis XIII*, p. 28, published in 1638.

time the second generation of antiquarians, Théodore and Denys Godefroy, Pierre Dupuy, and many others, initiated extensive research projects on the history of the *Lit de Justice* in part to identify the constitutional precepts which had regulated regency and majority in past times.[36] Despite the climate favoring a Law of Regency, however, Louis XIII did not issue such an ordinance in a *Lit de Justice* assembly. But he did take legal steps to assure royal control of the Inaugural *Lit de Justice*, which would propagate Bourbon dynastic ideology as the cornerstone of French succession. The following reassessment of circumstances surrounding Louis XIII's death and Louis XIV's accession shows how in those weeks the Parlement of Paris was caught up in a constitutional dilemma.

Louis XIII summoned deputies (presidents and councillors) from the Parlement of Paris to Saint-Germain-en-Laye for a bedside Council meeting on 20 April 1643, twenty-four days before his death. The next morning those deputies reported back to the *parlementaires* in the Grand-chambre on the events which had transpired at that meeting. At the Château of Saint-Germain, the deputies recounted, they spoke privately with Chancellor Pierre (III) Séguier and then entered the chamber of the king for the meeting. In the presence of the dauphin (the future Louis XIV), Queen Anne of Austria, Bourbon blood princes, other princes, Crown officers, and deputies from Parlement, Louis XIII pronounced two important regulations, one on the regency, the other on parlementary officeholding. First, Louis XIII issued a regency declaration for the dauphin and commanded that the Duke of Orléans, the Prince of Condé, and Chancellor Séguier take it to Parlement the next day (21 April) for registration. Then he restored the privileges of office to five *parlementaires* whose charges had been suppressed for disobedience two years earlier. Speaking for Parlement, First President Mathieu Molé assured the king that the Court would register the regency declaration and acknowledged the restoration of parlementary offices. Following this amicable exchange of favors, the deputies from Parlement went to an outer chamber and received further instructions from the chancellor. Chancellor Séguier ordered Parlement to assemble in the Grand-chambre the next day (21 April) when he would summon the *gens du roi* to the parquet for a reading of the regency declaration and request conclusions on the matter

---

[36] Consult Table One for the new works. According to Dupuy's analysis, *Traité de la majorité*, pp. 28-29, there was need for a legal procedure to establish regencies.

immediately thereafter. The deputies apparently assented to this procedure as did the *parlementaires* later.[37]

The regency declaration of Louis XIII designated Anne of Austria as
regent in France responsible for "the administration and government of
the kingdom during the minority of the king," but it restricted the
queen's authority by establishing a Regency Council which was charged
with resolving important affairs of state following majority opinion.[38]
According to one *parlementaire*, Anne of Austria opposed that limitation
but made no move to amend the declaraton either before or at the time
of registration.[39] The regency declaration was registered in the Parlement
of Paris without incident on 21 April 1643.[40] On the same day back at
the Château of Saint-Germain the dauphin was baptized.[41] The next
day following a request of the Duke of Orléans, the king annulled an
earlier royal *arrêt* (registered in 1642) which had excluded the duke from
regency power.[42] As his condition worsened Louis XIII no doubt felt
secure that these measures assured a proper succession for the dauphin.

When Louis XIII died around three o'clock on the afternoon of 14
May 1643, the Regency Council sent a *lettre de cachet* to the Parlement
of Paris in the name of the new king Louis XIV. The Court was ordered
to continue in its functions, but at the same time the *parlementaires* were
exhorted to exercise their offices with integrity until they received from
the king the "customary confirmation" of those offices.[43] The Regency
Council also notified First President Molé of this order and requested
his assistance if further commands were necessary.[44] The royal party left
Saint-Germain-en-Laye for the palace of the Louvre the next morning,
15 May, and the young king made a rather formal *Entrée* into Paris on
that occassion. At the gates of Paris the City officials rendered homage

[37] Dupuy, *Traité de la majorité* [Reg. Parl.], pp. 500-506; *Mémoires de Talon*,
III, 5-6; *Mémoires de Molé*, III, 41-45.

[38] Dupuy, *Traité de la majorité* [Declaration du Roy Louis XIII], pp. 509-510.
The Regency Council included the Duke of Orléans, the Prince of Condé,
Cardinal Mazarin, and Chancellor Séguier.

[39] *Mémoires de Talon*, III, 8-9.

[40] Dupuy, *Traité de la majorité* [Reg. Parl.], pp. 506-512, contains the whole
declaration and recounts the proceedings of 21 April during which it was
registered.

[41] *Mémoires de Molé*, III, 43, n. 1.

[42] *Mémoires de Talon*, III, 10; *Mémoires de Molé*, III, 48, n. 1.

[43] Isambert, *Recueil général des anciennes lois*, XVII, 2.

[44] *Mémoires de Molé*, III, 53-55, prints the text of the original letter from B.N.
Cinq Cents Colbert ms. 212, fol. 87r.

to the new king. Throughout the city acclamations of *Vive le roi!* resounded, and at the Louvre, Parlement and other Courts saluted Louis XIV.[45] All the while, however, the Parlement of Paris was incensed at the royal request for a "confirmation" of offices. They expressed great displeasure to Chancellor Séguier at the first opportunity. Attempting to appease the *parlementaires*, the chancellor deleted the word "confirmation" and substituted the word "oath" in the request, so the order finally demanded the continued exercise of office "until you [the *parlementaires*] have made and sworn the *customary oath* to us."[46] The substitution did not satisfy Parlement, and the Court refused to register the *lettre de cachet* of the king until its registers were searched for precedent. On the afternoon of 15 May, after the search was completed, Parlement sent the *gens du roi* to the Louvre with instructions to arrange a royal audience wherein the Court's deputies (four presidents and two councillors) could salute the new king and queen regent officially.[47] At this point it is instructive to note that the convocation of an Inaugural *Lit de Justice* assembly for Louis XIV had not been mentioned by either the royal party or the *parlementaires*.

At nine o'clock on the morning of 16 May the *gens du roi* went back to the Grand-chambre and reported to Parlement on the results of that meeting the day before at the Louvre. First of all, they reported that Chancellor Séguier was very annoyed at the Court's reluctance to swear an oath renewing offices. The chancellor referred them to excerpts from the registers of Parlement taken from his own library to prove that the royal request for oaths conformed to the procedure followed upon the death of Francis I in 1547. The *gens du roi* in turn presented the results of Parlement's research to the chancellor. The practice followed in the year 1547 was not necessarily applicable in 1643, they said, because rules on the conduct of public affairs had changed in the past hundred years due to the establishment of the *droit annuel*, which instituted a system of "public heredity" assuring the status of offices. They agreed that obedience to the king was required of officeholders but insisted that the *droit annuel* dispensed with old formalities such as oath-taking which had been observed when offices were simple royal commissions. Following this contentious interview with Chancellor Séguier, the *gens du roi* recounted, they were kept waiting in an antechamber of the palace all day long. Finally, at six o'clock they were admitted to the chamber of

[45] *Mémoires de Talon*, III, 14; *Mémoires de Molé*, III, 53.
[46] Dupuy, *Traité de la majorité* [Reg. Parl.], p. 515.
[47] Ibid., 515-516; *Mémoires de Talon*, III, 16-17; *Mémoires de Molé*, III, 55.

the young king Louis XIV, who was on his bed, and then to the cabinet of Queen Regent Anne of Austria, who was attended by the Regency Council. The *gens du roi* presented the queen with Parlement's request for an official royal audience and were told to await instructions from the chancellor. Once outside the chambers of the king and queen, the chancellor drew the *gens du roi* aside and informed them that the queen regent had made two announcements. First, she had decided to grant the Parlement of Paris a royal audience the next day, 16 May, at three o'clock, but requested that the whole Parlement appear in a body garbed in red robes, not just a few deputies as a representative group. Séguier defended the queen's request as one which conformed to past usage as recorded in the registers of Parlement. Second, the queen regent had decided to withdraw the royal request of 14 May for new oaths of office from the *parlementaires*.[48] When the *gens du roi* concluded this report in the Grand-chambre on the morning of 16 May, there was still no mention of an Inaugural *Lit de Justice*, that is, no mention of a *Lit de Justice* to be held in the Grand-chambre of the Parlement of Paris.

The *parlementaires* remained in session in the Grand-chambre on the morning of 16 May, but the deliberations of the meeting were not recorded. The results were that Parlement declined the queen's invitation to appear that day at the Louvre in red robes as a corporate body to salute Louis XIV as king. They decided instead to send deputies to the king and queen regent at the appointed hour and request that Anne of Austria "lead the king to his Parlement to hold his *Lit de Justice* [assembly] there."[49] Again the bargains struck at the Louvre on the afternoon of 16 May are not recorded, but the Court's request for a *Lit de Justice* assembly was granted. At noon the next day, 17 May, the Bishop of Beauvais informed the *avocat* Omer Talon that Anne of Austria would lead the king to Parlement for the *Lit de Justice* assembly on 18 May, and during that assembly the Duke of Orléans and the Prince of Condé would denounce the restrictive clauses of Louis XIII's regency declaration and propose that the queen undertake the regency with full power and absolute authority.[50]

[48] Dupuy, *Traité de la majorité* [Reg. Parl.], pp. 517-519; *Mémoires de Talon*, III, 15-16, 22-26. The *droit annuel*, or *paulette*, introduced by an edict of 1604, assured hereditary transmission of office for an annual payment, and the privilege was renewed in 1638, 1648, 1657, and 1669. For comments on the practice, consult the works in n. 1 above, especially Hamscher, *Parlement of Paris after the Fronde*, who shows how the *droit annuel* influenced the social cohesion of *parlementaires*.

[49] Dupuy, *Traité de la majorité* [Reg. Parl.], p. 520.

[50] *Mémoires de Talon*, III, 19.

SOME HISTORIANS have held that the Parlement of Paris won an important political victory in 1643 when the minority succession of Louis XIV forced a weakened monarchy into the Grand-chambre for a *Lit de Justice* assembly in order to modify the regency declaration of Louis XIII.[51] Yet a different approach to these events, combining a close reading of sources including registers of Parlement with the knowledge that ceremonial protocol defined many of the working axioms of government, or public authority, suggests a very different conclusion. The first point to be noted is that the aura of mutual accord which prevailed at Louis XIII's bedside Council meeting on 20 April and the parlementary assembly which registered the regency declaration on 21 April actually masked the contentious bargaining which took place behind the scenes throughout those weeks. Parlement agreed to register the regency document only after an important royal concession was granted in return. The terms of the bargain struck on 20 April were not recorded in the registers, but clearly they were worked out earlier and discussed by Parlement's deputies and the chancellor when they met just preceding the king's Council meeting. The pronouncements which Louis XIII made in Council revealed the terms of the agreement: the king promulgated a regency declaration and ordered its registration in Parlement the next day (21 April), and he restored the exercise of office to *parlementaires* whose charges he had suppressed for disobedience in 1641. An exchange had taken place which profited both parties. Louis XIII declared the regency for the dauphin well ahead of time, preventing Parlement from claiming legislative tutorship of the minor king at a future inauguration; and Parlement secured an important reversal of the royal *arrêt* which had rescinded the right of five colleagues to exercise offices several years earlier. The next morning, 21 April, the deputies went to the Grand-chambre and relayed to Parlement the king's orders for registration of the regency declaration and the chancellor's plan for registration without deliberations. The ensuing discussion was not recorded, but the speed with which Parlement registered the regency declaration suggests that accord prevailed among the *parlementaires* despite the suppression of deliberations. In the meantime, on the same day back at the Château of Saint-Germain, Louis XIII settled other public matters: the dauphin was baptized and the Duke of Orléans was declared capable of serving on the Regency Council. All the while the discord over the regency plan was carefully masked. Anne of Austria opposed the restrictive clauses of the declaration, which named

[51] Chéruel, *Histoire de France pendant la minorité de Louis XIV* (Paris, 1879), I, 55-60; and Glasson, *Parlement de Paris*, I, 177-182, give that version of the events based mainly upon memoirs.

Council members and required a majority decision, but she took no action at the time. Rather, the queen clandestinely prepared the ground for rescinding these clauses later. It was clear even this early, therefore, that another meeting with Parlement regarding the regency would be required upon the king's death.

The second point to be noted is that during these meetings of 20 and 21 April, and those which followed on 15 and 16 May, there was no discussion by either the royal party or Parlement regarding the convocation of a *Lit de Justice* assembly to celebrate Louis XIV's inauguration. On the surface such silence might appear to reflect simple propriety since Louis XIII lay on his deathbed; underneath it actually signaled the wary diplomacy practiced by the two parties. First of all, it is certain that a *Lit de Justice* assembly was in the offing but not certain where it would be located. Queen Anne informed the *avocat* Talon as early as 9 May that she intended to take the dauphin to Paris "to hold a *Lit de Justice*." The *avocat*'s services might be needed, the queen said, because she planned to amend the regency *arrêt* with the support of the Duke of Orléans and the Prince of Condé.[52] In addition the elaborate plans devised by the grand master and aide of ceremonies, the brothers Saintot, seem to indicate that the expanded inaugural program (the Parisian *Entrée*, the procession to Sainte-Chapelle, the mass, and the *Lit de Justice* assembly) was organized some weeks before Louis XIII's death.[53] It would seem, therefore, that both parties expected the convocation of a *Lit de Justice* after Louis XIII died but that the aims of those expectations differed.

[52] *Mémoires de Talon*, III, 8-12. Some time after 21 April, moreover, the queen enlisted the aid of the Bishop of Beauvais to plant spurious rumors to the effect that the regency restrictions would aid the favorites of Cardinal Richelieu (recently deceased), who intended to control the government surreptitiously, and that rumor apparently aroused support for cancellation of the restrictive clauses.

[53] Besides organizing the events themselves, the masters of ceremonies took pains to serve special summonses which specified the rank and order of each attendant. For instance, those called the *grands du royaume* were served in Paris on 17 May with such letters for the Inaugural *Lit de Justice*; Godefroy, *Cérémonial françois* [Autre relation (unidentified)], II, 642. According to an early eighteenth-century manuscript, the *grands du royaume* was a "notable expression" in the seventeenth century; B.N. ms. fr. n. a. 9750, fol. 42r. In fact the term was used increasingly to categorize those of the royal entourage who had the right to sit with the king in a *Lit de Justice* assembly. In addition to Godefroy see *Mémoires de Molé*, III, 55, n. 1, and Dupuy, *Traité de la majorité* [Reg. Parl.], p. 523. The Saintot brothers were masters of ceremonies from 1645-1729.

On the one hand, Parlement wanted to maintain its important role as the primary inaugural institution by hosting the *Lit de Justice* in the Grand-chambre, yet still wished to limit the legislative capacity of a minor king and play the role of legislative tutor. On the other hand, the queen regent and royal party wanted to reiterate dynastic ideology in the *Lit de Justice* assembly and intended also to demonstrate royal legislative power by having the young king amend his father's regency *arrêt* there without parlementary interference. As late as 15 May, therefore, the convocation of an Inaugural *Lit de Justice* in the Grand-chambre depended on Parlement's cooperation, or lack of it, in amending the regency *arrêt*.

Over these weeks the royal party had gambled that the threat to remove the Inaugural *Lit de Justice* from the Grand-chambre, along with other pressures, would convince Parlement to cooperate with the Regency Council and allow Louis XIV free rein. That is why Parlement did not receive notice to convoke a *Lit de Justice* assembly in the Grand-chambre immediately upon Louis XIII's death on 14 May but instead found itself caught in a situation which subtly eroded its inaugural prerogative. Straightaway on the morning of 15 May the young king participated in a Royal *Entrée* where he was publicly acclaimed as king at the gates of Paris by City officials, greeted in the streets by shouts of *Vive le roi!*, and saluted at the Louvre by *parlementaires* forced to share the inaugural stage with the City of Paris. Chafing at the inaugural tone of the Royal *Entrée* and the potential loss of parlementary status, the *parlementaires* must have wondered at this point just what place the *Lit de Justice* assembly would be assigned in this expanded inaugural celebration.

These events provide the proper context in which to situate the two extraordinary demands made by the queen immediately upon Louis XIII's death as well as the Court's reaction to them: first, the demand made on 14 May for royal confirmation of the Parlement of Paris, amended on 15 May to request instead new oaths of office from the *parlementaires*; and second, the demand made later on 15 May for the whole Parlement to appear red-robed at the palace of the Louvre on 16 May to salute the new king officially. The *parlementaires* balked at the first demand for oaths renewing their offices because it compromised both the corporate claim of Parlement to institutional integrity beyond the death of kings and the dynastic notions of individual *parlementaires* regarding the hereditary and proprietary nature of their offices. On the afternoon of 15 May, therefore, the *gens du roi* returned to the Louvre with instructions to present Parlement's case against oath-taking and to offer instead a salutation from representatives of Parlement on behalf of the whole body. The deputies presented Parlement's formidable case to the chancellor. They dismissed his precedent, the renewal of offices as practiced at Francis I's death (1547), and cited a more recent one, the introduction of the *droit annuel* (*paulette*, 1604) which legalized the hereditary principle in officeholding. They concluded on legal and historical grounds that offices which had been held in the sixteenth century as simple commissions from kings certainly required renewal, but that offices which were held in the seventeenth century as hereditary property were tenured over generations.

Chancellor Séguier was visibly irritated during this confrontation and withdrew afterward to confer with Anne of Austria and the Regency Council on Parlement's request for a royal audience. In the meantime the deputies were kept waiting all day long in an antechamber. Following this rude interval, the queen regent finally received the deputies in royal quarters at six o'clock. She heard Parlement's request that a simple salutation replace oath-taking and directed the chancellor to present a rejoinder. Once in the antechamber again, Chancellor Séguier relayed the queen's counter offer to the deputies: that the whole Parlement, not just deputies, appear at the Louvre the next afternoon, 16 May, in a red-robed body to salute the new king. At this point the *parlementaires* must have suspected that the first event of the inaugural celebration, the Parisian *Entrée*, might not be followed by a *Lit de Justice* assembly, at least not by a *Lit de Justice* held in the Grand-chambre. Anticipating complaints against such procedural innovation, Séguier presented evidence from the registers of Parlement to show that the queen's request for such an assembly did not defy French tradition. Although the particulars of his argument are not known, it is very likely that the chancellor, who possessed a formidable collection of extracts from the registers,[54] drew from those sources an argument based on the historical fiction of the medieval *Lit de Justice* (as amended around 1560) which declared that the Parlement of Paris had attended kings in *Lit de Justice* assemblies not only outside the Grand-chambre of the Palais de Justice (as in 1332 at the palace of the Louvre) but also outside the City of Paris

[54] Séguier had a small archive of his own; see B.N. ms. fr. 18411, fols. 146r-156v, and fols. 116r-144v in particular, as well as Column R in Table One, and he had access to the collection of Brienne, B.N. ms. fr. n. a. 7231 (in Table One, Column I).

(as in 1458 at Vendôme). As an inducement toward cooperation, the chancellor then announced that the queen had withdrawn the royal demand for oaths renewing parlementary offices.

The *parlementaires* certainly recognized the dangerous procedural implications of the queen's invitation. Any assembly held at the Louvre with the king and queen regent and the whole red-robed Parlement of Paris in attendance would surely include Bourbon blood princes, dukes and peers, Crown officers, royal officials, and others, constituting a veritable *Lit de Justice* assembly in the palace. In its final rendition, therefore, the queen's invitation contained a threat hard for the *parlementaires* to ignore: that the *Lit de Justice* assembly could be removed from its moorings in the Grand-chambre to a berth in the royal palace. At the same time it offered bait hard for them to resist: royal recognition of the dynastic character of parlementary office. In the Grand-chambre on the morning of 16 May, when the *gens du roi* had finished reporting all of this, the *parlementaires* remained in session to discuss the dilemma before them. No doubt the alternatives were posed as follows: whether Parlement should maintain the Inaugural *Lit de Justice* in its own quarters and at the same time secure a royal precedent recognizing the hereditary nature of offices, or whether Parlement should maintain its stance on the legislative incapacity of minor kings and either refuse to amend the regency *arrêt* or insist upon a co-legislative role in implementing an amendment. It was clear almost immediately which way the Court would turn. If the Inaugural *Lit de Justice* could be transferred to the royal palace, or even dismissed, the Majority *Lit de Justice* too could share the same fate. Moreover, it might follow in an age given over to ceremonial grandeur that the king would move the *Lit de Justice* permanently to royal quarters, compromising the whole ceremonial program which had supported the great stature and dignity of the Parisian Parlement vis-à-vis other competing corporate bodies in the polity such as the Church, the City of Paris, the Royal Council, and even the other Parlements. The royal party had gambled astutely. Parlement discussed the dilemma all morning on 16 May and then sent deputies back to the Louvre in the afternoon with instructions: the Court declined the queen's invitation to assemble as a body at the palace and requested instead that Louis XIV convoke a *Lit de Justice* assembly in the Grand-chambre of the Palais de Justice. At noon the next day Parlement's formal request for a *Lit de Justice* assembly was honored. For the time being at least the transfer of the *Lit de Justice* from Parlement's Grand-chambre to the king's royal palace had been averted. This complex set of maneuvers clearly exposes Parlement's formidable attachment to the *Lit de Justice* assembly, for in effect the Court traded its claim to act as legislative co-tutor of a minor king for the prestige of hosting the royal inauguration. The cost of that bargain was yet to be reckoned.

XIII

THE ABSOLUTIST MONARCHY IN FRENCH CONSTITUTIONAL IDEOLOGY: THE ROYAL *SÉANCE* AND THE *LIT DE JUSTICE* ASSEMBLY 1643-1713

> Some assumed that "urgent necessity of state" would au-
> thorize those financial edicts [promulgated in a Minority
> *Lit de Justice*]. Others admitted ... that such venerable
> maxims as *necessitas* were no longer recognized by all sub-
> jects. *Nicolas Saintot (c. 1648)*

THE INAUGURAL *Lit de Justice* of 1643 took place in circumstances quite different from its prototype of 1610. When Louis XIV succeeded to the Crown of France as a minor there was no pressing constitutional crisis, because the ideology of dynastic monarchy, introduced through the ritual of Louis XIII's Inaugural *Lit de Justice*, confirmed in the pre-Coronation *Entrée*, and propagated for decades, allowed no ceremonial or legal interregnum in theory or practice. Nor was there a regency issue to settle, because the regency had been declared by Louis XIII weeks before his death. Nor, finally, was the first *Lit de Justice* of Louis XIV uniquely associated with minority succession, because it shared the inaugural stage with other public events and was followed by three "Minority" *Lits de Justice* in the next five years.

Louis XIV's Inaugural *Lit de Justice* assembly finally took place on 18 May 1643,[1] four days after Louis XIII's death, three days after the

---

[1] The account from the registers of Parlement, A.N. X1a 8388 (18 May 1643) [17 unnumbered folios (6r-14r)], is printed in Dupuy, *Traité de la majorité* [Reg. Parl.], pp. 520-531, and in *Ordre observé à la seance du roy Louys XIV en son Lit de Justice* (Poictiers, 1643). Parts of the register account are printed (with some errors) in Godefroy, *Cérémonial françois* [Premiere seance du roy Louis XIV tenant son Lict de Justice en son Parlement le 18 May 1643], II, 635-642. In addition, other unidentified accounts of the assembly appear in Dupuy, *Traité de la majorité* [Autre relation de ce qui se passa en la seance du roy Louis XIV tenant son Lit de Justice en son Parlement, le 18 May 1643], pp. 531-536; and in Godefroy, *Cérémonial françois* [Autre relation de la mesme ceremonie], II, 642-643. Finally, there are some contemporary papers and letters on the assembly collected in *Mémoires de Molé*, III, 56-65.

young king's rather formal *Entrée* to Paris, and some hours after the triumphal procession to Sainte-Chapelle for a celebrative mass.[2] When assembled in the Grand-chambre, the red-robed Parlement of Paris deputized members of the Court to escort the four-year-old king (carried by the *grand écuyer*) from Sainte-Chapelle to the entrance of the Grand-chambre and then to conduct the young king (carried by the *grand chambellan*) inside the Grand-chambre to the parquet of Parlement. The *chambellan* placed the young king on the throne under the canopy, the queen regent took the seat to his right, and the chancellor left the bench of the presidents and took his decorated seat at the foot of the throne. In general the ceremonial ritual observed in the first Inaugural *Lit de Justice* of 1610 was repeated in 1643. But on this day the Bourbon blood princes were declared regency councillors by virtue of birth, were seated ahead of all others in the assembly, and were consulted individually; and three Bourbon blood princesses were seated in the assembly on a special bench inside the parquet of Parlement. Besides the numerous members of the royal party and the Parlement seated inside the parquet, there were many others crowded into the space outside, including women of the royal party seated in side balconies and men standing around the railing of the parquet; so the Inaugural *Lit de Justice* hosted an enormous audience that day.[3]

An engraving of the event (Figure 12) captures the archaeology of the scene, but contains numerous errors.[4] The anonymous artist was not familiar with the Grand-chambre of the Palais de Justice and had not witnessed the session or read the registers of Parlement recounting it. On the wall to the left of the king the engraving shows the lower half of the old crucifixion tableau of Virelay, which had hung in the Grand-chambre in the early fifteenth century, instead of the painting *Le Retable du Parlement*, which had been there since the mid-fifteenth century. The tapestry of fleurs-de-lis which extended from the throne and covered the chancellor's seat is missing, leaving a bare chair in the middle of the

[2] Dupuy, *Traité de la majorité* [Reg. Parl.], p. 522 (18 May 1643); *Ordre observé*, pp. 3-4; Godefroy, *Cérémonial françois* [Premiere seance], II, 636 and 642; and ibid. [Autre relation], II, 642-643.

[3] Dupuy, *Traité de la majorité* [Reg. Parl.], pp. 520-522 (18 May 1643); *Ordre observé*, pp. 2-4; Godefroy, *Cérémonial françois* [Premiere seance], II, 635-642. See also Dupuy, *Traité de la majorité* [Autre relation], pp. 531-532; Godefroy, *Cérémonial françois* [Autre relation], II, 642-645; and *Mémoires de Molé*, III, 56-57.

[4] B.N. Dépt. des Estampes; Bouchot Pd., fol. 32; and B.N. Clairambault ms. 718, fols. 154v-155r.

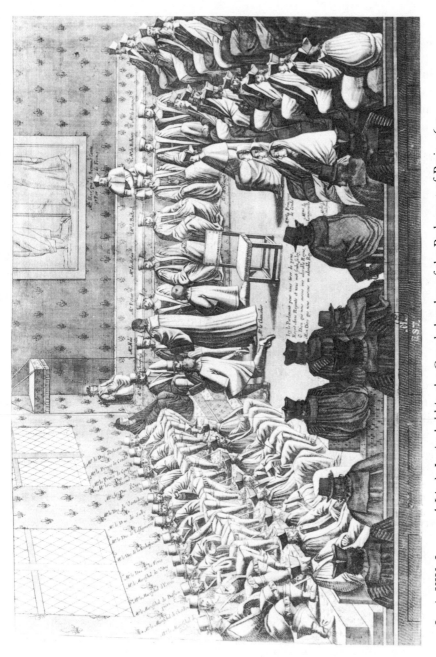

12. Louis XIV: Inaugural *Lit de Justice* held in the Grand-chambre of the Parlement of Paris, 1643.

parquet of the Grand-chambre. The king is enthroned beneath a canopy hung in the corner, but the usual backdrop behind him is missing.[5] The queen is properly seated at the right of the king but mistakenly placed in a lower tier of seats rather than beside him under the canopy as recorded in the registers. Surely the artist was furnished with a list of important persons present, because the labels are applied accurately in the print. In the series shown here, this engraving is the fourth to depict a *Lit de Justice* assembly and the second to show that assembly in the Grand-chambre of the Palais de Justice.

When the chancellor convened the session, the four-year-old king mumbled a few words which were interpreted as a message of good will toward Parlement. Queen Anne of Austria took the floor as regent and stated that the assembly was convoked because "they [the Parlement] requested him [the king] to come and hold his *Lit de Justice* here [in the Grand-chambre] and [thus] take the place of his ancestors, [an act] which is considered one of the signs of royalty. Since Louis XIII's regency *arrêt* divided sovereign authority and thus ran contrary to the Fundamental Law of the kingdom, she said, it must be amended by his successor. In a long discourse Chancellor Séguier repeated the inaugural theme of 1610 which linked the funereal and celebrative aspects of the ceremony and lauded dynastic monarchy as a system undisturbed by minority succession. In tones which recalled the phoenix and sun metaphors of 1610 and the proverb *The king never dies*, he noted that in France the king was not dead because "Nature" imbued his worthy successor with "seeds of [royal] virtue" guaranteed to generate the "rebirth of the dead king in the person of the king his son." Repeating warnings about the dangers to sovereignty posed by divided authority, the chancellor too requested that the restrictions in the regency *arrêt* be deleted.[6]

Just before consultation took place, the *avocat* Omer Talon gave his speech on the proper exercise of royalty. He described the young Louis XIV as carrying out a historic public act by "sitting for the first time in his *Lit de Justice* [assembly]" and taking "public possession of the throne of his ancestors." During that important ritual French kings were invested with "absolute power and sovereign authority" and imbued with

[5] Probably the thronal paraphernalia described by Master of Ceremonies Saintot for the *Lit de Justice* of 1635 was used in this inauguration of 1643.

[6] Dupuy, *Traité de la majorité* [Reg. Parl.], pp. 523-525 (18 May 1643); *Ordre observé*, pp. 4-8; and Godefroy, *Cérémonial françois* [Premiere seance], II, 637. See also Dupuy, *Traité de la majorité* [Autre relation], p. 532, and *Mémoires de Molé*, III, 59-62.

a God-given "secret unction," or divine grace, which distinguished them from other men as "visible divinities" on earth. The fact that Louis XIV was enthroned in the *Lit de Justice* and inaugurated in the presence of the Bourbons and the three orders of the kingdom, Talon said, gave him the legal power to amend the deceased Louis XIII's regency *arrêt* which improperly divided sovereign royal power. The original regency edict had been registered by Parlement (21 April) under conditions of "necessity" (the deceased king's illness), he explained, and now its restrictive clause must be canceled to allow the regent to choose members of the Regency Council (in addition to Bourbon blood princes born to the regency) and to allow the Council free decisions without a requisite majority vote.[7] The order of consultation which followed highlighted dynastic right and favored the royal entourage. The chancellor took advice first from the Bourbon blood princes individually, second from the other princes as a body, third from the rest of the royal entourage together, and last from the presidents and councillors of Parlement.[8] Chancellor Séguier pronounced the regency declaration as amended to give the queen regent "absolute, full, and entire administration of the affairs of his [the king's] kingdom during his minority," and the document was registered under the auspices of "the king sitting in his *Lit de Justice* [assembly]."[9]

In contrast to the first Inaugural *Lit de Justice* in 1610, which was held immediately to avert a constitutional crisis, this second one took place four days after Louis XIII's death and fit into a larger inaugural framework. Programmed and directed by the grand master of cere-

---

[7] Dupuy, *Traité de la majorité* [Reg. Parl.], pp. 525-530 (18 May 1643); *Ordre observé*, pp. 9-14; and Godefroy, *Cérémonial françois* [Premiere seance], II, 638-641. There is a précis of the speech given in Dupuy, *Traité de la majorité* [Autre relation], p. 533. The *avocat* Talon sent Parlement a copy of his speech; *Mémoires de Talon*, III, 20. Apparently one of the presidents also spoke on the indivisibility of the monarchy, an imitation of divine unity; Dupuy, *Traité de la majorité* [Autre relation], p. 535.

[8] Dupuy, *Traité de la majorité* [Reg. Parl.], pp. 530-531 (18 May 1643); *Ordre observé*, pp. 15-16; Godefroy, *Cérémonial françois* [Premiere seance], II, 641-642; and see also *Mémoires de Molé*, III, 63-65. One of the manuscript commentaries noted that odd procedure: ". . . ainsi monsieurs opine le premier et les presidens les derniers rien du plus singulier que cet ordre . . . et le prononcé nomme les princes du sang singulierement puis generiquement autres princes . . ."; B.N. ms. fr. n. a. 9750, fol. 41v.

[9] Dupuy, *Traité de la majorité* [Reg. Parl.], p. 531 (18 May 1643); and *Ordre observé*, p. 16. For the text of the regency *arrêt*, see Isambert, *Recueil général des anciennes lois*, XVII, 4-5.

monies, Rhodes, and the master and aide of ceremonies, the Saintots, the inaugural program of 1643 featured a series of events: the Royal *Entrée* to Paris on 15 May where the young king was acclaimed publicly by City officials and subjects, the triumphal procession which marched to drums and trumpets from the Louvre to Saint-Chapelle on the morn of 18 May for celebration of mass, and finally the convocation of the *Lit de Justice* assembly that same morning in the Grand-chambre. Buried beneath these ostentatious ceremonial trappings and delayed in the new lineup of inaugural events, the constitutional tone of Louis XIV's first *Lit de Justice* was dimmed. Furthermore, during negotiations over the convocation of this assembly a shift of cognizance over the *Lit de Justice* had occurred. To be sure, its convocation was a royal prerogative, but now its location too would be chosen by the monarch and its ceremonial ritual would be devised and controlled by the masters of ceremonies, the new guardians of a rising Bourbon cult of rulership. Finally, the dynastic hue observed in the mode of discourse adopted for the inaugural ceremony of 1610 was deepened considerably in 1643.

Regent Anne of Austria viewed Louis XIV's Inaugural *Lit de Justice* as publicizing a Fundamental Law, that is, an ancient prerogative of the dynasty bequeathed by Nature (not Public Law), and she intimated that its location in the Grand-chambre, rather than the royal palace, required a formal request from the Parlement of Paris. For the queen the ritual of the *Lit de Justice* assembly which symbolized Bourbon blood right was an attribute of the dynasty (not of the royal *dignité*) because in the assembly the successor king regardless of age (not subject to the Law of Majority) formally took the place of his ancestors (not his predecessors). In their speeches Chancellor Séguier and the *avocat* Talon elongated this shadow of dynasticism. Reiterating the metaphorical images and language of dynastic continuity rendered in 1610 (the phoenix and sun imagery, the proverb *The king never dies*), Séguier confirmed the peculiar biological foundations of Bourbon royalty. The *Lit de Justice* served both funereal and celebrative functions for Louis XIII and Louis XIV because the affinity of father and son was derived from the "seeds of [royal] virtue" through which "Nature" (not Public Law) generated the new king from the old. Adding the ingredient of divine grace to this dynastic matrix, the *avocat* Talon circumvented the Coronation ceremony and promoted the inaugural function of the *Lit de Justice*. When Louis XIV convoked the *Lit de Justice* assembly and took "public possession of the throne of his ancestors," the *avocat* said, he was imprinted with a "secret unction" distinguishing him from other men as a "visible divinity" and was guaranteed "absolute power and sovereign authority" as ruler. Increasingly the *Lit de Justice* assembly was treated by the royal party as a dynastic ritual focused on Bourbon royalty, and these speeches introduced a note into the discourse on public authority which recognized that transition.

Once again the shift of vocabulary noted in discourse is instructive. The idea of a "fundamental law" (of the kingdom) was introduced briefly by the Edict of Union in 1588, but the precept was quickly dismissed in favor of French Public Law. The idea of a "Fundamental Law" (of royalty) surfaced in 1610, and the precept maintained a dual link with Public Law (and Nature). The idea of the Fundamental Law (of royalty) was commonplace in 1643, but the precept now indicated axioms which were natural, or original, and retained no link with Public Law. During the later seventeenth century the notion of Fundamental Law placed two different perceptions of reality in opposition and discarded one of them. When the French constitution was perceived as Fundamental Law which emanated from a royal tradition and was observed from time immemorial, rather than as Public Law which emerged from French history and was observed from specific moments in time, the ideology of absolutist kingship had taken root in ground hostile to the historicist temperament. In all of this, the transforming potential of language is apparent. Over these centuries modes of discourse did not simply reveal constitutional ideologies; they helped to mold them.

As would be expected, the ritual of the inaugural assembly propagated Bourbon blood right, a veritable *mystique du sang*, and legislative authority. The *avocat* legally declared Bourbon blood princes as regency councillors by virtue of birth (not by appointment), and they were seated as a group before all others and consulted as individuals in the assembly to signal that elevated status. Indeed, Bourbon blood right superseded even gender on this day, as three Bourbon princesses were seated contrary to parlementary policy inside the parquet of Parlement without stirring overt criticism.[10] In addition to propagating the Bourbon *mystique du sang*, the ritual emphasized royal legislative authority. Although the modification of royal legislation by a minor king was a weighty action, it was not contested in the assembly, due to the careful coercion of Parlement weeks before. Resting the case against Louis XIII's regency

[10] In the *Lits de Justice* of December 1527 and January 1537 the queen mother, queens, and princesses of the royal entourage sat in the Grand-chambre on a platform but not inside the parquet; and the presence of women inside the parquet in the assembly of 1610 caused complaint.

arrêt upon the concept of sovereignty, Chancellor Séguier, the Duke of Orléans, the Prince of Condé, and the *avocat* Talon argued that the *arrêt* was illegal because the provision on majority opinion divided sovereign authority. Like the others, they called for its amendment to grant the queen regent "absolute, full, and entire administration" of public affairs during the minority of Louis XIV. At the same time, however, they attempted to dispel the glaring fact that Parlement had willingly registered a faulty regency *arrêt* on 21 April. Hence the *avocat* presented a legal case which rationalized both the deed and its undoing. Parlement had registered Louis XIII's regency declaration in the face of "necessity" (the king's illness); now Louis XIV as successor must modify that faulty legislation. According to Talon, Louis XIV's enthronement in the *Lit de Justice* assembly provided an eminent forum for issuing such an amendment, for the legislative act was witnessed publicly there by Bourbon royalty and by the three Estates of the kingdom. Following a method of consultation emphasizing Bourbon blood right, Chancellor Séguier read the regency *arrêt* as amended, and the document was registered under the auspices of Louis XIV in the *Lit de Justice* assembly.

ONCE again it is necessary to challenge the conventional interpretation of these events, which states that Parlement attained another political victory due to minority kingship in 1643 by forcing an abased monarchy to appeal to the Court for a modification of Louis XIII's regency *arrêt*.[11] The situation was quite the reverse. At mid century Parlement had a vested interest not only in the *Lit de Justice*, which associated Crown and Court in governance, but also in dynastic ideology, which legitimized family stakes in parlementary office. There was constant conflict over the nature of the *Lit de Justice*—whether or not it entailed a separation of legislative and judicial powers, was consultative or deliberative, comprehended the three Estates—but Parlement did not doubt the importance of that association. There was further conflict over the nature of a dynastic monarchy—whether there was a necessary link between blood right and legislative power—but Parlement depended on dynastic ideology itself to support the principles of inheritance contained in the *droit annuel*.

Finally, if the Inaugural *Lit de Justice* was removed from the Grand-chambre, then the Majority *Lit de Justice* also could be located elsewhere. Caught in this vise the Parlement of Paris bargained with the royal party

[11] Glasson, *Parlement de Paris*, I, 177-182; and Chéruel, *Histoire de France*, I, 55-60.

in order to protect its ceremonial prerogative and ideological support: the Court recognized the legislative capacity of a minor king and thus maintained the prestigious inaugural assembly in the Grand-chambre. In the end such a dependence upon ceremonial prerogative would not serve the Parisian Parlement well, although at the time the *parlementaires* no doubt were convinced that the trade was a prudent one under the circumstances.

MINORITY *Lit de Justice* ASSEMBLIES IN 1645 AND 1648

There occurred soon after Louis XIV's Inaugural *Lit de Justice* of 1643 a series of assemblies which demonstrated just how Bourbon dynastic ideology eventually extended royal legislative power and eased the transition to absolutist monarchy. In a most astonishing move the king while still a minor convoked three *Lit de Justice* assemblies in red-robed Parlements, one in 1645, two in 1648, and invoked the legal principle of *necessitas* there to legitimize the registration of royal edicts.[12] Louis XIV and the regent Anne of Austria convoked the first Minority *Lit de Justice* in 1645 and registered financial edicts which the Court had not examined. Although Parlement railed against the action, Louis XIII's Edict of 1641 (disallowing remonstrances at a *Lit de Justice*) prevailed that day.[13] Three years later Louis XIV convoked another Minority *Lit de Justice* in January 1648 to register an edict creating offices for immediate sale, and the *parlementaires* questioned the constitutional validity of the assembly itself.[14] Some assumed that "urgent necessity of state" would authorize

[12] For the heated debate over whether or not a minor king could hold a *Lit de Justice*, see Moote, *Revolt of the Judges*, pp. 71-74.

[13] A.N. X1a 8388 [14 unnumbered folios] (7 Sept. 1645), and the summons [2 unnumbered folios] (5 Sept.). There is another account in Godefroy, *Cérémonial françois* [unidentified source], II, 644-646. Glasson, *Parlement de Paris*, I, 207-208, confuses events and assumes that there were two assemblies in September. He reports that the king was in a "robe d'enfant" which caused a great scandal, as some wondered if a child "à la bavette" had authority to register edicts. Failing to recognize the role of the Inaugural *Lits de Justice* of 1610 and 1643, Kerviler, *Chancelier Pierre Séguier*, p. 220, remarks that before this event a minor king never held a *Lit de Justice*. A proposed medallic history, Claude-François Ménestrier, *Histoire du roy Louis le Grand* (Paris, 1691), p. 49, lists this event. For the political context, see Moote, *Revolt of the Judges*, pp. 103-104.

[14] The account is missing from the registers of Parlement, but it is copied in A.N. U 2101 (Le Nain), fols. 382v-391v (15 Jan. 1648). There is another account in Godefroy, *Cérémonial françois* [unidentified source], II, 647-650, the last *Lit*

those financial edicts.[15] Others admitted a dilemma in this regard. The problem was stated rather eloquently by Saintot. He noted that war had imposed financial burdens which justified extreme measures due to "necessity, the good of the state." Yet one had to face the fact that such venerable maxims as *necessitas* were no longer recognized by all subjects. As a result, the Regency Council convoked a *Lit de Justice* to create new offices, a "prompt and dependable recourse for raising money . . . , for the demand is great, the prices are high, and there is little financial expense to the king and none to the people."[16] The most radical *parlementaires*, obstreperous *maîtres des requêtes*, assembled the very next day to reexamine and deliberate on the legislation already registered in the *Lit de Justice*. The action caused a furor in royal quarters, where "it was assumed that the matter was settled since their majesties had taken the trouble to enter Parlement in person so that verification would take place in their presence."[17] Parlement raised a critical constitutional question, "whether or not the king during his minority could appoint sovereign judges."[18] That volatile issue over the sale of judicial offices was not resolved; furthermore, the discussion about it was expunged from the records two decades later. On royal command the appropriate registers of Parlement for 1648 were brought to Louis XIV in 1668 by the chief clerk Du Tillet, and the record of Parlement's deliberations on the constitutional question was removed on the spot.[19] One can recall with

---

de Justice in this treatise; and one in B. Mazarine ms. 2737 [Saintot, copied by Desgranges], fols. 122r-139r, containing decisions on organization and some details of the session. For the edict, see Isambert, *Recueil général des anciennes lois*, XVII, 66. On the missing registers, see below, n. 19. For the political context just preceding the *Fronde*, see Moote, *Revolt of the Judges*, pp. 107-109, who mistakenly denotes this session as the second rather than the third (including the Inaugural) *Lit de Justice* of Louis XIV.

[15] For that opinion, see A.N. U 336 [39] (Journal du Parlement pendant la minorité de Louis XIV, 1648-1649); and Le Bret had expressed the same opinion earlier.

[16] B. Mazarine ms. 2737 [Saintot, copied by Desgranges], fol. 124r.

[17] On Parlement's reaction, see Glasson, *Parlement de Paris*, I, 214-219; on the royal party's reply, see ibid., 219-221, and B. Mazarine ms. 2737 [Saintot, copied by Desgranges], fol. 132r. Mousnier fails to recognize the constitutional issue posed by Minority *Lits de Justice* which subverted French Public Law; "Comment les français du XVIIe siècle voyaient la constitution," pp. 23-24.

[18] B. Mazarine ms. 2737 [Saintot, copied by Desgranges], fols. 136r-137r.

[19] On 18 January 1668 Louis XIV ordered the volumes brought to him, according to a note in A.N. X1a 8395, fol. 226r; consult Madeleine Dillay, "Les registres secrets des Chambres des Enquêtes et Requêtes du Parlement de Paris,"

a sense of *déjà vu* a similar scene expunging parlementary registers which took place in 1563 in front of Charles IX, the regent, chancellor, and some *parlementaires*. But this time the deed took place before a crowd of two or three hundred people, including princes, dukes, marshals, and deputies of Parlement, clearly an affair to remember.[20] In these two Minority *Lit de Justice* assemblies Louis XIV carried out the policy set forth by Louis XIII in the Edict of 1641, which denied deliberations and remonstrances on legislation at such sessions. In June and July of 1648 Parlement defied that legislative policy, issuing a declaration which claimed that in the future all financial edicts not registered by Parlement would be revoked.[21] Six months later when the situation was repeated, however, the royal party remained undaunted.

The third and final Minority *Lit de Justice* was held in July 1648.[22] Although the year had been difficult with the beginning of the *Fronde*, Louis XIV and Regent Anne of Austria were determined to implement the legislative regulations of 1641 pertaining to the *Lit de Justice* assembly. In part this session was an effort to soothe a rancorous Parlement: Anne was quite willing "to scatter roses about its [Parlement's] head," and so the *droit annuel* demanded by the Court was renewed, guaranteeing the right of inheritance for officeholders.[23] On the question of legislation registered at a *Lit de Justice*, however, the young king and the regent stood firm.[24]

Sighs of relief from both quarters must have attended Louis XIV's Majority *Lit de Justice* of 7 September 1651 held in the Grand-chambre (Figure 13). As described earlier, the celebration was a gala fête, but as

---

Bibliothèque de l'École des Chartes, CVIII (1950), 78, n. 1. Jean Le Nain made copies of these sessions (see nn. 14 and 22), but how he requisitioned the accounts is not known. There are excerpts of the assemblies contained in the missing volumes (1648-1649) recorded in A.N. U 182, U 333 (1648-1649), U 334 (1649-1652), and U 335 (1652).

[20] B. Mazarine ms. 2737 [Saintot, copied by Desgranges], fols. 137r-140r.

[21] On the reforms which issued from the declaration of the Chambre Saint-Louis, see Moote, *Revolt of the Judges*, pp. 125-176. For the declaration itself, see Isambert, *Recueil général des anciennes lois*, XVII, 74-75 (Article 3).

[22] The account is missing from the registers of Parlement, but it is copied in A.N. U 2101 (Le Nain), fols. 460v-467r (31 July 1648). On the missing registers, see n. 19 above. In the political context, consult Moote, *Revolt of the Judges*, pp. 148-151, on the assembly.

[23] On the renewals, again in 1657 and 1669, see Hamscher, *Parlement of Paris after the Fronde*, pp. 8-14.

[24] Glasson, *Parlement de Paris*, I, 242-244. For the edict, see Isambert, *Recueil général des anciennes lois*, XVII, 86.

13. Louis XIV: Majority *Lit de Justice* held in the Grand-chambre of the Parlement of Paris, 1651.

the mere followup to an Inaugural and three Minority *Lits de Justice* it struck no constitutional chord. In fact Louis XIV's Majority Declaration rested uneasily on historical interpretation. When he announced the terms of his majority as being in accordance with the "Law of my state,"[25] the words vaguely recalled the Law of Majority, which had been discovered by Du Tillet and credited to Charles V, publicized by L'Hôpital and enacted in Charles IX's Majority *Lit de Justice*. But by 1651 the Law of Majority, which was observed by the juristic monarchy in 1563 and by the dynastic monarchy in 1614, had been displaced by a new precept, that of Bourbon *mystique du sang*, a Fundamental Law conferred by "Nature."[26] The consequences of that reinterpretation of the French constitution were formidable.

Louis XIII did not hold a *Lit de Justice* between his Inaugural and Majority assemblies, thus theoretically maintaining the axiom, albeit attenuated, that French kings were *legibus solutus* but *ratione alligatus*, above the law but bound by reason to observe it. Conversely, Louis XIV instituted Minority *Lits de Justice* which pronounced publicly that French kings were *legibus solutus*, subject not even to the French constitution (the Law of Majority in succession). The Crown thus stretched the legislative prerogative of kings minor and major to the utmost limit. In general, historians have agreed that the authority of French monarchs was limited by the so-called Fundamental Law, but that thesis must be qualified. While French Public Law prevailed in the sixteenth and first half of the seventeenth centuries, limitations were perceived. When French Public Law with its historical base was reinterpreted and then replaced by Fundamental Law with its traditional aura, limitations began to recede. It is this substantive transformation from a legal constitution to a traditional one which sets absolutist ideology apart. Indeed the lengths to which the constitutional absolutism of Louis XIV could be drawn were evident by the end of the century when the Sun King pronounced Bourbon consanguinity as the new rule of succession, in effect discarding the tenets of both juristic and dynastic kingship. In this way Louis XIV's Minority *Lits de Justice* of 1645 and 1648 marked the transition whereby dynastic monarchy was absorbed by absolutist monarchy characterized by Bourbon *mystique du sang*, supreme legislative authority, and finally,

[25] For the quotation, see above, Chap. VIII, n. 49.

[26] This comment exemplifies the shift from legal-hereditary succession (to public office) to a notion of dynastic right (in the office). But the statement does not connote proprietary ownership of the state per se, as suggested by Rowen, *The King's State*, pp. 70-121.

a cult of royal *gloire* which paid little heed to the quaint notion of Public Law or the historical underpinnings of the *Lit de Justice*.

The *parlementaires* criticized this constitutional shift and the unprecedented extension of royal legislative power manifested in Minority *Lits de Justice*, as well as the ostentatious ceremonial format now adopted for *Lits de Justice*, but their protests should be placed in proper context. Far from castigating the *Lit de Justice* itself, as is often assumed, they simply complained about the present corruption of that ancient French forum and recalled its pristine historical origins. Anticipating Louis XIV's intention to hold a *Lit de Justice* while still a minor, Omer Talon wrote that "it was an extraordinary action without precedent for a minor king to hold his *Lit de Justice* to verify edicts by absolute power."[27] After the assembly he criticized the action in a brief which recounted the history of the *Lit de Justice*. According to that brief, French monarchs had deliberated on affairs of state in the Parlement of Paris since 1369 (a reference to Charles V's *Séance*). That historical tradition was first breached in 1563 (a reference to Charles IX's Majority *Lit de Justice* at Rouen), and now Louis XIV overwhelmed the constitutional forum with ceremonial trappings, arriving with "pomp and circumstance and inspiring undue awe with the loud sounds of trumpets."[28] Another memoir deplored the disintegration of the *Lit de Justice* assembly into a theatrical spectacle where the enthroned king appeared as a "dieu de theâtre" rather than a "juste moderateur" and where the parquet of Parlement was a stage for the "inventions stériles" of those (presumably the ceremonial masters) who used "machines sur le theâtre" to hinder the proper judgment of participants. The *Lit de Justice* had become a "deus ex machina," more akin to an enemy attack than an act of justice, and Henry II was blamed for having initiated "surprise visits" to the Grand-chambre (probably a reference to the *Séance* of 1552) without giving the

---

[27] *Mémoires de Talon*, III, 287-313, quoted by Glasson, *Parlement de Paris*, I, 193. Here Talon reacted to the suggestion that such a Minority *Lit de Justice* might be held in 1644.

[28] Talon, *Harangue faite au roy [le 15 janvier 1648] par monsieur Talon, son advocat général au Parlement de Paris* (Paris, 1649), fol. 4r-v. The date 1379 is mistakenly given, but Talon meant 1369 because he noted Charles V's allegations against the English prince Edward on that date. The *Mémoires de Talon*, III, 209-212, contain no details as in the latter. Referring to the first Minority *Lit de Justice* of 1645, Claude Joly complained that the king's worst infraction of the constitution was to set himself above the law; *Recueil de maximes véritables et importantes pour l'institution du roy* (Paris, 1663).

Court adequate warning.[29] These comments demonstrate two facets of *parlementaire* opinion in the later seventeenth century: the tenacity of the constitutional legend of the *Lit de Justice* assembly in that circle and the resentment of the ceremonial programming which was steadily undermining the association between Crown and Parlement, which was symbolized by the *Lit de Justice* in the Grand-chambre. It was Parlement's symbiotic attachment to the *Lit de Justice*, a ceremonial forum which brought prestige to the Court, which accounts for the passion of these indictments and the plea for a return to the pristine past. It is that attachment which also accounts for the fact that Parlement over the preceding decades traded legislative prerogative for ceremonial privilege and thus made itself party to the advent of absolutist kingship. In any case, pleas for a reform of the ritual of the *Lit de Justice* fell upon deaf ears in the new era of absolutist monarchy. Louis XIV and his entourage considered the presence of "heralds and bearers of maces, trumpets, and drums" necessary to constitute a valid *Lit de Justice* assembly and eventually found the Grand-chambre cramped quarters for such baroque splendor.[30] The *Lit de Justice* assembly had been devised under the juristic monarchy and refashioned under the dynastic monarchy. But contrary to opinions which link the *Lit de Justice* with "absolutism" through several centuries, it was after all the absolutist monarchy of the later seventeenth century which readily discarded the assembly without a backward glance.

THE WANING OF THE *Lit de Justice* ASSEMBLY 1652-1713

In the chaotic turn of events which followed Louis XIV's unprecedented, some even cried illegal, Minority *Lits de Justice*, capped by a Majority *Lit de Justice* enacted in rote ritual, the king held a bewildering array of parlementary sessions which flouted traditional regulations. Some sessions were *Lits de Justice* and others Royal *Séances*, some were held in red-robed Parlements and others in black-robed Courts, some were convoked in the Grand-chambre and others in the royal palace, some

[29] A.N. U 336 (33), (6 Feb. 1648). Here Henry III is mistakenly denoted, but the suprise visit took place in 1552.

[30] By the next decade, according to the master of ceremonies, a royal visit to Parlement was not a valid *Lit de Justice* without such fanfare; see n. 40 below. The manner in which royal grandeur was highlighted by such instruments is shown in the *Lit de Justice* of 1664.

were held in the Parlement of Paris and others in provincial Parlements. Perhaps even more shocking than the convocation of Minority *Lit de Justice* assemblies was the removal of the *Lit de Justice* from the Grand-chambre of the Parlement of Paris to the palace of the Louvre, a move which Parlement had tried to avert at all costs in 1643. In 1652, a year after his majority, Louis XIV convoked a sixth *Lit de Justice*, a solemn event granting amnesty to participants in the *Fronde*, but it was located in the palace of the Louvre, not the Grand-chambre of the Palais de Justice,[31] breaking a tradition which Parlement had fought to maintain since 1563. From the moment that Master of Ceremonies Saintot ordered the *lit de justice* (throne paraphernalia) taken to the Louvre and set up for a *Lit de Justice* (assembly) attended by the Parlement of Paris, all three entities (the throne apparatus, the assembly, and the *parlementaires*) became exportable at royal whim.[32] As the century wore on, moreover, the term *"Lit de Justice"* itself took on new meaning. From the 1360's to 1527 the phrase had signaled the drapery paraphernalia which decorated the king's seat in the Grand-chambre of the Parlement of Paris; from 1527 to 1610 it had distinguished honorary Royal *Séances* from constitutional assemblies in Parlement (which featured red-robed *parlementaires* and a high royal throne from 1563); and from 1610 to 1652 it designated all royal visits to the Grand-chambre of Parlement. From 1652 to 1673, however, the term *"Lit de Justice"* signified either a legislative assembly held in quarters of royal choosing or the royal throne apparatus per se wherever situated. Clearly, the historicist *mentalité* which marked the juristic monarchy and colored the dynastic monarchy was on the wane.

A sample of Louis XIV's parlementary assemblies points to the gradual dwindling of favor accorded the *Lit de Justice* assembly in the 1650's and 1660's. Following the extraordinary *Lit de Justice* held in the Louvre,

---

[31] The registers of Parlement are missing, but they were copied in A.N. U 2105 (Le Nain), fols. 379r-391r (22 Oct. 1652), and the summons, fols. 376r-378r (21 Oct.). On the missing registers, see n. 19 above. For edicts, consult Isambert, *Recueil général des anciennes lois*, XVII, 296-299. As Moote, *Revolt of the Judges*, pp. 351-354, notes, the major concession made by the *parlementaires* was the registration of a declaration forbidding the Court cognizance of affairs of state. But the radical step taken here was the removal of the *Lit de Justice* from the Grand-chambre.

[32] Consult A.N. U 2105 (Le Nain), fols. 376r-378v (21 Oct. 1652), where Saintot ordered the *lit de justice* thronal paraphernalia delivered immediately to the Louvre and summoned a red-robed Parlement to attend the *Lit de Justice* assembly there the next day.

the king convoked two red-robed assemblies in the Grand-chambre in 1652 with pronounced legislative intent.[33] Two years later between January and March 1654 he issued summonses for three *Lit de Justice* assemblies to hear charges against the Prince of Condé, but he specified red robes for the *parlementaires* only for the last one pronouncing the verdict. On paper the clerk of Court drew attention to these ambiguities (royal summonses for the *Lit de Justice* assemblies, but red robes for only one) by refusing to acknowledge these three black-robed meetings as *Lit de Justice* assemblies.[34] The account is missing from the registers, but a red-robed *Lit de Justice* assembly was held on 20 March 1655 to register royal edicts.[35] Whether or not the tale about Louis XIV proceeding

[33] For the first session, see A.N. X1a 8389, fols. 202r-206r (13 Nov. 1652), placed out of order at the end of the register, and the summons, fols. 1v-2r (12 Nov.): "The king Louis XIV ... sitting in his *Lit de Justice* [assembly] ... all chambers assembled in red robes ... following his command of yesterday. ..." Thenceforth the new wording of the summons, ibid., indicates legislative intention: "We have resolved to go next Wednesday, the 13th of this month [November] into our Parlement to hold our *Lit de Justice* there *in order to apprise you of our will (pour vous faire entendre nostre volonté)* on the matters presented there. ... We command you [Parlement] to appear in a body in red robes and to receive us in the customary manner ... [and the master of ceremonies will provide you with the regulations] ..." [italics added]. For the second session, see A.N. X1a 8389, fols. 19v-20r (31 Dec. 1652), and the summons, fol. 19v (30 Dec.), presenting the same orders as above. For further discussion of the financial edicts, including those on offices, which were registered there due to the "necessity" of war, see Glasson, *Parlement de Paris*, I, 381-383; Moote, *Revolt of the Judges*, pp. 357-358; Hamscher, *Parlement of Paris after the Fronde*, p. 88, and Bonney, *The King's Debts*, chap. V.

[34] The sessions were as follows. (1) A.N. X1a 8389, fols. 240r-242r (19 Jan. 1654): "The king was in the high tribunal in the place where he holds his *Lit de Justice* ..."; and the summons, fol. 240r (17 Jan.), specifying a *Lit de Justice* assembly but no red robes for Parlement. (2) A.N. X1a 8389, fols. 278v-280r (21 Mar. 1654), the same ambiguous account as above; and the summons, fol. 277r (20 Mar.), with the same specifications; A.N. X1a 8389, fols. 284v-286r (27 Mar. 1654), the same ambiguous account; and the summons, fol. 282v (26 Mar.), with the same specifications. (3) A.N. X1a 8389, fols. 286v-288v (28 Mar. 1654): "The king Louis XIV sitting in his *Lit de Justice* ... all chambers assembled in red robes ..."; and the summons, fol. 286r (27 Mar.), noting that "the king would come tomorrow to hold his *Lit de Justice* and to pronounce the said *arrêt* [against Condé] ... the Court in red robes. ..."

[35] The summons appears twice in the registers of Parlement, A.N. X1a 8390, fols. 76r-v and 78r, but there is no account. A copy appears in A.N. U 2107 (Le Nain), fols. 453v-455r (20 Mar. 1655), but it is out of order at the end of the volume. On the registration of these fiscal edicts, as well as the Court's

directly from the Bois de Vincennes to the Grand-chambre for the *Lit de Justice* of 1655 while dressed in hunting attire is apocryphal,[36] the king's attention to ceremonial protocol in Parlement was waning and caused embarrassment for the Court. One by one these incidents multiplied, mocking the solemnity of the *Lit de Justice* which had been promoted for almost a century by Parlement as the main ritual symbolizing the Court's claim to represent the Crown and royal justice, or later in bolder terms, to represent the nation.

Louis XIV held a *Lit de Justice* assembly in 1657 to publish a papal bull against the Jansenists.[37] He followed it in 1658 with a visit to the Parlement of Dijon,[38] and he returned in 1662 to the Grand-chambre.[39] Then without explanation the king reinstituted Royal *Séances* in the Grand-chambre in 1663 and 1665 where royal edicts creating new dukedoms were registered in black-robed Courts.[40] In the end Parlement's

---

reexamination of them, see Moote, *Revolt of the Judges*, pp. 358-359, and Hamscher, *Parlement of Paris after the Fronde*, pp. 89-90.

[36] According to the registers, A.N. X1a 8390, fols. 89r-91r (13 Apr. 1655), and the summons, fol. 88r-v (12 Apr.), the *Lit de Justice* was held in a red-robed Parlement as usual. The incident on the hunting attire springs from Chéruel, *Histoire de France pendant la minorité de Louis XIV*, II, 255. Note that Glasson, *Parlement de Paris*, I, 398-399, mistakenly dates this incident as 10 April. This *Lit de Justice* became part of the proposed medallic history; see Ménestrier, *Histoire du roy Louis le Grand*, p. 49, who also adds a spurious *Lit de Justice* (20 April 1655) to the seventeenth-century legend. See also Moote, *Revolt of the Judges*, pp. 359-360, and Hamscher, *Parlement of Paris after the Fronde*, p. 90.

[37] A.N. X1a 8391, fols. 20v-28r (19 Dec. 1657), and the summons, fol. 20v (18 Dec.). On the papal bull, consult Glasson, *Parlement de Paris*, I, 404.

[38] A.N. KK 1428 and 1429, fols. 62r-74v (18 Nov. 1658, Dijon); some additional details are in B.N. ms. fr. 9750, fols. 46v, 72r, 88r, 143r-v. Ménestrier, *Histoire du roy Louis le Grand*, p. 49, cites this event for the medallic history, but dates it incorrectly as 28 November.

[39] There was a summons to convoke a *Lit de Justice* on 27 February 1662; A.N. X1a 8393, fols. 32r-34r (25 Feb.), but there is no account of the assembly. It is copied in A.N. U 2111 (Le Nain), fols. 84v-93r.

[40] These Royal *Séances* were recorded as follows. (1) A.N. X1a 8394, fols. 12r-28r (15 Dec. 1663): "... the king sitting in his Parlement ... black robes ..."; and the summons, fols. 11v-12r (14 Dec.), "... having resolved to hold our Parlement ... black robes. ..." (2) A.N. X1a 8394, fols. 8r-15r (2 Dec. 1665), and the summons, fol. 7v (28 Nov.), both worded as above. In the making of a medallic history (and stretching the legend in the process), Ménestrier, *Histoire du roy Louis le Grand*, p. 49, designated both these *Séances* as *Lit de Justice* assemblies. According to Master of Ceremonies Saintot, these sessions were not *Lit de Justice* assemblies because "There were no heralds, mace-bearers, drums or trumpets. Since he did not come as head of Parlement, the king [simply]

fading prestige in the ceremonial order was sealed by the *Lit de Justice* of 1664. After arduous argumentation on briefs drawn up by both sides, the king registered a declaration which stripped the Court of the right to precede the dukes-peers in consultation.[41] Already moved down the ladder of precedence behind Bourbon blood princes by the ceremonial protocol of Louis XIII, Parlement would now opine another step below. The last two *Lit de Justice* assemblies of the 1660's, legislative sessions duly orchestrated to the tune of drums and trumpets, were held in 1665 and 1667,[42] but the registers do not tell whether a final assembly planned for 1669 was ever actually convoked.[43] Throughout all these sessions of

placed himself upon the dais in the place which he ordinarily takes when he holds his *Lit de Justice*"; B. Mazarine ms. 2738 [Saintot, copied by Desgranges], fol. 112r ff. Consult Glasson, *Parlement de Paris*, I, 410, for the discussion there of the *droit annuel* and finances.

[41] A.N. X1a 8394, fols. 112r-119v (29 Apr. 1664), and the summons, fols. 111v-112r (28 Apr.). The master of ceremonies describes how the ceremonial grandeur was heightened by musical instruments when the king marched into the Grand-chambre to the tune of drums, fifes, and trumpets, which were sounded again when he arose to leave and during his exit; see B. Mazarine ms. 2738 [Saintot, copied by Desgranges], fols. 113v-115v. The decision against the presidents was recorded by Saintot, who recounts the briefs prepared by both sides in the controversy; ibid., fol. 115r-v. These two briefs may well be the ones drawn in 1664 and recorded in Institut de France, Collection Godefroy ms. 395, fols. 284r-299r (Parlement's case), and ibid., fols. 317r-323v (peers' case). Hamscher, *Parlement of Paris after the Fronde*, pp. 55-57, gives a nice summary of this argument between peers and presidents from 1662 to 1664. But there were no *Lits de Justice* held in January 1662 or January 1664, as he suggests, and such procedure was not purely ceremonial by the seventeenth century. In fact, this kind of dispute was rife throughout the long history of the *Lit de Justice* assembly from 1527 on, because ritual defined public authority. The presidents gave no precedents before 1597, since the facts for the sixteenth century would not have supported their case. For the social ramifications of such ranks, see Jean-Pierre Labatut, *Les Ducs et pairs de France au XVIIe siècle* (Paris, 1972).

[42] For the first, A.N. X1a 8394, fols. 25r-29r (22 Dec. 1665), and the summons, fols. 24v-25r (21 Dec.). The proposed medallic history, Ménestrier, *Histoire du roy Louis le Grand*, p. 49, lists this event but dates it incorrectly as 2 December 1663. For registration of the edict on the *paulette*, consult Isambert, *Recueil général des anciennes lois*, XVIII, 66-69. For the second, A.N. X1a 8395, fols. 89r-94v (20 Apr. 1667), and the summons, fols. 86v-87r (19 Apr.). The famed ordinance on the reformation of justice, the "Code Louis" or "Code Civil," was registered here; see Isambert, *Recueil général des anciennes lois*, XVII, 103-190. Glasson, *Parlement de Paris*, I, 412-429, discusses the event but says it was not a *Lit de Justice*.

[43] Although a summons for a *Lit de Justice* of 13 August 1669 was issued, A.N. X1a 8396, fol. 149r-v (12 Aug.), there is no account in the registers. There

the 1650's and 1660's the ritual reflected a royal policy which considered the Court's role as consultative, not deliberative, and the *"grands du royaume"* (the Bourbon blood princes and peers in concert with the monarch) as representatives of the nation.[44]

No doubt the dwindling attention given the *Lit de Justice* assembly at this time followed in some measure the attitudes of key advisers. One of the main architects of the new Bourbon cult of rulership, Jean-Baptiste Colbert, viewed royal visits to Parlement with skepticism. In the past they were undertaken most frequently, he said, by kings such as Charles IX and Louis XIII, whose rulership was so weak that they confronted Parlement just to demonstrate their power.[45] Earlier Richelieu and Séguier had despaired of the Estates General and contended that *Lits de Justice* comprehended them. Not long after, the Estates disappeared from the scene. Now Colbert and other royal advisers disdained *Lits de Justice* and Royal *Séances*, king and Royal Council carried out a program of judicial and administrative reform, and all looked to a royal cult of rulership which would symbolize Bourbon *gloire* in a variety of poses disconnected from the Grand-chambre. Not long after, these parlementary assemblies faded away. As Louis XIV's interest in the ritual of the *Lit de Justice* waned, his attention to legislative remedies waxed. Furthering the course begun by Louis XIII in 1641, the king wrote these ritualized patterns of authority into law. Once again parchment replaced ceremony to clarify the centuries-old confusion over the separation of powers. The case for Louis XIV's redefinition of the natural limits of Parlement's authority has been posed quite convincingly. To begin with the king issued an edict in 1661 which declared the decrees of Royal

---

is no account in A.N. U 2115 (Le Nain), fol. 392v, although a marginal note there lists the date without a record (this is the last entry in the Le Nain collection of *Lits de Justice*). The assembly was probably held. The master of ceremonies laid plans for it; B. Mazarine ms. 2738 [Saintot, copied by Desgranges]. Perhaps the register was "borrowed," since Colbert had advised the king to sequester registers of Parlement at will; Jean-Baptiste Colbert, *Lettres, instructions, et mémoires*, ed. Pierre Clément (Paris, 1861-1882), VI, 15-17 (memorandum of 1665). Colbert makes remarks about the assembly of 1669: Twenty-five edicts were read there, he says, and the king did not utter one word either during the session or as he left it; ibid., VI, 42, n. 1.

[44] For that presumption, see B.N. ms. fr. 14119, fols. 348r-353r.

[45] Colbert, *Lettres*, VI, 15-17. These off-hand remarks made in 1665 were probably devised to undermine *Lits de Justice* and Royal *Séances*, because they do not accurately describe the use of *Lits de Justice* by those two kings to support juristic and dynastic monarchies.

Councils superior to those of sovereign Courts. Then he promulgated the Code Louis in the *Lit de Justice* of 1667. That ordinance effectively limited Parlement's exercise of remonstrance. Finally, in 1673 the king issued *lettres patentes* which further curtailed Parlement's restricted remonstrance procedure. Since the Court had issued a mere six remonstrances between 1661 and 1667 on minor issues, the conclusion has been justly drawn that Parlement's prerogatives were redefined for one express purpose: to limit any future incursions of the Court into affairs of state which might injure the Crown's future plans for wider reforms. Judicial reform was the issue, not judicial review.[46] For Louis XIV Parlement's authority stopped at affairs of state, a point consistently held by French kings since the early sixteenth century and recently justified in Louis XIII's historical preamble to the Edict of 1641. Yet the difference in the times was a telling one: whereas Louis XIII had viewed the *Lit de Justice* assembly as the primary mode of royal enthronement, Louis XIV set loftier sights and acted accordingly.

In retrospect Louis XIV's increasing neglect of the ceremonial ritual of the *Lit de Justice* was a prelude to the king's abandonment of the assembly. The last *Lit de Justice* of the reign was held in 1673.[47] During the next forty years Louis did not visit the Grand-chambre of the Parlement of Paris again. When he reappeared there in 1713 the matter which drew him certainly touched French Fundamental Law, as it was termed. On the docket was the edict regarding the "Spanish succession," an agreement which disbarred the king's grandson Philip (and his descendants) from a future claim to the French throne in return for recognition of Philip as king of Spain by the European powers. Yet on this day Parlement wore black robes and the session was recorded as a Royal *Séance*.[48] When Charles IX legalized the succession compact of 1573, which allowed the legal successor (the future Henry III) to accept the Polish Crown without forfeiting succession rights to the French Crown, the action was carried out according to French Public Law in a *Lit de Justice* assembly. To the contrary, in legalizing this succession arrangement, Louis XIV freely subverted the two constitutions associated with

[46] Hamscher, *Parlement of Paris after the Fronde*, pp. 129-146. For these edicts of 8 July 1661, 20 April 1667, and 24 February 1673, see Isambert, *Recueil général des anciennes lois*, XVII, 403-405; XVIII, 105-106; and XIX, 70-73.

[47] A.N. X1a 8397 [19 unnumbered folios] (23 Mar. 1673), and the summons (21 Mar.).

[48] A.N. X1a 8429, fols. 358v-362r (15 Mar. 1713), toward the end of the register out of chronological order.

juristic and dynastic monarchies, Public Law (legal-hereditary succession) and Fundamental Law (dynastic right). In fact, that action, unconstitutional by any standard, served as a prelude to his outright reversal of Fundamental Law the next year. When the Sun King legally promoted his bastard sons to the status of blood princes in 1714 (which made them legal heirs to the throne),[49] Bourbon constitutional absolutism was confirmed. Interestingly enough, by chance or design, neither of these acts was carried out in a *Lit de Justice* assembly. During the seventy-two years of his reign Louis XIV convoked approximately nineteen *Lits de Justice* and five *Séances* before he abandoned both parlementary forums. During the last half of the seventeenth century the association of Crown and Parlement symbolized by the *Lit de Justice* in the Grand-chambre of the Palais de Justice was severed. The change of venue thus wrought was portrayed in the designs for a medallic history of the reign which depicted the Sun King enthroned in a variety of locations including the palace of Versailles.[50] Contrary to Charles V, who moved out of the Palais de Justice in the fourteenth century but left his throne apparatus there, and contrary to successor kings who lived in other palaces but maintained a throne room in the Grand-chambre, Louis XIV moved into the grand palace of Versailles where enthronement per se (with its former legal tenor) was replaced by a many-splendored cult of rulership. Clearly the ideology of absolutist monarchy was not sustained readily by the *Lit de Justice* assembly. The new Bourbon cult of rulership featured a galaxy of ceremonies which studded the firmament of Louis XIV's new universe at Versailles, and that multifaceted cult would have overshadowed the ritual of the *Lit de Justice* in the Grand-chambre even if the king had not first rendered it into oblivion himself.

[49] See Giesey, *Juristic Basis of Dynastic Right*, pp. 40-42.

[50] On that proposed medallic history, which likewise contributed to the legend of the *Lit de Justice* along with antiquarians and manuscript compilers, see Ménestrier, *Histoire du roy Louis le Grand*, plate 4 (no. 3) and plate 28 (no. 5), and *Médailles sur les principaux evenements du règne de Louis le Grand avec des explications historiques. Par l'Academie Royale des Médailles et des Inscriptions* (Paris, 1702), pp. 4, 5, 68, and 216. For the use of sun imagery in those medals and its connection with ceremony, see Kantorowicz, *Oriens Augusti-Lever du Roi*, pp. 119-177, and accompanying figures. The thesis recently advanced about medals, a combination of figure and word effecting representation and revelation and transcending time, offers interesting philosophical speculation but lacks solid historical grounding; see Marin, *Le Portrait du roi*, pp. 147-168. For the disposition of the palace, see Gaston Brière, *Le Château de Versailles* (Paris, 1907), especially I, 14, for the decoration of the new throne room completed in 1682.

XIV

EPILOGUE: THE BOURBON CULT OF RULERSHIP AT THE TURN OF THE EIGHTEENTH CENTURY

> ... one maxim alone ruled all ... [that of] proximity of
> blood. ... *Master of Ceremonies (c. 1670's)*

TOWARD THE END of the seventeenth century and at the turn of the eighteenth century the Bourbon cult of rulership comprehended a variety of disparate attributes—secular and sacred, classical and Christian, rational and magical—and was supported by the cultural system at large. Casting its net ever wider for French and foreign adherents, the royal cult first moved out of the Grand-chambre into the palaces, churches, and streets of Paris and then crossed international borders. The perpetrators of that phenomenon—ceremonial masters, writers, artists, historiographers, and propagandists—constructed a grand cultural edifice for Louis XIV. Only brief comments can be made on the enormous range of ceremonial spectacles which took place in the later seventeenth century, because the subject entails a whole study in itself. The rapid rise of a specialized ceremonial bureau staffed by masters of ceremonies has been traced. The ceremonial programs devised by that active bureau were numerous and varied: audiences for ambassadors, city representatives, provincial estates, and clergy; church celebrations such as devotions, communion, confirmation, funerals, baptisms (especially those of Bourbon blood), and the important Te Deum; ceremonies for public processions, *Entrées*, nameday *fêtes*, oath-taking, homage rituals; and the famous ceremonial ritual developed to regulate daily life at Versailles from sunrise to sunset, including the Apollonian *lever* and *coucher* of the Sun King, whose public behavior supposedly effected a mimesis of the eternal workings of the universe.[1]

[1] Consult B. Mazarine mss. 2737-2751 (covering the years 1645-1729). [Jean Dumont], *Corps universel diplomatique du droit des gens* (Amsterdam, 1726-1731), and *Le Cérémonial diplomatique des cours de l'Europe* (Amsterdam, 1739), which use some of the Saintot manuscripts; and André Félibien, *Relation de la feste de Versailles du 18ᵉ juillet 1668* (Paris, 1668), and *Les Divertissements de Versailles, donnés par le roy au retour de la conqueste de la Franche-Comté* (n.p., 1674). For

At the palace of Versailles royal ceremony flourished within a system of rigid social stratification. The copious notes left by Master of Ceremonies Saintot, whose research included memoranda on the ceremonial comportment of emperors,[2] give some indication of the lofty heights to which Louis XIV aspired. The system of ranks observed in the royal court applied even to the dynastic grandeur of the Bourbon family. Since it was agreed that "one maxim alone ruled all," that of *La proximité du sang* (*The proximity of blood*), persons of Bourbon lineage were delineated into three groups ranked in descending order: The *Famille du roy* (sons and daughters, grandsons and granddaughters of a reigning king), the *Famille royale* (the same relations of a deceased king), and the *Famille des princes du sang* (all princes and princesses of the blood).[3] Some sense of the complexity of this lineage system can be gleaned by viewing the subculture which issued from this milieu of assigned ranks and requisite etiquette. The subculture at court was stratified by reference to blood lineage (male and female) and to related values (sacred and profane, pure and impure), and the dual *homo hierarchicus* and *domina hierarchica* which emerged provided interlocking focal points for the political cabals soon fomented within it.[4] This rapid proliferation of ceremonial injunctions implemented by masters of ceremonies eventually fashioned a new panoply of symbols quite alien to the spirit of the sixteenth century, which had given rise to the *Lit de Justice* assembly, and at odds with the first half of the seventeenth century, which had promoted its grandeur in the Grand-chambre of the Parlement of Paris. As it turned out, the former thronal apparatus raised seven degrees in the Grand-chambre and attended by *parlementaires* remained empty, while the new one raised eight degrees in the throne room at Versailles (or elsewhere) and surrounded by Bourbon blood relations served for almost half a century as

recent studies of such phenomena, see Rule, ed., *Louis XIV and the Craft of Kingship*; Robert M. Isherwood, *Music in the Service of the King* (Ithaca, 1973); and the comments on the Te Deum, church processions, and bonfires in Joseph Klaits, *Printed Propaganda under Louis XIV: Absolute Monarchy and Public Opinion* (Princeton, 1976), chap. 1.

[2] A.N. K 1712 (17, 18, 24), extracts from Saintot's memoirs.

[3] A.N. K 1712 (3, 6), giving ranks to the Bourbon blood "orders," the *Famille du roy* taking precedence over all.

[4] Emmanuel Le Roy Ladurie, "Versailles Observed: The Court of Louis XIV in 1709," pp. 149-173, in *The Mind and Method of the Historian* (Chicago, 1978), trans. Siân Reynolds and Ben Reynolds; and ibid., "Auprès du roi, la cour," *Annales: Économies, Sociétés, Civilisations* (forthcoming).

the central stage for the ceremonial cult of rulership and the chief symbol of absolutist monarchy.[5] Still, the absolutist ideology manifested at Versailles, in churches, and on the streets of Paris through symbolism, ritual, and spectacle was a domestic commodity not easily exportable. And for that reason the ceremonial cult in these later decades was accompanied by a brilliant use of image and word.

A most vivid picture has been drawn of artifacts which propagated the royal image—portraits, statuary, and medals. Artists and engravers had tried to interest Henry IV in a medallic project, and those officiating at the Inaugural *Lit de Justice* of Louis XIII thought the idea worthy. But it was Louis XIV who initiated the first medallic history of a reign. Represented in almost every pose imaginable, many reminiscent of imperial Rome, the king's presence and thus royal *gloire* was disseminated to the public. Whether or not the royal image was made omnipresent by transcending ordinary space and time in this manner,[6] it surely was an image which sidestepped history. Along those same lines an engrossing tale has been told of the "artisans of glory," royal historiographers of the seventeenth century,[7] who helped mold the new cult of rulership. As discussed earlier, the historicist *mentalité* of the sixteenth century bred persons such as Du Tillet, Pasquier, L'Hôpital, and others who were active in public life. They adopted a historical perspective, criticized rhetoric as hostile to truth, and fortified treatises with documentary evidence. Guided by juristic ideology, in part the makers of it, they separated the "king's two bodies," discussed constitutional concerns in terms of the royal *dignité* and the *chose publique*, and "revived" the *Lit de Justice* assembly as a constitutional forum for treating issues of French Public Law. Conversely, writers of the later seventeenth century such as Mézerai, Pellisson-Fontanier, Racine, and others were artisans of royal *gloire* employed in niches of the royal patronage bureaucracy. They

[5] A.N. K 1712 (17, 18, 24) record events where Louis XIV was enthroned beneath a canopy upon a platform elevated by eight degrees with the Bourbon blood princes at his sides as early as 1669; and A.N. K 1712 (1, 5, 12) record the same through 1717.

[6] Louis XIV supported a grand project for a medallic history; see, for example, Ménestrier, *Histoire du roy Louis le Grand*, and *Médailles sur les principaux evenements du règne de Louis le Grand*. For the collection, consult Josephe Jacquiot, *Médailles et jetons de Louis XIV après le manuscrit de Londres* (Paris, 1968). On the role of images, see Marin, *Le Portrait du roi*.

[7] Orest Ranum, *Artisans of Glory: Writers and Historical Thought in Seventeenth-Century France* (Chapel Hill, 1980).

adopted the rhetorical heritage of antiquity to fashion a cult of kingship modeled on ancient heroes, replaced canons of historical evidence with panegyric, and fused literature and history.[8] Directed by absolutist ideology, the makers of it too, they neglected the distinction between the mortal monarch and his immortal office, emphasized the *gloire* of the dynastic incumbent, stressed service to Bourbon royalty, professed adherence to a natural, or traditional, Fundamental Law, and abandoned the *Lit de Justice* assembly.

The word was propagated widely by other means too. A recent study shows how government-sponsored propagandists of the later seventeenth and early eighteenth centuries attempted with some success to transmit royal grandeur beyond the narrow confines of the royal court. They influenced public opinion through propaganda printed in books, pamphlets, and the periodical press which crossed national boundaries. Admirably coordinated by Louis XIV's councillor, Colbert de Torcy, who wished to influence the views of dissidents and foreigners, this royal propaganda addressed a wide audience and spoke to those afflicted with that *crise de conscience* rife in Europe during the years just preceding the trenchant criticism of the French monarchy associated with the generation of Montesquieu.[9] All the while, the dissidents issued a stream of philosophical and political treatises which articulated opposition to the régime of Louis XIV. Those works dissected social, economic, and religious problems, traced the origins of the French nation, created complex plans for reform, and toyed with visions of utopia.[10] During this vigorous dissemination of the Bourbon cult of rulership, as well as the literature of opposition which it engendered, the *Lit de Justice* assembly figured not.

The ceremonial ritual of the *Lit de Justice* was neglected in the 1650's and 1660's and then abandoned after 1673. For almost half a century thereafter, a panorama of ceremonial spectacles and a plethora of printed propaganda struck the public eye at home and abroad, emitting a certain didactic quality. In the first decade of the eighteenth century, therefore, the times were not propitious for dredging up the old ritual of the *Lit de Justice* assembly. Yet that is precisely what happened.

[8] Ibid.

[9] Klaits, *Printed Propaganda*, chaps. I-IV.

[10] For the dissidents, consult Lionel Rothkrug, *Opposition to Louis XIV: The Political and Social Origins of the French Enlightenment* (Princeton, 1965); Keohane, *Philosophy and the State in France*, chaps. XI-XII; and Myriam Yardeni, *Utopie et révolte sous Louis XIV* (Paris, 1980).

THE REVIVAL OF *Lit de Justice* ASSEMBLIES IN 1715, 1718, AND 1723

On the morning of Louis XIV's death, 1 September 1715, the grand chamberlain appeared on the balcony of the deceased king's bedchamber wearing a black plume in his hat and cried out, "The king is dead!" He disappeared for a moment and then returned with a white plume in his hat and cried out three times, "Long live King Louis XV!"[11] The guardians of the royal cult of rulership had fashioned still another ritual announcing royal succession. The next morning, 2 September, the very specter which haunted Louis XIII and was avoided by Louis XIV settled on the premises when an assembly of Bourbon blood princes, dukes and peers, Crown officers, *parlementaires*, and others was convened in the Grand-chambre of Parlement without the young king Louis XV present. The constitutional collusion undertaken there satisfied the parties at the time: the Parlement of Paris declared the Duke of Orléans regent and reorganized the Regency Council to his specifications by amending Louis XIV's testament. Almost two weeks later, 15 September, the quid pro quo for Parlement's favorable action on the regency was effected: the new regent recognized pre-registration remonstrance as a valid facet of legislative procedure for the first time in French history.[12]

Squeezed in between these critical events, Louis XV's Inaugural *Lit de Justice* was performed rather perfunctorily in the Grand-chambre of the Parlement of Paris on 12 September, just one event in an inaugural program organized by masters of ceremonies. The proceedings of the *Lit de Justice* were recorded in the registers of Parlement,[13] but the most impressive account, published for public consumption that year, came from Saintot's ceremonial registers and included engravings of the Parisian *Entrée*, the *Lit de Justice* (Figure 14), and the seating plan drawn for the assembly (Figure 15).[14] Since the assembly itself had been defunct

[11] Jean Buvat, *Journal de la régence*, ed. Émile Campardon (Paris, 1865), I, 47-48, cited in James D. Hardy, *Judicial Politics in the Old Regime* (Baton Rouge, 1967).

[12] For the Remonstrance Edict of 1715, see Isambert, *Recueil général des anciennes lois*, XXI, 41.

[13] A.N. X1a 8431, fols. 431v-443v (12 Sept. 1715), and B. Mazarine ms. 2349 [8 unnumbered folios], with a seating plan ("Plan geometral de la Grand-chambre du Parlement de Paris . . . chez Poilly") included (see Figure 15 below). For the regency declaration, see *Arrest de la Cour de Parlement, le roy seant en son Lit de Justice* (12 Sept. 1715), pp. 1-3.

[14] This rare piece, *Extrait des registres de Parlement du jeudy 12 September . . . Louis XV du nom tenant son Lict de Justice en son Parlement* (Paris, 1715), pp.

14. Louis XV: Inaugural *Lit de Justice* held in the Grand-chambre of the Parlement of Paris, 1715.

for forty-two years, as an inaugural procedure for seventy-two years, most of the officials in attendance had never witnessed such a ceremony before. Few realized that this version of the ceremony in 1715 directly subverted the seventeenth-century tenets of succession associated with dynastic and absolutist ideologies. The symbolism of Louis XIII's Inaugural *Lit de Justice* had confirmed dynastic right and emphasized royal legislative authority, and the symbolism of Louis XIV's inauguration, when linked with unprecedented Minority *Lits de Justice*, had confirmed dynastic right and supreme legislative power. Conversely, this first *Lit de Justice* of Louis XV confirmed dynastic succession but recognized Parlement as legislative tutor of the minor king. Master of Ceremonies Saintot wrote a memoir on the day of the assembly which assessed this situation rather candidly: Parlement had already conferred the regency for Louis XV on 2 September, he pointed out, so the young king in the *Lit de Justice* of 12 September merely confirmed a legislative fait accompli.[15] Consequently, as performed in 1715 for Louis XV the Inaugural *Lit de Justice* actually marked the moment when the Bourbon claim to supreme legislative power could no longer be supported.

Out of sight and mind for generations, the ritual of the *Lit de Justice* assembly as revived in 1715 rotely acknowledged the regency, but it spelled out no constitutional axioms. To the contrary, the accompanying Edict of 1715 on remonstrance procedure set an astounding precedent. Louis XIII's important Edict of 1641 had disallowed remonstrance in *Lits de Justice*, and Louis XIV's Edicts of 1667 and 1673 had followed suit and then curbed remonstrance altogether. But the Edict of 1715 accorded Parlement the unprecedented privilege of pre-registration remonstrance for the first time and in addition contained no guidelines for legislation promulgated in the king's presence. These odd circumstances suggest that the parties involved had not only lost touch with precedent but also presumed that the *Lit de Justice* ceremony just revived would serve in this new era for the special Inaugural and Majority fêtes

---

1-11, includes three engravings and an attached drawing in manuscript of another seating plan for the event. The engraving of the Inaugural *Lit de Justice* (Figure 14) is one of François de Poilly from a design of Delamonce: B.N. Dépt. des Estampes; Collection Hennin, LXXXVII, fol. 38, and B.N. Clairambault ms. 719, fols. 594v-595r (and a copy of this print hangs in the Musée Carnavalet, Paris [D. 7013]). The engraving of the seating plan (Figure 15) is also one of François de Poilly: B.N. Dépt. des Estampes; B.N. Clairambault ms. 719, fol. 593r; B. Mazarine ms. 2349 (head of volume); and A.N. KK 1429, fol. 214r.

[15] B. Mazarine ms. 2349 [unnumbered folio (8v)] (12 Sept. 1715).

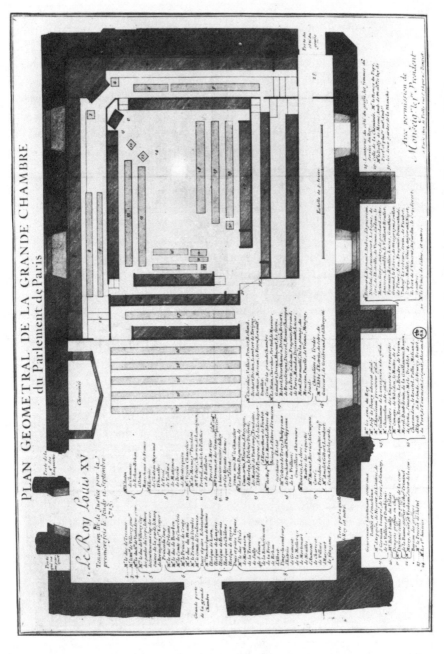

15. Louis XV: Plan of the Inaugural *Lit de Justice* held in the Grand-chambre of the Parlement of Paris, 1715.

only. In fact Louis XV's Majority *Lit de Justice* was held in 1723 (Figure 16), as discussed earlier, a gala celebration with the requisite fanfare and more. At this particular point in 1715, however, there was no reason to assume that *Lits de Justice* would be featured in Louis XV's reign, or any other reign for that matter. That factor has always been overlooked, but it is critical for understanding how the Crown's *Lit de Justice* and Parlement's remonstrance made a debut as legislative rivals in the eighteenth century. In fact, the stage was set for matching the two as procedural protagonists when the Duke of Orléans legalized pre-registration remonstrance in return for Parlement's support of his regency. It was not long, however, before the regency government became thoroughly enraged by Parlement's meddling in affairs of state, especially financial matters, and in 1718 the exasperated regent sent to Parlement for registration another edict which defined the remonstrance procedure more stringently.[16] The Court ignored the regent's command and continued its business as usual, intruding at every turn in legislative affairs. As a result, during the next three weeks the most bizarre *Lit de Justice* in French history was secretly planned and convoked for the express purpose of registering the Edict of 1718 regulating remonstrance.

Louis de Rouvroy, Duke of Saint-Simon, and the regent Duke of Orléans met secretly between 19 and 22 August 1718 to discuss the convocation of Louis XV's Minority *Lit de Justice*, not in the Grand-chambre of Parlement but in the Château of the Tuileries. Saint-Simon met clandestinely with the keeper of Crown furnishings, Moïse Augustin Fontanieu, and informed him of the plan. Fontanieu's cooperation was crucial because he would have to construct the thronal paraphernalia furtively and swiftly on command. Yet he was frightened of the venture for a practical reason: he had never witnessed a *Lit de Justice* assembly and did not know how to arrange the thronal apparatus. Saint-Simon assuaged such fears.[17] Obviously he had done some research, perhaps in the ceremonial registers or manuscript compilations, because he was familiar with the archaeological disposition of such sessions, as well as precedents for convoking the *Lit de Justice* outside the Grand-chambre.[18]

[16] For the second Edict of 1718 on remonstrance, see Isambert, *Recueil général des anciennes lois*, XXI, 159-162 (2 Aug. 1718).
[17] Louis de Rouvroy, Duke of Saint-Simon, *Mémoires de Saint-Simon*, ed. Arthur de Boislisle (Paris, 1923), XXXV, 32-45.
[18] The duke must have consulted the ceremonial registers before making these plans, and the manuscript compilations (Table One below) would have been very useful in establishing precedents for location.

16. Louis XV: Majority *Lit de Justice* held in the Grand-chambre of the Parlement of Paris, 1723.

Saint-Simon sketched a rough plan of the seating arrangements and coached Fontanieu on the fine points of constructing the *lit de justice* apparatus. Initiated into the secret pact, Fontanieu became a key figure in the conspiracy to surprise Parlement with a *Lit de Justice* assembly in the Tuileries.[19] In the meantime the regent Orléans grew exceedingly anxious and caused a series of vexing delays by wavering on simple decisions, but Saint-Simon persisted doggedly and finally prodded him into action.[20] When the secret plans for this strange Minority *Lit de Justice* at the Tuileries were finally arranged, the royal party turned to the problem of procedural strategy.

It was agreed that tactics must be devised to control procedure during the assembly in the event that Parlement refused to opine during consultation. Should the Court remain silent when consulted, Seals-keeper (acting chancellor) René-Louis de Voyer, Marquis of Argenson, would pretend to have received advice and continue on his rounds consulting others. Should the Court openly insist on deliberations before consultation, Argenson would declare outright that Parlement in a *Lit de Justice* assembly was allowed a consultative voice, not a deliberative one, and then admonish the Court to obey the king.[21] Should the Court attempt to make a remonstrance during the *Lit de Justice*, he would approach Louis XV and then swiftly announce that the king wished to be obeyed then and there.[22] Whereas the regent Anne of Austria had suffered little anxiety over convoking a Minority *Lit de Justice* for Louis XIV in 1645, the regent Duke of Orléans suffered great apprehension in 1718. These opposite regental reactions might be related to differences of character, Anne's aggressiveness and Orléans' timidity. But more important is the fact that the *Lit de Justice* assembly itself, whether held in the Grand-chambre or royal quarters, was so utterly obsolete by the turn of the eighteenth century that the regent and his advisers actually feared that the summons for its convocation might go unheeded or that the proceedings might incur open revolt.

Before dawn on 26 August the royal plan was implemented. Fontanieu

[19] *Mémoires de Saint-Simon*, XXXV, 45-46, and 328, for a copy of the hand-written plan drawn for Fontanieu.

[20] Ibid., 75-78, 97-98, 105. For instance, Orléans could not decide on the exact date; then he quarreled with Fontanieu over the height of the elevated seats as the latter struggled with the mechanical difficulties caused by raising that staging so high.

[21] Ibid., 155-156.

[22] Ibid., 201.

set up the thronal apparatus in the royal apartments of the Tuileries and the masters of ceremonies issued letters summoning attendants. At five o'clock that morning soldiers of the French and Swiss Guards were stationed in strategic places to announce the arrival of royal messengers bearing summonses. At six o'clock the master of ceremonies Michel Ancel Desgranges arrived in the Grand-chambre and delivered a summons for the Court to appear at the *Lit de Justice* assembly in the Château of the Tuileries.[23] Around nine o'clock (no doubt after three hours of heated discussion) the red-robed *parlementaires* marched with grim fortitude two-by-two through the streets of Paris to the Tuileries and took their places in the prepared chamber. Others traveled to the château by varied means and took seats after the *parlementaires*.[24] Just before the arrival of the king, the Duke of Saint-Simon sat in the high bench of the peers (to the right of the throne) and looked down upon the *parlementaires* with vengeful satisfaction. "I saw astonishment, silence, consternation ... which seemed a good omen," he said. "The first president was humbled, the other presidents were disconcerted, all were attentive. . . ."[25] Louis XV arrived at the assembly, preceded by the regent, Bourbon blood princes, and the royal party, and then the *Lit de Justice* of 26 August 1718 was officially convened.[26] Saint-Simon perceived the whole assembly as one pervaded by "an extreme silence which eloquently announced the fear, attention, uneasiness, and curiosity of the various spectators,"[27] but with characteristc obtuseness he failed to sense the ominous nature of that silence, especially on the part of *parlementaires*. When they protested the lack of deliberations prior to the registration

---

[23] Ibid., 160-169. For the summons, see A.N. X1a 8435, fols. 595v-596r (26 Aug. 1718). Desgranges was nominated as master of ceremonies on 24 August 1691.

[24] *Mémoires de Saint-Simon*, XXXV, 201-211.

[25] Ibid., 221.

[26] Oddly enough, there are two accounts in the registers of Parlement: A.N. X1a 8435, fols. 595r-606v [a short account], and fols. 606v-621r [a long account including discussion] (26 Aug. 1718). A printed version of these proceedings was planned right away and can be seen in varied stages: see A.N. KK 696 (no. 39), the first draft of the *procès verbal*, and A.N. KK 696 (nos. 40, 40 bis, and 40 ter), another corrected draft. The final printed version (which contains mistakes) appeared as *Procès-verbal de ce qui s'est passé au Lit de Justice, tenu par le roy au château des Tuileries, le vendredy 26ᵉ jour d'aoust 1718* (Paris, 1718), pp. 1-32. See also *Mémoires de Saint-Simon*, XXXV, 212-217, including a plan drawn of the seating and identification of the placement of participants.

[27] *Mémoires de Saint-Simon*, XXXV, 223.

of the Edict of 1718 on remonstrance, Seals-keeper Argenson demanded compliance, as planned.[28] There was compliance on the spot but not without future cost.

During most of the seventeenth century the *Lit de Justice* assembly (which associated king and Parlement in the Grand-chambre) was the most celebrated ceremony in the kingdom: it served as the primary inaugural institution and marked the royal majority, utilized ritual to define working axioms of government and legislative procedure, and supported the ideology of dynastic monarchy and with it the dynastic aspirations of parlementary officeholders. Thus when Parlement hosted Inaugural *Lit de Justice* assemblies for the minor kings Louis XIII and Louis XIV in 1610 and 1643 and allowed them to act as dynastic successors and as legislators there, the Court traded some legislative prerogative for institutional prestige conferred through ceremonial grandeur. Conversely, from the mid-seventeenth century the *Lit de Justice* (which associated Parlement with the king in the Grand-chambre or the royal palace) eventually became institutionally defunct: the dynastic mysteries formerly elucidated through ceremony had become secular axioms, hereditary succession for officeholders was assured within dynastic officialdom, and a more ostentatious Bourbon cult of rulership was propagated through a wide variety of rituals staged by ceremonial masters. In the Inaugural *Lit de Justice* of 1715, therefore, when the Parlement of Paris was allowed to act as legislative tutor of a minor king for the first time and pre-registration remonstrance was first legalized, the young Louis XV was displayed as dynastic successor but not as legislator. All the more incomprehensible was the Minority *Lit de Justice* of 1718, which attempted to turn back the clock of ceremonial symbolism.

WHITHER THE ANCIENT FRENCH CONSTITUTION?

A reading of the history of the *Lit de Justice* assembly from fictions and facts, ritual and discourse, between 1527 and 1673 suggests that constitutional ideologies—juristic, dynastic, and absolutist—were articulated in that forum; that those ideologies were formed and transformed through the consensus of Crown and Parlement; and that the vital consensus itself rested on a base which was historicist at the core. In two distinct phases, one coinciding with the introduction of the *Lit de Justice* in 1527, the other following the Inaugural *Lit de Justice* in 1610, the archival

[28] See the sources in n. 26 above.

research of historians produced a fiction, then a legend, about the pristine medieval origins of the *Lit de Justice* assembly held in the Grand-chambre of the Parlement of Paris. In turn the provocative legend underwrote numerous *Lits de Justice* in the seventeenth century until the gradual demise of the assembly after 1652.

The ceremonial rituals performed in these sessions, controlled by the Crown, manipulated by Parlement, framed and reframed constitutional precepts. The constitutional legitimacy of the *Lit de Justice* was not in question after the 1560's, but the ceremonies which structured the sessions and determined prerogative and place were continually contested. The Crown employed ritual to vest sovereign authority in the monarch, separate legislative (royal) and judicial (parlementary) functions, and provide a consultative, not deliberative, body of orders, or Estates, which included the Parlement of Paris. Parlement bent ritual to vest sovereign authority in the monarch but insinuate co-legislative capacity; assume superiority (as the seat of the *Lit de Justice*) over rival councils and Courts, and confirm its corporate continuity, as well as the hereditary tenure of individual officeholders. Overshadowing all contests, however, was the formidable stature of the *Lit de Justice* and the ritual bond which it forged between Crown and Parlement: hence, kings promoted the grandeur of the assembly in the Grand-chambre, and the *parlementaires* traded legislative prerogative to maintain the prestigious forum in their quarters.

The discourses associated with such sessions, prepared under separate auspices, revealed and shaped constitutional ideologies. Over the centuries Crown officers, *parlementaires*, historians, and others converted private-law maxims, classical and juridical metaphors, biogenetic doctrines, popular proverbs, and historical legends into a language expressing constitutional axioms. In the sixteenth century the juristic maxims, *Royal authority does not die*, *The kingdom is never vacant*, and *Crown and Justice never die*, described a monarchy in which the royal *dignité* was conferred upon kings by the Public Law of the kingdom, or *chose publique*. In the early seventeenth century the dynastic maxims, *The king never dies* and *Royalty is always replenished and never vacant*, described a monarchy in which royalty was conferred upon a series of corporeal incumbents by dynastic right and Public Law. In the later seventeenth century the absolutist maxims, *The king never dies* and *The proximity of blood rules all*, described a monarchy in which royalty was exercised by Bourbon incumbents through Fundamental Law, a veritable *mystique du sang* supported by nature and tradition. The tenets of juristic ideology limited royal legislative capacity (as shown in the Majority *Lit de Justice* of 1563);

those of dynastic ideology expanded it (through the Inaugural of 1610) but preserved some limits (as shown in the Majority of 1614); and the tenets of absolutist ideology left royal capacity unbounded (as seen in the Minority *Lits de Justice* of 1645 and 1648).

These discourses also shaped constitutional ideologies by countenancing different modes of perception. The historical method for comprehending the French past, nominalist and philological in conception, offered a new means for apprehending reality. The antiquarian treatise of Jean du Tillet deserved the inordinate attention it attracted, because the documentary evidence adduced there reconstructed the ancient constitution, and it provided the prototype for a new genre of historical writing. Conversely, the later appeal to tradition in time immemorial, idealist and rhetorical in orientation, became the guide to the French past, and the artisans of royal *gloire* set a different standard for the apprehension of truth, which was radically different though no less ambitious. All the while, the fortunes of the *Lit de Justice* assembly flourished on the vine of history, withered at the root of tradition.

Along those lines it has been pointed out that the ancien régime did not suppress its institutions. It superimposed new forms by allowing the old ones to remain dormant and atrophy without realizing that one day they might be resuscitated.[29] There is no better example of this process than that afforded by the various fortunes of the *Lit de Justice* assembly, the Royal *Séance*, and the Estates General in these decades. In the sixteenth century the Royal *Séance* and the Estates General, partners from medieval times, shared the stage for twenty-one years (1506-1527), until the *Lit de Justice* assembly appeared. These three forums then remained on the scene for eighty-three years (1527-1610), until the *Séance* faded away. In the seventeenth century the *Lit de Justice* and the Estates General shared a short five years (1610-1615), until the Estates also disappeared. At this point the *Lit de Justice* assembly surveyed the scene alone for thirty-nine years (1615-1654), until the *Séance* reappeared. These two shared quarters again for nineteen years (1654-1673), until the *Lit de Justice* disappeared. All three forums (except for the one *Séance* of 1673) were virtually dormant for forty-two years, until the old *Lit de Justice* was revived in 1715. Finally, in the eighteenth century the *Lit de Justice* assembly and the Royal *Séance* remained for seventy-three years (1715-1788), until both were rudely retired and the very aged Estates General was called to the fore on the eve of the Revolution.

[29] Pierre Goubert, *L'Ancien régime* (Paris, 1973), II, 16-17.

The revival of the *Lit de Justice* in 1715 was out of joint with the times; its procedural linkage with remonstrance set a problematic precedent. During the next half century a series of sporadic quarrels between Crown and Parlement caused untold enmity and turned the ritual and discourse of the *Lit de Justice* into an eighteeth-century farce, which was acted out on the stage of Versailles with written parody published for the public.[30] When Louis-Adrien Le Paige surveyed this turbulent scene around mid century and projected the query "You ask me what a *Lit de Justice* is?" the parties at bay looked back through the registers of Parlement and the ceremonial bureau, antiquarian treatises and manuscript compilations, and resurrected the legend of the *Lit de Justice* assembly. Over the centuries Parlement had come full circle, from silent negation to vociferous defense of the *Lit de Justice* in the Grand-chambre. The convocation of a *Lit de Justice* today, they asserted, was an occasion of mourning for the nation, because the French constitution had been corrupted by the death of the pristine *Lit de Justice* assembly of yore. In the beginning it was claimed that in the "Republic of France ... Crown and Justice never die," later on that "The king of France never dies," finally that "The proximity of blood rules all." In the end both the Crown and the Parlement were consumed by the same funeral pyre, which admitted no phoenix-like rebirth. In their turn the architects of the new French Republic sought historical justification for the state in the decades after 1789, but they deliberately leaped over the cold ashes of these ancient French constitutions and tapped the remains of Roman antiquity and other polities to mold another constitutional ideology from new legends, rituals, and discourse.

[30] For example, see the printed version of the speech given by the *parlementaire* Antoine-Louis Séguier, *Discours de M. Antoine-Louis Séguier ... prononcé au Lit de Justice ... au château de Versailles le treize avril 1771* (n.p., n.d.), and compare that with the parody issued on the speech (the two versions identified by italicizing Séguier's original comments) with its deadly criticism; *Discours de M. Séguier ... prononcé au Lit de Justice ... 13 avril 1771. Nouvelle édition ...* (n.p., n.d.). The proliferation of such published retorts did indeed make the staging of the *Lit de Justice* appear somewhat farcical in the later eighteenth century.

TABLE ONE. The Legend of the Lit de Justice Assembly

	A	B	C	D	E	F	G	H	I	J	K	L	M	N	O	P	Q	R	S	T	U	V	W	X	Y	Z
		Primary Sources		Secondary Sources																						
	King in Parlement	Registers of Parlement (original accounts) A.N. X1a 1315–1713	Registers of Parlement (copies & notes) A.N. U (Le Nain)	Du Tillet	La Roche-Flavin	ms. fr. 2881	ms. fr. 18522	ms. fr. 18410	ms. n.a. 7231	ms. fr. 4346	U 425-426	ms. 2912	ms. 16511	ms. fr. 23410	Dupuy mss. 513-514 Dupuy and B.N.	Godefroy	Clairambault 715	ms. fr. 18411	ms. fr. suppl. 11737	C.P. ms. 5046	ms. fr. 16512	ms. fr. suppl. 10948-10949	KK 1441	ms. n.a. 9749	ms. n.a. 9750	KK 1428-1429
				1563 Pub.	1615 Pub.	1616 B.N.	1627 B.N.	1632 B.N.	1633 B.N.	1634 B.N.	1638 A.N.	1641 Maz.	1643 B.N.	1643 B.N.	1645 Pub.	1649 Pub.	1650 B.N.	1662 B.N.	1665 B.N.	1673 B.V.P.	1673 B.N.	1680 B.N.	1684 A.N.	1723 B.N.	1723 B.N.	1725 A.N.
1	1315 4 July	[3]	2000																				●	●	●	●
2	1353 4 Mar.		2005																				●		●	●
3	1358 10 Dec.		513																				●	✻	●	
4	1364 12 Nov.	[1469][a]	2014	✻																						
5	1366 27 July	[1469] Saint-Pol[b]	2014														✻									

	Primary Sources			Secondary Sources																						
	A	B	C	D	E	F	G	H	I	J	K	L	M	N	O	P	Q	R	S	T	U	V	W	X	Y	Z
6	1369, 9, 11 May	[1469]	2014, 513	●	●			●	●	●	●	✳	●	●	●	●		●			✳	●	●	✳	●	●
7	1375, 21 May	[1470] [8602]	2014, 513	●	●										●			✳			✳			●	●	●
8	1378, 9, 10 Dec.	[1471]	2014, 513	●	●	●	●	●	●	●	●	●	●	●	●	●		●			●	●	●	●	●	●
9	1380, 2 Oct.	[1471]	2014, 513	✳	✳		●														✳				●	●
10	1387, 2 Mar.	[1473]	2015, 513	●	●			●	●	●	●	●	●	●	●	●	●	●		●	●	●	●	●	●	●
11	1392, 3 Dec.	1477	2016, 513	●	●	●								●												
12	1396, 10 Apr.	4784	2170, 513	●	●									●							●					
13	1407, 26 Dec.		513	●	●																				
14	1413, 26, 27 May	1479 4789	2018, 513	●	●		●				●	●	●						●	●	●	●	✳	●	●	●
15	1413, 5 Sept.	1479 4789 8602	2018, 513	●	●	●	●					●	●							●			●	✳	●	●	●
16	1458, 10 Oct.	Vendôme[c]	513[d]	✳	✳			●	●	●					●		●	✳			●	●		●	●
17	1484, 20 July	4825	2175, 513[e]																						●	
18	1487, 21, 22 Feb.	[1495]	513		●			●	●	●		●	●	●		●		●			●		●		●	●

	1	2	3	4	5	6	7	8	9	10	11	12
				•	•	❋	•	•	•	•	•	•
		•		•	❋	❋	•	•	•	•	•	•
	•		•		❋	❋		•	•	•	•	•	•
				❋	❋	•	❋	•	•			•	•
		•		•	•	•		•	•	•		•	•
	❋		❋		❋				•			
	•	❋		❋					•	•		•
								•	•		•	•
					•	❋	•	•	•		•	•
									•			•
					•		•	•	•		•	•
					•		❋	•	•			•
	•	•	•	•		•	•	•	•	•	•	•
	❋	❋		•		•	❋	•	•	•		•
	•			•	•		❋	•	•			•
								•	•		•	•
				❋		❋	•	•	•	•	
							•			•	•
							•	•			•
	❋			❋	❋	❋	❋	•	•			•
	•							•			•
❋		❋	❋	❋	❋	❋	❋	❋	•	•	•	•
❋		❋	❋	❋	❋	❋	❋	❋	•	•	•	❋

	2024		2181[f]	2024	2025	2026		2168	2168	2029	2169	2192	2038
	513		513[f]	2181	513	513		513	513	513	513	513	2169
				513									2196
													513

	[1500]	[1504]	[1504]	[1504]	[1517]	[1519]	[1524]	[1525]	[1526]	1530	1531	[1565]
				[4840]								

	1493	1498	1498	1499	1515	1517	1522	1523	1524	1527	1527	1537	1549
	8, 9, 11	17 May	7 July	13 June	14 Mar.	5 Feb.	15 Feb.	30 June	8, 9 Mar.	24-27 July	16, 20	15 Jan.	2 July
	July										Dec.		

| 19 | 20 | 21 | 22 | 23 | 24 | 25 | 26 | 27 | * 28 | * 29 | * 30 | 31 |

TABLE ONE. (cont.)

		Primary Sources							Secondary Sources																			
	A	B	C	D	E	F	G	H	I	J	K	L	M	N	O	P	Q	R	S	T	U	V	W	X	Y	Z
32	1551 12 Nov.	[1571]	2039 / 513	❋	❋		●	●	●	●	●	●	●	●	●	●	●	●	●	●		●	❋	●	●	●
33	1552 12 Feb.	[1571]	2039 / 513	❋	❋	●	●	●	❋	●	●	●	●	●	●	●	●	●	●	●		●	●	●	●	●
34	1558 5 Jan.	Salle Saint-Louis[g]	2046	❋								❋						●	●	●	❋	●	●	●	●	●
35	1558 15 Jan.	[1587]	2046 / 513	❋			●	❋	●	●	❋	●	●	●						●			●	●	●	●
36	1563 17 May	[1605]	513	❋	●	●	●	❋		●		●	●	●		❋	●		●	●		●	●	●	●	●
*37	1563 17 Aug.	Rouen[h]	513	—	❋			●	●	●	●		●	●	●	●	●	●				●	●	●	●	●
*38	1564 11 Apr.	Bordeaux[i]	513	—	●				●	●				●	●	●		●				●	●	●	●	●
*39	1565 1 Feb.	Toulouse[j]	513	—	●			●		●				●		●		●				●	●	●	●	●
40	1569 1 Aug.	5023[k]	2205 / 513	—																							
41	1571 12 Mar.	[1631] [5031]	2205 / 513	—																	❋					
42	1572 26 Aug.	[5039]	513	—																			●			
*43	1573 18 Sept.	1640	2063 / 513	—																			●			
44	1580 26 July	[1669][l]	513	—																						

No.	Date	Edition	Catalogue
45	1581 4 July	[1672]	2068 / 513
46	1583 7 Mar.	[1679]	2068^m / 513
47	1585 18 July	—	—
48	1586 15 June	—	—
49	1589 23 Mar.		513°
*50	1597 21 May	1749	2079 / 513
*51	1610 15 May	1829	2082 / 513
*52	1614 2 Oct.	1866	2085 / 513
*53	1615 10 Dec.	Bordeaux^p	
*54	1616 7 Sept.	1878	2085 / 513
*55	1619 12 Mar.	1896	2087 / 513
*56	1620 18 Feb.	1905	2087 / 513
*57	1620 4 July	1909	2087 / 513
*58	1620 11 July	Rouen^q	
*59	1620 28 Sept.	Bordeaux^r	513^s

TABLE ONE. (cont.)

	Primary Sources			Secondary Sources																							
	A	B	C	D	E	F	G	H	I	J	K	L	M	N	O	P	Q	R	S	T	U	V	W	X	Y	Z
* 60	1621 3 Apr.	1918	2087 / 513	|	|	|	•	•	•	•		•		•	•	•	•	•			•	•	•	•	•	•
* 61	1622 18 Mar.	1929	2087 / 513	|	|	|	•	•	•	•	|	•	|	•	|	•	|	•	|	•	•	•	|	•	•	•
* 62	1626 6 Mar.	1967	2090 / 513	|	|	|	•	|	|	•	|	•	•	•	•	|	•	•	•	|	•	|	•	•	•
* 63	1627 28 June	1982	2089 / 513	|	|	|	•	|	|	•	|	•	•	|	|	•	|	•	|	|	•	•	•	•	•
* 64	1629 15 Jan.	2009	2089 / 513	|	|	|	|	|	|	•	|	•	|	•	•	•	•	|	•	•	|	•	•	|	•	•	•
* 65	1631 13 Aug.	2044	2091 / 513	|	|	|	|	•	•	•	|	|	•	•	•	•	|	•	|	|	•	•	•	•	•	•
* 66	1632 12 Aug.	2055	2091 / 513	|	|	|	|	•	|	•	|	|	|	|	•	•	•	|	|	•	•	•	•	•	•
* 67	1633 12 Apr.	2064	2091 / 513	|	|	|	|	•	|	•	|	•	•	•	•	|	•	•	|	•	•	•	•	•	•
* 68	1634 18 Jan.	2074	2094 / 513	|	|	|	|	|	|	•	|	•	•	•	•	|	|	|	•	|	•	•	•	•	•
* 69	1635 20 Dec.	2101	2094 / 513	|	|	|	|	|	|	|	|	•	•	•	•	|	|	•	•	|	|	•	•	•	•
* 70	1641 21 Feb.	8387	2096 / 513	|	|	|	|	|	|	|	|	|	|	•	|	|	|	|	|	•	|	•	•	•	•
* 71	1643 18 May	8388	2098 / 513	|	|	|	|	|	|	|	•	•	•	|	•	•	•	•	•	|	|	•	•	•	•
* 72	1645 7 Sept.	8388	2098 / 513	|	|	|	|	|	|	|	|	|	|	|	|	|	•	|	•	•	•	•	•	•	•

No.	Number		Catalog	Date
*73	2101	513		1648 15 Jan.
*74	2101	513		1648 31 July
*75	2103	513	Louvre[t]	1651 7 Sept.
*76	2105	513	8389	1652 22 Oct.
*77	2105-6	513	8389	1652 13 Nov.
*78	2105	513	8389	1652 31 Dec.
79	2105	513[u]	8389	1654 19 Jan.
80	2105	513	8389	1654 21, 27 Mar.
*81	2105	513	—	1654 28 Mar.
*82	2107[w]	513	8390	1655 20 Mar.
*83	2107	513	8391	1655 13 Apr.
*84	2108	513		1657 19 Dec.
*85			Dijon[x]	1658 18 Nov.
*86	2111	513		1662 27 Feb.
87	2112	513	8394	1663 15 Dec.

Table One. (cont.)

		Primary Sources											Secondary Sources														
		A	B	C	D	E	F	G	H	I	J	K	L	M	N	O	P	Q	R	S	T	U	V	W	X	Y	Z
*	88	*1664* 29 Apr.	8394	2112	—	—	—	—	—	—	—	—	—	—	—	—	—	—	—	•		•		❋		•	•
	89	*1665* 2 Dec.	8394	513	—	—	—	—	—	—	—	—	—	—	—	—	—	—	—	•				❋		•	•
*	90	*1665* 22 Dec.	8394	2114, 513	—	—	—	—	—	—	—	—	—	—	—	—	—	—	—								
*	91	*1667* 20 Apr.	8395	2114, 513	—	—	—	—	—	—	—	—	—	—	—	—	—	—	—		•	•		❋		•	•
*	92	*1669* 13 Aug.	—	2114	—	—	—	—	—	—	—	—	—	—	—	—	—	—	—		•	•		•		•	•
*	93	*1673* 23 Mar.	8397	—	—	—	—	—	—	—	—	—	—	—	—	—	—	—	—					❋		•	•
	94	*1713* 15 Mar.	8429		—	—	—	—	—	—	—	—	—	—	—	—	—	—	—	—	—	—	—	—		❋	❋

a Account inserted by Du Tillet in 1545.
b Session held in the Hôtel Saint-Pol, Paris.
c Trial held in the Château of Vendôme, Vendôme.
d A.N. U (Le Nain) mistakenly dates as 18 December.
e A.N. U (Le Nain) mistakenly dates as 28 March.
f A.N. U (Le Nain) mistakenly dates as 5 July.
g Session an Assembly of Notables which functioned as an Estates General, the first in Paris in that century, convoked in the Salle Saint-Louis, Palais de Justice.
h Convoked in the Parlement of Rouen.
i Convoked in the Parlement of Bordeaux.
j Convoked in the Parlement of Toulouse.
k X1a 5023 mistakenly denotes a *Lit de Justice*; not cited by any commentator except A.N. U (Le Nain).
l Not cited by any commentator.

m A.N. U (Le Nain) mistakenly dates as April.
n No evidence that the session was held.
o A.N. U (Le Nain) gives no day.
p Convoked in the Parlement of Bordeaux.
q Convoked in the Parlement of Rouen.
r Convoked in the Parlement of Bordeaux.
s A.N. U (Le Nain) mistakenly dates as 1618.
t Convoked in the palace of the Louvre, Paris.
u A.N. U (Le Nain) mistakenly dates as March.
v Summons issued for a *Lit de Justice* on 19 March; account missing.
w A.N. U (Le Nain) places account out of order at end of volume.
x Convoked in the Parlement of Dijon.
y Summons issued for a *Lit de Justice* on 12 August; account missing.
z A.N. U (Le Nain) notes that the account has been added (A.N. U 2115); account missing.

TABLE Two. The *Lit de Justice* Assembly in
the *Recueil des roys de France* of Jean du Tillet (ed. 1607)

KEY

✳ Designated as a Royal *Séance*
by Du Tillet

● Designated as a *Lit de Justice*
assembly by Du Tillet

	Date		Location	Grands and [Roys], pages
1	1310	(Winter)	Unknown	35
2	1332	—	Louvre	42-45
3	1366	(21 Feb.)	Saint-Pol	48
4	1366	(27 July)	Saint-Pol	48-49
5	1367	(13 Feb.)	Saint-Pol	50
6	1367	(15 Nov.)[a]	Louvre	50-51
7	● 1369	(24 Apr.)	Saint-Pol	52
8	● 1369	(9, 11 May)	Parlement	51-52, [256]
9	✳ 1369	(10 Dec.)	Parlement	52
10	1374	(19 Mar.)	Saint-Pol	53
11	● 1375	(21 May)	Parlement	52-53, [277]
12	● 1378	(9 Dec.)	Parlement	11, 14, 18, 53-55, 65-66, [368-69, 371]
13	● 1387	(2 Mar.)	Parlement	12, 55, 66, [368-69, 371]
14	● 1392	(3 Dec.)	Parlement	58
15	● 1396	(10 Apr.)	Parlement	16, 20, 59
16	1404	(23 Aug.)	Saint-Pol	59
17	● 1407	(26 Dec.)	Parlement	60, [279]
18	1412	(18 Feb.)	Saint-Pol	60
19	● 1413	(26 May)	Parlement	60-61, 62
20	● 1413	(5 Sept.)	Parlement	61-62
21	1458	([10] Oct.)	Vendôme	13, 14, 15, 16, 19, 67-68, [314, 370-71]
22	✳ 1493	(22, 25 Feb.)	Parlement	75-76
23	✳ 1493	(8, 11 July)[b]	Parlement	76-77
24	✳ 1498	(7 July)	Parlement	78
25	✳ 1499	(13 June)	Parlement	78
26	✳ 1502	(24 Feb.)	Parlement	78
27	✳ 1504	(3 Dec.)	Parlement	78
28	✳ 1504	(5 Dec.)	Parlement	78
29	✳ 1504	(16 Dec.)	Parlement	78

TABLE TWO (*cont.*)

	Date		Location	Grands and [Roys], pages
30	✳ 1505	(2 Jan.)	Parlement	78
31	✳ 1508	(13 Nov.)	Parlement	79
32	✳ 1508	(16 Nov.)	Parlement	79
33	✳ 1510	(18 Mar.)	Parlement	79
34	✳ 1515	(14 Mar.)	Parlement	79
35	✳ 1515	(29 Mar.)	Parlement	79
36	✳ 1517	(5 Feb.)	Parlement	79
37	✳ 1522	(15 Feb.)	Parlement	80
38	✳ 1523	(30 June)	Parlement	80
39	✳ 1524	(8, 9 Mar.)	Parlement	81
40	● 1527	(24, 26, 27 July)	Parlement	14, 19, 81-86
41	● 1527	(16, 20 Dec.)	Parlement	14, 86-92
42	● 1537	(15 Jan.)	Parlement	12, 14, 15, 19, 93-95
43	✳ 1549	(2 July)	Parlement	98-99
44	✳ 1551	(12 Nov.)	Parlement	99-100
45	✳ 1552	(12 Feb.)	Parlement	100-101
46	1558	(5 Jan.)	Saint-Louis	68
47	✳ 1558	(15 Jan.)	Parlement	105-6
48	1559	(10 June)[c]	Augustins	106-7
49	✳ 1563	(17 May)	Parlement	107-8
50	1563	(17 Aug.)[d]	Rouen	[280]

[a] Listed incorrectly as 25 November 1367.

[b] Should be 8, 9, 11 July 1493.

[c] Parlement moved to the Convent of the Augustinians to hold this *Mercuriale* because the Palais de Justice was being decorated, and Henry II surprised the Court by arriving without warning to sit in the proceedings. Maugis, *Histoire du Parlement*, I, 602, n. 1, cites A.N., X1a 1592, fols. 369r-370r (24 Jan. 1560), when referring to 10 June 1559 and says the session was a "Mercuriale et lit de justice," although in fact there is no reference to a *"lit de justice"* in those folios.

[d] The Majority *Lit de Justice* assembly in Rouen is added to complete this list, but it is not treated by Du Tillet as a *Lit de Justice* assembly, as others in the *Recueil des grands*, and is simply mentioned in passing in the *Recueil des roys*.

BIBLIOGRAPHY

Manuscripts

I. Manuscript Sources and Antiquarian Treatises in Table One: The Legend of the *Lit de Justice* Assembly

A. *Primary sources (1315-1713) recording the events (Columns A-C)*

Column A: Dates of alleged royal appearances in Parlement.

Column B: A.N. Série X1a, Civil Registers, Parlement of Paris.
That series of registers runs as follows: (1) *Olim*, X1a 1-4 (1254-1319); (2) *Jugés I (Jugés, Lettres, Arrêts)*, X1a 5-156 (1319-1515), and *Jugés II*, X1a 157-1466 (1514-1779); (3) *Conseil (Conseil* and *Plaidoiries)*, X1a 1469-1477 (1364-1394), and *Conseil (Seul)*, X1a 1478-4779 (1400-1776); (4) *Plaidoiries-matinées*, X1a 4784-5033 (1395-1571); (5) *Plaidoiries*, X1a 5034-8282 (1571-1774); (6) *Aprés-dinées*, X1a 8300A-8386 (1373-1570); (7) *Conseil secret*, X1a 8387-8601 (1636-1786); (8) *Lettres patentes, Ordonnances, etc.*, X1a 8602-8843 (1337-1785); (9) *Registres du greffe*, X1a 8844-8851.

Column C: A.N. Série U, Copies of Civil Registers (X1a), Parlement of Paris, collected by Jean (V) Le Nain.
That series of copies of the registers runs as follows: (1) U 513, a table which records royal appearances in Parlement; (2) U 2000-2115 (1260-1673), copies of civil registers.

B. *Secondary sources (1563-1725) commenting on the events (Columns D-Z)*

Column D: Jean du Tillet, *Recueil des roys* and *Recueil des grands*, published in *Recueil des roys de France, leurs couronne et maison*. Paris, 1607 [work completed 1563]. (See Table Two.)

Column E: Bernard de La Roche-Flavin. *Treze livres des Parlemens de France*. Bordeaux, 1617 [work completed 1615].

Column F: B.N. ms. fr. 2881 (190 folios) [terminal date 1616].

Column G: B.N. ms. fr. 18522 (257 folios) [terminal date 1627].

Column H: B.N. ms. fr. 18410 (439 folios) [terminal date 1632].

Column I: B.N. ms. fr. n. a. 7231 (45 folios) [terminal date 1633].

Column J: B.N. ms. fr. 4346 (124 folios) [terminal date 1634].

Column K: A.N. U 425 (107 folios) and U 426 (147 folios) [terminal date 1638].

Column L: B. Mazarine ms. 2912, vol. II, pts. 1-3 [terminal date 1641].

Column M: B.N. ms. fr. 16511 (600 folios) [terminal date 1643].

Column N: B.N. ms. fr. 23410 (417 folios) [terminal date 1643].

Column O: Pierre Dupuy, *Traité de la majorité de nos rois et des régences du royaume*. Paris, 1655 [work completed around 1645]. B.N. Dupuy ms. 513 (131 folios) and B.N. Dupuy ms. 514 (103 folios) [terminal date 1633].

Column P: Théodore Godefroy [and Denys Godefroy], *Le Cérémonial françois*. 2 vols. Paris, 1649 [work completed 1648 or 1649].

Column Q: B.N. Clairambault ms. 715 (722 folios) [terminal date 1650].

Column R: B.N. ms. fr. 18411 (234 folios) [terminal date 1662].

Column S: B.N. ms. fr. suppl. 11737 (11 folios) [terminal date 1665].

Column T: B.V.P., C.P. ms. 5046 (241 folios) [terminal date 1673].

Column U: B.N. ms. fr. 16512 (202 folios) [terminal date 1673].

Column V: B.N. ms. fr. suppl. 10948 (273 folios) and ms. fr. suppl. 10949 (283 folios) [terminal date 1680].

Column W: A.N. KK 1441 (81 folios) [terminal date 1684].

Column X: B.N. ms. fr. n. a. 9749 (347 folios) [terminal date 1723].

Column Y: B.N. ms. fr. n. a. 9750 (256 folios) [terminal date 1725].

Column Z: A.N. KK 1428 and 1429 [terminal date 1725].

II. Other Manuscript Sources

Archives Nationales, Paris (A.N.)
 K 695, 696, 1712
 KK 336, 1428, 1429, 1441, 1448
 P 2306, 2606
 U 182, 333, 334, 335, 336, 425, 426, 492, 787, 790, 819, 822, 928, 960
 U 513, 2000-2115
 X1a 3-8630

Bibliothèque de la Ville de Paris (B.V.P.)
 C. P. mss. 5046, 5055

Bibliothèque de l'Institut de France, Paris (Institut de France)
 Collection Godefroy, mss. 395, 535, 536

Bibliothèque Mazarine, Paris (B. Mazarine)
 mss. 2349, 2737-2751, 2752, 2753, 2912

Bibliothèque Nationale, Paris (B.N.)
 Cinq Cents Colbert ms. 212
 Clairambault mss. 715, 718, 719, 1343
 Dupuy mss. 404, 513, 514
 Français mss. 2881, 4346, 6391, 9750, 13017, 14117-14120, 15524, 16511-16513, 16579, 16633, 17367, 18275, 18310, 18311, 18410, 18411, 18441, 18522, 18843-18883, 20821, 23061, 23285, 23410
 Français, nouvelles acquisitions mss. 3122, 3156, 7231, 9744, 9749, 9750, 20256
 Français, supplément mss. 10948, 10949, 11737, 11185

PRINTED WORKS

I. *Primary Sources*

Arnauld, Antoine. *La Justice aux pieds du roy pour les Parlemens de France.* N.p., 1608.

Arrest de la Cour de Parlement, le roy seant en son Lit de Justice [12 Sept. 1715]. N.p., n.d.

Baudoin, Jean. *Discours d'un fidelle françois sur la majorité du roy.* Paris, 1614.

———. *Les Feux de joye pour la resjouyssance publique par la déclaration de la majorité du roy, en sa Cour du Parlement de Paris, le jeudy deuxiesme de ce présent mois d'octobre 1614, ensemble les merveilles du ciel, envoyées le mesme jour à sa majesté.* Paris, 1614.

Baussonnet, Guillaume, Nicolas Bergier, and Jacques Dorat. *Inscriptions principalles des portes et arcs de triomphe faicts pour l'entrée, sacre et couronnement du roy Louis treizième en sa ville de Reims.* Reims, 1610.

Baye, Nicolas de. *Journal de Nicolas de Baye, greffier du Parlement de Paris, 1400-1417.* 2 vols. Ed. Alexandre Tuetey. *Société de l'histoire de France.* Paris, 1885-1888.

Beaune, Henri, and J. d'Arbaumont, eds. *Mémoires d'Olivier de La Marche.* 4 vols. *Société de l'histoire de France.* Paris, 1883-1888.

Bellaguet, Louis-François, ed. *Chronique du religieux de Saint-Denys, contenant le règne de Charles VI, de 1380 à 1422. Collection de documents inédits sur l'histoire de France.* 5 vols. 1ʳᵉ série, vol. VI, pts. 1-5. Paris, 1839-1844.

Belleforest, François de. *Histoire des neuf roys Charles de France.* Paris, 1568.

Bergier, Nicolas, and P. de La Salle. *Le Bouquet royal, ou le parterre des riches inventions qui ont servy à l'entrée du roy Louis le Juste en sa ville de Reims.* Reims, 1637.

Bernard, Pierre de. *Les Cérémonies qui ont esté observées en la déclaration de la majorité du roy.* Paris, 1614.

Bertrand, Nicolas. *Opus de Tholosanorum gestis ab urbe condita.* Toulouse, 1515.

Bignon, Jérome. *La Grandeur de nos roys et de leur souveraine puissance.* Paris, 1615.

Bodin, Jean. *Les Six livres de la république.* Paris, 1583.

Boulainvilliers, Henri de. *Lettres sur les anciens Parlements de France que l'on nomme États-Généraux.* 3 vols. London, 1753.

Bourgeois de Paris. *Journal d'un Bourgeois de Paris, sous le règne de Charles VII.* Eds. Joseph-François Michaud et Jean J. F. Poujoulat. *Nouvelle collection des mémoires pour servir à l'histoire de France.* 1ʳᵉ série, III, 237-300. Paris, 1837.

Bref discours des pompes, ceremonies, et obseques funebres de tres-haut, tres-puissant, tres-excellent prince Henry le Grand, par la grace de Dieu roy de France et de Navarre, tres-chrestien, tres-auguste, tres-victorieux et incomparable en mag-

nanimité et clemence, qui trespassa en son palais du Louvre, le vendredy qua-torziesme may mil six cens dix. [14 May 1610]. N.p., n.d.

Cappel, Jacques. *Plaidoyez de feu maistre Jacques Cappel, advocat du roy en la Cour de Parlement à Paris.* Paris, 1561.

Catalogue des actes de François Ier. 10 vols. Paris, 1887-1908.

Catalogue général des livres imprimés de la Bibliothèque Nationale. Actes Royaux. Ed. Albert Isnard. 7 vols. Paris, 1910-1960.

[Les]Ceremonies et ordre tenu au sacré et couronnement de la royne Marie de Médicis, royne de France et de Navarre, dans l'eglise de Sainct Denys le 13 may, 1610. (Ensemble la mort du roy, et comme monsieur le dauphin a esté declaré roy, et la royne regent par la Cour de Parlement). N.p., 1610.

C'est l'ordre qui a este tenu à la nouvelle et joyeuse entrée, que treshault, tresexcellent, et trespuissant prince, le roy treschrestien Henry deuzieme de ce nom, à faicte en sa bonne ville et cité de Paris, capitale de son royaume, le seizieme jour de juin, M.D.XLIX. Paris, 1549.

Chartier, Jean. *Chronique de Charles VII, roi de France.* 3 vols. Ed. Vallet de Viriville. Paris, 1858.

Chastellain, Georges. *Oeuvres de Georges Chastellain.* 8 vols. Ed. Kervyn de Lettenhove. Brussels, 1863-1866.

Chronique du religieux de Saint-Denys, contenant le règne de Charles VI, de 1380 à 1422. Ed. Louis-François Bellaguet. *Collection de documents inédits sur l'histoire de France.* 5 vols. 1re série, vol. VI, pts. 1-5. Paris, 1839-1844.

Cimber, Louis [Lafaist, Louis], and Félix Danjou. *Archives curieuses de l'histoire de France depuis Louis XI jusqu'à Louis XVIII.* 30 vols. Paris, 1834-1841.

Clément, Pierre. [Jean-Baptiste Colbert]. *Lettres, instructions, et mémoires.* 8 vols. Paris, 1861-1882.

Colbert, Jean-Baptiste. *Lettres, instructions, et mémoires.* 8 vols. Ed. Pierre Clément. Paris, 1861-1882.

Commentaires sur l'ordonnance de la majorité des rois. N.p., n.d.

Corbin, Jacques. *Le Code Louis XIII, roy de France et de Navarre, contenant ses ordonnances et arrests de ses Cours souveraines pour les droicts de sa couronne, police entre ses sujets. Reiglement de la justice; forme et abbreviation des procez.* Paris, 1628.

Corpus Juris Canonici.

Corpus Juris Civilis. Ed. Jean Vignon. Orléans, 1604.

[La] Declaration faicte par le roy de sa majorité tenant son Lict de Justice en sa Cour de Parlement de Rouen: Et ordonnance par luy faicte pour le bien et repos public de son royaume: Et ce qu'il dict en ladicte Cour avant la publication de ladicte ordonnance. Paris, 1563.

De la nature et qualité du Parlement de Paris et qu'il ne peut estre interdit ny transferé hors de la capitale du royaume, pour quelque cause ny pretexte que se soit. Paris, 1652.

Deschamps, Eustache. *Le Miroir de mariage. Oeuvres complètes de Eustache Deschamps*. Ed. Le Marquis de Queux de Saint-Hilaire. Paris, 1894.

Douët-d'Arcq, Louis Claude. *Comptes de l'argenterie des rois de France au XIVe siècle*. Paris, 1851.

———. *Comptes de l'hôtel des rois de France aux XIVe et XVe siècles*. Paris, 1865.

———. *Nouveau recueil de comptes de l'argenterie des rois de France*. Paris, 1874.

Du Chesne, André. *Les Antiquitez et recherches de la grandeur et majesté des roys de France*. Paris, 1609.

———. *Les Antiquitez et recherches des villes, chasteaux et places plus remarquable de toute la France, divisées en huict livres selon l'ordre et ressort des huict Parlemens*. Paris, 1609.

Du Haillan, Bernard de Girard. *De l'estat et succez des affaires de France*. Paris, 1571.

[Dumont, Jean]. *Le Cérémonial diplomatique des cours de l'Europe. Supplement au corps universel diplomatique du droit des gens*. Amsterdam, 1739.

———. *Corps universel diplomatique du droit des gens*. 8 vols. Amsterdam, 1726-1731.

Dupuy, Pierre. *Traitez touchant les droits du roi très chrestien*. Paris, 1655.

———. *Traité de la majorité de nos rois et des régences du royaume, avec les preuves tirées tant du Trésor des Chartes du roy que des registres du parlement, ensemble un traité des prééminences du Parlement de Paris*. Paris, 1655.

Du Tillet, Jean. *Pour la majorité du roy très chrestien contre les escrits des rebelles*. Paris, 1560.

———. *Pour l'entière majorité du roy très chrestien contre le légitime conseil malicieusement inventé par les rebelles*. Paris, 1560.

———. *Recueil des roys de France, leurs couronne et maison*. Paris, 1607.

Du Vair, Guillaume. *Actions et traictez oratoires*. Ed. René Radouant. Paris, 1911.

Edict du roy de l'erection d'une deuxiesme chambre au requestes du palais et de deux présidents et huict conseillers pour la composition d'icelle. Publié en Parlement, le roy y séant, le 26 juillet 1580. Saint Maur-des-Fossés, 1580.

[L']Entrée du roy dans son Parlement, pour la declaration de sa majorité. Paris, 1651.

Escouchy, Mathieu d'. *Chronique de Mathieu d'Escouchy*. 3 vols. Ed. Gaston Du Fresne de Beaucourt. *Société de l'histoire de France*. Nouv. édition. Paris, 1863-1864.

Extrait des registres de Parlement de jeudy, 12 septembre 1715 ... Louis XIV du nom tenant son Lict de Justice en son Parlement. Paris, 1715.

Fauquembergue, Clément de. *Journal de Clément de Fauquembergue*. 3 vols. Ed. Alexandre Tuetey. *Société de l'histoire de France*. Paris, 1903-1915.

Félibien, André. *Les Divertissements de Versailles, donnés par le roy au retour de la conqueste de la Franche-Comté*. N.p., 1674.

———. *Relation de la feste de Versailles du 18e juillet 1668*. Paris, 1668.

Froissart, Jean. *Oeuvres de Froissart.* 25 vols. Ed. Kervyn de Lettenhove. Brussels, 1867-1877.

Gillot, Jacques. *Relation faite par maître Jacques Gillot, conseiller d'Eglise à la Grand'chambre du Parlement de Paris, de ce que se passa audit Parlement séant aux Augustins, touchant le régence de la reine Marie de Médicis, mère du roi Louis XIII, les 14 et 15 mai 1610.* Eds. Joseph-François Michaud et Jean J. F. Poujoulat. *Nouvelle collection des mémoires pour servir à l'histoire de France,* 1ʳᵉ série, XI, 473-484. Paris, 1838.

Godefroy, Théodore. *Le Cérémonial de France.* Paris, 1619.

Godefroy, Théodore [and Denys Godefroy]. *Le Cérémonial françois.* 2 vols. Paris, 1649.

Godefroy, Théodore. *L'Ordre et cérémonies observées aux mariages de France et d'Espagne.* Paris, 1627.

Guillaume de Nangis. *Chronique latine de Guillaume de Nangis de 1113 à 1300 avec les continuations de cette chronique de 1300 à 1368.* 2 vols. Ed. Hercule Géraud. *Société de l'histoire de France.* Nouv. édition. Paris, 1843.

Harangue du roy Charles IX a messieurs de la Court de Parlement à Paris, tenant son siege royal et Lict de Justice. Rouen, 1574.

Haton, Claude. *Mémoires de Claude Haton contenant le récit des événemets accomplis de 1553 à 1582, principalement dans la Champagne et la Brie.* Ed. Félix Bourquelot. *Collection de documents inédits sur l'histoire de France.* 1ʳᵉ série. Paris, 1857.

Isambert, François-André et al., eds. *Recueil général des anciennes lois françaises depuis l'an 420 jusqu'à la révolution de 1789.* 29 vols. Paris, 1821-1833.

Isnard, Albert, ed. *Catalogue général des livres imprimés de la Bibliothèque Nationale. Actes Royaux.* 7 vols. Paris, 1910-1960.

Jaligny, Guillaume de. *Histoire de Charles VIII.* Ed. Théodore Godefroy. Paris, 1617.

Jolly, François-Antoine. *Projet d'un nouveau cérémonial françois, augmenté d'un grand nombre de pièces qui n'ont pas été publiées par M. Godefroy.* Paris, 1746.

Joly, Claude. *Recueil de maximes véritables et importantes pour l'institution du roy.* Paris, 1663.

Joly, Jacques, and Étienne Girard. *Trois livres des offices de France.* 2 vols. Paris, 1638.

Journal d'un Bourgeois de Paris, sous le règne de Charles VII. Eds. Joseph-François Michaud et Jean J. F. Poujoulat. *Nouvelle collection des mémoires pour servir à l'histoire de France.* 1ʳᵉ série, III, 237-300. Paris, 1837.

Juvénal des Ursins, Jean (II). *Histoire de Charles VI, roy de France.* Eds. Joseph-François Michaud et Jean J. F. Poujoulat. *Nouvelle collection des mémoires pour servir à l'histoire de France.* 1ʳᵉ série, II, 335-569. Paris, 1836.

La Buigne, Gaces de. *Le Roman des diduis.* Ed. Ake Blomqvist. *Studia Romanica Holmiensia,* III. Karlshamn, 1951.

La Marche, Olivier de. *Mémoires d'Olivier de La Marche.* 4 vols. Eds. Henri Beaune and J. d'Arbaumont. *Société de l'histoire de France.* Paris, 1883-1888.

La Place, Pierre de. *Commentaires de l'estat de la religion et république soubs les rois Henry et François seconds et Charles neufviesme* (1565). Ed. J.A.C. Buchon. *Choix de chroniques et mémoires sur l'histoire de France*, II, 1-201. Paris, 1836.

La Planche, Louis Regnier de. *Histoire de l'estat de France tant de la république que de la religion sous le règne de François II* (1576). Ed. J.A.C. Buchon. *Choix de chroniques et mémoires sur l'histoire de France*, II, 202-421. Paris, 1836.

La Roche-Flavin, Bernard de. *Treze livres des Parlemens de France.* Bordeaux, 1617.

Laurière, Eusèbe de, Denis F. Secousse et al., eds. *Ordonnances des roys de France de la troisième race.* 21 vols. Paris, 1723-1849.

Le Bret, Cardin. *De la souveraineté du roy.* Paris, 1632.

Le Févre, Jean. *Chronique de Jean Le Févre.* 2 vols. Ed. François Morand. *Société de l'histoire de France.* Paris, 1876-1881.

Le Paige, Louis-Adrien. *Lettre sur les Lits de Justice, 18 août 1756.* N.p., n.d.

———. *Réflexions d'un citoyen sur les Lits de Justice par Louis-Adrien Le Paige* [1787]. N.p., n.d.

L'Hôpital, Michel de. *Oeuvres complètes de Michel de l'Hospital.* 3 vols. Ed. P.J.S. Dufey. Paris, 1824-1825.

———. *Oeuvres inédites de Michel de l'Hospital.* 2 vols. Ed. P.J.S. Dufey. Paris, 1825-1826.

Loisel, Antoine. *Institutes coutumières.* Ed. Michel Reulos. Paris, 1935.

Loyseau, Charles. *Cinq livres du droit des offices. Les Oeuvres de Loyseau.* Paris, 1666.

Médailles sur les principaux evenements du règne de Louis le Grand avec des explications historiques. (Par l'Académie Royale des Médailles et des Inscriptions.) Paris, 1702.

Ménestrier, Claude-François. *Histoire du roy Louis le Grand par les médailles, emblèmes, devises, jetons, inscriptions, armoiries et autres monuments publics recueillis et expliqués.* Paris, 1691.

[Le] Mercure françois; ou La suite de l'histoire de 1605-1644. 25 vols. Paris, 1605-1644.

Molé, Mathieu. *Mémoires de Mathieu Molé.* 4 vols. Ed. Aimé Champollion-Figeac. *Société de l'histoire de France.* Paris, 1855-1857.

Mollat, Michel, ed. *Les Affaires de Jacques Coeur: Journal du procureur Dauvet.* 2 vols. Paris, 1952-1953.

Monstrelet, Enguerran de. *La Chronique d'Enguerran de Monstrelet.* 6 vols. Ed. Louis Claude Douët d'Arcq. *Société de l'histoire de France.* Paris, 1857-1862.

Montfaucon, Bernard de. *Les Monumens de la monarchie françoise.* 5 vols. Paris, 1729-1733.

[Nagerel, Jean]. *Description du pays et duché de Normandie, appellée anciennement Neustrie, de son origine et des limites d'iceluy. Extraict de sa Cronique de Normandie, non encores imprimée, faicte par feu maistre Jean Nagerel.* Rouen, 1580.

Nicot, Jean. *Dictionnaire françois-latin.* Paris, 1584.

Nicot, Jean, and Aimar de Ranconet. *Thresor de la langue francoyse, tant ancienne que moderne.* Paris, 1606.

Ordonnances des rois de France de la troisième race. 21 vols. Eds. Eusèbe de Laurière, Denis F. Secousse et al. Paris, 1723-1849.

Ordonnances des rois de France, règne de François Ier. 9 vols. to date. Paris, 1902-.

Ordre de la séance tenue au Parlement ... le roi séant en son Lit de Justice, pour la déclaration de sa majorité ... [1614]. *Le Mercure françois.* Vol. III, pt. II, pp. 579-595. Paris, 1614.

[L']Ordre et cérémonies observées à la majorité du roi, avec la réception de M. le Prince de Condé et la requête des prisonniers de sa majesté. Paris, 1614.

Ordre observé à la seance du roy Louys XIV en son Lit de Justice. Poictiers, 1643.

Orléans, Louis d'. *Les Ouvertures des Parlements faictes par les roys de France, tenant leur Lict de Justice.* Lyon, 1620.

Pasquier, Étienne. *Des recherches de la France, livre premier et second [1581].* Ed. Léon Feugère. *Oeuvres choisies.* 2 vols. Paris, 1849.

Peleus, Julien. *Le Premier president du Parlement de France.* Paris, 1611.

Picault, Pierre. *Traité des Parlements ou États Généreaux.* Cologne, 1679.

Piganiol de la Force, Jean-Aymar. *Nouvelle description de la France.* 6 vols. Paris, 1718.

Pisan, Christine de. *Le Livre des fais et bonnes meurs de sage roy Charles V.* Ed. Suzanne Solente. *Société de l'histoire de France.* 2 vols. Paris, 1936-1940.

Plancher, Le P. Urbain. *Histoire générale et particulière de Bourgogne.* 4 vols. Dijon, 1739-1781.

Procès-verbal de ce qui s'est passé au Lit de Justice, tenu par le roy au château des Tuileries, le vendredy 26e jour d'aoust 1718. Paris, 1718.

Recueil de ce que le roy Charles IX a dict en sa Cour de Parlement de Rouen, declarant sa majorité. Assisté de la royne sa mere, monsieur son frere, et tous les princes de son sang, et officiers de sa couronne, et seigneurs de son conseil, d'esquelz tous il a ésté declaré et recogneu pour tel. Rouen, 1563.

Recueil de lettres patentes concernant la discipline du Parlement [after 1770]. N.p., n.d.

Recueil et discours du voyage du roy Charles IX. Paris, 1566.

Response faicte par le roy et son conseil, aux presidens et conseillers de sa Cour de Parlement de Paris: Sur la remonstrance faicte à sadicte majesté, concernant la declaration de sa majorité, et ordonnance faicte pour le bien, et repos public de son royaume. Lyon, 1563.

Saint-Simon, Louis de Rouvroy, Duc de. *Mémoires de Saint-Simon.* 41 vols. Ed. A. de Boislisle. Paris, 1881-1928.

Séguier, Antoine-Louis. *Discours de M. Antoine-Louis Séguier, avocat général, prononcé au Lit de Justice, tenu par le roi au château de Versailles le samedi, treize avril 1771.* N.p., n.d.

[Séguier, Antoine-Louis]. *Discours de M. Séguier, avocat général, prononcé au Lit de Justice du samedi, 13 avril 1771. Nouvelle édition, revue et corrigée.* N.p., n.d. [A parody of the above, author anonymous.]

Séguier, Pierre (III). *Lettres et mémoires addressés au Chancelier Séguier (1633-1649).* 2 vols. Ed. Roland Mousnier. Paris, 1964.

Servin, Louis. *Action des gens du roy sur la déclaration de Louys XIII, roy de France et de Navarre, séant en son L'ict de Justice en sa Cour de Parlement au jour de sa majorité, faicte par M. Louis Servin, avocat général de sa majesté, le 2 octobre 1614.* Paris, 1615.

Seyssel, Claude de. *La Grant monarchie de France.* Paris, 1519.

⸻. *Les Louenges du roy Louys XIIe de ce nom, nouvellement composées en latin par maistre Claude de Seyssel docteur en tous droitz et maistre des requestes ordinaires de l'hostel du roy translatees par luy de latin en françois* [Paris, 1508]. Ed. Peter Richard. *La Langue française au seizième siècle: Étude suivie de textes.* Cambridge, 1968.

⸻. *La Monarchie de France.* Ed. Jacques Poujol. Paris, 1961.

Sully, Maximilien de Béthune, Duc de. *Mémoires de Sully, principal ministre de Henri-le-Grand.* 6 vols. Nouv. édition. Paris, 1814.

Talon, Omer. *Harangue faite au roy [le 15 janvier 1648] par monsieur Talon, son advocat général au Parlement de Paris.* Paris, 1649.

⸻. *Mémoires de feu M. Omer Talon, avocat général en la cour de Parlement de Paris.* 8 vols. The Hague, 1732.

Thou, Jacques-Auguste de. *Histoire universelle de Jacques-Auguste de Thou avec la suite par Nicolas Rigault.* 11 vols. The Hague, 1740.

Valladier, André. *Parénèse royale sur les cérémomies du sacre du très-chrestien Louis XIII, roy de France et de Navarre.* Paris, 1611.

Wavrin, Jehan de, Seigneur du Forestel. *Anchiennes cronicques d'Engleterre, par Jehan de Wavrin.* 3 vols. Ed. Émilie Dupont. *Société de l'histoire de France.* Paris, 1858-1863.

Secondary Sources

Albert-Buisson, François. *Michel de L'Hospital.* Paris, 1950.

Amphoux, Henri. *Michel de L'Hôpital et la liberté de conscience au XVIe siècle.* Paris, 1900.

Aubert, Félix. *Le Parlement de Paris, de Philippe le Bel à Charles VII (1314-1422).* 2 vols. Paris, 1886-1890.

Autrand, Françoise. *Naissance d'un grand corps de l'état: Les gens du Parlement de Paris, 1345-1454.* Paris, 1981.

Bak, Janos M. "Medieval Symbology of the State: Percy E. Schramm's Contribution." *Viator*, IV (1973), 33-63.

Beaucourt, Gaston du Fresne de. *Histoire de Charles VII.* 6 vols. Paris, 1881-1891.

Benedict, Philip. *Rouen during the Wars of Religion.* Cambridge, 1981.

Bloch, Marc. *Les Rois thaumaturges.* Paris, 1961.

Blondel, J.J.M. *Mémoires du Parlement de Paris, ou recueil de ses délibérations secrètes, arrêtés et remonstrances, avec les Lits de Justice qui y ont été tenus depuis que Phillipe le Bel l'a rendu sédentaire, jusqu'au moment où il a été supprimé par l'Assemblée Constituante.* 4 vols. Paris [1803?].

Boislisle, Arthur de. "Jean du Tillet et le Trésor des Chartes." *Société de l'histoire de France, Annuaire-Bulletin,* X (1873), 106-111.

Bonney, Richard. *The King's Debts: Finance and Politics in France, 1589-1661.* Oxford, 1981.

————. *Political Change in France under Richelieu and Mazarin, 1624-1661.* Oxford, 1978.

Bossuat, André. "Le Formule 'Le Roi est empereur en son royaume.' " *Revue Historique du Droit Français et Étranger,* 4me série (July-Sept. 1961), pp. 371-381.

Bouchot, Henri. *Bibliothèque Nationale. Inventaire des dessins exécutés pour Roger de Gaignières et conservés aux Départements des Estampes et des Manuscrits, par H. Bouchot.* 2 vols. Paris, 1891.

Bourbon de Parme, Sixte de. *Le Traité d'Utrecht et les lois fondamentales du royaume.* Paris, 1914.

Boutaric, Edgard. *Recherches archéologiques sur le Palais de Justice de Paris, principalement sur la partie consacrée au Parlement depuis l'origine jusqu'à la mort de Charles VI (1422).* Paris, 1862.

Brière, Gaston. *Le Château de Versailles, architecture et décoration.* 2 vols. Paris, 1907-1909.

Bryant, Lawrence M. *The French Royal Entry Ceremony: Politics, Society, and Art in Renaissance Paris.* Ann Arbor, University Microfilms, 1978.

————. "*Parlementaire* Political Theory in the Parisian Royal Entry Ceremony." *The Sixteenth Century Journal,* VII, 1 (April 1976), 15-24.

Chamberland, Albert. *Le Conflit de 1597 entre Henry IV et le Parlement de Paris.* Paris, 1904.

Champion, Pierre. *Louis XI.* 2 vols. Paris, 1927.

Chatelet, Albert. "Le Retable du Parlement." *Art de France* (1964), pp. 60-69.

Chéruel, Adolphe, *Dictionnaire historique des institutions, moeurs et coutumes de la France.* 2 vols. Paris, 1855.

————. *Histoire de France pendant la minorité de Louis XIV.* 4 vols. Paris, 1879-1880.

Church, William F. *Constitutional Thought in Sixteenth-Century France.* New York, 1969.

————. *Richelieu and Reason of State*. Princeton, 1972.

Clément, Pierre. *Les Grands hommes de la Bourgogne*. Paris, 1966.

Cuttler, Simon H. *The Law of Treason and Treason Trials in Later Medieval France*. Cambridge, 1981.

Dauvillier, Jean. "Histoire des costumes des gens de justice dans notre ancienne France." *Recueil des mémoires et travaux: Mélanges Roger Aubenas (La Société d'histoire du droit et des institutions des anciens pays de droit écrit)*, IX (1974), 230-240.

Declareuil, Joseph. *Histoire générale du droit français des origines à 1789*. Paris, 1925.

Delisle, Léopold. *Le Cabinet des Manuscrits de la Bibliothèque Impériale (Nationale)*. 4 vols. Paris, 1868-1881.

Delsol, Jean-Joseph. *Biographies aveyronnaises. Notice sur La Roche-Flavin*. Rodez, 1866.

Dent, Julian. *Crisis in Finance: Crown, Financiers and Society in Seventeenth-Century France*. Newton Abbot, 1973.

Desmaze, Charles. *Le Parlement de Paris, son organisation, ses premiers présidents et procureurs généraux. Avec une notice sur les autres parlements de France, et le tableau de MM. les premiers présidents et procureurs généraux de la cour de Paris (1334-1859)*. Paris, 1859.

Diefendorf, Barbara. *Paris City Councillors in the Sixteenth Century: The Politics of Patrimony*. Princeton, 1983.

Dillay, Madeleine. "Les registres secrets des Chambres des Enquêtes et des Requêtes du Parlement de Paris." *Bibliothèque de L'École des Chartes*, CVIII (1950), 75-123.

Dodu, Gaston J. *Les Valois: Histoire d'une maison royale (1328-1589)*. Paris, 1934.

Doucet, Roger. *Étude sur le gouvernement de François Ier dans ses rapports avec le Parlement de Paris*. 2 vols. Paris, 1921-1926.

————. *Les Institutions de la France au XVIe siècle*. 2 vols. Paris, 1948.

Doyle, William. "The Parlements of France and the Breakdown of the Old Regime." *French Historical Studies*, VI, 4 (Fall 1970), 415-458.

Du Cange, Charles Du Fresne. *Glossarium mediae et infimae latinitatis*. 10 vols. Paris, 1883-1887.

Ducoudray, Gustave. *Les Origines du Parlement de Paris et la justice aux XIIIe et XIVe siècles*. Paris, 1902.

Duplessis, Georges. *Inventaire de la collection d'estampes relatives à l'histoire de France, léguée à la Bibliothèque Nationale par M. Michel Hennin, rédigé par M. Georges Duplessis*. 5 vols. Paris, 1877-1884.

————. *Roger de Gaignières et ses collections iconographiques*. Paris, 1870.

Durrieu, Le Comte Paul. *Le Boccace de Munich*. Munich, 1909.

Egret, Jean. *The French Prerevolution, 1787-1788*. Trans. Wesley D. Camp. Chicago, 1977.

————. *Louis XV et l'opposition parlementaire, 1715-1774*. Paris, 1970.

Esmein, Adhémar. "La maxime *Princeps legibus solutus est* dans l'ancien droit public français." *Essays in Legal History*. Ed. Paul Vinogradoff. Oxford, 1913.

Fayard, Ennemond. *Aperçu historique sur le Parlement de Paris*. 3 vols. Paris, 1876-1878.

Flammermont, Jules. *Remonstrances du Parlement de Paris au XVIII siècle*. 3 vols. Paris, 1888-1898.

Ford, Franklin L. *Robe and Sword: The Regrouping of the French Aristocracy after Louis XIV*. Cambridge, Mass., 1953.

Foucault, Michel. *The Order of Things: An Archaeology of the Human Sciences*. New York, 1971.

Franklin, Alfred. *Les Rois et les gouvernements de la France*. Paris, 1978.

Franklin, Julian H. *Jean Bodin and the Rise of Absolutist Theory*. Cambridge, 1973.

Gaignières, Roger [Collection]. See Duplessis, Georges.

Geertz, Clifford. *The Interpretation of Cultures* (New York, 1973).

———. *Negara: The Theatre State in Nineteenth-Century Bali*. Princeton, 1980.

Giesey, Ralph E. "The French Estates and the *Corpus Mysticum Regni*." *Album Helen Maud Cam (Études présentées à la Commission Internationale pour l'Histoire des Assemblées d'États)*, XXIII (1960), 153-171.

———. *If Not, Not: The Oath of the Aragonese and the Legendary Laws of Sobrarbe*. Princeton, 1968.

———. *The Juristic Basis of Dynastic Right to the French Throne*. Transactions of the American Philosophical Society, LI, 5. Philadelphia, 1961.

———. "The Monarchomach Triumvirs: Hotman, Beza and Mornay," *Bibliothèque d'Humanisme et Renaissance*, XXXII (1970), 41-46.

———. "The Presidents of Parlement at the Royal Funeral." *The Sixteenth Century Journal*, VII, 1 (Apr. 1976), 25-34.

———. " 'Quod omnes tangit'—A Post Scriptum." *Studia Gratiana*, XV (1972), 319-332.

———. *The Royal Funeral Ceremony in Renaissance France*. Geneva, 1960.

———. "Rules of Inheritance and Strategies of Mobility in Prerevolutionary France." *American Historical Review*, LXXXII, 2 (Apr. 1977), 271-289.

———, and John H. M. Salmon, eds. *Francogallia by François Hotman*. Cambridge, 1972.

Glasson, Ernest D. *Le Parlement de Paris, son rôle politique depuis le règne de Charles VII jusqu'à la révolution*. 2 vols. Paris, 1901.

Godefroy, Frédéric. *Dictionnaire de l'ancienne langue française*. 10 vols. Paris, 1881-1902.

Godefroy-Ménilglaise, Denis-Charles. *Les Savants Godefroy, mémoires d'une famille pendant les XVIᵉ, XVIIᵉ, et XVIIIᵉ siècles*. Paris, 1873.

Goubert, Pierre. *L'Ancien régime*. 2 vols. Paris, 1969 and 1973.

Graham, Victor E., and W. McAllister Johnson. *The Royal Tour of France by*

Charles IX and Catherine de Médicis: Festivals and Entries, 1564-1566. Toronto, 1979.

Guenée, Bernard, and Françoise Lehoux. *Les Entrées royales françaises de 1328 à 1515.* Paris, 1968.

Guerout, Jean. "Le Palais de la Cité à Paris des origines à 1417." *Fédération des sociétés historiques et archéologiques de Paris et de l'Ile de France, Mémoires.* 3 vols. Paris, 1949-1951.

Hamscher, Albert N. *The Parlement of Paris after the Fronde, 1653-1673.* Pittsburgh, 1976.

Hanley, Sarah. "Constitutional Ideology in France: Legend, Ritual, and Discourse in the *Lit de Justice* assembly, 1527-1641," in *Rites of Power: Symbolism, Ritual and Politics since the Middle Ages.* Ed. Sean Wilentz. Forthcoming.

——. "L'Idéologie constitutionelle en France: Le Lit de Justice." *Annales: Économies, Sociétés, Civilisations,* no. 1 (Jan.-Fév. 1982), pp. 32-63.

——. *Discours Politiques des diverses puissances* (introduction, edition, and notes). Forthcoming.

——. "The *Discours Politiques* in Monarchomaque Ideology: Resistance Right in Sixteenth-Century France." *Annali della Facoltà de Scienze Politiche,* XIX, Quaderni di storia, 7, 1982-1983.

——. "The *Lit de Justice* and the Fundamental Law." *The Sixteenth-Century Journal,* VII, 1 (Apr. 1976), 3-14.

Hardy, James D. *Judicial Politics in the Old Regime.* Baton Rouge, 1967.

Hartung, Fritz, and Roland Mousnier. "Quelques problèmes concernant la monarchie absolue." *Proceedings of the tenth congress of the international committee for the historical sciences,* IV, *Storia Moderna* (1955), 1-55.

Henneman, John Bell. *Royal Taxation in Fourteenth Century France: The Captivity and Ransom of John II, 1356-1370.* Philadelphia, 1976.

Hennin, Michel [Collection]. See Duplessis, Georges.

Hirschman, Albert O. *The Passions and the Interests: Political Arguments for Capitalism before its Triumph.* Princeton, 1980.

Hudson, David. "The Parlementary Crisis of 1763 in France and its Consequences." *Canadian Journal of History,* VII (Apr. 1972), 97-117.

Huguet, Edmond. *Dictionnaire de la langue française du seizième siècle.* 7 vols. Paris, 1925-1967.

Huppert, George. *Les Bourgeois Gentilshommes: An Essay on the Definition of Elites in Renaissance France.* Chicago, 1977.

——. *The Idea of Perfect History: Historical Erudition and Historical Philosophy in Renaissance France.* Urbana, 1970.

Isherwood, Robert M. *Music in the Service of the King.* Ithaca, 1973.

Jackson, Richard A. "Elective Kingship and *Consensus Populi* in Sixteenth-Century France." *Journal of Modern History,* XXXXIV, 2 (June 1972), 155-171.

Jackson, Richard A. "Peers of France and Princes of the Blood." *French Historical Studies,* VII, 1 (Spring 1971), 27-46.

———. "The Sleeping King." *Bibliothèque d'Humanisme et Renaissance,* XXXI (Sept. 1969), 527-551.

———. *Vivat rex: Une histoire des sacres et couronnements en France, 1364-1825.* Forthcoming.

Jacquiot, Josephe. *Médailles et jetons de Louis XIV après le manuscrit de Londres.* 4 vols. Paris, 1968.

Kantorowicz, Ernst H. "The 'King's Advent' and the Enigmatic Panels in the Doors of Santa Sabina." *Selected Studies,* pp. 37-75. New York, 1965.

———. *The King's Two Bodies: A Study in Medieval Political Theology.* Princeton, 1957.

———. "Oriens Augusti—Lever du Roi." *Dumbarton Oaks Papers,* no. 17, pp. 119-177. New York, 1963.

Kelley, Donald R. *The Beginning of Ideology: Consciousness and Society in the French Reformation.* Cambridge, 1981.

———. *Foundations of Modern Historical Scholarship: Language, Law, and History in the French Renaissance.* New York, 1970.

———. "Jean du Tillet, Archivist and Antiquary." *The Journal of Modern History,* XXXVIII, 4 (Dec. 1966), 337-354.

Keohane, Nannerl O. *Philosophy and the State in France: The Renaissance to the Enlightenment.* Princeton, 1980.

Kerviler, René. *Le Chancelier Pierre Séguier.* Paris, 1874.

Kinser, Samuel. *The Works of Jacques-Auguste de Thou.* The Hague, 1966.

Klaits, Joseph. *Printed Propaganda under Louis XIV: Absolute Monarchy and Public Opinion.* Princeton, 1976.

Knecht, Robert J. *Francis I and Absolute Monarchy.* London Historical Association, no. 72. London, 1969.

———. *Francis I.* Cambridge, 1982.

Labatut, Jean-Pierre. *Les Ducs et pairs de France au XVIIᵉ siècle.* Paris, 1972.

Laborde, Léon-Emmanuel. *Les Ducs de Bourgogne: Études sur les lettres, les arts et l'industrie pendant le XVᵉ siècle.* 3 vols. Paris, 1849-1852.

Langlois, Monique. "Le Parlement de Paris." *Guide des recherches dans les fonds judiciares l'ancien régime,* pp. 66-160. Paris, 1958.

Lavisse, Ernest, ed. *Histoire de France depuis les origines jusqu'à la révolution.* 9 vols. Paris, 1900-1911.

Lemaire, André. *Les Lois fondamentales de la monarchie française d'après les théoriciens de l'ancien régime.* Paris, 1907.

Le Roy Ladurie, Emmanuel. "Auprès du roi, la cour." *Annales: Économies, Sociétés, Civilisations.* Forthcoming.

———. *The Mind and Method of the Historian.* Trans. Siân Reynolds and Ben Reynolds. Chicago, 1978.

Lewis, Andrew W. *Royal Succession in Capetian France: Studies on Familial Order and the State*. Cambridge, Mass., 1981.

Lightman, Harriet. *Sons and Mothers: Queens and Minor Kings in French Constitutional Law*. Ann Arbor, University Microfilms, 1980.

Littré, Émile. *Dictionnaire de la langue française*. 7 vols. Paris, 1968.

Lougee, Carolyn C. *Le Paradis des Femmes: Women, Salons, and Social Stratification in Seventeeth-Century France*. Princeton, 1976.

Major, J. Russell. *Representative Government in Early Modern France*. New Haven, 1980.

———. *Representative Institutions in Renaissance France, 1421-1559*. Madison, 1960.

Marin, Louis. *Le Portrait du roi*. Paris, 1981.

Marion, Marcel. *Dictionnaire des institution de la France aux XVIIᵉ et XVIIIᵉ siècles*. Paris, 1923.

Maugis, Édouard. *Histoire du Parlement de Paris de l'avènement des rois Valois à la mort d'Henri IV*. 3 vols. Paris, 1913-1916.

Mazerolle, Fernard. *Les Médailleurs français du XVᵉ siècle au milieu du XVIIᵉ siècle. Collection de documents inédits sur l'histoire de France*. 3 vols. Paris, 1902-1904.

Michaud, Joseph-François, and Jean J. F. Poujoulat, eds. *Nouvelle collection des mémoires pour servir à l'histoire de France*. 32 vols. Paris, 1836-1839.

Moote, A. Lloyd. *The Revolt of the Judges: The Parlement of Paris and the Fronde, 1643-1652*. Princeton, 1971.

Mousnier, Roland. "Comment les français de XVIIᵉ siècle voyaient la constitution." *XVIIᵉ Siècle*, nos. 25-26 (1955), 9-36.

———. *The Institutions of France under the Absolute Monarchy, 1598-1789*. Vol. I. Trans. Brian Pearce. Chicago, 1979.

———. *Les Institutions de la France sous la monarchie absolue*. Vol. II. Paris, 1980.

———. *La Vénalité des offices sous Henri IV et Louis XIII*. Rouen, 1945.

Muir, Edward. *Civic Ritual in Renaissance Venice*. Princeton, 1981.

Omont, Henri. "Jean du Tillet et le Trésor des Chartes (1562)." *Bulletin de la Société de l'histoire de Paris*, XXXI (1904), 79-81.

Picot, Georges. *Histoire des États Généraux considérés au point de vue de leur influence sur le gouvernement de la France de 1355 à 1614*. 4 vols. Paris, 1872.

Pinoteau, Hervé. "Quelques réflexions sur l'oeuvre de Jean du Tillet et la symbolique royale française." *Archives héraldiques suisses* (Lausanne, LXXᵉ année, 1956), pp. 1-24.

Pocock, John G. A. *The Ancient Constitution and the Feudal Law: A Study of English Historical Thought in the Seventeenth Century*. Cambridge, 1957.

———. *The Machiavellian Moment: Florentine Political Thought and the Atlantic Republican Tradition*. Princeton, 1975.

Pocock, John G. A. "The Origins of Study of the Past: A Comparative Approach." *Comparative Studies in Society and History*, IV (1961-1962), 209-246.

————. *Politics, Language, and Time: Essays on Political Thought and History.* New York, 1973.

Post, Gaines. *Studies in Medieval Legal Thought: Public Law and the State, 1100-1322.* Princeton, 1964.

Quicherat, Jules E. J. *Histoire du costume en France depuis les temps les plus reculés jusqu'à la fin du XVIIe siècle.* Paris, 1877.

Ranum, Orest. *Artisans of Glory: Writers and Historical Thought in Seventeenth-Century France.* Chapel Hill, 1980.

Rothkrug, Lionel. *Opposition to Louis XIV: The Political and Social Origins of the French Enlightenment.* Princeton, 1965.

Rowen, Herbert H. *The King's State: Proprietary Dynasticism in Early Modern France.* New Brunswick, 1980.

————. "Louis XIV and Absolutism." *Louis XIV and the Craft of Kingship*, pp. 302-316. Ed. John C. Rule. Columbus, 1969.

Rule, John C. ed. *Louis XIV and the Craft of Kingship.* Columbus, 1969.

Russell, Conrad S. R. "Monarchies, Wars, and Estates in England, France, and Spain, c. 1580-c. 1640," *Legislative Studies Quarterly*, VII, 2 (May 1982), 205-220.

Saenger, Paul. "Burgundy and the Inalienability of Appanages in the Reign of Louis XI." *French Historical Studies*, X, 1 (Spring 1977), 1-26.

Saint-Palaye, Jean Baptiste La Curne de. *Dictionnaire historique de l'ancien langage françois.* 10 vols. Ed. Lucien Favre. Paris, 1876-1882.

Salmon, John H. M. *Society in Crisis: France in the Sixteenth Century.* New York, 1975.

————. "Venal Office and Popular Sedition in Seventeenth-Century France." *Past and Present*, no. 37 (1967), pp. 21-43.

Salmon, John H. M., and Ralph E. Giesey, eds. *Francogallia by François Hotman.* Cambridge, 1972.

Scheler, Auguste, ed. *Oeuvres de Froissart: Glossaire.* Brussels, 1874.

Schramm, Percy E. *Herrschaftszeichen und Staatssymbolik.* Stuttgart, 1954-1956.

————. *Der König von Frankreich.* 2 vols. Weimar, 1960.

Shennan, Joseph H. *The Parlement of Paris.* Ithaca, 1968.

Skinner, Quentin. "Conventions and the Understanding of Speech Acts." *The Philosophical Quarterly*, XX, 79 (Apr. 1970), 118-138.

————. *The Foundations of Modern Political Thought.* 2 vols. Cambridge, 1978.

————. "Some Problems in the Analysis of Political Thought and Action." *Political Theory*, II, 3 (Aug. 1974), 277-303.

Spiegel, Gabrielle M. *The Chronicle Tradition of Saint-Denis.* Leyden, 1978.

Stocker, Christopher W. "Office and Justice: Louis XI and the Parlement of Paris (1465-1467)." *Mediaeval Studies*, XXXVII (1975), 360-386.

————. "The Politics of the Parlement of Paris in 1525." *French Historical Studies*, VIII, 2 (Fall 1973), pp. 191-212.

Sutherland, Nicola M. *The Huguenot Struggle for Recognition.* New Haven, 1980.

————. *The Massacre of St. Bartholomew and the European Conflict, 1559-1572.* New York, 1973.

Thibault, Marcel. *Isabeau de Bavière, reine de France.* Paris, 1903.

Tobler, Adolf, and Erhard Lommatzsch. *Altfranzösisches Wörterbuch.* 10 vols. Berlin, 1925-1979.

Vale, Malcolm G. A. *Charles VII.* London, 1974.

Wartburg, Walther von. *Französisches etymologisches Wörterbuch.* 25 vols. Bonn, 1928-1957.

Wilentz, Sean, ed. *Rites of Power: Symbolism, Ritual and Politics since the Middle Ages.* Forthcoming.

Yardeni, Myriam. *Utopie et révolte sous Louis XIV.* Paris, 1980.

Zeller, Berthold. *La Minorité de Louis XIII.* 2 vols. Paris, 1892-1897.

Zeller, Gaston. *Les Institutions de la France au XVIᵉ siècle.* Paris, 1948.

INDEX

absolutism, theory of, 4-6, 46n, 48n, 68n, 180n, 213n, 216, 226-27, 289, 300, 310-14, 319-21, 328

absolutist monarchy. *See* French constitutional ideologies

admirals, 92, 211n

advice. *See* consultation

Aegidius Romanus, 131n

affairs of state, 3, 55-56, 70, 74, 115n, 122, 126, 130-31, 136, 141, 150, 152, 170, 194-95, 199, 202n, 209-10, 215, 219, 232, 242-43, 276, 284, 293-95, 298, 320, 322n, 327, 337

Africa, 254

Agincourt, Battle of, 165n

Aix, Parlement of. *See* Parlement of Aix

Alençon, Jean (II), Duke of, 32-35, 37n, 39-41, 115-16, 124, 277, 304-5

Alexander Severus, Roman emperor, 135

Alexander Tartagna de Imola, 77

ambassadors, 58, 63-64, 329

Amboise, Peace of, 154

Anglicus, Bartholomaeus, 37-38

Ango, Guillaume, 171n

Anguien, Louis de Bourbon, Count of. *See* Bourbon

Anjou, Duke of, 220

Anne of Austria (1601-1666), 206, 227, 297-304, 314, 317, 339; Inaugural *Lit de Justice*, 308-12

Anne of Beaujeu, 42

Annunciation, 30

Antinor, 296n

Aquinas, Thomas, 248

Archangel Michael, 30

archbishops, 52, 58, 73, 141, 234n, 236n

Argenson, René-Louis de Voyer, Marquis of, 339-40

Aristotle, 248

Arnauld, Antoine, 229, 268

arrêts. *See* legislation

Artois, 46, 74, 86, 90-91

Artois, Robert (III) of, 32, 35-37, 116

Assemblies of Notables, 72n, 152, 224n, 275

Augustinians, Convent of. *See* Convent of the Augustinians

Aumale, Duke of, 136

Aurelian, Roman emperor, 61n

L'autorité royale ne meurt point. *See* maxims

avocats: Parlement of Paris, 89, 94-97, 99, 134-35, 140-41, 171n, 217n; Parlement of Rouen, 171n. *See also* gens du roi; procureurs général

Bagarris, Rascas de, 259n

baillis, 56, 58, 63-64, 167, 242

Baldus de Ubaldis, 77, 175n, 274n

Baudouin, François, 99

Baure, Jehan, 16n

Baye, Nicolas de, 14, 19, 21-25, 31n, 99, 104

Beauvais, Bishop of, 300, 302n

Belle, Pierre, 16n, 23

Bellièvre, Pomponne de, 258n, 281n

Benedicti, Guillaume, 66n, 178

Bergier, Nicolas, 254, 258-67, 270, 281n

Bernyer, Claude, 45n

Bertrand, Jean, 134n, 135-36

Bertrand, Nicolas, 59n

Béthune, Maximilien de, Duke of Sully. *See* Sully

Bignon, Jérome (I), 269

Bigot, Laurens, 171n

biogenetic doctrines. *See* maxims

bishops, 58, 73, 89, 130, 234-35, 236n, 247, 252, 256n, 257, 300, 302n

Blanche of Castile (1188-1252), 26, 156, 241, 249

Bodin, Jean, 84, 99, 171, 251, 263; discourse, 178-81

Bois de Vincennes, 147, 324

Bordeaux, Parlement of. *See* Parlement of Bordeaux

Boulainvilliers, Henri de, 279n

Bourbon, Antoine de, King of Navarre, 117n, 145, 153
Bourbon, Cardinal of, 76, 136, 196
Bourbon, Charles (II), Duke of, 46-47, 49-52, 56-58, 63-65, 74, 94, 116, 277
Bourbon cult of rulership, 312, 328-33, 341; *gloire*, 320, 326, 331-32, 343
Bourbon, Henry (II) de, Prince of Condé, 232n, 290-92, 297, 300, 302, 314, 323
Bourbon, Louis de, Count of Anguien, 236n
Bourbon, Louis de, Count of Soissons, 290-91
Bourbon, Philippe de, as King of Spain, 327
Brabant, 139n
Brétignières, 171n
Brienne, research collection, 279n, 304n
Brisson, Barnabé, 86, 110n
Brittany, Francis (I), Duke of, 43
Budé, Guillaume, 67n, 99
Burgundian-Armagnac conflict, 23n
Burgundy, Duchy of, 61n, 72, 74, 76-77, 178n; ceremonies, 33n, 49; drapery apparatus, 33n; Parlement in, 33n. *See also* Franco-Burgundian rivalry

Caen, city of, 186n
Caesar Augustus, Roman emperor, 135, 139
Calais, city of, 138
Cambrai, Treaty of. *See* Treaty of Cambrai
Canon Law, 54, 66n, 97, 248
Cappel, Jacques, *Lit de Justice*, discourse, 89-92, 94-97, 99, 106, 132, 141
cardinals, 123n, 234-35, 236n, 281, 287, 290-91, 298n, 302n. *See also* Mazarin; Richelieu
Carnavalet, Musée, 335n
Catherine de Médicis (1519-1589), 117n, 136, 145, 153, 155-56, 186n, 187-89, 190, 193, 196, 199, 200, 206, 317;*Lits de Justice*, 198n, 200n; at the Majority *Lit de Justice*, 163, 167, 170-71, 172n, 173; at the Royal *Séance*, 127-28
Catholics. *See* religious factions
ceremonies. *See* Assemblies of Notables; Bourbon cult of rulership; ceremonies, ritual of; coronation; *Entrées*; Estates General; funeral; *Lit de Justice* assem-

blies; Royal *Séances*; Sleeping King
ceremonies, bureau of, 252, 254-58, 260-61, 267-80, 284, 295, 302, 305, 311-12, 320-21, 328-30, 333-44
ceremonies, masters of, 127, 200n, 213, 268, 272, 283, 287-88, 290n, 293n, 297n, 310-12, 316, 320-22, 324-26, 329-30, 333-35, 340-41; aide, 279, 302, 312; grand master, 279, 302
ceremonies, ritual of, 6-10, 49, 51, 57-59, 63-64, 72-73, 80, 88, 92, 98-99, 121-27, 134-35, 152, 155, 159, 160-61, 163, 165-66, 170, 172-74, 177, 181, 183, 185, 193, 198, 200n, 203-8, 213-15, 218-19, 225-26, 228-30, 233-34, 236, 240, 244-45, 248-49, 251-58, 260-62, 272-73, 279-80, 282-91, 295-96, 301-3, 305, 307-8, 310, 312-13, 315, 320-21, 324-26, 328-37, 340-42, 344
chamberlains, 19, 24n, 52, 92, 234n, 236n, 293n, 308
Chambre de la Tournelle, 87
Chambre des Comptes, 107-9, 271n, 288n
Chambre des Enquêtes, 129, 292-93
Chambre des Requêtes, 129; maîtres des, 129, 235n, 316
Chambre du Roi, 53, 57
chancellery, 93-94, 189n; research depository, 108, 140, 172, 209, 273
chancellors, 122n, 123n, 169, 199n, 204n, 206, 215, 221
Charlemagne (742-814), 42, 90, 105
Charles, Duke of Burgundy. *See* Charles V, emperor
Charles I, King of Spain. *See* Charles V, emperor
Charles II, King of France (840-877), 90
Charles V, Holy Roman Emperor, 46, 49, 72, 74-75, 91, 94-96, 136, 139n; trial of, 86-96
Charles V, King of France (1364-1380), 25-26, 41, 110, 147, 151, 205n, 328; and Corbechon, 37-39; drapery apparatus, 15-19, 45, 118; in *Entrée* tableaux, 42; and the Estates, 276; Royal *Séances*, 6n, 15, 20, 24, 25n, 37-39n, 98, 115-18, 122, 131, 145, 166, 177, 181, 185, 226, 262, 276, 296, 320
Charles VI, King of France (1380-1422), 24n, 26, 147; Burgundians vs. Armagnacs, 23n; drapery apparatus, 16; and the Parlement at Poitiers, 27; Royal

Séances, 15-16, 19-22, 25n, 27, 34, 98, 115-19, 122, 145, 166, 173, 177, 185, 262n

Charles VII, King of France (1422-1461), 27n, 165n, 185n; Coronation, 28; *Entrées*, 28, 33; and the Grand Conseil, 32; and the Parlement at Poitiers, 28; Royal *Séance*, 32-35, 39-41, 124, 277, 304-5

Charles VIII, King of France (1483-1498), 185; *Entrées*, 42, 266; and the Estates, 54; and the Parlement of Paris, 61, 146; Royal *Séances*, 42-43, 98-99, 115n

Charles IX, King of France (1560-1574), 96, 153-54, 157-60, 163, 170-75, 201, 206, 209, 212n, 213n, 223, 226, 317, 319-20, 326-27; contest with the Parlement of Paris, 183-208, 210, 294; Coronation, 152; and Du Tillet, 110-11, 196; and the Estates General, 108n, 147, 175; *Lits de Justice*, 198-202, 211; and L'Hôpital, 205n; and Louis X, genealogy, 156; Majority *Lit de Justice*, 160-82; and regency, 145-59, 232; ritual, Sleeping King, 266; Royal *Séance*, 152, 155-57

Charles of Austria. *See* Charles V, emperor

Charles the Bold, Duke of Burgundy, 33n, 49

Chartier, Jean, 34-35

Chartres, city of, 222n, 223, 258

Chastellain, Georges, 33n

Chateauneuf, Charles de L'Aubespine, Marquis of, 289, 290-91

Châtelet, 28-29, 30

Cheverny, Philippe Hurault de, 128, 215, 219

Choppin, René, 67, 84

chose publique. See maxims

Chronicler of Saint-Denis, on Royal *Séance* (1413), 31

chronicles, 37, 47, 105, 117; of Chartier, 34-35; of Chastellain, 33n; Chronicler of Saint-Denis, 31; of Escouchy, 34n; of Froissart, 28-32; of Haton, 154n; of Herald Berry, 31n; of Jaligny, 43; of Juvénal des Ursins, 29, 31; of La Marche, 33n; of Le Févre, 31; of Monstrelet, 30-31, 151n; of Nangis, 37n; of Wavrin, 34

Church, Catholic, 76, 130, 136, 155-56, 249, 258, 305

Cicero, 54n, 67n

civil law. *See* Roman Law

clergy, 153, 274, 329

clerks, Parlement of Paris, 15, 16, 21-23, 24n, 25, 28, 34-35, 43, 53, 55-58, 70n, 71n, 72, 74, 86-89, 93, 96-100, 102-4, 106-7, 109-10, 118, 121, 136, 200n, 209-10, 211n, 215, 231n, 279, 292, 316

Clisson, Olivier de, 20

Coeur, Jacques, 39n

Colbert, Jean-Baptiste, 326

Coligny, Gaspard de, 211n

Combien que les rois soient morts, le royaume et la justice ... est inviolable. See maxims

Concordat of Bologna, 46

Condé, Henry (II) de Bourbon, Prince of. *See* Bourbon

Conseil étroit. See Royal Council

Conseil, Grand. See Royal Council

Conseil privé. See Royal Council

constable, 123n, 136, 169, 193, 234n

Constantine, Roman emperor, 240n

consultation, 3, 4, 92-93, 136, 148, 150, 156, 167, 171, 204n, 206, 216-18, 232-33, 238-39, 241n, 242-46, 274, 276, 283, 287, 290-91, 293, 308, 311, 313-14, 324, 326, 339, 342

Convent of the Augustinians, 114n, 231, 233, 235n, 236, 243, 252, 260

Coquille, Guy de, 202n, 222n

Corbechon, Jean, 37-38, 41

Corbin, Jacques, 269, 296n

coronation, 9, 46, 74, 84, 86, 91-92, 94-95, 104, 114n, 127, 134, 138-39, 144n, 145, 152, 160, 165-66, 174, 223, 229, 231, 249, 251-52, 254-67, 271, 280, 312

corps politique (corpus mysticum). See maxims

corpus mysticum (corps politique). See maxims

councillors: Parlement of Paris, 39, 53, 55-56, 63, 88-90, 92, 94, 122n, 123n, 127, 136, 153, 155, 194-95, 213n, 215, 220, 231n, 233, 235n, 284, 289, 297, 299, 311, 314; Parlement of Rouen, 163n

counsel. *See* consultation

counts, 260n

La couronne et la justice ne meurent jamais. See maxims
Craon, Pierre de, trial of, 17, 20, 119
Crécy, Battle of, 165n
Crown, 4, 8, 31, 42, 58, 64n, 66, 77, 83, 89, 90-92, 95, 99, 111, 139n, 145, 163, 166, 175n, 178, 181, 210-11, 220, 230, 240, 261, 264, 282n, 283-84, 287, 295, 305, 321, 324, 327-28, 337, 341-42, 344. *See also* French constitutions; officers of the Crown
Crown, laws of. *See* French constitutions
Crown, officers of. *See* officers of the Crown

dauphins, 27n, 34, 35n, 74-76, 84, 91, 252, 257, 296-98, 301-2; in the Estates General, 137, 139, 145; in *Lits de Justice,* 87, 89, 92-94, 137, 139, 253; in *Royal Séances,* 21, 136-37, 139, 145
declarations. *See* legislation; legislative procedure
Delamonce, 205n, 335n
Deschamps, Eustache, 26-27
Desgranges, Michel Ancel, 279, 287, 340
Desiré, Artus, 186n
Dieppe, city of, 186n
Dignitas non moritur. See maxims
dignité, royal, nature of, 42n, 53-54, 63-66, 74-75, 83-84, 93, 94n, 98, 117, 123-24, 134, 139, 144-45, 147, 149, 158-59, 166, 175-76, 178-81, 223, 234n, 235n, 247-48, 253. *See also* French constitutions; maxims; *royauté* (dynasty)
Dijon, Parlement of. *See* Parlement of Dijon
discourse, modes of, 6-11, 15, 47, 51, 66, 89-92, 94-99, 132, 141-43, 147, 160-61, 163, 173-81, 184-85, 201, 203, 220-21, 226-28, 249, 264, 267, 270-72, 310, 312-14, 342-44
Disque, François, 56n
domain, royal, 51, 58, 74, 77-78, 86, 90-91, 95-96, 111, 116, 130, 171, 199. *See also* French constitutions
Dominicus de Sancto Germiniano, 77
Dorat, Jacques, 258n, 263
Dormy, François, 192-94
drapery apparatus (thronal): Parlement of Bordeaux, 198n; Parlement of Paris, 15-18, 20-25, 27, 35n, 37-39, 41, 43-47,

52-53, 55, 57-59, 61, 64, 73, 73n, 78, 88-89, 108, 108n, 119n, 120, 127, 127n, 133, 206n, 284, 287, 287n, 291, 293n, 308, 310, 322, 328, 330, 331n, 337-40; Parlement of Rouen, 200n; Parlement of Toulouse, 287n. *See also* throne
drawings. *See* iconography
droit annuel (paulette). See legislation; Parlements, regulation of offices
Du Bourg, Antoine, 87-89, 92-94, 97
Du Chesne, André, 229, 268
duchesses, 235n
Dufresnoy, Lenglet, 296n
Du Haillan, Bernard de Girard, 68n, 99
dukes, 241-42, 260n, 287, 295, 296n, 305, 317, 325, 333
Dumesnil, Baptiste, 156
Du Moulin, Charles, 95n, 99, 182n
Duprat, Antoine, 53, 56n, 58, 63-64, 70n; in *Lit de Justice,* 73, 79-80
Dupré, Guillaume, 249-51, 259n, 260
Dupuy, Jacques, 270
Dupuy, Pierre, 3, 9, 12, 44n, 110n, 117n, 121n, 151n, 296n, 297; and Bergier, 258n; on the Law of Majority, 271; on the *Lit de Justice,* 270-72; research commissions, 270; on regencies, 297n; and Séguier, 273-74
Du Tillet, Elie, 106n, 107n
Du Tillet, Jean, 103n
Du Tillet, Jean, Sieur de la Bussière, 12, 50, 51n, 86, 89, 93, 96-98, 100, 102-21, 123, 126-27, 132, 136, 138, 152, 156, 180n, 195-96, 288n, 331
—appointed chief clerk, 102, 106-7, 121
—archival forays, 87n, 102-21, 142, 145, 147, 185, 209, 213
—cited by: Bergier, 262; d'Orléans, 229; Dupuy, 110n, 270-71; Godefroy, 272; La Roche-Flaven, 49n, 268; L'Hôpital, 104, 146-51, 172, 177
—constitutional theory, 111-21, 124-26, 138, 140, 147, 148-49, 150-52, 158-59, 172, 185, 201, 203-4, 209, 212, 225-26
—constitutional theory modified, 121-25, 159-61
—discourse, 105-6, 110-11, 179-81, 271
—fiction of the medieval *Lit de Justice,* 3, 8, 49, 110, 112-21, 172, 268
—historical works of, 3, 102-3, 105n, 110-16, 118, 145, 209, 213, 268

—memorandum of 1560, 121-25
—opinions on: coronations, 104, 113; *entrées*, 103-4, 111, 113; Estates, peers, Parlement, 103-5, 110-16, 120-21, 128, 141-42; funerals, 103-4, 113; Law of Majority, 105n, 116-18, 137n, 145, 164, 177, 188, 319; *lèse-majesté*, 20, 116-18, 277; *Lits de Justice*, 49, 104, 107, 110-21, 124-25, 141-42, 144, 185, 201; Royal *Séances*, 103-4, 107, 110-21, 276n; Salic Law, 105n, 116-18, 176, 178
—reconstructs French constitution, 102-21, 125, 343
—research commissions, 100, 101, 106-11, 121, 128, 140, 172, 213, 223, 226, 272
—research used by Olivier, 103, 108, 273
Du Tillet, Louis (II), Sieur de Senelles, 196, 231n, 316
Du Tillet, Séraphin, 50, 52, 55-56, 58-59, 71n, 72, 74, 93
Du Vair, Guillaume, 217n, 220-21, 222n
dynastic monarchy. *See* French constitutional ideologies
dynastic right. *See* succession

écuyer, grand, 308
edicts. *See* legislation; legislative procedure
Edinburgh, city of, 249n
Edward, Prince, 320n
Elbeuf, Duke of, 234n
Eleanor of Austria, 89, 94
emperors, Roman, 134-35, 139, 217, 241; ceremonies of, 330
England, 32, 155, 157, 164, 165n, 320; and *Dignitas non moritur*, 176; monarchy and absolutism, 227; "parlement" in, 148; Queen of, 16, 165n
engravings. *See* iconography
Entrées, 9, 27-42, 46, 63, 103-4, 108, 113, 123, 127-28, 132, 138-39, 152n, 155, 173, 198, 210, 214n, 229, 240n, 249, 280, 302-4, 333-36; provincial, 139n, Reims, 42, 104n, 258-67, 281, 298-99, 307-8, 312; Rouen, 158, 167; tableaux, 28-30, 31n, 32, 42, 139, 259-63, 266; Tours, 41n, 42n; Vendôme, 33
Épernon, Duke of, 232, 244
Épernon, Louis de Nogaret d', Cardinal of La Valette. *See* La Valette
Escouchy, Mathieu d', 34n

Estates, 3-4, 45n, 46n, 54, 75, 79, 81, 83, 98, 104, 108, 111, 113, 116, 128-29, 146-49, 151, 214, 222, 274-75, 278, 287, 311, 342-43
—comments on, 151n; by Boulainvilliers, 279n; by Du Tillet, 103-4, 111, 113; by Richelieu, 275; by Séguier (III), 225, 270-77
—four estates: in *Entrée* tableau, 139n; in Estates General, 137n, 274
—General. *See* Estates General
—*Lits de Justice* and, 48, 74, 78, 80-81, 83, 96, 98, 137n, 274-79, 314, 326
—and "parlements," 148, 274
—and Parlement of Paris, 75n, 81, 274-75, 278
—of Pepin, 104n
—provincial, 329
—and regencies, 144n, 147, 148n, 170
—and Royal *Séances*, 104n, 137, 137n, 274, 276
—and taxation, 78, 274, 276-77
Estates General: (1468), 104n, 147n; (1484), 4, 41, 42n, 54, 147n; (1506), 147n; (1558), 137n, 138-39, 147n, 274; (1560-1561), 45n, 108, 144n, 147, 149, 152, 175; (1588-1589), 104n, 220, 222-23; (1593), 223; (1596-1597), 224; (1614-1615), 284; (1789), 5, 278
Europe, and European powers, 128, 327, 332

Fauquembergue, Clément de, 28, 99, 104
feudal law, 83, 90-91, 94-95, 97
Feuilloy, Guillaume de, 15-17
Flanders, 46, 74, 86, 90-91
Fontainebleau, 152, 182n
Fontanieu, Moïse Augustin, 337, 339
Fouquet, Jean, 33, 37n, 39-41
France, law of. *See* French constitutions
France, Republic of, 171n, 193, 344
Francis I, King of France (1515-1547), 47, 89-101, 109n, 115-16, 122, 125, 137-39, 144-45, 150, 163, 185, 223, 244n, 294, 299, 304; and the drapery apparatus, 45n, 52, 73n, 89; and Du Tillet, 100, 103, 106, 109; *Entrée*, 46; *Lit de Justice*, 48-50, 51-72, 74-76, 80-82; research commission, 100, 106, 108, 226; and the Royal Council, 49-50, 55-56, 67-70, 72-85, 86-101; Royal *Séances*, 46-

Francis I (*cont.*)
    47, 61, 68, 225-26; and Treaty of Ma-
    drid, 50, 81; and venality, 67n
Francis II, King of France (1559-1560),
    45n, 46n, 116-17, 137n, 144-45, 175,
    226; as dauphin, Estates General, 136,
    139; as dauphin, Royal *Séance*, 137n,
    139, 145; drapery apparatus, 45n, 61;
    research commission, 109, 111, 223;
    summons the Estates General, 147, 175
Franciscus de Acoltis de Aretrio, 77
Franciscus Zabarella, 77
Franco-Burgundian rivalry, 27, 33, 35,
    41, 61n
Franco-imperial rivalry, 49-50, 61n, 75,
    86, 99, 138-39, 142
French constitutional ideologies, 6-7, 10-
    11, 47, 118, 160, 212, 230, 261-67, 313,
    341-42, 344; absolutist monarchy, 11,
    180n, 227, 272, 307-44; dynastic mon-
    archy, 11, 180n, 227, 231-307, 310, 314-
    15, 319, 321-22, 326n, 328, 335, 341;
    judicial monarchy, 14-47, 277; juristic
    monarchy, 11, 48-230, 249, 252-54, 261,
    267, 270-72, 295, 319, 321-22, 326n,
    328, 331, 341-42
French constitutions, 3, 8-12, 14, 50, 81-
    82, 98, 101, 145, 202, 229, 254, 266,
    268, 272, 296, 319, 327-28, 344
—Fundamental Law, 22n, 223, 271n,
    272, 310, 327; associated with Public
    Law and nature, 261, 263, 312-13;
    comprehended in Bourbon blood
    right, 316, 319-20, 327-28, 331-32, 342;
    Law of Regency proposed, 296-97;
    linked with Public Law, 222, 313;
    lodged in nature and tradition, 310-14,
    319-20, 332, 342; subverts Public Law,
    296, 312. *See also royauté* (dynasty);
    maxims
—Public Law, 9, 48-50, 86, 89, 94, 95n,
    98-99, 130-31, 139-47, 151, 161, 163,
    170-73, 177, 229, 327, 331; as "ancient
    laws and constitutions of the king-
    dom," 261; as "fundamental," 165n,
    174n; as "fundamental and irrevocable
    law," 222, 313; as "immutable law,"
    165, 174, 262, 272; as "Law of
    France," 91-92, 95, 97, 272; Law of In-
    alienability, 51, 67n, 71-78, 80-81, 83,
    91-92, 95-97, 261, 263, 272; as "Law of

the Kingdom," 149, 175, 178, 181;
    Law of Majority, 117-18, 137n, 145,
    148n, 165-66, 174-77, 181, 198, 205-8,
    226, 266, 271, 296, 312, 319; Law of
    Succession, 116, 165, 174-77, 179n, 181,
    198, 202, 211-12, 221, 223, 226, 228,
    241, 249, 251-53, 261-63, 266, 272, 328;
    as "Laws of Crown," 77, 83, 90, 96;
    reconstructed by Du Tillet, 102-25;
    Salic Law, 42, 74, 77, 83, 95-97, 105,
    111, 116, 118, 165n, 174, 238, 261, 266,
    272, 296; as "special law . . . unique
    and particular to this kingdom," 179,
    212, 272; subverted by Fundamental
    Law, 261, 267, 270, 272, 295, 312-14,
    319. *See also dignité*
French Revolution, 5, 203, 343
Froissart, Jean, 28, 32
Fronde, 282n, 317, 322
Fundamental Law. *See* French constitu-
    tions
funeral, 64, 123, 139, 166, 177, 229, 234n,
    249, 252, 254-56, 261, 278; Du Tillet
    on, 103-4, 113; effigies, 139, 234n,
    235n, 255-56; red-robed presidents of
    Parlement, 41n, 63-64, 123, 144, 158-
    59, 179; slogans, 180, 264n

Gagnières, Roger de, 35n, 37n
Gaillon, city of, 187, 189n
Gartres, P.L.D., 264
genealogy, French kings, 42, 156, 238-49
gens du roi, 89, 134, 232, 243, 244n, 297,
    299, 300, 303, 305. *See also avocats; pro-
    cureurs général*
Gillot, Jacques, 231n
Godefroy, Denys, 9, 12, 297
Godefroy, Théodore, 9, 12, 51n, 124, 270-
    73, 279n, 291n, 297; and Denys Gode-
    froy, 9, 12, 297; and Dupuy, Saintot,
    Séguier, 272-74; reseach commissions,
    270
governors, provincial, 123n, 136, 186n,
    188n, 189n, 232n
Grand-chambre (Palais de Justice). *See*
    Parlement of Paris (Grand-chambre)
Grand Conseil. *See* Royal Council
Grand Salle (Palais de Justice), 25n, 29n,
    57, 65n, 87
grands du royaume, 4, 302n, 326

Grassaille, Charles de, 84
greffiers. See clerks
Grégoire, Pierre, 84
Grenoble, Parlement of. *See* Parlement of
 Grenoble
guards, royal, 53, 56, 58, 89, 100n, 116,
 124, 235n, 340
Guillart, Charles, 57, 65-71, 96-97, 99,
 106, 132, 141, 216, 274; *Lit de Justice*,
 discourse, 53-55
Guise, Dukes of, 134, 232, 244; faction,
 144

Harlay, Achille (I) de, 212-13n; Inaugural *Lit de Justice*, 231-51, 269; in Royal
 Séance, 209, 216-21, 289; speeches collected by Du Vair, 220-21
Harlay, Achille (III) de, 269n
Haton, Claude, 154n
Helêne (wife of the Roman emperor
 Constantine), 240n
Hennequin, Christophe, 56n
Henry II, King of France (1547-1559),
 126, 133-36, 138-43, 151, 165n, 213n,
 228n, 320; as dauphin, 89, 92-93; *Entrées*, 104n, 108, 127-28, 132, 138-39,
 139n; Estates General, 137n, 139; and
 the *Lit de Justice*, 108, 125; Parlement
 of Paris, 274; research commission,
 107-12, 128, 140, 172, 223, 226; Royal
 Séances, 103, 104n, 106, 108, 114n,
 115n, 120, 123, 126-48, 150-51, 155n,
 199n, 226, 253, 273, 274, 294, 320; and
 venality, 217n
Henry III, King of France (1574-1589),
 179, 211, 219, 222n, 223-24, 226, 232,
 253, 279, 321n, 327; *Lit de Justice*, 212-
 13, 217n, 219-23; research commission,
 213; Royal *Séances*, 209, 212-18, 220,
 221n, 226
Henry IV, King of France (1589-1610),
 209, 223, 226, 231, 241, 244, 252-53; assassination and mourning, 230-33, 256;
 Coronation, 223-24; and Dupré, 251;
 and the Estates General, 223-24; Funeral, 255-56; funereal commemoration, *Entrée*, 254-56, 258-61, 263-66; funereal commemoration, Inaugural *Lit
 de Justice*, 236-41, 247-53; as Henry of
 Navarre, 220-22; medallic history,

259n, 264n, 331, 366n; ritual, Sleeping
 King, 266
Henry VI, King of England, 28
Henry VIII, King of England, 75
Herald Berry, 31n
Herisset, Antoine, 205n
Herouval, Monsieur Vyon d', Sieur, 19,
 271n
historiography: French institutions and
 the French constitution, 3-12, 14, 17-
 25, 30-35, 43-44, 45n, 46n, 47-51, 53-
 54, 59-60, 67-72, 75, 84, 90-91, 97-99,
 100, 102-43, 145-53, 157, 160-61, 165,
 172-73, 180n, 183-85, 188, 190n, 197-
 99, 201, 203, 205, 212, 213n, 216, 226-
 29, 241n, 243, 254, 259n, 267-80, 283-
 84, 289, 296n, 310-14, 319-21, 325n,
 328, 331-32, 342-44; historical fiction of
 the medieval *Lit de Justice*, 6n, 8-9, 12,
 14, 17n, 19, 24, 44n, 49, 65, 99-100,
 105-9, 114-22, 124-25, 131, 138, 145,
 147, 172, 181-83, 185, 190, 201-2, 205n,
 206, 226, 247-48, 251, 268-69, 271-72,
 276, 283, 296, 304, 320-21, 331, 342;
 historical legend of the *Lit de Justice*,
 6-9, 11-12, 34, 37n, 47-49, 98, 251, 267-
 83, 296-97, 320-21, 324n, 328n, 342,
 344; rhetoric and, 90, 105-6, 141-44,
 155-56, 161, 185, 331, 332, 343. *See
 also*: research commissions
Hôtel Saint-Pol, 15, 23n, 24n, 25, 27n,
 114n
Hotman, François, 84, 178, 182n
Huguenots. *See* religious factions
huissiers. See ushers

iconography: drawings of *Lits de Justice*,
 234n, 236-37, 287n, 335n, 339, 340n;
 engravings, 59-62, 204-5, 249-51, 264-
 65, 280; engravings of *Lits de Justice*,
 161, 204-5, 279-80, 285-86, 308-9, 333-
 34, 335n, 336-39, 340; illumination, 37-
 39; jetons and coins, 241, 242n, 251,
 266n; medallic history, 241n, 258n,
 259n, 264n, 266n, 315n, 324n, 325n,
 328, 331; medals, 211n, 240, 242n, 246,
 249-51, 259n, 260; miniatures, 26n, 33,
 35-41, 59; paintings, 24n, 44n, 45n,
 161n, 238n, 308; portraits, 39, 249,
 266n, 331; statuary, 29, 331. *See also*

iconography: (*cont.*)
    drapery apparatus; *Entrées,* tableaux
illumination. See iconography
Ils [rois] ne sont morts pour la justice. See
    maxims
L'image vive du défunt. See maxims
Inalienability, Law of. *See* French consti-
    tutions
l'interest . . . concernant l'utilité publique.
    See maxims
Isabel of Bavaria (1371-1435), 28

Jaligny, Guillaume de, 43
Jansenists. *See* religious factions
Jean II, King of France (1350-1364), 126,
    130-31, 294
jetons and coins. *See* iconography
Joan of Arc, 28
Joly, Claude, 320
judicial monarchy. *See* French constitu-
    tional ideologies
Judicium Francorum. See maxims
juristic monarchy. *See* French constitu-
    tional ideologies
jus sanguinis. See succession, legal-heredi-
    tary
La justice ne cesse pas. See maxims
Justinian. *See* Roman Law
Juvénal des Ursins, Jean (II), 29, 31

king: as chief judge, 14-47, 59, 92, 94n,
    130-31, 147, 171, 202, 277; as legislator,
    231-315; as legislator (and judge), 48-
    230; as supreme legislator, 315-32
kingdom, law of the. *See* French consti-
    tutions, maxims
king's two bodies. See maxims
knights, 53, 73, 89, 92, 134, 136-37, 163n

La Barre, Jean de, 55
La Buigne, Gaces de, 25-27
La Guesle, Jacques de, 171n
La Marche, Olivier de, 33n
Lansac, Louis de Saint-Gelais, sieur de,
    184, 186, 192
La Place, Pierre de, 117n, 151n
La Planche, Louis Regnier de, 104n,
    106n, 118n, 151n
La Popelinière, Lancelot Voysin, sieur
    de, 100n

La Roche-Flavin, Bernard de, 9, 49, 268
La Salle, P. de, 258n
L'Aubespine, Charles de, Marquis of
    Chateauneuf. *See* Chateauneuf
La Valette, Cardinal of, Louis de No-
    garet d'Épernon, 290-91
law, customary (private), 30, 91, 130-31,
    165, 171, 173, 182, 264; divine, 30, 54,
    91, 264; natural, 30, 54. *See also* Canon
    Law; French constitutions; feudal law;
    Roman Law
Law, French. *See* French constitutions
L'Aubespine, Charles de, Marquis of
    Chateauneuf. *See* Chateauneuf
League, Catholic. *See* religious factions
Le Bret, Cardin, 232, 243, 277, 292n
Le Clerc, Alfondet, 15-16
Le Clerc, Ernoulet, 16
Le Coq, Nicole, 56n
Le Févre, Jean, 31
legal-hereditary succession. *See* succession
Le Gendre, P., 45n
legislation, 33n, 63, 71, 111, 113, 117n,
    130-31, 138n, 150-51, 167, 169, 171,
    174, 180n, 182-84, 194-96, 199, 202n,
    211n, 214-20, 223-36, 276, 278, 282-95,
    301-3, 307, 315-17, 320, 323n, 324,
    326n; (1318), 18n, 19, 271n; (1343),
    68n; (1345), 19n, 68n, 119n; (1375), 20,
    24, 118n, 125, 130-31, 184-85; (1392),
    20, 117, 118n, 184-85; (1407), 20, 117,
    118n, 184-85; (1413), 21-22, 31n;
    (1454), 28; (1483), 185n; (1493), 43;
    (1498), 180n; (1499), 43, 115n; (1527),
    55-58, 63-64, 69-71, 142, 244n, 294;
    (1537), 92-93; (1558), 137-39; (1560,
    Romorantin), 153; (1561, Saint-Ger-
    main, or Toleration), 153-54; (1562,
    Pacification), 109; (Mar. 1563, Am-
    boise, or Pacification), 154, 157, 164,
    185, 187n, 188n, 189, 192; (Aug. 1563,
    Pacification), 157, 161n, 164, 170-71,
    173, 183-98, 199n; (1563, Rouen), 183-
    98, 201; (1563), 294; (1566, Moulins),
    150n; (1576), 253; (1588, Union), 222,
    313; (1604, *droit annuel,* or *paulette*),
    299, 300n, 304; (1610, regency), 232-33,
    238-43, 245-47, 252, 257, 281; (1614,
    Majority), 205, 206n; (1629, Code Mi-
    chaud), 292-93; (1638, *droit annuel,* or
    paulette), 300n; (1641), 294-95, 315, 317,

323, 326-27, 335; (1642), 298; (1643, regency), 227, 297-98, 300-303, 305, 310-14; (1645), 315-16; (1648, *droit annuel,* or *paulette*), 300n, 315-17; (1651, Majority), 205-6, 319; (1657, *droit annuel,* or *paulette*), 300n; (1661), 326-27; (1664), 325; (1667, Code Louis), 325n, 327, 335; (1669, *droit annuel,* or *paulette*), 300n; (1673), 327, 335; (1715, regency), 333-37, 341; (1718), 337-40; (1723, Majority), 205-6

legislative procedure: evocation, 32, 55, 67, 69, 134, 189n; legislative and judicial functions separated, 4-5, 46, 50, 59, 70, 81-82, 98, 130-33, 140-43, 145, 147-48, 150-52, 160-61, 163, 167, 170, 172-73, 182-84, 190, 194-96, 199, 202-3, 210, 216, 228, 252, 267, 280-81, 283-96, 303, 305-6, 313-19, 320, 326, 335, 337, 342; *lettres closes,* 186-87, 188n, 189, 190, 193n, 194, 259n; *lettres de cachet,* 287n, 288n, 298-99; *lettres de jussion,* 48n, 140, 224; *lettres patentes,* 44, 45n, 195, 232, 244, 327; remonstrances, Parlement to king, 4-6, 46, 48-49, 61, 66n, 67n, 134-35, 140-41, 146, 151, 153-54, 157, 167-68, 182, 187-90, 192, 201, 210, 216, 218-19, 291-95, 317, 327, 333, 337, 339, 344. *See also* legislation

Le Havre, city of, 155, 157-58, 164, 165n

Le Jay, Nicolas, 289, 290n, 291

Le Maistre, Gilles, 133n, 134, 137-38, 140-41, 156n; Royal *Séance,* discourse, 134-35

Le Maistre, Pierre, 86-89, 93, 96-97

Le Nain, Jean (V), 7, 44n, 270, 271n, 317n, 326n

Le Noir, Raoul, 16, 20

Le Paige, Louis-Adrien, discourse of, 3-6, 278, 344

lèse-majesté, 20, 32-35, 46-47, 51, 57-58, 65, 71, 94, 115n, 116, 118, 164, 174, 277. *See also* peers, trials of

lettres de cachet, lettres de jussion, lettres patentes. See legislative procedure

lex animata: debitor justitiae, legibus solutus, ratione alligatus. See maxims

L'Hôpital, Michel de, 121, 148, 156, 161n, 170, 172, 189, 193, 196, 202, 206, 317, 319, 331; constitutional theory, 145-53, 157, 159, 166-69, 173-74, 181-82, 201-3,

209-10, 212; and Du Tillet, 117n, 146-51, 164-65, 172, 273; on the estates, Parlements, and Public Law, 104, 148-49, 159, 167-70, 175, 199, 274; *Lits de Justice,* 197-200; Majority *Lit de Justice,* 160, 164-69, 174-82, 186, 197, 205, 262, 271, 319; the memorandum of 1560, 152; parlementary assemblies, discourse, 149-55, 197; Royal *Séance,* 155, 197

lit de justice (phrase), 7, 31, 59, 132; adopted by clerks, Parlement of Paris, 19-25; adopted by ushers, Parlement of Paris, 17, 19, 20, 119; as drapery apparatus in Royal *Séances,* 19-26, 32, 47; meaning conflated with *Lit de Justice,* assemblies, 322; metaphor for king and the Parlement of Paris in the Grand-chambre, 99, 106, 132-33, 185, 214n, 215n, 216n; signifies the drapery apparatus, 14, 16-17, 20-30, 34-35, 41, 44-47, 88-89, 93, 97, 99, 118-20, 322, 337; signifies the funeral effigy, 256; signifies the Grand-chambre, Parlement of Paris, 99, 132-33, 141, 185, 214n; signifies jurisdiction, Parlement of Paris, 14, 21-25, 34-35, 43, 47; symbolizes royal justice, *Entrée* tableaux, 27-42. *See also* drapery apparatus (Parlement of Paris)

Lit de Justice assemblies: distinction from Royal *Séances* blurred, 282-95, 322, 327, 332; distinguished from Royal *Séances,* 3, 8, 14, 47-85, 86-101, 106-43, 147-48, 152, 159, 185, 197-98, 202-3, 209, 212, 219, 223, 228-29, 234, 295-96, 322, 328; and the Estates, 48, 74, 78, 80-81, 83, 96, 98, 274-79, 326; Inaugural assemblies, 261, 300, 303, 305, 310-12, 314-15, 335, 341, 344; location outside the Grand-chambre, 124-25, 158-59, 183-204, 303-6, 312, 314, 322, 337-41; location outside Paris, 152, 157, 160-82, 190, 197, 201-3, 211, 225, 304-5, 312, 314, 322; Majority assemblies, 160, 166, 177, 181, 184, 188, 204-8, 254, 257, 261, 279, 305, 314, 335, 341; Minority assemblies, 307, 315-21; revival of, 333-44; waning of, 321-30. *See also* Charles IX; Francis I; Henry IV; Louis XIII; Louis XIV; Louis XV

Lizet, Pierre, 87-88, 93, 106, 138, 141; Royal *Séance*, discourse, 132-33
Loisel, Antoine, 180, 266
lords, 63-64, 156, 193, 260n
Louis IX, King of France (1226-1270), 26, 42, 129, 147, 156, 165n, 240n, 241, 249, 254
Louis XI, King of France (1461-1483), 28n, 41-42; *Entrée*, 104n; in *Entrée* tableaux, 42; and the Estates, 41n, 42n, 104n; and the *Grand Conseil*, 54; and the Parlement of Burgundy, 33n, 34n
Louis XII, King of France (1498-1515), 42, 54-55, 161n, 214n, 302; drapery apparatus, 44-45, 61, 236n, 240, 251; renovates the Grand-chambre, 44-45, 59; Royal *Séances*, 43, 115n, 123, 155n
Louis XIII, King of France (1610-1643), 174n, 204, 230, 233-35, 248, 263-65, 267-69, 277, 279, 281-82, 284, 287, 289, 290-93, 296-301, 303, 307, 311-12, 315, 317, 319, 325-27, 333, 341; ceremonial programs, 267-80; Inaugural *Lit de Justice*, 231-53; inaugural plan for 1643, 295-306; *Lits de Justice*, 281-84, 287, 288n, 289-95, 326, 335; Majority *Lit de Justice*, 204-8, 282-84; pre-Coronation *Entrée*, 254-67, 281; research commissions, 270; revision of constitutional ideology, 267, 281-95; ritual of the "Sleeping King," 266
Louis XIV, King of France (1643-1715), 225-27, 278-79, 297-307, 310-12, 314-17, 319-23, 326-29, 332-33, 335, 339, 341; Inaugural *Lit de Justice*, 307-15; *Lits de Justice*, 322-27; Majority *Lit de Justice*, 204-8; medallic history, 259n, 266n, 331; Minority *Lits de Justice*, 315-21; regency plan for, 295-306; research commission, 270; Royal *Séances*, 323-24, 327
Louis XV, King of France (1715-1774), 5, 204, 279; Inaugural *Lit de Justice*, 333-37; *Lit de Justice*, 337-41; Majority *Lit de Justice*, 204-8, 257
Louis XVI, King of France (1774-1793), 5
Louise of Savoy (1476-1531), 56n, 70n; attends *Lit de Justice*, 73, 79
Louvre, palace, 25, 35-37, 39, 41, 52, 59, 114n, 116, 207, 225, 232-33, 235n, 243-

44, 249, 256-57, 260, 298-300, 303-5, 312, 321, 322
Loyseau, Charles, 180, 266, 270, 272
Lucas de Penna, 84, 95n, 131n

Madrid, Treaty of. *See* Treaty of Madrid
Magistri, Jean, 99
Maillot, A., 205n, 337-38
maior pars. *See* maxims
maîtres des requêtes (Royal Household), 52-53, 56, 92
majority, law of. *See* French constitutions
majority, royal, 20, 24, 105, 117, 125, 144-45, 154-58, 160-208, 226, 262, 297, 319-41. *See also* French constitutions, Public Law; legislation; *Lit de Justice* assemblies, Majority assemblies
Malon, Nicolas, 51n, 56, 58, 96-97
Mantes, city of, 188, 190, 192n
Marguerite of Angoulême, 89, 94
Marie de Médicis (1573-1642), 204n, 206, 231-33, 235-36, 238-39, 242-45, 249-52, 257; Inaugural *Lit de Justice*, 233, 235-38, 240, 243-46, 249
Marillac, Michel de, 293; discourse, 288n
marshals, 58, 169, 317
masters of ceremonies. *See* ceremonies, masters of
Mathonière, Nicolas de, 204n
maxims of the kingdom, 10, 11, 180-81, 216, 228, 262, 307, 316, 329, 330, 342

On King and Kingdom:
—authority: from French Public Law, 149, 181; from God, 90, 94, 97, 139, 149n, 171n, 181
—characteristics, 4, 47, 53, 66, 66n, 97-98, 131, 134-35, 139, 171n, 186n, 216-17, 217n, 227, 319
—incorporation of king and kingdom, 77, 82n, 83, 97
—the king's two bodies, 77, 82-83, 176n, 179-80, 228, 331-32
—marriage metaphor, 77-78, 82n, 83-86, 91-92, 94-97, 139, 171, 171n, 181, 228
—succession: and acclamation, 166, 177, 180n, 249, 255, 257, 260, 264n, 299, 303; and biogenetic affinities, 231-40, 247, 247n, 248, 255, 310, 312; and phoenix metaphors, 251, 259n, 263-64, 264n, 265-66, 266n, 267, 310, 312, 344; and the royal *dignité*, 160, 165, 174-76,

178-79, 180n, 181, 262, 264, 271; and the *royauté*, 178-81, 228, 259, 262-64, 266-67, 272, 310, 312, 329-30, 342, 344; and sun metaphors, 54, 90, 231, 240, 248, 251, 254, 259-60, 262-65, 310, 312, 328n
—tutorship, 54, 66, 67, 97, 140n, 146, 156, 158, 171, 190, 223, 244

On Kingdom as a Body Politic:
—body metaphor, 53, 66, 67n, 77, 82n, 83, 84n, 97, 171n, 193, 344
—necessity (emergency), 75, 78, 82, 154-56, 184, 189n, 191, 215-18, 225-26, 292-93, 307, 311, 314-16, 323n
—public nature, 54, 66-67, 74-75, 78, 80, 82-83, 86, 91, 95, 97, 180, 228, 261, 272, 331, 342
—public welfare, 90, 97, 278n

On King and Parlement:
—associated, 188, 190n, 216, 268-69, 278
—continuity, 64n, 158-59, 179, 256, 342, 344
—representation, 67n, 80, 80n, 82, 99, 188

Cited:
L'autorité royale ne meurt point, 175-76, 178, 181, 267, 342; *chose publique*, 54, 66-67, 74-75, 78, 80, 82-83, 86, 91, 95, 97, 180, 228, 261, 272, 331, 342; *Combien que les rois soient morts, le royaume et la justice . . . est inviolable*, 179; *corpus mysticum*, 53, 66, 67n, 77, 82n, 83, 84n, 97; *La couronne et la justice ne meurent jamais, La justice ne cesse pas*, 64n, 342, 344; *Dignitas non moritur*, 175-76, 178, 181; *Ils [rois] ne sont morts pour la justice*, 158-59, 179, 256; *L'image vive du défunt*, 231, 240, 248, 255, 310, 312; *l'interest . . . concernant l'utilité publique*, 90, 97, 278n; *Judicium Francorum*, 278; *lex animata: legibus solutus, ratione alligatus, debitor justitiae*, 4, 47, 53, 66, 66n, 97-98, 131, 134-35, 139, 171n, 186n, 216-17, 217n, 227, 319; *maior pars*, 188, 190n; *le mary et époux politique de la chose publique, ledit domaine en dot de la République, les dauphin et duc d'Orléans . . . sont enfans du peuple François et de la chose publique*, 77-78, 82n, 83-86, 91-92, 94-

97, 139, 171, 171n, 181, 228; *Le mort saisit le vif*, 174-78, 181, 264, 271-72; *Mortuus aperit oculos viventis*, 160, 165, 174-76, 178-79, 180n, 181, 262, 264, 271; *necessitas, casus necessitatis*, 75, 78, 82, 154-56, 184, 189n, 191, 215-18, 225-26, 292-93, 307, 311, 314-16, 323n; *Occasum Gallia nescit*, 254, 259-60, 262-63; *le pétit phoenix*, 264; *phoenix Francorum*, 264-65; *La proximité du sang*, 329-30, 342, 344; *quod omnes tangit*, 67n, 80, 80n, 82, 99, 188; *République de France, corps politique*, 171n, 193, 344; *Rex est imperator in regno suo*, 90, 94, 97, 139, 149, 149n, 171n, 181; *Rex et Lex*, 268-69, 278; *Le roi de France ne meurt jamais*, 259, 262-63, 344; *Le roi est mort! Vive le roi!*, 166, 177, 180n, 249, 255, 257, 260, 264n, 299, 303; *Le roi meurt, mais un autre est né*, 264; *Le roi ne meurt jamais*, 178-81, 228, 263-64, 266-67, 310, 312, 342; *Le roi n'est pas mort*, 264; *Les rois en France ne meurt point*, 263; *Le royaume est au roy et le roy est aussi au royaume*, 77, 82n, 83, 97; *Le royaume n'est jamais vacant*, 160, 165, 174-76, 178, 180n, 181-82, 228, 262-63, 267, 271, 342; *La royauté est toujours remplie et non jamais vacante*, 180, 266-67, 342; *Le roy est fait marit du royaume qu'il espouse, Il fiance la royauté que la loy et la nature luy donnent*, 261-63; *Le roy ne meurt point en France*, 272; *sol Franciae*, 264; *Vivit morte refecta*, 263

Mayenne, Duke of, 234n, 236n
Mazarin, Jules, 279n, 298n
medals, medallic history. *See* historiography, iconography
memorandum of 1560. *See* research commissions
Ménestrier, Claude-François, 324n, 325n, 328n
mercuriales. See Parlement of Paris; Parlements, provincial
metaphors. *See* maxims
Meulan, city of, 192-94
Mézerai, François Eudes de, 331
miniatures. *See* iconography
Molé, Mathieu, 121n, 288n, 289n, 290n, 293n, 297-98

monarchomaques, 67n
Monstrelet, Enguerran de, 30-31, 151n
Montagu, Girard de, 110
Montargis, city of, 33, 35n, 124
Montesquieu, Charles de Secondat, 332
Montfort, Jean (IV) of, 32, 65, 115-16
Montluc, Jean du, Bishop of Valence, 189-90
Montmorency, Anne de, 136
Montmorency, Duke of, 134
Le mort saisit le vif. See maxims
Mortuus aperit oculos viventis. See maxims
mystique du sang. See succession, Bourbon bloodright

Nangis, Guillaume de, 37n
Navarre, Charles (II), King of, 19-20, 32
Navarre, King of, 92, 156. *See also* Bourbon, Antoine de, King of Navarre; Navarre, Charles (II)
necessitas, casus necessitatis. See maxims
Netherlands, 139n
nobles, 3, 26, 52, 56, 76, 136, 235n, 274
Normandy, 164, 165n, 171, 173, 185n, 186n, 287n. *See also* Parlement of Rouen; Rouen
notaries (Parlement of Paris), 45n, 53, 102, 109-10. *See also* Bernyer
Notre Dame, 235n, 249, 258

oaths, 28n, 53, 64-65, 73-74, 79, 92, 95, 134, 136, 155, 167, 181-82, 249, 258, 274, 299-300, 303-5, 329
Occasum Gallia nescit. See maxims
office (*dignité*). *See dignité* (office)
officers of the Crown, 3, 52, 63, 89, 92, 97, 115, 134, 137, 139n, 153, 163n, 167, 182, 213, 228, 234, 235n, 236n, 241-42, 287, 288n, 295, 296n, 297, 305, 333, 342
Oldradus de Ponte, 217n
Olivier, Alexandre, 211n
Olivier, François, 145, 150, 202, 219; and Du Tillet's research, 103, 108, 172, 273; Royal *Séance*, 126-42, 148, 199n, 219, 294
orders. *See* Estates
ordinances. *See* legislation; legislative procedure
Orléans, Charles, Duke of, 23n
Orléans, Charles, Duke of (son of Francis I), 78

Orléans, city of, 149, 152
Orléans, Gaston, Duke of, 297-98, 300-302, 314
Orléans, Louis d', 229, 268
Orléans, Louis (II), Duke of, 43, 65, 98-99
Orléans, Philippe, Duke of, 206n, 333, 337, 339

paintings. *See* iconography
Palais de Justice, 15, 29, 41, 52, 61, 136-37, 159, 207, 229, 236n, 260, 280, 284, 304-5, 308-10, 322, 328. *See also* Grand-chambre; Grande Salle; Salle Saint-Louis; Salle Verte; Tournelle Civile; Tournelle Criminelle; Tour Ronde
Palais Royal, 207
papacy, papal court, 155, 269n
Paris, city of, 28, 121, 124, 127-28, 164n, 184, 186n, 190, 194-95, 198, 207, 210, 214n, 223, 235n, 240n, 249, 255, 257, 259, 260, 298-99, 302-5; city officials of, 73, 76, 79, 81, 137, 298-99, 303-4, 331. *See also* provost of Paris
Parlement of Aix, 76-77, 79-80
Parlement of Bordeaux, 76-77, 79-80, 198-200, 283n, 292; drapery apparatus, 198n; habit, red robes, 199n; a judicial body, 199-200; presidents, 200
Parlement of Dijon, 76-77, 79-80, 324
Parlement of Grenoble, 76-77, 79-80
Parlement of Paris, 3-7, 14-32, 37, 41-52, 55-67, 70-71, 76, 79-80, 86-104, 108-67, 170, 173, 179, 182-98, 205-11, 214-34, 236n, 238n, 241-45, 255-57, 268-70, 274-305, 308-30, 333-44; claim to a co-legislative, co-tutorship, role, 54-56, 66-67, 80-81, 140n, 146, 151, 153-54, 156-58, 161, 171, 183-98, 201-2, 216, 218-19, 228, 244, 257, 269-70, 278, 281-95, 301, 303, 305-6, 315, 317n, 321, 335, 341-42; as a Court of peers, 32-35, 108n, 109n, 114-15, 120, 124, 128, 130-31, 185, 241, 284, 294-95; drapery apparatus, inventories of, 15-18, 44-46; and the Estates, 4, 41n, 42n, 79, 81, 128-29, 137n, 148, 274-75, 278; Grand-chambre as a "throne of justice," 44, 61, 66n, 90, 96-97, 132, 141, 156, 269, 280, 282, 295, 328; habits, black robes, 63n, 64n, 65,

72-73, 79, 122-24, 136, 138, 155, 212n, 213-14, 226, 321, 323-24, 327; habits, red robes, 57, 63, 64n, 65, 87, 89, 93, 122-24, 127, 134, 140-41, 144, 155, 158-59, 172-73, 179, 200n, 213-14, 219, 224-26, 233, 235n, 255-56, 282n, 300, 303-5, 308, 315, 321-23, 340; history of, 6, 54-59, 65, 68n, 99, 103-5, 113-14, 120, 125, 128-33, 140-48, 197, 271n, 274-75, 278, 284; institutional continuity, procedural autonomy, 44, 68, 159, 216-17, 243-44, 282, 292-93, 301, 303-5, 342; a judicial body, 46, 111, 129-32, 134-35, 141-42, 145-54, 156, 158, 167-69, 171, 181-82, 185, 190, 199, 210, 293-94; jurisdiction of, 6n, 32, 33n, 44, 54-55, 130, 134, 190, 294, 297-306, 320, 322n, 326-27; likened to the Senate of Rome, 44, 47, 61, 135, 140n, 217; *Mercuriales*, 169, 182; at Poitiers, 27-28; registers of, 7-8, 13, 20-23, 24n, 25, 28, 32-34, 42-43, 46, 49-50, 52, 56, 58, 61, 65, 69-71, 78, 86, 87n, 89, 93, 96n, 97-100, 103-4, 107-8, 110-11, 113n, 114, 119n, 120, 127, 138, 157, 161, 183, 184n, 187, 189, 190, 192-93, 195-96, 199, 204n, 205n, 210n, 211n, 214, 215, 219-20, 224-25, 234, 243, 246, 269-70, 273, 278, 283n, 289, 299-301, 304, 308, 310, 316-17, 325, 344; as the supreme court, 43-44, 54, 67, 80, 90, 108n, 109n, 114, 131, 140n, 142, 149, 173, 183-85, 197-99, 201-3, 228, 241, 244, 269; at Tours, 222; trials of peers, 15n, 16, 19-20, 32-37, 39-41, 43, 51-72, 86-101, 114n, 116, 118-20, 122, 124, 277, 304-5
Parlement of Rouen, 76-77, 79, 80, 159, 161-63, 170-71, 173, 183-84, 185n, 188, 190-91, 195, 206, 226, 257, 273, 283n, 287, 291n, 294, 320; discourse of president, 170; drapery apparatus, 287n; habit, red robes, 163n; judicial role, 171-73, 181-82
Parlement of Toulouse, 59, 76, 198-200
Parlement of Tours, 204n, 232n
Parlements, provincial, 59, 73, 136, 149, 159, 164, 167, 170, 173, 183, 197, 201, 283, 305, 322; judicial role, 167-69, 181-82; *Mercuriales*, 182; presidents, 169. *See also* Parlement of: Aix, Bordeaux, Dijon, Grenoble, Rouen, Tou-louse, Tours; Parlements, regulation of offices
Parlements, regulation of offices, 41, 56, 68n, 169, 182, 195-96, 199, 274, 281, 289, 294n, 297, 299-301, 303-5; and the *droit annuel (paulette)*, 281-82, 299, 300n, 303-6, 314, 317, 325n; the dynastic character of, 272-74, 281-82, 291-92, 295, 298-300, 303-5, 314-16, 341-42; and *survivance*, 196, 281; venality, 55, 67, 69, 134, 146, 214-15, 217, 219-20, 223, 284, 291-93, 316. *See also* legislation
Pasquier, Étienne, 68n, 99, 331
paulette (droit annuel). *See* legislation; Parlements, regulation of offices
Pavia, Battle of, 50
peers, 3, 97, 105, 114, 117n, 122n, 123n, 127, 129-30, 132-34, 136-37, 153-56, 163n, 198n, 206, 228, 234-35, 236n, 241-42, 247, 252, 257, 284, 287, 288n, 295, 296n, 325-26, 333, 340; trials, ad hoc parlementary sessions, 277; trails, Parlement of Paris, 15n, 16, 19-20, 32-37, 37n, 39-41, 43, 51-72, 86-101, 114n, 115-16, 118-20, 122, 124, 277, 304-5. *See also lèse-majesté*
Peiresc, Fabri de, 259n
Peiresc, Nicolas-Claude, 258n
Peleus, Julien, 269
Pellisson-Fontanier, Paul, 331
Pepin, King of France (751-768), 104n
le pétit phoenix. *See* maxims
Petrus de Ancharano, 77
Pharamond, 42, 105, 296
Philip II, King of France (1180-1223), 164n
Philip II, King of Spain, 139n
Philip III, King of France (1270-1285), 129, 254
Philip IV, King of France (1285-1314), 54, 68, 120, 129, 131n, 141
Philip V, King of France (1316-1322), 214n
Philip VI, King of France (1328-1350), 35-37, 41, 114, 129-30, 249, 304
Philippus Decius, 77
Philip the Good, Duke of Burgundy, 33n, 34, 35n
phoenix Francorum. *See* maxims
Picault, Pierre, 278n

Pinchon, Nicole, 102
Pisan, Christine de, 27n
Plato, 67n
Plutarch, 171n
Poilly, François de, 333, 335n
Poitiers. *See* Parlement of Poitiers
Poland, 211, 232, 327
Pons, Michel de, 178n
Pontac, Jacques de, 198n, 200n
portraits. *See* iconography
prelates, 130, 156, 242
presidents (Parlement of Paris), 52-55, 57, 63, 70, 73, 76-78, 87-89, 90, 92-94, 96-97, 99, 122n, 123, 127, 129, 132, 134, 136, 141, 151, 155-56, 158, 169-70, 171n, 172n, 190, 195, 204n, 209, 215, 231n, 234-36, 240n, 242n, 256n, 269, 273n, 284, 287-99, 308, 311, 325n, 340
Prévost, Nicole, 187n
princes, 3, 23n, 58, 64, 73, 92, 115-16, 129-30, 136-37, 156, 163n, 171, 176, 213n, 232, 235n, 236n, 241-42, 260n, 284, 287, 288n, 295, 296n, 297, 311, 317; princes of the blood, 33n, 58, 64, 89-94, 115n, 117n, 122n, 123n, 127, 134, 144-45, 153-55, 191-94, 198n, 206, 211, 213, 234, 241-42, 252-53, 260n, 278, 281, 284, 287, 290-91, 297, 305, 308-13, 325-26, 328, 330, 331n, 333, 340
princesses, 89, 127, 207n, 235n, 313n; princesses of the blood, 308, 313, 330
procureurs général (Parlement of Paris), 56n, 87, 89, 204n, 220, 242. *See also avocats; gens du roi*
Protestants. *See* religious factions
proverbs. *See* maxims
provost (Royal Household), 57
provost of Paris, 28, 52, 55, 58, 89, 122n, 136, 189n, 236n, 293
La proximité du sang. See maxims
Public Law. *See* French constitutions

Quesnel, François, 249-51
quod omnes tangit. See maxims

Racine, Jean, 331
Rebuffi, Pierre, 67n, 99
regalia, 36-39, 59, 251, 257
regency, 115n, 116-18, 136, 138, 141, 173, 181, 183, 190, 231-43, 255, 271n, 296-97; for Charles VI, 20-21; for Charles

VIII, 42-43; for Charles IX, 145-59, 170; for Francis II, 144-45; for Henry III (in Poland), 211-12; for Louis IX, 26; for Louis XIII, 231-53; for Louis XIV, 295-321; for Louis XV, 333-41
regency council, 145, 152, 155-57, 158, 167, 170, 227, 298-304, 308, 311, 316, 333
regents, 26, 42, 70n, 136, 156, 163n, 170n, 173, 241, 257, 271n, 298, 313, 317, 335, 337, 339-40
Reims, city of, 41n, 138, 223, 258-60, 263. *See also* coronation
religious factions, 117n, 144, 153-54, 157, 164, 186, 190n, 191, 193, 210, 211n, 219-20, 222-23, 228, 324
remonstrances (exhortations): king to Parlement, 75, 188-89, 199, 200n; Parlement to king, 55, 68-69, 87, 93, 140-41, 150, 187, 189, 192-95, 200n, 278n
remonstrances (legislative). *See* legislative procedure
research commissions, royal, 100-101, 106-12, 121-25, 128, 138, 140, 155, 158, 172, 188, 213, 223, 226, 270
Rex est imperator in regno suo. See maxims
Rex et Lex. See maxims
rhetoric and history. *See* historiography
Rhodes, François Pot de, Sieur du Macquet, 213n, 279, 287n, 311-12
Rhodes, Guillaume Pot de, 213, 219, 279
Richelieu, Armand Jean du Plessis, Cardinal of, 270, 287, 288n, 290-91, 302n, 326; and the Estates General, 275; and Le Bret, 277; on *lèse-majesté*, 174n, 277; and the *Lit de Justice*, 275-76, 279n; and research commissions, 270
Robertet, Jean, 70
Roger, François, 56n, 87, 89, 242
Le roi est mort! Vive le roi! See maxims
Le roi meurt, mais un autre est né. See maxims
Le roi ne meurt jamais, Le roi de France ne meurt jamais. See maxims
Le roi n'est pas mort. See maxims
Les rois en France ne meurt point. See maxims
Roman Law, 32n, 54, 66n, 67n, 77, 97, 103, 117, 144, 156, 166, 180n, 188,

215n, 215-18, 225-27, 247n, 248, 292
Rouen, city of, 157-59, 163-64, 167, 186n; city officials, 158
Rouen, Parlement of. *See* Parlement of Rouen
Royal Council, 3, 14-15, 20-22, 23n, 25n, 32, 53-56, 67, 69-70, 88, 115-16, 117n, 123n, 136, 141, 144, 150, 152, 163n, 169, 170, 172-73, 175, 188-89, 190, 192-96, 199, 200n, 201, 207n, 213, 219-21, 233n, 244-45, 257, 284, 293, 296n, 297, 301, 305, 326-27
Royal Household, 15, 17, 52-53, 56, 63, 89
Royal *Séances*, 7, 14-47, 59-60, 65, 71, 86, 91-92, 98-99, 103, 106-8, 110-24, 126-48, 150-51, 152, 155-57, 173, 185, 199n, 201, 209-28, 253, 273-74, 277, 294, 304-5, 320-28, 343; and the Estates, 24, 276; incorrectly cited as *Lits de Justice*, 6n, 17n, 20n, 22n, 27n, 32n, 37n, 44n, 46, 47n, 48n, 52n, 115, 127n, 133n, 135n, 137n, 153n, 157n, 209-11, 212n, 213n, 214n, 216n, 217n, 219-22, 224, 325n; and the *lit de justice*, 15, 19-20, 24-25, 47, 50, 115-16, 118-19, 122
royalty (dynasty). *See royauté* (dynasty)
Le royaume est au roy et le roy est aussi au royaume. See maxims
Le royaume n'est jamais vacant. See maxims
royauté (dynasty), 180, 255-56, 260-63, 264n, 267, 272, 297, 310, 312-14, 331-32, 342. *See also dignité*; maxims
La royauté est toujours remplie et non jamais vacante. See maxims

Saint-André, François de, 187, 190; parlementary discourse, 150-51, 216
Saint Anne, 29
Saint-Anthot, Antoine de, Majority *Lit de Justice*, discourse, 170
Saint Bartholomew's Day massacres, 210
Saint-Denis, 39n, 127, 235n, 255-57
Sainte-Chapelle, 94, 127, 289, 302; mass in, 135, 308, 312
Saint-Germain, château, 297-98, 301
Saint-Germain-en-Laye, 213n
Saintot, aide of ceremonies, 312
Saintot, Nicolas, 207n, 272, 279, 288, 290n, 293n, 302, 307, 310n, 312, 316,

322, 324n, 325n, 326n, 329n, 330, 333, 335
Saint-Simon, Louis de Rouvroy, Duke of, 337-40
Salic Law. *See* French constitutions
Salle Saint-Louis (Palais de Justice), 23n, 25, 31n, 32n, 114n, 137, 147
Salle Verte (Palais de Justice), 55-56, 67-71, 244n
Scotland: King of, 87, 89, 92; Parlement in, 148
seals-keepers. *See* chancellors
Séguier, Antoine-Louis, 344n
Séguier, Pierre (I), 134-35, 140, 186n, 192-94, 217n
Seguier, Pierre (III), 170n, 273n, 289-90, 298n, 299-301, 326; and Brienne, 304n; contest over oaths of office, 297-300, 303-6; Dupuy and Godefroy, 273-74; Inaugural *Lit de Justice*, 307-15; library of, 273-74, 299, 304; on *Lits de Justice* and Estates General, 225, 270-77
Selve, Jean (II) de, 95-97; *Lit de Justice*, discourse, 76-78, 81-82, 83-84
Seneca, 156n
sénéschals, 56, 58, 63-64, 167, 242
Servin, Louis, 204n, 205n, 232, 241, 242n, 243, 244n, 247; Inaugural *Lit de Justice*, discourse, 248-49, 263n, 269
Seyssel, Claude de, 35n, 48n, 59-62, 98
Sillery, Nicolas (II) Brulart de, 232, 241-42, 245-46, 249; Inaugural *Lit de Justice*, 235-36, 238-40, 241-42, 245-47
Sleeping King, ritual of, 266
Soissons, Louis de Bourbon, Count of. *See* Bourbon
sol Franciae. See maxims
Solomon, biblical king, 61n
Spain, 50-51, 63, 74
Spanish succession, 327
stag, white, 29; winged, 39
statuary. *See* iconography
Succession, Law of. *See* French constitutions
succession, 20, 42, 105, 116, 211, 222-24, 226, 241, 270-72, 310, 327; Bourbon blood right, 253, 263-64, 266-67, 310-14, 319, 328-33, 335, 342; dynastic right (law and nature), 239, 241, 247-48, 251-53, 260-61, 263-64, 266-67, 282-97, 342; legal-hereditary, 149, 161, 174-

succession (*cont.*)
81, 202, 211, 222-24, 228, 247, 252-53, 263-64, 266-67, 319n, 328, 342
Sully, Maximilien de Béthune, Duke of, 231n, 232, 251-52, 256, 281n

Talon, Omer, 227, 300-2; Inaugural *Lit de Justice*, discourse, 310-14; Minority *Lit de Justice*, discourse, 320-21
taxation, 75, 82, 137, 155-56, 215-18, 223-26, 274, 276, 277n, 291-93, 295, 307, 315-17
Te Deum, 123, 329
Terre Rouge, Jean de, 66n, 175, 247n, 248
Theopompus. *See* maxims
Thou, Augustin (II) de, 218n
Thou, Christophe de, 158-59, 182n, 186n, 187-88, 190-91, 192n, 195-96, 218; Royal *Séance*, discourse, 155-56, 179
Thou, Jacques-Auguste de, 210n, 231n
throne, 41n, 52-53, 58-59, 61-64, 72-73, 76, 87n, 89, 92-94, 97, 119, 122, 127, 134-35, 138, 140, 161n, 163n, 170, 173, 198n, 234-35, 236n, 308, 310, 312, 322, 328, 330, 337, 340
Tiraqueau, André, 175n, 176n
Torcy, Colbert de, 332
Toulouse, Parlement of. *See* Parlement of Toulouse
Tournelle Civile (Palais de Justice), 24n
Tournelle Criminelle (Palais de Justice), 22
Tour Ronde (Palais de Justice), 87
Tours, city of, 147, 222
Tours, Parlement of. *See* Parlement of Tours

Treaty of Cambrai, 91-92
Treaty of Madrid, 50, 72-78, 81, 83, 91-92
Trésor des Chartes, 108-111, 121n, 270
trials. *See lèse-majesté*; peers, trials of
Tuileries, palace, 225, 337, 339, 340
tutorship. See maxims

unigenitus. See maxims
university, 153
Ursins, Jean (II) Juvénal des. *See* Juvénal des Ursins
ushers (Parlement of Paris), 15-16, 19, 25, 35, 43, 57, 87-89, 119
ushers (Royal Household), 53, 56-57, 65, 122n, 161n

Valence, Jean du, Bishop of, 189
valet, royal. *See* Guillaume de Feuilloy
Vendôme, city of, 33, 52, 59, 114n, 116, 124, 305
Vendôme, Duke of, 76
Vernon, city of, 187, 189n
Versailles, 328-30, 344
Viole, Guillaume, 187n, 192n
Virelay, Jean de, 24n, 308
Vivit morte refecta. See maxims

Wavrin, Jehan de, Seigneur du Forestel, 34
Willequin, Jean, 19, 21, 25
William the Conqueror, 164n
women, in the Grand-chambre, 73, 87, 89, 94-95, 127, 163n, 207n, 235, 308, 313

Library of Congress Cataloging in Publication Data

Hanley, Sarah, 1937-
The lit de justice of the kings of France.

(Studies presented to the International Commission for the History of Representative and Parliamentary Institutions = Études presentées à la Commission internationale pour l'histoire des assemblées d'états   ; 65)
Bibliography: p.   Includes index.
1. Lit de justice—History. 2. France—Constitutional history. 3. Rites
and ceremonies—France—History.   I. Title.   II. Series: Études
présentées à la Commission internationale pour l'histoire des assemblées d'états; 65.
LAW   342.44'029   82-61374
ISBN 0-691-05382-0   344.40229